CREATING AND CAPTURING VALUE

Perspectives and Cases on Electronic Commerce

To
Max and Rachel
and Monica

UH
University of
Hertfordshire

WITHDRAWN

CREATING AND CAPTURING VALUE

Perspectives and Cases on Electronic Commerce

Garth Saloner

A. Michael Spence

Stanford Graduate School of Business
Center for Electronic Business and Commerce

JOHN WILEY & SONS, INC.

Acquisitions Editor Jeff Marshall
Associate Director of Development Johnna Barto
Production Manager Jeanine Furino
Production Editor Sandra Russell
Marketing Manager Charity Robey
Designer Madelyn Lesure
Cover Illustration David Flaherty
Production Management Services Argosy

This book was typeset in 10/12 Janson by Argosy and printed and bound by R.R. Donnelley (Crawfordsville). The cover was printed by Lehigh Press, Inc.

The paper in this book was manufactured by a mill whose forest management programs include sustained yield harvesting of its timberlands. Sustained yield harvesting principles ensure that the number of tress cut each year does not exceed the amount of new growth.

This book is printed on acid-free paper. ∞

Library of Congress Cataloging-in-Publication Data
Saloner, Garth
Creating and capturing value: perspectives and cases on electronic commerce/Garth Saloner, A. Michael Spence.
p. cm.
Includes bibliographical references and index.
ISBN 0-471-41015-2 (cloth: alk. paper)
1. Electronic commerce. 2. Electronic commerce—Case studies. I Spence, A. Michael (Andrew Michael) II. Title.
HF5548.32 .S186 2001
658.8'4—dc21

2001026641

Printed in the United States of America.

10 9 8 7 6 5 4 3 2 1

PREFACE

We have had the great privilege of spending the past decade at Stanford University's Graduate School of Business in the heart of Silicon Valley. As the 1990s drew to a close, we were surrounded by students, alumni, managers, corporations, executive education students, and friends grappling with the actual and potential impacts of dramatic technological change on their current and future businesses.

We found ourselves drawn to these problems. One reason is that we are in constant awe of the rate of technological change and what it can do to improve all of our lives, both in developed and developing economies. Another is that some of the most important challenges and opportunities presented by electronic commerce are managerial rather than technical. They are at least as much about how industries and firms will be restructured and what strategies new and established firms should pursue, as about how to engineer faster and better computers and networks—though it is true that the latter drives the former. These are hard problems because they involve thinking about nonincremental change and as industrial organization economists and strategic management scholars we find them fascinating.

Teaching is one of the best ways of learning, and to that end we decided to put together an MBA elective on electronic commerce in early 2000. Since we could not approach this subject with an established set of conceptual frameworks and theories on electronic commerce—since none existed—we decided to make a set of business cases the basis of the course.

The cases and what we have learned from teaching them became the core of this book. Part I of the book contains some of the perspectives we have developed on electronic commerce from teaching the course several times to MBAs and business executives. Part II contains the cases that were written for the course, augmented by cases written by some of our colleagues.

We owe a great debt in this venture (and adventure) to Stanford's MBA students; those who took the course with us and those in prior years who helped put us in a position where we could teach it. Most of the cases were written by second-year students, usually just in time for class in the winter of 2000. For their dedication to this effort, we are extremely grateful to our MBA case writers Kasey Craig, David Doctorow, Katie Gray, Tyee Harpster, Katherine McIntyre, Jamie McJunkin, Michelle Moore, Trae Neist, Ezra Perlman, Todd Reynders, Kostas Sgoutas, Cara Snyder, Chris Thomas, Meredith Unruh and Liz Urban, and to GSB case writers Eric Marti and Philip Meza. The mammoth case writing task was managed with poise and equanimity by Margot Sutherland, the Executive Director of the Center for Electronic Business and Commerce and Case Writing Manager at the Stanford GSB.We thank her both for the accomplishment as well as the way it was carried out. We are also thankful for research assistance generously provided by Daniel Guhr of the Boston Consulting Group and by McKinsey & Company's Palo Alto office.

We are grateful to our colleagues Dave Baron, Robert Burgelman, and Haim Mendelson who have graciously contributed cases to this volume. Haim has also contributed to our thinking on the subject in many conversations over the past year. Severin Borenstein at the Haas School of Management co-authored a paper with Garth on electronic commerce that appeared in the *Journal of Economic Perspectives*. That paper was a precursor of some of what appears in the "Perspectives" section of the book. We are grateful to Severin for his collaboration and for permitting us to draw on that work here. We have also benefited from conversations with David Brady, David Brown, Ray Conley, Andy Grove, Paul Romer, and Mark Wolfson as well as fellow board members and managers at a variety of companies with which we have had the privilege of working.

A number of executives spoke to our classes about their experiences in electronic commerce and their insights have helped to shape this book. We thank Tom Siebel, founder and CEO of Siebel Systems; John Simon, CEO of QRS; Yoav Shoham, a Stanford colleague and founder of Trading Dynamics; Sir John Browne, CEO of British Petroleum; Karen Brown, founder and CEO of Karen Brown Books; Mike Volpi, Chief Strategy Officer of Cisco Systems; Matt Glickman, founder of Babycenter.com; and Peter Johnson, founder of Tradeweave and founder and Chairman of QRS.

Our work has been supported by the Center for Electronic Business and Commerce at Stanford University's Graduate School of Business. The Center was established with major contributions from three founding partners: eBay, the Charles Schwab Corporation, and General Atlantic Partners. Generous support was also provided by BP Amoco, General Motors, Jeffrey S. Skoll, and Carl D. and Marilynn J. Thoma. We are grateful for this support which has made this work possible.

The editors and staff at Wiley have been wonderful partners. Brent Gordon guided the project from its inception, Johnna Barto managed development, and Gerald Lombardi's careful editing significantly improved the manuscript.

Our greatest debt, as always, is to our families who cheerfully indulge our enthusiasm for technological change and our fascination with what it will do for all of our futures, while keeping us firmly and happily grounded in the here and now.

Garth Saloner
A. Michael Spence
Stanford University

CONTENTS

PART I

PERSPECTIVES

INTRODUCTION

We live in an extraordinary time. The Internet and related technologies have opened new forms of communication, caused the costs of many kinds of market interactions to plummet, and have brought firms and consumers around the globe into closer proximity than ever before. At the same time, many of the frictions that impede efficient market performance—for example, imperfect information about who is willing and able to supply which goods and services and at what price—are being swept aside.

This is creating a tremendous amount of economic value. As with any dramatic technological change, the most obvious and earliest effects are incremental: we find easier and less costly ways of doing the things we were already doing. Over time, however, the shifts are more drastic: we discover that we can do new things, or completely restructure how we conduct age-old business. So, too, the current technological change will drastically affect business transactions. Although change will take time to work its way through the system, it is restructuring entire supply chains and markets, and the industries, firms, and labor forces that participate in them.

As with prior major technological developments, such as the railroad, telegraph, and electric power, the current technological change is creating new industries, transforming existing ones, and giving birth to new firms that will be household names and industry giants a century from now. Consequently, who captures the value that is created—whether it be firms or end-consumers, and if firms, which firms—will also change.

Technological changes of this magnitude don't simply change things at the margin. Many incremental changes add up to nonincremental change. In the language of economics, we shift from one equilibrium to another. The complexity of the changes that are taking place makes it difficult for managers to see far ahead and plan accordingly. When the entire landscape is changing, navigating by just peering ahead on the road you are currently on is dangerous! You need to head for higher ground to try to understand the major forces at work and their likely impact.

Through the text and cases in this book, we have tried to give general managers a perspective on those key forces and their likely impacts. Given the complexity and uncertainty of the many markets and industries that technology is affecting, it would be foolhardy to attempt to cover all situations. That would require analyzing the idiosyncrasies of each specific case. Our goal, instead, is to provide some perspective that

This Introduction draws heavily on Severin Borenstein and Garth Saloner, "Economics and Electronic Commerce," *Journal of Economic Perspectives*, 15, 1, Winter, 2001, 3–12. The authors thank Severin and the American Economic Association for their permission to do so.

helps the general manager get to the starting gate in thinking strategically about electronic commerce.

THE CHALLENGE: LOOKING AHEAD

We begin the class that we teach on electronic commerce by examining how the pottery industry in England evolved in the 1700s and the role that Josiah Wedgwood played.[1] This old tale illustrates several challenges that the analysis of major technical or industrial change poses. One of the most important is the difficulty of forecasting the nature of the change. As prescient and visionary as he was, even Josiah Wedgwood would have had difficulty during the 1750s or 1760s predicting the character of his own industry five years hence.

The problem is that in such periods of ferment, so many things are changing and so many different strategies are being pursued that there are numerous paths that firms and industries can go down. With hindsight we can see which path was taken and can often explain why the firm in question took it; however, to those living at the time, neither the path forward nor the reasons for taking it are clear.

Part of the complexity is typical for the emerging stage of an industry. Scholars of the early history of the automobile industry, for example, will recall that hundreds of new firms were pursuing different strategies. Some firms tried steam engines, others electric or gas. Some concentrated on engines and outsourced the purchase of bodies while others sought competitive advantage in bodies and procured their engines. Over time, however, the uncertainty about which approaches would be the most successful was resolved, and the industry entered a "shake-out" period. Before long the hundreds of aspiring firms were winnowed down to a few pursuing similar strategies. Successful firms absorbed the less successful, and the industry consolidated.

This evolutionary process in which firms experiment and only a few survive and are imitated is a natural process of the emergent phase of new industries. It is also reminiscent of competition among different "business models" that fledgling electronic commerce companies are pursuing. But just because it has happened before does not make it easier for managers to deal with uncertainty.

Moreover, predicting the long-term impacts of technological change is particularly difficult for electronic commerce. For one thing the markets are currently far from equilibrium. The rapid pace of technological change has created a wealth of entrepreneurial opportunities that in many markets has spawned large-scale entry and further innovation. Although it is always difficult to know when an industry is near a long-run equilibrium, in many of these new markets, we know that they are not.

In many markets, firms are pursuing strategies that are not sustainable in equilibrium. In an attempt to survive, much of their activity aimed to gain and secure market position amounts to the payment of one-time, largely sunk entry costs. The focus

[1] For a description see Nancy F. Koehn, "Josiah Wedgwood and the First Industrial Revolution," in Tom McCraw, *Creating Modern Capitalism* (Boston: Harvard University Press, 1997), pp. 19–50.

of these expenditures is often on "customer acquisition" or building infrastructure to achieve minimum efficient scale. These expenditures—fueled by the largest inflow of venture capital ever—may represent reasonable investments for a chance of a future stream of profits that might accrue to the resulting market positions. Nonetheless, we cannot see them as equilibrium long-run expenditures or part of the permanent competitive landscape in most markets.

A clear example is expenditure on banner advertising when a firm quickly funnels the revenue it garners from the banner advertising on its own site into its own advertising on others' sites, showing up as a source of revenue there. Yet the demand for banner advertising is diminishing, not least because many of these nascent market participants clamoring for visibility are disappearing while the brands of the survivors become more prominent. Indeed banner advertising rates have already plummeted. As this occurs, "business models" that depend on such revenue become unsustainable.

The continuing entry into electronic commerce of firms that have an established offline presence also affects current market structures. These "traditional" firms bring tremendous strategic assets, including brand names, geographic locations that are often synergistic with an online presence, logistics and fulfillment infrastructure, and so forth, to bear on their electronic commerce operations. Yet in some cases the online initiatives of these firms are in their infancy or still on the drawing board, and their implementation will affect equilibrium market structures.

Despite the uncertainty and complexity of this environment, managers need a clear, albeit changing and evolving, view of the landscape. It is difficult to plan without such a view, or at least scenarios of the possible futures the firm may confront. Moreover, although strategy must evolve in response to market and competitors, having a strategy is critical. This book seeks to provide tools, frameworks, and perspectives to help map the landscape and set strategy.

OVERVIEW OF THE BOOK

The book has two parts, "Perspectives" and "Cases." "Perspectives" provides an overview of some of the important issues in electronic commerce. "Cases" provides case studies that we, our colleagues, and students have compiled. The cases contain a wealth of information about technologies, industries, issues, firms, strategies, and organizational structures. They also pose issues that the challenge of electronic commerce confronts for students and practitioners. The two parts of the book work in tandem. "Cases" provides context for "Perspectives," which accordingly often refers to the cases, and "Perspectives" seeks to help the reader address many of the challenges the cases pose. A brief overview of the chapters in Part I follows.

In Chapter 1 we begin with an overview of the technological drivers of the changes that have given rise to electronic commerce. We have found in teaching the subject to both MBA students and executives that to analyze electronic commerce strategic options one must understand the underlying technologies. Although the most relevant developments relate to the Internet and World Wide Web, the development of the computer platforms on which they rest is equally important. Moreover, any electronic commerce strategy must take into account both the enterprise systems already in place in large firms and the economy-wide distribution infrastructure. In addition, earlier technologies like electronic data interchange can teach important lessons.

In the subsequent chapters we examine how these technological changes create value in the economy and what determines who captures that value. In Chapter 2 we discuss how electronic commerce can increase the amount of value created in the economy by reducing cost, enhancing products and services, and ensuring that goods and services are allocated to the people who value them most.

In Chapter 3 we examine which competitors within a particular industry are best situated to capture value that is created, and the extent to which competition will cause downstream buyers rather than the competing firms to capture value. Since industry structure influences the extent of competition, we examine conventional determinants of market structure and the role of demand-side increasing returns. We also examine the determinants of competitive intensity within the industry, including product differentiation and price competition.

In Chapter 4 we broaden the discussion to include a more holistic look at the entire industry supply chain in which firms operate. This is important both because some of the most interesting ways that electronic commerce can create value are by improving the coordination of supply chains and because the adoption of electronic commerce can determine which firms in the supply chain have the power to capture the value in the chain. Moreover, the emergence of new intermediaries that seek to replace bilateral transactions between firms with broad marketplaces in which all firms participate is reengineering some supply chains. Chapter 4 discusses the role of such intermediaries and the potential disappearance of existing ones.

Part II of the book begins with an overview of the cases that follow and relates them to the concepts in the "Perspectives" section.

CHAPTER

1

TECHNOLOGICAL DRIVERS OF CHANGE

The economic and strategic disruptions being wrought by electronic commerce are the result of dramatic recent technological changes, especially the Internet, World Wide Web (WWW), and advances in broadband and wireless technologies. However, these technologies stand on the shoulders of prior and continuing advances to the computer platforms on which they depend. Moreover, especially in the business-to-business (B2B) realm, the computing systems inside large firms and the logistics and fulfillment systems available to them enable and sometimes limit electronic commerce. Because technological history conditions its future, this chapter discusses the history and describes the status of some of the most important underlying technologies and infrastructure.

KEY TECHNOLOGY COMPONENTS

As we proceed, a simple conceptual map of the technological terrain may be useful. Figure 1-1 illustrates the latter part of an industry supply chain in the pre-Internet era. It includes two firms and end-consumers [so that we can discuss both B2B and business-to-consumer (B2C) settings]. Most medium-sized and large firms have at the core of their information technology infrastructure an enterprise computing system. For

FIGURE 1-1 A Simple Conceptual Map of the Pre-Internet Technological Terrain

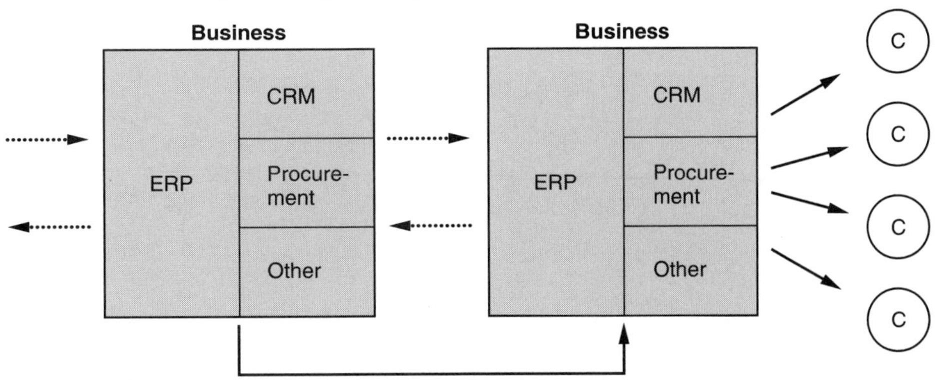

each of the entities labeled "Business" in the figure, we have indicated this with a base enterprise resource planning system (ERP) of the kind that, say, SAP or Oracle offers, augmented with special-purpose modules for procurement, customer relationship management (CRM), and so on. Although these systems vary, this basic architecture is prevalent enough to warrant discussion, especially since those systems affect the speed and type of further technology that firms will adopt.

The arrows indicate interconnections between end-consumers and firms. Solid arrows refer to physical flows (e.g., the shipment of goods or paper orders); dotted arrows denote electronic flows (e.g., electronic purchase orders). In electronic commerce parlance, the solid arrows track the movement of "atoms" while the dotted ones track the movement of "bits." Note that even in the pre-Internet era significant data flowed between firms. In addition to data exchanged using telephone and fax lines, face-to-face communication, and so on, electronic data interchange (EDI) facilitated other electronic exchanges, as we discuss in more detail later. Second electronic flows between end-consumers and firms were minimal. Figure 1-2 illustrates how the Internet affected these direct flows. Interfirm interactions (B2B) could now occur over the Internet in addition to EDI. More importantly, the Internet enabled electronic interactions between consumers and firms (B2C).

Even more significant is the Internet's potential for restructuring industries and supply chains as opposed to simply changing how they operate. Figure 1-3 illustrates two important categories of ways in which this can occur. The first is the potential for various electronic markets to serve as new intermediaries, whether B2B markets or other intermediaries, B2C intermediaries (both markets and portals), or consumer-to-consumer (C2C) electronic forums (such as eBay). Second, as the figure also shows, is the potential for firms to use the Internet to bypass a segment of the supply chain, either via a new B2C intermediary or directly. We will have more to say later about this phenomenon, called "disintermediation," and the role of new intermediaries.

In this chapter we present an overview of the components in Figure 1-2 and their origins. We begin with the Internet and WWW because they are the lenses through

FIGURE 1-2 B2B and B2C Internet Information Flows

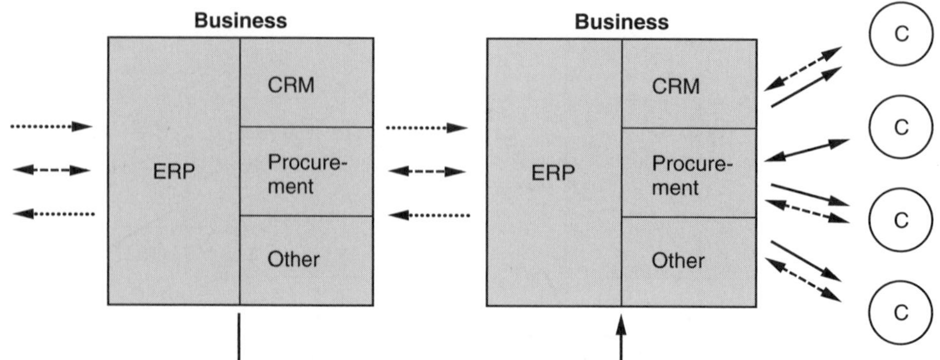

FIGURE 1-3 A Conceptual Map of the Post-Internet Technological Terrain

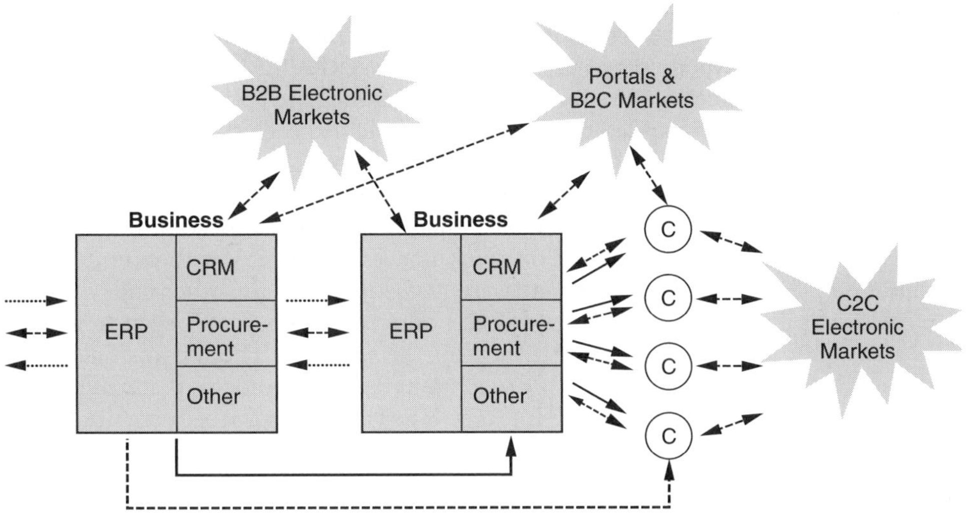

which we must view the impact of technology on electronic commerce. We then discuss underlying computer platforms and enterprise systems, and logistics and fulfillment (the solid arrows in the figures).

THE INTERNET AND THE WORLD WIDE WEB

The Internet and WWW are by far the most important technological enablers of electronic commerce, for the physical network and information architecture are the sources of global interconnectivity and ubiquity. We provide a brief history of the Internet and WWW because knowledge of how their architecture evolved and what lies behind their tremendous growth can help us understand their impact on electric commerce.

The Internet

The Internet has unlikely origins.[1] In response to the launching of Sputnik I by the Soviet Union in 1957, the United States established the Advanced Research Projects Agency (ARPA) within the Defense Department to keep the U.S. military on the cutting edge of technology. Since ARPA drew on a large network of scientists and subcontractors, it quickly sought to facilitate communication among them using direct links among computers. Fortunately, this was becoming technologically feasible.

[1] For more information on the history of the Internet see Vinton Cerf, "A Brief History of the Internet and Related Networks," at http://www.isoc.org/internet-history/cerf.html, September 13, 2000, and Richard T. Griffiths, "Internet for Historians, History of the Internet" at http://www.let.leidenuniv.nl/history/ivh/frame_theorie.html, September 13, 2000, on which this summary draws.

By the early 1960s computer scientists had developed a vision for networked computers accessible to everyone, and in 1965 the first experimental link on dial-up telephone lines was created between Berkeley and MIT; by the end of the decade an ARPANET linked several computers together. The ARPANET used a standardized "interface message processor" to connect computers through telephone lines. The interface message processor provided the interface that enabled each computer to treat the signals being sent over the telephone line as though they were coming from a local terminal. Another important feature of the ARPANET was that it was based on packet switching technology. Messages from one computer were broken down into "packets," each with the address of the destination computer. Each packet was then routed over the most efficient path, and the packets were reassembled on the other end.

Following the success of the ARPANET, other networks soon began to appear. This created the next problem—how to *inter*link the *net*works. The system of networks that resulted from the development of the communications protocols that made interlinking possible became known as the Internet. The two key protocols were the "transmission control protocol" and the "internet protocol," collectively known as *TCP/IP*. The guiding philosophy behind TCP/IP, developed in 1974 in an effort led by Robert Kahn and Vinton Cerf, is one of "open architecture." Developers can design and operate each network independently without having to consider the desire to connect to the Internet. Instead, each network has a gateway (at the time typically a mainframe computer) that links it to the Internet and houses the software required to transmit and direct packages. These gateways link a local network to the Internet and accept and redirect traffic to computers on other networks. Because the gateways were designed to always be open and to route traffic in a nondiscriminatory fashion, any network adhering to TCP/IP can "join" the Internet, immediately have access to the most efficient routing of data traffic, and contribute to its speed, performance, and growth.

By 1984, a thousand "host" computers had been connected to the Internet. The overall volume of traffic was far greater than had originally been forecast, partly because e-mail, developed in 1972, had become very popular and because researchers were using it extensively to transfer files using the file transfer protocol (FTP). Seeing the advantages to higher education, the British government and the United States's National Science Foundation (NSF) decided to construct networks (JANET and NSFNet) for universities in the United Kingdom and the U.S., respectively. To deal with the expected increase in traffic, NSFNet agreed to build a huge "backbone" for the U.S. Internet. The network utilized five supercomputers and could carry 56K bytes/sec initially. It was upgraded in 1988 to carry 300,000 times as much traffic. Even though the NSFNet could be used only for research and education (a restriction dropped in 1991), its impact was explosive. Five thousand hosts were connected to the Internet by 1986, 28,000 the following year, and 300,000 by 1990 (see Figure 1-4).

The World Wide Web

Although the Internet was growing rapidly, it was cumbersome to use. That changed when Tim Berners-Lee at CERN designed the World Wide Web (WWW) in 1989. The first step was the development of the hypertext transfer protocol (HTTP) which

FIGURE 1-4 Growth in Number of Host Computers on the Internet

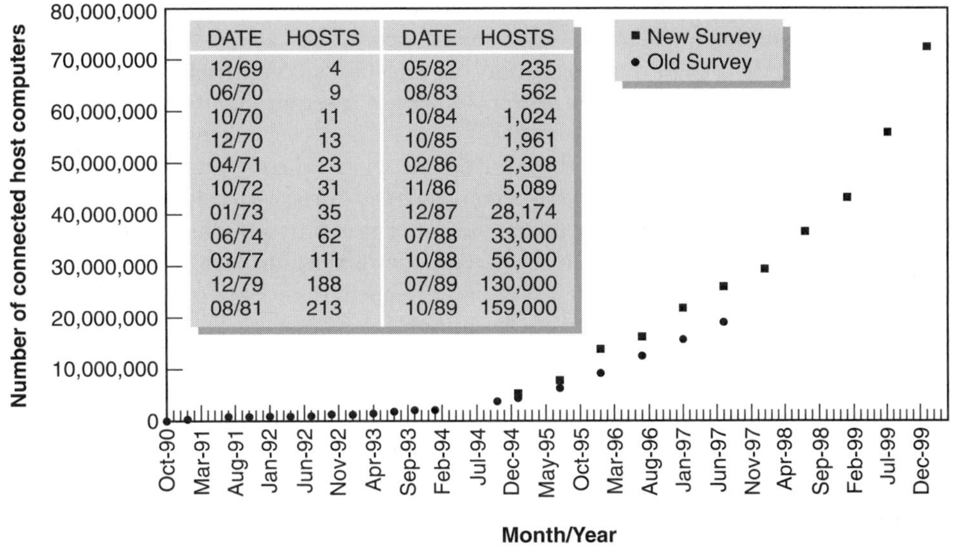

DATE	HOSTS	DATE	HOSTS
12/69	4	05/82	235
06/70	9	08/83	562
10/70	11	10/84	1,024
12/70	13	10/85	1,961
04/71	23	02/86	2,308
10/72	31	11/86	5,089
01/73	35	12/87	28,174
06/74	62	07/88	33,000
03/77	111	10/88	56,000
12/79	188	07/89	130,000
08/81	213	10/89	159,000

Source: Robert H. Zakon, *Hobbes' Internet Timeline*, http://www.isoc.org/guest/zakon/Internet/History/HIT.html, September 13, 2000.

created a simplified protocol for writing document addresses and then calling them up automatically. Soon elementary browsers had been developed that facilitated the use of HTTP. The next step was the development of a hypertext markup language (HTML) that allowed the addresses to be hidden behind text and for the embedded link to be activated by the click of a mouse. More sophisticated browsers soon followed, most notably Mosaic launched by Mark Andreesen at the National Center for SuperComputing Applications at the University of Illinois.

Mosaic represented a breakthrough in the adoption of the WWW because it was easy to use, had enhanced graphics capabilities, was backed by 24-hour customer support, was distributed free, and was downloadable. The WWW in turn vastly increased the Internet's usefulness. Since end-users are fundamentally interested in the content that they can obtain from other computers and not in how they obtain it, suppressing the plumbing and providing an intuitive and easy-to-use method to access and view pages directly vastly increased the Internet's utility. Similarly, introducing intuitive and easy-to-use user interfaces enormously improved e-mail and spurred its widespread adoption.

Java

Early browsers only enabled one-way communication in which Web pages stored on one computer (the server) were displayed on another (the client). Two-way communication, which is necessary for something as simple as having a customer complete an order form, required additional functionality. The initial approach provided for a common gateway interface (CGI) to manage communications between the computer where the Web page was stored and the end-user's computer: data entered on the client could be sent back to the server. However, it required a lot of communication between the server and client.

An alternative approach is for the page that is sent to the client's browser to itself contain a program. Then the user can interact back-and-forth with the program, receiving different browser views in response to the data entered without having to get additional direction or information from the server. This is the approach taken by the Java programming language that Sun Microsystems developed. In this approach Java "applets" are written to run within the browser. An important feature of Java is that the Java applets will run on a wide variety of operating systems. The reason is that the browser or associated server software contains a Java virtual machine (JVM) that translates from Java into the operating instructions that the specific operating system requires. This is why a user using the same browser on different computers has virtually the same experience.

Java represents an important innovation not just because it enables far greater functionality for Web browsing than was possible before, but also because it potentially changes the paradigm for computing. If a browser anywhere in the world can quickly call up an application, if that application can run on any computer, and if files can be stored on servers connected to the Internet, a user can have the same experience regardless of where he or she is or what computer he or she is using. This idea has given rise to the notion that "the network is the computer."[2] Of course, enabling users to have the same experience using any browser on any computer requires a certain amount of standardization, both in the protocols that browsers deploy, the programming language that is used, and how that language is implemented. Concern that these standards might either fragment or become proprietary was a consideration in the antitrust suit that the Justice Department brought against Microsoft.

Search Engines, Portals, and Growth

The WWW is already so ubiquitous that it is hard to believe that at the end of 1992 there were only 50 Web sites in existence and a mere 600 at the end of 1993. The hockey-stick shaped curves of adoption, like those in Figure 1-5, illustrate the dramatic growth since then.

[2] Taking the networking of computers one step further, it is possible for separate computers connected only by the Internet to share computing power. In that way the unused computing power on idle machines can be put to productive use. In addition to sharing computing power it is possible to share data and applications. As the Napster and Scour cases brought to the fore, this raises difficult intellectual property issues. Developing the capability for "peer-to-peer" networking to enable sharing of all kinds over the Internet is an active area of technological and business development.

FIGURE 1-5 Growth in the Number of WWW Sites

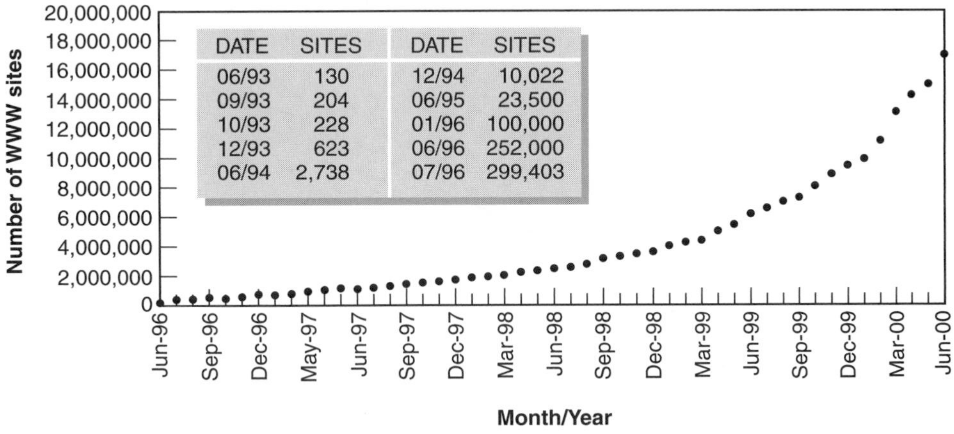

DATE	SITES	DATE	SITES
06/93	130	12/94	10,022
09/93	204	06/95	23,500
10/93	228	01/96	100,000
12/93	623	06/96	252,000
06/94	2,738	07/96	299,403

Number of WWW sites

Month/Year

Source: Robert H. Zakon, *Hobbes' Internet Timeline*, http://www.isoc.org/guest/zakon/Internet /History/HIT.html, September 13, 2000.

The proliferation of sites quickly brought with it a need to navigate through them. Early search engines like Yahoo! enabled users to search for words or phrases of interest. However, since the search engines attracted a lot of traffic of their own, they soon discovered that they could provide roadmaps and indexes to sites by organizing them into categories and providing links among them. From that position it was a small step to becoming an aggregator of content and a "community center" for users with similar interests who wished to exchange ideas through chat or bulletin boards. This in turn made them attractive "shopping malls" for firms attempting to reach large numbers of potential shoppers. Through this evolution these sites emerged into full-fledged portals (see the AOL case in Part II for details on the portals' evolution).

A similarly dramatic growth in the number of users has accompanied this growth in infrastructure and organization. Although there is some controversy surrounding measures of the number of users (the numbers vary dramatically depending on the kind of survey done), any method of measurement shows similar dramatic growth rates. A typical example is illustrated in Figure 1-6, which shows the growth in the number of U.S. households with Internet access. (This type of data is usually more reliable than estimates of individual users for the obvious reason that it is easier to measure household access than individual use.) The data show a six-fold increase in connected households from 1994 to 1999. Although that number is expected to almost double in the next four years, it represents a reduction in the rate of growth. Such a reduction is inevitable as penetration rates increase.

Figure 1-7, which compares the number of years it took several innovations to reach 30% penetration in U.S. households, contains another and perhaps more compelling picture of the speed of adoption. By these estimates, the Internet took half as long as the personal computer and one-fifth the time of the telephone to reach that level.

FIGURE 1-6 U.S. Households with Internet Access (Actual to 1999 and Projected to 2003)

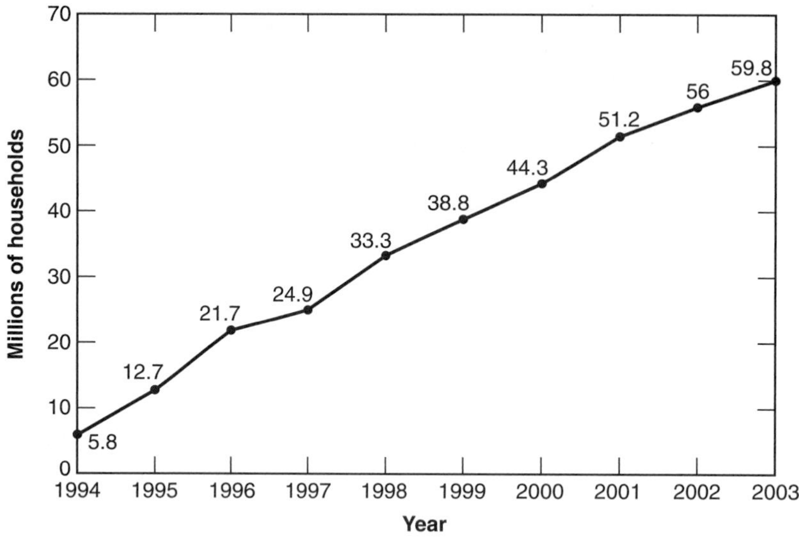

Source: U.S. Internet Council, "State of the Internet: USIC's Report on Use and Threats in 1999," citing Forrester Reports, at http://www.usic.org/, September 13, 2000.

Although North America accounted for more than 40% of the world's Internet users at the end of 1999 (see Figure 1-8), that percentage is dropping rapidly as the growth rate in the United States slows relative to that in countries with lower penetration

FIGURE 1-7 Number of Years to Reach 30% Penetration of U.S. Households

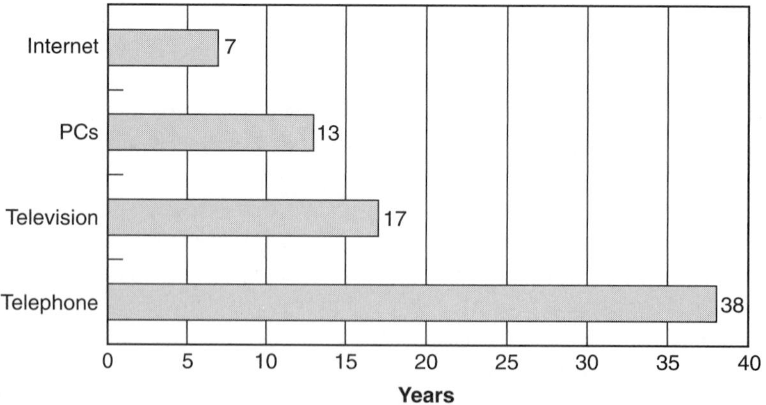

Source: U.S. Internet Council, "State of the Internet: USIC's Report on Use and Threats in 1999," citing Morgan Stanley Research Group, at http://www.usic.org/, September 13, 2000.

FIGURE 1-8 Percentage of World Internet Users by Region

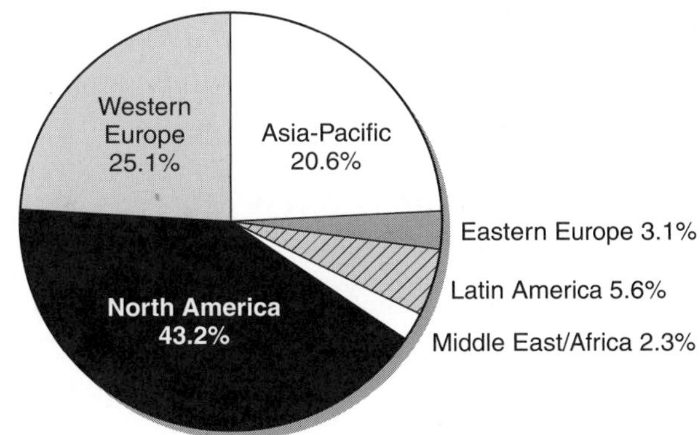

Source: Stacy Lawrence, "The Net World in Numbers," *The Standard*, February 7, 2000, at http://www.thestandard.com/research/metrics/display/0,2799,10121,00.html, September 13, 2000.

rates (see Table 1-1). Still, analysts predict that by 2005 the 15 countries with the most users will account for 82% of the world's users and that by year-end 2002 only in 14 countries will more than 30% of the population be Internet users.[3] By contrast, Vietnam

TABLE 1-1 Internet Usage by Country and as a Percentage of Total Population

	Online Population in Millions, 1999	*Total Population in Millions, 1999*	*Percentage of Total Population Online*
United States	110.8	273	40.6%
Japan	18.2	126	14.4%
United Kingdom	13.9	59	23.6%
Canada	13.3	31	42.9%
Germany	12.3	82	15.0%
Australia	6.8	19	35.8%
Brazil	6.8	172	4.0%
China	6.3	1,247	0.5%
France	5.7	59	9.7%
South Korea	5.7	47	12.1%
Taiwan	4.8	22	21.8%
Italy	4.7	57	8.4%
Sweden	3.9	9	43.3%
Netherlands	2.9	16	18.1%
Spain	2.9	39	7.4%

Source: Stacy Lawrence, "The Net World in Numbers," *The Standard*, February 7, 2000, at http://www.thestandard.com/research/metrics/display/0,2799,10121,00.html, September 13, 2000.

[3] *Computer Industry Alamanac*, at http://www.c-i-a.com/, December 1, 2000.

in 2000 only had an estimated 40,000 Internet users among its 78 million people, due to inadequate infrastructure and low incomes.[4] If penetration rates are to increase appreciably in developing countries where about 80% of the world's population lives and where even more (96%) of the world's future population growth is going to occur, a tremendous amount of infrastructure must be built.[5]

THE INTERNET AND WORLD WIDE WEB AS A PLATFORM FOR ELECTRONIC COMMERCE

That the Internet and WWW are ubiquitous and growing rapidly does not necessarily imply that they should provide a good platform for electronic commerce. However, several of their characteristics do indeed underlie the potential for electronic commerce to create value.

• ***Reach.*** For both consumers and firms, the Internet provides unprecedented reach. This is the result, of course, of its rapid growth, due in turn to its open architecture. For electronic commerce, the Internet's reach is greater when physical distance does not greatly constrain users' ability to realize value. For example, where a transaction or interaction is consummated entirely through bits rather than atoms, reach is limited mainly by governmental regulation and the costs of matching potential parties to the interaction. Financial transactions (both banking and investing) are probably the most important transactions where no physical product is involved (except for the requirement of a real signatures on many legal documents and difficulties in exchanging cash—two problems that are currently the focus of a great deal of R&D). Other cases ultimately involve a physical "product," but prepurchase evaluations can be conducted electronically. Screening of job applicants is a good example. Where the transaction involves bits as well as atoms, but the cost of moving the atoms is relatively low, the reach of the Internet is still typically far greater than the competing alternatives. For example, a classified advertisement on the Internet has far greater reach than the same advertisement in a local newspaper.

• ***Flexibility and ease-of-use.*** The WWW provides a flexible programming environment and combines several media. These characteristics are partly responsible for the tremendous range of uses to which Web sites have been put. Moreover, compared to most computer technologies in even the recent past, the Web is easy to use, both for those building Web sites and those using them.

• ***Personalization.*** The Internet offers the ability to personalize transactions and offerings at low cost. Amazon.com's tailoring its book recommendations to the characteristics of its customers is an example. Another is BabyCenter.com's ability, simply by

[4] See http://cyberatlas.internet.com/big_picture/geographics/article/0,1323,5911_151291,00.html, December 1, 2000.
[5] "World Population Profile" at http://www.census.gov/.

knowing just the stage of pregnancy of an expectant mother, to provide individually-tailored information and products that are particularly relevant to the situation faced by the consumer (see the BabyCenter case in Part II for details).

• ***Interactivity.*** The advantages of flexibility and personalization are significantly enhanced by interactivity. The ability of users to tailor the information they receive, to search for information they want, or to provide cues to enable computer-generated tailoring, increases the value of information and the likelihood of a good match between potential trading partners. To see how interactivity supports personalization, return to the BabyCenter.com example and note that the ability to personalize is not limited to electronic transactions. Providers of baby products can and do tailor their direct marketing in similar ways. However, the ability of the user to electronically interact with a database—by providing information or making queries—makes this a much more valuable form of interaction than one-way direct marketing.

• ***Asynchronous communication.*** A great advantage of the Internet is that it is "open" 24 hours a day, 7 days a week. Thus users can access it, place orders, or send messages at almost any time. Of course this is something of an overstatement since there is not always someone on the other end of an interaction, and if the matter is urgent, there is usually little reliability as to when a query will be dealt with. Still, it is often far more efficient for consumers to be able to place orders at their convenience and then for the firm to process them over time. As long as the customer is willing to put up with a small delay in the firm's response, the firm can rationalize its order-processing rather than gear itself up to respond instantaneously to the arrival of orders that typically wax and wane. Asynchronous communication is also a major strength of bulletin boards and e-mail and is especially valuable when communications occur across widely differing time zones.

• ***Encyclopedic nature.*** Information and content build up on the WWW over time. Except when Web sites are not maintained or content is removed, content development on the WWW is cumulative. Given that storage costs are low and falling, most content placed on the Web stays there. And more and more content is added all the time. Consequently end users have an extraordinary and growing amount of information at their fingertips. The increase in and ready availability of information for investors is an example. Investors now have access to SEC filing, analysts' reports, CEO interviews, and so on. By the middle of 2000, the Web contained more than two billion pages and was growing at the rate of 7 million pages per day.[6] At that rate the Web would double in size in a year!

• ***Richness.*** The combination of links, search capabilities, multimedia, and personalization results in an extremely rich medium. Coupled with low (and falling) dissemination costs, it is possible to provide end-users with unprecedented quality of content.

[6] See http://cyberatlas.internet.com/big_picture/traffic_patterns/article/0,,5931_413691,00.html, November 20, 2000.

The richness of the Web is likely to increase enormously as higher bandwidth raises the quality of streaming media, and computer platforms improve in video capabilities, speed, and resolution.

These characteristics combine to create a medium of unprecedented scope, depth, ubiquity, and reach. As we explore in some detail, the implications for electronic commerce are profound. As Table 1-2 shows, between 1998 and 2000, Internet use by AOL's users for commerce increased dramatically. Moreover, 80% of online users say they research products online before buying.

Although forecasts of the impact of electronic commerce on B2B transactions are controversial, most analysts expect the extent of B2B transactions to grow rapidly and significantly. For example, a study by Jupiter projected that the percentage of B2B commerce transacted electronically will grow from 3% to 42% in the United States in five years (see Table 1-3 for Jupiter's projections for several industries). A Boston Consulting Group study expects less dramatic—but still rapid—growth, with B2B electronic commerce in the United States growing from $1.2 trillion to $4.8 trillion between 2000 and 2004.[7]

Although we focus in this book on the impact of the Internet on electronic commerce and firm performance and strategy, its implications for economic development and global education may be even greater. Even for countries that have limited infrastructure, the ability of communities to access such a wealth of information potentially gives every village a fully stocked library. Add to that the ability to communicate at low cost and to access markets that were previously too costly to enter, and the potential for economic and educational advancement is enormous.

TABLE 1-2 Increase in Online Transactions by AOL Users, 1998–2000

Use	*1998*	*2000*
Shopping	31%	56%
Intending to shop online in future	14%	28%
Planning to increase online purchases	41%	49%
Banking	16%	25%
Trading stocks	11%	16%

Source: AOL study cited by CyberAtlas at http://cyberatlas.internet.com/big_picture/geographics/article/0,,5911_494701,00.html#table, December 1, 2000.

[7] CyberAtlas at http://cyberatlas.internet.com/markets/b2b/article/0,,10091_454041,00.html, December 2, 2000.

TABLE 1-3 Projected Growth in B2B Spending by Industry

Industry	*2000*	*2005*
Computer/Teleco Equipment	$90	$1,028
Food and Beverage	$35	$863
Motor Vehicles and Parts	$21	$660
Industrial Equipment and Supplies	$20	$556
Construction and Real Estate	$19	$528

Source: A Jupiter study cited by CyberAtlas at http://cyberatlas.internet.com/markets/b2b/article/0,,10091_475401,00.html, December 2, 2000.

ADVANCES IN COMPUTERS AND ENTERPRISE SYSTEMS

Although the emergence of the Internet and the WWW are the main technological developments that provide the platform for electronic commerce, those innovations owe much to advances in the computers on which they run. Moreover, as we shall discuss in more detail later, many of the potential advances in electronic commerce will leverage the enormous investments that firms have made in their enterprise systems over the past decades. Looking forward, the development of electronic commerce will also depend on advances in logistics and fulfillment, increases in bandwidth, and developments in and adoption of wireless technologies.

Advances in Computing

The most important factor facilitating the popularization of computing over the past two decades is the realization of Intel's Gordon Moore's prophesy that computing power would double every year or two. This staggering accomplishment of technological innovation, which has become known as "Moore's Law,"[8] implies that the same computing power that would have cost $1 million to produce in the early 1970s costs just over $30 three decades later. The fulfillment of Moore's Law has taken computing power out of the corporate glass house and put it, literally, in the palm of individual users' hands. It has made computers (both in the conventional sense and as microprocessors embedded in appliances) cheap and ubiquitous.

Although advances in microprocessors were at the heart of the personal computer revolution, other components have also seen considerable innovation. It is important to recognize here that the rate of technological progress across components was in part due to the reorganization of the computer industry, as Andy Grove of Intel has pointed

[8] See Haim Mendelson, "Moore's Law," at http://www.gsb.stanford.edu/CEBC/pdf/Moore'sLaw.pdf, September 17, 2000, for a chronicle of the development of Moore's Law. As Mendelson describes, in 1965 Moore first observed that in the prior six years, the number of components that engineers were able to fit on a chip had roughly doubled every year and predicted that this remarkable rate would continue. In 1975, with additional evidence from microprocessors, Moore revised his prediction to a doubling every two years, which has pretty much been borne out empirically.

out.[9] In the mainframe era, large vertically integrated firms produced (on their own or in close collaboration with suppliers with whom they had long-term relationships) all the components required to operate a computer, including the operating system and many of the applications.

Partly because of time-to-market pressures facing Apple's competitors (particularly IBM), the PC industry instead became organized into separate component "layers," for example, memory chips, microprocessors, disk drives, operating systems, applications, and distribution. Firms competed within each layer, producing components, so that a firm could assemble the components of any set of manufacturers to produce a final product. The key architectural feature that enabled this was the presence of *standardized interfaces* between each layer.

This organization of the industry had several virtues. First, a computer assembler could mix-and-match the best of each component rather than have to rely on its own in-house division to produce a quality product. Second, competition among component producers was intense because they all competed for the entire market rather than having a captive in-house buyer. This pressure kept component prices low. Third, and perhaps most important, technological innovation in each component was rapid because the reward for innovation was being first to the entire market.

We stress this feature of the organization of the personal computer industry here because this structure is an important indicator of the efficiencies that electronic commerce might bring to a variety of other markets. The essence of the change in the computer industry was that it became reorganized from a "vertical" structure in which large vertically integrated firms performed almost all of the functions required to produce a computer, to a "horizontal" structure in which specialists competed to produce components. For the change from a vertical to a horizontal organization of industry to be efficient, it must be relatively easy for firms to transact across firm boundaries and the countervailing efficiencies of internal coordination must not be too great.

These conditions are important to highlight because, as we will note later, they will often be met or enhanced by electronic commerce. Where these conditions are met, in circumstances that go well beyond the personal computer industry, it will sometimes be efficient for industries to adopt a horizontal organization. For that to happen, however, some firms must still "put the pieces together." We call such firms *vertical architects* because they provide the "glue" and organization for the supply chain.

Enterprise Resource Planning Systems

While the personal computer industry was coping with a new structure, the end-users of computer technology, and large enterprises in particular, were dealing with the new challenge of tying together disparate technological components and systems. The

[9] See Andrew S. Grove, *Only the Paranoid Survive* (New York: Doubleday, 1996), as well as interviews in *Fortune* ("How Intel Makes Spending Pay Off," February 22, 1993, pp. 56–61) and the *Wall Street Journal* ("Intel Plans to Consolidate Industry Lead with Salvo of Price Cuts," January 18, 1993, pp. B3 and B5).

tremendous advantages in the power and performance of mid-range comput had already led to significant decentralization of computing within corporat advent of the personal computer accelerated the centripetal forces, and firms migrate to "client-server" architectures. Accustomed to the ease-of-use and siveness of the personal computer, end-users in enterprises became frustrated difficulty of extracting crucial data from unwieldy mainframes. At the departmen level in firms, managers quickly realized that they could implement their own client-server systems cheaply and eliminate some of the dependency on the mainframes in the "glass house." At the same time most organizations, especially those that had very large databases or large transaction processing requirements, found they could not rid themselves of the mainframes.

Thus firms found themselves facing great information technology complexity. Although departments were happy with the stand-alone functionality of their systems, the data they contained were often either unavailable to other users in the firm or poorly integrated with other corporate databases. To deal with these problems, many corporations adopted large enterprise software applications to harmonize systems and make data more efficient to re-use (so that data used in several applications can be entered once and automatically re-used where appropriate). Later, improvements in networking, and especially the adoption of Internet and Web technology in internal corporate "intranets," enabled companies to further improve their internal systems.

Although most of the world's attention has been on the development of the Internet, the less flashy, methodical work of improving enterprise systems should not be underestimated in thinking about the technological platform for electronic commerce. Although electronic commerce opens up new frontiers for firms, to leverage the enormous strategic and operational assets that they bring to bear, large firms will need to tie their electronic commerce initiatives back into their enterprise systems. At the heart of these systems are the enterprise resource planning (ERP) systems that often include modules that cover everything from accounting and controlling, to production planning and materials management, to quality management, plant maintenance, and human resource and project management. (See the "ERP Overview" and "SAP and the Online Procurement Market" cases in Part II for detailed discussions of ERP systems.) Something as simple as an online procurement system must be tied into the ERP system to take advantage of synergies with the existing accounting and production planning systems.

Customer Relationship Management

More recently, firms have begun to turn their attention from the "back-end" enterprise systems to information technology that helps them serve their customers. By the late 1980s packaged software on the market was aimed at two different "front office" challenges. *Sales force automation* addressed functionality, such as managing marketing sales leads and customer contacts, generating proposals, and configuring products for price quotations. *Consumer service and support* was aimed at improving after-sale services like help desks, call centers, and field service operations.

These packages achieved their functionality by accessing and analyzing data from disparate databases within the company, drawing heavily on data already available in

ERP systems. As described in the Siebel Systems case in Part II, "a sales rep could direct an automated system to request all the records for customers in a particular city, which might be drawn from database X. Then she could view the purchase histories of those customers, the data for which might come from database Y. She could then analyze the profit from each customer, a task that would require additional data from database Z, plus various computations. The sales force automation application tied together these multiple, disparate databases and provided the rules and logic to perform the analysis."

By the mid-1990s firms had begun to merge the sales force automation and customer service and support segments into the overall category of customer relationship management (CRM) software. However, the segment still only had sales of around $200 million compared to $6.4 billion for ERP. In the second half of the 1990s, however, this market exploded and exceeded $5 billion by 2000.

The demands and increased functionality of the Internet and WWW fueled this meteoric growth in demand for CRM. One important factor in this is the fact that customers increasingly interact with the company in a multitude of ways—via the Web, through a call center, etc.—and the company needs a single view of that relationship so that any customer-facing employee has current information about all of the customer's interactions with it. Moreover, customers increasingly expect to be able to use the Web to serve themselves, drawing on information in the company's systems (for example, by downloading credit card purchases). Also, the points of contact between a firm and any business customer have potentially increased enormously. Finally, the amount of information about its customers that the firm can analyze so as to be able to customize its sales effort based on the attributes of each customer has also increased. These factors have helped to increase both demand for CRM systems and the range of functionality that they offer.

Electronic Data Interchange

While on the subject of existing systems that are important to understand before thinking about the likely impact of the Internet and Web on electronic commerce, we should not neglect to mention electronic data interchange (EDI). It is important to recognize that although the Internet provides a superior technology to what has heretofore been available, technology has been available for a long time to enable firms and their suppliers to coordinate electronically. In particular, they have used EDI to exchange electronic data over proprietary networks for decades. (See the QRS Corporation case in Part II for a discussion of the evolution of EDI.)

Now, to be sure, the WWW holds significant advantages over EDI: the fixed costs of adopting the WWW are lower, variable transaction costs are lower, it is easier to use, it is a more flexible and richer medium, and so on. Still, EDI is important for at least two reasons. The first is that companies have made large investments in implementing electronic interactions with suppliers and customers over EDI, and in some cases there is significant inertia resulting from those cumulative expenditures of time and effort. The second is that there is much to learn from the EDI experience about what kinds of electronic interactions among companies are likely to be adopted and the processes by which adoption might take place. We will have more to say about these issues later.

LOGISTICS AND FULFILLMENT

In addition to the infrastructure to deal with the "bits" part of electronic commerce that is inherited from prior systems, the evolution of electronic commerce—at least for that part of electronic commerce that deals with the manufacture and distribution of goods to consumers—will also be importantly affected by the infrastructure to deal with the movement of the "atoms."[10] The three main components of processing a customer's purchase (order processing, fulfillment, and shipping) account for around 13% (1.5%, 4%, and 7.5%, respectively) of the cost of an average order.[11]

Although catalog companies have performed these functions effectively for some time, electronic commerce companies have been struggling with them. For example, in attempting to purchase 480 gifts online, Andersen Consulting found that a quarter of the sites they accessed could not take an order.[12] Consumers found that they could not get accurate estimates of when items would be delivered, that items were not delivered when promised, and that it was often difficult to ask about order status. Moreover, customers return a much higher percentage of goods ordered online (estimates in advance of the 1999 holiday season were 12% for online orders versus 5–7% for catalog sales).[13] These issues have to be resolved because the volume of packages delivered to the home is likely to grow significantly. Forrester Research projects that the number of packages shipped to consumers daily will increase from 3 million in 1999 to 6.5 million in 2003 and that online orders will account for all of the growth while the number of parcel shipments from traditional channels (essentially catalogs) will stay steady at 2.3 million per day.[14]

Ordering and Fulfillment

The various elements of the process face different challenges. The front-end order processing, which includes the elements outlined in Table 1-4, has the least to inherit from existing systems and the steepest learning curve for both new and established firms. It is also, consequently, the area in which firms have the most potential to develop capabilities that might become significant sources of competitive advantage in the future. We shall say more about the ability of firms to differentiate from their rivals in this way in Chapter 2.

[10] This section draws extensively on "Electronic Commerce Logistics," Stanford Business School Case EC-3, by Ted Haynes under the supervision of Garth Saloner, January 14, 2000.

[11] *ibid.*

[12] Andersen Consulting press release (via NewsWire), December 21, 1999.

[13] The *Wall Street Journal*, December 31, 1999.

[14] The Forrester Report, Mastering Commerce Logistics, August 1999.

TABLE 1-4 Steps in Online Order Processing

- Capture the items and quantities desired (often requires "shopping cart" software).
- Apply promotional pricing or other terms, if applicable, and advise customer.
- Advise customer of items in or out of stock, and date of likely shipment.
- Check with suppliers if necessary.
- Obtain shipping and billing addresses (check/update customer record if old customer).
- Determine special requirements (gift wrap, enclosed card).
- Offer delivery options to customer and gain agreement to choices.
- Determine required delivery timing (standard or expedited).
- Determine acceptability of partial deliveries.
- Determine acceptability of back-ordering.
- Compute shipping and handling costs, plus any applicable taxes.
- Compute total cost to customer.
- Determine credit-worthiness and commitment to pay.
- Obtain credit card or debit card information from consumers.
- Advise customer if credit is rejected and solicit alternatives.
- Complete transaction and provide customer with order number.
- Clear transaction with credit card or debit card processor.
- Update inventory or ERP system.
- Deliver order to shipping or to fulfillment house.

In contrast, many traditional firms, especially catalog companies, have considerable experience in the next stage of the logistics process, fulfillment. (Table 1-5 describes fulfillment at one of these companies, Lands' End.) Fulfillment is either done in-house or outsourced. An estimated 70 third-party fulfillment companies served electronic commerce companies in 1999. Each had an average of nine customers with average revenues per customer of around $1 million.[15]

Whether firms do fulfillment themselves or outsource it depends on various factors, especially economies of scale and specialization. As Table 1-5 illustrates, running an efficient pick, pack, and ship operation can entail significant economies of scale. The fixed cost of building the necessary infrastructure can be spread as volumes increase. It is therefore not surprising that firms with established state-of-the-art facilities have become third-party fulfillment houses for others and that fulfillment houses have made major investments in sophisticated systems.

Economies of specialization are important because most firms regard fulfillment as a noncore activity. They prefer to concentrate on the distinctive parts of their business such as the interface to the customer, and outsource fulfillment to fulfillment specialists. This tendency is mitigated when customer service is a key element of the firm's competitive advantage and the firm believes that in-house control of fulfillment will give it the necessary flexibility and responsiveness.

As a result, there tends to be a U-shaped relationship between firm size and the likelihood of outsourcing. The largest firms can reap economies of scale with their own

[15] "e-Fulfillment: The Industry Behind the Button," Stephens Inc., Industry Report, November 15, 1999.

TABLE 1-5 Anatomy of an Electronic Commerce Order

Consider what happens on what retailers call the "back end"—the customer-fulfillment side—of Lands' End's operation. Say you go to the company's Web site one afternoon and order a blue 32-16 oxford-cloth button-down shirt and a pair of size-9 Top-Siders. At midnight, the computer at Lands' End combines your order with all of the other orders for the day: it lumps your shirt order with the hundred other orders, say, that came in for 32-16 blue oxford-cloth button-downs, and lumps your shoe order with the fifty other size-9 Top-Sider orders of the day. It then prints bar codes for every item, so each of these hundred shirts is assigned a sticker listing the location of blue oxford 32-16 shirts in the warehouse, the order that it belongs to, shipping information, and instructions for things like monogramming.

The next morning, someone known as a "picker" finds the hundred oxford-cloth shirts in that size, yours among them, and puts a sticker on each one, as does another picker in the shoe area with the fifty size-9 Top-Siders. Each piece of merchandise is placed on a yellow plastic tray along an extensive conveyer belt, and as the belt passes underneath a bar-code scanner the computer reads the label and assembles your order. The tray with your shirt on it circles the room until it is directly above a bin that has been temporarily assigned to you, and then tilts, sending the package sliding downward. Later, when your shoes come gliding along on the belt, the computer reads the bar code on the box and sends the shoe box tumbling into the same bin. Then the merchandise is packed and placed on another conveyer belt, and a bar-code scanner sorts the packages once again, sending the New York-bound packages to the New York-bound U.P.S. truck, the Detroit packages to the Detroit truck, and so on.

. . . Before the popularization of the bar code, in the early nineteen-eighties, Lands' End used what is called an "order picking" method. That meant that the picker got your ticket, then went to the shirt room and got your shirt, and the shoe room and got your shoes, and then put your order together. If another shirt-and-shoe order came over next, she would have to go back to the shirts and back to the shoes all over again. A good picker under the old system could pick between a hundred and fifty and a hundred and seventy-five pieces an hour. The new technique, known as "batch picking," is so much more efficient that a good picker can now retrieve between six hundred and seven hundred pieces an hour. Without bar codes, if you placed an order in mid-December, you'd be hard pressed to get it by Christmas . . .

. . . The head of operations for Lands' End is a genial man in his fifties named Phil Schaecher, who works out of a panelled office decorated with paintings of ducks which overlooks the warehouse floor. When asked what he would do if he had to choose between the two great innovations of the past twenty years—the bar code, which has transformed the back end of his business, and the Internet, which is transforming the front end—Schaecher paused, for what seemed a long time. "I'd take the Internet," he said finally, toeing the line all retailers follow these days. Then he smiled. "But of course if we lost bar codes I'd retire the next day."

Source: Excerpted from Malcolm Gladwell, "Clicks and Mortar," *The New Yorker*, December 6, 1999 (Available at http://www.gladwell.com/1999_12_06_a_clicks.htm.)

captive operations and therefore often do their own fulfillment, especially if it is integral to competitive advantage. For example, both of these considerations led Amazon.com and Webvan.com to in-house fulfillment. On the other hand, medium-sized firms are more likely to get better terms from a large fulfillment house that can achieve economies of scale that they cannot achieve on their own. Finally, the smallest firms tend to run simple pick, pack, and ship operations in-house because they are too small to justify the transaction costs of setting up a relationship with a third-party fulfillment house. Forrester recommends that firms shipping between 100 and 10,000 packages a day outsource, while firms below and above that range do fulfillment themselves.

Shipping

Both specialty fulfillment firms and those that do their own in-house fulfillment also need to decide on the number and locations of their fulfillment facilities. These decisions in turn are related to the nature of shipping costs. Ground shipping is the quintessential example where the economics of a hub-and-spoke system drive logistics. Simplistically stated, shipping costs are minimized when full, densely packed trucks are driven long distances. Since few manufacturers ship more than a few packages from one manufacturing facility to the same neighborhood, consolidating truckloads that are going in the same direction increases efficiency. These truckloads, each containing packages with a variety of destinations, converge at a hub. At the hub the truckloads are then broken down and reassembled into new truckloads, each again with a common destination. This process is repeated until the goods arrive at a depot close to their final destination where they are again consolidated for delivery (in vans rather than trucks) for particular neighborhoods.

In such a system, routing as many packages as possible in a coordinated fashion offers huge advantages. For example, if all the packages being shipped between two regions are shipped together, a single truckload could be shipped. In contrast, if 10 separate and uncoordinated shippers divide the load among them, one or more intermediate hubs (with an increase in handling costs) may be needed to achieve full truckloads.

An important implication of these basic observations about the economics of ground transportation is that the market for shipping goods to individuals is extremely concentrated. For example, in the United States where business-to-residence parcel delivery accounts for $5 billion in revenue[16] (in contrast to approximately $40 billion for intercity freight trucking to retailers), United Parcel Service (UPS) and the United States Postal Service (USPS) together account for about 90% of home deliveries. In many other countries the state-mandated postal service dominates this market, even where competition is allowed. One reason for this, of course, is that competing for the business of shipping a parcel between any two points against a firm that has an elaborate hub-and-spoke system and can ship full truckloads large distances, almost regardless of the points of origin and destination, is difficult.

Another reason is that the infrastructure (information technology, distribution centers, and trucks) required to reap these economies of scale is significant. For example, in the United States, UPS operates 29 package operating facilities, owns about 730 smaller operating facilities, and leases another 873. It maintains 51,000 letter drop boxes and provides service through 30,000 independently owned shipping locations. Its ground

[16] SJ Consulting Group, Inc. in *Air Cargo World*, March 1999.

fleet includes 149,000 delivery vehicles ranging from its familiar brown panel trucks to large tractor-trailers.

As a consequence, almost all firms engaged in electronic commerce use a third-party shipping company for at least part of their shipping needs. However, exactly how a firm ties into the third-party network depends on the volumes it ships and, if it is a firm with its own retail outlets, the nature of its retail and logistics networks. For example, a firm that has a large volume of shipments to consumers may find it more economical to do some of the long-haul stages itself, connecting to hubs of one of the major shipping companies at points somewhat closer to the customer. This is especially the case for firms that ship large volumes to regional distribution centers that feed their retail stores. Trucks carrying full loads can then drop part of their load at a corporate distribution center and part at a shipping company's depot.

The "Last Mile"

Although the anticipated growth is likely to affect all elements of shipping and logistics, getting the parcel from a local depot into the hands of the consumer is the area that faces the most significant challenges and the most innovation. Like the "last mile problem" involved in getting data to and from the home, this is in some respects the most difficult part of the process because delivering small numbers of parcels (often only one) to individuals located blocks or miles apart is inherently expensive. Indeed, the local delivery route accounted for 42% of the total cost of delivery to consumers versus only 17% for the long-distance transportation component.[17] Since these costs fall dramatically as the "stop density" (i.e., the number of end-customers receiving parcels per region) increases, this too is a highly concentrated segment of the business (see the Webvan.com case in Part II for details).

Another major problem is that often no one is at home to receive the parcel. In the United States, for example, between 9:00 A.M. and 5:00 P.M., some 70% of Americans are not at home to receive packages.[18] Leaving packages on doorsteps encourages theft, not only of the package, but also of the contents of the apparently unoccupied house, and redelivering increases costs. A recent survey of 600 homeowners indicates that their use of home delivery would go up 23% for prescriptions, 22% for groceries, 25% for dry cleaning, 21% for prepared meals, and 15% for alcoholic beverages if secure deliveries could be made when they were not at home.[19] Problems with home delivery are cited as one reason the catalog business has never grown to more than about 4% of total retail sales to consumers.

One approach to the problems of home delivery is to provide higher service levels. This is the approach that the grocery-delivery company, Webvan, took in the United States. Webvan offered extended hours of service and allowed customers to schedule their delivery times. It could offer this higher (and more expensive) level of service, because the revenue and margin per stop were significantly greater than for standard

[17] "Electronic Commerce Logistics," *ibid.*

[18] The *New York Times*, March 30, 1998.

[19] The *Wall Street Journal*, August 17, 1999.

parcel delivery. Although Webvan did not achieve the dollar volume per order and density of stops to sustain this approach, if it had been successful it could have leveraged its position by delivering packages for others as well. In addition, since most deliveries involve human contact, it could have been able to solve another difficult issue confronting home delivery, namely returns of items to the manufacturer.

A variety of other possible approaches to the home-delivery problem have been floated. One is to provide secure residential boxes in which parcels can be left (in the United States only the USPS can legally leave packages in home mailboxes). Most designs are expected to cost about $300. However, this solution works less well for apartments, especially in urban areas, that lack sufficient space.

Another possibility is to deliver parcels to the workplace. However, this adds significant cost and inconvenience for the employer and inserts a gap in the delivery cycle during which the consumer cannot track the package using the delivery company's tracking number. Moreover, bringing a package home from the office could be more bothersome than bringing it home from a store (e.g., when commuting via mass transit).

A variety of retail outlets seem to hold the potential for secure parcel pick-up. For example, oil and gas executives have pointed out that their customers might use the several minutes spent filling their gas tanks to pick up their parcels. Moreover, retailers like Wal-Mart that have an extensive logistics network of their own could offer parcel pick-up to leverage their logistics networks and draw customers repeatedly to their stores.

Most of these ideas are in their infancy, and for now the pre-existing carriers are picking up most of the incremental traffic. The number of parcels being delivered will probably have to increase significantly to change that.

SUMMARY

In this chapter we have examined some of the technologies that constitute the antecedents to electronic commerce. Since the future of electronic commerce is conditioned on its technological past and present, it is important to understand these building blocks before formulating an electronic commerce strategy. Foremost among these technologies, of course, is the Internet and WWW. However, changes and advances in the computer platforms on which they operate are just as important to the viability of electronic commerce. We also stressed the importance of leveraging existing enterprise systems, such as ERP systems, CRM software, procurement systems, and so on. Finally, for the distribution of goods, the infrastructure for moving the "atoms" is ultimately a driver or inhibitor of change.

Other current and future developments will also influence the evolution of electronic commerce. Chief among these are probably developments in broadband and wireless technologies. Especially for home and mobile users, the rate at which they can access the Web, and the relaxation of limits on where they can access it, will influence the utility of the Web in general and its use as a platform for electronic commerce in particular.

A detailed examination of these technologies is beyond the scope of this book. However, at the time of writing bandwidth seems to be about to increase dramatically, fall in price, and become ubiquitous. We realize there are many caveats to these general conclusions. For example, by fall 2000 only 11% of Internet connections in the United States were broadband connections. A major limiting factor in the diffusion of broadband is still the "last mile" problem: the time-consuming and costly task of connecting individual homes to the network. Still the penetration rate was almost double that of just six months earlier, and the number of households with high-speed access was expected to double again in a year.[20] Moreover, firms have invested significantly in adding capacity, so that prices are likely to continue to fall. Furthermore, advances in wireless technologies are likely to increase the share of broadband access via wireless technologies, and the rapid spread of handheld wireless devices is increasing the reach and utility of the Web.

In attempting to think about the likely evolution of electronic commerce, we should, therefore, think about scenarios in which users can access the WWW virtually anywhere at high speeds at virtually no cost. Although this nirvana is unlikely to be realized (at least soon), it is still useful to imagine what it will be like when almost any piece of information can be available to almost anyone almost anywhere because, directionally at least, that is where we are headed. And preliminary indications are that the quality of access matters a lot. For example, whereas the average American spends 33% of his or her time devoted to media in front of TV and only 11% accessing the Internet, in homes with broadband Internet access, the Internet's share is almost twice as high, at 21% (134 minutes a day).[21] These users are also much more likely to download and stream content from the Internet.

The technological changes discussed in this chapter have been made in a relatively short time, and the rate of change shows no sign of slowing. They set the stage for firms to create and capture a tremendous amount of value by leveraging these technologies in new and existing industries. We take up the issue of value creation in the next chapter.

[20] For details see http://cyberatlas.internet.com/markets/broadband/article/0,1323,10099_481071,00.html, November 21, 2000.

[21] *ibid.*

CHAPTER

2

CREATING VALUE: ECONOMICS OF INTERNET-BASED COMMERCE

The extraordinary attributes of the Internet described in the previous chapter provide many opportunities for firms to create value. Value is created whenever the value of a product or service to a consumer is greater than the cost of the resources used to produce it. In this chapter we focus on how the Internet, and electronic commerce in particular, enables firms to create value in ways that they could not create value before. These fall into three main categories: enhancing value to consumers; reducing costs; and improving the match between what consumers want and what is provided.

Value to consumers can be increased by improving existing products and services, by introducing new ones, or by providing consumers with information that enables them to make better decisions about what to buy or better appreciate what they do buy. Examples might be when a consumer is able to sample a music CD on the Internet before deciding whether to buy it or has access to others' reviews of items he or she is considering purchasing.

The cost of goods and services can be reduced when firms can manufacture them more efficiently or distribute them at lower cost. In practice, the latter, not the former, has accounted for most of the gains from cost reduction to date. For example, distributing music over the Web eliminates the cost of manufacturing a CD and of shipping and handling it, but does little to alter the cost of producing the music in the first place.

However, the largest gains come from improving the match between what consumers want and what they get. Most standard textbook discussions of supply and demand ignore the mechanisms that bring supply and demand into equilibrium. If a consumer is willing to pay $A for a product and the cost of producing it is $B, textbooks assume that the economic system will "somehow" ensure that the potential value of $(A–B) is realized.

In practice, however, many frictions impede the realization of this potential value. Consumers may not even know that a product exists for which they would have a high willingness to pay. And if they do, they may not know that there is a supplier who is able to supply it for less than they are willing to pay or where to find him or her. Or the costs of figuring all of that out and carrying out the transaction may be prohibitive. And, perhaps most frustrating, if they do locate a supplier who sells what they want for less than they would be willing to pay, they may well find that the supplier is out of stock.

These frictions include transaction costs involved in economic exchange and costs related to uncertainty. The latter costs arise from the difficulty of predicting who will want what and where and when they will want it, which inevitably results in consumers having to compromise in their choices. Although electronic commerce can create value by increasing willingness to pay or reducing manufacturing and distribution costs, it mostly creates value by reducing these frictions. Many of the successful business models that firms have implemented involve, at their core, understanding and removing impediments to the "somehow" by which the economic system is supposed to clear markets.

We begin by briefly considering value creation that arises from increasing value to consumers and reducing distribution costs. We then discuss how electronic commerce can eliminate or reduce transaction costs and how the Internet can lessen uncertainty and thereby reduce compromise.

CREATING VALUE TO CONSUMERS AND REDUCING DISTRIBUTION COSTS

The Internet and World Wide Web (WWW) can increase the value of goods and services to buyers, whether end-consumers or business buyers, in many ways.

• ***Product Information.*** What we know about something conditions what we are willing to pay for it. Increasing the quantity and quality of product and service information is one of the great strengths of the WWW. For example, consumers have ready access to reviews of products and services both by independent third-party evaluators and by previous purchasers. Most consumers with Internet access now use the Web to help buy automobiles, for example. In some cases, such as software, music, books, and videos, the consumer can also sample the product before purchase. Moreover, consumers can often compare products via product comparison engines.

• ***Personalization.*** As mentioned in the previous chapter, online distribution can increase consumers' willingness to pay because the Internet can *personalize* the content to the user's specific tastes. For example, a user can see news feeds about only the issues that interest him or her, thus increasing the value and the amount he or she might be willing to pay. In many cases a relatively small amount of demographic information (for example, age and location) can accurately predict which products and services are likely to interest a particular person. Past purchase histories (which tell a lot about taste) enable firms to make even more precise predictions. Coupled with other distribution economies described next, the potential exists to present a customer with a virtual store stocked only with items of interest to him or her and in relevant sizes.

• ***Customization.*** Whereas personalization filters available information so that the firm only presents information of interest to the consumer, customization makes it possible for the item itself to be tailored to the consumer's preferences. Customized personal computer assembly of the kind offered by Dell Computer is an example, but ultimately it may be possible for customization to extend to other areas such as cars (discussed in Chapter 4) or apparel (so far clothing produced "to fit" has met with limited success).

• ***Convenience.*** The convenience that asynchronous communication and/or automated fulfillment of customer queries affords, often translates into a far superior customer experience. Placing orders for stock trades or buying airline tickets without having to be connected to someone on the other end of a phone line are examples. It can also lower the costs of shopping, especially when the buyer knows, or can easily ascertain, what he or she wants to buy.

• ***Complementary services.*** Providing online services that are complementary to the product, such as online instruction manuals and other assistance tools and support, can enhance the value of physical products. In the case of software, the value of applications is enhanced by the availability of online upgrades. Another example is running shoes, which are surprisingly complex products. Matching running shoes to the runner's needs, running style, and physique is difficult and the cost of a mismatch in terms of potential physical injury is high. Moreover, few salespeople know enough to ensure a good match. In these and many other cases, a centralized online repository can provide superior product information.

As is evident from this list, providing superior information and channels about existing products and services rather than changing the goods and services themselves accounts so far for most of the increase in value to consumers. Similarly, on the cost side, most of the increase in value comes from how those goods and services reach us.

For goods and services that can be delivered over the Internet—many financial services, music, software, and so on—there are obvious cost savings in distribution. However, electronic commerce can also reduce distribution cost savings for goods that cannot be delivered electronically. At first blush this seems surprising given the enormous economies of scale in fulfillment and shipping discussed in the prior chapter. It is surely less expensive to distribute full boxes of goods to the store than to ship those same items to end-consumers one or two at a time. Yet it turns out that shipping direct can actually be less expensive for many items, especially if the consumer already knows what he or she wants (or can easily figure it out).

One obvious reason is that the consumer is spared the cost (in time and transportation) of picking up the good at the store. However, that alone does not balance the efficiencies of mass distribution. Rather, the main reason is that there are many costs of distribution through the store that can be avoided through direct delivery. These include the reduction of handling within the store (unpacking, stocking, and maintaining shelves), theft (which can account for 3% of a retailer's sales), rent (low-cost distribution centers replace expensive urban or suburban real estate), and selling costs (automated and telesales replace relatively expensive in-store salespeople). (See the cases on The Gap and Nike.com for details.) In addition, in the United States (for the moment anyway) online purchases often avoid sales taxes.

Although most of the cost savings are in distribution, important cost savings can be obtained in services for which specific functions can be parceled out for execution to locations that are less expensive or have a time zone advantage, for example, handing off code in software projects to engineers in India at the end of a business day in the United States. However, the possibilities extend to other business functions. For example, Sun Microsystems set up a site that enables programmers to bid on fixing customers' software problems, and many low-skilled, labor-intensive tasks tend to flow to regions with low labor costs.

INCREASING MARKET EFFICIENCY BY REDUCING TRANSACTIONS COSTS

We turn now to the value that the efficiencies from electronic commerce create not by altering either the attributes of the products or services or how firms produce then, but by making market exchange function more effectively.

In offline transactions we pretty much take for granted our ability to buy and sell what we want. However, the ease of transacting is possible only because our institutions (legal, organizational, and reputational) have evolved to eliminate many potential impediments. Conversely, to the extent that transacting is difficult, we largely take that for granted too. We have become used to the limitations that our institutions place on us.

Because it is in its infancy, electronic commerce is still developing the institutions to support it. However, because it is built on such radically different technology, it also can sweep aside many of the impediments to transacting that have previously encumbered us.

Because we take so much of what is necessary to transact for granted, it is useful to break out some of the main steps that must be accomplished for efficient transacting to take place (as we have done in Table 2-1). This table also highlights some of the areas in which transaction costs can be eliminated through the use of improved technology and where the institutions that support electronic commerce need to improve as the medium matures. Although these steps differ depending on whether the transaction is business-to-business (B2B) or business-to-consumer (B2C), in this chapter we discuss them at a general level. We drill down into some particular features of B2B transactions in Chapter 4.

The sections that follow discuss how electronic commerce eliminates or reduces impediments to the frictionless completion of these steps and raises new impediments, at least during its adolescence.

Increasing Product Awareness

The first potential impediment to realizing value is that consumers may be unaware in the first place that there are products and services available that they might value highly. Internet information technology has great potential to make this information

TABLE 2-1 Steps in Transacting

- Buyers (either end-consumers or downstream firms) must decide what they want to buy, and sellers must decide to whom they would like to sell.
- Buyers must identify low-cost suppliers.
- Buyers must "qualify" those suppliers, that is, validate that they have the ability to produce goods or services of the appropriate quality in the appropriate quantities in a timely manner.
- Buyers and suppliers may have to make investments in processes or even in plant and equipment to enable or facilitate trade between them.
- The mechanics of transacting (ordering, paying, etc.) must take place.
- Routines and policies must be established for after-sales service and support.

available because of the relative ease of using histories of prior consumer purchase behavior and of linking electronic data that reside in different databases. It does not take much knowledge of demographic information and preferences—as revealed through prior purchase decisions—for firms to be able to make pretty good predictions about what consumers might like. Of course, the undesirable consequences of direct marketing are also likely to grow, although the ratio of desired to undesired unsolicited offers might increase. And, as mentioned earlier, for consumers who want to investigate a product or product class in more depth, the Web provides a wealth of information and tools.

Matching Buyers and Sellers

A potentially willing buyer and seller must first find one another before a trade can take place. Here the reach of the Internet makes it different and superior to anything that preceded it. Put somewhat simplistically, for the most part electronic data interchange (EDI), for example, enables firms that have already identified potential trading partners through other means to connect with one another to carry out electronic transactions, but does little to help them find one another in the first place. In contrast, because of the ease of establishing a presence on the Web and for searching for the presence of others, the Web is far better suited to bringing parties together. Of course, many intermediaries seek to make this even easier by aggregating potential partners in one place and facilitating trade among them.

The enormous outpouring of used consumer durables onto the market and into the hands of willing buyers through eBay is ample testament to the power of this phenomenon (see the Online Auctions case in Part II for more on eBay). Tremendous value is unleashed when a consumer with a high willingness to pay for an item that is wasting away unused in someone's closet is matched with that item. Value is created because a buyer in California, say, can be matched with a seller in Singapore. Thus, at first blush anyway, the value seems to be that the seller's geographic scope is increased. However, the key underlying attribute of the Internet and WWW that is so powerful here is their ability to provide a universally accessible, content-rich, searchable repository of product information and availability.

The impediment before was not that the buyer and seller couldn't have dealt with the mechanics of the transaction (i.e., payment and shipping), but that it was prohibitively costly for the seller to make the availability of the item known to buyers all over the world, or for the buyer to seek out sellers all over the world. The networked nature of the Web makes the information available from anywhere; powerful search tools allow the buyer to select a product from millions of listings, and richness gives the buyer access to much more information than most competitive media (e.g., classified advertisements). Of course sites like eBay add centralization to the mix, so that the buyer need access only a few sites, but the WWW itself (coupled with search) solves most of the problem.[1]

Although eBay represents the most striking example of this phenomenon involving person-to-person transactions, the efficient matching of buyers and sellers for B2B transactions can unleash even more value. Transactions between corporations are often long-term ones, and the transactions that occur at any point in time are similar to those that have occurred before. Those kinds of transactions might seem to offer little potential for gain because buyers and sellers are already well matched. However, in many B2B transactions what is desired or available changes so much that matching is very important. For example, as fashions and seasons change it is difficult for apparel retailers to predict precisely what will sell. Consequently they routinely sell out of some "hot" items and have excess of others. The broad reach of the Internet can help them find potential suppliers who can replenish the items in short supply and buyers who will take the surplus off their hands on reasonable terms (see the Tradeweave case for a discussion of these issues).

The Web can also facilitate the emergence of new intermediaries that bring willing buyers and sellers together. For example, iMotors.com provides a site where buyers can order a used car (at a fixed price), and iMotors, through a network of geographically dispersed procurement agents, finds a car that meets those specifications, which it then refurbishes and delivers to the buyer. The unique functionality provided by the Web that enables this kind of intermediation is the ability for buyers to demonstrate their "willingness to pay" before anyone has identified a specific item for sale. Whereas most traditional offline markets clear by having consumers choose from a menu of available items, here the process is turned on its head by registering the willingness to buy first. "Reverse auctions" such as those Priceline.com offers (discussed in the next chapter) that allow sellers to bid for the right to supply a demonstrated consumer desire are an elaboration of this concept (see the Pricing and Branding case for a discussion of Priceline.com).

The Web can also sometimes make it possible to avoid the costs involved in physically bringing buyers and sellers together. An example is the approach to B2B used car sales taken by Autodaq.com. Since a dealer who acquires a used car as a trade-in or when a leased car is returned is usually not the most appropriate dealer to resell it, at least in the United States, most cars are resold on the wholesale market. The standard way of accomplishing this is to physically transport the cars to an auction house

[1] Auction aggregators like AuctionWatch.com add even more centralization by enabling participants to view multiple auction sites in one place.

where dealers, who have often traveled a long way, bid on them. The acquiring dealer must then transport the cars for resale to consumers.

Autodaq instead enables a dealer to make a used car available to other dealers on the Web. Independent appraisers assess the car's value, and, exploiting the richness of the Web, a great deal of information about it (including appearance) can be made available to possible buyers. In addition to potentially reaching many more buyers than a single auction could, this method lowers transactions costs by reducing transportation (the car is shipped once rather than twice) and by saving buyers the costs in time and transportation of attending an auction.

Authenticating and "Qualifying" Buyers and Sellers

Another step in the purchase process that can involve significant transactions costs is ensuring the legitimacy and reliability of the party with whom one is transacting. Many offline B2C transactions are "spot" transactions in which goods are exchanged for cash at the time of the transaction. In those settings consumers' risks are limited by the fact that they take possession of the item at the time of the transaction and they are at risk only for after-sales service performance, warranties, and so on. In others, such as when items must be made-to-order, risks of performance on both sides of the transaction are introduced.

In online settings the risks are particularly high because there is typically a delay between the time the good is ordered and when it is received and because so many vendors are new that they do not have established reputations for quality of service, time to delivery, returns policy, and so on. In B2C settings, the fact that credit card companies can be called on to help settle disputes has been an important factor in emboldening consumers to try relatively unknown online vendors. But while this has facilitated trade, it merely shifts the transactions costs associated with online fraud to the financial intermediaries (who, to be sure, are better equipped to deal with it). Nor does it eliminate the costs of underperformance (late shipments, supplying the wrong item, etc.) or the costs that customers must bear in dealing with those problems (for example, trying to rectify an incorrect order with a vendor that lacks the call center capacity to respond adequately).

To help fill the informational and reputational void that gives rise to these transaction costs, intermediaries have arisen to provide independent certification of merchants. Third-party certifiers like Gómez or intermediaries like AOL certify that merchants meet particular standards or rate their performance. Criteria include how quickly merchants respond to e-mail, whether they monitor out-of-stock products and can report on it when a customer places an order, how quickly merchants process orders, whether and how quickly they confirm orders, conditions of delivery, returns, and so on.

Also, as we discuss in more detail in the next chapter, brand has emerged as an important guarantor of reliability. Customers can assume that a nascent Internet supplier would not risk tarnishing a good reputation that it has worked hard to establish. It thus serves as a "bond" that the vendor posts. Similarly, and quite surprisingly to many observers given its somewhat informal nature, the online reputation mechanisms of the kind supported by eBay have proven quite successful in authenticating buyers and sellers for the same reason. In B2C commerce, the Web has matured more rapidly than many commentators expected. The combination of reputation, brand, third-party certification, and the elimination of many marginal suppliers in the shake-out have increased consumers' confidence in purchasing online. And, of course, the share of online sales that traditional stores account for is increasing, and their established offline reputations carry over to their online operations.

B2B settings introduce additional complexity because orders are large and the failure of one supplier can jeopardize an entire manufacturing operation. Consequently not only is it even more important to be able to ensure that a supplier is legitimate, but it is necessary to ensure that the supplier is qualified, that is, their customers can rely on them to produce quality goods on time. The cost of doing this often restricts the set of suppliers with whom a buyer will deal.

In the near term, firms like Freemarkets.com are streamlining the process by which suppliers can respond to requests for quotations (RFQs) by buyers (see the Online Auctions case for details). Although this lowers the costs of issuing and processing an RFQ, it does not significantly alter the process of qualifying suppliers. In the longer term it is conceivable that if these processes become sufficiently standardized, online reputation mechanisms may arise to help with the qualification process as well.

Comparing Prices

Shop bots and other automated price comparison engines reduce the cost of comparison shopping among online sellers (see the Pricing and Branding case for a discussion of mySimon). Even for products that price comparison engines do not cover well, a price comparison is just a few clicks away. Moreover, even when consumers consummate transactions at a traditional offline store, the ability to use the Internet for comparison shopping still reduces transactions costs. Knowing the available range of prices on the Internet is often a good substitute for visiting a second store to compare prices.

Making Investments to Facilitate Trade

Especially in B2B settings, firms often need to make relationship-specific investments that are somewhat idiosyncratic to their relationship. However, once firms have made investments that tie them (at least partially) to one another, either one can potentially take advantage of the other. In the offline world, inefficiencies that creep into the relationship because of this constitute one of the most important sources of transactions costs that impede transactions across firm boundaries.

A classic—if somewhat remote—example of this in a traditional setting is when a coal-fired electric power plant is located in close proximity to a coal mine to take advantage of low transportation costs from co-location. A problem arises, however, if the power plant and the mine have separate ownership, because once they are co-located the power plant owner has an incentive to lower the price he or she is willing to pay for the coal and the mine owner has an incentive to raise the price he or she charges. In extreme circumstances, fear of such *ex post* exploitation may make one or both unwilling to make the investment to get its operation going in the first place. In this particular setting it usually requires a long-term contract or vertical integration (in which the same firm owns both operations) to overcome such difficulties. In other settings, however, fears are resolved by establishing long-term relationships or, especially in B2C settings, by relying on reputations.

Electronic commerce is unlikely to ameliorate these transaction costs, except at the margin. There is little the Internet can do about the co-location problem of a mine and power plant. In a few cases, however, such as when buyers and suppliers must invest in compatible inventory management systems that give each visibility into the needs of the other, instituting industry-wide standards for exchanging electronic information can eliminate the potential *ex post* hold up problem. We discuss this issue further in Chapter 4 (see also the Online Auctions and E-Markets 2000 cases).

The Mechanics of Purchasing

There are significant potential cost savings in the actual process of making a purchase online in both B2C and B2B transactions. In some B2C transactions, for example, inexpensive asynchronous electronic communication can replace costly synchronous telephone transactions (e.g., how many hours of telephone "hold time" will communication via the Internet save?).

In the B2B realm electronic transactions can replace paper ones. The manual costs of processing paper transactions are high, and most orders involve several kinds of information flows. For example, a buyer must typically send a purchase order to the supplier to initiate the transaction; the supplier often sends an advance ship notice to notify the customer that the goods are on their way; both sides must update inventories; and the supplier must generate a bill that the customer has to pay. Automating these processes can lead to considerable savings, especially when they are integrated with existing ERP systems (estimates are that replacing a paper order with an electronic one can save $50 *per transaction*, or even two or three times that). The potential for reducing these fairly mundane transactions costs has been a big impetus for online procurement and electronic markets (see the SAP and the Online-Procurement Market and E-Markets 2000 cases).

After-Sales Service and Support

The final step in transacting in which impediments can arise is dealing with problems that come up after purchase: for example, returns and after-sales service. Offline channels usually hold an edge in this regard, although as we discuss in more detail in Chapter 4, online merchants who have an offline presence (either their own stores or a relationship with an offline merchant) can ameliorate this deficiency. For example, J Crew and The Gap handle online returns at their offline outlets.

Implications and Firm Scope

Reducing transactions costs, especially by making it easier for buyers and sellers to find one another, is the main way in which electronic commerce will create value. However, while the institutions for transacting on the Web are maturing rapidly, they are still not equal to those offline.

Reduced transactions costs will not just affect the ease of transacting, but will affect the scope of the firm itself. As economist Ronald Coase has pointed out, a firm's boundaries are determined in part by whether particular transactions can be carried out at lower cost within the firm or between the firm and another. To the extent that electronic commerce can reduce the costs of transactions between firms, firms may elect to outsource functions that they previously did in-house. For example, if firms can find, qualify, and transact with specialists at low cost, they will choose to do so and instead will focus on doing in-house only what they are particularly good at. Lower costs and more effective cross-boundary transactions could lead to smaller, more focused firms, such as occurred when the personal computer industry was reorganized along horizontal lines, a process we described in Chapter 1.

In some cases there may also be a vertical architect that coordinates the activities of firms, each performing a separate function in the supply chain. Benetton is a spectacular example of a firm that coordinates a supply chain that includes every step in the manufacture and distribution of its clothes, all the way from styling and sourcing of materials through the operation of the retail stores. Yet, although Benetton coordinates all of these steps, it actually performs very few of them in-house. Apart from dyeing (which is a core capability necessary to produce the hallmark Benneton colors), running a very large automated distribution center in Italy, and ensuring that designs embody the Benetton "look," Benetton owns none of the many firms that form its supply chain. For example, it outsources manufacture; independent agents do sales; and most stores are independent franchises. Benetton mostly serves as a vertical architect, coordinating the functioning of the rest of the chain.

This form of supply chain governance enables the vertical architect to focus on what it is good at and select input suppliers that are best of breed for each of the other steps. In an increasingly global market, a horizontal market structure enables the vertical architect to choose suppliers for each part of the supply chain from those regions that specialize in them and where factor costs are the lowest. To the extent that electronic transactions can further reduce those frictions, it is possible to envisage vertical architects with tremendous geographic scope moving production to the most efficient provider of each component while maintaining a well-functioning and coordinated chain.

Of course we don't want to overstate the ease with which firms can switch among suppliers since, as we have already argued, there are often relationship-specific factors that tie firms together. Moreover, while transactions costs *between* firms are falling, they are also falling *within* firms thanks to the very same technologies. Nonetheless, the effect on interfirm transactions will often be greater than intrafirm ones, and supply chain improvements are likely to involve both the efficiency of the firms in them and their scope.

CREATING VALUE BY REDUCING COMPROMISE

Whether online or offline, any system for facilitating the purchase and sale of goods and services has to deal with uncertainty. Given that most consumer goods must be manufactured well in advance of their purchase, uncertainty about future demand inevitably leads to a mismatch between what consumers want and what is available. By the time the consumer goes shopping, even if she knows exactly what product and service attributes are potentially available and precisely which ones she would choose given her preferences and the prevailing prices, too often she has to compromise on the attributes of the products she purchases.

This occurs, for example, when a consumer leaves a store with a red item when he would have preferred blue, or a large when a medium would have been more appropriate, or simply leaves the store empty-handed when another store in the chain has exactly the item he wants. The problem in this case is not that the consumer doesn't know what he wants, or that it isn't possible for the vendor to provide it, but that the costs of ensuring a perfect match are so high that the consumer has to compromise or buy nothing. Although it is difficult to measure the costs of this misallocation of resources, they are undoubtedly very large.

The Web can do a better job of matching preferences to products because online stores benefit from enormous economies of centralized inventories. As an example, consider a company like The Gap that has close to 2,000 stores in the United States alone and that carries shirts in many styles, colors, and sizes (and in the case of men's trousers has both waist and length sizes). Since the cost of ensuring that demand can be met in every store for every item is prohibitive, a certain amount of customer disappointment is inevitable. Moreover, the cost of ensuring enough (albeit imperfect) inventories to meet an acceptable level of "stock outs" is high. In contrast, it is much less costly for an online operation to make a given level of product available because it aggregates the purchases for a large region at a centralized distribution center rather than on a store-by-store basis.

The reason for this is that there are enormous statistical economies of scale in centralizing inventories. This phenomenon is, of course, not new to online distribution and is well documented and has been extensively studied in the operations management literature on inventory policy. The canonical version of this problem is the "newsvendor" problem and relates to the question of how many newspapers should be delivered to each of a number of geographically distributed newsvendors.

The trade-off involved in making this decision is that sales are lost if demand exceeds the available newspapers at any location, whereas if the reverse is true, the newspapers are wasted. The benefit to carrying an extra newspaper is the probability the paper will be sold multiplied by the value of the sale (which includes avoiding ill-will from being out of stock). The cost is the expense of producing an extra paper (which has no value if it isn't sold). The "solution" in this simple case is to increase the inventory as long as the probability of an additional sale exceeds the ratio of the cost of the extra unit to the value of an extra sale.[2]

From our point of view, what is interesting is not the optimal inventory level for an individual newsvendor, but rather what would happen if it suddenly became possi-

[2] See Harold Bierman, Charles P. Bonini, and Warren H. Hausman, *Quantitative Methods for Business Decision* (Homewood, Ill: Irwin), 1986, for a more general treatment. If the probability of an additional sale is p, the value of a sale is V, and the cost of having an additional unit on hand is C, it pays to have the extra unit as long as $pV > C$, or $p > C/V$.

ble to quickly distribute the newspapers to each newsvendor from a central warehouse. The inventory problem is similar because the central warehouse would also increase inventory as long as the probability of an additional sale multiplied by the value of the sale exceeded the cost of producing an extra paper. What is different, however, is that the probability of an additional sale is now the probability of an additional sale *at any of the vendors* not just one of them. A marginal unit of inventory is much more valuable because it can be applied to randomly high demand in any of a number of different newsvendors' locations rather than just one.

To see how this logic plays out in a firm with multiple stores, consider the simple example of two potential buyers for a particular item at any store, each of whom has a 50-50 chance of wanting the item in any particular week. The chance that there will be demand for zero items is 25%; for one item, it is 50%; and for two items, it is 25%.[3] Any store therefore has a choice of a number of inventory policies. If it carries only one item in the store (and cannot replenish it within the week), it has a 25% chance of missing a sale. Alternatively it can carry two items and never miss a sale, but have a 75% chance it will carry one item on its shelves unsold for the week and a 25% chance it will carry two. Suppose that the value of selling an item is $30 and the cost of having it available for sale but not selling it is $10. It is easy to show that under these circumstances a store will choose to carry one item (see the footnote for details).[4] Since the firm faces the same problem at each of its stores, a firm that has two stores carries two units of inventory (one in each store), and its expected revenue in each store is $15 (a 50% probability of a sale yielding $30) and its expected profit in each store is $5 (the $15 expected revenue minus the $10 cost).

Now suppose instead that an online store serves the same region. Using the same logic, Table 2-2 shows the distribution of demand. An online store that has two units of inventory on hand at the beginning of the period (the equivalent of the two separate stores in the example), will sell two items if there is aggregate demand for two or more items.[5] Table 2-2 shows that it should now expect to sell two items with probability 3/8 + 1/4 + 1/16 (that is, the probability that two, three, or four items are demanded) and one item with probability 1/4. Its expected revenue is therefore (3/8 + 1/4 + 1/16) × 60 + 1/4 × 30 = $48.75 and its expected profit is $28.75. Holding inventory at the same levels as the separate stores, sales increase by 62.5% and profits by 287.5%!

When there is demand for two units at one location and none at the other, the centralized online store with two units of inventory can satisfy demand for both, but geographically distinct stores carrying one unit each bear the same inventory costs

[3] There are four equally likely outcomes: Buyer 1 wants the item and buyer 2 does not; 2 does and 1 does not; both do; neither does.

[4] If it carries one item, the probability of a sale is 50%, so its expected revenue is $15, which exceeds its cost of $10. The probability of a second sale is 25%, so its expected revenue from carrying a second unit is $7.50, which is less than the cost of $10.

[5] In fact it is easy to see that optimal policy is to carry two units of inventory. If it were to carry a third unit of inventory, the probability of a sale would be the probability that there was demand for three or four units. From the table this is equal to 1/4 + 1/16 = 5/16. The expected revenue from that is $150/16, which is less than the additional cost of $10. (Conversely it is easy to see that carrying two units of inventory is better than carrying just one.)

TABLE 2-2 Demand Across Two Stores

Number of Items	*Probability of Demand*
0	1/16
1	1/4
2	3/8
3	1/4
4	1/16

but sell only one unit. Although there are many particular assumptions in this example that one can take objection to (for example, no cross-store transfers are possible), the effect in general is quite robust. Statistical averaging allows centralized distribution to deal more effectively with local fluctuations in demand than local distribution can. The effect is even stronger with more stores because the centralized inventories can be applied to even more local demand variations.

This effect is particularly compelling for products such as books and music CDs. In most bookstores many items—perhaps even half—do not even sell once a year on average. Demand for low-selling books is uncertain, and bookstores must carry many books to stock the one that the customer wants. For such low-demand items, the gains from centralized inventories are enormous. It makes more sense for a central repository to hold a few copies of those rarely demanded books than for thousands of bookstores around the country to each hold enough to meet random local demand.

Of course, there are many more books that local booksellers do not carry at all because the chance they will be demanded is even lower. Again a centralized online store will have incentive to carry a much broader range. This effect holds for any product for which there is a large range, for many of which demand is sporadic. The effect is even greater for more expensive items (like consumer electronics) where the inventory carrying costs are higher, both because the items are more expensive and because the costs of obsolescence are higher. The result is that stores carrying those items carry many fewer stock-keeping units (SKUs).

Exploiting these economies of centralized inventories presupposes that buyers already know the menu or can easily ascertain what they want from an electronically provided menu. This is probably a reasonable assumption for most books and CDs (especially since samples and previews can influence the purchase decision). However it is a dubious assumption when fit, touch, sound quality, and so on are issues. Even then, however, hybrids in which stores function like a showroom, albeit with limited range, coupled with an online delivery capability can offer great gains.

For items like clothing where the number of SKUs is so high because of variations in size and color, a showroom could have an item in each size and color, but not necessarily each combination of size and color. By ensuring that it has at least one of each size and color, the store can enable a shopper to select the appropriate product, which he or she can get fulfilled online (either from a kiosk within the store or from home). If consumers are willing to accept delayed fulfillment (potentially at a significant cost saving), stores—serving mainly as showrooms—can carry smaller inventories of each item and broader ranges of items. As stores adapt to such a model, they are likely to alter their rules both for inventory and product breadth decisions. Of course, they will often do this only at the margin, for example, carrying fewer colors in sizes that sell in low volumes, rather than moving to a complete showroom model.

As with many other changes that electronic commerce affects, stores were already moving toward a hybrid model. After all, many stores were willing to order an out-of-stock item from a central warehouse or call around to neighboring stores. Moreover, some were setting up electronic repositories of store-by-store inventory data accessible to all salespeople. However, increased functionality of the new technologies, increasing customer acceptance of electronic ordering, and growth in home delivery infrastructure have accelerated this trend.

Another important technological development is the rapid reduction in costs and improvements in performance of radio frequency identification technology. A low-cost radio frequency emitter on an article's tag can, in essence, tell the system where the article is. These technological trends are likely to create a considerable amount of value as consumers have to compromise less and vendors can get the most out of every item of inventory, regardless of where it is located.

SUMMARY

Electronic commerce holds the promise of adding significantly to the creation of value. As a repository and channel of information, it will make consumers much more knowledgeable about what goods and services are available and enable them to evaluate them better. This is a crucial first step because the target audience has to appreciate the value of a product or service to unleash the potential value it can provide. Reducing the cost at which firms can place the desired goods and services in consumers' hands can also create value. So far most of these savings have come from distribution and not from manufacturing.

However, by far the most important area in which electronic commerce will create value is in reducing transactions costs involved in bringing buyers and sellers together. In reducing these transactions costs, in its emergent stage, electronic commerce on the Web has had to confront many of the impediments to transacting that we have long taken for granted in the offline world and to develop institutions, experience, and reputation to deal with them. As the Web matures, it is providing a more robust platform for market exchange, and firms that do not have, or cannot develop, the infrastructure and systems to keep pace are falling by the wayside. In contrast, firms that have already developed that infrastructure or bring with them reputations and consumer trust from their offline operations, are strongly positioned to compete in a mature exchange environment.

Another important area is improving the match between what consumers want and what they can get, so that consumers have to compromise less. In this regard we are in an awkward transition, with the "old" distributed inventory system in offline stores competing with a "new" centralized inventory management system in online stores, while some hybrid systems try to marry the two. In the short term, some outcomes may actually be worse than in the pre-Internet era. Some online stores do not have enough expected sales to carry efficient levels of stock both because they are currently in competition with too many other online stores and because of competition from offline stores, and some offline stores will carry lower levels of inventory, expecting to lose sales to online stores. In the longer term, however, as inefficient online stores exit, as online and offline firms find the right balance, and as hybrid stores mature, "out of stock" occurrences and compromise are likely to decline significantly.

Consumers will be tremendous beneficiaries of electronic commerce as much of the value created ends up being captured by them. They will have the information to make better choices about their purchases and investments, will be able to make those decisions and transactions at much lower cost, and will have to compromise much less in their choices.

CHAPTER

3

CAPTURING VALUE: MARKET STRUCTURE AND COMPETITION

For the general manager engaged in electronic commerce, the value the firm can *capture* is at least as important as the value it can *create*. Although many factors determine how much value a firm can capture, among the most important is the degree of competition among the firms in the industry or market segment in question. For example, highly competitive industries tend to compete so vigorously that downstream buyers largely capture the value that is created.

The degree of competition, in turn, depends largely on the structure of the industry; in particular, the number and size distribution of firms. Industries with many similar competitors tend to be more competitive than those with a few large firms, especially if the latter pursue different strategies. Although the structure of the industry or market segment in which the firm competes is important (that is, the horizontal structure of the industry, alluded to previously), the vertical organization of industry also matters. Powerful upstream suppliers or downstream buyers will capture value even if the horizontal structure of the industry is otherwise conducive to capturing value. In this chapter we examine how horizontal market structure and competition affect capturing value. We discuss the vertical organization of industry in the next chapter.

First we examine factors that mold market structure in electronic commerce markets. Many of these are the same factors that structure conventional offline markets. Others, however, concern so-called demand-side increasing returns (DSIR). Although these also affect many offline markets, especially telecommunications and computers, they are particularly prevalent and important in electronic commerce, and we discuss them in the subsequent section.

Market structure is only one factor that determines how vigorous competition is, however. The way that firms behave is itself an important determinant of their profitability. We discuss competition, strategy, and pricing before concluding the chapter.

"CONVENTIONAL" DETERMINANTS OF MARKET STRUCTURE

In considering market structure we are interested in a variety of factors: the number of firms in the industry, their size distribution, and the nature of their respective strategies. Several factors determine offline market structures, many of which continue to be relevant in online markets, although the nature of these factors and their relative importance may be different.

One of the main factors that drives traditional analyses of the determinants of market structure involves comparing the size that a firm must be to compete efficiently to the overall size of the market in which it competes. Roughly speaking, absent other barriers to entry, we would expect to see no more firms in an industry than the number that can operate at efficient scale. If the industry has more than that number, a subset of the firms currently in it could operate at lower cost than the average firm in the industry, and competition should encourage some firms to grow and force others to shrink and eventually exit. Conversely, if the industry has so few firms that a new firm could enter it and by stealing share from the incumbents reach a scale that makes it no less efficient than the others, the drive for profitably should lead to more entry (absent other entry barriers).

Thus factors relating to increasing returns help determine market structure. All else the same, factors that give larger firms a cost advantage will lead to those markets having fewer, larger firms. To the extent that, at least for a while, electronic commerce is likely to involve mainly distribution, the relevant increasing returns are those that relate to distribution rather than manufacturing. Three aspects of distribution have the potential for increasing returns. The first involves the design and development of the Web site itself. A second concerns the infrastructure of the ordering process (including call centers, payment processing, and so on). A third encompasses functions related to getting the product to the customer, including fulfillment and logistics.

What is most notable about increasing returns originating from the fixed costs of establishing a business and developing a Web site is how small they are relative to the fixed costs of entering and establishing most traditional businesses. For many fledgling electronic commerce companies, first-year start-up costs are in the relatively low \$10–15 million range. Moreover, many firms need not build a complete in-house engineering team because they can outsource the Web development to a specialist firm. They can also outsource many of the functions relating to order processing, fulfillment, and logistics. In other cases, at least in the start-up phase, these functions are fairly rudimentary, and the firms can manage them in-house at fairly small scale without suffering significant cost disadvantages (see the E-Commerce Building Blocks case for details.)

Thus the fixed costs of entry and start-up on their own are unlikely to drive nascent online markets toward significant levels of market concentration. Indeed, the tremendous amount of entry that has already occurred testifies to the ease of entry and the small scale (relative to potential demand) that a start-up requires.

However, this analysis of increasing returns has four important caveats that substantially alter this picture and suggest that the equilibrium structure for many of these markets is likely to be significantly more concentrated. The first is that many firms are finding that, while they do not have to be large to have a rudimentary Web presence, providing competitive levels of service (especially for firms whose strategies depend on differentiating their offerings) generally involves much more than a Web site and simple fulfillment operation. The infrastructure that is required—sophisticated fulfillment technology, efficient call centers, Web sites that offer accurate in-stock information, order tracking, comparison engines, and product configurators—creates significant increasing returns.

Second, many business models simply cannot be implemented via a "minimalist" organizational structure. For example, Webvan.com had to invest in sophisticated warehousing, trucks, and logistics systems (see the Webvan.com case for more details), and Amazon.com has concluded that it must perform fulfillment in-house to achieve the differentiation it seeks. Even firms that started out at much smaller scale (see the BabyCenter.com case) found that existing outsourcing options did not meet their needs, and that they had to invest in in-house operations.

Third, and perhaps most important, is that other sources of increasing returns exist beyond these basic infrastructure ones. First, as discussed in the previous chapter, for many firms that sell a lot of items (batteries, contact lenses, books, music CDs, and so on), there are substantial economies of centralized inventories. As Figure 3-1 illustrates, there is a virtual cycle in which the firms with the most comprehensive inventories experience the fewest "stock outs," leading to higher customer satisfaction that in turn increases their market share at the expense of smaller rivals, enabling them to more efficiently carry larger inventories, and so on.

FIGURE 3-1 Virtual Cycle with Increasing Returns in Inventories

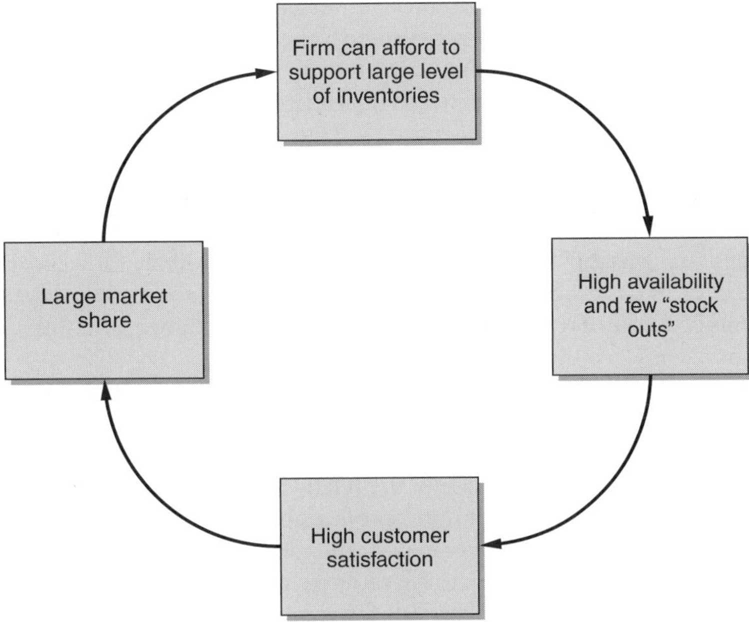

Fourth, although it may not take much work to establish a Web presence, driving traffic to the site typically requires a lot more. As consumers initially try to figure out which online stores to visit and return to, firms must expend resources on customer acquisition and brand development. As many failing dot-coms have discovered, most markets can support only a few firms with significant brand development and maintenance budgets.

A variety of sources of increasing returns, then, are likely to lead to a positive feedback cycle in which the strong get stronger and the weak wither. Other factors that create *incumbency advantage* for the early movers that attain strong market positions and entrench them further are likely to reinforce these trends toward concentration.

One of the most important of these is that early successful brands are likely to become stronger over time. Not only can the successful brands afford larger marketing budgets, which reinforce their market positions, but reputation and word-of-mouth add to their brand equities. As with the development of many consumer brands during the last industrial revolution and early twentieth century, some of the brands developed in these early years of electronic commerce are likely to become and remain household names for decades.

Experience effects or *learning economies* will also become more important in electronic commerce. The early successful firms develop capabilities that give them an enormous advantage over later potential market entrants. These range from incremental improvements in logistics and fulfillment to better techniques for exploiting information on consumer purchase histories to improvements in speed and quality of the Web interface upgrades.

An effect that is similar in that it increases over time originates in the fact that information itself is subject to increasing returns. Information is an unusual resource in that its consumption by one user does not diminish the amount of it available for others (and often doesn't even diminish the value to others). For information that is encyclopedic (in contrast to current news, which depreciates rapidly), established sites develop incumbency advantages as their content grows. Examples are search engines that develop databases of available Web sites and organize them by content and usefulness.

Because the sources of conventional increasing returns and incumbency advantages are numerous, we should not focus excessively on start-up costs or those of maintaining a rudimentary "virtual" Web presence in thinking about likely future market structures. Moreover, as described previously, concentration is subject to positive feedback. As some firms become more successful, they become better known, and word-of-mouth and reputation reinforce their market positions.

Indeed, as online market structures evolve, many market segments will probably look a lot like the market for online books looks today: a few large players with a "fringe" of smaller competitors: Amazon, Borders, and Barnes and Noble account for around 90% of online book sales. However, because of the relative ease of maintaining a rudimentary Web presence, there are a significant number of competitors, none of which accounts for many sales. Although the book market may be more concentrated than most other markets, the same basic structure is likely to characterize many markets. This "oligopoly plus fringe" structure has important implications for competition, which we discuss next.

Although we have taken a conventional view of what determines the structure of horizontal markets, we also want to stress that, particularly in these emerging electronic commerce markets, it is insufficient to take a simple perspective that considers these markets in isolation. There are some important ways in which adjacent markets are likely to importantly condition the way in which any market for electronic commerce and its competition develops. First, upstream firms can enter downstream markets and eliminate intermediaries. For example, in the market for home stereos, branded manufacturers like Sony may increasingly sell their products direct to consumers. Disintermediation, which we discuss in more detail in Chapter 4, can dramatically affect market structures.

Second, several factors blur horizontal boundaries. Successful Web-based firms can often exploit "economies of scope" by leveraging their infrastructure and brand by increasing the number of product lines they carry. Amazon.com's expansion from books into videos, music, and other lines is an example.

Also, many electronic commerce markets are becoming hybrids of pure online "e-tailers" and traditional "bricks-and-mortar" firms that have added an electronic commerce channel. So, for example, eToys finds itself competing with the online arm of Toys"R"Us. We discuss competition among these different kinds of online entities later in this chapter. However, it is clear that the ability of an offline store to have an online presence must significantly affect the analysis of those market structures. Online and offline firms will often be direct competitors in the online market (as the book competitors undoubtedly are), or online entities will compete in such different ways that they constitute another market segment (or "strategic group"). The online discount brokerage firms are arguably a case in point because the "discount" end of the spectrum (which characterizes most of the pure online firms and some hybrid firms) is so different from the "full-service" end of the spectrum (see the Broker.com case for more detail).

We return to the subject of competition later in this chapter. However, from a structural point of view, this discussion suggests that any analysis of competition must consider not just competition among firms within a given online market or market segment, but must also consider competition from upstream or downstream firms, and between online and offline firms.

It is also important to recognize that online markets are not in equilibrium now, and the equilibrium distribution of firms will depend on exactly how these markets shake out. In particular, there is a very real danger that in some cases the "wrong" (i.e., less efficient) stores may survive in equilibrium. For example, many pure play e-tailers do not sell enough or have the financial strength to support what their equilibrium levels of inventory would be if they grew. Consequently they may enter a "death spiral" of the kind discussed in Chapter 2 (where inadequate inventories alienate customers, which leads to lower sales, which supports even lower inventory levels). If that happens, they will ultimately exit, yielding the market to offline and hybrid stores, and only a brave new entrant will test the waters again. Yet if some of these firms had survived until they had achieved critical mass, they might have become efficient enough to drive out marginal offline stores.

DEMAND-SIDE INCREASING RETURNS[1]

Although "conventional" increasing returns will remain determinants of electronic commerce market structures, demand-side increasing returns (DSIR) are likely to be at least as important. DSIR are important because they frequently create "winner-takes-all" markets that a single firm eventually dominates even though initially several well-positioned rivals heavily contested them. Although many industries go through a period of consolidation after the emergent phase of their life cycle, this pattern is more pronounced in markets where an underlying characteristic accentuates it: when *the product's or service's benefits to each user increase along with the number of other users*. When this happens, consumers or firms want to choose the product that others are choosing.

Buyer preferences in markets with this characteristic are different from those for more conventional products. For many products or services, a buyer is worse off if everyone else wants what he or she wants. For example, when driving to work, a commuter prefers that other drivers choose a different road so that his or her route has less traffic-slowing congestion. Similarly, when people go to a movie, they might prefer that others attend at another time, so that they get a good seat. For many other goods, buyers don't care how many others buy or use them.[2] The products or services we are considering here, however, exhibit increasing returns to the size of the user population: the more people who use them, the more valuable they are.

Although we prefer (and use) the label "demand-side increasing returns" for this phenomenon, it is also sometimes referred to as "demand-side economies of scale," "network externalities," "network effects," or "positive feedback economics." We prefer the DSIR label because, as we argue next, the phenomenon does not always involve a network. The following quote from Bill Gates, CEO of Microsoft, who uses the label "network externalities," illustrates the strategic importance of DSIR:

> *We look for opportunities with network externalities—where there are advantages to the vast majority of consumers to share a common standard. We look for businesses where we can garner large market shares,* not just 30–35%.[3]

Microsoft's strategy is to offer products that have DSIR and find ways to be the "big winner."

DSIR have two main sources: compatibility and networks. Compatibility means that the products one consumer uses "work" with the products others use. Networks facilitate transactions among users by connecting them to each other.

[1] Much of this section is drawn from Chapter 12 of *Strategic Management* by Garth Saloner, Andrea Shepard, and Joel Podolny (New York: Wiley, 2000) with the permission of the co-authors.

[2] Of course, for all products, increasing demand (holding supply constant) tends to drive up prices. For simplicity, we ignore this pricing and focus on cases where, implicitly, the positive effect of more users is stronger than the pricing effect.

[3] *Microsoft, 1995*, HBS Case 9-795-147, by Tarun Khanna and David Yoffie. Emphasis added.

Compatibility Benefits

The benefits of compatibility are familiar to anyone who uses a computer. Computer users want to share files and programs with others and to use the same applications and peripherals on different computers. They value *compatibility* among computers, applications, and peripherals. For example, someone who uses Microsoft Word can share documents more easily when everyone else also uses Microsoft Word. Compatibility benefits imply that *standardization* has benefits. Each user of Word benefits from its status as the word processing standard.[4]

As we described in Chapter 1, standardized protocols and the compatibility they provide are crucial to the architecture of the Internet and World Wide Web (WWW) and to their dramatic growth. However, compatibility issues are equally important for many products and technologies that use the Internet as a platform. For example, AOL has come under scrutiny because its two instant messenger products, AIM and ICQ, are largely incompatible with other instant messaging products (see the AOL case for a description of instant messaging). Similarly, compatibility issues also arise between video and music media and players of those media (e.g., Windows' Media Player, RealNetworks' RealPlayer, and Apple's QuickTime).

Although compatibility issues are important for the functioning of the Internet and WWW, when it comes to DSIR as a determinant of market structure for electronic commerce, it is the second source of DSIR, network benefits, that is the more important.

Network Benefits

Perhaps the clearest examples of network benefits come from physical networks, such as a telephone system. The owner of the only telephone in the world would have just an interesting knickknack. The value of a telephone depends on one's ability to use it to communicate with other people who also own telephones, and its value increases enormously as the network of telephone users grows.

It is easy to see the benefit from network size in telephones. Using Figure 3-2, imagine that "A" is the only person who owns a telephone. He cannot use the equipment to communicate with anyone. When "B" also buys a phone, they can make calls in two directions: from "A" to "B" and "B" to "A." Adding the second user creates two directions in which messages can be sent. Adding a third user, "C" creates four additional directions in which users can send messages (from "A" to "C," from "C" to "A," from "B" to "C," and from "C" to "B"). Adding "D" creates six additional message routes, and so on. The number of directions in which users can send messages grows at an increasing rate as the system adds users. "B" added two, "C" added four, and "D" added six.

[4] The benefits of compatibility are not limited to the computer industry. Cameras and lenses (for cameras with interchangeable lenses, the lens must be compatible with the lens mount), VCRs and tapes, typewriter keyboards, railway gauges, language, nuts and bolts, autos and auto parts, bicycles and bicycle parts, and electric current and outlets are a few of the many other markets where compatibility issues arise.

FIGURE 3-2 The Network Effect

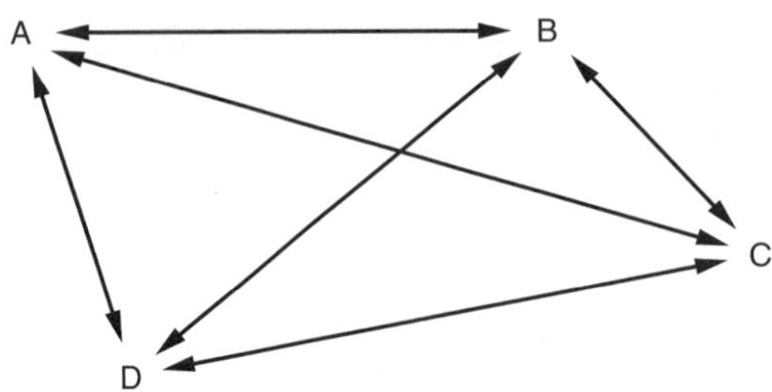

Because the value of the network to any user increases with the number of directions in which messages can be sent, the value increases at an increasing rate. In general the number of directions in which calls can be sent is equal to $n \times (n - 1)$, where n is the number of "nodes" in the network. This means that the number of directions in which a message can be sent increases by roughly the square of the number of nodes. This is sometimes called the *rule of squares*, also known as *Metcalfe's Law*.

Networks are often more complex than the simple telephone example suggests, however. In particular, the value of the network can depend on who is in it and how it is structured. For example, consider an electronic commerce network that connects retailers and their vendor suppliers, as in Figure 3-3. There are a number of mechanisms that might serve as the gateway that connects the retailers and their vendors. They might interact through an electronic marketplace. They might use a hub to process transactions between any two of them. Or, as is often the case, they might use a common electronic catalog in which the vendors keep a current list of their products (for an example of such a catalog see the QRS Corporation case).

There are two features of such a system that differ from the telephone example and that are worth noting here. First, typically there are potential trading relationships between each retailer and each vendor, but not between one retailer and another retailer or one vendor and another vendor. Thus the number of potential links here is V × R, where V is the number of vendors and R the number of retailers. Second, a network that large retailers use might be more valuable to vendors than one small retailers use, even if an equal number of retailers participate in each network. Thus V × R is unlikely to represent the value of the network: it should be weighted by the relative importance of the participants.

In some networks all users interact via a central nexus. Figure 3-4 illustrates these "star" networks. A clearinghouse is a star network. Banks increasingly rely on central clearinghouses to facilitate interbank transfers of funds, and physicians rely on information clearinghouses that the National Institutes of Health (NIH) maintains to track new developments in medical research. In both cases, the value of the clearinghouse to its users increases with the size of the network. As more banks use the system, a larger share of any single bank's transactions can go through the clearinghouse. As more publications cooperate with the NIH clearinghouse, it will include more relevant research. This means that physicians have access to more information and journals reach more researchers.

FIGURE 3-3 An Electronic Commerce Network Connecting Vendors and Retailers With and Without an Intermediary

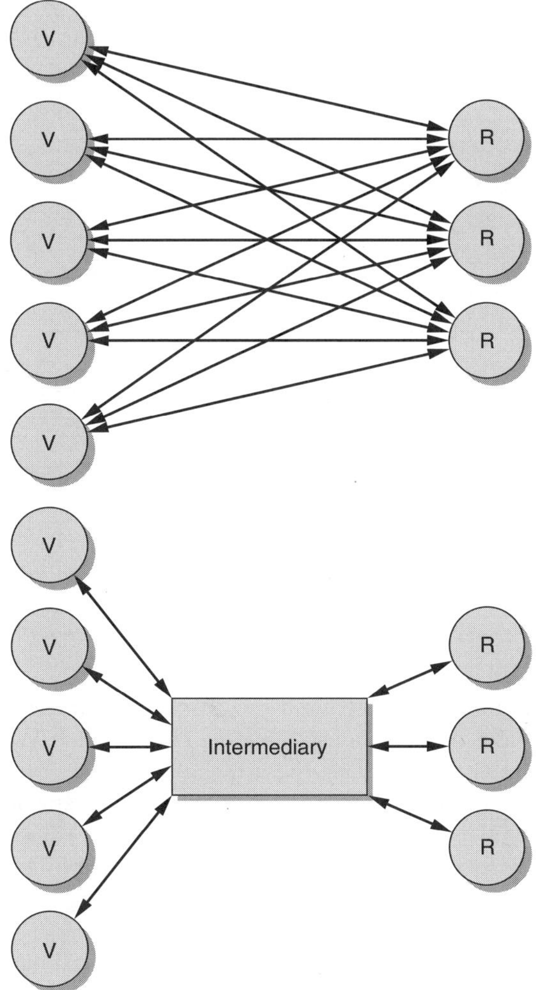

In yet other cases, some participants are both buyers and sellers, and others are only (or predominantly) buyers or sellers. Regardless of the exact composition of the network, however, when the network brings together buyers and sellers, the primary DSIR benefit is increased market liquidity. The larger the network, the more buyers a seller can find, and vice versa. Such DSIR are at the heart of the rationale for many of the electronic markets and exchanges that have sprung up and which are discussed in some detail in the next chapter.

The WWW itself is a technology with even more rapidly increasing DSIR than the simple networks we have described. Each new Web site (or the addition of information to an existing site) increases the value of the Web to every existing user. Thus

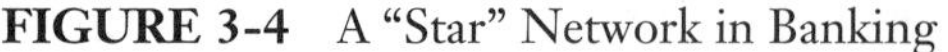

FIGURE 3-4 A "Star" Network in Banking

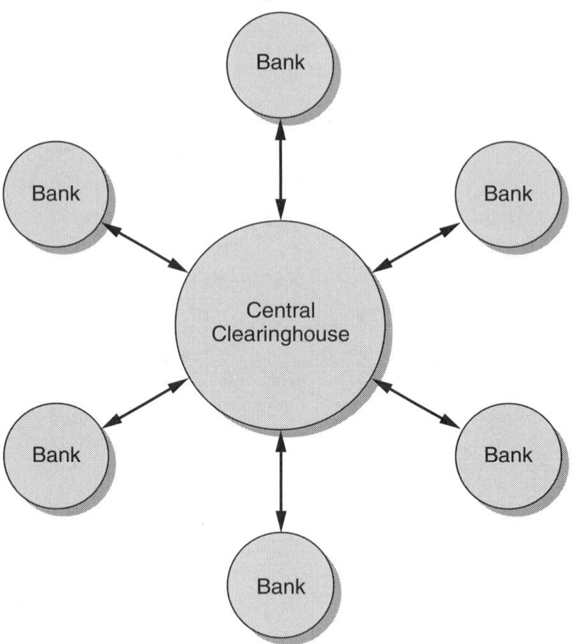

the value of the Web increases both with the amount of content on it and with the number of people who use it. Since each user can access each Web site, the value of the content that is available grows along with the user base. Thus the overall social value of the Web is increasing both with the amount of content on it and the number of people who surf it.

Although we have discussed them separately, both compatibility and network effects can be present in the same technology. For example:

• ***E-mail.*** Network effects are particularly strong for e-mail because the same message can be sent to multiple recipients. But the value of some e-mail features requires compatibility between the sender's and receiver's software.

• ***Peer-to-Peer Networks.*** Applications that allow users to share content typically benefit from a large network of users, but require them to have compatible software. Putting issues of legality and intellectual property aside for the moment, sites like Napster or Scour offer benefit to their users from the content each user brings to the community, and that value generally increases with the number of users, both because the amount of music available is greater if there are more users, and because the number of potential links that are active and available increases with the size of the network.

• ***Payment Clearinghouses.*** As in the offline world, payment clearinghouses (e.g., PayPal and Billpoint, which permit individuals to make credit card payments to one another—see the Online Auctions case for details) are subject to strong DSIR. Parties to both sides of the transaction desire common (that is, compatible) methods of transacting financially. Moreover, since both parties must establish a relationship with the payment service, there are benefits to all parties being part of the same community.

Whether the underlying source of DSIR is compatibility, a network effect, or some combination, it has dramatic implications for market structure because DSIR can turn small advantages in market share into a large, enduring positional advantage. This is the subject to which we turn now.

DEMAND-SIDE INCREASING RETURNS AND MARKET STRUCTURE

If a product has DSIR, potential buyers care about how many people use it. Whether DSIR come from compatibility, network benefits, or both, buyers want to purchase the same product that others purchase. A consumer deciding between VHS and beta VCRs in the 1980s would want to know how many others had already purchased each format and how many were likely to purchase each in the future. Similarly, if a consumer were choosing between Napster and Scour, he or she would want to know how many people were using each.

How many people already use a service with DSIR heavily influences a consumer's belief about how many people will use it. The buyers who already use a product or technology are called its *installed base* of users. If people can easily switch among products, installed base will be less important; the number of people using a brand of toothpaste today may not indicate how many will use it two years from now. However, many DSIR products have high switching costs that induce buyers to stay with their initial choice. As a result, a service with a large share of the installed base will retain most of those customers. A new buyer, then, will assume that most of the installed base for a given product will contribute to the benefits she would get if she chooses to buy it. This gives the service with a larger installed base a competitive advantage: all else equal, she would rather use the service with the largest installed base. Furthermore, she knows that other new users will also prefer the service with the largest installed base. As a result, all the new buyers will choose the one with the largest installed base (again, assuming nothing else differentiates the services in the buyers' minds).

Because installed base looms large for potential buyers of products, technologies, or services that have DSIR, markets for these products are inherently unstable: *they tend to "tip" toward a winner*. For example, consider the competition between VHS and beta in the market for videocassette recorders in the 1980s. In the early years, the market share advantage of VHS was not large. Suppose a consumer noticed that VHS had a 55% share. For many products, he or she would correctly interpret a 55-45 split as a stable configuration and assume that the two products would continue to enjoy a large market share. But, since VCRs have DSIR, the larger share would make VHS the more attractive choice. The consumer and others would therefore choose VHS. As new users disproportionately adopted VHS, its lead grew, making it even more attractive to new buyers. As this cycle repeats itself, the product with a small installed base advantage becomes ever more dominant; the market tips toward a winner. Eventually, this cycle drove beta VCRs from the market.

As this example suggests, the strong firms or technologies that compete in markets with DSIR tend to become even stronger. This tendency is known as *positive feedback*: a large installed base yields current strength in the market place, which results in stronger sales, which feeds back to increase the installed base. Figure 3-5 illustrates this positive feedback cycle. For the loser, of course, the feedback is negative. It loses some market share, so its installed base grows more slowly, and the slow growth in market share leads to a greater loss, and so forth. The feedback loop for the loser, like beta, is a death spiral.

These positive feedback effects have benefited portals like AOL and Yahoo! (see the AOL case for details). One element of DSIR is the benefit the users themselves derive from being members of a large community. Almost any aspect of electronic commerce where community is important (e.g., chat, message boards, etc.) benefits from DSIR if users would rather belong to a large community (and thus benefit from more content and more people to interact with) than a smaller one.

More importantly, users would like to be at a site like a shopping mall that has lots of merchants, and the merchants would like to be at a site that has lots of traffic. Similarly, users want access to content (e.g., news feeds, travel guides, etc.), and the providers of content want large audiences. Many portals augment their sites with other services that are themselves subject to DSIR. For example, some sites provide product reviews that have DSIR because buyers interested in others' views would rather visit a site that has many opinions rather than a few. AOL's Instant Messenger is another ploy along

FIGURE 3-5 Positive Feedback

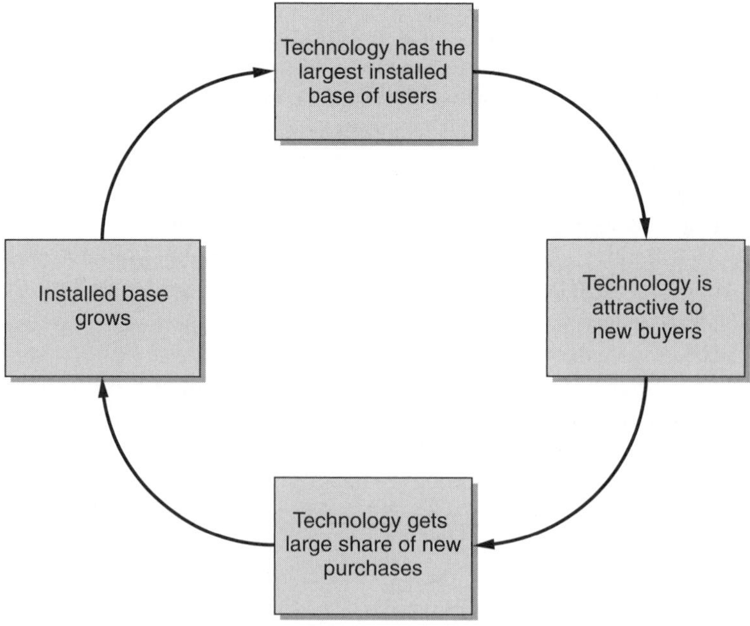

these lines. Users want to be on the same instant messaging network that their friends and colleagues are on.

The tremendous growth of the Web and its relative lack of organization have benefited Internet intermediaries. For example, at least in the early stages of electronic commerce, the firms that dominate the gateways to commerce and channels, in particular the portals but also to a lesser degree the shopping bots (sites like mySimon) and to an even lesser degree the search engines (such as Lycos and Google), can extract some of the value created. (Anchor tenancy on a shopping site on AOL can cost tens of millions of dollars over a few years, for example. See the AOL case for details.)

However, if as suggested in the previous chapter, market concentration increases until a few competitors dominate each market segment, those firms are likely to become household names, so that consumers can easily bypass other intermediaries, reducing the slice of the pie intermediaries can take. However, the many new sites, or those that find it difficult to establish brand identity, will continue to value relationships with the portals and search engines.

The assertion that DSIR products have high switching costs is crucial to our argument. Installed base affects DSIR because people who are using the product, technology, or service today will continue to use it tomorrow because it is costly for them to switch. Because they will use it in the future, they contribute to the installed base that today's users expect to see in the future. If users could switch with no cost, today's installed base might have little effect on tomorrow's. Often, switching costs are high because individual users customize the product or service to their own needs, such as when users of AOL's Instant Messenger create personal "buddy" lists that they do not want to have to redo if they switch to another service.

Moreover, switching costs for products with DSIR can be high even if no individual switching costs are significant. That is, even when none of the potential switching costs we have described is large enough to create lock-in, DSIR can still create lock-in because no user wants to switch unless most other users also switch. An analogy might be helpful here. Suppose cowboys have to camp overnight in the desert. They need to keep their horses from wandering off, but cannot find anything in the barren landscape to tie the horses to. They could hobble each horse (tie its front legs together), or they could tie the horses to each other. This second solution would be effective because horses are not good at coordinating an escape. In a similar way, DSIR ties users together. Unless users of a particular product with DSIR can coordinate a move to another product, they will be stuck with the one they have.

A similar phenomenon occurs in the co-location of nightclubs. Nightclubs want to locate close to other nightclubs, so that patrons can easily go "club hopping." If an area where a group of nightclubs is co-located loses favor (perhaps because rents are rising), even if it is not that costly for any individual nightclub to relocate, none of them is likely to move unless the nightclub owners can coordinate a joint move.

eBay is a striking example of how DSIR can create switching costs. Communities of traders have developed who regard eBay as the premier electronic site on which to trade. They share information about items and about each another. Individuals have developed reputations for trustworthiness that make others who frequent the site willing to deal with them. eBay thrives precisely because its auction has attracted a large, loyal following. Although any individual participant can switch to a competing site, he would leave behind almost everyone with whom he wants to trade. Like the horses tied together, mutual interdependence ties eBay's users together, and they would have to make a coordinated effort to move to another auction site.

eBay achieved this position even though it has no proprietary technology standard. It gained an initial advantage primarily by being a first mover in Internet auctions, but it could not prevent other firms from imitating its technology. Many competitors (including some with considerable resources, such as Yahoo! and Amazon) have attempted to enter eBay's space with little success. DSIR made eBay's first-mover advantage sustainable and propelled its market capitalization to over $8 billion within months of its initial public offering. The positive feedback loop illustrated in Figure 3-5 creates big winners and endows them with a positional advantage that challengers have difficulty overcoming.

Even a superior new technology may be unable to displace one that has created large DSIR benefits. In appraising the new technology, new users will compare the value of its inherent superiority with the benefits of the larger installed base on the inferior, old technology. Unless the enhancements the new technology offers can compensate new users for the loss of compatibility with the installed base, they will choose the old technology. Their decision means that the installed base on the old technology continues to grow, making it even more attractive to the buyers who follow them. It is therefore hard for the new technology to get off the ground, and it may fail to gain market acceptance, despite its superiority.

In summary, DSIR are a crucial determining factor in many online market structures. They are critically important because they are one of the most important sources of sustainable competitive advantage in electronic commerce. A very large fraction of electronic commerce business plans rely on some form of DSIR for competitive advantage. However, not all electronic commerce opportunities possess them. Finding those that do and using first-mover advantages to seize them are often key to long-term success.

COMPETITION

Horizontal market structure is an important determinant of the value the firms in the market can capture because it affects how vigorously they compete, but it is not the only factor. Even firms in highly concentrated industries sometimes compete vigorously because other factors promote competition. Many industry segments for trading goods and services on the Internet seem, at least at first blush, to have many of the characteristics that would tend to lead to intense competition even in market structures where competition might be blunted if the firms competed in the offline world.

Chief among these distinctive characteristics of electronic commerce competition is the fact that the competitor's "store" is just a few clicks away. That is, at least for consumer products, the travel costs between stores that are usually required to compare prices and that blunt price competition in the offline world is absent in online competition. Moreover, the costs of finding competing firms, and this point holds for goods and services sold both to businesses or to consumers, are much lower on the Internet, and buyers are considerably aided by the existence of shop bots and other intelligent agents that seek out and list offerings by price (including shipping costs).

These observations suggest that price competition should be vigorous and that prices should soon converge to competitive levels. A high priced "store" is easily revealed as such by a little bit of search, and as long as switching costs are low, we should expect buyers to abandon any but the lowest-priced vendors. These arguments suggest than online markets should tend to behave like the textbook examples of perfectly competitive markets, even if there are relatively few incumbents.

The theory of "contestable markets" reinforces this argument. Markets are "contestable" if a new firm can relatively easily enter a market and quickly gain share if prices are above competitive levels. In contestable markets prices are forced to competitive levels, not just by competition among actual rivals, but also by the threat of potential competition. As we discussed earlier, the costs of entry into many electronic markets are modest. The costs of setting up a Web site are fairly modest and if the firm outsources fulfillment or runs a rudimentary pick, pack, and ship operation, it can limit infrastructure costs. Although the presence of other sources of increasing returns that we have discussed may prevent all of these firms from becoming major players, the threat of entry from these firms, or the threat of expansion from those that are present but small, exerts downward price pressure on the major market participants.

The effects of actual and potential competition suggest that electronic markets should tend toward the "law of one price." Instead, so far price dispersion seems to characterize online markets. For example, one study found that prices for books and CDs among online retailers differed by an average of 33% and 25% respectively.[5]

Of course, ultimately we are interested in not simply the dispersion of prices at which firms offer products and services, but the dispersion of prices at which significant numbers of transactions occur. The (temporary) existence of firms that post high prices but get no takers is not particularly interesting. Still, there seems to be significant price dispersion even if only "meaningful" prices, that is, prices at which transactions do occur, are considered. Moreover, if some of the high prices at which little trading occurs persist as an equilibrium phenomenon, that in itself is interesting.

One obvious reason for the degree of observed price dispersion is simply that firms are still offering a fair amount of introductory pricing to build long-term market share. That is, there is significant price discounting taking place as part of customer acquisition strategies. Firms may not be able to sustain these prices in the long run but, instead, are offering them now in hopes of recouping these "investments" through the lifetime of their relationship with the customer.

Another reason for current levels of price dispersion is that most electronic markets are still far from equilibrium. Many buyers are still unsophisticated in their search,

[5] See Erik Brynjolfsson and Michael D. Smith, "Frictionless Commerce? A Comparison of Internet and Conventional Retailers," *Management Science*, 46 (April 2000), pp. 563–585. For other analyses of price dispersion, see the following and the references therein: Erik Brynjolfsson and Michael D. Smith, "The Great Equalizer? Consumer Choice Behavior at Internet Shopbots," National Bureau of Economic Research Working Paper, 2000; Dennis Carlton and Judith Chevalier, "Free Riding and Sales Strategies for the Internet," National Bureau of Economic Research Working Paper, 2000; and Karen Clay, Ramyya Krishnan and Eric Wolff, "Pricing Strategies on the Web: Evidence from the Online Book Industry," National Bureau of Economic Research Working Paper, 2000.

and reputational mechanisms that drive out less efficient high-priced firms have not yet had the time needed to work their way through the system.

A more important reason for price dispersion, and one that may persist, is that although electronic commerce eliminates many of the geographic impediments to search and to the frictionless functioning of markets, it does not eliminate all sources of differentiation. Indeed, it introduces new ones.

For example, there is significant differentiation in the Web sites themselves (superior look and feel, quality of product information, ease of use, and so forth). Differentiation of this kind should not necessarily lead to price dispersion because consumers can separate the decisions of what to purchase and where to purchase (because "locations" are just a click or two apart). Nonetheless, we suspect that many consumers value these attributes and will return to sites that offer them and will not bother to search elsewhere for lower prices, especially for relatively inexpensive items like books. Ease of use and a user-friendly interface are surely part of the explanation for Amazon.com's popularity (see the Pricing and Branding case for more on Amazon.com and on product differentiation).

However, differences in site design and functionality are neither the only nor the most important source of differentiation. Factors such as trustworthiness, after-sales support and service, reliability of delivery, likelihood of in-stock products, and accuracy of in-stock forecasts are all dimensions along which online offerings can differ. As we discussed in the previous chapter, many of these aspects of the purchase experience are vendor-specific, resulting in different valuations for consumers depending on whom the product is purchased from (and for firms that have an offline presence, many of these characteristics carry over from the offline world).

Once one admits the possibility of significant differentiation among the offerings of firms on the Web, prospects arise for firms to pursue different strategies and to blunt the intensity of competition among them, because of the fact that they do not compete directly for the same customers. So, for example, a generalist book vendor like Amazon.com can coexist with sellers of specialist books (technical books or collector's items, for example) without competing directly.

Moreover, because they can differ on the basis on which they compete, firms whose competitive advantage is that they have very low costs (and hence can sell profitably at a discount) compete with firms who charge a premium for the superior quality of their service. Since firms pursuing those kinds of strategies appeal to somewhat different customer segments, they again do not compete head-to-head. (See the Pricing and Branding case for a comparison of the strategies of Amazon.com and Buy.com along these lines.)

Firms naturally seek novel sources of competitive advantage as they strive for strategies that will sustain them in the face of intense competition. Some of these are simple extensions of familiar strategies from the offline world. The strategy of being the low-cost leader just discussed is an example, and the tactics undertaken to pursue it are just as familiar (exploiting economies of scale and managing a very "tight ship").

However, there are also a number of kinds of competitive advantage which, although they may have counterparts in the offline world, are particularly relevant in the online world. One of these that is becoming increasingly important is developing the capability to analyze histories of prior customer behavior to personalize offerings to the consumers, both to give them the information and content they want, but also, as discussed previously, to offer a menu of products and services and to price them so as to maximize revenue. We discuss this further in the next section.

While new online firms must develop new sources of sustainable competitive advantage, existing firms can leverage existing ones. These firms have demonstrated competitive advantage in their traditional markets or they would not have survived. As with the kinds of competitive advantages just discussed for online firms, these can be capability-based or positional. Either way, these firms bring tremendous strategic assets to bear, many of which they can transfer when they enter online markets. Moreover, they can often enjoy synergies between their online and offline strategies, such as when an online site handles returns through its offline store. We take up the subject of the electronic commerce strategies of traditional firms in the next chapter.

As this discussion suggests, as electronic commerce matures, strategy, structure, and competition are starting to more closely resemble what we see in the offline world. Product differentiation remains important, and even with price competition just a click away, many of the survivors will have found ways to differentiate themselves from their rivals. Others will succeed by pursuing classic low-cost strategies. And some of the biggest winners will be those that have managed to exploit DSIR to build sustainable competitive advantage by attracting buyers and sellers to a common site, by building a community, or by establishing a portal that attracts vendors and users.

Nonetheless, despite the familiarity of many of the industry structures to which electronic commerce seems to be evolving and of the continued importance of differentiation, price competition among the many aspiring online firms that do offer similar merchandise will continue to erode margins and winnow out all but the most efficient firms. Although the survivors may gain some respite from the current intense competition, many of these market segments will remain structurally unattractive.

Moreover, as venture capital–backed customer acquisition dollars decline and consumers become increasingly indifferent to banner ads, unless a significant technological breakthrough renders online ads more compelling (for example, 3-D animated banners could liven up this space), advertising rates will continue to fall. Charging for content also faces challenges. Most consumers have shown little willingness to pay for online content, in part because of an expectation (that may or may not change) that it should be free and in part because the transactions costs of doing so are high.

Consequently, until the likely technological advances are made that will enable the widespread use of "micro payments" (for example, automatic payments that enable users to be automatically charged a few pennies for downloading an article) or unless portals can ultimately get away with charging a small subscription fee, few sites will be able to rely on significant revenue streams from content. Therefore, most commercial sites that survive will have to rely on revenue from the purchase of goods and services.

Although it is as yet hard to predict exactly which firms will "win" (apart from those that have already gained sustainable competitive advantage from DSIR), it is safe to say that in most markets competition will increase. Not only are there strong competitive forces in electronic commerce markets themselves, but many of them are in

partial competition with existing offline markets, and online and offline mar-
l create competition for one another.

TURING VALUE THROUGH PRICING

Firms that are in a position to capture value ultimately do so largely through their pricing behavior. For electronic commerce what is interesting about pricing is not just what will happen to the levels of prices, but what opportunities the medium of electronic commerce opens up for pricing. From this point of view, several things are interesting about pricing on the Internet: prices can be updated dynamically, they can (at least in principle) be somewhat tailored to the individual buyer, buyers can negotiate prices, prices can be determined by groups of buyers, and auctions are relatively easy to implement.

Each of these characteristics has potentially important implications for how much value is captured and by whom. In order for firms to come close to capturing the value created in their markets, they must be able to charge buyers something approximating their individual willingness to pay. If, instead, they charge a common price to all buyers, the optimal price surrenders value to those buyers with the highest willingness to pay and, if they have any market power at all, results in a price being charged that exceeds marginal costs. As a result some consumers whose valuations exceed costs are deprived of the item.

To avoid these outcomes (especially the first), most firms that can price discriminate do. Price discrimination on the Internet is interesting because, on the one hand, it is easier when sellers can retain and quickly access detailed information about the customer's buying habits and easily customize price to the individual, and, on the other hand, more easily undermined when the customer can use intelligent shopping software to find the best price available (including, possibly, by hiding his or her identity). That is, although it is certain that the amount of information that is available and will be used in pricing will increase, whether this will increase or reduce information asymmetries between buyers and sellers is unclear. Buyers know much more about competitive prices, but sellers also know more about individual buyers.

The use of the electronic information that e-commerce retailers (and, increasingly, conventional stores) gather is already controversial, as Amazon.com discovered when it was accused of offering lower prices to new customers than it offered to its longstanding customers. Interestingly, Amazon.com responded to the charge by claiming that it was actually varying prices randomly in order to better estimate the price elasticity of demand for each item it sells.

Although there are a number of instances in which the offers that customers receive sometimes depend on the sites they visited immediately before receiving the price quote, individually tailoring prices in this way is only one of many means of price discriminating on the Web. A more subtle means, for example, is to tailor product recommendations to the individual. So, for example, a firm might offer consumers who have demonstrated a general high willingness to pay items that carry larger markups than others or bundles of items that are the higher end of the range of available products. Alternatively, firms might offer consumers who have demonstrated price sensitivity coupons by e-mail that they do not offer to less price-sensitive buyers.

There are a variety of other pricing strategies which at first appear to have nothing to do with price discrimination but when one takes a larger view of the market are probably best understood in those terms. Consider, for example, MobShop.com where an item's price falls as more and more buyers make purchases (see the Pricing and Branding case for details). Buyers can supposedly obtain lower prices because they reap the advantages of increasing their buyer power through group buying.

To understand the phenomenon, however, it is necessary to step back and look at it from the perspective of the manufacturer whose item is being sold in this way. To them MobShop represents just another channel, and in most cases not a particularly large one. Presumably, then, the aggregation of buyer power does not account for the lower prices to end-consumers. A more plausible explanation is that the end-consumers who end up buying in this manner are different from those who purchase through more conventional channels. They are willing to expend more time on the purchase process and wait for the process to run its course. They are therefore probably relatively price-sensitive consumers. Providing a channel where price sensitive consumers can pursue low prices but which less price-sensitive consumers would not choose to use (because of inconvenience and delay) is an excellent way for the manufacturer to achieve price discrimination!

Looked at from the point of view of the manufacturer, "reverse auctions," in which consumers post the prices at which they would be willing to buy, have similar characteristics. In equilibrium, price-sensitive consumers who are willing to expend the time to get a deal do indeed pay lower prices than others. Particularly for time-sensitive items like airline tickets, channels like Priceline.com help solve a thorny problem. Airlines prefer not to fly with empty seats because the marginal cost of carrying an additional passenger is low. However, if they make inexpensive seats available at the last minute to fill those seats, some consumers who now pay higher prices would wait for the lower fares, thwarting the airlines' attempt at revenue management. By making those same seats available through a less convenient channel and one where prices are less easily observable, however, the airlines dissuade most consumers who would have purchased at higher prices from defecting and instead pick up extra revenue on exactly those seats they are eager to fill.

Auctions represent another interesting pricing mechanism that has flourished in electronic commerce. This is a particularly interesting phenomenon because, although auctions are an important feature of the offline world, they are more prevalent in online commerce. The most important reason is that the interactive nature of the Internet makes it much easier to implement auctions there than in offline markets. Buyers and sellers do not have to come together—either in place or time—and yet it is easy to provide a centralized site that keeps participants apprised of progress and lets them change their bids. That is, reductions in transactions costs have made it possible to make markets in individual items.

Moreover, as described earlier, the expanded reach of the Internet is particularly valuable for goods that are not routinely purchased but which are somewhat idiosyncratic in nature, such as surplus merchandise, used consumer durables, and collectibles. However, it is precisely for goods like these that it is also unclear what the "right" price is. Because these goods are not "standard," it is unclear what price the market will bear. An auction market relieves the seller of the burden of figuring out what the "right" price is. Instead competitive bidding reveals the valuation. To be more precise, competitive bidding reveals what the bidder with the second-highest valuation is willing to pay because the bidder with the highest valuation need only bid up to that level to win the auction.

This pricing mechanism has a couple of features that are important to the success of the auction format. On the one hand, if there are many bidders, the seller can extract most of the buyers' willingness to pay, which makes it an attractive format for sellers. On the other hand, the winning bidder does receive the product for less than he or she is willing to pay. This feature is important because otherwise bidders would have no incentive to participate (see the Online Auctions case for more on this subject).

SUMMARY

As in offline markets, online market structures will vary enormously. In many cases they will also look very little like they do today. As is typical of industries in their emerging stage, less efficient firms will whither while others, many of which will become household names if they aren't already, will blossom. Some of the winners will pursue low-cost strategies while others rely on brand to support premium pricing. Although some of the basis for the differentiation that supports the branding will be different from that in traditional markets (ease of use of a Web site, for example), much of it will be familiar (reputation for reliability and quality of service, for example).

Some market structures will be relatively fragmented while others are likely to be quite concentrated. Some of the determinants of these market structures are familiar from conventional markets, but DSIR are a particularly important determinant in many online markets. Whatever the source, however, the fluidity of the markets is likely to decrease as barriers to entry increase, and incumbents entrench themselves and develop unassailable advantages.

Overall, however, although some firms will be lucky or smart enough to find and dominate market niches, competition will be the overriding characteristic of electronic commerce in many markets. The ease of price comparison among firms on the Web will mean they are less insulated from competition, even as the Web consolidates. Moreover, in those many sectors where online and offline firms compete, each will feel the effects of competition from the other. The competitive pressures will drive the survivors to continue to innovate in pricing. "Revenue management"—the euphemism for using information about consumers and dynamic pricing to maximize the amount of value that a firm captures—is likely to flourish as a result.

CHAPTER

4

CREATING AND CAPTURING VALUE IN THE SUPPLY CHAIN

Goods and services flow down supply chains from the most basic input providers (raw materials manufacturers, for example) to final consumers, with value being added along the way. While this flow of goods and services is largely unidirectional, information must flow both up and down the chain. Information about what is—or is expected to be—demanded at successive stages must pass up the chain. Moreover, as later-stage firms select their suppliers, they must obtain information about potential suppliers and their qualifications, and firms who have established suppliers must pass information about supply conditions (availability, pricing, time-to-manufacture, etc.) down the chain.

The efficiency of supply chains and corresponding minimization of transactions costs depends as much on the right information being in the right hands at the right time as it does on the productive efficiency of the firms along the way. It is precisely because this is an information-intensive process that the Internet holds the potential to significantly increase the amount of value that is created. Imperfections in supply chains squander value as firms produce goods that no one wants while they could have deployed the capacity used to produce those goods to make products that end up being in short supply. Moreover, to avoid shortages, firms in each segment of the supply chain carry buffer inventories. As researchers have documented,[1] this tendency can become conflagrated as each layer overcompensates for the inventory-buffering demands of later stages, which produces a "bullwhip effect" in which larger and larger buffer inventories are carried up the chain, leading to large excess aggregate inventory levels. Exploiting the low cost of transmitting information over the Internet can ameliorate these and other supply chain inefficiencies.

[1]See, for example, H. L. Lee, P. Padmanabhan, and S. Whang, "Information Distortion in a Supply Chain: The Bullwhip Effect," *Management Science*, 43, 4, 1997, pp. 546–558, and H. L. Lee, P. Padmanabhan, and S. Whang, "The Bullwhip Effect in Supply Chains," *Sloan Management Review*, 38, 3, Spring, 1997, pp. 93–102.

Vertical market structure matters not just for value creation but for value capture as well. In particular, firms that can build powerful positions in the vertical supply chain can capture value from those that precede or succeed them in the chain. While some intermediaries might hold significant power, others will lose it. Indeed, many firms will disappear altogether as downstream buyers and end-consumers find they are able to bypass them and go directly to an upstream manufacturer, disintermediating some firms along the way. At the same time electronic commerce will create opportunities for some new intermediaries even as others are being disintermediated. Although some information that is on the World Wide Web (WWW) will depreciate, much of it is long lived. Therefore, the amount of it will just continue to grow, providing ample room for those who would help to organize it and creating opportunities for intermediaries who do that.

We first examine why, so far at least, electronic commerce has affected distribution more than manufacturing and what it will take for that to change. We then discuss the Internet as an alternative channel for existing firms before proceeding to a discussion of how electronic commerce might change existing supply chains. Finally, we discuss the possibility that electronic commerce might not just improve existing supply chains but rather restructure the vertical organization of entire industries by establishing electronic markets and other new forums for exchanging goods and information.

MANUFACTURING VERSUS DISTRIBUTION

The vision of firms and managers pursuing improvement in supply chain management has long been that information about what end-consumers want would be rapidly relayed to manufacturers who, using just-in-time manufacturing techniques and flexible manufacturing technology, would quickly produce exactly what was demanded and deliver the product to the customer. This is in contrast to the current system in which firms guess what the consumer is likely to want, and put goods where and when they hope he or she is likely to want them.

This vision cited is not new and neither are attempts to realize it. By linking all the relevant economic actors (including end-users) electronically, the Internet makes this vision much more plausible. Note, however, that fulfilling this vision requires much more than changing the way people decide what to buy and the way in which those chosen goods and services get to them. It requires gearing manufacturing (or at least assembly) operations to custom production and, for many products, replacing batch manufacturing and assembly processes with more flexible just-in-time ones.

One of the best examples of implementing this approach is Dell Computer's custom assembly and distribution of personal computers.[2] The traditional approach to producing products like personal computers is to forecast which models will be demanded in which locations, produce them in batches, and hold inventories of finished goods at various levels of the supply chain to accommodate variances from expected demand. More sophisticated variants of this approach involve producing and assembling a common chassis and then assembling those models that consumers actually demand, using

[2] For details see "Dell Direct," Stanford GSB Case EC-17, June 2000.

just-in-time assembly techniques. Dell takes this process several steps further by selling direct to end-consumers. This approach has several advantages: it largely avoids having to estimate demand; by producing to order, Dell can customize the product attributes to precisely what the customer wants; and it essentially eliminates finished goods inventories throughout the supply chain.

Several attributes of the Internet and WWW that we have discussed particularly lend themselves to this kind of process. For example, the fact that a product configurator can check for personal computer component compatibility in real time is particularly valuable and appropriate. Also, the ease with which a menu-driven interface can serve up exactly the information needed to assist in the purchase decision (product attributes and comparison, for example) is very hard for retail salespersons, with varying degrees of skills, to match. Moreover, the Internet store is always open, facilitating an asynchronous transaction that is convenient to the purchaser and enables the manufacturer to smooth peaks in order arrival (customers don't have to wait for an available salesperson).

What is striking about the Dell example, however, is not how successful a model it is in the personal computer industry, but how few other examples there are that deploy the new technologies to restructure the entire process by which supply chains operate (including the manufacturing layers). So far, most electronic commerce has involved changing how existing goods and services find their way to end-consumers, rather than how they are produced in the first place. Electronic commerce has largely been a "distribution revolution" rather than a manufacturing one. So, for example, while the way books, apparel, and consumer electronics are distributed has been affected, the way they are made has not.

However, personal computers are not the only products that would seem to be amenable to the process Dell employs. Cars are another. First, distribution costs comprise a large fraction (by some estimates one-third) of the final cost of a car. Second, many consumers end up compromising on options because of what is available on the dealer's lot. Third, few consumers relish the buying process itself. (See the case on Disintermediation in the U.S. Auto Industry for more details.)

Yet, in most countries, and in the United States in particular, we are still far from the online customized order and made-to-order manufacturing in the automobile industry that we have in personal computers. Although the buying process has changed and Internet intermediaries can now help with that part of the process, car manufacturing itself remains virtually unaffected. There are many contributing factors to this. One of the most important is that car manufacturing is currently optimized to batch production, so that the typical delay from order to manufacturing ranges from three weeks on the low end (Toyota) to close to eight weeks (General Motors) on the longer end. Moreover, at least in the United States, consumers have not been willing to defer instant gratification. Although the Internet arguably provides a far better medium for customizing a product like a car, buyers have long been able to get a built-to-order car through a dealer. Despite that, most consumers (around 85%) prefer to take a car off the lot than to wait. Another important factor in the United States is that legislative protection for the existing dealer network makes disintermediation difficult.

Our main point, however, is that if value is to be created from electronic commerce in the manufacturing as well as the distribution of goods, unlocking that potential is likely to require significant restructuring of manufacturing. Consequently it is likely to occur relatively slowly, at least compared to changes in distribution.

Before leaving the auto and personal computer examples, we should point out that the discussion of them blurs two different classes of benefit from supply chain improvement using the Internet. One is the benefit to end-consumers from customization; the other is the benefit from improving information flows through the supply chain for noncustomized products and services. There are relatively few products for which the first of these, benefits from customization, are likely to lead to supply chain restructuring. For most products the benefits of customization are small relative to the efficiencies of mass production.

Indeed, for most electronic products, for example, it is more economical to include a wide range of features and functionality in all products than it is to provide for customized manufacture, especially when the production volumes are large. Nonetheless there are some categories where increased customization will become possible over time as manufacturing processes adapt to custom ordering. Textbooks that individual instructors can customize to their own idiosyncratic needs and preferences are an example. Travel books that are customized to the traveler's itinerary are another.

Most of the benefits from supply chain reengineering for manufactured goods are therefore likely to involve improving how goods are manufactured and distributed rather than changes in what is made. We describe the significant potential for making supply chain improvements by changing existing channel structures later in this chapter. First, however, we examine the Internet as an alternative to existing channels.

THE INTERNET AS A NEW CHANNEL

It is now widely accepted that for the vast majority of goods and services, the Internet will supplement rather than replace existing channels of distribution. The relative impact of the Internet channel on traditional existing channels will vary with the product and service. In products for which factors like fit, touch and feel, and immediacy are important, traditional stores have an obvious advantage and will be less affected. For others such as music and books, which are easily sampled and, in some cases, delivered online and for which the economics of direct delivery are favorable, the impact is likely to be greater, although the business models of those online firms are still unproven (see the Amazon.com section of the Pricing and Branding case for more information).

However, even for products like books and music for which the online channel looks like a good alternative, few predict that the existing traditional channels will disappear altogether (at least not any time soon). To be sure, some disintermediation is already occurring. Many marginal offline intermediaries will not be able to withstand even a relatively small amount of siphoning off of sales by online channels. However, other intermediaries will survive, serving those product and consumer segments for which online transactions are not a good substitute.

For most existing upstream manufacturers and vendors, therefore, the challenge of the Internet is less how to respond to a completely different channel structure than how to manage a more complex one in which a new Internet channel sits beside pre-existing channels and in which Internet technology alters how the existing ones function.

Firms that have chosen to exploit the Internet as a complementary channel have learned that although it may enable them to exploit synergies among channels, it also raises customers' expectation that the firm will integrate those channels. The history of Schwab's online offerings is instructive on this point.[3] Schwab's first response to online discount brokers was to launch its own online discount offering, but to keep it separate from its existing service. Customers essentially had to choose between a discounted online offering without being able to talk to a person and the pre-existing offering with a broader range of products and higher service levels. Users who wanted both to trade online and the ability to speak to a broker were not offered the same deep discount that Schwab offered to pure online traders.

However, Schwab soon discovered that its customers wanted the best of both worlds and were confused when they could not have it. Moreover, customers expected brokers to be able to answer questions about the discount trades they had completed on their own; that is, they expected their existing relationship with the firm to extend to the new services. The necessity of providing this kind of cross-channel integration is causing a mini-boom in the market for enterprise software applications that can tie together disparate data bases and customer-facing applications like customer relationship management software, in particular (see the Siebel Systems case for a discussion).

Another important issue is ensuring that incentives are aligned across multiple channels. In principle this is no different from what multichannel firms encounter in the offline world between, say, low-service discount retailers and high-service premium-priced retailers. In these cases the issue is that high-service retailers rely on their high premiums to offset the costs of providing high service. Consumers then have an incentive to get the sales advice from one store and make the purchase at another.

The problem is even more severe, however, for firms that want to employ a hybrid model in which goods are only showcased in offline stores but can also be purchased online, as discussed in Chapter 2. To separate the purchase of goods from their fulfillment in that way, organizational and interfirm incentives will have to be significantly altered because incentives for sales effort are usually tied to measures of actual sales. Firms base commissions, bonuses tied to store sales, and profit-sharing schemes on the notion that actual sales are a signal of unobservable sales effort. If sales effort in a showroom pays off in online sales or online sales effort pays off in offline sales, and if the connection between the sales and the sales effort is hard to establish, it becomes difficult to induce (online and offline) sales effort using performance-based incentives. Some stores are experimenting with providing compensation to store managers based on Internet sales that originate from the store's neighborhood (on the theory that some in-store sales effort is responsible for at least some of the online sales). But such methods are crude, and significant effort is likely to be put into finding better ones.

The Internet channel also adds to the channel conflict problem in a variety of other ways. One is that the price-conscious consumer can easily search for the lowest price using a price bot on the Internet, having consumed the in-store sales advice or simply

[3] For details see "Schwab.com," Stanford GSB Case EC-18, April 2000.

perused, touched, and felt the merchandise in an offline store. Another is that the Internet has thwarted one of the main devices that firms have used to deal with this problem. In the offline world many manufacturers give their retailers exclusive territories, so that price-conscious consumers must bear significant travel costs if they want to seek out the same product at a lower cost. Since a distant store cannot easily attract the customers who are geographically closer to its rival, it has less incentive to discount, ameliorating the problem even further. However, the Internet's lack of geographic boundaries obviates the benefits of exclusive territories.

Finally, the temptation for manufacturers to sell direct over the Internet further compounds the problem. Most manufacturers have resisted the temptation or have done it in a way that does not threaten their existing channels (by, for example, selling at relatively high prices or selling direct only in collaboration with an existing downstream channel). If electronic commerce continues to grow, however, the relative profitability of direct sales is likely to cause many firms to revisit their online channel strategies.

CHANGING EXISTING CHANNELS AND SUPPLY CHAINS

Improving the efficiency of supply chains involves not only attempting to reduce the kinds of transaction costs we described in Chapter 2 (and illustrated in Table 2-1), but also improving information flows and coordination. In particular, to be effective, supply chains must also accomplish the following:

- Ensure that information about what is needed, what has been produced, and what is in process is available wherever it is needed in the chain; and
- Configure production processes to produce components when and where it is most efficient.

Attempts at using the electronic transmission of information to improve supply chains in this way are not new. As we described in Chapter 1, firms have long used electronic data interchange (EDI) over proprietary networks to improve the flow of information and to automate paper processes (see the QRS Corporation case for details).

In the retail industry, Wal-Mart has been a leader in the use of integrated data systems to optimize its supply chain. In particular, its information systems are often well integrated with those of its suppliers. For example, Wal-Mart transmits point-of-sale information to them so that they can use it to forecast future sales. For some items stores like Wal-Mart and their suppliers use collaborative replenishment schemes that automatically generate (electronic) orders to replenish the depleted stock when in-store inventory of particular items falls below certain levels. (Indeed the desired stock level itself is adjusted as statistical models utilizing actual sales data forecast likely future sales.) Wal-Mart and some of its partners, such as Procter & Gamble, even put the responsibility (and financial cost) for maintaining and replenishing inventory in the hands of the supplier.

When a store carries many stock keeping units (SKUs) because of variety in sizes, colors, and products, it is difficult for store managers to manually track out-of-stock items and reorder in time. For example, the authors know of an instance when a store manager complained that a collaborative replenishment system that had been installed two weeks earlier "wasn't working" because he had noticed that a particular item was out of stock and had not been replenished. Closer investigation, however, revealed that the product had been sold and replenished several times during that two-week period without the store manager having been aware of it! The point is that although automating these processes can save costs, a far bigger efficiency is that the product consumers want is more likely to be in the store when they want it. Stores often report increased sales of some items by as much as 30% when they introduce automated replenishment systems.

Tightening the link between actual sales and production to optimize inventory and production is only one potential efficiency gain from sharing information through the supply chain. A second is that a manufacturer and retailer typically have different signals of final demand. A retailer of blue jeans, for example, knows both how a particular manufacturer's jeans are selling and how rival jeans are selling. It may therefore know more about demand, including demand for styles and sizes the manufacturer may not provide. Conversely, a manufacturer knows both how its jeans are selling in a particular retailer's stores and how they are selling in rival stores. It therefore has a different set of signals about demand and a better estimate of aggregate demand for its jeans. Because they have different signals of demand, their aggregate planning is likely to improve if that information is pooled. There are thus potential gains to jointly planning what assortment of products to offer.

Accurate transmission of information can generate particularly high savings in the production of expensive items like cars and planes for which both the savings in inventory from just-in-time production and the costs of not having a part when it is needed in the production process are high. By integrating their information systems, Johnson Controls is able to drop its car seats into Toyota's assembly line just when they are needed.[4] Conversely Boeing incurred tremendous losses when its information systems failed to deliver the necessary parts to its plane assembly process during a period of particularly high plane demand.

Although significant improvement has been made in the efficiency of supply chains through improving the flow of information and automating the transmission of information, in many areas the rate of progress has been painfully slow. It would be wonderful to believe that the Internet and related technologies will make all prior impediments disappear. Unfortunately that is unlikely. To be sure, many of the advantages of the Internet and the WWW that we have described earlier have great potential for improving the flow of information through supply chains as well. In particular, the ubiquity of the platform, its richness and ease of use, and the low costs of transmission and connection render it a superior and lower-cost medium than EDI.

However, many of the impediments to the effective adoption of information technology (IT) to improve supply chain operation are not technical. The inertial forces relate more to organizational issues, the importance of compatibility with legacy systems, and nontechnological transactions costs. As the previous examples suggest,

[4] See Paul Milgrom and John Roberts, "Johnson Controls, Inc.—Automotive System Group—The Georgetown, Kentucky Plant," Standford Business School Case BE-9, 1993.

obtaining efficiencies by more closely coordinating the activities of sequential firms in a supply chain generally requires changes in business process in addition to merely adopting new technology. For example, the effective implementation of collaborative replenishment requires restructuring information flows, incentives, roles, and responsibilities. Such changes are time consuming and costly. More importantly, they require adaptation and change by multiple firms, each of which has its own routines, organizational structure, strategy, and objectives. Change across the boundaries of firms is notoriously more difficult than within a single firm.

In addition, many of the adaptations that adjacent firms in the supply chain must make are specific to the relationships between those firms. Once the firms have invested in the technology and processes required to reap supply chain efficiencies between them, they have created costs to switching to other partners. The presence of switching costs increases the extent to which firms are "locked in" to one another, at least in the short run. Because of the considerable danger of being exploited by another in the presence of lock in, these relationships can only be formed in the presence of considerable trust among the parties or where other safeguards are in place to prevent exploitation through opportunistic behavior by one of the parties. Fear of the effects of lock in from switching costs often makes firms reluctant to enter into these relationships in the first place, even if they potentially offer great efficiencies. It is no wonder, then, that considerable effort is going into technical solutions that lower these switching costs.

Second, as we described in Chapter 1, firms have made significant investments in their enterprise IT systems, which enable integration of databases, re-use of data, facilitate queries, and so on. To be effective, IT innovations in supply chain management must interface well with these systems. Although technologies like XML provide templates that enable firms to share information while maintaining compatibility with legacy systems, each industry has to agree on industry-specific implementations of such templates tailored to that industry.[5] As with most consensus standards processes, these are lengthy and often political (see the E-Markets 2000 case for details).

These arguments should not be taken to imply that we don't believe the new technologies will have a significant impact on supply chains. They will. However, the presence of these inertial forces suggests that adoption is going to take time and technical advances, and much painstaking relationship-by-relationship business process improvement is going to have to take place for firms to fully realize the potential gains.[6]

[5] In brief, XML, like HTML, inserts tags that enable browsers to interpret the data in Web pages. However, in addition to using the HTML tags, such as P for paragraph, XML also enables the creator of a Web page to add his or her own tags. The trick, of course, is to ensure that others know how to interpret them. That requires standards. W3C, a working group of the WWW Consortium, developed XLM. However, particular industries or other groups need to define their own tags. A variety of initiatives are under way, both proprietary and open, to develop such standards. An example is RosettaNet, a nonprofit organization attempting to set XML standards primarily in the electronics industry.

[6] The Hurwitz Group estimated that less than one-third of Fortune 500 companies were ordering "strategic goods" online. (For details see CyberAtlas at http://cyberatlas.internet.com/markets/b2b/article/0,,10091_524631,00.html, December 2, 2000.) A study by Financial Executives Institute/Duke University Corporate Outlook Survey in Sepetember 2000 found that B2B Internet purchases still represented only 4.5% of total purchases and had not increased in the prior 18 months. (For details see http://cyberatlas.internet.com/markets/b2b/article/0,,10091_475401,00.html#table, December 2, 2000.)

ELECTRONIC MARKETS

While the new technologies facilitate the steady, and incremental, improvement of existing supply chains, they can also dramatically restructure those supply chains. The enormous proliferation of "electronic markets" over the past few years represents the highest profile attempts to do this. As we shall discuss, however, other lower profile changes are likely to have at least as great an impact.

There is a variety of different market forms and they tackle different sets of problems. To get a handle on this, look at the vertical supply chains in Figure 4-1 where we depict partial chains for Boeing and Airbus in the aerospace industry and for General Motors (GM) and Toyota in the automobile industry. The important part of this figure is that firms share many of the same suppliers. Note that this is true both within each industry and across them. Of course, the shared suppliers within an industry are different across industries. GM and Toyota typically share auto parts suppliers, whereas the common GM and Boeing suppliers typically sell more generic items that many industries use, such as paper, pens, personal computers, and so on. More generally this category includes administrative supplies; maintenance, repair, and operations (MRO) products; HR services; and so forth.

It appears that there are significant opportunities for value creation from systematizing and automating the transactions between each layer of the supply chain. In the previous section we focused on creating value by improving a firm's interactions with its own suppliers. However, if each of the firms undertakes similar transactions with a common set of suppliers, having a common intermediary for those transactions could create significant value. Figure 4-2 illustrates three such potential intermediaries.

There has been a flurry of activity around the creation of new intermediaries of this kind and their number has grown rapidly (see the E-Markets 2000 case for details).[7] Within this general trend, however, many different kinds of intermediaries are emerging.

FIGURE 4-1 Automobile and Aerospace Supply Chains

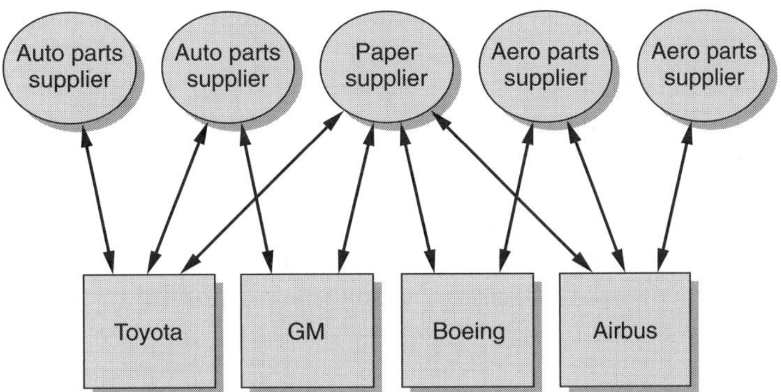

[7] The Gartner Group estimates that by 2005 more than 500,000 companies will be participating in electronic marketplaces. (See CyberAtlas at http://cyberatlas.internet.com/markets/b2b/article/0,,10091_505151,00.html, December 2, 2000.)

FIGURE 4-2 Common Intermediaries for Transactions

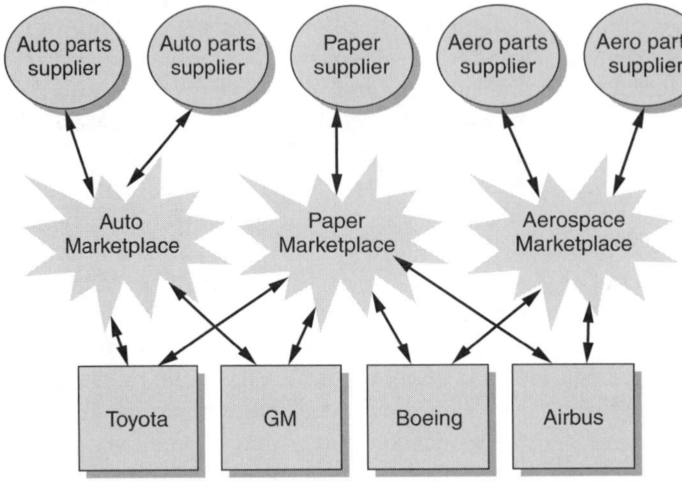

We can see the first important distinction from the two kinds of intermediaries illustrated in Figure 4-2. Some are hubs that focus on transactions between firms in successive layers *within the same industry supply chain* while others focus on transactions among firms in different industry supply chains. We call the first of these *vertical* markets because they relate to transactions (sometimes called "direct" procurement) within a "vertical" industry. We call the second *horizontal* markets because they cut across industry verticals, that is, they involve goods and services that more than one industry vertically purchases (e.g., autos and airplanes). These purchases are also sometimes called "indirect" purchases.

Another important distinction, which can relate to either horizontal or vertical markets, is whether the intermediary enables transactions or simply provides information that facilitates interaction. Many sites provide both content and transactions, but some focus only on content (see the E-Markets 2000 case for details). Finally, some intermediaries attempt to facilitate existing purchasing and sales practices rather than changing them. Figure 4-3 illustrates these two dimensions along which intermediaries differ and the corresponding intermediary types. It shows the range of strategies these new intermediaries are pursuing and the different functions they perform. (See the E-Markets 2000 case for definitions of the terms in the figure.)

The more important of these different types of intermediaries are clearly those that can in fact facilitate transactions rather than simply provide information, and the opportunity to create value from trading hubs like these is potentially huge. One reason for this is that buyers and sellers who have already found one another can transact more efficiently, that is, there is an attendant reduction in transaction costs. Of course we argued in the prior section that the Internet can be used to cut transactions costs among parties within existing supply chains without inserting a common hub. Although that is true, to achieve those gains, the firms must each work with their buyers and suppliers to institute appropriate systems through a set of bilateral negotiations and

FIGURE 4-3 A Functional Categorization of E-Markets

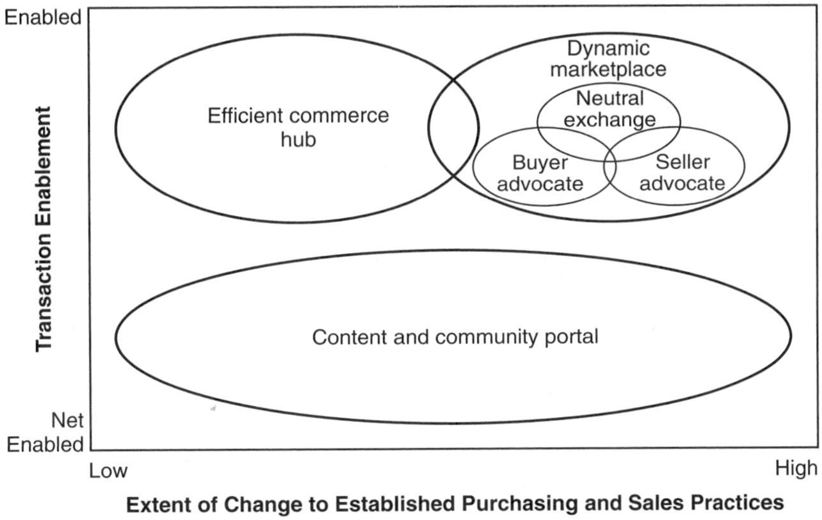

Source: Adapted from "The E-Market Maker Revolution," Gartner Group, September 27, 1999 in E-Markets 2000 case in this book.

adoptions of technology. In contrast if a hub can be put in place to which a large set of firms interconnect, each firm pays the costs of setting up its system to connect to others only once and yet enjoys the potential gains of thereby transacting with all of the others who have similarly joined the hub.

This is a form of demand-side increasing return (DSIR): the value of the hub increases with the number of users who connect to it. For example, if there are S connected suppliers and B connected buyers, there are S × B potential trading relationships. Consequently the number of trading relationships increases in both S and B, and more importantly, the number of trading relationships increases at an increasing rate as S and B increase. So, for example, if there are 10 suppliers and 10 buyers, there are 100 potential trading relationships, and if one more buyer joins the network, that number increases by 10 to 110 (11 × 10). On the other hand, if there are 100 buyers and suppliers, the number of potential trading relationships is 10,000, and, more importantly, now if one more buyer joins the network, that number increases by 100 to 10,100 (101 × 100). Now a single buyer adds 100 trading relationships, whereas with the smaller network the incremental impact is much less.[8]

The important point, however, is that if the 100 buyers and suppliers had to set themselves up to trade with one another bilaterally, 10,000 trading relationships would have to be established if any buyer were to have the ability to interconnect to any seller.

[8] Note that this is slightly weaker than the magnitude of the DSIR when all users connect to one another, of the kind illustrated in Figure 3-2. This is because here we have supposed that there is no benefit to sellers (buyers) from communicating with other sellers (buyers), whereas in Figure 3-2 users benefit from interacting with all others.

Conversely if they connect through a common hub, only 200 total trading relationships need be established, since each buyer and seller needs to create a connection to one common hub.

This reduction in transactions costs creates tremendous value. However, it is related to another that is potentially even greater in its impact. In particular, if it becomes significantly less costly for firms to enter into trading relationships they may enter into many more than they otherwise would. More buyers and sellers will find one another. This has at least two implications. First, it will likely create more competition because buyers have a broader range of options and lower switching costs in moving from one to another. Even when firms decide to stay with their existing suppliers, however, the potential competition from new sources of supply may also cause existing suppliers to lower prices. Second, over time it may potentially change the structures of some of the supplier industries. To the extent that access to distribution has been a gating factor that has inhibited entry, providing open, centralized markets may lead to more firms in equilibrium and not just more intense competition among existing firms.

Although the value that can be created would therefore seem to be greatest toward the top right part of Figure 4-3, there has been a somewhat gradual and evolutionary shift in this direction in the strategies of those seeking to establish intermediaries. The earliest approaches, which were the antecedents to e-markets, focused on "procurement" rather than "markets" and on indirect rather than direct purchases. They sought to automate and rationalize existing procurement processes. To get maximal leverage for their efforts, they focused on horizontal markets because the suppliers of those items serve many verticals, and thus any supplier that could transact with downstream buyers in this way could also potentially reach many buyers. Moreover, indirect purchases seem to be a more natural starting point than direct purchases because they are less intimately tied to the manufacturing processes of the firms and therefore need to be less sensitive to issues of supply chain coordination and integration.

Typically, as we described in Chapter 1, firms pursuing this approach offered a procurement module that their customers could add to an existing ERP system. Besides enabling electronic transactions, they also integrated with management systems that could ensure both that disparate purchases were aggregated to yield bulk discounts as well as ensure that purchasing agents were adhering to corporate policies and staying within their budgets. Ariba's ORMS product is an example.

With the spread of the Internet and WWW, however, the rhetoric soon began to change toward the establishment of trading hubs as firms realized they could use the Internet to exploit the network effects described previously. Firms like Ariba introduced the idea of linking users of ORMS in a centralized hub. A similar approach was taken by providers of the ERP systems, who sought to provide a collaborative transactions environment for firms that had already implemented their ERP systems by adding additional products and functionality (SAP's mySAP offering is an example—see the ERP Overview in Part II for details). Figure 4-4 illustrates a typical evolutionary path that this approach envisions. Others, like Commerce One, sought to exploit expertise, experience, and assets in electronic catalogs to provide electronic marketplaces.

More interestingly, however, the focus started to shift from horizontal to vertical hubs. This trend is especially interesting because, for reasons described previously, at

FIGURE 4-4 The Evolution from ERP to E-Markets

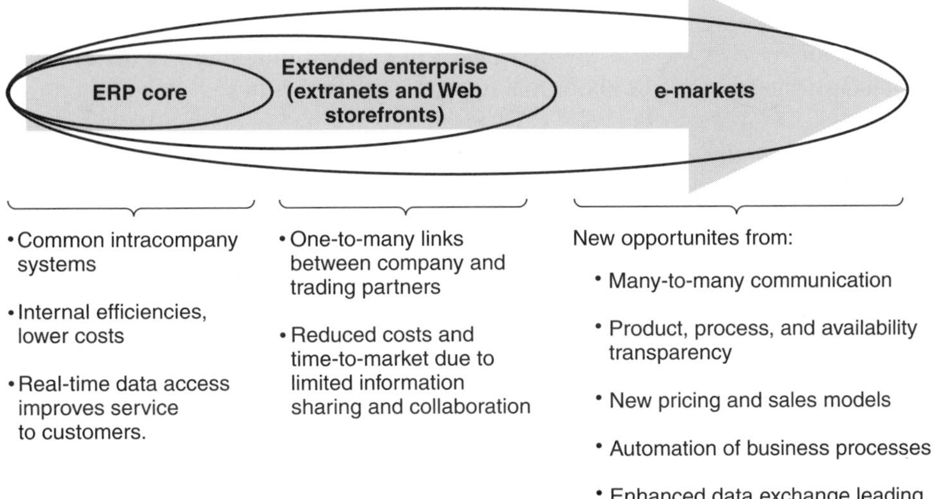
ERP core
Extended enterprise (extranets and Web storefronts)
e-markets
• Common intracompany systems
• Internal efficiencies, lower costs
• Real-time data access improves service to customers.
• One-to-many links between company and trading partners
• Reduced costs and time-to-market due to limited information sharing and collaboration
New opportunites from:
• Many-to-many communication
• Product, process, and availability transparency
• New pricing and sales models
• Automation of business processes
• Enhanced data exchange leading to collaboration

Source: E-Markets 2000 case in this volume.

first blush these would seem to be less amenable to the early adoption of e-markets. The reason for this trend can be found in the nature of markets subject to network effects described in Chapter 3. Since buyers want to be where the sellers are and the sellers want to be where the buyers are, there is a premium to liquidity. Consequently the markets that have the largest share of transactions tend to grow at the expense of smaller ones. That is—as is typical of markets with network effects—they tend to tip toward the winners. The network effects also tend to tie the participants together once they are in established relationships. You cannot defect to a new marketplace unless you can take many of the existing participants with you. Thus these are often "winner-takes-all" markets, and many vertical markets will end up with only one or two marketplaces even though they currently have many contenders. It also means, however, that if an early mover manages to establish itself as a "gatekeeper"—that is, as the organizer of the marketplace—it may have a sustainable position that will last for a long time.

This would not be the first time that firms have used a period of technological disruption to capture value that other firms upstream or downstream from them in the vertical industry structure or their own rivals within their layer of that structure had previously captured. A classic example of this occurred in the airline industry when electronic reservations became possible. American Airlines and United Airlines launched electronic customer reservation systems (CRSs), the Sabre and Apollo systems respectively, that enabled travel agents to book seats on their flights as well as those of other airlines that chose to participate. Since travel agents do not wish to use many different systems, CRSs were subject to strong network effects, and soon there were only a few competing systems. Competitors of American and United soon complained, however, that those airlines were using their systems to unfair advantage.

One of the most difficult parts of creating and dominating a marketplace, however, is getting critical mass in the first place. Because of the effects we described in Chapter 3, firms are nervous about making the investments necessary to join a marketplace in case others do not join. (Who wants to be stuck with the market equivalent of an 8-track tape player?) Thus there are conflicting motives of fear and greed at play. No one wants to invest in a marketplace that no one else joins; yet anyone would love to own a marketplace that everyone joins.

One way to get momentum in such situations is to enlist the support of a large player who brings both a large volume of transactions to the marketplace and by virtue of its importance to the industry is a focal point that others will want to join. While few firms have this stature in the global economy as a whole, many have it within their own vertical markets. Thus large industry leaders (like General Motors, for example) began to emerge as contenders to form marketplaces, typically prodded and supported by particular providers of the underlying technology (firms like Ariba, CommerceOne, i2, IBM, and Oracle, for example). Once industry leaders began to put a stake in the ground, others were quick to follow suit, or at least to take a position, for fear of looking like they were being left out.

The industry market structures of the buying and supplying sides of the marketplace are therefore important factors both because of the amount of value that such marketplaces are likely to provide and how they are likely to be organized. The greatest value can be created in markets in which both the buying and selling sides are fragmented because that is where buyers and sellers have the hardest time finding one another. Unfortunately, these are also likely to be the hardest markets for an intermediary to organize because the chicken-and-egg problem is the greatest in them. In contrast, markets that have just a few buyers and sellers are likely to be the easiest to organize. However, the value created more easily is of the lowest value since these firms already know one another and can arrange for bilateral interconnections.

Markets in which one side is concentrated and the other is fragmented are probably the most likely early candidates to form marketplaces. At least if there are a few large players on one side of the market, it is possible to use a hub-and-spoke strategy, using a large player to encourage its many suppliers (or buyers, as the case may be) to join. Since the hubs are the key to the success of such ventures, they are likely to end up capturing much of the value that is created; it is also a setting in which it is very hard for a neutral third party to wrest control. Figure 4-5 summarizes these observations.

Although the flurry of activity around vertical markets is understandable in this context, these nascent intermediaries must confront the fact that since they are dealing largely with direct purchases, they are operating in the part of the market where supply chain coordination issues are the most difficult. As we have discussed previously, the creation and capture of value through electronic transactions in supply chains entail more than simply bringing buyers and sellers together in a convenient setting. In particular, they include all the obstacles to close supply chain integration that we discussed previously.

FIGURE 4-5 Marketplace Outcomes Depending on Numbers of Buyers and Sellers

		Sellers: *Few*	Sellers: *Many*
Buyers	*Few*	Less value created Less need for marketplace Difficult for third party to enter	Intermediate levels of value created Intermediate need for marketplace Buyers best positioned to establish market
	Many	Intermediate levels of value created Intermediate need for marketplace Sellers best positioned to establish market	Huge value created Hard to get traction (chicken-and-egg problem) Role for third party

However, the multilateral nature of the marketplaces introduces additional complexities. For example, late movers and smaller firms are worried that they will be subject to an uneven playing field and become locked in to a marketplace that others own. Consequently the governance structure of marketplaces has become a contentious issue. Also the sources of inertia that even two parties in a supply chain face (for example, change can be organizationally threatening to employees who are using the legacy systems) are magnified when many parties must agree to move. It is well known that adoption of new technology is faster when an individual makes the decision, and becomes progressively more difficult and slower as that decision-making entity moves to a group, enterprise, or interenterprise.

We do not mean to suggest that these obstacles are so great that electronic intermediaries will not play a significant role. Indeed we believe that in many industries they will. However, especially for vertical markets, many technical, organizational, and interorganizational issues will have to be overcome. Consequently the road there will often be long, slow, and difficult. That road will also often be evolutionary, rather than the "big bang" that proponents hope for, in which all the industry players move simultaneously.

Indeed, individual firms will often take the first step with their own suppliers or buyers, using the Internet and the WWW to get these efficiencies among themselves. Many firms are deploying extranets of that kind. Of course, since buyers and suppliers are members of many such groups, as long as the technologies they are using are compatible, these extranets may eventually become joined, forming a larger marketplace. Because compatibility requires open standards or interoperability, however, the technology adoption decisions will often be overlaid on complex politicized standards battles. (See the E-Markets 2000 case for more on this issue.)

SUMMARY

Creating and capturing value from B2B supply chain improvements are fascinating areas of opportunity and frustration for electronic commerce. On the one hand, the new technologies provide evolutionary (gradual improvement in existing supply chains) and revolutionary (restructuring of supply chains through electronic markets) approaches to seamlessly coordinating information and production throughout the chain. On the other hand, they often butt up against the organizational forces that have slowed progress in the past, and the bolder attempts at restructuring markets introduce a host of new political, technical, and organizational issues.

Some analysts expect the already large number of marketplaces that have been established to continue to grow for at least the next few years. However, as many of these nascent exchanges fail to get traction, their funding is likely to dry up, and the consolidation that has already swept through the B2C sector is likely to follow too. The survivors may well be those that have the domain expertise to help firms overcome the organizational and political inertial forces that plague markets attempting to build critical mass, rather than those that have the "coolest" technology. Moreover, the firms that do succeed may well be those that follow incremental strategies, like building out extranets, for example, rather than those that attempt to get entire industries to coalesce at once.

The financial difficulty in which so many firms in this space find themselves is not necessarily an indictment of the phenomenon nor an indication that value will not be created here. First, value may be created but captured by others (existing suppliers and buyers, for example). Second, and more likely, as these markets shake out, there will often be at most one or two marketplaces in each industry or market sector left standing. In a few cases, the victors may well be the "winners" that "take all." Either way, in this area we are closer to the beginning of the road than to the end.

PART II

CASES

OVERVIEW OF THE CASES

The cases in Part II contain a wealth of information about technologies, industries, issues, firms, strategies, and organizational structures. They also pose issues that the challenge of electronic commerce confronts for students and practitioners. The objective of the cases is to provide some context and background to stimulate in-class discussion of the open issues in the cases. However they are also useful resources for readers simply wanting to learn more about an area that interests them. The cases are grouped into four sections.

The first section, Technology and Logistics, examines in more detail each of the most important technological and logistical components of the electronic commerce landscape discussed in Chapter 1. The ERP Overview and SAP and Online Procurement cases discuss enterprise software systems and analyze how one of the leading firms, SAP, is positioned to compete in the online procurement market. The Siebel Systems, Inc. case describes the booming customer relationship management market and its leading firm. The QRS Corporation case provides background on electronic data interchange and examines the role of an important intermediary. AOL: The Emergence of an Internet Media Company examines the role of portals, and the Webvan.com case discusses the "last mile" problem in fulfillment and delivery.

The second section, Markets and Channels, contains cases that examine issues related to changes in market structure and function, including the growing role that online auctions (Online Auctions in 1999), electronic markets (E-Markets 2000), and pricing and branding (Pricing and Branding on the Internet) play. Channel structure and channel conflict (GAP.com and Nike: Channel Conflict) and disintermediation (Disintermediation in the U.S. Auto Industry) are also included.

The third section, Strategy and Organization, examines the opportunities and challenges that electronic commerce poses for both established and new companies, and the markets for talent and advice that these companies can draw on (including Web development, consulting, venture capital, and so on in E-Commerce Building Blocks). The Karen Brown case describes the opportunities and risks involved in a possible deal between a travel portal and a traditional publisher of travel guides. The Broker.com case discusses the evolution of competition in the brokerage industry, including both online and traditional firms, and provides the context for understanding each group's competitive strategy.

The BabyCenter.com case shows how a firm can exploit the Internet to create a novel business strategy and discusses partnering, global expansion, and acquisition issues. HP E-Services.Solutions examines the challenges a traditional information technology provider faces in responding to electronic commerce opportunities and the strategic response of one of the leading firms. An established company wanting to acquire new technology or develop an electronic commerce operation has to decide how to organize that activity, in particular whether to organize as an internal venture or as a new, separate firm. The Cisco Systems case examines the novel approach that company has taken to fund and then "spin in" new technology. Finally, the Tradeweave case integrates many of the topics described in this section and analyzes the opportunity, strategy, and organization involved in launching an electronic commerce venture.

The final section, Strategy and Public Policy Issues, examines how firms' nonmarket environments affect their electronic commerce strategies and behavior. These cases, written or supervised by our colleague David Baron, consider privacy issues (DoubleClick and Internet Privacy), intellectual property (eBay and Database Protection), and taxation (Internet Taxation).

ERP OVERVIEW[1]

Large organizations often spread information across many homegrown computer systems in different functions or organizational units. While each of these "information islands" can support a specific business activity, the lack of integrated information hampers enterprisewide performance. Further, maintaining these systems can be costly. For example, many of the older programs could not handle dates beyond the year 2000 and were expensive to fix or replace.[2]

While firms fixed the Y2K bug (at an estimated cost of $600 billion worldwide), the lack of integration is still pervasive. For example, Boeing relies on hundreds of internal and external suppliers for the millions of components it needs to build an airplane. Boeing used four hundred disparate systems that were designed in the 1960s to try to put the right parts in the right airplane in the right sequence at the right time. Information inconsistencies were rife and the systems were not synchronized. As a result, parts often arrived late, idling partially built airplanes on Boeing's assembly lines. In 1997, these problems became unbearable, and Boeing had to shut down two major assembly lines and take a $1.6 billion charge against earnings. An integrated Enterprise Resource Planning (ERP) system based on commercial, off-the-shelf software has replaced these systems at Boeing.

With the advent of e-business and the need to leverage multiple sources of information within the enterprise, ERP software has become important for many businesses. Back-office enterprise software has its roots in the 1960s and 1970s, when companies became able to automate materials planning through MRP (Material Requirements Planning) and financial processing through payroll and general ledger software. MRP converts forecasted demand for a manufactured product into a requirements schedule for the components, subassemblies, and raw materials that comprise it. MRP only controls the flow of components and materials and is not effective for more complete production control and coordination. The next generation of manufacturing software, MRP II, integrates business activities into a common framework to address this shortcoming. MRP II divides the production control problem into a hierarchy based on time scale and product aggregation. It coordinates the manufacturing process and links together such tasks as capacity planning, demand management, production scheduling, and distribution.

However, even MRP II primarily serves a company's manufacturing needs. Its data and processes are not integrated with those in the rest of the enterprise, such as

[1] January 2000. By Haim Mendelson, Graduate School of Business, Stanford University, Stanford, Calif. 94305-5015. Send comments to haim@stanford.edu.

[2] This problem is known as the Y2K bug.

marketing, finance, and human resources. ERP facilitates information sharing and integration across these different functions, allowing the enterprise to use a unified data store and consistent processes to operate more efficiently and effectively.

WHAT IS ERP?

ERP provides the backbone for an enterprise-wide information system. Its software architecture facilitates the flow of information among the different functions, units, and locations within an enterprise.[3] It enables decision makers to get the enterprise-wide information they need in a timely, reliable, and consistent fashion.

At the core of this enterprise software, a central[4] database draws data from and feeds it into modular applications that operate on a common computing platform, thus standardizing business processes and data definitions into a unified environment. With an ERP system, data need to be entered only once. The system provides consistency and visibility—or transparency—across the entire enterprise. It makes reliable, integrated information easier to get, eliminates redundant data, and rationalizes processes, which cuts costs.

The integration among business functions facilitates communication and information sharing, leading to dramatic gains in productivity. Cisco Systems, for example, harnessed ERP to help it become the market leader in the global networking industry. Cisco's ERP system enabled its new business model—Global Networked Business—to build interactive, knowledge-based relationships with its customers, business partners, suppliers, and employees. In the process, Cisco doubled in size each year and reaped hundreds of millions of dollars in cost savings and revenue enhancements. An ERP system at Autodesk, a computer-aided design software company, cut order fulfillment times from two weeks to 24 hours. Similar examples abound in other businesses.[5]

Based on the promise of tightly integrated corporate functions, globally optimized decisions, and fast and easy access to accurate information, enterprise software has become essential to many large businesses. By 1998, over 20,000 firms around the world had spent $17 billion on enterprise software, following annual growth rates that ranged from 30% to 50%[6] (see Figure 1). Companies are using enterprise software to automate front-office activities such as sales and marketing, call center operations, product configuration, lead tracking, and customer relations.

GROWTH OF THE ENTERPRISE SOFTWARE INDUSTRY

Four trends increased the enterprise software market. First, as discussed previously, an integrated information architecture improves business performance. Once a major company in an industry adopts enterprise software, its competitors often must follow suit

[3] In recent years, ERP systems also started supporting interorganizational linkages.

[4] The database may be physically centralized, as in earlier mainframe-based systems, or distributed.

[5] As discussed later, not all ERP implementations are as successful.

[6] Based on data in AMR Research, *ERP Software Report*. As discussed later, the ERP market experienced a substantial slowdown in 1999.

FIGURE 1 ERP Software Market Revenues, 1993–2000

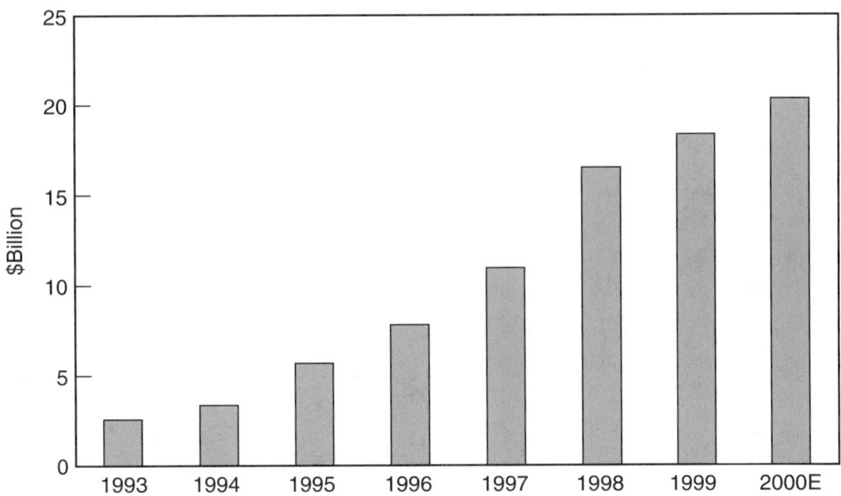

to stay competitive. Second, firms are using more packaged applications. This was partly related to the "Y2K bug" and the European Union's conversion to a single currency, which induced companies to replace their legacy systems with packaged software, effectively "outsourcing" the solution to the ERP vendor. Third, many companies abandoned legacy software due to the demands of e-commerce and front-office applications on the front end and the need to link to suppliers and business partners at the back end. Similarly, many companies have purchased ERP packages because of the emergence of ERP-based "vertical applications" that address the needs of a specific industry. Finally, many companies have had to put more emphasis on their use of information technology (IT) and invest in a more robust enterprise architecture because of rapid advances in computer and software technologies combined with the explosive growth of the Internet.[7]

Hundreds of software producers fight for market share in the enterprise software business. Some companies offer an integrated suite of applications; others address specific business processes. Five companies known in industry parlance as JOPS—J. D. Edwards, Oracle, PeopleSoft, and SAP AG—made up the first group. They attempt to create "end-to-end" solutions for an entire enterprise, so that their customers will purchase most of their critical enterprise applications from them. The reasoning behind this strategy is twofold. First, enterprise applications increasingly need to communicate and interact with each other seamlessly. For example, a company's delivery time becomes more reliable if it integrates its sales order entry and manufacturing software packages; if the company buys all of the software from the same vendor, it can integrate

[7] Additional recent trends are discussed in the last section of this case.

FIGURE 2 ERP and ERP-Related Packaged Application Market, 1998–2003

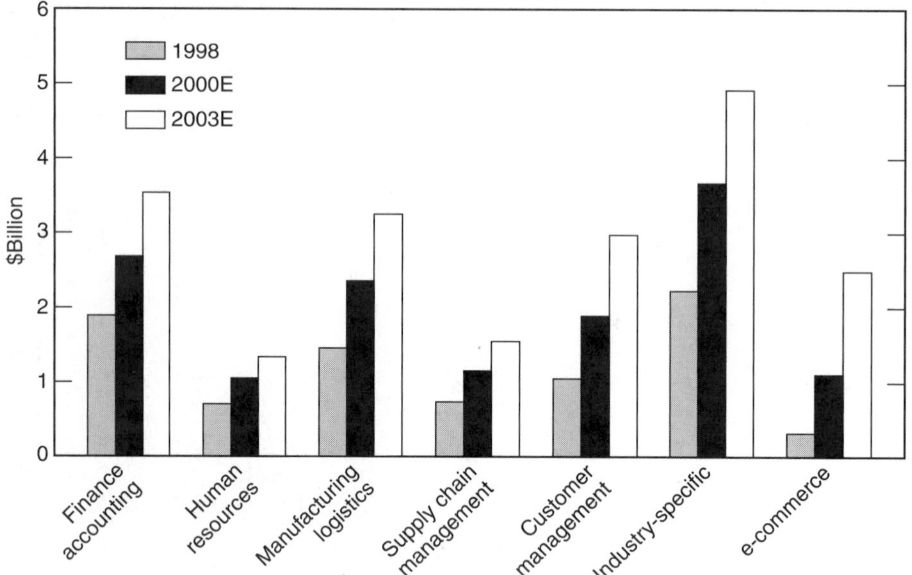

applications more tightly. Second, customers may prefer to rely on one major vendor for most of their software needs, because that simplifies contracting and makes that vendor accountable for all of the firm's software problems.

On the other hand, scores of companies make innovative products to provide software solutions to manage customer relations, supply chain, e-commerce, and purchasing applications. Their software can be "bolted on" to the existing ERP backbone to provide a flexible "best-of-breed" portfolio of solutions in different areas. Players in customer relationship management include Siebel Systems, Clarify, Remedy, Epiphany, Broadvision, and Trilogy. Their software helps with customer support, product configuration, one-to-one marketing, and sales-force automation. Leaders in e-commerce software are too numerous to list (and the list changes daily), but some examples are GE Information Systems, Sterling Communications, Ariba Technologies, and Commerce One. Supply chain management software helps companies optimize their production processes and logistics across the entire supply chain; i2 Technologies and Manugistics are leaders in this area. Figure 2 shows the size of the packaged application market by category and market forecasts for the years 2000 and 2003.[8]

These approaches are not mutually exclusive. Some ERP companies are acquiring smaller players to fill the gaps in their "end-to-end" solutions, while others are developing interfaces at the front and back end of their ERP offerings.

[8] Source: Adapted from Forrester Research reports.

ERP SOFTWARE VENDORS

Throughout the 1990s, SAP led the ERP market. Figure 3 shows total revenues of the top five ERP firms.[9]

SAP AG

The leading ERP package vendor, with a 32% market share in 1999, is SAP AG (SAP stands for Systems, Applications, and Products in Data Processing). Five engineers who wanted to produce integrated business application software for manufacturing founded SAP AG in Germany in 1972. Seven years later, the company launched its first enterprise software, R/2, designed around a centralized, mainframe-based database. SAP introduced its client/software product, R/3, in 1992, and it quickly dominated the ERP software market.[10] In 1999, SAP AG was the third largest independent software vendor in the world, serving more than 11,000 customers (with more than 20,000 installations) in over 100 countries.

Leveraging its leading position in the ERP market, SAP developed vertical, industry-specific business solutions for 19 industries that provide functionality from SAP and its partners for complete, end-to-end industry-specific processes.[11] Following the lead of focused niche players, in 1999 SAP extended its ERP offering to include customer relationship management, data warehousing, and supply chain management modules. SAP recast its entire set of offerings around the Internet, borrowing the "business portal"

FIGURE 3 Sales of Leading ERP Vendors

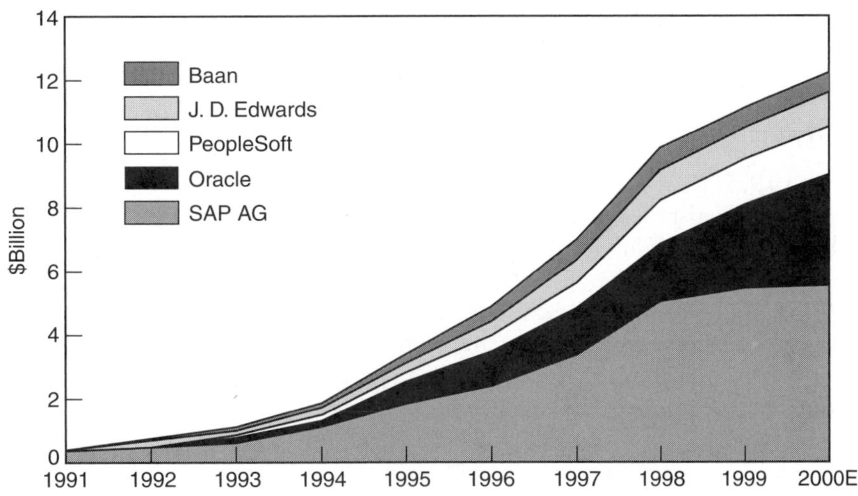

[9] Source: Company annual reports and author's analysis.
[10] The structure of SAP R/3 is discussed in the next section.
[11] Examples are SAP Automotive, SAP High-Tech, SAP Aerospace and Defense, SAP Banking, SAP Insurance, and SAP Utilities.

concept (called mySAP.com Workplace in SAP parlance) to organize all information around the user's role in the enterprise, and adding functionality for business-to-business and business-to-consumer electronic commerce. SAP started the mySAP.com Marketplace, an electronic intercompany trading community for buying, selling, and collaborating within and across industries.

Oracle

The heavyweight of the database software market, Silicon Valley-based Oracle is the world's second largest software company. It has built a solid enterprise applications business, which accounted for $2.5 billion of the firm's $9.3 billion 1999 revenues. Second to SAP in the enterprise software market, Oracle applications serve over 5,000 customers in 140 countries. Oracle has refocused its ERP solutions around the Internet and launched a barrage of electronic-commerce and Internet-based business-to-business software applications while the other JOPS companies were slow to react to the changing marketplace. Oracle was also the first JOPS company to integrate front-office applications with its ERP offering.

PeopleSoft

Started as a software firm for human resource management in 1987, PeopleSoft expanded its software to cater to other corporate functions. Its revenues grew to $1.3 billion in 1998—from $32 million in 1992 (sales were expected to remain flat in 1999). PeopleSoft's ERP system provides enterprise solutions for finance, materials management, distribution, supply chain planning, manufacturing, and human resources. In 1996, PeopleSoft acquired Red Pepper, a producer of supply chain management software, and in 1999, it acquired Vantive for its customer relationship management offering.

J. D. Edwards

Founded in 1977, J. D. Edwards addresses business processes in finance, manufacturing, distribution/logistics, and human resources and encompasses the entire supply chain from planning and scheduling through execution. Growing from $120 million in revenues in 1992 to $944 million in 1999, it has served more than 5,000 customers in more than 100 countries. Many firms consider its OneWorld system more flexible than its competitors' offerings, and the company sold it to many smaller enterprises. Rather than build its own customer relationship management system, J. D. Edwards developed tight integration with Siebel's leading offering.

Baan[12]

Baan was founded in The Netherlands in 1978 to make financial software. Because its products were simpler to use than SAP's, the company grew in the early 1990s to serve

[12] JOPS was called JBOPS until 2000, when Baan was acquired by Invensys.

more than 2,800 customers in 80 countries. Baan's net revenues have increased from $47 million in 1992 to $736 million in 1998. Its primary enterprise system, the Baan Services, incorporates a variety of functionalities from sale order management and manufacturing to supply chain management. Beginning in October 1998, management turmoil, accounting irregularities, multiple-quarter losses, and CEO turnover hurt Baan, and Invensys PLC acquired it in 2000.

Choosing the right ERP package is difficult. First a customer must identify system scope and its business objectives and processes. Some ERP packages provide better solutions in certain functional areas. For example, SAP excels in manufacturing software. Moreover, different ERP vendors have experience in different industries and offer solutions geared to those industries. Figure 4 summarizes the recommendations of Benchmarking Partners' consultants on industries that the different ERP packages served well.

In choosing a package, firms must also consider their management style. Even the most flexible ERP packages are based on a model of doing business that may not align with a firm's desired business model. For example, Dell Computer found that the SAP R/3 system it had licensed would not fit its highly decentralized management style. Time-to-implementation may also be critical. Moreover firms need to consider technical issues ranging from the hardware platform that the ERP package will run on to currencies and tax rules. The stability and future viability of the ERP vendor are also important.

Implementing of ERP packages is a major effort. Costs include licensing the package, consulting, process redesign, data conversion, training, integration, and testing. A Gemini Consulting survey of 220 companies found that the average SAP R/3 implementation effort consumed 141 person-months and cost $7.5 million. While most companies surveyed were pleased with the outcome, many ERP implementations are cancelled, or scaled back, or involve late deliveries, budget overruns, and hampered

FIGURE 4 ERP Packages and the Industries They Serve

	Aerospace/Defense	*Automotive*	*Consumer Packaged Goods*	*Electronics*	*Industrial/Manufacturing*	*Oil/Gas*	*Pharmaceuticals*
J. D. Edwards OneWorld		*	*	*	*	*	*
Oracle Applications	*	*	*	*	*	*	*
PeopleSoft		*	*	*			
SAP R/3	*	*	*	*	*	*	*
% ERP Penetration	10–15	5–10	35+	40+	35	30	20

processes. Hershey Foods, the United States's largest candy maker, went live in July 1999 with a companywide $112 million ERP system that left many retailers with empty shelves. Hershey incurred significant losses when it could not fix its order fulfillment problems in time for Halloween or Christmas. When Whirlpool switched to a new SAP platform over the 1999 Labor Day holiday, the system lost about 10% of the orders entered in it.

It can get worse. FoxMeyer Drug, once the fourth largest distributor of pharmaceuticals in the United States, went out of business after it implemented an SAP system projected to save it $40 million a year. After two-and-a-half years and more than $100 million in costs, FoxMeyer could process less than 1/40 of its orders—with multiple problems. In August 1996, FoxMeyer, once a $5 billion company, went bankrupt. Its bankruptcy trustee sued SAP AG and Andersen Consulting, the systems integrator in charge of the effort, for half a billion dollars each (both deny misconduct).[13]

THE LEADING ERP PACKAGE: SAP R/3

SAP R/3 is a general-purpose platform with options that enable each company to configure it for its specific needs without changing the R/3 code. This is a complex process that can take years to implement. The organization, the business process, and all transaction details must be explicitly modeled and entered as settings in about 8,000 configuration tables.[14] The user defines precisely the organizational units, processes, transactions, different SAP R/3 screens, reports, and so forth.

SAP R/3 consists of modules that customers may use separately or together. It allows third-party solutions that provide other functionalities to be "bolted on" to the SAP backbone. All the modules are integrated, so different parts of the enterprise use the same data at the same time. The software can also link business processes between companies worldwide, for example, between a supplier and a customer in different countries.

Example: Integrated Order Process

The SAP R/3 database integrates all data items, so entire processes use the same data, seamlessly passed from step to step. Consider, for example, how SAP R/3 manages the order fulfillment process. As Figure 5 shows, when a customer inquires about a potential purchase (Stage 1), SAP R/3 creates a quote (Stage 2) that includes price and delivery date. The quote takes into account what the system already knows about the customer (Stage 3), the item, and inventory and materials availability (Stage 4), which are in the SAP R/3 database. As a result, the prices and delivery times and delivery terms are based on up-to-date information and may be specific to a customer or an order. If the customer accepts the quote, SAP records a sales order (Stage 5), including pricing and delivery terms. The order then triggers the entire order fulfillment process. SAP automatically sends the relevant data where it needs to go, so delivery can be automatically

[13] See "FoxMeyer's Delta Project" case study by Haim Mendelson, January 2000.

[14] The tables have standard default settings, but companies typically need to change them, and each change affects other values and tables.

FIGURE 5 SAP R/3 Order Process Stages

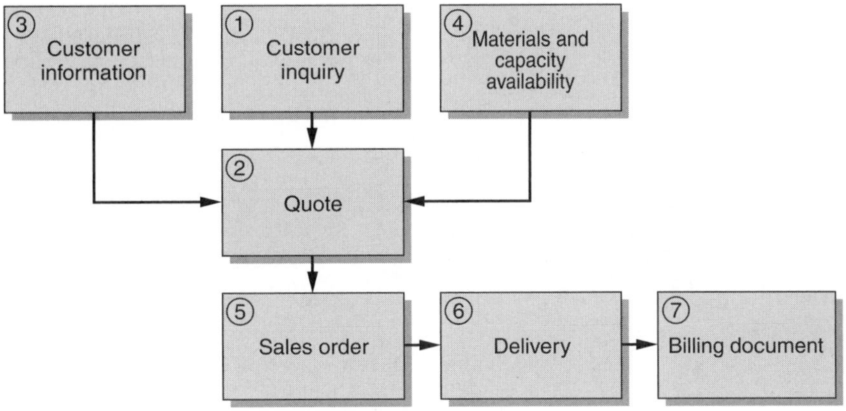

scheduled (Stage 6). The system can automatically check the customer's credit limit and manage the collection process (Stage 7).

Linking SAP R/3 to Other Applications: BAPIs

SAP does not solve everything. For example, the firm's forecasting or customer relationship management processes may not be modeled within SAP. Where SAP does not provide a solution, it is possible to "bolt on" another application to attain the required functionality.

SAP has an open, component-based architecture that enables integration with other applications. This architecture consists of two key elements:

1. **SAP Business Objects** are essentially "black boxes" that contain SAP R/3 data and business processes, while suppressing the details of their data structure or specific implementation details.
2. **BAPIs (Business Application Programming Interfaces)** define how the application links to SAP R/3. The result is a standard method of communication between SAP R/3 and other applications.

Business objects are the business-application versions of real-world entities, such as a sales order or an employee. The core of the business object is the actual data (for instance, an employee's name and ID number). The interface is a set of clearly defined methods, each specifying what operations can be performed on this data (including the possibility of altering it).

A BAPI is a method of an SAP business object, which enables external access to SAP R/3 data and processes. Figure 6 illustrates how business objects and BAPIs function. For instance, if an application performs demand forecasting by exponential smoothing,

FIGURE 6 Interfacing to SAP R/3

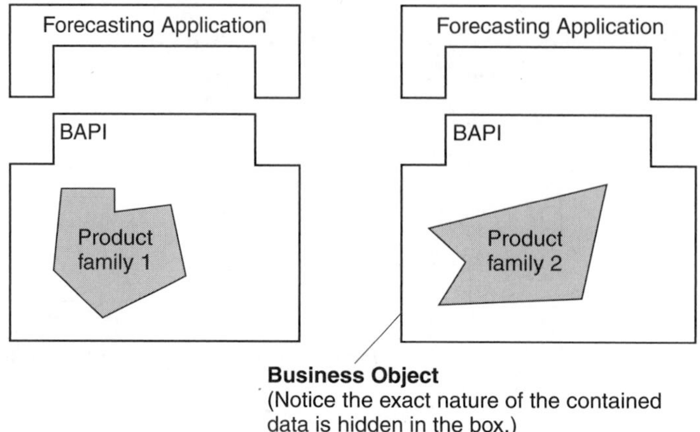

the application can examine quantity demanded in the past, product by product, even if products have different data items.

FROM ERP TO E-BUSINESS

In the last decade, ERP software has exploded around the world. To remain competitive, companies must leverage their information assets across the entire enterprise, and ERP packages promise to let them do that. The unified framework ERP packages provide and the business processes they support are the result of a balancing act between standardization and discipline on the one hand, and flexibility and agility on the other. The increasing emphasis on front-end, customer-focused applications and the growing importance of e-commerce and interenterprise business networks are tipping this balance. As a result, the traditional inward focus of the large ERP players had to change. Oracle's chief executive, Larry Ellison, put it bluntly:

> *We blew it in the 1990s. By running applications on the client, client/server was meant to put information at your fingertips. But all we did was to create distributed complexity and fragmented data. CEOs have come to hate IT, because they can't get what they want from it. Burger King put an SQL Server database in every hamburger store, but they still couldn't answer the question, "how many Whoppers are we selling each day?" ERP as an industry missed the boat. It focused on automating processes, not on getting information to key decision makers. So how do we do it now? We've learned from the Internet that you don't put shared applications on the client and that you centralize complexity. You consolidate your data. The unchanging appliance accesses the dynamic applications of the network.*[15]

[15] Ellison's comments (*The Economist*, June 26, 1999) refer both to the leading ERP vendors and the client/server computing paradigm they follow.

With the advent of e-business, companies are using the Internet to link with their suppliers, customers, and trading partners. This shifts the emphasis from the traditional internal focus of the ERP vendors to an external orientation, increasing the importance of both business-to-business and front-office applications, which have been traditionally bolted on to companies' ERP backbones. The fortunes of the leading ERP vendors changed along with the changing marketplace: ERP package sales slowed (see Figure 3),[16] and the stocks of traditional ERP vendors lost value. The ERP package vendors promised to broaden their offerings to fulfill the promise of e-business, but only time will tell whether they can extend their architectures to satisfy the new demands—or whether today's ERP systems will become tomorrow's legacy systems.

[16] The maturation of the ERP market (by 1999, about half of the potential large-company ERP market had been penetrated) and the Y2K problem, which caused IT managers to shy away from major new installations, also contributed to the slowdown.

STANFORD
GRADUATE SCHOOL OF BUSINESS

SAP AND THE ONLINE-PROCUREMENT MARKET

A NEW STRATEGY

As 1999 ended, German software giant SAP AG was trying to execute a corporate strategy that it had forged earlier that year. Faced with slowing growth for its core product—enterprise resource planning (ERP) software that automated corporate processes such as manufacturing, accounting, and human resource management—SAP management devised a new business plan that involved three main thrusts. One was to continue expanding its offerings beyond ERP by developing enterprise software for the fast-growing customer relationship management (CRM) and supply chain management (SCM) markets, an initiative that the company first conceived in 1996 but had been slow to act on. Second was to recast its entire product line with a unified Internet focus. Third, SAP had decided to enter the market for electronic-commerce software and services, including the creation and management of online trading communities. This represented a far-reaching departure from its traditional ERP business.

A major target of SAP's new e-commerce strategy was the market for online-procurement software and services—tools that enabled companies to automate and manage their purchases of "operating resources" (i.e., goods and services, such as office supplies, furniture, travel services, etc., that were not direct inputs into a company's products). The online-procurement market was still in its infancy—worldwide sales of online-procurement software and services were just $62 million in 1998 (compared to $16.6 billion for ERP software sales that year).[1] But analysts estimated that the pro-

---

Case Writer Eric Martí prepared this case under the supervision of Professor Garth Saloner and Professor A. Michael Spence as the basis for class discussion rather than to illustrate either effective or ineffective handling of an administrative situation. Margot Sutherland, Executive Director, Center for Electronic Business and Commerce, Stanford Graduate School of Business managed the development of the case.

[1] "Procurement Pays Off," Charles Waltner, *Information Week*, 7/26/99, p. 65; AMR Research.

curement market could exceed $14 billion by 2003: sales of software and related services (e.g., support, consulting, training) would generate $5 billion,[2] and transaction fees from online trade could generate $9 billion more.[3]

Several companies had already established leading positions in the nascent market, notably Ariba, Inc. and Commerce One, Inc., both of which had been started within the last five years and focused exclusively on the procurement opportunity. Neither company had yet produced a profit—for the quarter ending September 30, 1999, Ariba had a loss of $9.9 million on sales of $17.1 million, Commerce One lost $10.4 million on revenues of $10.4 million, and neither had more than a few dozen customers (Exhibits 1 and 2). By contrast, SAP had operated for more than 25 years and was now the world's third largest software company, with 1998 profits of $631 million (on sales of $5.1 billion). Thousands of organizations used its ERP software. Still, SAP was a relative newcomer to the online-procurement market, and its credibility was in question: on December 23, 1999, SAP's market value stood at $5.3 billion, while Ariba and Commerce One—which had become publicly traded companies just months before—each had values exceeding $14 billion. Clearly, investors regarded Ariba and Commerce One, not SAP, as the most credible contenders for the online-procurement market (Exhibits 3, 4, and 5).

SAP was driven to its new strategy by the need to find new sources of growth. The company commanded 30% of the market for ERP software, more than twice the share of the second-place vendor, Oracle Corporation. But SAP had begun to stumble. In January 1999, the company reported that pretax profits for 1998 increased just 15% over the year before—a performance that paled against profit growth that had averaged 46% a year (compounded annually) over the previous five years (1992–1997). In October 1999, SAP reported that despite a 14% increase in sales from the previous year's period, profits for the first nine months had fallen by 24%. The company reduced its sales growth forecast for 1999 and predicted that profits would be less than the year before. However, SAP management expected the new strategy to turn the company around in 2000 and beyond.

SAP BACKGROUND

SAP was started in 1972 by five former IBM engineers who wrote programs for mainframe computers to help industrial companies control their manufacturing processes. When IBM transferred the project they were working on to another unit, they left and founded SAP. By the 1980s, SAP's flagship product, R/2, was a leading mainframe application powering corporate information systems. But from the mid-1980s onward, corporations were shifting from mainframe computing to so-called distributed computing, using client/server architecture: client computers (desktop PCs and workstations) were connected by local- or wide-area networks to multiple servers (powerful computers that housed data and applications that the client computers could access).

[2] "Oracle Paves Procurement Path," M. A. Farmer, CNET News.com, 8/27/99.

[3] Based on Forrester Research's projection of $900 billion of online indirect purchases in 2003, and estimating average transaction fees of 1%.

SAP navigated this transition with flying colors. In 1992 it released R/3, a client/server version of its software that fueled tremendous growth: the company's sales soared from $513 million in 1992 to $5.1 billion in 1998, and profits grew even faster, from $40 million to $631 million (Exhibit 6). SAP's workforce also mushroomed, from 3,200 employees in 1992 to nearly 17,500 by the end of 1998. By 1999, some 12,000 companies around the world were using R/3 software at more than 20,000 sites. The next closest competitor, Oracle Corporation, had only 7,100 customers for its ERP software.

Though SAP's original focus was on manufacturing processes, its R/3 software encompassed a wide range of features and components for automating and controlling many aspects of corporate operations. The software comprised a core system, to which various modules could be added that extended its functionality. The complete product line included 12 modules for:

- Accounting and controlling;
- Production planning and materials management;
- Quality management and plant maintenance;
- Sales and distribution;
- Human resources management; and
- Project management.

Each of the modules incorporated features that controlled processes associated with the relevant corporate activity. Corporations could customize the modules to reflect their specific processes, practices, and business rules.

Because ERP system requirements varied among industries, SAP organized its product development and marketing around industry business units that it called "Centers of Expertise." The company had 19 such units, addressing specific industries ranging from aerospace to healthcare to retail.

ERP OVERVIEW

Like SAP's R/3, ERP software in general had its roots in programs first written in the 1960s and 1970s for mainframe computers that manufacturing organizations employed to help automate production planning. A car maker, for example, could use such software to calculate the precise type and quantity of parts required for various production runs of a particular vehicle. These programs were known initially as material requirements planning (MRP) systems and later as manufacturing resources planning (MRP II) systems.

These applications evolved to incorporate a broad array of functions beyond manufacturing operations. In addition to automating a company's preferred business practices, ERP systems also enabled companies to capture and analyze extensive internal data—such as inventory flow, production patterns, compensation levels, expenditures on equipment, investment and asset management statistics, and so on—which helped to inform managerial decisions. ERP systems thus served as the backbones of corporate information systems: they controlled core aspects of business operations and provided managers with key data to make strategic decisions (Exhibit 7).

Implementing an ERP system was expensive and complex. The cost of licensing the ERP software itself often represented less than 20% of the overall cost of implementing the system: additional costs included expenditures on hardware and, most significantly, fees paid to programmers, systems integrators, consultants, and other service providers. For large corporations—for example, a Fortune 500 company—installing an ERP system could cost $30 million in license fees and $200 million in professional services (plus millions more on hardware), and it could take three or more years to complete.[4]

Companies installed a system in stages, beginning with an assessment and design phase: analysts identified and deconstructed the thousands of business processes that constituted the company's operations—manufacturing procedures, inventory management rules, accounting practices, and so on—so that the ERP system could adapt and automate them. The system was generally installed on one area of operations at a time, such as manufacturing or accounting, and was rolled out in successive stages.

While ERP software was designed to standardize range of business processes, each installation typically required extensive customization to reflect a company's unique procedures and situation. An ERP system also had to interact with other software in the company's information system ("legacy applications")—such as, messaging systems, manufacturing control software, and database programs—which required further customization. Before an ERP system could go online, its various components needed repeated testing and debugging.

THE ERP SOFTWARE MARKET

The ERP software market exploded from worldwide sales of $2.1 billion in 1993 to $16.6 billion in 1998—a compound annual growth rate of 51.2%. Five companies accounted for nearly two-thirds of total sales (see Table 1).

These five firms—sometimes referred to by the acronym JBOPS—had increased their collective ERP market share from 44% in 1994 to more than 60% in 1998. SAP had remained the market leader, though its advantage over the second-place competitor had narrowed (from more than a 4-to-1 lead in 1994 to less than a 3-to-1 margin in 1998; Exhibits 8 and 9).

By late 1998, however, the ERP party had begun to wind down for three main reasons. First, the market was maturing: analysts estimated that ERP installations had penetrated as much as 50% of the potential customer base. The manufacturing sector, which accounted for three-quarters of ERP revenues in 1998, had a penetration rate of 56% (versus 43% for the nonmanufacturing sector).[5] Motivated buyers had already bought ERP systems; the remaining prospects would adopt ERP software more slowly. Analysts' forecasts for ERP sales growth over the next three to five years ranged from 17%

[4] "The E-Ware War: Competition Comes to Enterprise Software," David Kirkpatrick, *Fortune*, 12/7/98, p. 103.

[5] "ERP's Rough Waters," Eric Knorr, *Upside Today*, 11/18/99.

TABLE 1 Leading ERP Providers

Company	*1998 ERP Revenues ($B)*	*Market Share, Worldwide (%)*	*Number of ERP Customers*[6]
SAP AG	5.1	30.1	12,000
Oracle Corporation[7]	2.1	12.7	7,100
PeopleSoft Corporation	1.3	7.8	3,300
J. D. Edwards Company	1.1	6.6	5,000
The Baan Company	.743	4.5	3,700
Worldwide ERP Market[8]	16.6	100.0	

to 36% (compound annual growth rates); most researchers predicted a rate of 30% or less. Second, companies were siphoning dollars from ERP budgets to address the Y2K problem. Though analysts expected this to be a temporary drain on ERP spending, most predicted that post-Y2K funding for ERP systems would not reach its prior levels. Third, the explosive emergence and growth of the Internet that began in the mid-1990s was shifting corporate IT priorities toward Internet-based e-business software, an area of fervent innovation. Companies were rushing to build intranets and extranets, install e-mail systems, and establish online stores. Whole new categories of e-business software had emerged—commerce platforms, Web servers, Web application servers, search engines, catalog engines, and e-tail storefronts. New products and companies were announced every day.

A fourth factor also had potential to affect the fortunes of ERP vendors—the emerging market of application service providers (ASPs). These firms provided companies with various IT services on a contract basis: the ASP maintained both the software and hardware systems, and its clients would essentially rent their use as needed. This saved client companies from purchasing and installing their own systems. While most large corporations viewed ERP systems as mission-critical resources that they had to own and administer themselves, outsourcing ERP appealed to many midsize firms—an underpenetrated market segment. The ASP industry was in its infancy, but already several ASPs were offering ERP services. Some ERP vendors themselves had also begun to offer their own hosting services. While the emerging ASP market opened a potential new opportunity for ERP developers, particularly with small and midsize companies, it also threatened to reduce the number of ERP systems that could be sold and installed.

By early 1998, several of the JBOPS companies started to feel the effects of the slowing ERP market, and investors turned on their stocks. Beginning in May, Baan and PeopleSoft saw their share prices implode; each company lost three-quarters of

[6] *Enterprise Resource Planning Software*, R. J. Schwartz, A. C. Brosseau, and D. Gremmels, S. G. Cowen Securities Corp., 9/8/99, p. 9.

[7] Among these firms, Oracle was the only one that derived the majority of its revenues from outside the ERP category. As the world's leading vendor of corporate database software, Oracle received three-quarters of its sales from database products and related services. The company's total 1999 sales were $8.83 billion.

[8] AMR Research (figures published in *Computer Reseller News*, 4/19/99).

its market value in a few months. By year end, every JBOPS firm except Oracle had seen investors lop off 50%–80% of its share price. Oracle's shares gained value in 1998 because of its dominance in the database market: the boom in e-commerce was fueling demand for high-end databases to store rapidly expanding quantities of corporate data. Oracle was also increasing its share of the ERP market—which was still growing at 20%–30% a year—and the company was making credible bids for a share of the fast-growing CRM and electronic-commerce markets.

Reacting to these unfavorable ERP market trends, the firms had begun to extend their product lines into other areas of enterprise software. Three fast-growing markets were particularly attractive:

- Customer relationship management (CRM);
- Supply chain management (SCM); and
- E-commerce (EC) applications and services.

However, ERP firms' expansion plans faced major problems. First, other companies—many of them start-ups or young concerns—had staked out significant leads in each of these areas. In CRM, for example, six-year-old Siebel Systems had captured 35% of the $2.3 billion market; the company was highly profitable and growing at 80% a year. Two established companies dominated the $2.6 billion SCM market, i2 Technologies and Manugistics, whose combined market share exceeded 35%. The emerging EC market was a hotbed of competition among scores of new and established companies. For example, in the commerce platform segment—the technology that enabled companies to build online stores—leading providers included household names like IBM and America Online (via its Netscape unit), as well as lesser-known new entrants such as BroadVision and Blue Martini.

Second, many of the business processes involved in these areas—such as customer service and supplier relationship practices—were well outside ERP firms' expertise. Third, ERP software was designed so that only a limited number of trained, internal specialists at a corporation could use it. On average, for example, only 15%–20% of a SAP customer's workforce ever used the R/3 software.[9] By contrast, untrained, infrequent users—including individuals outside of the corporation, such as prospects, customers, and suppliers—often used CRM and e-commerce applications, and, to a lesser degree, SCM software.

Nonetheless, ERP firms viewed these opportunities as natural extensions of their expertise in building corporate information systems and all five of the leading ERP players were moving into these segments.

THE ONLINE-PROCUREMENT OPPORTUNITY

While many companies had automated (to a degree, at least) the purchasing of direct resources (i.e., materials and services that are directly used to produce a company's goods),

[9] "SAP AG," B. Skiba and M. Johnson, Lehman Brothers, 5/24/99, p. 6.

few companies had automated procurement of so-called operating resources (OR). These were the nonproduction goods and services that every company required to run its business—paper, pens, desks and chairs, janitorial and repair services, and so on. Though virtually all businesses purchased a common set of operating resources—for example, standard office supplies—demand for other categories of indirect products and services varied by industry, location, and other factors. FedEx, for example, was a large buyer of specialized printed materials (airbills and other forms), while IBM spent more than $3 billion annually on software.[10]

As a whole, U.S. businesses spent 33% of their revenues on nonproduction goods and services—approximately $1.4 trillion.[11] Analysts estimated that a disproportionate share of the average company's purchase transactions—80%—was for indirect goods and services. In addition, 95% of these purchases were transacted using paper-based manual processes.[12] The overhead costs associated with these transactions totaled as much as 10% of the value of the purchases themselves.

The OR purchasing process was filled with time consuming manual labor, multiple transfers of documents, and lengthy waits for approvals, processing, and fulfillment. In a typical scenario, an employee would fill out a requisition form, submit it to a supervisor, and wait for approval. The approved requisition was then routed to a purchasing department, where it was transferred to a specialist, who searched the approved vendor catalogs to ensure that orders went to suppliers with whom the company had negotiated favorable terms. Once the right item was found, the purchasing specialist made out the purchase order and mailed, faxed, or phoned it to the vendor. The vendor routed the purchase order to an order processor, who rekeyed the data into the vendor's order-fulfillment system.

To avoid this burdensome process, many departments purchased items from vendors with whom the employer had not negotiated special terms. These so-called maverick or rogue purchases represented about one-third of all indirect procurement. The National Association of Purchasing Managers estimated that companies paid a 17%–27% premium on maverick purchases.[13]

The OR procurement process was not automated for several reasons. First, demand for OR purchases was spread across a company's operations, diffused among its many departments and divisions. Second, a large company typically purchased OR items from hundreds or thousands of different suppliers across many industries: unlike production operations, the nature and timing of OR demand was irregular. Third, and perhaps most critical, companies viewed OR procurement as an administrative detail rather than a strategic operation. Many companies were unaware of the inefficiencies of their procurement process or regarded purchasing overhead as a cost of doing business.

Prior to the Web, electronic purchasing of operating resources was impractical for most organizations. Electronic data interchange (EDI), the technology that many large enterprises used to purchase production materials, was not efficient for most OR purchases. For two organizations to employ EDI between them, each had to install spe-

[10] "Who Spends How Much on What?" *Purchasing*, 11/4/99, p. 59.

[11] "Online-procurement: The Rise of the Market-Makers," *Electronic Commerce World*, 11/99, p. 24.

[12] "Ariba," R. J. Schwartz and D. Gremmels, S. G. Cowen Securities Corp., 9/9/99, pp. 5 and 15.

[13] Ariba prospectus filed with SEC, 6/24/99.

cial software that enabled their computer systems to communicate with each other. Further, each had to write complex programs that translated their business documents into a format that the other company's computer could understand. Each of the dozens of different document types that a company used required a separate translation procedure.

Further custom programming was needed to connect the company's EDI translation programs with the internal information system that ran its various back-office functions, such as billing and inventory management.

In addition to these setup costs, EDI transactions required a special communications network—either a dedicated phone line or a private network maintained by a third-party company specializing in EDI services—to connect the trading partners' computers securely and reliably. Most EDI users opted for a third-party network (called a "value added network," or VAN) that charged both subscription and transaction fees. Given these costs, companies typically conducted EDI with only a few of their largest and most frequent suppliers or customers, that is, with other organizations that could justify the high cost and complexity of EDI. As a result, few enterprises conducted EDI with more than 15%–20% of their trading partners.[14]

Nonetheless, there had been efforts to make OR procurement more efficient. For example, many supplier companies and third-party services had created electronic product catalogs that were distributed on CD-ROM or could be accessed via a dial-up modem. This made it easier for buyers to search a vendor's product list. Stand-alone procurement software had also been developed to help purchasing specialists search for products and initiate orders. And when the Web first appeared, many suppliers set up Web sites where buyers could search their catalogs and enter orders. But none of these methods reached every employee in a large company or fully integrated with the enterprise's information system.

In the mid-1990s, however, entrepreneurs realized that Web technology could automate OR procurement. The Web browser provided an easy-to-use way for any employee to make a transaction, and the Web created the infrastructure for a digital marketplace, with easy access to products from multiple suppliers. With an affordable, easy-to-use technology now available, companies could reduce procurement costs and use the savings to improve their bottom line: a 5% savings from automated procurement could bump profits by 28%.[15]

Online-procurement systems produced savings in four ways. First, they eliminated manual, paper-based procedures. According to AMR Research, processing a purchase transaction cost the typical corporation \$75–\$175.[16] Ariba claimed that its software could reduce that to between \$10 and \$30. Second, by reducing maverick buying, companies could eliminate the 17%–27% premium they paid on one-third of their purchases. Third, automation reduced the order-to-receipt cycle time and improved productivity. Fourth, with less effort spent processing forms manually, purchasing personnel could devote more time to building relationships with suppliers and negotiating better contracts.

[14] "The EDI Legacy," Eric Knorr, *Upside Today*, 10/26/99.

[15] "The Young Pretenders," *Supply Management*, 10/8/98, p. 23.

[16] *Business-to-Business E-Commerce*, Douglas J. Crook, Prudential Securities, 9/28/99, p. 22.

Anecdotal accounts of user experiences corroborated the dramatic cost savings. At Cisco Systems, for example, online-procurement reduced the cost of processing a purchase order from $130 to $25, while Microsoft reported that its cost fell from $60 to $5.[17] And according to a study by Deloitte Consulting, companies averaged 300% returns on their investments in online-procurement system, over the first two to three years of deployment. The average implementation cost was between $2 and $4 million, and firms shaved about 9% from their annual procurement costs in the first two years of use.[18]

FROM ENTERPRISE TO INTERENTERPRISE: THE GENESIS OF MYSAP.COM

Even before SAP encountered sales and profits turbulence in late 1998, it had expected that the frothy ERP growth of the 1990s would not last. In 1996, SAP internally launched an initiative dubbed "New Dimension" to expand the company's product line beyond ERP systems into customer relationship management, supply chain management, and procurement. SAP expected New Dimension products to generate some 30% of its sales within a few years. However, New Dimension progress was plagued by internal dissension and development delays. But by 1998, SAP had started to ship a handful of New Dimension products. Two of the early products, SAP Business Information Warehouse (BIW) and SAP Advanced Planner and Optimizer (APO), were focused on supply chain management functions and met with initial success. Release of a suite of CRM applications, however, had been delayed until at least December 1999.

By the beginning of 1999, SAP management determined that New Dimension alone would not solve the company's problems and that SAP needed to focus on the opportunities the Internet presented. In May it unveiled mySAP.com and planned to spend 25%–30% of its revenues to promote it.[19] SAP also shifted its R&D efforts—which consumed 14% of its annual revenues—to concentrate on automating interenterprise business processes.[20]

The mySAP.com strategy was intended to provide a unifying framework for SAP's entire range of products and services, under the company's new focus on the Internet. It included four main components:

1. **mySAP.com Business Scenarios.** These were templates that SAP customers could use to create and customize processes using R/3 modules and other SAP applications.
2. **mySAP.com Application Hosting.** This offered hosting services for R/3 and other SAP applications. Rather than install and maintain R/3 software on their

[17] "Revolution, or E-volution?" Conrad Nowikow, *Supply Management*, 9/23/99, p. 26.
[18] "Massive Returns on e-Procurement Investments Aren't Just e-Business Hype, According to New Study," Canada NewsWire, 11/11/99.
[19] "SAP to Spend 30% of Revenue to Promote mySAP.com," P. S. Menon, *Financial Express*, 10/11/99.
[20] "SAP," G. Gilbert, D. Clayton, B. Thill, and M. Hammond, Credit Suisse First Boston Corp., 5/14/99, p. 4.

own information systems, clients could access (via the Internet) R/3 resources from a computer system that SAP and its hosting partners maintained.

3. **mySAP.com Workplace.** This was a Web-based enterprise portal, through which an organization could access the company's R/3 system, as well as information and other services, using a standard Web browser. Corporations could customize mySAP Workplace to reflect each employee's role, activities, authorizations, and other attributes.

4. **mySAP.com Marketplace.** This was a Web-based online marketplace to enable business-to-business commerce. Participating vendors could connect their online sales operations, including catalogs and ordering systems, to mySAP.com Marketplace. Buyers could search mySAP Marketplace for vendor offerings and transact purchases online. SAP.com also intended to partner with other companies to create similar digital marketplaces to serve industry-specific vertical markets. In late 1999, SAP reported that more than 2,000 supplier companies participated in the mySAP.com Marketplace.

SAP'S ENTRY INTO ONLINE PROCUREMENT

SAP's entry into the online-procurement market began with the launch of its Business-to-Business Procurement (B2BP) application, as part of the New Dimension initiative. SAP released an early version of B2BP for pilot testing in December 1998 and the first commercial version in March 1999. By the year's end, SAP had delivered B2BP to more than 200 customers, but only a handful had actually gone live with it. In October, SAP launched the mySAP.com Marketplace, which gave it a platform to develop an e-commerce network. B2BP now served as a complement to the company's strategy for the online-procurement market: customers could use B2BP to transact purchases over mySAP.com Marketplace. B2BP incorporated functions to automate purchasing—such as, catalog search, requisition, approval, purchase order generation, and so on—and firms could customize it to fit each employee in the organization.

Marketplace was SAP's most aggressive bid to enter the market for e-commerce services. SAP believed that it was well positioned to take advantage of e-commerce opportunities because full-scale e-commerce between large enterprises required complex interaction between companies' ERP systems: to trade efficiently online, buyers and sellers had to integrate their ERP functions such as inventory control, billing and payments, production planning, logistics, and distribution—that is, the very functions that SAP's market-leading R/3 software handled. Moreover, SAP argued that customers benefited from having a single company provide their internal and interenterprise technology, to ensure interoperability of the various pieces. Some SAP customers agreed. "This is complicated stuff," said Colgate-Palmolive CIO Ed Toben, "and you have to do anything you can to simplify it."[21] A Raytheon Aircraft manager, who emphasized that

[21] "SAP Announces Customer Relationship Management Tools," Craig Steadman, *Computerworld Online News*, 11/10/99.

integration was critical even if it meant compromising on features, agreed: "What you might give up in functionality ain't worth fighting about."[22]

SAP management further argued that the need for interenterprise integration was even more urgent if companies were to take full advantage of e-commerce to become collaborative trading partners—that is, to routinely and seamlessly exchange critical business information. The groundwork for creating this interconnected ecosystem was, in SAP's view, already in place because its R/3 software had more than 10 million users in thousands of organizations around the world—a customer base that employed approximately 100 million workers. And many of the world's largest buyers and sellers of commercial goods and services already used R/3 software for their order processing and fulfillment.

In SAP's estimation, these factors gave it an unrivaled advantage to extend its influence into business-to-business e-commerce. And, in late 1999, the company appeared to be making headway on this front.

In mid-December 1999, SAP announced two deals in which it would create business-to-business e-commerce networks based on the mySAP.com Marketplace platform. One venture focused on establishing an OR-procurement marketplace for chemical and pharmaceutical companies, which would begin operating in mid-2000. Participants included BASF, Bayer, and Siemens. The other deal involved a partnership with Neoforma.com, which provided e-commerce services for medical products. SAP and Neoforma.com would build a global online network to enable healthcare providers and medical suppliers to exchange information and buy and sell medical products. SAP planned to announce more of these "Internet portal" deals and stated that within five years, e-commerce would generate 10%–20% of its revenues.

Though SAP was gaining momentum in the procurement market, its two leading competitors, Ariba and Commerce One, were making their own gains—and in late 1999, at least, the stock market continued to reward them. SAP did not have first-mover advantage in this market and would have to play catch-up.

ARIBA OVERVIEW

Ariba was founded in September 1996 by a group of entrepreneurs, many of whom had worked with co-founder and CEO Keith Krach at Rasna Corporation, a maker of software to automate computer-aided design. Ariba was an early mover into the market for OR procurement software and services. It launched its first product in 1997, signing up chip maker Advanced Micro Devices, Inc. as its first customer in May of that year. In less than three years' time it had assumed the lead position in this nascent industry. The company went public in June 1999.

Ariba based its business on two main offerings. First was its flagship online-procurement software, Ariba ORMS (Operating Resource Management System). Running over a company's intranet, Ariba ORMS enabled employees throughout an organization to initiate OR purchases from their desktop computers. Companies could customize ORMS software to enforce their specific purchasing rules and procedures. Purchas-

[22] "SAP Takes Next Steps Beyond R/3," Craig Steadman, *Computerworld Online News*, 9/20/99.

ing administrators could set up a profile for each employee in the organization that included, for example:

- Preapproved vendors from which the employee could order;
- The employee's spending limits;
- Instructions for automatically routing the employee's requisitions to the appropriate supervisor for approval; and
- The account against which the employee's purchases would be charged.

Via ORMS, users were able to track and check the status of their orders.

A company could also integrate the ORMS software with its back-office applications, such as its accounting program that handled payments. With this capability, procurement purchasing data automatically entered the company's information system without having to be manually rekeyed. This streamlined issuing purchase orders and reconciling them with incoming invoices.

Ariba derived its revenues from selling licenses for its ORMS software and from services such as installation, maintenance, and support. The number of line items the licensee expected to purchase using the system determined the licensing fee. If the number of line items exceeded the expected amount, the licensee paid more. In mid-1999, the average license fee surpassed $1 million. More than 40 major customers used Ariba ORMS, including Hewlett-Packard and Cisco Systems. Ariba targeted corporations with more than $500 million in annual revenues, believing that the potential savings on their procurement volume justified the price tag of the ORMS software, plus several million more in implementation fees. As of October 1999, 50 customers used Ariba's procurement software.[23]

Ariba also offered ORMX (Operating Resource Management Exchange), an outsourced version of the procurement application that companies could access on a subscription basis rather than install Ariba ORMS on their internal system.

The second major piece of Ariba's offerings was the Ariba Network, launched in March 1999. This was a single global network over which all Ariba customers could purchase goods and services from any participating supplier. Companies could customize the Ariba Network so that their employees could access only those suppliers that the company authorized. Buyers could search authorized vendors' catalogs and initiate a purchase request that, after online approval, would directly enter the vendor's sales system. These efficiencies shortened the cycle time between purchase request and fulfillment. By late 1999, Ariba reported that ORMS users application could access products from nearly 85,000 suppliers via the Ariba Network.[24] Ariba did not charge suppliers to join the Ariba Network, nor did it charge transaction fees. Ariba designed its network as a proprietary closed system that only users of Ariba ORMS procurement software could access.

[23] "B2B E-commerce Battles Get Bloody," Om Malik, Forbes.com, 10/4/99.

[24] Ariba Web site, http://www.ariba.com, 12/99.

COMMERCE ONE OVERVIEW

Commerce One was founded in January 1994 as DistriVision Development Corporation (DDC) to create product catalogs on CD-ROM. CEO Mark Hoffman, who joined the company in 1997, had started the database maker Sybase in 1984 and led it to over $1 billion in sales by 1996. Under Hoffman's guidance, DDC reinvented itself as a provider of online-procurement software and services and relaunched in April 1997 as Commerce One. The company's solutions automated the procurement cycle between multiple buyers and suppliers. Commerce One's solutions consisted of the BuySite enterprise procurement application, the MarketSite Platform, and its MarketSite Commerce Services. Its customers included large enterprises in the public sector and in the utilities, finance, telecommunications, information services, travel, and transportation industries. It released its first products in 1998 and went public in July 1999.

Commerce One had aggressively pursued opportunities to franchise its MarketSite technology and had signed up several large partners, including MCI WorldCom, British Telecommunications, Cable and Wireless, Nippon Telegraph and Telephone, and Singapore Telecommunications. Under these arrangements, franchisees would use the MarketSite platform to host digital marketplaces in their regions and would share 10%–30% of the transaction fees with Commerce One. Each of these companies had invested in Commerce One, and several held board seats.

Commerce One's emphasis on building marketplaces was a key component of its strategic focus, as stated in its public offering prospectus:

> *Our objective is to create the leading global business-to-business trading Web comprised of marketplaces . . . operated by both our strategic partners and us in targeted regional and industry-specific markets. . . . Our strategy is to deliver the world's largest and most valuable business-to-business marketplace.*[25]

Ariba, on the other hand, had focused its early efforts on developing and marketing Ariba ORMS. This difference in emphasis reflected a key divergence in their respective strategies. Ariba's tactic was to accumulate an extensive base of powerful buyers who would use the ORMS buying application. Commerce One, in contrast, believed that creating marketplaces built on its MarketSite platform would allow it to control the trading network and establish a recurring source of transaction fee revenue, no matter which procurement application trading partners used. Hence Commerce One designed MarketSite as an open platform: any type of procurement system could operate over a MarketSite network.

Commerce One derived revenues from four sources:

- License fees (70% from BuySite, 30% from MarketSite);
- Maintenance and support fees;

[25] Commerce One Prospectus, filed with SEC 7/2/99.

- Fees for professional services (installation, consulting, training); and
- Transaction fees and royalties.

In 1999, revenues from software (license fees plus maintenance and support fees) accounted for 55% of total receipts; professional services generated the balance of revenues. Due to the still low volume of transactions over MarketSite.net, transaction fees were a negligible revenue source (but were expected to generate significant revenue as network transactions ramped up).

A RACE FOR DIGITAL MARKETPLACES

In November 1999, Commerce One received a major boost when General Motors selected it to build GM TradeXchange, an online marketplace that would connect GM with its 36,000 suppliers of both direct and indirect materials. The companies expected TradeXchange to start operating in the first quarter of 2000. The world's largest industrial enterprise and biggest car maker, GM spent $87 billion on direct and indirect purchases in 1999. But GM's purchasing chief said that TradeXchange would not be limited to GM's transactions with its suppliers: the company expected its trading partners to conduct non-GM business over the network as well. The potential volume of those transactions exceeded $500 billion. GM also planned to open the site to businesses outside of GM's trading community. Commerce One and GM did not specify how they would share transaction fee revenues from the site.

In December 1999, Commerce One announced more e-marketplace joint ventures. In one deal, Commerce One, ERP vendor PeopleSoft, and clothing maker Guess, Inc. created the Apparel Buying Network (www.apparelbuy.com). Sponsored by Guess and powered by MarketSite, the site would facilitate e-commerce among Guess and its network of suppliers and retailers. PeopleSoft would provide the buyer application, PeopleSoft eProcurement (PeopleSoft's rebranded version of Commerce One's BuySite). Commerce One also entered separate deals to build digital marketplaces for Toronto Dominion (a large Canadian bank) and Grupo Financiero Banamex-Accival (a Mexican financial powerhouse).

On the same day that the GM–Commerce One deal was made public, Ford Motor Company announced a similar initiative in partnership with Oracle Corporation. Dubbed the Auto-Xchange, it would link Ford with its supplier base of 30,000 businesses, with which Ford spent $80 billion in 1999. As with GM TradeXchange, Ford's suppliers would also use Auto-Xchange to transact non-Ford business; the extended supply chain represented some $300 billion in purchasing volume. Oracle predicted that Auto-Xchange would produce fee revenues of $1 billion in its first two years of operation and would eventually generate fees of $5 billion a year. Oracle and Ford did not disclose how they would share those fees.

GM was a user of Ariba's procurement software, and it had considered asking Ariba (and others, including Oracle) to build the TradeXchange site. But GM determined that Commerce One was better positioned do that job. Analysts suggested that GM passed over Ariba because Commerce One had developed more powerful technology for building digital marketplaces. On January 4, 2000 GM announced that it had also selected Commerce One for its online auction services, and Commerce One announced its acquisition of Mergent Systems. Analysts believed that the acquisition would enable Commerce One to provide its users with product catalog information culled from a variety of vendors, as well as advanced search tools that it had lacked.[26]

Ariba management had perceived this relative weakness in its product line and had tried to address it. In September 1999, it unveiled the Ariba Internet Business Exchange (IBX), a service for building online corporate exchanges. Then in November, it acquired TradingDynamics, Inc., a developer of online-auction technology. A month later, it acquired Tradex Technologies, Inc., a privately held developer of technology for creating "Net markets," Internet-based vertical markets for business-to-business commerce. The all-stock deal was valued at $1.86 billion. Tradex's software provided the platform for 18 digital marketplaces, including Chemdex, PlasticsNet, and MetalSite. Following the Tradex acquisition, Ariba rolled its IBX technology into the Tradex Commerce Center and formed a Net Markets Business Unit to focus on market-making opportunities.

In December 1999, Ariba announced two deals involving the use of its marketplace technology. One was with Spain's Telefonica, under which the telecommunications giant would use Ariba's e-commerce platform to create business-to-business exchanges throughout the Portuguese- and Spanish-speaking countries in which Telefonica operated. The exchanges would be connected to Ariba Network. Telefonica would also resell Ariba's buy-side solutions (ORMS and ORMX). The other deal was with American Management Systems (AMS), a Virginia consulting firm with many government clients. AMS would create an Ariba-powered network called Buysense.com, a marketplace for connecting state and local agencies and higher-education institutions to their suppliers. (See Exhibit 10 for an overview of types of digital marketplaces.)

RISING COMPETITION FOR THE ONLINE-PROCUREMENT MARKET

Many other firms were competing in the market for online-procurement software and services. Like Ariba and Commerce One, many of these companies focused exclusively on the procurement market, and often on a specific vertical market. Most of them offered both a buy-side procurement application and a buying network service, but few provided high-end platform technology comparable to Commerce One's MarketSite or Tradex Technologies' Commerce Center (acquired by Ariba).

Every major ERP vendor—as well as many second- and third-tier players—had also entered the procurement market. Two JBOPS companies, J. D. Edwards and PeopleSoft, had partnered with the established leaders, Ariba and Commerce One, respectively, rather than develop their own procurement offerings. Baan offered a buying application, E-Procurement, which was an extension to its E-Enterprise suite of Internet-enabled ERP software. It did not have a marketplace-platform product.

Oracle, on the other hand, offered a suite of products that included a buy-side application (Oracle Internet Procurement), a trading network (Oracle Supplier Network),

[26] Commerce One, First Union Securities, 1/5/00.

and a marketplace platform (Oracle Exchange). Oracle was an early convert to the Internet: it had shifted its focus to Internet-related opportunities, including a massive effort to "Webify" its entire product line. Like SAP, Oracle was extending its product line beyond ERP and had entered the SCM, CRM, and EC markets. As evidenced by its deal with Ford to develop the Auto-Xchange site, Oracle wanted to become a major player in the online-procurement market. Like SAP, Oracle's ERP business provided a large customer base for potential procurement business: 7,100 customers and 11,500 installations. Moreover, with some 120,000 database customers, Oracle had extensive reach into corporate IT systems. Indeed, a large chunk of its database customer list overlapped with SAP's: 75% of all R/3 installations used Oracle as the database engine.

TECHNICAL CHALLENGES OF ONLINE PROCUREMENT

Developers of online-procurement systems faced three technical challenges in creating well-functioning products.

• ***Integration with other enterprise applications.*** To reap the full benefits of automation, online-procurement systems had to connect with the organization's networking system and financial software. Procurement documents—requisitions, approvals, and the like—needed to travel electronically among various individuals and departments of the organization and had to pass to the accounting system. In addition, the exchange of documents between enterprises (i.e., the buyer and seller) required a standard format that their respective information systems could read and process. No dominant standard yet existed. Procurement-system vendors, therefore, created their own standards (typically based on an emerging technology called XML, extensible markup language).

• ***Ability to adapt to different business processes and workflows.*** Every organization had unique rules and procedures for purchasing that were often complex. Procurement systems needed to have the tools and customization capability to reflect these processes, which meant that their implementation generally required extensive custom programming.

• ***Management of supplier catalog content.*** One of the thorniest challenges concerning procurement systems was how to manage catalog content, which changed frequently, and who would do it. Several issues were involved. First was the need to standardize the format of catalog files from the multiple suppliers on a system. These files contained data such as product name, SKU number, price, and description. There was no single standard for catalog file format (though the Catalog Interchange Format was fairly common). Second was the issue of who was responsible for updating catalog content—the buyer, the seller, or a third party. Some buying organizations preferred to maintain a customized catalog on their intranet, drawing product data from a list of preferred vendors. Others relied on supplier catalogs maintained on vendors' Web sites. Managed procurement networks, however, enabled suppliers to post their catalogs on the network, where they were accessible to buyers. Under this arrangement, suppliers were still responsible for keeping catalog contents up to date.

XML: PART OF THE STANDARDS SOLUTION

To operate efficiently, digital marketplaces required a set of standards to present and exchange information, including product data and transaction documents (e.g., invoices, purchase orders, requests for proposal, etc.). The Web was a new medium for commerce, however, and standards were still being developed. One promising technology for addressing the information-standards issue was XML. Adopted by the World Wide Web governing body in 1998, XML was a flexible means for defining different types of documents. Similar to the hypertext markup language (HTML) that was widely used to create Web pages, XML employed pairs of tags to define the types of data in a business document. For example, the tag-pair "<INVOICE NUMBER> </INVOICE NUMBER>" indicated that the numerals between the two tags represented an invoice number. When an XML-enabled application encountered this document, it would correctly interpret the invoice number and handle it appropriately.

But while XML provided a standard *method* for defining data types, it did not actually *define* data types themselves or specify what an XML-enabled application should do once it encountered a defined data element. That was left to various industry groups—including buying organizations, sellers, and developers of e-commerce software and services—who had to agree on the kinds of documents and data definitions required for e-commerce in their industries. There was still much competition to set standards. Ariba, for example, had developed a set of definitions, which it called cXML (for Commerce XML), while Commerce One was propounding an XML-based standard called CBL (for Common Business Library).

Vendors of e-commerce technology wanted their own XML variant to become the standard, because it would enhance the value of their software. E-commerce buyers and suppliers wanted their e-commerce applications to be fully interoperable with those of their trading partners, which required a common standard.

PUTTING THE PAST BEHIND

In addition to its sales and profit woes and its stock market misfortunes, SAP had also been plagued in 1999 by highly publicized glitches with its software. A newly installed R/3 system at Whirlpool Corporation had hiccuped, causing Whirlpool to delay shipment of some of its most popular appliances. Problems with its R/3 system prevented Hershey Foods Corporation from fulfilling some candy orders for Halloween. Though the problems were soon resolved, the unflattering headlines hurt SAP's image at a challenging time.

Even more troubling was the continuing hemorrhage of personnel from the company. Dozens of managers and salespeople had fled SAP's ranks, many to join direct competitors such as Oracle and Siebel Systems. Though SAP management downplayed the loss, many analysts considered the exodus of talent a serious problem. One reason for the problem was stock options: German law made it difficult for German corporations to award stock options. By contrast, American competitors were using stock options to attract and retain talent. In December 1999, SAP devised a plan to offer stock options to key personnel, but the plan required shareholder approval; SAP had scheduled a special shareholder meeting in January 2000 to vote on the proposal.

Though 1999 had been an unfortunate year SAP management remained sanguine about the company's future. It believed that its new strategic focus on the Internet and e-commerce would lift the company to new highs: it planned to double its sales within three or even two years. Though the company's stock had rallied in late 1999, it still remained about 20% lower than its high in mid-1998. Meanwhile, Ariba's and Commerce One's stock appeared to defy gravity, giving the companies the means to make acquisitions and lure talent. Nonetheless, if the market research firm Gartner Group was right in predicting that 7,500–10,000 new digital marketplaces would arise over the next few years,[27] SAP management appeared determined to take what it considered its rightful share of that business.

EXHIBIT 1 Ariba Income Statement ($000)

	Annual			*Quarterly*			
	9/30/97	*9/30/98*	*9/30/98*	*12/31/98*	*3/31/99*	*6/30/99*	*9/30/99*
Revenue:							
License	630	6,040	3,540	4,827	5,673	6,439	9,829
Maintenance/ service	130	2,323	1,145	2,025	3,813	5,454	7,312
Total revenue	760	8,363	4,685	6,852	9,486	11,893	17,141
Cost of license	13	165	61	53	197	331	143
Cost of maintenance	927	1,373	501	902	1,607	2,113	3,467
Sales/marketing	2,235	10,311	3,938	4,399	6,903	9,796	12,761
Research/ development	1,899	4,499	1,339	1,649	2,200	3,462	4,309
General/ administrative	588	2,580	1,149	1,201	1,497	2,396	2,823
Amortization	50	956	473	1,113	2,932	5,285	5,254
Total expenses	5,712	19,884	7,461	9,317	15,336	23,383	28,757
Interest, net	289	568	149	106	81	197	1,835
Other income	(16)	0					
Income before taxes	(4,679)	(10,953)	(2,627)	(2,359)	(5,769)	(11,293)	(9,781)
Income taxes	0	0	0	0	0	0	98
Income after taxes	(4,679)	(10,953)	(2,627)	(2,359)	(5,769)	(11,293)	(9,879)

Source: Company reports.

[27] Ariba press release, December, 1999.

EXHIBIT 2 Commerce One Income Statement ($000)

	Annual					*Quarterly*				
	12/31/94	*12/31/95*	*12/31/96*	*12/31/97*	*12/31/98*	*9/30/98*	*12/31/98*	*3/31/99*	*6/30/99*	*9/30/99*
Revenue:										
License fees	112	90	152	742	1,633	450	678	1,456	2,270	7,778
Services	108	349	660	1,004	930	276	336	648	1,932	2,585
Total revenue	220	439	812	1,746	2,563	726	1,014	2,104	4,202	10,363
Cost of revenues	181	232	782	2,887	4,369	1,352	1,382	1,668	3,096	4,768
Sales and marketing	89	146	862	6,055	13,108	3,329	3,895	4,078	6,319	9,361
Product development	179	314	516	2,172	6,839	1,724	2,464	3,362	3,609	5,353
General/administrative	25	57	432	1,805	1,941	534	615	827	923	1,226
In process R&D		0	0	0	0	0	3,037	0	0	
Amortization dfrd.comp.	0	0	0	0	1,102	348	429	584	663	531
Amortization intangibles		0	0	0	0	0	0	875	1,049	1,053
Total expenses	474	749	2,592	12,919	27,359	7,287	8,785	14,431	15,659	16,697
Interest, net	0	(31)	(25)	9	156	73	144	16	217	15,737
Income before taxes	(254)	(341)	(1,805)	(11,164)	(24,640)	(6,488)	(7,627)	(12,311)	(11,240)	(10,356)
Income taxes	0	0	0	0	0	0	0	0	586	0
Income after taxes	(254)	(341)	(1,805)	(11,164)	(24,640)	(6,488)	(7,627)	(12,311)	(11,826)	(10,356)

Source: Company reports.

EXHIBIT 3 SAP Stock Price Chart

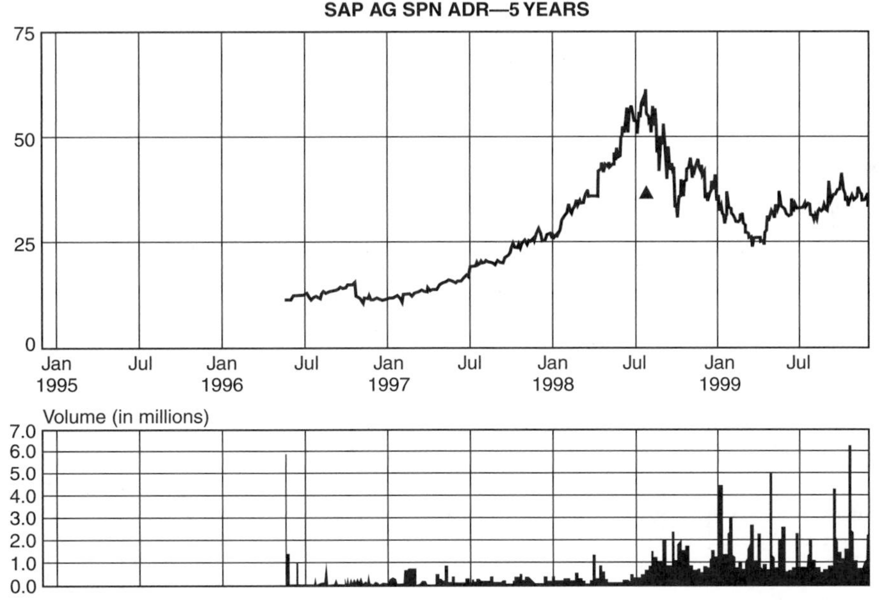

Source: Netscape Netcenter. Reproduced with permission from CSI.

EXHIBIT 4 Ariba Stock Price Chart

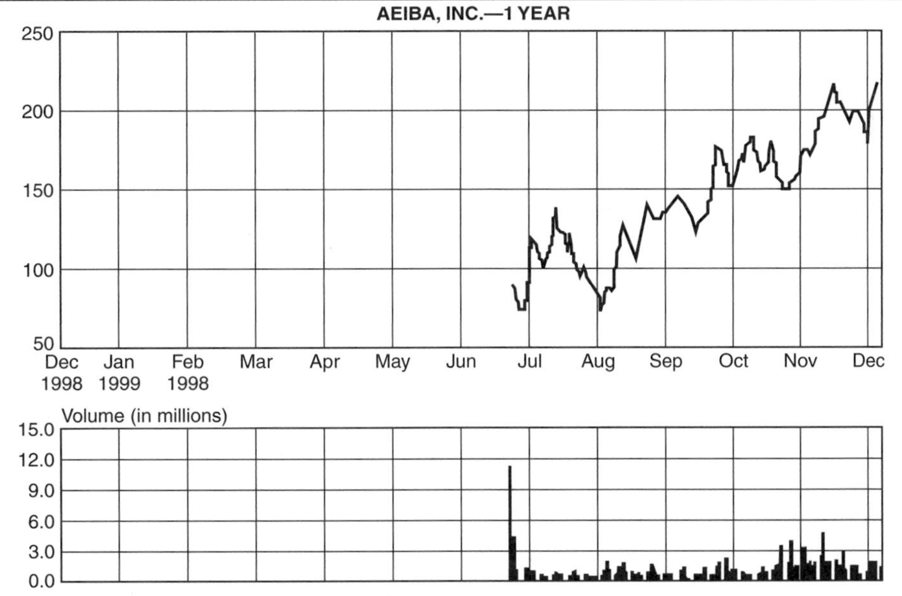

Source: Netscape Netcenter. Reproduced with permission from CSI.

EXHIBIT 5 Commerce One Stock Price Chart

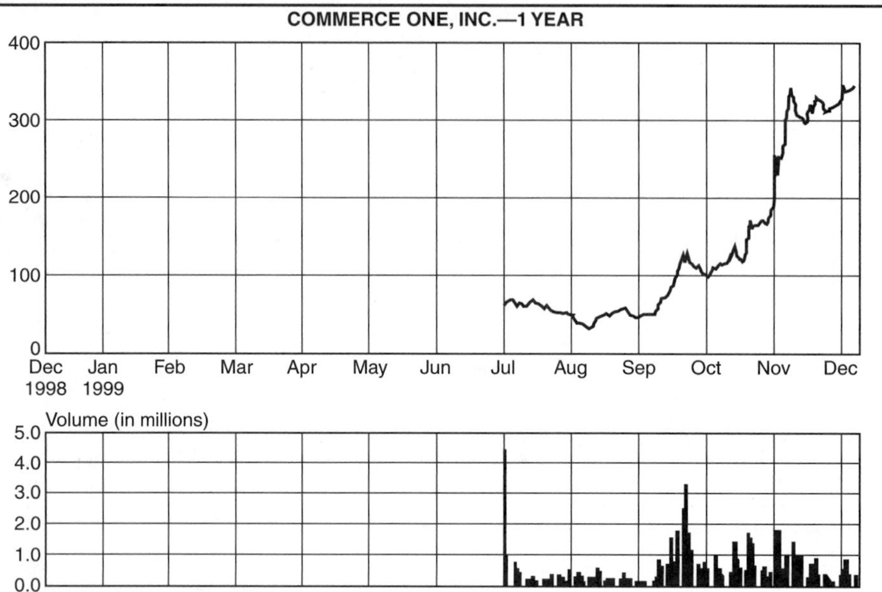

Source: Netscape Netcenter. Reproduced with permission from CSI.

EXHIBIT 6 SAP Income Statement

Annual Income (Currency = German Marks, 000s)

	12/31/96	*12/31/97*	*12/31/98*
Revenue:			
Sales revenues	3,722,150	6,017,466	8,465,294
Income in inventories	961	2,472	20,300
Other income	73,712	79,966	169,271
Total revenue	3,796,823	6,099,904	8,654,865
Supplies/goods	13,967	16,485	23,604
Purchased services	380,417	589,234	1,156,539
Personnel expenses	1,338,473	2,074,920	3,043,564
Depreciation/amortization	164,591	195,321	271,348
Travel	191,973	292,029	424,008
Other operating	658,954	1,110,484	1,520,289
Licenses/commissions	104,819	209,215	322,363
Total expenses	2,853,194	4,487,688	6,761,715
Interest expense	(2,618)	(3,782)	(6,923)
Other, net	26,202	58,502	33,995
Income before taxes	967,213	1,666,936	1,920,222
Income taxes	399,677	741,582	867,874
Income after taxes	567,536	925,354	1,052,348

Quarterly (Currency = Euros, millions)

	3/31/99	*6/30/99*	*9/30/99*
Product revenue	615	736	611
Service revenue	453	504	488
Other revenue	8	20	24
Total revenue	1,076	1,260	1,123
Cost of product	96	107	103
Cost of service	389	417	401
Research and developmt	138	170	173
Sales and marketing	225	278	287
General and administrative	42	59	67
Other expenses	12	6	10
Total expenses	1,790	1,037	1,041
Other non-op inc/exp, net	–6	–7	–6
Finance income, net	4	32	3
Income before taxes	172	248	79
Income taxes	74	105	33
Minority interest	0	1	1
Net income	98	142	45

Source: Company reports.

EXHIBIT 7 Extending the Enterprise Information System

From their traditional focus on internal corporate processes—manufacturing, distribution, financials, and human resources—ERP firms were extending their business strategies and product development to the interenterprise functions of supply chain and demand chain management, including e-commerce.

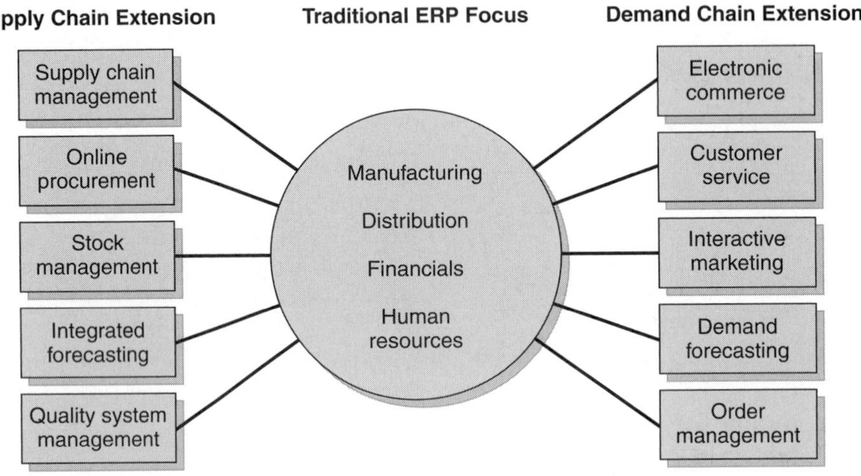

EXHIBIT 8 Selected Financial Data, Leading ERP Vendors ($000)

Oracle Corp.	*5/31/96*	*5/31/97*	*5/31/98*	*5/31/99*
Revenue:				
Licenses	2,296,572	2,896,696	3,193,490	3,688,366
Services	1,926,728	2,787,640	3,950,376	5,138,886
Total revenue	4,223,300	5,684,336	7,143,866	8,827,252
Total expenses	3,318,409	4,421,351	5,899,666	6,954,371
Income after taxes	**603,279**	**821,457**	**813,695**	**1,289,758**
PeopleSoft Corp.	*12/31/95*	*12/31/96*	*12/31/97*	*12/31/98*
Revenue:				
License fees	137,808	252,799	433,195	576,467
Services	94,331	197,253	382,456	737,206
Total revenue	232,139	450,052	815,651	1,313,673
Total expenses	190,151	394,228	649,475	1,092,164
Income after taxes	**27,338**	**35,861**	**108,263**	**143,218**
The Baan Co.	*12/31/95*	*12/31/96*	*12/31/97*	*12/31/98*
Revenue:				
License revenue	118,894	226,135	367,101	285,778
License rev.-parties	0	14,532	66,325	50,600
Maintenance/service	84,434	174,875	246,170	399,271
Hardware/other	23,357	0	0	0
Total revenue	226,685	415,542	679,596	735,649
Total expenses	207,562	355,358	568,061	1,067,719
Income after taxes	**10,899**	**36,612**	**77,156**	**(315,192)**
J. D. Edwards Co.	*10/31/95*	*10/31/96*	*10/31/97*	*10/31/98*
Revenue:				
License fees	134,138	180,366	248,707	386,081
Services	206,628	297,682	399,105	547,901
Total revenue	340,766	478,048	647,812	933,982
Total expenses	311,888	434,421	587,556	827,344
Income after taxes	**18,209**	**26,326**	**37,228**	**74,468**

Source: Company reports.

EXHIBIT 9 Stock Price Charts for Leading ERP Vendors

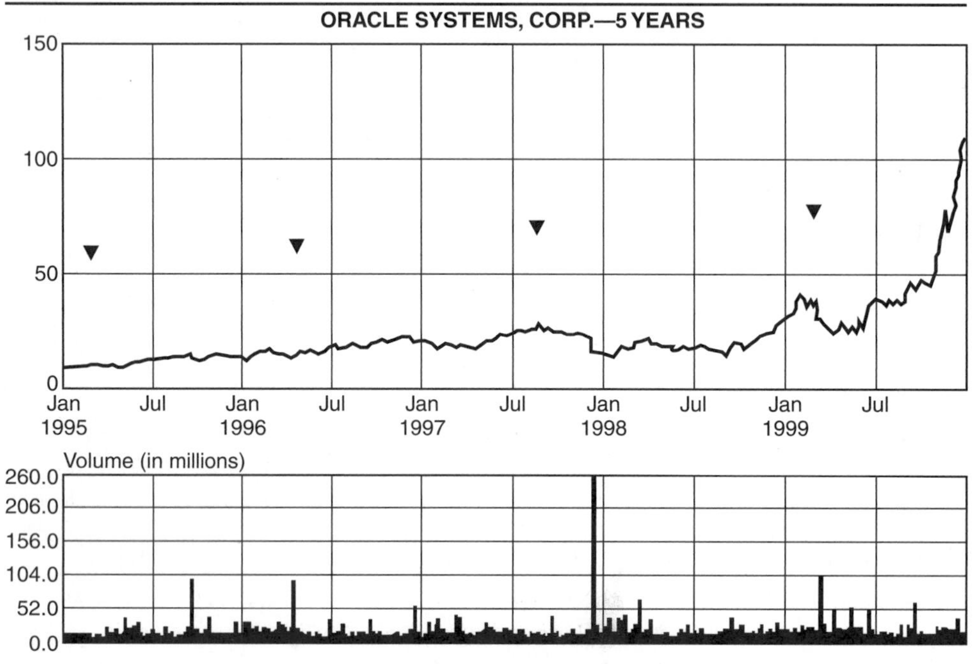

Source: Netscape Netcenter. Reproduced with permission from CSI.

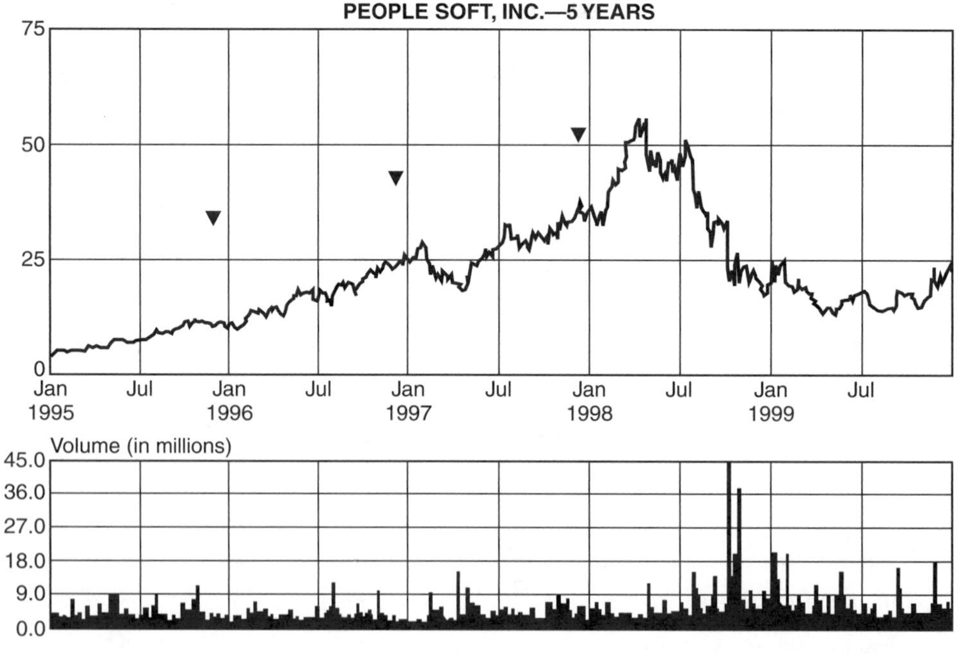

Source: Netscape Netcenter. Reproduced with permission from CSI.

(continues)

EXHIBIT 9 Stock Price Charts for Leading ERP Vendors *(continued)*

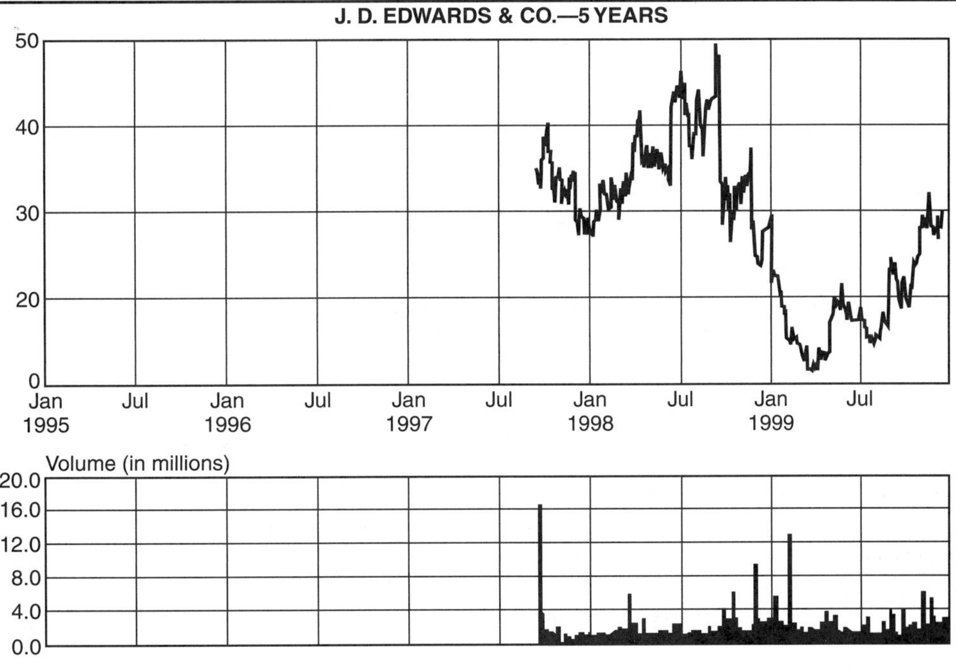

Source: Netscape Netcenter. Reproduced with permission from CSI.

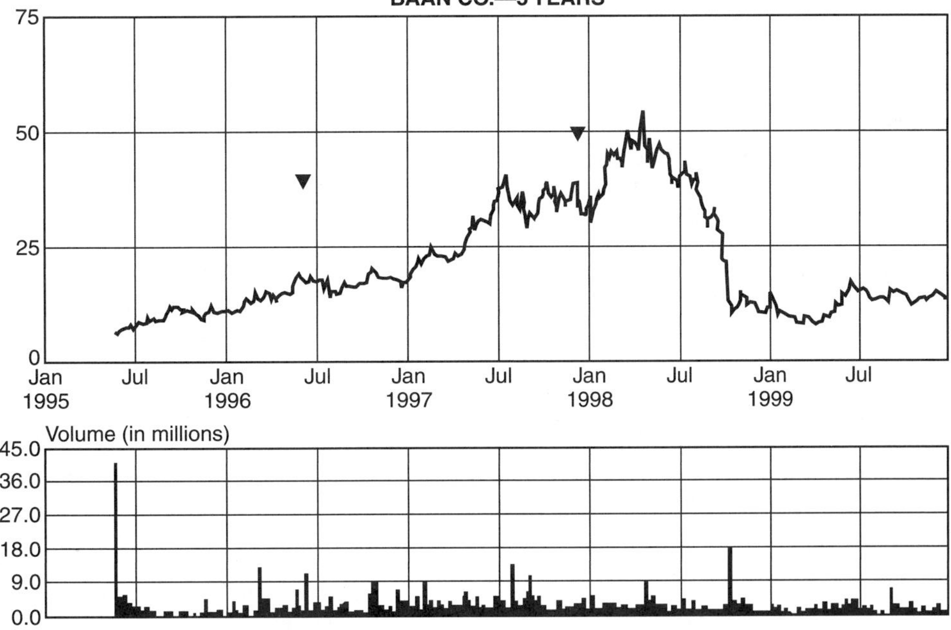

Source: Netscape Netcenter. Reproduced with permission from CSI.

EXHIBIT 10 Types of Digital Marketplaces

Multi-Vendor Catalogs

Use	Aggregates multiple independent suppliers
Product Types	Specific items, whether simple or complex
Price	Defined by seller
e-Revenue	Transaction-based or by referral fee
Benefits to Buyers	• Wider product selection • Allows product and price comparisons • Convenient • Single purchase order for multiple vendors
Benefits to Sellers	• Access a larger pool of buyers • Reduces marketing expense

Auctions (Forward and Reverse)

Use	Sell unique products
Product Types	Perishable goods, excess inventory, discontinued goods, collectibles
Price	Dynamic bid/offer to identified point in time
e-Revenue	Transaction-based
Benefits to Buyers	• Access to unique or hard-to-find items • Reduced search cost • Competitive bidding brings best price (reverse auction) • Potential to buy below retail price
Benefits to Sellers	• Access to a larger pool of buyers • Competitive bidding brings best price (forward auction) • Speeds transaction process • Move excess inventory quickly

Exchanges

Use	Sell standardized products
Product Types	Well-defined commodity products
Price	Continuous price discovery
e-Revenue	Transaction-based, membership fee and/or advertising
Benefits to Buyers	• Speedy access to goods and services in a volatile market • Real-time price information • Provides most competitive price
Benefits to Sellers	• Accelerates process of finding buyers • Broadens customer base • Real-time pricing information

SIEBEL SYSTEMS, INC.

With the rise of e-business, successful business people are obliged to adapt their practices to an electronic, distributed, real-time model. They are forced to think about customers in entirely new ways, to alter their production, marketing, and delivery scenarios, and to adopt new strategies for ensuring customer satisfaction. Some will succeed at this challenge, and many will fail. But no one—not even the "Internots"—will be unaffected by the change.[1] —*Tom Siebel and Pat House*

On August 3, 1999, Siebel Systems Chairman and CEO Tom Siebel stood at the entrance of company headquarters in San Mateo, California, surrounded by a photo team from *Fortune* magazine who were taking pictures for the upcoming September 6 cover story on the nation's 100 fastest-growing companies. Siebel Systems was ranked number one on the list. In the company's six-year existence, it had rocketed to the top of the fast-growing, $2.3 billion worldwide market for customer relationship management (CRM) software—a market expected to reach $16.8 billion in 2003.[2] The 46-year-old Siebel was delighted by the *Fortune* accolade. However, his thoughts focused not on the past success of his company but on its future strategic challenges. Recently, he had spent hours analyzing how the Internet was changing companies' relationships with their customers. The continued success of his own company, he knew, depended on how well he and his executives could respond to those changes, because many of

---

Case Writer Eric Martí prepared this case under the supervision of Professor Garth Saloner and Professor A. Michael Spence as the basis for class discussion rather than to illustrate either effective or ineffective handling of an administrative situation. It draws on an earlier case prepared by Nick Mansour. Margot Sutherland, Executive Director, Center for Electronic. Business and Commerce, Stanford Graduate School of Business, managed the development of this case.

[1] Thomas M. Siebel and Pat House, *Cyber Rules: Strategies for Excelling at E-Business* (New York: Doubleday, 1999), p. 12.

[2] *Customer Relationship Management Report, 1998–2003*, AMR Research, Inc., press release, 9/29/99. AMR further projected CRM sales of $25 billion by 2005. Estimates of current and future market size varied among research firms. International Data Corporation, for example, estimated CRM sales of $2.95 billion in 1999 and predicted sales of $8.98 billion in 2002 (versus AMR's forecast of $11.5 billion in 2002).

the world's leading corporations relied on Siebel Systems software to manage their own customer relationships.

As businesses rushed to establish e-commerce capabilities, their information technology (IT) priorities shifted from optimizing internal processes to managing enterprise relationships with customers, suppliers, and partners. This shift fueled the enormous growth of the CRM software market. Over the past few years, Siebel Systems had captured a dominant 35% share of this market. While several factors accounted for this success, Tom Siebel pointed to a corporate culture that emphasized reverence for the customer, embodied in the slogan "100% customer satisfaction." Now Siebel Systems faced competition from the larger companies, including software giants Oracle Corporation and SAP AG. In addition, other firms were developing new categories of e-business applications to enable companies to conduct their business over the Internet: many of these new generation applications incorporated CRM functions and thus could compete with, or even supplant, Siebel System products. For Tom Siebel, continuing his company's consolidation of the CRM market required staying ahead of these competitive threats, while maintaining a strong corporate culture.

TECHNOLOGY'S IMPACT ON CUSTOMER RELATIONSHIPS

Prior to the Internet, in industry after industry, technological innovations had profoundly affected companies' relationships with their customers. The telephone, for example, led to telemarketing and telesales. Computer technology enabled corporations to establish sophisticated call centers and customer service operations. And automated teller machines (ATMs) enabled banks to provide self-service capability around the clock.

Behind-the-scenes applications of IT had equally dramatic effects on customer relationship management. Customer information databases, for example, enabled companies to analyze customer preferences and purchases. Companies could develop marketing and product development strategies to target their most profitable customers. Wireless data technology, coupled with laptop and handheld computers, helped companies improve field service operations.

The Internet, however, provided a powerful new means for companies to reach customers, and for customers to interact with companies. It also gave customers a new and efficient mechanism to interact with one another, outside a company's channels. Usenet newsgroups, for example, provided an early, pre-Web medium for customer groups—that is, users of a particular software application—to exchange information about a company's products and services. (Newsgroups also enabled proactive companies to gather market information.) The advent of the Web in the early 1990s allowed companies to interact and conduct commerce with customers 24 hours a day, 365 days a year. It also gave customers more information and choices. Customers could search the Web for prices and competitive product information. They could exchange market knowledge and advice via chat rooms and other online forums. These developments shifted power from producer to consumer.

By removing the barriers of time and distance, the Web enabled companies to reach widely dispersed customers across geographical boundaries and time zones—and vice versa. Companies had more customer contact and customers could seek out new vendors via Web searches, automated shopping assistants ("bots"), third-party intermediaries (e.g., car buying services such as autobytel.com), and a proliferation of Web-based information sources and services. This transfer of power to the customer gave customer relationship management a higher priority. Indeed, for many companies, it became the highest priority. To deal with more customer relationships, companies required a more sophisticated CRM system. Ideally, companies wanted to be able to track, manage, and coordinate all their contacts with a customer—by letter, phone, fax, e-mail, online, or in person—across time.

Tom Siebel characterized this historical trend, in which the Internet was the latest and most powerful catalyst, as the "dissolution of structured markets." He explained:

> *In the past companies operated in structured markets through discrete channels, and customers' contact with companies was limited to those channels. Today, those structures—based on time or distance or location—are collapsing. Conventional distribution channels are being wiped out. Customers can interact with companies 24-hours a day, from anywhere in the world. They're not restricted to any specific channel anymore. Now companies must be prepared to do business in whatever way the customer chooses. This presents companies with a multidimensional balancing problem.*

To succeed, Siebel contended, companies had to solve that balancing problem. A major part of the solution would be the use of IT to manage customer relationships. "Organizations will need to reach and maintain relationships with their customers across all channels at the same time," he noted, "and they will need software that simultaneously supports all of these points of customer contact."

THE EMERGENCE AND EVOLUTION OF CRM TECHNOLOGY

Businesses began applying IT to their general operations in large numbers during the 1960s and 1970s, with the automation of internal processes such as manufacturing, purchasing, and payroll. The software to automate these back-office functions was first written as custom programs for mainframe computers and eventually evolved into the packaged-applications category known as enterprise resource planning (ERP) —a $13.2 billion market worldwide in 1998.[3] By the mid-1980s, packaged software aimed at front-office customer relationship functions began to appear. These were two main categories of products: sales force automation (SFA) and customer service and support (CSS). SFA software addressed selling and marketing functions such as managing leads and customer contacts, generating proposals, configuring products for price quotations, and telemarketing. CSS software addressed after-sale activities such as help desks, call centers, and field service operations. The market for these products, however, was so small and fragmented that until the mid-1990s market analysts viewed the two CRM segments (SFA and CSS) as separate, minor markets, overshadowed by the much larger ERP

[3] "Clarify, Inc.," by William P. Lanzon and Monica P. Gullickson, Dain Rauscher Wessels, 2/24/99.

market. In 1994, sales of CRM software were only $200 million compared to $6.4 billion for ERP.[4]

CRM software was a subcomponent of the overall market for enterprise software, that is, applications that served key corporate functions and involved centralized information that many users shared. These applications involved combinations of (a) one or more databases, and (b) a set of programs enabling users to act on elements in those databases. For example, a sales rep could direct an automated system to request all the records for customers in a particular city, which might be drawn from database X. Then he or she could view the purchase histories of those customers, the data for which might come from database Y. Next, using database Z plus various computations, he or she could analyze the profit from each customer. The CRM application tied together these disparate databases and provided the rules and logic to do the analysis.

The first wave of CRM applications, in the mid- and late-1980s, typically focused on specific, narrow functions such as laptop-based contact managers, and many were designed for a particular industry or customer group. Created by small independent software developers, these applications were intended to improve the efficiency of customer-facing employees (e.g., customer service representatives, salespeople, and field service technicians). Unlike ERP applications, however—which companies adopted primarily to control their operating costs—CRM technology enabled firms to generate more sales.

These tools gave early adopters of CRM technology a competitive advantage. SFA systems, for example, enabled salespeople to find and retrieve product information far more quickly than they could by consulting paper catalogs or datasheets; this greater efficiency translated into the ability to make more calls and increase sales. In 1985, for example, Blue Bell's Wrangler division spent $400,000 to equip a 72-person sales force with portable computers running a customized sales information system. In a single selling season the system paid for itself, reducing the unfilled order rate from 13% to 3% and cutting the order processing time by two weeks.[5] By the mid-1990s, corporations considered CRM technology a competitive necessity.

During the early phase of CRM technology, individual applications generally were not integrated with each other. Customer service, for example, was not connected to the sales system. Each function had its dedicated, discrete application: a company's tools for different aspects of managing customer relationships would often be from different vendors. But with the rapid adoption of client/server computer networks, which had begun in the mid-1980s, companies wanted to integrate both their CRM functions and their front-office operations (i.e., CRM) with their back-office systems (i.e., ERP).

CRM MEETS THE WEB

The latest phase of CRM evolution began with the explosive rise of the World Wide Web in the mid-1990s, which changed CRM technology in three critical respects.

[4] *ibid.*

[5] "The Wrangler Laptop Experiment," *Sales & Marketing Management*, Thayer C. Taylor, 5/13/85.

First, the Web transformed how companies and customers interacted, both in the quality and quantity of their contacts. Companies needed to manage a proliferating number of Web-based customer relationships, and CRM technology had to meet those needs. For example, companies wanted their information systems to provide customer-facing employees—a call center operator, for instance—with a single, real-time view of a customer's relationship with the company, incorporating all relevant information about past purchases, service calls, and so forth.

Second, the Web empowered customers: they now had rapid access to information and could perform more transactions online. These rising expectations of self-service—e.g., the ability to view a credit card statement or to book an airline reservation over the Web—pressed companies to make their own information systems accessible to customers. But conventional CRM tools were not designed to enable customers to serve themselves. In the new era of Web-based interactivity, however, CRM technology would have to extend more control to the customer.

Third, the Web presented a new platform for corporate computing, one that many companies were adopting. The easy-to-use Web browser was becoming the universal tool for accessing computing resources. Web-based computing differed from client/server computing in several respects. The typical client/server model divided an application into server-side and client-side components: to access and use the server-side application, a client computer (e.g., a worker's desktop PC) had to have the associated client application installed on it. The client application usually employed a nonstandard, proprietary interface: that is, the "look and feel" of the interface and its navigational features were unique to that particular application and often did not resemble the other programs a worker used. Users had to be specially trained to operate the software. Moreover, upgrading the server-side application often required upgrading the client software as well, which meant servicing each client computer on which the software was installed.

By contrast, with the Web the application software resided entirely on a network server: the client computer only needed a standard browser. The browser—a "thin client," as opposed to the "fat client" of client/server computing—provided a window to the server-based applications, through which the user could access those applications to manipulate data (which were also remotely stored on network databases). Corporations derived two benefits from Web-based computing: users did not have to learn to navigate multiple interfaces; and the cost and administrative burden of keeping each desktop in the firm up-to-date were reduced because fewer applications needed to be stored and maintained on them. Web-centric applications also allowed hundreds of thousands of clients to be served simultaneously.

The transition to Web-based computing meant that developers of client/server CRM technology, such as Siebel Systems, had to re-engineer their software. "By 1996," Tom Siebel recalled, "we had determined that the Internet was changing things and that it was here to stay in a big way." Siebel Systems quickly began building Web capabilities into its products, but it only released a fully Web-based version of its entire product line, Siebel 99, at the end of 1998. In the meantime, a new generation of e-business applications, designed expressly for the Web, had begun to appear.

TOM SIEBEL'S BACKGROUND: THE SEED OF AN IDEA

As a graduate student in business and computer science at the University of Illinois in the early 1980s, Siebel had decided to pursue a career in relational database technology. He joined a young West Coast company, Oracle Corporation, in 1984. His job was to help customers use database technology to solve their information problems. In six months, Siebel was promoted to district sales manager. After several more rapid promotions, Siebel became vice president of direct marketing in May 1988. He determined that the sales force needed tools to quickly access customer, product, and competitor information and to forecast revenues. "We evaluated all the products that were commercially available," Siebel recalled, "and honestly they were not very good." So he decided to build a system in-house. In 1989, his unit deployed the new software, dubbed OASIS (Oracle Automated Sales and Information System). Productivity increased 40%, and the division achieved 149% of its quota. Direct Marketing became Oracle's largest sales division.

Siebel sensed that there was a market for OASIS: "We were running a call center, and every day someone new was visiting the facility to look at the system. Jim Edwards, the president of AT&T; Mitchell Watson, the president of ROLM; and David Norman, the CEO of BusinessLand took a tour of the center." But Oracle refused to develop OASIS as a commercial product.

In 1990, Siebel left Oracle. The next year he signed on as chief operating officer of Cayenne Systems, a developer of office automation systems for the Japanese market. The company was employee owned. "Like Oracle," Siebel recalled, "it was financed by selling good products to its customers, not by professional risk capital. That makes a big difference in the culture of the company, the employees' motivation, and how the management operates." With Siebel's help, the company repositioned itself into multimedia software, changing its name to Gain Technology. Siebel eventually became CEO, and he sold the company to Sybase in September 1992 for $104.7 million.

Siebel then turned to private investing in software start-ups. In July 1993, after a meeting with the CEO of the leading sales force automation company, Siebel realized that no one was taking advantage of an enormous opportunity. "The current 400 competitors were just blowing it," he remembered thinking. "In my opinion, they were using obsolete technology with horrible user interfaces, and the products could not scale to accommodate large organizations. They also had ineffective development and customer service strategies." Immediately after that meeting, Siebel contacted Patricia House, a former Oracle marketing colleague. Within days the two launched Siebel Systems.

THE START-UP

To get the company off the ground, Tom Siebel put up $50,000. Rather than seek funding from venture capital firms, Siebel Systems looked to its employees: they could receive their salaries—which constituted most of the start-up costs—in stock, cash, or a combination of the two. Most opted for stock. Tom Siebel and some friends made periodic cash infusions, but the company had spent only $1.8 million when it released its first product in April 1995.

The company designed its software expressly to meet the needs of high-end, large, typically multinational corporations. Besides designing the product, the Siebel start-up team spent months interviewing sales and information executives at large corporations to determine their needs and desires. Because it was a new entrant Siebel Systems could employ state-of-the-art tools and design principles in engineering its applications, without having to support a legacy system. So it optimized the software for the latest generation of client/server network environments and the proliferating mobile computing devices that field sales personnel used.

EARLY STRATEGY: THE POWER OF PARTNERSHIPS

Tom Siebel recognized the power and value of strategic partnerships, and he formed alliances with key players before the company released its first product. He knew, for example, that to implement his company's products within customers' enterprises would require more time and expertise than his company possessed. Siebel Systems therefore would leave the implementation of its products—a lucrative business in its own right—to its systems integrator and consulting partners and reserve its own personnel for engineering, support, and sales. In 1995, when it released its first product, Siebel Systems signed Andersen Consulting as its first major partner—a move that paid handsome dividends. One of the world's largest IT consulting firms, Andersen had extensive relationships with corporate IT executives. Most of Siebel Systems' major customers were Andersen clients, and in 1999 Siebel's top 10 customers (out of more than 700) accounted for nearly one-quarter of Siebel's total revenues. The relationship between Andersen Consulting and Siebel Systems was further cemented in October 1995, when Andersen took a 10% equity stake in the company, and Andersen's chief executive, George Shaheen, joined Siebel's board of directors.

By mid-1999, Siebel's roster of technology and marketing partners included major players in software (e.g., Microsoft, J. D. Edwards), systems integration (e.g., Cambridge Technology Partners, Keane), and IT consulting (e.g., Deloitte Consulting, Pricewaterhouse Coopers), more than 250 partners in all. By contrast, Siebel's two main rivals, Vantive Corporation and Clarify, Inc., each had fewer than 65 partners.

GROWTH

The company's growth was phenomenal. While its first-year sales of $8 million (1995) were impressive for a new entrant, revenues were $39.2 million. In 1997, Siebel Systems tripled its sales from the year before, eclipsing all other vendors. In just two and a half years, it had become the SFA leader. By mid-1999, the company was on track to generate annual sales of $600 million. It had 2,200 employees and offices in 24 countries. Its 35% share of the CRM market was three times as large as that of the second-place vendor[6] (Exhibits 1 and 2).

In addition to the SFA market's 50% annual growth rate and the partnership with Andersen, a well-executed marketing and sales strategy helped drive the company's

[6] "Siebel Systems," by Rob Schwartz and David Gremmels, S. G. Cowen Securities, 9/2/99.

growth. From the start, Siebel Systems intended to create a strong brand. The company spent aggressively on advertising and tradeshows. In 1995, when Digital Consulting, Inc. (DCI) launched its regional SFA trade shows, Siebel Systems signed on as a charter sponsor. The company put up large booths, and the charismatic Tom Siebel served as a keynote speaker (a role that he continues to play), becoming well recognized in the industry. As the DCI expos became important industry events, Siebel's early and ongoing association with the shows enhanced the company's visibility.

Another key component of Siebel Systems' marketing strategy was its goal of 100% customer "referenceability": that is, to have every one of its customers serve as a reference for other potential buyers of its products. References were critical in the high-tech, high-ticket business of CRM applications: faced with an average price tag of $600,000, customers needed to evaluate the software before buying it, and a sale generally took months to complete. The customers for Siebel's products—those who actually made the buying decisions—were high-level executives responsible for sales, marketing, customer service, or information systems. A committee of decision makers typically oversaw an evaluation process, part of which involved checking the experiences of other companies who used the software.

Customer referenceability was so critical for the sales process that Siebel Systems based its company culture on the principle of "100% customer satisfaction." The company backed its commitment "to do whatever it takes to assure that our customer is successful" with concrete procedures and policies. Every quarter, an independent firm monitored the company's customers' level of satisfaction. Employee rewards and bonuses were based in part on customer satisfaction; one-quarter of salespeople's compensation depended on the results of the surveys. Reverence for the customer pervaded the Siebel organization in other ways, as well. For example, at its headquarters in San Mateo, Siebel named conference rooms after its customers and adorned walls with their logos and posters. Siebel Systems also did not permit shorts, sandals, or T-shirts—the standard attire of programmers at other Silicon Valley high-tech firms—and prohibited employees from eating at their desks. These elements were part of a conscious effort to maintain a culture of professionalism and respect for the customer. Indeed, one of the key issues that Tom Siebel believed was that instilling company values into new employees, particularly as Siebel Systems expanded globally, would be a major challenge.

He also recognized a further human resources challenge: developing the "human capital" to maintain and manage a fast-growing company. Like every technology company, Siebel Systems faced a tight labor market for technical and managerial personnel, a market made tighter by the allure of the dot-com Internet start-ups. Nonetheless, Siebel Systems attracted strong performers, and in recent months Tom Siebel recruited the former CEO, president, and two other high-level executives from SAP America, and two senior IBM executives.

CONSOLIDATION

By early 1997, Tom Siebel had concluded that over the next few years, SFA and CSS firms would consolidate their markets into a merged industry for customer relationship management applications. In the end, he believed, the combined market—with

1996 sales of $600 million and projected sales of $3.5 billion by 2000—would support only three major vendors. The leader would have 50% of the market; the second- and third-place vendors would have 15% and 10%, respectively, and numerous small, niche firms would have the rest of the market. He also believed that the CRM market's fast growth would attract the large ERP firms, such as SAP, Oracle, and Baan: they would eventually develop their own CRM products or acquire existing vendors (Exhibits 3 and 4).

Siebel was right. The consolidation that he anticipated began in 1997, when Baan bought Aurum Software; the second largest SFA vendor, Vantive Corporation—a leading vendor of CSS software—acquired Innovative Computer Concepts, a developer of field service software; and Clarify, Inc., another leading CSS vendor, bought SFA developer Metropolis. Later that year, IBM's Tivoli Systems unit—a major vendor of systems-management applications—announced that it was acquiring Software Artistry, which specialized in help desk technology.

In March 1998, Siebel Systems leveraged its $2 billion stock market valuation to make its own consolidation move: in a stock-for-stock transaction valued at $460 million, Siebel Systems acquired Scopus Technology, a leading vendor of help desk software (primarily for the high-tech industry). The Scopus acquisition catapulted Siebel Systems far above the consolidating CRM pack: the companies' combined 1997 revenues of $208 million were nearly twice those of second-place Vantive. The acquisition also added 500 customers to Siebel's 200.[7] At the end of 1998, Siebel Systems had stretched its lead even further—its sales of $391.5 million more than doubled Vantive's and tripled those of third-place contender Clarify—and by mid-1999, Siebel's market share was three times as big as the closest competitor. Worldwide sales of CRM applications were $2.3 billion. Despite this rapid growth, however, only 5% of potential users had installed CRM systems.[8]

SIEBEL PRODUCT EVOLUTION

While the 1999 Siebel product line covered the entire CRM spectrum, the company's roots were in sales force automation. Released in April 1995, Siebel Systems' first product, Siebel Sales Enterprise (SSE), targeted the high-end SFA market. Designed to run on client/server networks, SSE enabled users to automate sales-related activities, such as organizing customer information, accessing product data, writing sales proposals, and generating quotes. In December 1996, Siebel released Siebel Service Enterprise, which added customer service capabilities: tools to automate call centers, help desks, and customer support operations. In March 1998, Siebel released a third basic application, Siebel Marketing Enterprise (SME), to enable managers to monitor the effectiveness of sales and marketing programs by providing tools to extract and analyze data from their sales and marketing information systems. Siebel also introduced a line of vertical market versions of its applications, tailored for specific industries.

[7] "Siebel's Pre-emptive Strike," by J. Thomas Gormley III, Forrester Research, 3/24/98.
[8] "Is Siebel the Next SAP?" by Kim Girard, CNET News.com, 5/12/99.

While the early releases of Siebel products could operate over an Internet-based network, they were not designed as Internet-based applications and hence were not optimized for the Web. By 1996, however, the company built greater Internet functionality into its products and began to redesign its software to make it more Internet-centric. In 1997, Siebel released several products that, for the first time, incorporated a Web browser interface: the user could access the application from Microsoft Internet Explorer and use the browser's familiar tools to navigate the program.

In March 1998, Siebel 98 extended the browser interface to the entire product line, and in December, the company released Siebel 99, a fully Web-based version of the product suite. Besides providing a browser interface, this release allowed customers to "configure once, deploy everywhere." That is, rather than loading copies of the applications onto each employee's desktop PC, customers could store the applications on a network server (or servers), and individual users could access Siebel software via their Web browser. To upgrade or modify application software, customers only had to make the changes to the server-based applications, rather than having to upgrade hundreds or thousands of copies on individual PCs. In June 1999, Siebel 99.5 extended the company's product line to include Siebel eBusiness—a family of electronic commerce and service tools—as well as new applications for incentive compensation, professional sales management, database marketing, and other functions.

The first generation of Siebel products had a two-tier client/server architecture: part of the application software was stored locally on the "client" computer (i.e., the user's desktop PC), while the other part resided on a network server. In 1996, however, Siebel redesigned its software based on an "n-tier" client/server architecture: the programs' fundamental elements—data stores, business logic, information presentation, and other application layers—were separated into modular components that could be distributed among multiple servers within a network. The new architecture made the software far easier for customers to deploy and customize and improved its efficiency and versatility.

Looking "under the hood" of the Siebel product line, one would see more than 2,000 "business objects" (modules of software code, each designed to perform a specific function, such as generate a price quote or log a service request). One would also find thousands of tables and indexes (containing customer information, product information, competitor information, price data, rules for configuring products, etc.). This enormous underlying complexity—the result of more than 1,300 person-years of software engineering—attempted to embed the world's best sales, marketing, and customer service practices into the applications. The interface, which neatly presented information to the end user via some 2,000 different screens, overlaid the internal engine of the software.

In early 1999, following the release of Siebel 99, Siebel Systems unveiled a new corporate initiative called "Siebel Everywhere." The program included many aspects, including Sales.com (a portal site for salespeople) and Siebel Sales (a free, single-user version of its software). But the overarching goal was to make Siebel 99 applications ubiquitously available, so that any device, mobile or stationary, connected to the Internet or a company's intranet could access Siebel applications.

THE SIEBEL PRODUCT LINE

Like most vendors of enterprise applications, Siebel Systems derived its revenues from two main activities: sales of its software products (so-called license fees) and sales of services, such as maintenance and support, consulting, implementation, and training. In many enterprisewide installations of Siebel applications, the cost of the software represented less than 20% of the total implementation costs, which also included services and hardware. License fees generated 68% of Siebel's revenues, a ratio that reflected the company's primary emphasis on software sales and its reliance on partners to provide most of implementation services. (By comparison, Vantive derived 55% of its revenues from software sales.) Revenues from existing customers—via sales of maintenance and support, upgrades, and additional software licenses—accounted for 45%–60% of Siebel's sales in an average quarter.

The Siebel product line comprised more than 100 separately priced items, the broadest line of any CRM vendor. Siebel offerings fell into six categories:

1. Enterprise applications (including industry-specific versions for vertical markets)
2. E-business products
3. Mid-market products
4. Tools
5. Products for individuals
6. Services

1. Enterprise Applications

Enterprise applications, the core of Siebel's product line and its main source of revenue, were targeted to Global 2000-size corporations, the company's primary customer base. In addition to Siebel Sales Enterprise, the company's flagship product, this group also included Siebel Service Enterprise and Siebel Marketing Enterprise, as well as applications for call centers, field service, and product configuration. The company also marketed its enterprise applications in separately branded versions configured for various vertical markets. Targeted industries included pharmaceuticals, consumer goods, telecommunications, insurance and financial services, high technology, utilities, and government. Each base application listed for $1,350 per user, with add-on modules priced between $250 and $500 per user. The average deal for enterprise applications ranged between $500,000 and $600,000. Siebel Systems also provided interfaces to connect its front-office applications to the major back-office systems from companies such as SAP, Oracle, and PeopleSoft.

2. E-Business Products

Issued in June 1999 with the Siebel 99.5 release, these products were the latest additions to the company's portfolio. The group included four applications:

- eSales
- eMarketing
- eChannel
- eService

Together, they provided tools for companies to conduct commerce, perform marketing, and provide customer service over the Web.

3. Mid-market Products

Intended for mid-size customers (companies with $50–$500 million in sales), Siebel Sales for Workgroups was the company's primary offering in this category. Customers could extend this base application with several modules. Siebel Advanced Selling Pack, for example, added sales libraries and product catalogs, quoting, and organizationwide forecasting. Siebel distributed its mid-market products primarily through reseller partners, such as Great Plains Software (a provider of financial systems to mid-size companies) and Compaq Corporation.

4. Tools

Siebel Tools included five applications for customizing, upgrading, or otherwise modifying Siebel products.

5. Products for Individuals

In February 1999, as part of its "Siebel Everywhere" initiative, the company announced two products for individuals: Siebel Sales, a single-user version of its sales management software, and Sales.com, a Web site for sales professionals. Siebel Sales had a list price of $199, but the company initially gave it away for free. Individuals could obtain a copy by downloading the software from Siebel's Web site, or requesting it to be mailed to them on CD. In either case, Siebel captured the recipient's identity. The give-away enhanced awareness of the Siebel brand, seeded the market, and created interest in the company's products. The Sales.com site, which Siebel billed as "*the* premier destination for sales professionals on the Web today," offered salespeople information and productivity tools and information, such as a contact manager and calendar, e-mail, news, maps, sales advice, and job postings. Membership was free, but individuals could also buy a premium subscription that included access to specialized content such as customized news briefings. Users could also purchase sales leads from a Dun & Bradstreet database. Siebel estimated that Sales.com would help build awareness among roughly 40 million professional salespeople.

6. Services

Service products included technical support, consulting, and education, as well as SiebelNet, an application hosting service. Several third-party companies, including USinternetworking and Qwest Communications, also provided hosting of Siebel applications. Services, primarily maintenance and technical support, accounted for about one-third of Siebel's revenues.

COMPETITION

In mid-1999, Siebel Systems faced competition from four directions:

1. Established top-tier CRM firms;
2. Smaller, second-tier CRM firms;
3. Developers of "e-business applications," including numerous start-ups; and
4. Major ERP firms.

1. Top-Tier CRM Firms

Three major CRM firms—Vantive, Clarify, and Baan Front Office Systems (formerly Aurum Software)—competed against Siebel for the same high-end, global corporate customers. In this category, Siebel's most frequent head-on competitor was Vantive.

Founded in 1990 by Roger Sippl, Vantive began as a developer of customer service and support (CSS) software, with a focus on call center and help desk systems for the software industry. It shipped its first product in 1992. The company sought to offer a full suite of integrated CRM tools. It quickly filled out its product line with SFA and other modules, but its primary focus remained on CSS: Vantive Support, the company's flagship product, accounted for 50% of the company's revenues. Vantive's sales force concentrated on selling the CSS product; sales of the other modules typically came as add-ons to Vantive Support.

By 1995 Vantive led the CRM market with sales of $25 million (versus $20.9 million for Clarify and $8 million for Siebel). By 1997, however, Siebel had overtaken Vantive by offering a superior product in the fast-growing SFA segment. Reacting to Siebel's challenge, Vantive shifted its focus from CSS and aggressively pursued the SFA segment. But Vantive stumbled. Its sales force fared poorly in the SFA market, and by neglecting the CSS market, it missed opportunities there as well. As a result, Vantive's growth rate plummeted in 1998: sales increased by less than 40%, down from an annual average of 84% over the previous three years. In contrast, Siebel's 1998 revenues nearly doubled from the year before (adjusted for an acquisition). Turnovers and shake-ups in Vantive's management and sales force made things worse. In the first half of 1999, revenue grew only 26%. To help turn its business around, Vantive hired Thomas L. Thomas, former Chief Information Officer at 3Com Corporation, as its CEO in April 1999 and refocused its efforts on CSS, its original area of strength.

Despite its troubles, Vantive's product had a strong reputation; the company had more than 850 customers, most of them large, blue-chip corporations. Sales of its software outside of the North American market were strong. The company had solid partnerships with several of the largest IT consultants and systems integrators. Vantive had also begun building Internet capabilities into its products in 1996, and in 1998 it acquired Wayfarer Communications, which specialized in Web-based information delivery. Vantive used the acquired technology to develop Web front ends for its software, enabling users to access Vantive applications via a Web browser. Some market observers predicted that either an ERP firm or another CRM developer, and possibly even Siebel, would acquire Vantive.

2. Second-Tier CRM Firms

More than 30 smaller CRM developers—firms that primarily targeted the low-end, middle, and niche markets—frequently competed with Siebel, particularly for Workgroups, the company's mid-market offering that it released in mid-1999. Leaders in this segment included Onyx Software Corporation (1998 sales: $35.1 million), Pivotal Corporation (1998 sales: $25.3 million), and SalesLogix Corporation (1998 sales: $15.6 million). Siebel's primary focus remained on large corporations, a market that encompassed thousands of potential customers. But it was also interested in the mid-market (i.e., companies with revenues of $50–$500 million), with potential customers numbering in the tens of thousands. The company had several initiatives to promote Siebel for Workgroups. For example, it partnered with Great Plains Software—a major vendor of back-office applications for mid-size companies—to market Siebel for Workgroups through Great Plains' network of 1,400 resellers. And ERP developer J. D. Edwards, which catered largely to mid-size customers, marketed both the Enterprise and Workgroup versions of Siebel's sales applications as integrated components of its OneWorld suite. Siebel Systems also targeted mid-market customers with its outsourcing solution, SiebelNet, and by hosting partnerships with USinternetworking and Qwest, which also hosted the Enterprise versions of Siebel applications.

3. E-business Application Developers

Many recent entrants and start-ups offered a new generation of e-business applications—the tools for creating dot-com enterprises—many of which included components for managing Web-based customer relationships (Exhibit 5). This emerging market for e-business applications was fragmented and growing. In 1998, total revenues for e-business applications were $444 million and were expected to exceed $13 billion by 2003.[9] Not all of these firms' products competed with those of Siebel Systems, but many were in the CRM market. Some, for example, developed narrow point solutions to specific e-business requirements, such as tools for handling incoming customer e-mail (e.g., eGain, Kana, Mustang), content management systems (e.g., Interwoven, Vignette), catalog engines (e.g., Requisite, Mercado, Aspect), and product configurators (e.g., Calico, Selectica). A few offered more comprehensive products. Silknet Software, for example, marketed a suite of Web-based e-commerce and customer service applications that attracted considerable press and analyst coverage—both Forrester Research and Aberdeen Group cited the company as a promising vendor of next-generation cus-

[9] *E-Business Technology Forecast*, PriceWaterhouseCoopers, May 1999.

tomer management software[10]—and it raised $46.9 million in its May 1999 initial public offering. Though its revenues were small, it was growing quickly: its 1999 fiscal-year sales were $13.9 million (with a loss of $9.4 million) compared with just $3.6 million the year before (and a loss of $6.9 million).

Another company that gained attention with a comprehensive product line was BroadVision, Inc., whose products provided Web-based personalized sales, service, and support. Its One-to-One suite of applications was the leading packaged software for business-to-consumer e-commerce, with a 1998 market share of 13.5% (nearly double second place Open Market's 7% share).[11] BroadVision also sold a business-to-business version of its software. The company marketed its software to a broad range of companies across many industries, from Global 2000 corporations to start-ups, and had more than 350 customers. With 1998 sales of $50.9 million versus $27.1 million in 1997, BroadVision was also growing quickly. Its 1996 initial public offering had raised $20.8 million; by mid-1999, the company's market value exceeded $1.5 billion.

In addition to these small and relatively young firms, several large and established companies were also aggressively pursuing the market for e-business applications, such as IBM and Sun Microsystems (through its iPlanet alliance with America Online unit Netscape). Both companies were leading vendors of so-called commerce platforms, that is, application suites that enabled companies to set up and operate high-end e-commerce Web sites. Commerce platforms typically provided many built-in functions, including various CRM features (such as self-service sales and technical support) and were designed to allow third-party products to connect to them. IBM had partnered with Siebel and other vendors to extend the CRM capabilities of its products.

None of these firms had yet emerged as a significant competitor in the high-end, CRM space that Siebel dominated. But Tom Siebel recognized that a new company with a compelling product based on the latest technology could leapfrog existing vendors as his own company had already done. In many respects, keeping an eye on one's known competitors was easier than monitoring the frenetic activity among these small but aggressive companies.

4. Major ERP Firms

Five companies dominated the market for ERP software: SAP, Oracle, PeopleSoft, J. D. Edwards, and Baan. After Baan acquired Aurum in 1997, other ERP vendors, notably SAP and Oracle, had entered the CRM market. After impressive growth since the early 1990s, ERP vendors faced slowing demand for their products. Most large corporations had already committed to an ERP system, and their IT priorities were shifting to other projects, including the Y2K problem, the Internet, and CRM. From the ERP firms' perspective, the progression from back-office to front-office product development was natural, especially because front-office applications had to integrate with corporate ERP systems. All the major CRM applications—those from Siebel, Vantive,

[10] "Silknet's eBusiness System: Customer Relationship Management Software for the Web," Hugh Bishop and Christopher Fletcher, Aberdeen Group, 3/11/99; "Web-Centric Customer Service," J. Thomas Gormley III, Forrester Research, 2/99.

[11] *E-Business Technology Forecast*, PriceWaterhouseCoopers, May 1999.

Clarify, and others—connected to most ERP systems, through a variety of methods such as application programming interfaces (APIs) or "middleware" packages. But the ERP companies believed that they could deliver CRM products that worked more effectively with their own back-office applications.

• ***SAP.*** Based in Germany, SAP had 30% of the ERP market—three times as much as second-place Oracle. It had 12,000 customers worldwide and 19,500 site installations.[12] The company was founded in 1972 by ex-IBM engineers to develop process automation software that ran on mainframe computers. It rose to worldwide prominence in the early 1990s, when it shipped R/3, the client/server version of its flagship ERP system: revenues skyrocketed from $513 million in 1992 to $5.1 billion in 1998, and profits rose from $78 million to $631 million. As early as 1994, SAP management saw the need to expand from the ERP market to other enterprise applications. The success of R/3, however, kept the company focused on ERP, and SAP did not announce its intentions to enter the CRM market until 1997.[13] However, internal debates over product strategy held up its development efforts. In 1998, SAP released a limited set of CRM products under the New Dimensions banner and took control of Kiefer & Veittinger GmbH, a leading German vendor of SFA software.

Sales of R/3 had begun to sag in the last two quarters of 1998, and the slump continued into 1999. In May 1999, the company announced a new, Internet-based strategy, an initiative called mySAP.com, to bring all of its enterprise applications—ERP, CRM, supply chain management, procurement, and e-commerce—into an integrated, Web-based environment. It planned to ship additional CRM products as part of mySAP.com and expected much of its customer base to choose its CRM offerings. However, observers questioned how quickly SAP could implement this ambitious plan: SAP had a reputation for moving slowly, and its products were considered complex and difficult to implement. Tom Siebel doubted SAP's ability to develop CRM products. "They know manufacturing very well and have embedded the world's best practices in their software—after all, the Germans are world-class manufacturers," Siebel observed, "but SAP doesn't have the same understanding of sales, marketing, and customer service."

• ***Oracle.*** Oracle Corporation, Tom Siebel's former employer, had 61% of the corporate database market and 120,000 customers worldwide.[14] It had also become the second largest ERP company behind SAP, with 7,100 customers using its ERP software at some 11,500 sites.[15] Software accounted for 42% of its fiscal 1999 (ended May 31) sales of $8.8 billion, while most revenues came from professional services (consulting, training, and education). Microsoft, IBM, and others were attacking Oracle's database business, and like SAP, the growth of its ERP sales was slowing. CRM presented a new fast-growth

[12] "Enterprise Resource Planning Software," by Robert J. Schwartz, Andrew C. Brosseau, and David Gremmels, S. G. Cowen Securities Corp., 9/8/99.

[13] "Problem Child: SAP Is Struggling to Give Its Lineup a New Dimension," by Matthew Rose, *Wall Street Journal Europe*, 6/22/99.

[14] "Larry Ellison: Oracle at Web Speed," by Brent Schendler, *Fortune*, 5/24/99.

[15] "Enterprise Resource Planning Software," by Robert J. Schwartz, Andrew C. Brosseau, and David Gremmels, S.G. Cowen Securities Corp., 9/8/99.

opportunity. Oracle CEO Larry Ellison committed 900 programmers to CRM product development and vowed to unseat Siebel Systems' lead. Oracle also acquired three CRM firms: call center software maker Versatility; configuration software maker Concentra; and Tinoway Nederland, a Dutch developer of field service applications.

In December 1998, Oracle rolled out its CRM product suite, followed by more offerings in March 1999. Though the products received lukewarm reviews, Oracle reported that it had received $90 million in orders by mid-year.[16] Oracle had a sales force of more than 7,000; an R&D budget approaching a billion dollars; and a strong balance sheet boasting more than $2.5 billion in ready funds. However, Oracle's large consulting operation made it a major competitor of companies that would be important potential partners in trying to win CRM business, and Oracle had strained relationships with some of them. Despite Oracle's bold statements, Tom Siebel remained confident of his company's ability to lead the market. "If and when Oracle releases a functionally complete product, we'd expect them to become a competitor," Siebel told *Barron's*. "But Oracle today is just not a factor in the market."[17]

• ***Baan.*** Though still an occasional competitor, Baan's CRM unit—Baan Front Office Systems (formerly Aurum)—had lost much of its momentum after the acquisition, due to challenges in integrating the two companies' technologies. In 1996 Aurum had sales of $27.6 million, and through the first eight months of 1997—before the acquisition by Baan—it posted revenues of $24.2 million. Aurum's strength had been in sales force automation. Founded in 1990, the company was an early leader in client/server SFA software for large enterprises. Aurum was one of many companies Baan, a Netherlands-based company with 1997 revenues of $680 million, acquired. However, after several years of phenomenal growth and impressive earnings, the difficulties of digesting its acquisitions caught up with Baan: in 1998 the company lost $315.2 million against revenues of $735.6 million. Accounting irregularities were also discovered—revenues had allegedly been recorded before products were delivered—that resulted in a shareholder lawsuit. The company lost 80% of its market value in the second half of 1998. Baan undertook a major reorganization, cutting its workforce by 20% and closing or consolidating offices. In May 1999, the company appointed a new CEO and chairman: Mary Coleman, the former Aurum CEO, who had stayed with the company after its acquisition. In the first six months of 1999, Baan's revenues decreased 15% from the year earlier period, and the company posted a loss.

• ***PeopleSoft.*** Founded in 1987, PeopleSoft started out making client/server software to manage human-resource functions and eventually included financial, manufacturing, inventory, and distribution applications. It targeted the high-end market and had more than 2,900 customers. PeopleSoft was the only top ERP firm that did not offer its own CRM applications. However, since 1996, it had codeveloped with Vantive CRM products that tightly integrated with PeopleSoft applications, and PeopleSoft's 2,200

[16] "Grudge Match," by Julie Pitta, *Forbes*, 9/20/99.

[17] "Software Hardball: More Than Egos Are at Stake as Oracle Takes on Fast-growing Siebel," by Bill Alpert, *Barron's*, 8/23/99.

salespeople marketed the CRM products. In mid-1998, PeopleSoft expanded its relationship with Vantive and also entered a partnership with Siebel Systems.

At various times over the previous years, rumors about a PeopleSoft/Vantive merger had circulated. In 1998, PeopleSoft's growth rate slowed to 60%, from nearly 100% a year over the prior six years, and it cut its workforce for the first time, by 6%. The slump continued in 1999: first half sales were flat over the year before, and profits (excluding one-time charges) were down 85%. In less than a year's time, PeopleSoft had lost three-quarters of its market value. Like other ERP firms, PeopleSoft was concentrating its product strategy on the Internet. In addition to Web-enabling its ERP software, it began to roll out a suite of e-business applications that provided e-commerce capabilities, such as online selling and procurement. It also launched a Web marketplace for third-party merchants called the PeopleSoft Business Network, and it was positioning its Web-enabled ERP applications as the "PeopleSoft eBusiness Backbone."

• ***J. D. Edwards.*** J. D. Edwards focused primarily on small to mid-size companies, and had more than 4,700 customers worldwide. While some of its customer-service applications competed with Siebel products, it lacked an SFA component: in 1999, it signed a deal to market Siebel's sales applications as part of its flagship OneWorld product line. The deal, however, did not prevent J. D. Edwards from developing or acquiring a competitive product.

Tom Siebel had long expected the ERP firms' entry. However, he did not yet consider them imminent threats. In his view, their CRM offerings were not complete. Moreover, he believed that his company's leadership position, market knowledge, and technical experience enabled it to outpace competitors' offerings.

THE NEXT CHALLENGE

The *Fortune* team wrapped up the photo shoot. The article crowning Siebel Systems the country's fastest-growing company would not appear for several weeks. But for Tom Siebel, the story was yesterday's news. As the leading player in a fast-growing market, Siebel Systems operated from a position of strength—its sheer size and market dominance guaranteed that its products would be considered for any large deal—but market leadership also had its disadvantages. The acculturation and human capital issues facing the company, for example, were not problems that could ever be solved once and for all, especially given its furious growth. Siebel told one interviewer,

> *My concern is that—absent a concerted effort to drive a wholesome corporate culture—we will become yet another pathological corporate environment. Or become yet another company with a parking lot filled with Ferraris, where the CEO presents himself to the market as this creator of insanely great technology, or this great visionary, or this great entrepreneur, or this great technologist. We don't want to have all kinds of self-important, arrogant people engaging in e-mail wars while meeting customers in blue jeans and a T-shirt. We're here to do whatever it takes to make the customer successful with the highest level of professionalism. So my concern is to make sure we don't become another pathological Silicon Valley story.*[18]

[18] "Selling Siebel," by M. Vizard and K. Bull, *Infoworld Electric*, 11/30/98.

But the number one challenge facing Tom Siebel was the need to consolidate the company's market position: the company's growth had to keep pace with, or exceed, that of the CRM market itself. Though weaker competitors had fallen away and others were stumbling, Siebel knew that both Oracle and SAP—because of their size and resources—could not be dismissed. The proliferating e-business application developers were also potential competitors. And Siebel Systems, like every other business, had to adapt its practices to the new "electronic, distributed, real-time model." As he steered his company toward the billion dollar sales mark, Tom Siebel realized that he would have his own multidimensional balancing problem to solve.

EXHIBIT 1 Siebel Systems Operating and Financial Data, 1994–1998 and 1–2Q99

	2Q99	*1Q99*	*1998**	*1997*	*1996*	*1995*	*1994*
Operating Data							
Sales							
Software (license fees)	110,005	93,432	290,890	100,700	35,658	7,636	50
Services	54,411	40,618	100,649	18,075	3,494	402	0
Total revenues	164,416	134,050	391,539	118,775	39,152	8,038	50
Cost of revenues							
Cost of licenses	2,270	1,331	5,600	2,272	106	41	0
Cost of services	34,492	24,186	61,547	7,617	2,113	385	0
Total cost of revenues	36,762	25,517	67,147	9,889	2,219	426	0
Operating expenses							
Product development	16,950	16,678	42,698	13,349	5,894	2,816	868
Sales and marketing	60,390	52,168	172,946	55,983	19,577	3,232	718
General and administrative	11,397	8,210	28,401	9,682	4,748	1,192	243
Other	0	0	13,500	22,740	0	0	0
Total operating expenses	88,737	77,056	257,545	101,754	30,219	7,240	1,829
Other income, net	1,959	2,395	6,283	2,892	1,391	156	13
Income before taxes	40,876	33,872	73,130	10,024	8,105	528	(1,766)
Net income (loss)	25,752	21,340	42,875	(2,427)	5,025	317	(1,766)
Number of employees	2,200		1,418	473	213	67	20

(continued)

EXHIBIT 1 *(continued)*

	2Q99	*1Q99*	*1998**	*1997*	*1996*	*1995*	*1994*
Cash Flow Data							
Net cash from operating activities	38,163	(5,306)	85,936	22,726	3,447	2,811	(1,704)
Net cash used in investing activities	(9,609)	(1,167)	(98,659)	(20,148)	(57,664)	(865)	(191)
Net cash from financing activities	19,627	11,220	26,622	6,008	65,497	8,428	2,209
Balance Sheet Data							
Current assets							
Cash and equivalents	132,889	84,708	79,961	31,257	22,671	11,391	1,017
Short-term investments	156,981	145,756	151,888	62,894	49,716	0	0
Marketable equity securities	62,500	0	0	0	0	0	0
Accounts receivable	173,254	147,676	122,818	33,246	12,855	3,066	0
Other	29,608	27,196	27,028	8,030	5,325	754	29
Total current assets	555,232	405,336	381,695	135,427	90,567	15,211	1,046
Total assets	604,306	468,312	441,946	149,312	99,501	16,091	1,203
Liabilities and stockholders' equity							
Current liabilities	181,622	136,566	150,608	36,585	18,105	6,129	14
Debt	0	0	0	0	0	0	0
Other liabilities	204	642	710	162	205	28	0
Stockholders' equity	422,480	331,104	290,628	112,565	81,191	9,934	1,189
Total liabilities and stockholders' equity	604,306	468,312	441,946	149,312	99,501	16,091	1,203

Source: Siebel Systems annual reports and SEC filings. All figures are in thousands of dollars, except employee data.

*Data for 1998 have been restated to reflect the merger of Scopus Technologies with Siebel Systems in May 1998. Prior years' data have not been restated.

EXHIBIT 2 Siebel Systems Stock Price, 1996–1999

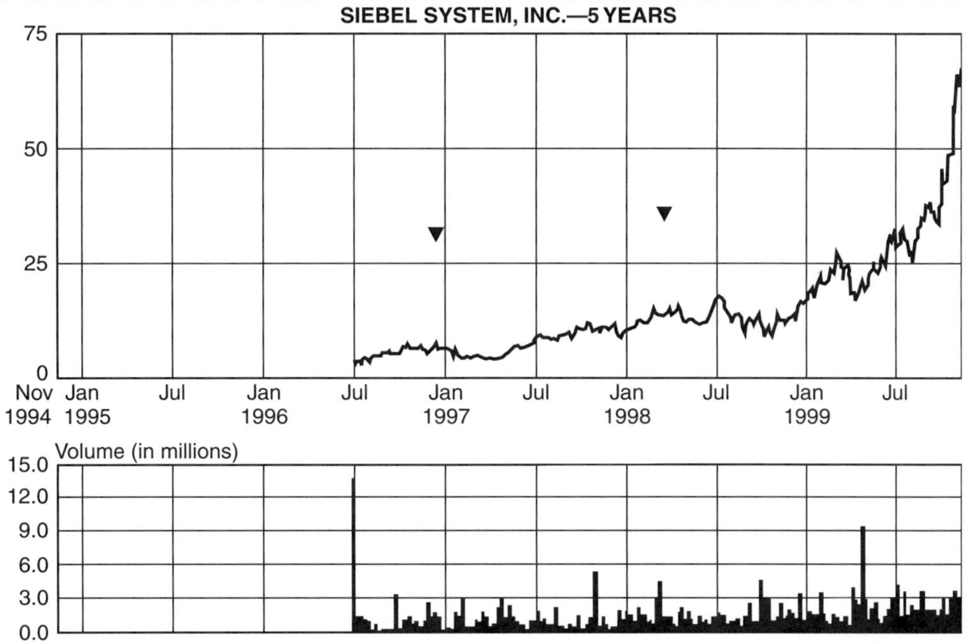

Source: Netscape Netcenter. Reproduced with permission from CSI.

EXHIBIT 3 CRM Software Market, 1997–2003

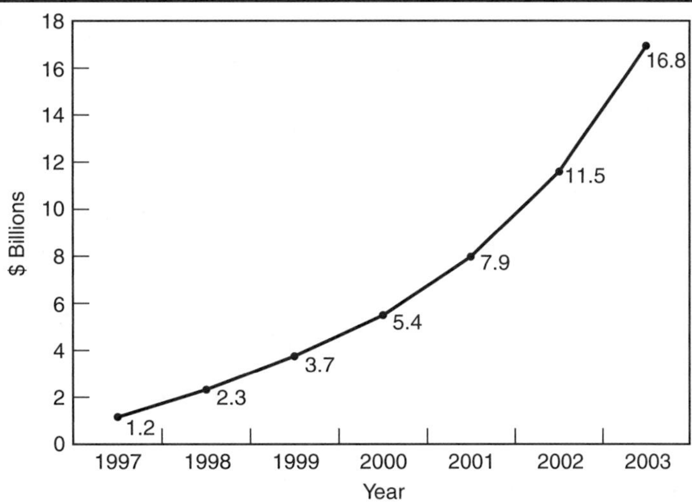

Reproduced with permission from AMR Research, Inc.

EXHIBIT 4 ERP Software Market, 1997–2003

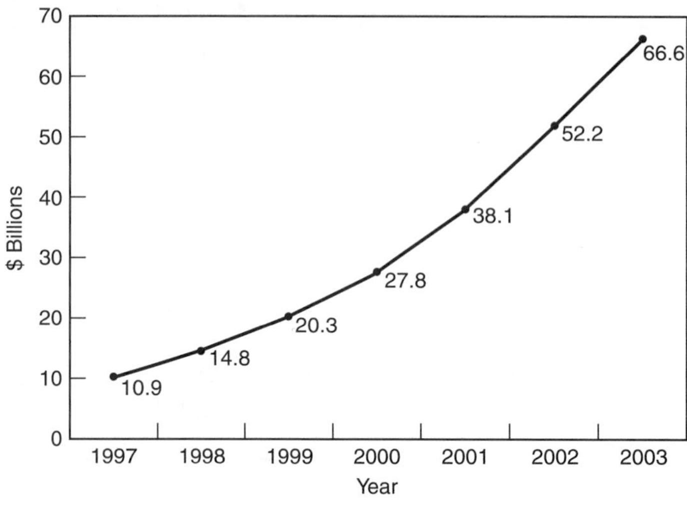

Reproduced with permission from AMR Research, Inc.

EXHIBIT 5 E-business Infrastructure

When the World Wide Web first came onto the scene in the early 1990s, few applications were available for enabling electronic commerce. Early Web technology included a limited set of tools:

- Web servers (i.e., the platforms for making Web pages accessible over the Internet via the hypertext transfer protocol [HTTP]);
- Web browsers (programs such as Netscape Navigator and Microsoft Internet Explorer, which enabled users to view Web pages stored on Web servers);
- Web page development tools (programs such as Microsoft FrontPage and Adobe PageMill, which enabled users to create Web pages formatted with the hypertext mark-up language [HTML], the lingua franca of the World Wide Web); and
- Tools for making Web pages interactive (for example, Sun Microsystem's Java programming language, which enabled developers to write small applications—so-called applets—that could be downloaded to a browser to perform a specific function, such as calculate a loan rate).

These basic technologies provided the foundation that enabled companies to create a presence on the Web (allowing them to post so-called brochureware on their sites, i.e., primarily static information and promotional content). But they lacked sophisticated functions that were essential to conducting e-business, such as interactive catalogs, online shopping management, and payment processing. Companies that wanted to do business over the Web had to custom-build their e-commerce systems, using various programming and development tools.

The explosive growth of the World Wide Web that began in the mid-1990s sparked the creation of whole new categories of e-business applications. Dozens, if not hundreds, of new or reinvented software companies started to provide the technological infrastructure for e-commerce. By 1999, the market for e-business technology had grown to encompass a broad range of functions, described in the following table with a sampling of companies and products in each major category:

Technology/Description	*Representative Vendors*	*Representative Products*
Catalog Engines		
Tools for creating, managing, and distributing online product catalogs	Actinic Software	Actinic Catalog
	Aspect Development	eDesign, eSource
	Mercado Software	IntuiFind Merchant Catalog; IntuiFind Procurement Catalog (tool for aggregating multiple supplier catalogs into one searchable entity)
	Requisite Technology	Unified Catalog (incorporates BugsEye search engine)
Commerce Platforms/Servers		
Bundled software integrating multiple e-business functions into one package: Web server, database server, and application servers, along with development tools to customize and maintain a commerce Web site	Allaire	Spectra, ColdFusion
	Art Technology Group (ATG)	Dynamo
	BroadVision	One-to-One Commerce
	IBM	Net.Commerce Pro, WebSphere
	INTERSHOP	enfinity
	Microsoft	Site Server Commerce Edition
	Open Market	Transact, FutureTense IPS
	Silknet Software	eCommerce System
	Sun Microsystems/Netscape (America Online)	iPlanet (ECXpert, BuyerXpert, etc.)
Configurators		
Tools for configuring complex products online, enabling customers to select from various components, modules, or other options	Calico Commerce, Inc.	Calico eSales Configurator
	SAQQARA	Genifer Configurator
	Selectica	ACE Internet Selling Systems

(continued)

Technology/Description	*Representative Vendors*	*Representative Products*
Content Management Systems		
Tools for creating, organizing, and distributing information to customers, employees, partners, and other constituents	Documentum	Documentum 4i
	Interwoven	TeamSite, OpenDeploy
	Vignette	StoryServer, Syndication Server
E-mail Management Systems		
Inbound e-mail: Tools for analyzing, routing, and responding to incoming e-mail	Brightware	Brightware Contact Center, Brightware Advice
Outbound e-mail: Tools for creating and targeting e-mail messages to prospects, customers, and other audiences	EGain Communications Corp.	E-mail Management System, Web Collaboration System
	Kana Communications	Kana Connect, Kana Response, Kana Classify, Kana Commerce
	Mustang.com, Inc.	Mustang Message Center
Marketplace Technologies		
Tools for creating and operating online marketplaces, such as exchanges, auctions, and trading networks	Moai Technologies	LiveExchange
	TIBCO Software, Inc.	TIB/ActiveEnterprise
	TRADEX Technologies	TRADEX Commerce Center
Payment Technologies		
Tools to enable e-businesses to collect, make, or process payments online	CyberCash	Secure Payment/SET, PayNow
	eCharge Corp.	eCharge Internet Purchasing Account, eCharge My Phone!
	Qpass	Qpass Network, PowerWallet
Personalization Tools		
Tools for capturing or developing customer profiles; analyzing customer behavior; recommending items for purchase; and predicting customer preferences	Engage Technologies	ProfileServer
	Net Perceptions	Recommendation Engine
	Personify	Personify Essentials

(continued)

Technology/Description	*Representative Vendors*	*Representative Products*
Procurement Systems		
Tools for automating corporate purchasing of indirect materials (e.g., office supplies, computers, janitorial products and services, etc.)	Ariba	Operating Resources Management System (ORMS); Ariba Network
	Commerce One	BuySite, MarketSite
	Intelisys Electronic Commerce, LLC	IEC-Enterprise
	ProcureNet, Inc.	OneSource
Search Engines		
Tools enabling customers to find information about products, services, technical support, and other topics from disparate corporate databases	Excalibur Technologies	Excalibur RetrievalWare
	PC DOCS/Fulcrum	SearchServer
	Verity	Verity Information Server; Verity Profiler; Verity Query Language; Verity Profiler; Verity Intranet/Internet Spider
Security Technologies		
Tools for authenticating identities, protecting privacy, and preventing fraud	CyberSource	CyberSource Internet Fraud Screen
	TriStrata, Inc.	TriStrata Secure Information Management System
	VeriSign	VeriSign OnSite
Shopping Engines		
Tools for online comparison shopping	Frictionless Commerce	Frictionless Value-Comparison Engine
	Inktomi Corp.	Inktomi Shopping Engine
Streaming Multimedia		
Tools for delivering graphics, audio, and video (e.g., product illustrations or demos) in a stream of small chunks, enabling customers to perceive content almost immediately upon requesting the download	LivePicture	LivePicture Zoom Server
	Microsoft	Windows Media Services
	RealNetworks	RealServer G2
Web Application Servers		
Specialized servers for running and managing Web applications and e-commerce transactions (in conjunction with Web servers and application servers)	Bluestone Software	Sapphire/Web
	HAHT Software	HAHTsite Application Server
	IBM	Lotus Domino
	Inktomi Corp.	Inktomi Traffic Server
	Oracle Corp.	Oracle Web Application Server

QRS CORPORATION

The hardest thing to accomplish strategically is watching for the person or company that comes out of left field with a new idea or innovative product. —*John Simon, Chief Executive Officer, QRS Corporation**

On a July morning in 1999, John Simon, CEO of QRS Corporation, reviewed figures for the quarter that had just ended on June 30: another ringing performance, with revenues and profits up more than 40% over the prior year's quarter. It was the latest chapter in the impressive growth of the Richmond, California company: over the last five years, sales and profits had increased at a compound annual rate of more than 30%, and the company's stock price had doubled in the last 12 months (Exhibit 1). QRS was a leader in its field, providing business-to-business (B2B) electronic commerce and merchandising management services to the U.S. retail industry. Simon believed that to continue its success, both in the industry and the stock market, the company would have to maintain its high growth rate. However, he also recognized the law of large numbers: growing at 30% a year would become increasingly difficult. He attributed QRS's past success to its ability to execute a strategy that focused solely on the electronic commerce needs of the retail industry and emphasized services that generated a high rate of recurring revenues. Simon and his staff had identified several opportunities for significant growth. Though many market analysts were predicting a dramatic rise of Internet-based B2B commerce—some expecting it to reach $1.3 trillion by 2003[1]—Simon doubted that the retail industry would move significantly in that direction. He was keeping an eye on Internet-related developments, but his near-term growth plans were focused elsewhere.

Case Writer Eric Martí prepared this case under the supervision of Professor Garth Saloner and Professor A. Michael Spence as the basis for class discussion rather than to illustrate either effective or ineffective handling of an administrative situation. Margot Sutherland, Executive Director, Center for Electronic Business and Commerce, Stanford Graduate School of Business, managed the development of the case.

* Wall Street Transcript Corporation, "CEO Interview: John Simon, QRS Corporation," 4/29/99.

[1] Forrester Research, "Resizing Online Business Trade," 11/98.

JOHN SIMON'S BACKGROUND

For more than 20 years, Simon had been involved with the retail industry. During his MBA studies at Harvard, he won the business school's Retailing Prize in 1980. Before coming to QRS, Simon had spent 10 years at Carter Hawley Hale Stores, Inc., then a major department store operator (whose assets were eventually acquired by Federated Department Stores, Inc.). He served as a buyer, store manager, and division vice president for its Broadway Stores operation in southern California. Later, he worked for the company's Information Services division, where he became a senior program manager. In that position, he supported the outsourcing of retail systems to clients such as Neiman Marcus, Woodward & Lothrop, and Holt H Renfrew.

Simon joined the QRS founding team in 1987. Since then, he had worked in nearly every part of the company, from customer support to product development. In the early days, he had been instrumental in developing business and operating plans, market strategies, and application development plans. In 1994, Simon was made executive vice president. Four years later, he was named CEO. From his days at Carter Hawley Hale, then at QRS, Simon had witnessed the retail industry's adoption of supply chain automation and electronic commerce.

THE U.S. RETAIL INDUSTRY AND SUPPLY CHAIN AUTOMATION

The U.S. retail industry, which accounted for nearly one-half of all consumer spending, was characterized by slow growth and low margins.[2] U.S. retail sales grew at an average annual compound rate of 5.5% from 1986 to 1997 and increased just 5% from 1997 to 1998.[3] Net profit margins for most retail segments were typically in the low to middle single digits: department and discount stores, for instance, averaged 3.1%; grocery stores, 2.2%; home improvement stores, 4.7%; drug stores, 2.6%; and apparel retailers, 6.9%.[4] These economics made cost reduction a key concern for retailers: a typical grocer, for instance, could nearly double its bottom line by cutting costs by just 1% of sales (Exhibits 2 and 3).

To reduce inventory costs and improve supply chain efficiency, major retailers began in the 1980s to adopt "quick response"—the industry's term for a just-in-time approach to inventory management—as well as other techniques. Additional initiatives included efficient customer response (ECR), vendor managed inventory (VMI), continuous replenishment process (CRP), and collaborative planning, forecasting, and replenishment (CPFR). Each of these depended critically on capturing and tracking product-specific data throughout the supply chain in order to get the right mix of goods to the right location at the right time, thus minimizing stock outs (i.e., missed sales

[2] Retail sales in 1998 totaled more than $2.7 trillion, out of $5.8 trillion in consumer expenditures. [Sources: Census Bureau, http://www.census.gov/svsd/retlann/view/artssal.txt and Bureau of Economic Analysis, http://www.bea.doc.gov/bea/dn/nipatbls/NIP2-2.HTM].

[3] Census Bureau.

[4] Retail profitability data from Market Guide, Inc. (published by OneSource Information Services, 8/99).

opportunities) and overstocks (i.e., markdowns). Two key elements of these initiatives were the use of universal product codes (UPCs) and electronic data interchange (EDI).

The Uniform Code Council (UCC),[5] a nonprofit organization first established by grocery-industry manufacturers and retailers to standardize product codes, created the UPC in the 1970s. The UCC expanded its activities beyond groceries, bringing UPCs to all industries and retail segments. The standard UPC in North America was a 12-digit code that identified the product by manufacturer and other attributes. Moreover, a symbol composed of a series of parallel lines, called a "bar code," could uniquely represent each code. Using a device hooked to a computer, a merchant could scan the bar code printed on a price tag or package, and the information would immediately enter the retailer's information system. This improved retailers' ability to track merchandise as it entered inventory and was sold, enabling them to quickly analyze sales data at the store level for both fast- and slow-moving items.

Electronic Commerce Before the Internet: EDI

Major retailers also implemented EDI, an automated approach to conducting transactions between trading partners. Well before the general public knew about the Internet—and years before creation of the World Wide Web—organizations had been conducting electronic commerce via EDI, facilitated by companies like QRS. Indeed, while B2B commerce over the Internet totaled $43 billion in 1998, EDI-based transactions amounted to $250 billion.[6]

EDI enabled companies to exchange business documents (such as purchase orders and invoices) via computer over a network, using predefined formats and standards. A typical EDI transaction—a purchase order (PO), for example—encompassed five steps:

1. Document preparation: In some companies a purchasing system might generate the PO automatically; in other companies a person might key the information into the ordering system.
2. Outbound translation: The system converted the PO file into standard EDI format. Third-party translation software usually handled these steps.
3. Transmission: Typically, an EDI document was sent over a private value-added network (VAN), which provided a reliable and secure communications medium through which confidential information could flow. The document arrived at the recipient's electronic mailbox.
4. Inbound translation: The recipient retrieved the document, and the internal information system converted it from the EDI. Third-party software usually handled this function as well.

[5] Uniform Code Council Web site, http://www.uc-council.com/about_ucc/uc_history_timeline.html, 8/99.

[6] *Business Week*, 6/22/98.

5. Document processing: The recipient acted on the contents of the document; depending on the type of transaction, this step could trigger further EDI transactions (for example, receipt of the PO might cause the recipient's system to issue a PO to its supplier).

EDI technology originated in the late 1960s (the U.S. government was an early user), and it was refined during the next decade. By the late 1970s, many government agencies and large corporations had started to adopt EDI. Over time, each business sector—finance, health care, manufacturing, retail, and so on—established standard EDI "transaction sets," reflecting the nuances of commerce that are characteristic of that industry.

EDI provided several benefits. First, it reduced the cost of processing a document manually by up to a factor of 20. Second, it speeded up operations: transmission of an EDI document over a network is virtually instantaneous, and the receiving party can (if set up to do so) process the information immediately, cutting response cycles by days if not weeks. Third, EDI helped reduce transaction errors by eliminating the need to rekey data.

The transmission of EDI documents required not only a communications medium but also a system to enable computers of many different kinds to exchange information. VAN providers developed services to address this fundamental need. Besides providing the basic connectivity for network transmission, the VAN operators offered electronic mailbox accounts, administration services, EDI translation and communication software, and other EDI-enabling services. Major VAN operators included telecommunications firms (e.g., AT&T, Sprint, MCI WorldCom), computer services firms (e.g., IBM, EDS), and firms specializing in EDI (e.g., GE Information Services, Sterling Commerce, Kleinschmidt). VANs also guaranteed high levels of security and reliability. They generally charged customers a monthly subscription fee (which varied with level of service) plus transmission charges.

All industries eventually developed EDI-based trading networks that took the form of interconnected "hubs and spokes": large firms, generally the first to adopt EDI, became the hubs, while their many trading partners (who varied in size) were the spokes. EDI VANs sought to extend the reach of the trading networks they served: the more trading partners that used the provider's service, the less need there was for any partner to use a competitor's EDI service. Each partner that joined the network thus increased the network's value.

Though EDI had been available for over two decades, only a small percentage of businesses used it. In 1998, for example, J. P. Morgan estimated that only about 50,000 U.S. companies employed EDI (including virtually the entire Fortune 1,000), and in 1997 International Data Corporation counted about 195,400 companies worldwide using EDI service.[7] Analysts estimated that EDI had penetrated only 10%–20% of the potential market.[8] For a large company processing tens of thousands or more documents each year (invoices, purchase orders, shipping notices, etc.), the savings from EDI easily

[7] *Computerworld*, "EDI vs. the New Kids," (posted on CW's "emmerce" Web site, 4/6/98); BT Alex Brown research report, "Sterling Commerce, Inc.," 6/2/99.

[8] BancBoston Robertson Stephens, "QRS Corporation," Richard A. Jaurez, 1/29/99.

exceeded its costs. For smaller companies, however, the cost and complexity of EDI impeded its adoption.

To become EDI-enabled, a company first had to purchase proprietary software that—for a small to mid-size company—could cost $10,000 or more (for larger companies, it can cost millions of dollars). If the software needed to be integrated with the company's back-office applications, this generally required costly custom programming. Ongoing upgrade and support cost several thousand dollars more a year. The company also had to subscribe to a VAN to transmit EDI documents: monthly fees and connection charges ranged from a few hundred to several thousand dollars a month. Other possible costs included expenditures on hardware to run the EDI system as well as initial and periodic training of EDI operators. Working with EDI-compliant partners also often required investing in expensive equipment such as bar code scanners and printers.[9] A small or mid-size company might have to pay $45,000 per year on EDI-related expenses.[10]

Rather than use third-party EDI services, some very large organizations built their own EDI systems in-house (though typically purchased or outsourced at least part of the system). In the retail industry, for example, Wal-Mart—the nation's largest retailer, with 1998 sales of $139.2 billion—was legendary for the internal development of its information systems. In the 1980s, it built its own satellite communications system, at a cost of some $20 million, to relay sales and inventory information between its stores and distribution centers.[11] And to integrate its suppliers into its inventory management system, Wal-Mart had invested some $4 billion in its Retail Link network: this system enabled suppliers to estimate demand more accurately by accessing specific sales data for their products at each Wal-Mart store on a daily basis. Most retail companies, however, had neither the resources nor in-house expertise to build their own EDI systems.

QRS HISTORY

QRS Corporation was founded in 1985 to provide software and related services to the retail industry. In 1987 it formed an affiliate company to develop and market a database of UPCs[12] to help retailers and suppliers manage their purchasing and fulfillment operations: suppliers could upload current UPCs to the database, and retailers could retrieve accurate UPCs for their ordering and inventory management systems.

While the adoption of UPCs had helped retailers and suppliers manage inventory, it also presented a logistical problem: to use UPCs, retailers had to maintain a database of suppliers' current codes in their information systems. Traditionally, suppliers provided their UPCs via paper catalogs or magnetic tapes, which were frequently updated and sent to their retail trading partners. Retailers would then transfer the information

[9] *Infoworld*, 4/6/98.

[10] *The Business Journal* [San Jose, CA], "Partnerships: The Big and Small of It," 9/2/98.

[11] *Wal-Mart: A History of Sam Walton's Retail Phenomenon*, Sandra S. Vance and Roy V. Scott, New York: Twayne Publishers, 1994 (p. 95).

[12] Peter R. Johnson, an entrepreneur with prior retail experience, started the original company named PRJ & Inc. The new affiliate changed its name from Quick Response Services, Inc. to QRS Corporation in May 1998.

from the catalogs or tapes into their internal databases. To address this cumbersome system QRS's UPC database provided a central repository, where suppliers could post their UPCs so that any authorized retailer could access and download them directly into its information system.

To enable customers to access the catalog, QRS negotiated a deal to resell IBM Global Network (IGN) services, including messaging and electronic data interchange services, rather than invest in creating its own VAN. IGN was part of IBM's worldwide data networking services, a highly secure and reliable system for transmitting corporate data. Subscribers had one or more electronic mailbox accounts on the system, which could store messages that other IGN subscribers and users of other VANs sent to them. The network took care of translating messages to a format that could be read by the recipient's computer, thus enabling trading partners with different computer systems to communicate with one another. The system operated under a set of IBM proprietary protocols.

QRS sold its software-related business in 1993, and the company focused solely on providing EDI and UPC catalog services to the retail industry. That same year QRS went public. QRS's timing was right: its EDI and UPC catalog offerings caught the retail industry's wave of supply chain automation just as it was gathering momentum. Over the following six years, the company's customer base increased from 2,800 to 7,764, including 270 retailers and nearly 7,500 manufacturers and carriers (Exhibit 4). Revenues increased to $91.9 million in 1998, while earnings rose to $12.1 million. And with 1999 first-half sales of $58.9 million and earnings of $7.5 million, QRS was on line for another year of better than 30% growth. At the same time, the company had grown from fewer than 75 employees in 1993 to 470 by mid-1999 (plus 400 part-time workers). This record had not gone unnoticed: two years in a row, *Forbes* placed QRS on its list of the "200 Best Small Companies in America," and in 1999 QRS made the *Business Week* roster of "100 Hot Growth Companies—The 100 Best Small Corporations" (Exhibits 5–9).

The company had become a leading provider of EDI services to the U.S. retail industry—with a 40% market share for EDI services in the soft goods sector (apparel, accessories, and footwear)—and its UPC catalog was the largest and most widely used by retailers.

THE QRS PRODUCT LINE

QRS derived revenues from six lines of business:

1. Network services (EDI and messaging services);
2. Catalog services (the UPC database);
3. Inventory management services (replenishment, sales analysis, and forecasting);
4. Logistics management services;
5. Professional services (consulting and training); and
6. Syndicated retail price information.

Analysts estimated that roughly 95% of the company's revenues came from network and catalog services, with network services alone accounting for 55% to 65% of total sales.[13] Inventory management services accounted for most of the remaining revenues. Network services were less profitable than its value-added services (such as the UPC catalog and inventory management services). One analyst estimated that the gross margin on network services was 30%–35%, while value-added services enjoyed gross margins of 60%–80%.[14] Network services had lower gross margins in part because basic connectivity had become a commodity-type business, with many vendors competing on price. By contrast, value-added services offered more differentiation (e.g., the size and make-up of QRS's UPC catalog distinguished it from competitors' catalogs).

Network Services

Network services included QRS Concourse, the company's connectivity offering, a secure wide-area network over which customers could send and receive EDI documents and other electronic messages. As mentioned earlier, QRS did not own or maintain the underlying physical network; rather, the company contracted to buy network services in bulk from IBM Global Network, subject to volume discounts and annual minimum purchases, and it resold service to QRS customers. QRS Concourse usage billed on a metered basis: each transaction was charged per thousand characters transmitted (i.e., by the "kilocharacter"); rates varied with higher peak time and lower off-peak rates.

Network services also included QRS Quickstep, QRS Passkey, and QRS EC Service Bureau. These services enabled small retailers and vendors to conduct EDI transactions with larger partners, without the start-up investment traditional EDI required.

QRS Quickstep and QRS Passkey were the company's offerings to small vendors and retailers, respectively, who wanted to do EDI-based business with hub partners. Quickstep, for instance, typically involved a large retailer that bought products from non-EDI vendors: the hub retailer "sponsored" a Quickstep program for these spokes. Under the program, QRS provided a desktop application that enabled the spokes to connect to the QRS network via the Internet. The hub used its normal EDI process to send documents (e.g., POs) to a spoke's mailbox on the QRS network; the vendor retrieved the messages (again, over an Internet connection), using the QRS Quickstep application, which downloaded the data into the vendor's own information system. Moreover, the vendor could use Quickstep to send messages to the hub account (e.g., invoices, shipping notices) that were delivered as EDI documents to the hub's mailbox on the network. QRS charged the Quickstep spokes a monthly mailbox fee and a per-transaction fee (based on the number of characters transmitted in the document). QRS Passkey operated similarly to Quickstep, but in this case the sponsoring hub was a large vendor doing business with small retailers who were not EDI-enabled.

[13] CIBC Oppenheimer, for instance, estimated that network services accounted for revenues of $61.2 million (or 67% of total sales); catalog services for $26.3 million (29% of sales). [Source: CIBC Oppenheimer Equity Research, "QRS Corporation," 1/29/99.] Robinson-Humphrey pegged 1998 revenues from EDI services at 55% of total sales, with 40% from catalog services and 5% from inventory management services. [Source: Robinson-Humphrey Research Brief, "QRS," 1/14/99.] And according to Advest, network services produced 68% of revenues; catalog services, 23%; and inventory management, 9%. [Advest, "QRS Corp." 5/5/99.]

[14] Lehman Brothers, "QRS," 5/19/99; 5/19/98.

The QRS EC Service Bureau was designed for the smallest spokes, for whom even the Quickstep and Passkey products were beyond their resources or capabilities. These businesses (mostly vendors seeking to sell to larger retailers) could fax their documents to a QRS service bureau, where human operators converted the documents into EDI format and forwarded them over the QRS network to the designated trading partner. Likewise, the bureau converted return EDI transactions from the large partner to the small partner back into paper forms. The average charge per document was $2 (versus $1 for the Web-based Quickstep or Passkey service, and less than $.50 for the standard Concourse service). QRS acquired its service bureau operations by purchasing two firms (see "Acquisitions"). "The service bureau is a good business, but the challenge there is scalability," Simon observed. "It's labor intensive, so to grow that business you have to keep adding people to keypunch the data."

Catalog Services

QRS Keystone was the company's flagship UPC catalog product. It was widely cited as the leading UPC catalog for the retail industry, containing some 73 million codes (as of mid-1999), more than any competitive product. Development started in 1987, and each year QRS added more vendors' UPCs, while increasing the number and type of data fields available (more than 40 fields, as of mid-1999). For instance, QRS added an image field to each UPC record, enabling vendors to upload a picture of their product along with its UPC and descriptive information (e.g., size, color, etc.).

The concept was straightforward: suppliers uploaded their UPC catalogs to the QRS Keystone database, maintained at QRS's Richmond, California data center, and retailers downloaded UPCs from any vendor's catalog to which they had access (each vendor controlled the retailers that had access to its catalog). QRS charged a fee for each "trading partnership" that occurred during the month: when a retailer accessed a vendor's UPCs from the QRS database, the retailer and vendor were each charged $145 for that month, with no limit on how often the retailer accessed the vendor's catalog during the month. Moreover, no customer was charged more than $2,700 per month for catalog access. (Network usage fees for uploading or downloading UPC data were an additional, per-kilocharacter charge.)

Inventory Management Services

The inventory management services (IMS) portfolio included three products: QRS Catalyst, QRS Mariner, and QRS Horizon. QRS Catalyst enabled retailers and vendors to track sales data, by various attributes, at the store level. Retailers uploaded store data to a QRS database, which authorized vendors accessed to identify store-level sales trends of their products. QRS Mariner was an outsource inventory replenishment service for retailers for whom an in-house system would have been too costly to purchase and manage: QRS collected daily sales data (at the UPC level) from the retailer's stores and, by prior agreement with vendors, generated purchase orders to replenish the stock. QRS Horizon enabled retailers to forecast sales, for up to 53 weeks, using input variables such as seasonal factors and promotional events.

The company measured the activity of its IMS business by the number of "extensions" under management. An extension was one instance of a UPC at a specific store; for example, the UPC for a particular style of size 8 white tennis shoes stocked at 100 stores in a chain counted as 100 extensions. By mid-1999, QRS had approximately 24 million extensions under management, double the number for 1998. Customers paid a monthly fee for the service, plus a charge per extension under management. According to Simon, QRS had no service-based competition in this area; rather, competition tended to be big-ticket enterprise software applications.

Logistics Management Services

Logistics management services (LMS) enabled retailers and suppliers to arrange and track shipment of goods. For example, a customer could post a load tendering message (via an EDI transaction) on the QRS network to solicit quotes from carriers on price and availability, then follow up with a shipping order to the carrier offering the best terms. As with other QRS services, the company charged customers a monthly subscription fee plus EDI transaction fees billed per kilocharacter. In 1998, approximately 150 customers subscribed to the service.

Professional Services

QRS consultants provided strategic consulting, readiness studies, operational analysis, implementation management, and educational services.

Information Syndication

The acquisition of Retail Data Services (RDS) in July 1999 brought this product into the QRS portfolio (see "Acquisitions"). The company's primary services, targeted at grocery retailers, included the in-store collection of retail prices, scan price verification, and pricing data analysis. Among its 117 customers were Wal-Mart, Kroger, and Safeway, as well as e-grocers Grocery Express and Homegrocers. The acquisition, Simon explained, "allows us to further extend our reach into the grocery retail segment, giving us a new value-added service and set of customers that QRS can use to expand our electronic commerce services across all major retail sectors."[15] Revenue and other operating data for this line of business were not available.

THE MARKET FOR EDI SERVICES TO THE RETAIL INDUSTRY

North American expenditures on EDI services were approximately $706 million in 1998, out of worldwide expenditures of about $1 billion.[16] (QRS estimated that retail accounted for 25% of the market.) From 1996 to 1998, the worldwide market for traditional EDI

[15] QRS press release, 7/26/99.

[16] Dataquest, "1998 Worldwide Digital Commerce Software and Services Market Share," 8/2/99.

grew at an average annual rate of 9.6%.[17] Forecasts of future growth varied: IDC projected worldwide revenues of $2.4 billion in 2002 (a 24.2% compound average growth rate), while Gartner Group expected a one-year increase in 1999 of 15%, with the growth rate declining to 5% over three years.[18] QRS's own market analysis forecasted 12% per year growth through 2002.[19]

By 1999, virtually every large firm in the retail industry used EDI. Moreover, relationships between hubs and their EDI providers tended to be "sticky": switching systems from one provider to another was time consuming and costly. EDI service firms typically had high customer retention rates, which made it difficult for EDI service providers to win established customers from a competitor. Hence, hubs that were encouraging (or forcing) their smaller trading partners to become EDI compliant largely drove growth in EDI services. Hub partners pressed these smaller companies to adopt EDI: some hubs charged their partners to process non-EDI transactions, while many would not do business with noncompliant firms.

EDI AND THE INTERNET

With the sudden rise of the Internet in the mid-1990s, a new form of EDI appeared: Internet EDI (also called Web EDI). While traditional EDI had been conducted over proprietary VANs, Internet EDI used the public Internet to send and receive EDI documents. Responding to the growing popularity of the Internet, providers of traditional EDI services, including QRS and its competitors, developed Internet-based EDI services. Moreover, a growing number of companies were formed to focus specifically on the market for Internet EDI services.

The Internet offered several advantages over the use of VANs for EDI. First, Internet access and usage costs were 50%–80% lower than the fees VAN operators charged. Second, the Internet was far more pervasive than any single VAN, providing easy access to any trading partner. Third, the Internet employed open standards, whereas VANs typically operated under their own proprietary protocols. Therefore, EDI software had to be custom-tailored for different VANs, making the software costly and often complex to operate. EDI software developed for the Internet, on the other hand, cost less than EDI software running on VANs and was simpler to operate.

However, companies had two major reservations about using the Internet for B2B commerce: security and reliability. The Internet was an open, public system that millions of users could access, and stories abounded about hackers stealing data, intercepting messages, and committing fraud. In addition, data sent over the Internet could be corrupted—or even lost altogether—and messages were sometimes delayed. In contrast, VANs controlled access to the network and were designed to be reliable. While advances in encryption, authentication, and other protective technologies eventually addressed companies' concerns about Internet security, Internet reliability remained

[17] Dataquest, "The EDI Market: Stellar Growth in Internet EDI, Traditional EDI Growth Slows Down as Predicted," 7/5/99.

[18] *Upside*, "EDI Vendors Spin a New Web," 5/99.

[19] QRS corporate presentation, summer 1999

an issue. Nonetheless, the pervasiveness of the Internet and the low cost of Internet access ensured its future in B2B commerce.

Within the IT community the big question was whether the Internet would kill EDI. Some claimed that a new set of B2B standards for electronic commerce would replace EDI standards altogether, and that the public Internet—or virtual private networks such as intranets and extranets that used Internet standards—would replace more costly proprietary VANs. Under this scenario, even the large hubs that had invested extensively in EDI-based systems would migrate to the Internet. Others predicted that EDI would remain the basic standard of B2B electronic commerce, with the Internet extending EDI to the smallest trading partners. Transactions would still be done via EDI-formatted documents, but they would be transmitted inexpensively over the Internet; and low-cost, easy-to-use software—embedded in familiar Web browser software—would handle the complexities of generating and translating EDI-formatted documents.

The Internet versus EDI debate often included mention of an emerging technology called extensible markup language (XML) that the World Wide Web Consortium was developing. This was the same group that set standards for the Hypertext Markup Language (HTML), the formatting language for creating Web pages. XML extended the capability of Web-based documents, by providing features for describing data types and document structures. For example, an XML document might include the numeral 4356 that was "tagged" with the data-type label "purchase order number." When the trading partner's computer received the document, its decoding software (called an XML parser) would recognize "4356" as a PO number and could insert that number, and other similarly tagged data, into its order processing system. In this respect, XML was far more flexible than EDI, which adhered to rigid document definitions. Some observers believed that XML would supplant EDI as the standard format for B2B transactions. Others viewed XML as a complement to EDI: XML would be a means of delivering EDI-based documents. Indeed, the XML/EDI Group, a task force composed of companies in the EDI business, had been formed to integrate the two technologies.

With the rise of the Internet and the enormous expectations for Web-based commerce, many firms had developed B2B electronic commerce products and services. Companies ranging from America Online's Netscape unit to lesser known startups were vying for a piece of the market. Netscape's ECXpert, for instance, enabled corporations to build Internet-based trading networks. On the services side, for example, a privately held firm called R-Net EDI (founded in 1996) offered retailers and suppliers access to a UPC catalog over the Internet: using R-Net's PC-based software, a customer could upload or retrieve UPCs for a monthly fee and no transaction charges. The software also enabled customers to conduct EDI transactions with members of the network. The company targeted small independent retailers; its vendor base included Wrangler, Nike, and Lee Apparel, and its UPC catalog had more than 25 million codes.[20]

Simon watched the development of Internet EDI, and its potential impact on VANs, with great interest: QRS was an established EDI provider, and most of its revenues came from reselling VAN services. He was skeptical, however, that the retail industry would quickly adopt the Internet for B2B electronic commerce. He based his view on

[20] *Sacramento Bee*, 7/23/99.

his company's experience. "Over a three year period, we invested five to ten million dollars in building Web interfaces for our products [Quickstep and Passkey]. If we're lucky, Web-based revenue *might* hit half a million this year," he said. "Meanwhile, our service bureau businesses, which we acquired for less than $5 million altogether, are doing $5 million a year in sales—*and* they brought us a thousand new customers. The Internet is here, but nobody's really climbing on board—at least not in retail." Indeed, worldwide sales of Internet EDI services totaled $52.4 million in 1998 (across all industries), compared to $1 billion for traditional EDI (an increase in Internet EDI of 355% from the year before versus a 7.5% increase for traditional EDI[21]). And while Forrester Research predicted B2B electronic commerce would total $1.3 trillion in 2003, it estimated that consumer goods would account for just $51.9 billion of that amount.[22]

Contrary to the predictions of many market analysts, Simon was not persuaded that the ease and low cost of the Internet would cause the retail industry to adopt electronic commerce en masse. "It's true, for example, that with fax machines, everybody eventually got on board when a critical mass had been reached," Simon said. "But electronic commerce isn't the same: fax machines don't require businesses to think or behave differently. They simply allow people to send letters more quickly, and they're not complicated to operate. Doing electronic commerce requires businesses to act in a different way, and computers still aren't that simple." According to Simon, while top-tier retail companies had embraced electronic commerce to some degree, the rest of the industry was slow to adopt. "Most companies are focused on coming up with the next hot item that will fly off the shelves," he observed, "not on reducing operating costs."

"What does it take to get mass conversion to electronic commerce in the retail industry?" Simon asked. "That's the question we'd like to have the answer to. For years we tried using the 'carrot' approach to get trading partners to adopt electronic commerce, with limited success. Now we're using the 'stick' approach, and it's far more effective." By the "stick" approach, Simon was referring to the "mandate" programs QRS hub clients were rolling out. To get their trading partners to adopt electronic commerce, hub accounts would have QRS send letters to their spokes instructing them to become EC-enabled or face penalties. Federated, for example—owner of the Macy's and Bloomingdale chains—charged trading partners $50 to send a non-EDI advance shipping notice and $25 for a non-EDI purchase order. QRS would send the letters printed on the hub's letterhead. "We discovered that most of these spoke accounts would rather pay our service bureau to handle the EDI transaction than do it themselves over the Web," Simon observed. "Maybe we're not communicating the value proposition of electronic commerce clearly or strongly enough. Or maybe it's a far harder problem—a problem of industrial psychology that really doesn't have a solution."

Though QRS did not see a large-scale adoption of its Web-based EDI services, Simon believed that making its service available over the Internet had an indirect payoff. "Once we had the Internet and the service bureau options in place," he said, "our

[21] Dataquest, "The EDI Market: Stellar Growth in Internet EDI, Traditional EDI Growth Slows Down as Predicted," 7/5/99.

[22] Forrester Research, Inc., "Resizing Online Business Trade," 11/98.

hub accounts realized that their trading partners had no excuse for using paper rather than EDI. It gave the hubs confidence in rolling out their mandate programs."

EDI COMPETITORS

In addition to QRS, three other companies occupied substantial positions in EDI services: GE Information Services (GEIS), a unit of General Electric Company; Sterling Commerce; and Harbinger Corporation. (IBM also marketed EDI services, but QRS and IBM did not compete; by signed agreement, the two companies operated as marketing partners in the retail industry.) Several other companies also provided EDI services—including AT&T and EDS—but they were less significant competitors in the retail industry, where QRS was focused.

GE Information Services

Established in 1964, GEIS was the oldest major EDI firm in continuous existence—and the largest. It was part of GE's Technical Products and Services division, which had 1998 revenues of $5.32 billion; GE did not publish revenue data for the unit, but according to a GEIS spokesman, sales for 1997 were approximately $700 million.[23] GEIS offered a broad range of electronic commerce services to a broad range of industries. According to company literature, its EDI services, including the flagship product EDI*Express, served more than 100,000 trading partners throughout the world (25% of the company's revenues came from international operations).[24] GEIS had offered a UPC catalog database since 1988; the current version, UPC*Express II, incorporated 46 million UPCs and had more than 1,200 commercial users. The company also offered a Web-based EDI service, GE TradeWeb, that enabled smaller trading partners to conduct EDI transactions, via Web-browser software and an Internet connection. Launched in mid-1996, the service cost less than $1,000 per year to use; by mid-1998, 3,000 customers had signed up.

Sterling Commerce

Sterling Commerce was also a long-time player in the EDI space.[25] With 1998 revenues of $490.3 million (23% from international sales), it trailed only GEIS in size. Sterling had acquired several companies in the 1990s, including its 1998 purchase of XcelleNet, a developer of remote computer management software, for $200 million. And with more than $600 million in cash and marketable securities, the company was

[23] *Computerworld*, "EDI vs. the New Kids," (posted on the *Computerworld* "emmerce" Web site, 4/6/98).
[24] Corporate Technology Information Services, "GE Information Services Corporate Overview," published by OneSource Information Services, Inc., 8/99.
[25] Before it was spun off as a separate company in 1996, Sterling Commerce had been a unit of Sterling Software, a major developer of systems management and application development tools and other products and services. Though Sterling Software was founded in 1981, the EDI unit that became Sterling Commerce was assembled from several older firms that had been acquired. The company's literature reported 1974 as the year it was founded.

well armed for further acquisitions. Sterling developed and marketed EDI software and other business automation software; sold EDI network services; and provided value-added services—such as its COMMERCE:Catalog (UPC database)—to the many trading partner communities that it managed. The company served more than 15 industries and had more than 45,000 customers worldwide, including nearly all the Fortune 500 corporations. It was particularly well established in financial services, and counted 99 of the top 100 U.S. banks among its customers. Revenues came from four main sources: software licenses, product support, transactions, and managed services. About 50% of the company's revenues were recurring. In the quarter ending June 30, 1999, 33% of Sterling's sales were from Internet-related sources ($49.9 million), up from $33.5 million in the year-earlier quarter;[26] these included Web-based versions of its EDI translation and communication software, Internet-based network services, and other EC-management services delivered via intranet or extranet configurations. Sterling expected to grow its Internet-related business at 30%–35% per year over the long term.[27]

Harbinger Corporation

Founded in 1983 by two former McKinsey & Co. consultants, Harbinger initially tried to market electronic cash management services to consumers, but that business went nowhere. The firm then switched its focus to small and mid-size companies, and by the late 1980s it was offering these segments EDI products and VAN-based transaction services. Harbinger grew from $5.5 million in 1991 to $135.2 million in 1998 (a 58% compound annual growth rate) and garnered more than 40,000 customers worldwide in a broad range of industries. In recent years, Harbinger had focused on migrating customers to Internet-based commerce, where it saw the greatest growth potential, especially for small and mid-size businesses. It had introduced a number of Internet-based products and services, including harbinger.net, a portal site that enables customers to transact B2B commerce over the Web. By mid-1999, 17% of its customers had shifted from VAN-based transactions to the Internet, representing 15% of the firm's total traffic, and Harbinger felt it would reach its target of moving 50% of its customers to the Internet by the end of 1999.

QRS COMPANY INFORMATION

Buyers and the QRS Sales Organization

The buyer of QRS services was generally an executive or senior manager at the client company, whether a retailer or manufacturer. For network services, typical buyer titles were Chief Information Officer; VP, Information Services; Director of Network Communications; VP, Electronic Commerce; or Director of Vendor Relations. For catalog services, typical titles were VP, Information Services; UPC Manager; or Merchandising Manager. Because the purchase of QRS services generally involved long-term goals

[26] Sterling Commerce, 10-Q Report, 8/5/99.
[27] PaineWebber Research Note, "Sterling Commerce," 5/14/99.

and contractual agreements, as well as changes in the customer's business procedures, buying decisions took several months or longer.

The QRS sales force was organized into east and west regions, each with its own sales director who reported to the VP for sales. Each region was divided into territories (15 to 20 nationwide), and each territory had a locally based account executive, who was responsible for all accounts in the territory. Account executives focused most of their time and efforts on large accounts. At corporate headquarters in Richmond, an inside sales force called on smaller accounts. Inside sales also concentrated on rollout campaigns—that is, on efforts to sign up hub customers' smaller trading partners, so that they could conduct EDI with their hub partners over the QRS network. Typically, QRS account executives furnished the leads on these smaller companies, which they received from their hub accounts. These rollout efforts represented a major thrust in QRS's growth strategy. Given that EDI had highly penetrated the top tier of retailers, which made it increasingly difficult to sign up new hub accounts for EDI service, bringing EDI services to smaller trading partners who were not yet EDI-enabled could generate significant business.

QRS Data Center and Network Operations

Located at company headquarters, the QRS data center involved a vast array of computing and storage systems, purchased from multiple hardware and software vendors. This equipment housed the company's critical databases (all standardized on software from Oracle), including its crown jewel: the UPC catalog. The center operated 24 hours a day, 365 days a year. Each day, data were backed up and shipped to an off-site location. Maintaining the data center was paramount to QRS's ability to guarantee service levels to its customers.

The IBM Global Network, from which QRS purchased network services, had a reputation for reliability, which was a key concern for QRS customers. Under its current agreement with IBM (effective January 1, 1998), QRS had committed to buy $250 million in network services over three years. In 1998, QRS met the minimum purchase requirements. On December 8, 1998, IBM agreed to sell IBM Global Network and its corporate networking business to AT&T. That transaction was completed in 1999. QRS did not consider the new arrangement a problem; it expected to continue to receive some network services from IBM (primarily messaging) and some from AT&T (connectivity). Given that AT&T's data network was far more extensive than IBM's, QRS viewed the new arrangement as a potential benefit.

Human Resources

As a technology-based services company, QRS depended on recruiting skilled workers in research, engineering, and product development; technical support and customer service; finance, human resources, and administration; and sales and marketing. Indeed, one issue that weighed on Simon's mind was the bench strength of his management team, and the company's ability to attract and keep critical talent. He felt confident about the executives at his side, but he knew that fast growth required the firm to develop talent. Of the current 10-person executive team, for instance, only two (including Simon) had been with the company for five or more years. And over the last five and a half years, the total number of employees had grown from 73 to 470 (plus 400 part-time workers).

The company's location in Richmond, California (across the bay from San Francisco and Silicon Valley) was at times a drawback in recruiting personnel, especially key technical talent. Still, Simon knew that if the company provided competitive compensation, opportunities to learn and grow, and the right atmosphere, it could attract good people. To that end, QRS employed various techniques to keep the workplace lively and interesting, including the use of cross-functional teams to address company objectives. Team members were recruited from different areas—engineering, marketing, human resources, and so on—and focused on a particular issue; for example, a recent team had been assembled to come up with ideas to improve communication throughout the company. QRS managers believed that such teamwork helped build a sense of camaraderie across the company.

OPPORTUNITIES FOR GROWTH

The 100% EC Initiative

QRS saw a major growth opportunity in extending EDI to the lower tiers of the retail industry. Though large retailers and suppliers were EDI-enabled, EDI had not significantly penetrated mid-size and small companies. Hence, QRS's largest customers (its hub accounts) still conducted paper-based transactions with many of their trading partners. "Over the last five to ten years," Simon said, "companies have made good progress in terms of moving the bulk of their unit volume to electronic purchase orders, for example. But retailers still have to conduct electronic commerce with the last 20% of their vendors, which may represent 50% of their orders. Why? Because retailers process just as much paper to buy one unit from a tertiary manufacturer as they do to purchase 100,000 units from a major vendor. In order to achieve some of the benefit of electronic commerce, vendors must become 100% EC enabled by eliminating paper processing in business documents such as invoices. We see that as a big trend among our more advanced customers."[28]

To quantify the potential return on investment from electronic commerce, QRS described the implementation of electronic commerce as a series of five stages, each achieving greater EC sophistication.

1. Electronic exchange of basic documents, such as purchase orders and invoices
2. Marking of merchandise at the vendor source (e.g., ticketing individual items with UPCs, marking cartons with scannable codes), prior to arrival at the retailer
3. Electronic exchange of "advanced" business documents (e.g., load tendering, freight status, advance shipping notices)

[28] Wall Street Transcript Corporation, "CEO Interview: John Simon, QRS Corporation," 4/29/99.

4. Collaborative inventory management between vendors and retailers (e.g., by sharing sales data and forecasts)
5. Outsourcing of functional applications (e.g., load tendering, inventory replenishment management)

According to QRS analysis, a retailer who fully implemented EC through stage 5 would typically see a return on sales of 5%. However, while top-tier retailers and suppliers (i.e., the hubs) had moved to stages 1 or 2 with a subset of their vendors—thereby achieving a 1%–2% return on sales—few had progressed to the more advanced levels. The further customers progressed through the stages, the more QRS services they used, such as its inventory and logistics management services, which were among the company's highest margin and fastest-growing lines of business.

Acquisitions

Acquisitions also played a role in QRS's growth strategy. In 1995, QRS made its first acquisition when it purchased ShipNet Systems, Inc., a provider of transportation logistics services, for $4.9 million. The ShipNet acquisition provided the basis for QRS Logistics Management Services, which filled a gap in the company's product line: now customers could use QRS's network to arrange for shipment and tracking of goods via EDI transactions.

In late 1998, QRS spent $4.2 million to buy Custom Information Systems Corporation and EDI Connection, two separate service bureaus—an area in which Simon suggested that the company might pursue further acquisitions. The bureaus were part of QRS's strategy to provide EDI-enabling services to small retailers and suppliers who still used paper forms for business transactions but who wanted to trade with large EDI-based partners.

QRS's largest acquisition came in July 1999, when it bought Virginia-based Retail Data Services, Inc. (RDS), which provided price information to grocery retailers for $17.76 million. Prior to the RDS acquisition, QRS had a small presence in the grocery segment, but its primary focus was on the soft goods sector (apparel, accessories, and footwear); it also served department stores and retailers of sporting goods and health and beauty products. Grocery stores, with 1998 sales of nearly $415 billion, were the second-largest retail segment, surpassed only by motor-vehicle dealerships (which had 1998 revenues of $631.7 billion).[29] With the RDS addition, QRS's client portfolio included 22 of the top 25 grocery, department store, and mass merchant retailers.

International Expansion

QRS's revenues came from the U.S. and Canadian markets. The company's first expansion into international sales came in 1997, with the creation of QRS Canada, a wholly owned subsidiary. In July 1999, QRS entered the Korean market through an agreement with Shinsegae I&C Co. Ltd., an IT-services affiliate of Korea's largest retailer.

[29] Census Bureau Web site, http://www.census.gov/svsd/retlann/view/artssal.txt.

Under the pact, Shinsegae I&C sold and marketed QRS Keystone (the UPC catalog) to Korean manufacturers and retailers. The move also gave QRS a foothold in Asian markets.

Simon saw two additional vehicles for expanding QRS's business beyond North America. One was to move into the international supply chain that extended out from U.S. manufacturers, who subcontracted most if not all of their work to factories based in low-cost markets (e.g., Central America, the Asia Pacific region). This would entail bringing these overseas trading partners of QRS customers into the EDI-based QRS trading community. A second opportunity was to establish hub customers as "anchor points" in foreign countries with developed retail infrastructure. In Simon's view, "anchor retailers in these markets desire to automate through electronic commerce and drive efficiency through their supply chain."[30]

Data Syndication

Data syndication offered another opportunity for growth. QRS first entered this area in a limited way with its inventory management services, which provided suppliers with information on sales of their products in retail stores. The RDS acquisition represented a significant advance into data syndication, and Simon was considering further opportunities. Acquisition of additional data-oriented businesses was one possibility, but Simon believed that the company already possessed potentially valuable data assets. "For example, we have 75 million UPCs in our database," he said. "By watching how our customers search the database, we can get a pretty good idea about what's going to show up in stores three months later." This was just one example of the kind of information that the company collected—or could collect—while managing its trading community. In addition to marketing data directly to customers, QRS could also sell or license data to third parties, such as market research companies, for consolidation into their products. The company had no precise measurement of the market for data services, but it cited the data-syndication companies AC Nielsen and Information Resources, Inc. (1998 sales of $1.43 billion and $511.3 million, respectively) as indicators of potential market size.

LOOKING TO THE FUTURE

As he pondered the company's future, Simon believed that QRS had created a powerful model to drive its growth. Key ingredients included a vertical focus on the retail industry and a transaction-based, service-oriented product line that generated recurring revenues of more than 90%. By building a trading network that the nation's leading retailers and their suppliers used, QRS now occupied the number one gateway position in the retail industry. The company's future success depended on extending its community of trading partners, making it even more difficult for competitors or would-be entrants to duplicate the value of the network. But a new product or competitor could come "out of left field." In the near term, Simon did not think the Internet

[30] Wall Street Transcript Corporation, "CEO Interview: John Simon, QRS Corporation," 4/29/99.

would significantly affect the company's EDI business. Nonetheless, he knew it required monitoring, because electronic commerce was on a course of rapid change. The Internet might represent some sort of opportunity for the company, Simon thought; but for now, he concluded, growth would come from other avenues.

EXHIBIT 1 QRS Corporation, Stock Price Chart, September 1994–September 1999

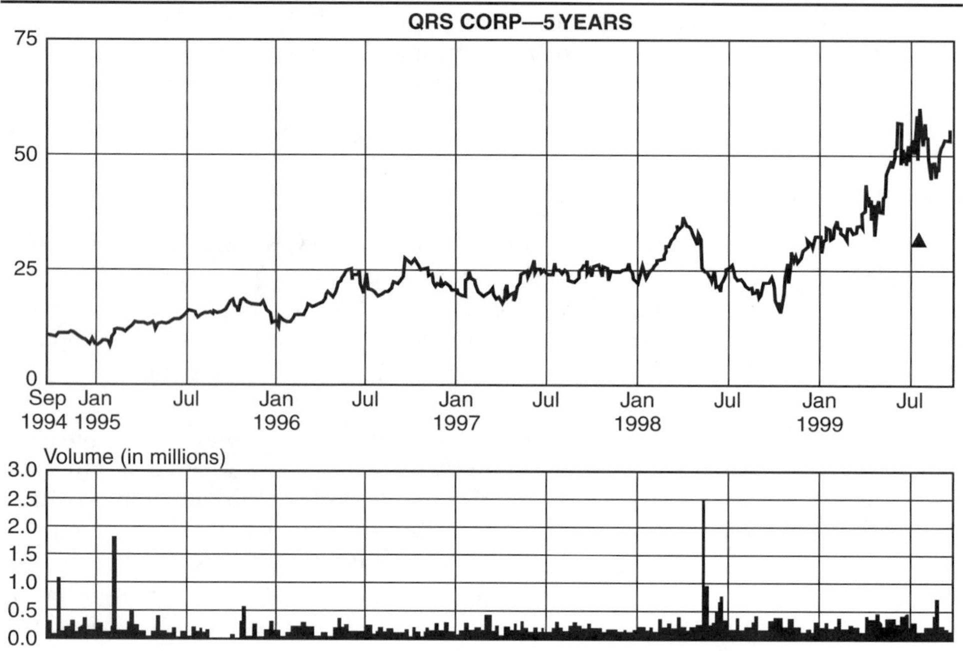

Source: Netscape Web site, http://quote.netscape.com/chart/. Reproduced with permission from CSI.

EXHIBIT 2 U.S. Retail Industry Sales, 1986–1998 (amounts are in millions of nominal dollars)

	1986	*1987*	*1988*	*1989*	*1990*	*1991*	*1992*
Retail sales, total	1,449,636	1,541,299	1,656,202	1,758,971	1,844,611	1,855,937	1,951,589
Total (excluding automotive dealers)	1,123,498	1,198,403	1,283,632	1,372,960	1,457,006	1,483,290	1,544,654
Durable goods, total	540,688	575,863	629,154	657,154	668,835	649,974	703,604
Building materials group stores	77,104	83,454	91,056	92,379	94,640	91,496	100,838
Building materials and supply stores	56,510	61,302	66,796	67,457	70,341	68,196	75,358
Hardware stores	10,734	11,036	11,894	12,637	12,524	12,148	12,729
Automotive dealers	326,138	342,896	372,570	386,011	387,605	372,647	406,935
Motor vehicle and misc automotive dealers	301,083	316,274	343,217	356,485	356,764	343,018	377,118
Auto and home supply stores	25,055	26,622	29,353	29,526	30,841	29,629	29,817
Furniture group stores	75,714	78,072	85,390	91,301	91,545	91,676	96,947
Furniture and home furn stores	43,030	44,477	47,617	51,202	50,524	49,469	52,348
Household appliance, electronics stores	27,037	27,121	30,608	32,666	33,035	33,569	35,802
Nondurable goods, total	908,948	965,436	1,027,048	1,101,817	1,175,776	1,205,963	1,247,985
General merchandise group stores	169,397	181,970	192,521	206,306	215,514	226,730	246,420
Dept. stores (excluding leased depts.)	134,486	144,017	151,523	160,524	165,808	172,922	186,423
Variety stores	7,447	7,134	7,458	7,936	8,306	8,341	9,516
Misc. general merchandise stores	27,464	30,819	33,540	37,846	41,400	45,467	50,481
Food group stores	297,019	309,461	325,493	347,045	368,333	374,523	377,099
Grocery stores	280,833	290,979	307,173	328,072	348,243	354,331	358,148
Gasoline service stations	102,093	104,769	110,341	122,882	138,504	137,295	136,950
Apparel and accessory stores	75,626	79,322	85,307	92,341	95,819	97,441	104,212
Men's and boys' clothing stores	8,646	9,017	9,826	10,507	10,450	10,435	10,197
Women's clothing, accessory stores	28,600	29,208	30,567	32,231	32,812	32,865	35,750
Shoe stores	13,947	14,594	15,444	17,290	18,043	17,504	18,122

(continued)

EXHIBIT 2 *(continued)*

	1986	*1987*	*1988*	*1989*	*1990*	*1991*	*1992*
Nondurable goods, total *(continued)*							
Eating and drinking places	139,415	153,461	167,993	177,829	190,149	194,424	200,164
Drug and proprietary stores	50,546	54,142	57,842	63,343	70,558	75,540	77,788
Liquor stores	19,929	19,826	19,638	20,099	21,722	22,454	21,698
GAF, total[31]	368,262	393,142	423,036	455,688	471,597	485,439	519,230

	1993	*1994*	*1995*	*1996*	*1997*	*1998*
Retail sales, total	2,083,029	2,250,033	2,361,793	2,506,141	2,615,669	2,746,011
Total (excluding automotive dealers)	1,623,712	1,724,654	1,798,926	1,897,360	1,982,784	2,077,353
Durable goods, total	782,264	887,443	948,652	1,020,861	1,066,087	1,138,286
Building materials group stores	111,014	125,868	131,711	141,935	150,482	165,331
Building materials and supply stores	96,501	95,209	99,181	120,848	114,187	124,365
Hardware stores	13,066	13,852	13,793	13,989	14,039	14,630
Automotive dealers	459,317	525,379	562,867	608,781	632,885	668,658
Motor vehicle and misc. automotive dealers	428,636	492,662	529,138	573,557	597,069	631,689
Auto and home supply stores	30,681	32,717	33,729	35,224	35,816	36,969
Furniture group stores	105,545	119,171	128,437	135,149	140,776	152,044
Furniture and home furn. stores	54,741	59,013	60,790	63,887	67,537	71,377
Household appliance, electronics stores	41,397	49,745	56,572	59,792	61,735	68,532

(continued)

[31] GAF represents stores that specialize in department store types of merchandise (general merchandise, apparel, furniture, and miscellaneous shopping goods stores).

EXHIBIT 2 *(continued)*

	1993	*1994*	*1995*	*1996*	*1997*	*1998*
Nondurable goods, total	1,300,765	1,362,590	1,413,141	1,485,280	1,549,582	1,607,725
General merchandise group stores	264,147	282,332	297,996	313,342	330,216	351,436
Dept. stores (excluding leased depts.)	199,845	217,499	231,303	244,783	259,985	276,697
Variety stores	9,729	9,464	9,750	10,481	11,120	11,480
Misc. general merchandise stores	54,573	55,369	56,943	58,078	59,111	63,259
Food group stores	382,930	394,671	403,205	415,390	425,170	438,212
Grocery stores	363,625	374,730	382,378	393,568	402,540	414,667
Gasoline service stations	141,603	148,673	156,939	168,320	171,527	162,095
Apparel and accessory stores	107,588	110,735	111,970	116,101	120,575	126,939
Men's and boys' clothing stores	9,986	10,064	9,353	9,592	10,123	10,922
Women's clothing, accessory stores	36,426	35,117	29,075	34,055	34,222	34,330
Shoe stores	18,509	19,349	19,755	20,609	20,802	21,227
Eating and drinking places	212,690	221,882	229,526	238,474	253,551	266,544
Drug and proprietary stores	79,784	82,156	86,093	92,169	99,301	106,713
Liquor stores	21,561	22,136	22,053	23,216	24,147	25,114
GAF, total	553,360	594,947	625,497	656,527	685,577	729,178

Source: U.S. Census Bureau, "Annual Retail Trade Survey: 1986 to 1998," www.census.gov/svsd/retlann/view/artssal.txt.

EXHIBIT 3 Selected North American Retail, Wholesale, and Manufacturing Statistics

TABLE 1 North American Manufacturing Firms with 1998 Sales of $5 Million or Greater

	Firms with 1998 Sales > $5 Million	*Firms with 1998 Sales > $100 Million*
Primary Manufacturing Activity		
Apparel/accessories	4,249	289
Appliances/tools	802	84
Audio/video equipment	479	41
Auto and truck (including parts)	5,309	700
Beverages	2,238	249
Food processing	11,722	1,161
Footwear	304	45
Furniture and fixtures	2,585	108
Jewelry/silverware	859	35
Personal and household products	3,439	339
Recreational products	1,535	90
Tobacco	292	47

Compiled from OneSource Information Services, Inc., 9/99.

TABLE 2 North American Retail Firms with 1998 Sales of $5 Million or Greater

	Total Number with 1998 Sales > $5 Million	*Number with 1998 Sales > $100 Million*
Primary Company Activity		
Apparel stores	602	77
Department/discount stores	342	31
Drug stores	263	27
Grocery stores	6,731	556
Home improvement stores	2,363	36
Specialty nonapparel stores	4,510	535
Technology stores	1,899	101

Compiled from OneSource Information Services, Inc., 9/99.

TABLE 3 Value of Shipments, U.S. Manufacturers in Selected Consumer Goods Industries, 1992–1999* (amounts are in millions of nominal dollars)

	1992	*1993*	*1994*	*1995*	*1996*	*1997*	*1998*	*1999*
Apparel/textile products	71,658	74,010	76,979	78,103	77,628	79,025	80,053	80,933
Consumer audio	n/a	n/a	6,190	6,378	5,949	5,914	6,158	5,984
Consumer video	n/a	n/a	15,104	15,376	15,216	14,419	14,884	15,052
Drugs	67,792	70,985	75,804	80,907	86,532	91,291	95,033	98,645
Food and beverages	406,963	422,220	430,963	446,869	461,324	477,791	480,513	499,879
Footwear (nonrubber)	3,898	3,974	3,923	3,688	3,605	3,352	3,139	3,270
Household appliances	18,633	20,435	22,829	21,776	22,157	22,a108	22,086	22,288
Household furniture	20,507	21,906	23,603	24,458	25,426	27,033	28,508	29,514
Jewelry, costume	1,444	1,429	1,627	1,660	1,525	1,562	1,573	1,605
Jewelry/precious metal	4,190	4,278	4,459	4,444	4,443	4,483	4,500	4,545
Lawn/garden equip	5,164	5,828	6,836	6,971	6,823	7,369	7,590	7,742
Luggage and leather goods	2,207	2,106	2,070	1,891	2,030	1,915	1,806	1,798
Musical instruments	982	1,037	1,062	1,144	1,173	1,222	1,280	1,330
Recreational equip	18,904	20,969	21,459	23,065	23,665	24,490	25,104	25,841

*Data for 1998 are estimates; data for 1999 are forecasts.

Source: *U.S. Industry & Trade Outlook '99* by DRI/McGraw-Hill, and Standard & Poor's, and U.S. Department of Commerce/International Trade Administration.

EXHIBIT 4 QRS Corporation, Selected Company Data, 1993–1999

	1993	*1994*	*1995*	*1996*	*1997*	*1998*	*1999**
Total number of customers	2,799	3,823	4,900	5,178	6,180	7,719	8,034
Retailer customers**	n/a	106	156	205	241	240	270
Number of UPCs in catalog (millions)	22.9	33.2	42.5	48.0	57.0	67.0	73.2
Number of full-time employees***	n/a	73	120	148	216	292	470

Source: Company reports and interviews.
*Customer data for 1999 are for period ending 6/30/99; UPC data for 1999 are as of 5/13/99; employee data for 1999 are as of 8/13/99.
**The balance of customers are manufacturers (who sell to retailers) and carriers.
***QRS also employed 400 part-time employees, as a result of its acquisition of Retail Data Services in July 1999.

EXHIBIT 5 QRS Corporation, Operating Results, 1993–1998 (amounts are in millions of dollars)

	1998	*1997*	*1996*	*1995*	*1994*	*1993*
Sales	91.9	71.6	56.7	42.1	31.4	22.5
Cost of goods sold	51.1	40.5	33.8	25.5	19.1	14.5
SG&A expense	19.4	14.2	10.4	7.8	6.0	4.0
Research and development	4.3	4.4	3.1	2.0	1.0	0.9
Unusual income/expense	1.0	0.0	0.0	4.3	0.0	0.0
Total expenses	75.8	59.0	47.3	39.7	26.1	19.3
Interest net, nonoperating	2.2	2.0	1.6	1.5	0.7	–1.2
Pretax income	18.3	14.6	11.0	4.0	6.0	1.9
Income taxes	7.1	5.9	4.4	1.6	–8.0	0.0
Income after taxes	11.2	8.8	6.6	2.4	14.0	1.9
Net income (excluding E&D)	11.2	8.8	6.6	2.4	14.0	1.9
Discontinued operations	0.9	0.0	0.0	0.0	0.0	1.4
Extraordinary items	0.0	0.0	0.0	0.0	0.0	–0.8
Net income	12.1	8.8	6.6	2.4	14.0	2.6

Source: Company reports.

EXHIBIT 6 QRS Corporation, Quarterly Operating Results (amounts are in millions of dollars)

	For quarter ending:				
	30-Jun-99	*31-Mar-99*	*31-Dec-98*	*30-Sep-98*	*30-Jun-98*
Sales	29.5	29.3	27.4	23.6	20.8
Cost of goods sold	15.0	15.2	14.9	13.3	11.7
SG&A expense	6.6	6.9	6.1	4.7	4.3
Research and development	2.1	2.0	1.2	1.2	1.0
Unusual income/expense	0.0	0.0	0.0	1.0	0.0
Total expenses	23.7	24.1	22.2	20.2	17.0
Interest income, nonoperating	0.5	0.6	0.5	0.5	0.6
Interest expense, nonoperating	0.0	0.0	0.0	0.0	0.0
Pretax income	6.3	5.8	5.7	4.0	4.4
Income taxes	2.4	2.2	2.2	1.5	1.8
Income after taxes	3.9	3.6	3.6	2.5	2.7
Net income (excluding E&D)	3.9	3.6	3.6	2.5	2.7
Discontinued operations	0.0	0.0	0.0	0.0	0.0
Extraordinary items	0.0	0.0	0.0	0.0	0.0
Net income	3.9	3.6	3.6	2.5	2.7

Source: Company reports.

EXHIBIT 7 QRS Corporation, Balance Sheet, 1993–1998 (amounts are in millions of dollars, for years ending December 31)

	1998	*1997*	*1996*	*1995*	*1994*	*1993*
Assets						
Cash and equivalents	36.6	16.1	16.0	6.5	8.6	8.2
Other short-term investments	7.0	17.7	8.6	18.0	11.9	8.7
Accounts receivable	19.1	14.6	9.3	8.0	5.6	3.7
Prepayments and advances	1.2	1.3	1.1	0.8	0.5	0.5
Other current assets	0.8	0.9	4.1	4.9	0.0	0.0
Total current assets	64.7	50.5	39.2	38.1	26.6	21.1
Long-term investments	1.5	1.0	10.0	0.0	0.0	0.0
Property plant and equipment	13.9	11.6	5.7	5.3	2.9	2.5

(continued)

EXHIBIT 7 *(continued)*

	1998	*1997*	*1996*	*1995*	*1994*	*1993*
Accum. depr. and amort.	–5.7	–4.1	–2.6	–1.9	–1.4	–1.1
Property plant & equipment, net	8.2	7.5	3.1	3.4	1.5	1.5
Goodwill/intangibles	6.9	2.2	0.0	0.0	0.0	0.0
Other long-term assets	1.7	2.8	3.7	5.1	11.9	0.7
Total assets	**83.0**	**64.0**	**55.9**	**46.6**	**39.9**	**24.6**
Liabilities						
Accounts payable	7.9	3.7	5.5	3.6	1.8	1.5
Curr. LT debt and CLOs	0.0	0.0	0.0	0.0	0.0	0.0
Other current liabilities	5.8	4.2	4.3	4.3	1.7	1.9
Total current liabilities	13.8	7.9	9.8	7.9	3.6	3.5
Long-term debt	0.0	0.0	0.0	0.0	0.0	0.5
Other long-term liabilities	1.3	1.3	2.6	3.3	4.9	3.7
Total liabilities	15.1	9.3	12.4	11.2	8.5	7.7
Stockholders' equity						
Redeemable preferred	0.0	0.0	0.0	0.0	0.0	0.0
Common stock	66.0	63.9	61.4	59.9	58.3	56.3
Retained earnings	2.6	–9.1	–17.9	–24.5	–26.9	–40.8
Treasury stock	–0.7	0.0	0.0	0.0	0.0	0.0
Other equity	0.1	0.0	0.0	0.0	0.0	0.0
Total shareholders' equity	68.0	54.7	43.6	35.4	31.4	15.5
Total liabilities + shareholders' equity	**83.0**	**64.0**	**55.9**	**46.6**	**39.9**	**23.1**

Source: Company reports.

EXHIBIT 8 QRS Corporation, Quarterly Balance Sheet (amounts are in millions of dollars)

	For quarter ending:				
	30-Jun-99	*31-Mar-99*	*31-Dec-98*	*30-Sep-98*	*30-Jun-98*
Asset					
Cash and equivalents	47.1	44.0	36.6	30.6	36.9
Other short-term investments	4.3	4.3	7.0	6.7	4.0
Accounts receivable	19.0	19.3	19.1	18.4	13.9
Prepayments and advances	1.2	1.3	1.2	1.3	1.2
Other current assets	0.8	0.8	0.8	0.9	0.9
Total current assets	72.4	69.7	64.7	57.8	56.8
Long-term investments	7.4	3.9	1.5	1.5	2.5
Property plant and equipment	16.3	14.9	13.9	14.1	13.3
Accum. depr. and amort.	–7.3	–6.5	–5.7	–5.9	–5.4
Property plant and equipment, net	9.0	8.5	8.2	8.2	8.0
Goodwill/intangibles	7.0	7.0	6.9	3.6	3.2
Other long-term assets	6.3	1.4	1.7	5.0	0.3
Total assets	**102.0**	**90.5**	**83.0**	**76.2**	**70.9**
Liabilities					
Accounts payable	8.6	9.1	7.9	7.7	7.1
Curr. LT debt and CLOs	0.0	0.0	0.0	0.0	0.0
Other current liabilities	4.5	4.1	5.8	4.5	2.0
Total current liabilities	13.1	13.2	13.8	12.2	9.2
Long-term debt	0.0	0.0	0.0	0.0	0.0
Other long-term liabilities	1.3	1.3	1.3	1.2	1.2
Total liabilities	14.4	14.5	15.1	13.4	10.4
Stockholders' equity					
Redeemable preferred	0.0	0.0	0.0	0.0	0.0
Common stock	78.3	70.4	66.0	64.3	64.3
Retained earnings	10.2	6.3	2.6	–0.9	-3.1
Treasury stock	–0.7	–0.7	–0.7	–0.7	–0.9
Other equity	–0.1	0.1	0.1	0.2	0.1
Total shareholders' equity	87.7	76.0	68.0	62.8	60.5
Total liabilities + shareholders' equity	**102.0**	**90.5**	**83.0**	**76.2**	**70.9**

Source: Company reports.

EXHIBIT 9 QRS Corporation, Cash Flow Statement, 1993–1998 (amounts are in millions of dollars)

	1998	*1997*	*1996*	*1995*	*1994*	*1993*
Net income	12.1	8.8	6.6	2.4	14.0	2.6
Depreciation	3.4	1.7	1.2	0.6	0.4	0.3
Deferred taxes	1.7	3.9	3.9	1.3	–8.3	0.0
Other noncash items	0.2	0.0	0.0	–4.0	–3.1	–8.4
Other operating cash flows	1.9	–7.3	0.8	–0.6	–1.6	–10.5
Cash from operations	19.3	7.2	12.4	–0.3	1.4	–16.0
Capital expenditures	–5.7	–7.2	–1.8	–2.4	–0.7	–0.4
Other investing cash flows	7.3	–1.4	–1.7	0.0	0.0	1.2
Cash from investing	1.6	–8.6	–3.5	–2.5	–0.7	0.8
Dividends paid	0.0	0.0	0.0	0.0	0.0	–0.5
Purchase or sale of stock	–0.3	1.5	0.6	0.6	0.4	40.6
Purchase and retirement of debt	0.0	0.0	0.0	0.0	–0.7	–19.2
Other financing cash flows	0.0	0.0	0.0	0.0	0.0	0.0
Cash from financing	–0.3	1.5	0.6	0.6	–0.3	20.9
Net change in cash	20.6	0.1	9.6	–2.2	0.5	5.6
Cash interest paid	0.0	0.0	0.0	0.0	0.1	1.4
Cash taxes paid	5.7	1.1	0.5	0.3	0.1	0.0

Source: Company reports.

AOL: THE EMERGENCE OF AN INTERNET MEDIA COMPANY

INTRODUCTION

On January 10, 2000, AOL Chairman and CEO Steve Case and Time Warner Chairman and CEO Gerald Levin announced the $165 billion merger of their two companies—the largest corporate takeover to date. Internet service provider AOL owned valuable Internet real estate frequented by 23 million subscribers visiting 59.8 million times a month, and boasted a market capitalization of $125 billion (see Exhibits 1 and 2). Time Warner owned a host of venerable media brands and the second largest cable system in the United States with 13 million subscribers[1] (see Exhibit 3). At the press conference announcing the deal Case said, "This merger will launch the next phase of the Internet revolution." Still, within five weeks of the announcement, even before the NASDAQ slide in March, the two companies had lost almost $50 billion of market capitalization.[2] Some thought the attempt to combine Internet assets with media brands was reminiscent of Barry Diller's failed $22 billion attempt to merge his USA Networks with the Internet portal Lycos and Disney's struggle to convince investors of the value of its $1.6 billion acquisition of Internet portal Infoseek. Others believed that the AOL/Time Warner merger would mark the beginning of an inevitable convergence

---

Professor Robert A. Burgelman and Philip Meza prepared this case as the basis for class discussion rather than to illustrate either effective or ineffective handling of an administrative situation.

[1] "How Can Tim Koogle Stay So Cool in the Face of AOL's Assault?" *Business Week*, Steve Rosenbush, May 15, 2000. Note: Yahoo! is the second most visited site, receiving 48.3 million visits per month.
[2] "Will Markets Ever Accept an Internet/Content Marriage?" *The Investment Dealers' Digest*, Jeffrey Keegan, February 28, 2000.

of old and new media, a combination of hitherto separate Internet service providers (ISPs), portals, and content providers, and that AOL was uniquely suited to lead this convergence (see Exhibit 4).

Conduit versus Content

While Time Warner brought AOL a number of proven and valuable assets, none was more important to AOL than Time Warner's cable assets: the company owned 3,300 cable franchises that served 12.6 million customers and passed 21.3 million homes.[3] In 2000, some analysts believed the growth outlook for the cable network industry was very good. In 1999, total cable network revenues for advertising and subscription fees were about $24 compared to the $16 for broadcast network advertising. By comparison, in 1992 broadcast TV networks generated $10 billion in advertising revenue versus $6 billion in total revenues for the cable network business.[4] Still, the paramount reason for the merger may have been plumbing rather than programming. Time Warner's cable properties would give AOL control of valuable broadband distribution assets.

AOL had grown nervous about its lack of broadband distribution capability. It feared being relegated to a backwater of some other company's broadband distribution network, or worse, being excluded completely. Since 1998, AOL earned substantial revenue from the fees it charged companies for the privilege of carrying their content and accepted shares and options in exchange for attractive placement in AOL's real estate. Companies that failed to pay risked getting lost in the "noise" of the Internet—getting overlooked by AOL's millions of users who instead noticed the companies that occupied the superior anchor positions on AOL screens. The specter of broadband Internet access controlled by others threatened to change the balance of power AOL had enjoyed.

For over a year, AOL led the effort to force cable companies to provide "open access" (nondiscriminatory access) for content providers to America's cable lines. AOL needed fast, inexpensive connections to its customers to remain competitive as broadband delivery increased in popularity. AOL invested $1.6 billion in Hughes Electronics Corporation, which offered the possibility of high-speed wireless connections. It also struck deals with regional Bell operating companies (RBOCs) for digital subscriber lines (DSL) packages. But in 1998, when AT&T announced mergers that would give it 60% of the U.S. cable capacity, AOL felt threatened, and began lobbying to ensure open access.[5] Thus, AOL joined and helped fund a group of consumer advocates lobbying state and national legislatures to ensure that whoever controlled the broadband distribution channel (e.g., cable companies) could not exclude programming and Internet services from cables, phone lines, or satellites. However, following the announced merger with Time Warner, AOL seemed to change its position about the importance of open access. Risking corporate whiplash, Case was quoted as saying, "We need to take [open access] off the table."[6] AOL has since publicly reaffirmed its support of open access.

[3] "Disney Campaigns Against AOL-Time Warner," *Wall Street Journal*, Kathy Chen, May 18, 2000.
[4] "Viacom," by E. Hatch, S. G. Cowen, April 26, 2000.
[5] "AOL's Access Saga," *Chief Executive*, Sally C. Pipes, March 2000.
[6] "A Media Monopoly in the Making?" *Business Week*, Ronal Grover, May 15, 2000.

One of the most vocal opponents to the AOL/Time Warner merger was The Walt Disney Company. Disney feared that the new AOL Time Warner would have ample motivation and power to steer customers to its own sites. Indeed, in September 1999, CNN abruptly blocked scheduled advertising from online magazine Salon, citing a CNN policy of not running advertising from competitors. Salon claimed fewer than 2 million unique visitors per month while CNN consisted of six cable and satellite networks that reached 800 million homes worldwide and ran nine Web sites.[7] Without its own broadband distribution assets, Disney feared that AOL, acting as a broadband gatekeeper, could choke off access to Disney's crown jewels—its content. During the all-important "sweeps weeks" in May 2000, when ratings were determined for prime time broadcasts, a spat between Disney's ABC and Time Warner over an ABC price hike resulted in Time Warner blocking ABC programming on Time Warner cable stations in critical markets such as Los Angeles and New York for two days. Two months later, broadcaster NBC, owned by conglomerate General Electric, joined Disney in filing its merger concerns with the U.S. Federal Communications Commission (FCC). NBC sought "meaningful, enforceable commitment by AOL Time Warner to provide nondiscriminatory access" to Time Warner's cable networks by other providers of programming.[8]

Now a Word from Our Sponsor

Advertising and e-commerce would be the lifeblood of the merged AOL Time Warner. Revenue from advertising and e-commerce increased by 23% at Time Warner in the second quarter of 2000. During AOL's fiscal fourth quarter 2000 ending June 30, advertising and e-commerce revenues increased more than 80% from the previous year. Speaking about the revenue generating prospects of a combined AOL and Time Warner, Gerald Levin said:

> *If you combine [Time Warner's advertising and e-commerce revenue] with where AOL is going, you have the predicate for a new model. . . . We're not just talking about measured media advertising that's brand promotion. We're talking about information that leads to transactions where you are really partnering with advertisers, where there is event marketing and where you are in effect renting your third-party facilities. . . . When you see it in that sense, you're not just talking about the $165 billion measured media universe. You are talking about the $256 billion universe of how companies market themselves, and suddenly you are in the $6 trillion transactional dome. The old ad model was based on the eyeballs television guaranteed at any given moment during a particular program to deliver an advertiser's one-way message. The new ad model is based on the consumers reached and then transformed into interactive buyers in a two-way learning and communication process that is punctuated by a transaction. It's not just the pitch; it's the sale.*[9] *(See Exhibits 5 and 6.)*

[7] "CNN Rejects Dot-Com Ads," *The Standard*, James Ledbetter, October 6, 1999.

[8] "NBC Warns on Merger Plans," *Financial Times*, July 26, 2000.

[9] "AOL-Time Warner Creates New Rules for Advertising," *Electronic Media*, Diane Mermigas, July 24, 2000.

Some new technologies, such as interactive TV, in which viewers using personal video recorders and other devices can skip over advertisements, threatened the traditional advertising model. To combat this, AOL Time Warner could develop new forms of ad-based revenue generated through e-commerce and ad-supported content featured in a closed AOL Time Warner universe.

Calling AOL

AOL undertook a series of acquisitions in order to make it easy to access the service via any medium. AOL enabled access to its service via digital subscriber lines (DSLs), announcing alliances with GTE, Ameritech Communications, and Bell Atlantic, where AOL offered asymmetric DSL (ADSL) service to subscribers. The same fiber and coax cable that delivered Time Warner's cable service could also be used to deliver voice service (VoIP). AOL owned a 5.4% stake in Internet telephony company Net2Phone and a 10% stake in Palm.com, which sold AOL-branded long distance to AOL subscribers.[10]

Several of AOL's key businesses are essentially telecommunications assets. Operations such as AOL Instant Messenger (AIM), ICQ (a play on the words "I seek you"), and buddy lists made the company a telecommunications player. ICQ had 62.4 million registered users who used the service an average of 75 minutes per day (see Appendix 1)—the potential for advertising revenue was substantial.[11] Together, AOL's AIM and ICQ software claimed to have 130 million users, while Microsoft reported 18 million users. Yahoo!, another leader in the field, does not reveal its total instant-messaging user base.[12]

Until 1999, most users could send messages only to users of the same software. Competitors then added interoperability features that enabled their users to send messages to AOL's users. AOL repeatedly blocked those attempts. AOL claimed that allowing competitors to create clients that access its instant messaging (IM) servers and customers jeopardized the security and privacy of its system.

AOL's policy of not allowing other ISPs to link to its ICQ system brought charges of anticompetitive behavior from ISPs and attention from the Federal Trade Commission (FTC). Competitors ranging from big players like Microsoft and AT&T to smaller players like iCast and Tribal Voice criticized AOL for its refusal to allow people using other products to trade instant messages with its users. They charged that AOL tried to block competition. The issue took on renewed urgency for AOL as its rivals' complaints of alleged anticompetitive practices received the attention of regulators at the FTC and the FCC, who were reviewing the Time Warner deal.[13]

[10] "Why AOL Is on the Case," *America's Network*, Shira Levine, May 15, 2000.
[11] "AOL," S. Rimmer, S. G. Cowen, April 19, 2000.
[12] "Point-Counterpoint on Instant Messaging," *The Standard*, Aaron Pressman, July 21, 2000.
[13] "AOL Offers IM Sharing Plan," *The Standard*, Aaron Pressman, June 14, 2000.

Regulatory Uncertainty

In addition to the regulatory issues surrounding open access that Disney and NBC raised, the FCC also had to wrestle with a potential reclassification of Internet over cable lines as a telecommunications service, with concomitant regulation implications. In June 2000, the 9th U.S. Circuit Court of Appeals ruled that Internet service over cable should be classified—and potentially regulated by the FCC—as a form of telecommunications service, which would give the FCC jurisdiction over broadband cable services. The appeals court ruled that the service is no different from high-speed Internet traffic traveling over phone lines. The ruling struck down a lower court decision concerning open access in Portland, Oregon, in which Internet over cable was classified as a form of cable TV service and thus subject to less stringent control based on cable franchising rules.[14]

The service classification was important because providers of telecommunications services were regulated as "common carriers," forbidden from discrimination, while cable providers operated under a looser regime that allowed companies to select which channels their customer receive. Cable companies limited access to their broadband pipes to only Internet service providers they own. Telecommunications rules requiring interconnection and prohibiting discrimination of ISPs could compel cable companies to share lines even beyond voluntary agreements struck by AT&T and Time Warner allowing limited open access in a few years.

Legal battles between ISPs and cable operators could drag on for years, creating substantial uncertainty for investors and consumers. FCC Chairman William Kennard said the FCC might decide to conduct its own proceeding to reclassify Internet service over cable as something other than a telecommunications service or the agency might adopt the court's classification but exempt such service from telecom rules. Cable companies welcomed Kennard's remarks because they expected that the FCC would follow Kennard's lead and continue to avoid regulating cable-broadband services. "In light of the way some are trying to spin the decision, clarification from the FCC would be expected and welcome," an AT&T spokesman said.

AMERICA ONLINE

Company Vision[15]

Walking the halls of AOL's corporate headquarters in Dulles, Virginia, employees and visitors were constantly reminded of the company's vision, which was prominently displayed in glossy frames in almost every hallway: To build a global medium as central to people's lives as the telephone or television . . . and even more valuable.

From the outset, Steve Case envisioned AOL as a consumer services company, not a technology company. Unlike many Silicon Valley companies that set out to bring the

[14] Discussion of regulatory implications of the appeals court ruling and FCC action is from "FCC to Examine Cable Broadband," *The Standard*, Aaron Pressman, June 30, 2000.

[15] The sections discussing AOL's history were excerpted from "America Online: The Online Giant in 1999," by Jason Goldberg, EC-4, Stanford Graduate School of Business.

latest technology to the market, AOL had focused on the customer experience. The relentless focus on customer experience led to a graphical user interface (GUI) for the service that was so easy to use that many observers derided it as the "Internet on training wheels." AOL realized early that the overwhelming majority of U.S. consumers wanted their online service to be easy to use above all else.

Chip Bayers, Internet analyst for *Wired* magazine, commented on AOL's consumer focus:

> *AOL's mass-market style and its unsophisticated look may not be sexy, but they're keys to its success. Over the years, the company has masterfully created a likeable, homey interface for its customers. When you look at AOL today, you're looking at the future of the Internet: where technology companies riding cool new hacks succumb to relentless marketing machines that are endlessly patient about building brand loyalty.*[16]

AOL's company vision was to provide online users with a service that was fundamental to their lives. For millions of Americans who spent time online, AOL had already become a fact of life—a medium as central to their daily lives as the telephone or television. The average AOL user in 1999 spent 54 minutes on the service per day.[17] Indeed, surveys showed that for millions of Americans, AOL was far more than a company that connected people to the Internet—for millions of people, AOL was the Internet.

Company History

Steve Case was designing new types of pizza for Pizza Hut in the early 1980s when he began using an online service called the Source. At the time, dial-up computer bulletin board services (BBSs) such as the Source featured text-based interfaces, enabling users to share information via message boards. The service was used almost exclusively by early tech-savvy adopters interested more in the ability to connect with others online than with the ease with which they accessed the service. Case believed that user-friendly technology had the potential to attract mass consumer usage.

In 1983, Case took a marketing job with Control Video, which ran an online service similar to the Source for users of Atari computers and games. Control Video soon ran into trouble and Case helped the new CEO, Jim Kimsey, raise money to resurrect the company. In 1985, Control Video was renamed Quantum Computer Services, and it launched the Q-Link online service (see Exhibit 7). Four years later, with Case as the top visionary, the company unveiled a nationwide service called America Online. First available only for users of Commodore computers, in 1989 the company debuted America Online for the Macintosh. Much like the Macintosh computer, the AOL service featured an easy-to-use graphical interface with large buttons that directed users

[16] Quoted in "Over 17 Million Served," *Wired*, Chip Bayers, October 1999, p. 134.
[17] Source: AOL Annual Report, 1999.

to categories such as news, sports, entertainment, and chat rooms—which quickly became the service's most popular feature.

In 1991, the company formally changed its name to America Online. From the beginning, America Online was a dial-up online service that utilized a proprietary technology platform, which the company called Rainman. Rainman was a software package used to create the GUI that allowed images and text to be seen by users connected to America Online. Rainman did not operate on or link to the World Wide Web, which had not yet been adopted for wide consumer use.

Users dialed into the America Online service by using modems attached to their personal computers. Once connected to America Online, users were able to read news, sports, and entertainment content, or chat with other users online—all presented in the Rainman format. Like most other online services at the time, America Online could only be accessed by members supplying a registered username and a password, and the company charged a monthly subscription fee as well as a fee for usage time.

AOL went public in 1992, and Case became the company's CEO. AOL spent heavily on marketing in an effort to pass rival online services Prodigy and CompuServe, while it also worked to expand its content lineup. Prodigy and CompuServe focused on technology enthusiasts and business users by accentuating features such as message boards for computer service help, online bill payment, and forums for discovering the latest technologies. AOL targeted mainstream users by making the service easy and fun to use and by heavily promoting its user chat rooms. At the end of fiscal year 1992, AOL had 181,000 paid subscribers—less than half the number of Prodigy. In January 1993, AOL began distributing a Windows-based version of its online software, which, with AOL's own easy-to-use interface, attracted even more subscribers.

Silver Coasters

In 1994 and 1995, AOL launched a major direct marketing blitz. While Prodigy and CompuServe ran television ads promoting their services and sold their software in retail stores, AOL went directly to consumers and gave away AOL software disks and CD-ROMs just about everywhere imaginable. AOL disks were found in the seat pockets of airplanes, inside the covers of almost every major computer magazine, at thousands of retail stores, and in the mailboxes of millions of American households. Each disk included a copy of the AOL software that enabled the user to log on to AOL, as well as a trial three months of AOL service. In all, AOL distributed more than 300 million disks. In January 1994 alone, the company gained 70,000 new members. By August 1994, AOL had more than 1 million subscribers, twice that of its closest rival, Prodigy.

Steve Case declared that the first 1 million subscribers were just the beginning. "The challenge now for America Online is to move this medium into the mainstream by reaching out to the 97 million households not online," Case wrote in a letter to AOL's customers, "It's 1 million down, 97 [million] to go."[18]

[18] Quoted by Kara Swisher in *AOL.Com*, Random House, 1998, p. 103.

In 1994 and 1995, AOL faced increasing threats to its business model from the growing number of ISPs offering direct dial-up access to content on the Internet using either the Netscape browser or Microsoft's Internet Explorer. Unlike AOL's proprietary service, which served up specific content to AOL users, ISPs afforded their users the freedom to browse the World Wide Web (WWW) to find any content they chose. As the number of ISPs grew from 1,800 in 1994 to 3,200 in 1995, many analysts predicted that the reigning kings of the online world, CompuServe, America Online, and Prodigy, with their closed proprietary services, were bound to be put out of business by the ISPs.

In addition to competition from ISPs, AOL recognized the threat posed by Internet browsers. After talks broke off to purchase start-up Netscape Communications in 1994, AOL took action to stave off this burgeoning threat by purchasing multimedia developer Redgate Communications and Internet browser software maker Booklink Technologies, which made a browser rivaling the increasingly popular Netscape Navigator Web.[19] The Booklink browser was quickly integrated into the America Online service, enabling AOL members to surf the Web. While AOL members had easy access to the Internet, however, America Online's proprietary Rainman content and chat rooms remained closed to nonservice members.

Case stated emphatically at the time that most consumers would prefer to use AOL as their gateway to the Internet because the America Online service was more user-friendly and trustworthy than ISPs that just connected users directly to the Internet. "I think the conventional wisdom is dead wrong, because we deliver what consumers care about—community and information; and what they don't care about is the underlying system they get it on."[20] Case also realized that AOL's Rainman technology was better suited for the slower consumer modems used at the time; Rainman pages loaded on the consumer's computers in a matter of seconds, while Internet hypertext markup language (HTML) pages often took several minutes to load.

While ISPs focused on providing Internet access at a fixed price of $19.95 a month, AOL focused on making the online experience more than just a connection to the WWW. AOL made the online experience fun through such simple things as a friendly voice greeting members each time they logged on to the service, with the message "Welcome." Moreover, when users received an e-mail, the same friendly voice told them, "You've got mail." Another popular user-friendly feature was the "buddy list" that enabled members to know when their friends were on the service. The service promoted a new type of simple communication, the "instant message," which enabled users to send quick messages to other users in real time. AOL also addressed growing consumer concerns about Internet safety and child usage by creating parental controls for its service, which had not yet been widely developed or used by ISPs.

By February 1995, AOL's mass-market, user-friendly strategy paid off. The AOL service had registered 2 million paid subscribers and was averaging 250,000 new sub-

[19] NB: AOL won the bidding war with Microsoft for the Booklink Web browser. Microsoft intended to use Booklink as the browser for its MSN online service.

[20] Quoted by Kara Swisher in *AOL.Com*, Random House, 1998, p. 103.

scribers per month. An Internet user survey by FIND/SVP in late 1995 found that AOL was responsible for more than 30% of all Internet access—by far the market leader.[21]

All You Can Eat

A year later, in February 1996, AOL, with 5 million members, had more than doubled its membership over the course of one year. However, the company faced a new threat: price pressure. At the time, AOL based its subscription fee on a combination of a monthly fee as well as a per hour charge: $9.95 per month for five hours of service, with a $2.95 hourly fee for usage in excess of five hours per month. For moderate AOL users, monthly fees amounted to about $30. Heavy users often received bills in excess of $100 or $200. The ISPs, however, charged a flat fee of $19.95 a month for unlimited access. On October 10, 1996, the Microsoft Network (MSN), which had surpassed Prodigy and CompuServe to be AOL's number one competitor in online services, announced a switch to $19.99 unlimited service.

To face the growing price pressure, on December 1, 1996, AOL started charging its members a flat rate of $19.99 for unlimited access. The effect was dramatic. Membership instantly shot up—more than 1 million new members joined in the first month of the change. At the same time, however, users vastly increased the amount of time they spent online. Whereas under the old pricing scheme AOL members constantly watched the clock, under the new pricing scheme members could stay on the AOL service for days at a time without paying extra charges. On December 1 alone, the first day of the pricing change, more than 2.5 million hours of member sessions were logged, an enormous increase over the 1.6 million member session hours on an average day. E-mail doubled from 12 million to 24 million pieces per day. AOL service levels plummeted. Hundreds of thousands of users were unable to log on because the AOL network could not handle the increased traffic. In the press, America Online became known as "America On Hold," as hundreds of thousands of users got nothing but busy signals as they tried in vain to access the America Online network.[22] Case saw positives even in this time of crisis.

> *What was happening for really the first time, was that we impacted people's daily lives in a significant way. Suddenly, almost overnight, we became part of everyday life. That's why there was this national outrage and tremendous passion and frustration, because people needed us, and many of them loved us, and we had disappointed them. It was a coming of age for the medium.*[23]

By 1996, AOL's business model started to include significant, new streams of revenue (see Exhibit 8). Ten percent of AOL's first quarter 1996 revenue came from new

[21] As reported by by Kara Swisher in *AOL.Com*, Random House, 1998, p. 131.

[22] *ibid.*, p. 208.

[23] *Fortune*, March 30, 1998.

revenue streams including advertising, transaction royalties, and merchandising.[24] Advertising emerged as a large potential revenue source as both the Web and online services enabled targeted advertising, something highly coveted by marketers. By 2000, 60%–70% of AOL's revenue came from members.[25] Most observers expected that percentage to decrease as access increasingly became a commodity.

Evolution of Strategy

On the cost side, the industry had three primary expense categories: (1) telecommunications, (2) customer acquisition, and (3) content royalties. Telecommunications expenses were substantial in the industry because the online service paid Telcos for a variety of access fees, including connecting local calls from users to their locations and connecting their servers to the Internet backbone. In an effort to control these expenses, AOL bought ANS, a company that provided AOL with a proprietary backbone through which it could connect its customers to the Internet.[26] Customer acquisition became increasingly more expensive due to competition, both among the online service providers and from other Internet-related companies. Content royalties had traditionally amounted to 15%–30% of overall revenues in aggregate based on the usage patterns of each content site. Microsoft and other Internet content aggregators put a crimp in this part of the business model when they began paying their content partners 60%–80% of subscriber revenues, relying much more on advertising as a source of revenues.[27]

As a way to both avoid content charges and keep users in the company's cyber neighborhoods, AOL flirted with content development. AOL launched the "Greenhouse Program" in which the company took equity stakes in over 50 start-up studios. AOL invested $200,000 to $1 million to select studios in exchange for 19%–50% of the equity. AOL also provided the studios with marketing, ad sales, engineering and production support, and a platform to access over 5 million customers. In early 1996, AOL had 23 Greenhouse services running and planned to have over one hundred by June 1996. Motley Fool was one Greenhouse studio success. Started by two brothers in their mid-twenties who had an idea for a new financial advice service, within 90 days it had become one of the top three finance sections on the service.[28] This success encouraged AOL to aggressively pursue other Greenhouse programs.

Ted Leonsis, then President of AOL Services, directed the Greenhouse services. Leonsis was an extremely successful executive at AOL. When he was in charge of sales, marketing, and business development, AOL's membership increased tenfold and revenues jumped from less than $100 million to more than $1.5 billion.[29] While AOL had agreements with some major media players, such as its 50-50 joint venture for The

[24] *Digital Media*, March 12, 1996.

[25] "The View from AOL," *Wall Street Journal*, Nick Wingfield, April 17, 2000.

[26] A backbone consists of a number of high-speed lines and a series of connections that form a major pathway within a network.

[27] Excerpted from and informed by "Note on the Consumer Online Services Industry in 1996," Matthew Murphy, Stanford Graduate School of Business, SM-33, July 1997.

[28] *Digital Media*, March 12, 1996.

[29] http://thestandard.com.

Hub with New Line Cinemas (a Time Warner subsidiary), it downplayed the importance of its relationships with traditional media companies. When AOL lost NBC content to Microsoft, which was developing its own entertainment division, and also lost some Time Warner content to CompuServe, Leonsis said, "We don't think established brands are that important because we're the brand. We're MTV or HBO. People tune into HBO or tune into MTV. They don't tune into the CBS music video on MTV."[30] By 1996 Leonsis gave up his job as president of services to focus exclusively on content creation as president of a new division called AOL Studios.

The benefit to content partners was clear. According to one Greenhouse studio, "Our site would never have taken off without AOL. What AOL provides its content partners is an audience. In cyberspace, that's difficult to come by any other way."[31] Less clear was AOL's ability to consistently pick content hits.

In 1996, the AOL board brought in Bob Pittman, founder of MTV, to run AOL's day-to-day operations as the company's president, while Case stayed on as company CEO, focusing on corporate strategy and product development. Pittman declared two goals for AOL: to make the company profitable and to make AOL one of the leading brands in the world.

Under Pittman, the company scaled back its direct marketing campaign, reducing customer acquisition costs from $375 to $90.[32] In addition, Pittman focused on solving AOL's network traffic problems. Facing possible lawsuits from states' attorneys general, AOL agreed to pay refunds to customers who had experienced difficulty getting online. In 1997, the company spent over $1 billion to improve its network.

By February 1998, Pittman oversaw all of AOL's major divisions. It was then that AOL's new strategy was enacted. With almost 14 million subscribers, but not many content hits or obvious talent for content development, AOL scaled back its efforts at developing and producing entertainment. Instead of buying or developing its own content, AOL used its massive audience to force content providers to pay for the privilege of carriage.

AOL Partnership Deals

The partnership deals that Pittman forged with providers and advertisers generally involved a combination of cash payments and cross-marketing provided to AOL by the partner in exchange for carriage on the AOL Service and a guaranteed number of impressions by AOL users (see Appendix 2).

The price tag associated with a particular deal was determined by a number of factors, including:

- The level of exclusivity on AOL (e.g., First USA paid AOL a premium in order to be the exclusive credit card marketer on AOL).

[30] *Digital Media*, March 12, 1996.
[31] "The Internet is Mr. Case's Neighborhood," Marc Gunther, *Fortune*, March 30, 1998.
[32] *ibid.*

- The areas in which placement was guaranteed on AOL (e.g., the Personal Finance Channel carried a high CPM because of the demographics and habits of channel users, whereas chat rooms carried a low cost per thousand [CPM] because audiences were less targeted and usage history showed that chatters rarely left chat rooms in order to visit promotional content or commerce seen in their chat rooms).
- The AOL brands on which a content partner gained carriage (e.g., CompuServe carried a high CPM because its 2 million users were generally much more educated and older than typical online users; Digital Cities also carried a high CPM because its content was locally targeted to specific cities and therefore more relevant to its users).

There were generally four types of partnership deals with AOL: anchor tenancy, exclusive provider, primary provider, and premier provider.

• ***Anchor tenancy.*** Each of AOL's 18 channels typically had up to four anchor tenants. As opposed to rotational ad banners or promotional links, anchor tenants had fixed placements on their respective pages. For example, AOL's personal finance channel featured anchor tenant buttons for four separate online brokerage houses—each of them paying AOL over $25 million for their fixed placements. Anchor tenancy spots either linked to a special AOL area for that anchor tenant or to the anchor tenant's own Web site.

• ***Exclusive provider.*** Exclusivity on AOL came at a steep price. First USA paid $500 million for that honor. Barnes & Noble paid over $100 million for its exclusive relationship with AOL.

• ***Primary provider.*** An AOL primary provider was the featured provider in a particular space, but without the guarantee of being the only provider. For instance, eToys paid AOL $18 million over three years to be the primary commerce provider of toys on AOL. Even though AOL has since struck a deal with Toys "R" Us, eToys will retain greater levels of promotion because of its prior "premier" status deal.

As another example, Preview Travel agreed in 1997 to pay AOL a minimum of $32 million over five years to become the primary provider of travel services on America Online's travel channel. As part of that deal, Preview Travel achieved exclusivity in the "reservations service" space across AOL's properties but was not given exclusive rights to all travel information and promotions on AOL's brands. It received only a guarantee of continued premier placement. As part of that deal, AOL and Preview Travel shared advertising and transaction revenues upon the achievement of thresholds specified in the agreement.

• ***Premier provider.*** Being a premier AOL provider generally included a combination of anchor tenancy, some exclusive content, and multifaceted placement and promotion. For instance, by paying AOL $21 million in 1999, CBS MarketWatch became the premier provider of business and financial news across several of the largest AOL brands (the America Online Service, Netscape, CompuServe, and AOL.COM). Under the three-year agreement, CBS MarketWatch provided business and financial news and analysis on the AOL properties. In addition, CBS MarketWatch became an anchor tenant in AOL's Business News Center, Investment Research, and Active Trader areas of AOL's personal finance channel. Links across several AOL brands provided instant and direct access to a CBS MarketWatch/AOL cobranded site. CBS MarketWatch headlines were provided through AOL, AOL.COM, Netscape Netcenter, and CompuServe, linked back to stories on the cobranded site. As part of the deal, MarketWatch.com produced daily multimedia correspondent packages, executed in a "slide show" format for AOL's users, as well as provided business and financial radio news. As was typical with such AOL deals, both companies involved shared advertising revenue generated through designated areas on the AOL brands that incorporated CBS MarketWatch programming.

In another deal announced in November 1999, computer game maker Electronic Arts (EA) paid AOL $81 million to program AOL's games channel with EA content. In order to execute this large transaction, EA created a separate division, EA.com, and issued a tracking stock for EA's online gaming businesses.[33] At the time of the deal, 42% of AOL's audience played online games on a regular basis.[34]

Partnerships/Acquisitions

Through the 1990s, AOL had established strategic alliances with dozens of companies including Time Warner, ABC, Knight-Ridder, Tribune, Hachette, IBM, American Express, AT&T, Netscape, and Microsoft to provide content, distribution, and the latest technology to its users. AOL's most notable alliances had occurred in early 1996 with Microsoft and AT&T. AOL made Microsoft's Explorer their featured Internet browser in exchange for an AOL icon in every copy of Windows 95. In an alliance with AOL, AT&T agreed to offer a link to AOL from its WorldNet Internet access service providing AOL with potential access to AT&T's 80 million customers.

AOL pursued a strategy to boost its market share on its own and through deals with distributors like AT&T. AOL bet that people would flock to a few known brands in cyberspace and struggled to make sure AOL was one of them. The company also believed that most consumers would stick with AOL branded and organized content rather than roam through the "digital clutter." At the same time, AOL believed the market was becoming increasingly segmented between two primary groups. One segment was comprised of "the masses," either new or non-Web-savvy users who wanted a condensed and organized way to view online content. The second segment was made

[33] A tracking stock is a special type of stock issued by a publicly held company to track the value of one segment of that company. By issuing a tracking stock, the different segments of the company can be valued differently by investors. Companies choose to issue tracking stocks for several reasons. The issuer can retain operating control over the subsidiary company. The subsidiary might also be able to reduce its cost of capital by using the parent's credit rating. Further, if the value of the tracking stock increases, the parent company can make acquisitions with its new currency. Source: invest-faq.com.

[34] "Big Week for Games Deals, But Online Games Not Yet Big Business," Anya Sacharow, Jupiter Communications.

up of more Web-savvy users who had diverse needs and liked the variety offered on the Web. AOL felt that many basic users would stay loyal due to the ease of use of its proprietary service while hoping that the more sophisticated users would graduate to its Global Network Navigator (GNN) Internet access service. AOL planned to offer services that catered to both segments. AOL had differentiated itself through its aggressive marketing, its user-friendly, attractive interface, and its breadth of content. Finally, AOL littered the country with millions of computer disks offering 10 free trial hours of its service. AOL simplified its interface and developed popular proprietary content.

In 1998, AOL sold the ANS Communications transmission network to telecommunications provider WorldCom (later MCI WorldCom) in exchange for rival CompuServe's content operations, 2 million subscribers, and $175 million in cash. With a top competitor out of the way, AOL announced a rate increase to $21.99—$2 more than typical ISPs. AOL saw little to no effect from the rate increase; AOL users were willing to pay more to stay with AOL.

In November 1998, AOL announced an agreement to purchase Netscape Communications at a price of about $4 billion in stock. By the time the deal closed in April 1999, AOL paid $10 billion.

International

In fiscal year 1999, AOL International (including AOL and CompuServe) had topped 3 million members outside the United States—just two and a half years after the first AOL International service was founded in Germany in partnership with Bertelsmann AG, one of the world's largest media conglomerates, with over $14 billion in revenue in 1999. In addition, in fiscal year 1999, AOL partnered with Mexico's Cisneros group to launch AOL Latin America services in Brazil, Mexico, and Argentina in 2000. According to International Data Corporation (IDC), the number of Internet subscribers in Latin America will grow by an average of 41% per year from 1998 to 2003, and e-commerce in the region will grow by an annual 122%.[35] Indeed, AOL estimated that average user time is 35–45 minutes per day in Brazil and Mexico, respectively, which exceeded usage in Europe where the average was only 23 minutes per day.[36] The company also launched AOL Japan and AOL Australia, and made a strategic investment in China.com to strengthen AOL's role in that region and to set the stage for the launch of AOL Hong Kong in 2000. By August 2000, AOL operated in 17 countries worldwide.[37]

Despite an attempt to be local in the markets where it operated—something "Yahoo!" has done with great success—AOL ran into problems in Europe.[38] AOL's partnership in Germany with Bertelsmann was devalued by the AOL/Time Warner merger. The media conglomerate, which owns significant media assets in publishing (Random House), music (BMG Entertainment), and the Internet (41% of barnesandnoble.com and several other Web properties), felt jilted by AOL's proposed takeover of Time

[35] "AOL's Perilous Journey South," *Financial Times*, Tim Jackson, July 25, 2000.
[36] "AOL Stands by Latin American Strategy," *Financial Times*, Raymond Colitt, August 9, 2000.
[37] *ibid.*
[38] "AOL's Perilous Journey South."

Warner. Following the AOL merger announcement, Bertelsmann became a "strategic partner" with Terra Networks, which had spent $12.5 billion to purchase Lycos. Bertelsmann committed to purchase $1 billion worth of advertising and services from Terra Lycos over the next five years. In return, Terra Lycos would get access to Bertelsmann content on preferential terms.[39] While plans for a listing of America Online Latin America progressed on schedule in 2000, the prospectus warned of potential management problems stemming from the minority ownership stakes controlled by AOL and Cisneros, creating two sets of bosses, as well as difficult operating conditions in Latin America. Still, the company's bankers estimated the per share price from $15 to $18, which would give the listing a valuation ranging between $3.9 billion and $4.4 billion.[40] By August 2000, the IPO launched at $8 per share, raising $200 million, roughly half of the amount initially expected. One analyst was quoted, "The business plan has not been well accepted by the market. . . . Having the AOL brand name is not enough. They do not have strong local content and without the content it is difficult to get heavy traffic."[41]

TIME WARNER

In 2000, Time Warner was the world's largest media company (see Exhibit 9a).[42] It published and distributed books and magazines; produced and distributed recorded music, movie, and television programming; owned and operated retail stores; owned and administered music copyrights; and operated cable TV systems. The company owned 75% of Time Warner Entertainment (MediaOne Group owned 25%),[43] which was comprised of Warner Bros., Time Warner Cable, and several other entertainment holdings.

Time Warner's Businesses

At the time that the merger was announced, Time Warner operated five businesses. These were cable networks, publishing, music, filmed entertainment, and cable systems.[44]

• ***Cable networks.*** Time Warner's cable networks group included Turner Entertainment's basic cable networks (TBS Entertainment), CNN News Group, and Home Box Office.

[39] "The Internet—Portal Plays," *The Economist*, May 20, 2000.

[40] "AOL's Perilous Journey South."

[41] "AOL Latin Arm Price Cut," *Financial Times*, Geoff Dyer and Christopher Grimes, August 2, 2000.

[42] Hoover's online.

[43] NB: On June 15, 2000, AT&T closed its purchase of MediaOne for $44 billion. The acquisition gave AT&T 16 million cable subscribers, potentially reaching 28 million homes. The purchase was made with the blessing of Time Warner. Due to regulatory and tax reasons, AT&T may be forced to divest its newly acquired interests in Time Warner Entertainment. "AT&T Closes Its $44 Billion Purchase of MediaOne," *Wall Street Journal*, Rebecca Blumenstein, June 16, 2000.

[44] Source of company information is http://www.timewarner.com.

- ***TBS Entertainment.*** The Turner entertainment networks housed TBS Superstation, TNT, Cartoon Network, Turner Classic Movies, and the new Turner South.
- ***CNN News Group.*** CNN featured more than 77 million U.S. subscribers and over 600 news affiliates in the United States and Canada.
- ***Home Box Office.*** This division featured both HBO and Cinemax, with 35.7 million subscribers in the United States and 10 branded channels.

• ***Publishing.*** Time Inc. featured 36 magazines with a total of 130 million readers. The company published 36 *New York Times* bestsellers in 1999.

• ***Music.*** Time Warner's Warner music group labels comprised Warner Music International, Atlantic, Elektra, Rhino, Sire, Warner Bros. Records, and their affiliate labels. Warner Music International had a roster of more than 1,000 artists and was expanding its efforts to sign local artists and devoting greater resources to marketing U.S. artists overseas. The group had 38 of the top 200 U.S. albums in 1999 and owned one million music copyrights.

• ***Filmed entertainment.*** Time Warner's filmed entertainment group consisted of Warner Bros. and New Line Cinema. Warner Bros. owned 5,700 feature films, 32,000 television titles, and 13,500 animated titles, including 1,500 classic cartoons. New Line Cinema produced four of 1998's top 25 box-office hits.

• ***Cable systems.*** Time Warner Cable featured the Road Runner high-speed online service. Time Warner cable had more than 12.6 million customers and passed 21.3 million homes.

Cross-promotion

When Time Inc. and Warner Bros. merged in 1989, it was with the idea of bringing together different media platforms so that the same piece of content could be used in different ways, and so that different products could promote each other.[45] The Time and Warner merger, which tried to combine the different cultures of publishing and movie production, was thought to have been troubled. In addition to integration problems, Time Warner failed to exploit its central strategy of leveraging its media assets, until the 1996 acquisition of Turner Broadcasting System (see Exhibit 9b).

Richard Parsons, president of Time Warner, described Turner assets as the third side of the Time Warner triangle. For example, Turner cable networks buy content from Warner Bros., and cobrand cable television shows with *Time* magazine and *Sports Illustrated*. Similarly, Turner could finally structure deals to show movies before they appeared on broadcast television, changing the old order whereby cable television was

[45] "One House, Many Windows," *The Economist*, August 19, 2000.

at the bottom of the entertainment food chain, after United States, foreign, pay-per-view, and video exhibition, and thus increased cable viewership and advertising rates.[46]

Time Warner's Earlier Efforts on the Internet

While Time Warner owned valuable media brands generating predictable free cash flow, the company failed to leverage these brands over the Internet.

In 1994, Time Warner launched Pathfinder, a portal to its various media properties. Pathfinder helped evolve the concept of the Web portal as an organized gateway that sites like Yahoo! and search engines like Excite and Infoseek later exploited far more successfully. Initially popular, Pathfinder was soon plagued with problems, including management changes and a graphically rich interface that took too long to download. By May 1999, Time Warner dropped the site. "The problem was that they buried their many great brand names under Pathfinder, a nameplate that no one had ever heard of," said Mark Mooradian, a senior analyst at Internet market-research firm Jupiter Communications.[47] The company was estimated to have spent $15 million on the portal.

In the wake of Pathfinder, Time Warner changed its Internet strategy to emphasize five vertical "hub" Web sites featuring news, sports, entertainment, lifestyle, and money. By the time the AOL/Time Warner merger was announced, only the entertainment hub, called "Entertaindom," which had been the original Warner Bros. online site, had launched. While Levin singled out that hub as one Time Warner Internet offering that would carry over postmerger, the company was tight-lipped on the status of the other hubs. Some employees suggest they had been abandoned altogether.[48]

According to February data from Nielsen NetRatings, Entertaindom ranked 664 overall and 66 in the entertainment category—just ahead of Backstreetboys.com.[49] Perhaps disappointed by a lackluster launch, Time Warner soon announced top management shake-ups at the hub when its president and another key executive were forced out.[50]

OTHER PLAYERS IN AN INTERNET MEDIA ECOSYSTEM

Six months after the announcement of the merger, few details were known. The press debated the merits of the deal. Some pointed out that Time and Warner had not made much of their earlier merger a decade ago.[51] Others pointed to Disney's failure to make much of its November 1999 takeover of Infoseek as an indication of how difficult it was to successfully merge content and Internet assets into an Internet media entity. "From any standpoint, this kind of marriage has not been a success to date," said Jeff Mallett, Yahoo!'s President and COO. "Controlling access and packaging content is

[46] *ibid.*

[47] "Pathfinder, Rest in Peace," *U.S. News and World Report*, Jack Egan, May 10, 1999.

[48] "A New World Order," *The Standard*, James Ledbetter, January 14, 2000.

[49] "What's Next for Entertaindom?" *The Standard*, Laura Rich, March 20, 2000.

[50] "Entertaindom's Cliff-Hanger Episode," *The Standard*, Laura Rich, April 24, 2000.

[51] "Don't Overestimate AOL Time Warner's Clout or Business Model," Jupiter Communications, David Card, January 17, 2000, and "AOL Time Warner: What's the Big Deal?" *Upside*, Loren Fox, March 2000.

more of a cable model than an Internet model."[52] Yahoo!, second in traffic only to America Online, had committed to remaining independent. However, analysts pointed out that Yahoo! was a strong narrowband player without an obvious broadband strategy. Industry watchers speculated about the possibility of other significant mergers in the space, with a Yahoo! takeover of Disney often proposed, in spite of the fact that Disney already owned the Go network, Disney's Internet portal.

Once AOL's main competitor was the MSN network. Microsoft had since sent mixed signals in this space. The company bought into cable, investing $1 billion in Comcast and $5 billion in AT&T. However, Microsoft's motivation for the cable alliances may have been to help keep Windows, which generated most of Microsoft's $19.75 billion in sales in 1999, and was an integral part of next-generation media devices like digital cable set-top boxes and wireless Web gadgets.[53]

Rupert Murdoch's News Corp. had structured itself around a future in which consumers would demand wireless Web access and interactive TV. News Corp. owns a movie studio, network and cable TV stations in the United States, and vast overseas holdings, including satellite TV networks and print assets. However, with nearly $19 billion in fiscal year 1999 revenue, News Corp.'s market capitalization is less than a quarter of Yahoo!'s. The company is tightly controlled by Murdoch, who is considered unlikely to relinquish control.

Consumer electronics giant Sony, with fiscal year 1999 revenue of $56.6 billion, had been building an online empire. But its many autonomous divisions meant Sony was more fractured than focused. Video games, which in 1999 accounted for more than 10% of revenue, could unify many of Sony's assets. Its new Play Station 2 could serve as a hub for games, music, and other digital entertainment, via broadband.

Viacom, which already stood as one of the world's largest entertainment companies, extended its leading global media position with its merger with CBS. Operations included MTV Networks, Blockbuster, Paramount Pictures, Paramount Television, Paramount Parks, Showtime Networks, Spelling Entertainment, 19 television stations, United Paramount Networks (UPN), and movie theatres located in 12 countries. Viacom also owned 50% of Comedy Central. With the CBS acquisition, Viacom added the CBS Television Network and television stations; Infinity radio stations and outdoor systems; CBS Productions and King World Productions.[54]

With MSNBC, CNBC, and NBC, General Electric, which earned $100 billion in 1998 revenue, owned leading network and cable brands and their mildly successful Internet counterparts. General Electric purchased NBCi, a conglomerate of NBC's Internet interests with Xoom.com and Snap.com, in 2000. CEO Jack Welch consistently denied speculation that the network properties were on the block.

AT&T was the largest telecom company in the United States, with more than 80 million customers. AT&T provided long distance, wireless, and local telephone service, along with Internet access (AT&T WorldNet), and a full range of telecom services for businesses. The company sold a stake in its wireless unit to the public, in

[52] "AOL Time Warner: What's the Big Deal?" *Upside*, Loren Fox, March 2000.

[53] The following evaluation of postmerger competitors is informed by "And Now for the Competition," *The Standard*, Kenneth Li and Bernhard Warner, January 14, 2000.

[54] "Viacom," by F. W. Moran, Jefferies & Company, Inc., April 5, 2000.

the form of a tracking stock. Driving toward domination of the cable TV market, AT&T became the largest cable operator in the United States with its purchase of MediaOne. The company intended to use cable to offer local phone service. Concert, AT&T's joint venture with British Telecommunications, targeted multinational corporations.[55]

The cost to AT&T of putting together its cable empire had been enormous, with an estimated $9 billion in upgrades to fix the aging cable plant that it inherited from TCI—costing as much as $200 million in key markets like Denver alone. But the company was still confident the big cable bet would pay off. Internet access, video, local telephone service, and other services were being piped into homes on cable lines, while competitors try to do the same thing with their DSL and wireless offerings. (See Exhibits 10 and 11 for a financial overview of selected ecosystem companies.)

CONCLUSION

Soon after the merger was announced, the key roles were already determined. Case, in effect the acquirer, declined the role of CEO in favor of the chairmanship of AOL Time Warner. Case said he planned to concentrate on long-term strategy, leaving the day-to-day operation of the company to Levin, who would keep his current position as CEO.[56] Bob Pittman, AOL's president and COO would share a co-COO role with Time Warner's president, Dick Parsons. Pittman was assigned subscription, advertising, and commerce businesses, while Parsons was to run content from film, television production, music, and books. Ted Turner, Time Warner's vice chairman, was to retain that role in the merged company, acting as a senior advisor across all of the new company's operations, but with no operational duties.[57]

The merger tested the ability of AOL (an Internet pure play with 12,000 employees) to make something greater than AOL and Time Warner (a 67,000 employee, traditional media conglomerate) would otherwise produce independently.

APPENDIX 1

AOL's Features in 2000[58]

AOL's array of communications, content, commerce, search, and access features included:

• ***E-mail.*** America Online's e-mail feature remained the world's most popular online application among home users, with members sending 70 million e-mails every day.

• ***AOL Instant Messenger (AIM).*** A pioneering innovation that was faster and more direct than e-mail, America Online's instant message feature generated more than 474

[55] http://www.thestandard.com.

[56] Steve Case quoted on "The Charlie Rose Show," May 17, 2000.

[57] "Management Team and Organization Announced for AOL Time Warner," Time Warner Press Release, May 4, 2000.

[58] Review of AOL's brands in 2000 was excerpted from "America Online: The Online Giant in 1999," by Jason Goldberg, EC-4, Stanford Graduate School of Business.

million real-time, one-on-one conversations a day. AIM enabled AOL members to send "instant messages" to other AOL members on the American Online Service, as well as to non-AOL members who downloaded AIM free from the AOL.COM Web site and on the company's other brands and services, including CompuServe and Netscape Netcenter. AIM was packaged into the Netscape Navigator Web Browser as well as the popular RealPlayer and RealJukebox from RealNetworks.

• ***ICQ.*** AOL gained ICQ (a play on the words "I seek you") when it purchased the Israeli company Mirabelis in 1998 for $400 million. At the time, ICQ—which provided free instant messaging over the Internet to anyone who downloaded the ICQ software—had 25 million registered users worldwide. As of September 1999, nearly two-thirds of ICQ's 45 million registrants were based outside the United States. ICQ's members were extremely active Web users: over 7 million ICQ registrants in 1999 averaged more than one hour of daily use.

• ***Keywords.*** America Online's service was designed so that members could type "keywords" into the America Online browser window instead of having to memorize URL addresses.

• ***Content.*** The America Online service featured 18 content areas known as "channels."

• ***Commerce.*** Relevant commerce opportunities were presented on each of America Online's content channels. For example, fantasy sports games and sports memorabilia were sold on the Sports Channel and on the Shop@AOL Shopping Channel.

• ***Parental controls.*** America Online was widely known for creating a family-friendly service where parents could limit access to the Web, e-mail, and the AIM feature.

• ***Additional security features.*** "Notify America Online" provided members with quick help from a trained America Online professional; the Download Sentry Alert let members know when downloadable files were coming from non-AOL members; and AOL's Integrated Web Security Browser guaranteed that online shopping via AOL was 100% secure.

• ***You've got pictures.*** In 1999, America Online joined with Eastman Kodak to offer a service that made sharing pictures with family members and friends as easy as sending e-mail.

• ***My calendar.*** The service included an interactive calendar that allowed members to plan and manage important parts of their life by tracking appointments, key dates, and other personal events online.

• ***AOL search.*** AOL search enabled AOL members to search America Online's content and the entire Internet at the same time.

• ***Broadband connectivity.*** America Online version 5.0, released in September 1999, was AOL's first software that supported DSL, T1, cable, and satellite broadband connectivity. The software automatically detected whether a member was accessing the service with broadband or narrowband connectivity and provided those with high-speed access rich interactive content and features including enriched video and games, and online catalog shopping.

• ***AOL.COM.*** The company's AOL.COM Web site functioned as a portal for America Online members when they ventured from the proprietary service onto the Internet, as well as a general portal for nonmembers. AOL.COM offered content, features, and tools, including AOL NetFind, an Internet search and rating tool, and added functionality for the AIM service. AOL.COM also offered AOL members the opportunity to access and exchange e-mail on the Internet, without signing onto the service, through AOL NetMail.

• ***CompuServe.*** The company's CompuServe online brand, which targeted businesses and tech-savvy users, drew 2.5 million worldwide subscribers. In mid-1999, through an agreement with eMachines, AOL offered CompuServe subscribers $400 rebates on selected eMachine computers—including one model priced at $399—which made the computer free to consumers as long as they committed to paying for the CompuServe online service. Over 300,000 new members were added to CompuServe in the first four months of the eMachines deal.

• ***Netscape/iPlanet.*** AOL's 1999 acquisition of Netscape Communications for about $10 billion in stock significantly expanded the company's profile. Through the acquisition, AOL gained control of the number two Web browser, Netscape Communicator (second to Microsoft's Internet Explorer); Netscape's Netcenter Web portal, which claimed 18 million members and was consistently one of the top five most frequented Web sites per month; as well as Netscape's burgeoning Web server systems business.

AOL believed that Netscape's brand complemented and extended its own mass-market audience appeal among Netscape's Netcenter portal users.[59] The Netscape acquisition also paved the way for AOL's joint venture with Sun Microsystems through which the two companies began developing enterprise software and business-to-business e-commerce solutions under the iPlanet name. In the fall of 1999, over 50% of the Fortune 100 companies were Sun-Netscape alliance customers.

• ***MovieFone.*** In 1999, AOL purchased MovieFone, the leading provider of online movie times and ticket purchases. MovieFone was the premier U.S. movie information and ticketing brand. It was available in more than 60 markets nationwide, covering more than 19,000 movie theaters. In 1999, AOL-MovieFone boasted 12 million weekly users and served one out of every five moviegoers in the United States.

[59] Source: Customer Cast: Web Site Visitor Survey (WSVS-6/99), Cyber Dialogue: American Internet User Study (AIUS-6/99).

• ***Digital City.*** The company's subsidiary, Digital City, Inc., owned in part by the Tribune Company, was a local online content network that offered a network of local content and community guides in over 60 American cities. Local content provided by DCI included original and third-party news, sports, and weather, a local guide service with directory and classified listings, and an interactive forum. As of June 1999, DCI had more than 5 million unique visitors monthly. In the first half of 1999, 85% of DCI users shopped online.

• ***Spinner.com, Winamp, and SHOUTcast.*** The company acquired several Internet music brands in May 1999 through the acquisition of Spinner Networks Incorporated and Nullsoft, Inc. The Spinner.com Web site offered more than 100 channels of programmed music in various formats. Content included over 175,000 songs and related material. The music players provided links that enabled real-time listener feedback and instant purchasing of the music being played. Nullsoft, Inc. was the developer of both Winamp, a branded MP3 player for Windows, and SHOUTcast, a MP3 streaming audio system. The SHOUTcast streaming audio system enabled individuals to broadcast their own content over the Internet. The company planned to make these music features available to consumers across its brands, as well as to customize them for the audience and partners of the company's brands. Nullsoft also developed Gnutella, a software application that enables peer-to-peer exchange of MP3 files. AOL discontinued work on Gnutella; however, the software was leaked onto the Web and has been widely distributed and improved by rogue groups of programmers.[60]

• ***AOLTV.*** AOLTV aimed to advance America Online's "AOL Anywhere" strategy of making its brands and features available to online consumers anywhere, anytime, through a range of devices. In 2000, the service was available via a set-top from Philips Electronics for a suggested retail price of $249.95. The service cost AOL members $14.95 per month in addition to the unlimited use AOL subscription price of $21.95 per month. Non-AOL members could subscribe to AOLTV for $24.95 per month.

APPENDIX 2[61]

The CPM and Advertising on AOL

The CPM, a standard media measure used in both offline and online advertising, equals the cost per thousand sets of eyeballs that have an opportunity to see an advertiser's ad. In online advertising, the opportunity equals an impression, which is the standard term for what happens when a Web page containing a banner ad is served as a result of a user's request. Serving, or displaying, the ad counts as an impression whether or not the user looks at or clicks on the advertisement. Banner advertisers (advertisements

[60] "Nightmare for the Music Industry," *Financial Times*, Tom Foremski, June 7, 2000.
[61] Aspects of this section are from "America Online: The Online Giant in 1999," by Jason Goldberg, EC-4, Stanford Graduate School of Business.

on the top or sides of Web pages) were priced according to a CPM rate for a particular Web site. The CPM rate was a market-advertising rate for the page based on a combination of factors such as the number of unique visitors per month, the demographics of the visitors, and usage behaviors of the visitors.

As Web advertising developed, the CPM became a crucial element in evaluating a site's possible success or failure. Those sites with the most traffic demanded the highest CPM, since they could deliver viewers. While revenue models could use e-commerce measures like transaction fees, ad revenue and the value of a site's CPM remained a significant source of income for Web sites. In 1999, Internet advertising was a small ($2.9 billion) but growing proportion of total US advertising spent ($151 billion), and was expected to increase to $33 billion by 2003.[62]

Because 75% of online ad revenues flowed to the top 10 Web publishers,[63] it was critical that these sites delivered the value expected by their advertisers. Not surprisingly, as the number of sites available to advertising increased, the average CPM decreased from $37.78 in June 1998 to $34.23 in June 1999.[64] While the list price of CPM was expected to decrease, some analysts expected the effective CPM to rise.[65]

While AOL sold some banner advertisements (on a CPM basis) that rotated throughout portions of the America Online Service and on AOL's other brands, the majority of the advertisements on AOL's properties were negotiated as part of much larger content or commerce partnership deals. For instance, in exchange for paying AOL millions of dollars to be the exclusive online greeting card provider on the America Online service, American Greetings also received a guaranteed number of monthly ad impressions on the service. FirstUSA, eBay, eToys, and other major AOL partners had similar promotional deals that included banner advertising. Impressions were the number of times an advertisement, promotion, or link either to content or commerce was seen by AOL users, as opposed to click-through percentage, which is the ratio of clicks per impressions. AOL rarely did deals based on click-throughs.

[62] Li, Charlene, et al., "Internet Advertising Skyrockets," Forrester Research, August 1999.

[63] Internet Advertising Board.

[64] Ad Knowledge 2000, eMarketer. http://www.emarketer.com.

[65] Effective CPM is the rate if all space is sold. Thus list CPM of $20–$40 with a 20% sell-out yields an effective CPM of $4. Source: "Internet Advertising and Direct marketing," Michael J. Russell, Morgan Stanley Dean Witter.

FIGURE 1 Internet Advertising Is a Small but Growing Proportion of Total U.S. Advertising Spent

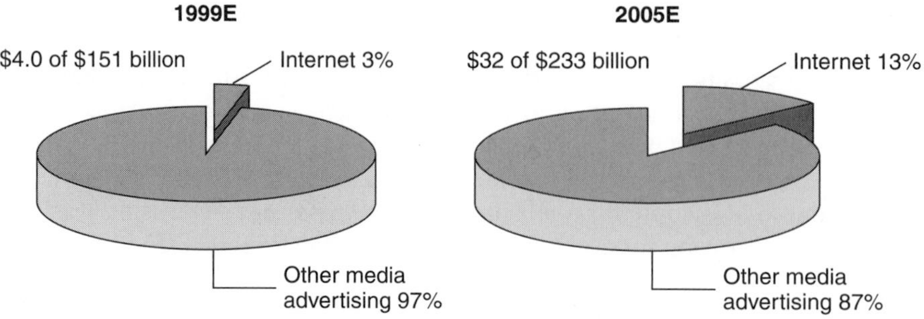

Source: Morgan Stanley Dean Witter.

TABLE 1 Internet Advertising, Measured by Effective CPM, Is Comparatively Inexpensive

Media	*CPM*
Daily newspapers	$19
Prime time broadcast TV	$16
Radio	$6
Magazine	$6
Daytime broadcast TV	$5
Internet-effective CPM	$4

Source: Morgan Stanley Dean Witter.

EXHIBIT 1 Overview of Key Data

	America Online	*Time Warner*
CEO	Steve Case	Gerald Levin
Market capitalization, Jan 7, 2000, $b	163.2	83.5
Sales,* $b	5.2	26.6†
Net income,* $b	0.53‡	1.19†
Employees, ´000	12.1	67.5
Paying customers	23.4 million members	13 million U.S. cable subscribers; 120 million magazine readers

*12 months to Sept. 99, †Consolidated, restated. ‡Fully taxed.
Sources: Company reports; Reuters, Primark Datastream; *The Economist*.
NB: Market capitalizations prior to slide in share prices.

EXHIBIT 2a AOL's North American Combined Subscriber Growth,, 1999–2009

	1999	*2000E*	*2001E*	*2002E*	*2003E*
Slow speed	16.010	19.435	23.793	26.324	27.002
Cable	0.000	0.043	1.024	1.865	6.467
DSL	0.000	0.200	0.990	1.665	2.945
Other	0.579	0.478	0.573	0.613	0.616
Total	19.465	23.339	29.819	34.239	41.258
Brand growth	33.3%	19.9%	27.8%	14.8%	20.5%

Source: Sanford C. Bernstein & Co., Table Base.

EXHIBIT 2b Overview of AOL Subscriber Data

America Online's forecast number of North America subscribers for each of six ancillary Internet services in 2002 to 2009, with AOL's forecast revenues in dollars from each of those online services

Ancillary Subscriber Revenue Components, 2002–2009

	2002E	*2003E*	*2004E*	*2005E*	*2006E*	*2007E*	*2008E*	*2009E*
Picture Albums								
Percentage of AOL HHLDS taking	3.0%	5.0%	7.0%	9.0%	11.0%	13.0%	15.0%	17.0%
Album subscribers	0.85	1.69	2.72	3.77	4.82	5.95	7.17	8.50
Monthly revenue	$1.00	$1.15	$1.32	$1.52	$1.75	$2.01	$2.31	$2.66
Picture album revenue to AOL	10	23	43	69	101	144	199	271
Voice Mail Conversion								
Percentage of AOL HHLDS taking	3.0%	5.0%	7.0%	9.0%	11.0%	13.0%	15.0%	17.0%
Subscribers	0.85	1.69	2.72	3.77	4.82	5.95	7.17	8.50
Monthly revenue	$1.00	$1.00	$1.00	$1.00	$1.00	$1.00	$1.00	$1.00
Voice mail conversion revenue to AOL	10	20	33	45	58	71	86	102
Ancillary Device								
Percentage of AOL HHLDS taking	2.0%	3.0%	7.0%	11.0%	15.0%	19.0%	23.0%	27.0%
Subscribers 0.57	.57	1.01	2.72	4.60	6.57	8.69	11.00	13.51
Monthly revenue	$2.30	$2.65	$3.04	$3.50	$4.02	$4.63	$5.32	$6.12
Ancillary device revenue to AOL	16	32	99	193	317	483	702	992

(continued)

Ancillary Subscriber Revenue Components, 2002–2009 (continued)

	2002E	2003E	2004E	2005E	2006E	2007E	2008E	2009E
Simultaneous Usage								
Percentage of AOL HHLDS taking	1.0%	3.0%	6.0%	8.0%	10.0%	12.0%	14.0%	16.0%
Subscribers	0.28	1.01	2.33	3.35	4.38	5.49	6.69	8.00
Monthly revenue	$10.00	$10.00	$10.00	$10.00	$10.00	$10.00	$10.00	$10.00
Simultaneous usage revenues to AOL	34	121	280	402	526	659	803	961
Software Services								
Percentage of AOL HHLDS taking	—	2.0%	4.0%	6.0%	8.0%	10.0%	12.0%	14.0%
Subscribers	—	0.67	1.56	2.51	3.51	4.58	5.74	7.00
Monthly revenue	—	$3.00	$3.30	3.63	$3.99	$4.39	$4.83	$5.31
Software services revenues to AOL	—	24	62	109	168	241	333	447
Television Services								
Percentage of AOL HHLDS taking	—	—	5.0%	10.0%	17.0%	24.0%	31.0%	38.0%
Subscribers	—	—	1.95	4.18	7.45	10.98	14.82	19.01
Monthly revenue	—	—	$10.00	$11.00	$12.10	$13.31	$14.64	$16.11
Television services revenues to AOC	—	—	233	552	1,082	1,754	2,604	3,674

Source: Sanford C. Bernstein & Co., Inc.

EXHIBIT 3 Time Warner Selected Businesses, Brands, and Products

Time Warner Cable Assets

Clusters of more than 100,000 subscribers:
Divisions/Clusters—Subscribers (thousands)

Region	*Subscribers (000)*	*Region*	*Subscribers (000)*
New York City	1,177	Charlotte	374
Tampa Bay	903	Los Angeles	360
Florida	669	Greensboro	343
Houston	665	Hawaii	340
Raleigh/Fayetteville	441	Syracuse	332
Milwaukee	426	Cincinnati	328
Western Ohio	415	San Antonio	327
Northeast Ohio	393	Kansas City, Missouri	313

(continued)

EXHIBIT 3 Time Warner Selected Businesses, Brands, and Products *(continued)*

Region	*Subscribers (000)*	*Region*	*Subscribers (000)*
Columbia, South Carolina	305		
Columbus	305	Green Bay	146
Rochester	304	Wilmington	141
Albany	296	Palm Springs	124
Austin	285	Indianapolis	121
Suburban New York	256	El Paso	120
Memphis	230	Jackson/Monroe, Mississippi	113
San Diego	205	Waco	110
Binghamton	166	Portland, Maine	102

Local News Channels

- Bay News 9, Tampa, Florida
- Central Florida News 13, Orlando, Florida
- NY1 News, New York, New York
- R/News, Rochester, New York
- Austin 8 News, Austin Texas

Joint Ventures

- Road Runner
- Time Warner Telecom, LLC

Warner Music Group Incorporated

- Atlantic Recording Corporation
- Elektra Entertainment Group, Inc.
- Rhino Entertainment Company
- Sire Records Group
- Warner Bros. Records, Inc.
- Warner Music International
- Warner/Chappell Music
- Warner Bros. Publications
- WEA, Inc.
- WEA Corp.
- WEA Manufacturing
- Ivy Hill Corp.

Warner Special Products

Joint Ventures

- Columbia House
- 143 Records
- Alternative Distribution Alliance
- Giant (Revolution) Records
- Maverick Recording Company
- Qwest Records
- RuffNation Records LLC
- Tommy Boy Music

(continued)

EXHIBIT 3 Time Warner Selected Businesses, Brands, and Products *(continued)*

Warner Bros. Assets

- Warner Bros. Pictures
- Warner Bros. Television
- Warner Bros. Animation
- Looney Tunes
- Hanna-Barbera
- Castle Rock Entertainment
- Telepictures Productions
- The WB Television Network
- Kids' WB! Warner Home Video
- Warner Bros. Consumer Products
- Warner Bros. Studio Stores
- Warner Bros. International Theatres
- Warner Bros. Online
- *DC Comics*
- *MAD Magazine*

New Line Cinema Assets

- New Line Cinema
- Fine Line Features
- New Line Home Video
- New Line International
- New Line New Media
- New Line Television
- New Line Cinema Studio Store

Time Inc. Assets

- *Time*
- *People*
- *Sports Illustrated*
- *Fortune*
- *Life*
- *Money*
- *Parenting*
- *In Style*
- *Entertainment Weekly*
- *Cooking Light*
- *Baby Talk*
- *Bébé*
- *Fortune Small Business*
- *Coastal Living*
- *Health*
- *People en Español*
- *Progressive Farmer*
- *Southern Accents*
- *Southern Living*
- *Sports Illustrated for Kids*
- *Sports Illustrated for Women*
- *Sunset*
- *Teen People*
- *This Old House*
- *Time Digital*
- *Time for Kids Mutual Funds*
- *AsiaWeekDancyu*
- *President*
- *Wallpaper*
- *Who Weekly*
- *Family Life*
- *Real Simple* (March 2000)
- *eCompany Now* (April 2000)
- Time Life Inc.
- Book-of-the-Month Club
- Time Warner Trade Publishing; Little, Brown and Company; Warner Books
- Oxmoor House
- Leisure Arts
- Sunset Books
- Media Networks, Inc.
- Time Inc. Custom Publishing
- Targeted Media, Inc.
- Time Inc. Interactive
- Time Distribution Services
- Warner Publisher Services
- First Moments

(continued)

EXHIBIT 3 Time Warner Selected Businesses, Brands, and Products *(continued)*

Turner Entertainment Group Assets

- TBS Superstation
- Turner Network Television
- Cartoon Network
- Turner Classic Movies
- Turner South
- TNT Europe
- Cartoon Network Europe
- TNT Latin America
- Cartoon Network Latin America
- TNT & Cartoon Network/ Asia Pacific Atlanta Braves
- Atlanta Hawks
- Atlanta Thrashers
- World Championship Wrestling
- The Goodwill Games
- Boomerang (Spring 2000)
- Joint Ventures
- Cartoon Network Japan
- Court TV (TWE-owned)

Cable News Network Assets

- CNN
- CNN Headline News
- CNN International
- CNNfn
- CNN/Sports Illustrated
- CNN en Español
- CNN Airport Network
- CNNRadio
- CNNRadio Noticias
- CNN Interactive
- CNN Newsource
- CNN+
- CNN Turk

Home Box Office Assets

- HBO
- HBO Plus
- HBO Signature
- HBO Family
- HBO Comedy
- HBO Zone
- Cinemax
- MoreMAX
- ActionMAX
- ThillerMAX
- HBO en Español

Joint Ventures
- Comedy Central
- HBO Ole
- HBO Brasil
- HBO Asia
- HBO Hungary
- HBO Czech
- HBO Poland
- HBO Romania

Source for all Exhibit 3: Time Warner.

EXHIBIT 4 Ownership Structure of Selected AOL and Time Warner Media Assets (as of January 2000)

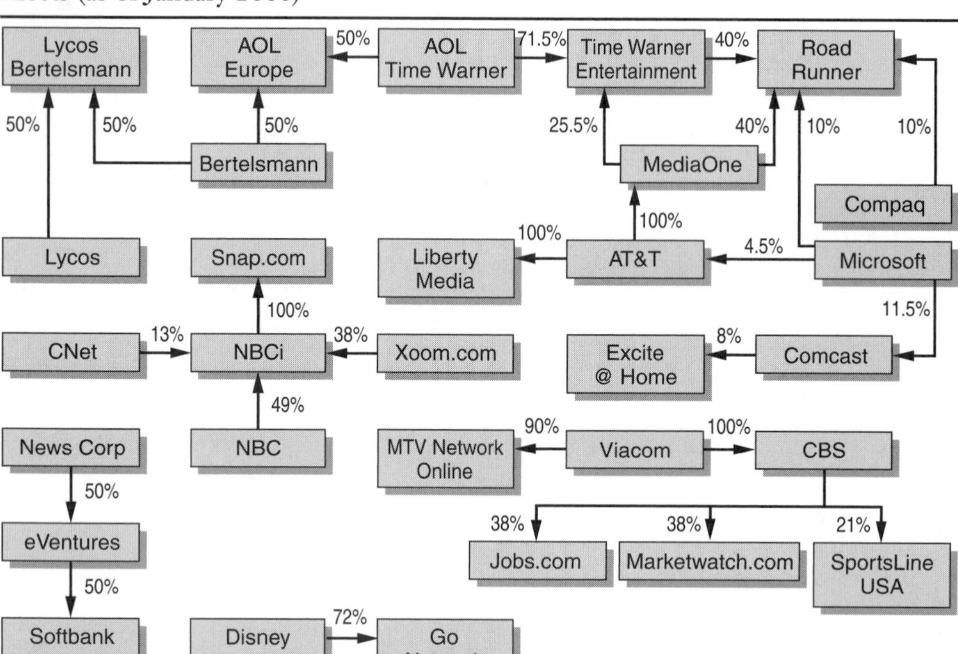

EXHIBIT 5 Selected Time Warner Advertising Expenditures

U.S. advertising spending by Time Warner by media and by brand (operation), and global and U.S. sales and earnings for both years in dollars

U.S. Ad Spending ($000)

By Media	*1997*	*1996*	*% Chg*
Magazine	$180,057	$157,313	14.5
Sunday magazine	3,379	4,857	–30.4
Newspaper	134,519	124,030	8.5
National newspaper	9,159	9,320	–1.7
Outdoor	3,656	2,109	73.4
Network TV	192,774	208,592	–7.6
Spot TV	86,345	90,947	–5.1
Syndicated TV	41,536	36,090	15.1
Cable TV networks	105,682	100,917	4.7
Network radio	6,576	7,906	–16.8

(continued)

EXHIBIT 5 Selected Time Warner Advertising Expenditures *(continued)*

By Media	*1997*	*1996*	*% Chg*
National spot radio	$15,424	$15,538	–0.7
Internet	2,054	938	119.0
Measured media	781,162	758,558	3.0
Unmeasured media	232,018	279,141	–16.9
Total	1,013,181	1,037,699	–2.4

By Brand	*1997*	*1996*	*% Chg*
Warner Bros. studios	$243,900	$241,500	1.0
New Line Cinema	118,400	97,700	21.1
HBO cable TV	112,062	111,240	0.7
Time-Life multimedia	52,766	77,880	–32.2
Sports Illustrated	36,694	47,081	–22.1
Warner Bros. entertainment	21,624	17,534	23.3
Pay-per-view cable TV	19,461	15,873	22.6
TNT cable TV	16,582	9,042	83.4
Warner Bros. TV network	13,386	18,211	–26.5
CNN cable TV	13,206	18,018	–26.7
Time Warner Cable	12,946	5,917	118.8
TBS cable network	11,335	11,752	–3.5

Sales and earnings ($ in millions)

Worldwide	*1997*	*1996*	*% Chg*
Sales	$24,622	$23,660	4.1
Earnings	246	–317	na

U.S.	*1997*	*1996*	*% Chg*
Sales	$19,255	$15,989	20.4
Operating income	NA	732	NA

Division sales	*1997*	*1996*	*% Chg*
Publishing	$4,290	$4,117	4.2
Music	3,691	3,949	–6.5
Cable TV	997	909	9.7
Cable TV networks—TBS	2,900	680	326.5
Filmed entertainment—TBS	1,531	455	236.5
Filmed entertainment	5,472	5,648	–3.1
Broadcasting—WB	136	87	56.3
Cable networks—HBO	1,923	1,763	9.1
Cable	4,243	3,851	10.2

Source: Crain Communications, Inc., Table Base.

EXHIBIT 6 Worldwide Advertising Spending

Worldwide Internet Advertising Spending, by Region ($M)

	1999	*2000*	*2001*
North America	2,831.0	5,410.0	8,773.0
Europe	286.0	621.0	1,217.0
Asia/Pacific	166.0	346.0	691.0
Latin America	51.0	121.0	259.0
Rest of world	2.0	4.0	8.0
Total	3,336.0	6,502.0	10,948.0
	2002	*2003*	*2004*
North America	12,740.0	17,482.0	22,589.0
Europe	2,169.0	3,589.0	5,480.0
Asia/Pacific	1,235.0	2,070.0	3,322.0
Latin America	517.0	949.0	1,647.0
Rest of World	14.0	23.0	37.0
Total	16,675.0	24,113.0	33,075.0

Source: Forrester Research, Table Base.

EXHIBIT 7 Important Historical Dates for AOL

06/29/00	AOL completes acquisition of MapQuest.com
06/22/00	Winamp surpasses 25 million registrants
06/16/00	AOL Service surpasses 23 million members
05/11/00	ICQ tops 65 million registered users
03/21/00	AOL surpasses 22 million members
02/15/00	Netscape Netcenter passes 25 million registrant milestone
02/02/00	AOL surpasses 21 million members
01/20/00	AOL Latin America files registration statement for IPO
01/10/00	America Online and Time Warner announce plans to merge
12/17/99	AOL surpasses 20 million members
12/01/99	ICQ surpasses 50 million registered users
11/22/99	Splits stock two-for-one
11/16/99	AOL Brasil launches
10/25/99	AOL surpasses 19 million members
10/20/99	AOL and Gateway announce strategic partnership
10/19/99	Netscape breaks 20 million registrant milestone
10/14/99	AOL Germany surpasses one million members
10/13/99	Motorola and AOL plan to develop wireless application for AOL Instant Messenger (AIM)
09/28/99	Launch of AOL Hong Kong
09/22/99	Netscape Search ranked #1 by *Search Engine Watch*

(continued)

EXHIBIT 7 Important Historical Dates for AOL *(continued)*

08/24/99	AOL Instant Messenger (AIM) surpasses 45 million users; launches next generation AIM version 3.0
08/17/99	AOL surpasses 18 million members
08/09/99	ICQ exceeds 40 million registered users, 14 months following its acquisition by AOL, more than tripling the number of registered users
07/27/99	AOL and GTE partner to provide ADSL service
06/22/99	AOL and 3Com Corporation announced a strategic relationship to give AOL members access to their e-mail via a handheld computer for the first time
06/21/99	AOL and Hughes Electronics form a strategic alliance to market unparalleled digital entertainment and Internet services
06/21/99	AOL signs pacts with DIRECTV, Inc., Hughes Network Systems, Philips Electronics, and Network Computer, Inc. to help bring connected interactivity to TV experience
06/15/99	AOL acquires Digital Marketing Services, Inc., the leader in online incentive marketing programs and online custom market research
06/01/99	AOL acquires leading Internet music brands Spinner.com, Winamp, and SHOUTcast
05/21/99	AOL completes its acquisition of MovieFone, Inc.
04/14/99	AOL surpasses 17 million members
04/05/99	AOL acquires When, Inc.
03/24/99	AOL announces a new organization to integrate Netscape's operations and build on the strengths of the Netscape brand
03/17/99	AOL completes its acquisition of Netscape Communications Corporation
03/11/99	AOL and SBC Communications announce partnership to deliver high-speed DSL access
02/22/99	Splits stock two-for-one
02/17/99	AOL announces that Marc Andreessen of Netscape Communications Corporation will become Chief Technology Officer
02/09/99	AOL surpasses 16 million members
02/03/99	AOL and First USA announce agreement that represents the Internet's largest advertising and marketing partnership to date, valued at up to $500 million
02/01/99	AOL announces intention to acquire MovieFone, Inc. the nation's number one movie listing and ticketing service
01/26/99	AOL, Inc. surpasses 3 million AOL and CompuServe members outside of the United States
01/12/99	AOL and Bell Atlantic announce partnership to deliver high-speed DSL access
12/30/98	AOL surpasses 15 million members
12/22/98	Standard and Poor's announces that America Online will be added to the S&P 500 Index
12/15/98	AOL and the Cisneros Group announce Latin America joint venture
11/24/98	AOL announces acquisition of Netscape; strategic partnership with Sun Microsystems
11/17/98	Splits stock two-for-one
11/12/98	AOL exceeds 14 million members
10/07/98	AOL and Bertelsmann launch AOL Australia
08/27/98	AOL surpasses 13 million members

(continued)

EXHIBIT 7 Important Historical Dates for AOL *(continued)*

06/08/98	AOL announces intention to acquire Mirabilis LTD and its ICQ Technology
04/16/98	AOL passes 12 million members
03/16/98	Splits stock two-for-one
02/10/98	AOL and CIC announce plans to launch online service in Hong Kong
02/02/98	AOL completes acquisition of CompuServe
01/20/98	AOL passes 11 million members
12/16/97	AOL passes one million member mark outside of United States
11/17/97	AOL passes 10 million members
10/27/97	AOL Studios launches Entertainment Asylum
10/07/97	AOL and Bertelsmann AG announce plans to launch an online service in Australia
09/08/97	AOL announces intention to acquire CompuServe Online Services
09/02/97	AOL passes 9 million members
06/16/97	AOL passes 750,000 member mark internationally
04/15/97	Launches AOL Japan
03/10/97	Acquires Lightspeed Media to create original content for Greenhouse Entertainment Network
03/04/97	Chat rooms opened to advertisers
02/25/97	Multiyear, $100 million marketing deal announced with Tel-Save Holdings
01/16/97	AOL passes 8 million members
12/01/96	Introduces unlimited use pricing plan of $19.95 per month
11/25/96	Excite becomes AOL's exclusive Internet search and directory service
11/13/96	AOL reaches 7 million members
09/16/96	Moves from Nasdaq to the New York Stock Exchange, where it is listed under symbol "AOL"
08/06/96	Acquires ImagiNation Network (INN) to expand multiplayer games offering
07/01/96	Launches version 3.0 for Windows
05/30/96	AOL exceeds 6 million members
05/08/96	Announces joint venture with Mitsui and Nikkei to launch service in Japan
03/18/96	Launches AOL France
03/12/96	Marketing distribution alliances announced with Apple and AT&T. Browser partnerships announced with Microsoft and Netscape Communications
	Licensing and developing agreement announced with Sun Microsystems
02/06/96	AOL passes 5 million members
01/31/96	Launches AOL UK and AOL Canada
12/28/95	AOL exceeds 4.5 million members
11/28/95	Third two-for-one stock split in just over one year (closing price, post-split: $39 7/8)
11/28/95	Bertelsmann AG and America Online launch AOL Germany
11/08/95	The Developers Studio launched to provide AOL software tools to third-party developers
11/08/95	*PC Magazine*, *Family PC Magazine*, *Online Access Magazine*, and the Information Industry Association rate AOL "Best Consumer Online Service"
10/19/95	Completes sale of previously registered shares at $58.38
10/30/95	Launch of GNN , AOL's direct Internet service

(continued)

EXHIBIT 7 Important Historical Dates for AOL *(continued)*

09/22/95	Acquires Ubique, Ltd., creator of Virtual Places
09/19/95	Registration filed for secondary offering of 3,500,000 shares
07/06/95	AOL passes 3,000,000 members
06/01/95	Acquires Global Network Navigator (GNN) as platform for direct Internet service; acquires WebCrawler search tool
05/22/95	Acquires WAIS, an Internet publisher, and Medior, a developer of interactive media
05/03/95	Exceeds 2.5 million members
04/27/95	Splits stock two-for-one
04/03/95	First participants of the Greenhouse announced: The eGG, Health ResponseAbility Systems, InterZine Productions, The Motley Fool, NetNoir, and Health Zone
03/01/95	Joint venture with Bertelsmann AG announced to create European online services
02/21/95	Passes 2 million members
02/17/95	Acquires ANS, a commercial Internet access provider
12/29/94	Acquires BookLink Technologies, developer of Internet applications
11/30/94	Acquires NaviSoft, developer of Internet publishing tools
11/28/94	Splits stock two-for-one
11/17/94	The Greenhouse launched to develop original content online
08/19/94	Acquires Redgate Communications, a multimedia publishing company
08/16/94	Reaches 1 million members
12/07/93	Secondary offering for 1 million shares
12/93	Exceeds 500,000 members
01/93	Windows version of America Online launched
03/19/92	America Online goes public on the NASDAQ market at original price of $11.50, under symbol AMER
10/91	Quantum Computer Services changes name to America Online, Inc.
02/91	DOS version of America Online launched
06/90	Quantum's Promenade service launched for the IBM PS/1
10/89	America Online service is launched for Macintosh and Apple II
08/88	Quantum's PC-Link launched through a joint venture with Tandy Corporation
11/85	Quantum's first online service, Q-Link, launched on Commodore Business Machines
05/24/85	Date of incorporation under original founding name, Quantum Computer Services, registered in Delaware

Source: AOL

EXHIBIT 8a AOL Financial Data

America Online, Inc.
Supplemental Consolidated Statements of Operations Fully Taxed

	Year ended June 30		
	1999	*1998* *(Amounts in millions, except per share data)*	*1997*
Revenues:			
Subscription services	$3,321	$2,183	$1,478
Advertising, commerce, and other	1,000	543	308
Enterprise solutions	456	365	411
Total revenues	4,777	3,091	2,197
Costs and expenses:			
Cost of revenues	2,657	1,811	1,162
Sales and marketing	808	623	608
Write-off of deferred subscriber acquisition costs	—	—	385
Product development	286	239	195
General and administrative	408	328	220
Amortization of goodwill and other intangible assets	65	24	6
Acquired in-process research and development	—	94	9
Merger, restructuring, and contract termination charges	95	75	73
Settlement charges	—	17	24
Total costs and expenses	4,319	3,211	2,682
Income (loss) from operations	458	(120)	(485)
Other income, net	638	30	10
Income (loss) before provision for income taxes	$1,096	$(90)	$(475)
Reconciling items:			
Gain on sale of Excite	(567)	—	—
Special charges	95	186	491
Transition costs	25	—	—
Adjusted net income before taxes	649	96	16
Assumed tax provision at 39%	(253)	(37)	(6)
Adjusted net income fully taxed	$396	$59	$10
Fully taxed earnings per share:			
Earnings per share—diluted	$0.34	$0.06	$0.01
Weighted average shares outstanding—diluted	1,182	1,070	1,004
Earnings before interest, taxes, depreciation, and amortization (EBITDA)	968	302	111

Source: AOL

EXHIBIT 8b AOL Revenue Breakdown

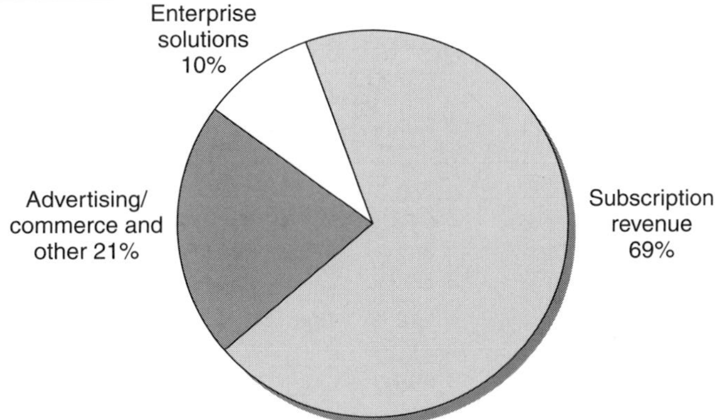

NB: The Netscape Enterprise Group is the primary product group in the Enterprise Solutions business of AOL. The company formed Netscape Business Solutions to sell AOL and Netscape products and services. The Netscape Enterprise group develops, markets, sells, and supports a broad suite of enterprise software, which consists of electronic commerce infrastructure and electronic commerce applications targeted primarily at corporate intranets and extranets, as well as the Internet. The Netscape Enterprise Group also provides a variety of services to support its software products, including technical support, professional services, and training. Following the merger with Netscape in March 1999, the Netscape Enterprise Group began contributing to the company's strategic alliance with Sun Microsystems, Inc.
Source: InfoTech Trends; AOL.

EXHIBIT 9a Time Warner Financial Data

Annual Income Statement
(Millions of U.S. Dollars)

	December 31				
	1999	*1998*	*1997*	*1996*	*1995*
Sales—core business	27,333.0	14,582.0	13,294.0	10,064.0	8,067.0
Total sales	27,333.0	14,582.0	13,294.0	10,064.0	8,067.0
Cost of goods sold	14,940.0	8,210.0	7,542.0	5,922.0	4,682.0
SG&A expense	7,513.0	3,698.0	3,187.0	2,188.0	2,129.0
Depreciation	1,298.0	1,178.0	1,294.0	988.0	559.0
Other operating expense	–2,344.0	0.0	0.0	0.0	0.0
Unusual income/expense	–109.0	0.0	0.0	0.0	0.0
Total expenses	21,298.0	13,086.0	12,023.0	9,098.0	7,370.0
Interest expense, nonoperating	–1,897.0	–1,180.0	–1,044.0	–1,174.0	–877.0
Other—net	–638.0	270.0	605.0	212.0	182.0
Pretax income	3,500.0	586.0	832.0	4.0	2.0
Income taxes	1,540.0	418.0	531.0	160.0	126.0

(continued)

EXHIBIT 9a Time Warner Financial Data *(continued)*

Annual Income Statement
(Millions of U.S. Dollars)

	December 31				
	1999	*1998*	*1997*	*1996*	*1995*
Income after taxes	1,960.0	168.0	301.0	–156.0	–124.0
Preferred dividends	–52.0	–540.0	–319.0	–257.0	–52.0
Net income (Excluding E&D)	1,908.0	–372.0	–18.0	–413.0	–176.0
Discontinued operations	0.0	0.0	0.0	0.0	0.0
Extraordinary items	–12.0	0.0	–55.0	–35.0	–42.0
Net income (including E&D)	1,896.0	–372.0	–73.0	–448.0	–218.0
Primary EPS excluding E&D	1.51	–0.31	–0.02	–0.48	–0.23
Primary EPS including E&D	1.50	–0.31	–0.06	–0.52	–0.28
Dividends per common share	0.18	0.18	0.18	0.18	0.18
Shares to calculate primary EPS (millions of shares)	1,267.0	1,194.7	1,135.4	862.4	767.6

Source: OneSource Information Services.

EXHIBIT 9b Time Warner Financial Data

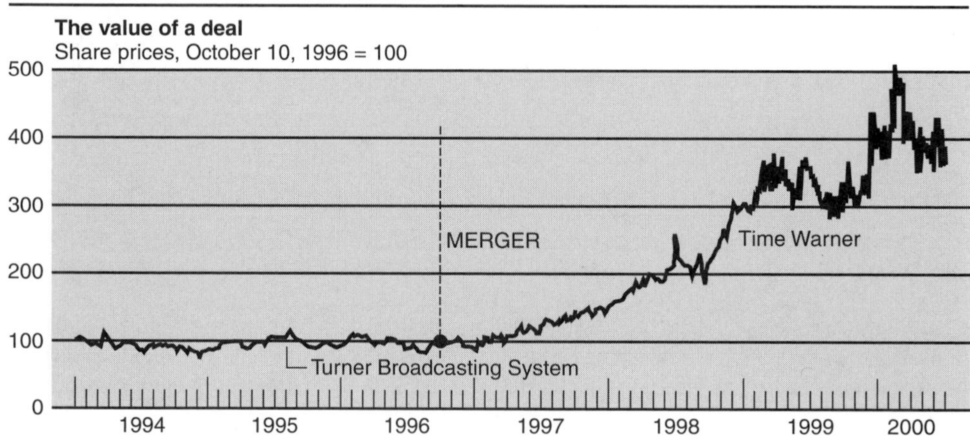

EXHIBIT 10 Share Price Data for Selected Companies

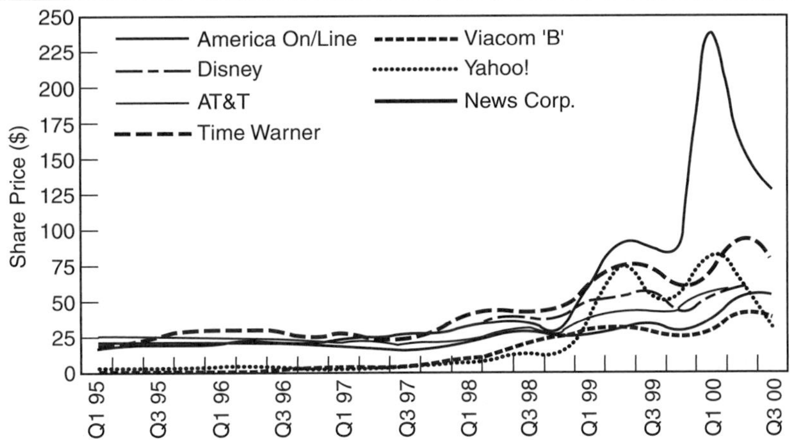

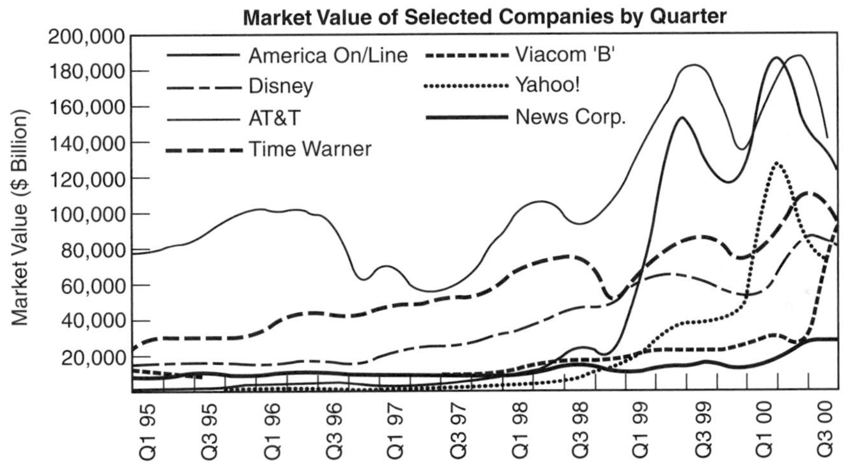

Source: DataStream

EXHIBIT 11 Financial Data for Selected Companies

AT&T Corporation Annual Income Statement
(Millions of U.S. Dollars)

			31 December		
	1999	1998	1997	1996	1995
Sales—core business	62,391.0	53,223.0	51,577.0	50,688.0	48,445.0
Total sales	62,391.0	53,223.0	51,577.0	50,688.0	48,445.0
Cost of goods sold	29,071.0	25,823.0	26,388.0	24,625.0	25,375.0
SG&A expense	13,516.0	12,770.0	14,371.0	14,535.0	14,366.0
Depreciation	7,439.0	4,629.0	3,982.0	2,819.0	3.520.0
Research & development	0.0	0.0	0.0	0.0	0.0
Other operating expense	0.0	0.0	0.0	0.0	0.0
Unusual income/expense	1,506.0	2,514.0	0.0	0.0	0.0
Total expenses	51,532.0	45,736.0	44,741.0	41,979.0	43,261.0
Interest expense, nonoperating	−1,651.0	−427.0	−307.0	−417.0	−490.0
Other—net	−2,523.0	1,247.0	443.0	405.0	284.0
Pretax income	6,685.0	8,307.0	6,972.0	8,697.0	4,978.0
Income taxes	3,257.0	3.072.0	2,723.0	3,239.0	1,943.0
Income after taxes	3,428.0	5,235.0	4,249.0	5,458.0	3,035.0
Preferred dividends	0.0	0.0	0.0	0.0	0.0
Misc. earnings adj.	2,022.0	0.0	0.0	0.0	0.0
Net income (excluding E&D)	5,450.0	5,235.0	4,249.0	5,458.0	3,035.0
Discontinued operations	0.0	1,300.0	166.0	355.0	−2,896.0
Extraordinary items	0.0	−17.0	0.0	0.0	0.0
Accounting change	0.0	0.0	0.0	0.0	0.0
Net income (including E&D)	5,450.0	6,398.0	4,415.0	5,793.0	139.0
Primary EPS excluding E&D	1.77	1.96	1.59	2.07	1.28
Primary EPS including E&D	1.77	2.39	1.65	2.19	0.06
Dividends per common stock	0.88	0.88	0.88	0.88	0.88
Shares to calculate primary EPS (millions of shares)	3,082.0	2,676.0	2,671.5	2,640.0	2,376.0

Source: OneSource Information Services.

EXHIBIT 11 Financial Data for Selected Companies *(continued)*

Sony Corporation Annual Income Statement
(Millions of Japanese Yen)

	2000	*1999*	*31 March* *1998*	*1997*	*1996*
Sales—core business	6,618,718.0	6,754,786.0	6,715,866.0	5,611,831.0	4,547,102.0
Sales—other	67,943.0	49,396.0	45,138.0	51,303.0	45,463.0
Total sales	6,686,661.0	6,804,182.0	6,761,004.0	5,663,134.0	4,592,565.0
Cost of goods sold	4,954,474.0	4,955,107.0	4,889,696.0	4,138,928.0	3,419,331.0
SG&A expense	1,491,560.0	1,500,863.0	1,345,584.0	1,153,876.0	937,910.0
Unusual income/expense	0.0	0.0	0.0	0.0	0.0
Total expenses	6,446,034.0	6,455,970.0	6,235,280.0	5,292,804.0	4,357,241.0
Interest expense, nonoperating	–42,030.0	–48,275.0	–62,524.0	–70,892.0	0.0
Other—net	65,713.0	77,554.0	–3,937.0	12,991.0	–97,165.0
Pretax income	264,310.0	377,691.0	459,263.0	312,419.0	138,159.0
Income taxes	94,644.0	176,973.0	214,868.0	163,570.0	77,158.0
Income after taxes	169,666.0	200,718.0	244,395.0	148,859.0	61,001.0
Minority interests	–10,001.0	–12,151.0	–16,813.0	0.0	0.0
Misc earnings adj.	–37,830.0	–9,563.0	–5,514.0	–9,399.0	–6,749.0
Net income (excluding E&D)	121,835.0	179,004.0	222,068.0	139,460.0	54,252.0
Primary EPS including E&D	144.58	218.43	278.85	183.87	72.53
Dividends per common share	25.00	25.00	30.00	27.50	25.00
Shares to calculate primary EPS (millions of shares)	842.7	819.5	796.4	758.5	748.0

Source: OneSource Information Services.

Viacom, Inc. Annual Income Statement
(Millions of U.S. Dollars)

	1999	*1998*	*31 December* *1997*	*1996*	*1995*
Sales—core business	12,858.8	12,096.1	10,684.9	9,683.9	10,915.9
Total sales	12,858.8	12,096.1	10,684.9	9,683.9	10,915.9
Cost of goods sold	8,337.9	8,506.3	7,476.3	6,340.2	6,689.5
SG&A expense	2,358.6	2,060.9	1,750.6	1,442.0	2,111.0
Depreciation	844.7	777.3	772.6	654.3	716.7
Unusual income/expense	70.3	0.0	0.0	50.2	0.0
Total expenses	11,611.5	11,344.5	9,999.5	8,486.7	9,517.2

(continued)

EXHIBIT 11 Financial Data for Selected Companies *(continued)*

Interest expense, nonoperating	–448.9	–622.4	–772.9	0.0	0.0
Other—net	45.5	8.1	1,266.0	–787.1	–818.9
Pretax income	843.9	137.3	1,178.5	410.1	579.8
Income taxes	411.4	138.7	646.4	243.3	367.1
Income after taxes	432.5	–1.4	532.1	166.8	212.7
Preferred dividends	–12.4	–27.2	–60.0	–60.0	–60.0
Misc earnings adj.	–60.8	–42.1	–158.6	–14.6	–62.2
Net income (excluding E&D)	359.3	–70.7	313.5	92.2	90.5
Discontinued operations	0.0	–4.2	420.1	1,095.7	72.0
Extraordinary items	–37.7	–74.7	0.0	0.0	0.0
Accounting change	0.0	0.0	0.0	0.0	0.0
Net income (including E&D)	321.6	–149.6	733.6	1,187.9	162.5
Primary EPS excluding E&D	0.52	–0.10	0.44	0.13	0.13
Primary EPS including E&D	0.46	–0.21	1.04	1.63	0.22
Dividends per common share	0.00	0.00	0.00	0.00	0.00
Shares to calculate primary EPS (millions of shares)	695.2	708.7	705.8	728.0	725.0

Source: OneSource Information Services.

Walt Disney Company Annual Income Statement
(Millions of U.S. Dollars)

			30 September		
	1999	*1998*	*1997*	*1996*	*1995*
Sales—core business	23,402.0	22,976.0	22,473.0	18,739.0	12,151.0
Total sales	23,402.0	22,976.0	22,473.0	18,739.0	12,151.0
Cost of goods sold	19,715.0	18,466.0	17,722.0	15,406.0	9,685.0
SG&A expense	196.0	236.0	367.0	309.0	239.0
Depreciation	456.0	431.0	439.0	0.0	0.0
Other operating expense	–345.0	0.0	–135.0	0.0	0.0
Unusual income/expense	132.0	64.0	0.0	525.0	0.0
Total expenses	20,154.0	19,197.0	18,393.0	16,240.0	9,924.0
Interest expense, nonoperating	–612.0	–622.0	–693.0	–438.0	–110.0
Other—net	–322.0	0.0	0.0	0.0	0.0
Pretax income	2,314.0	3,157.0	3,387.0	2,061.0	2,117.0
Income taxes	1,014.0	1,307.0	1,421.0	847.0	737.0
Income after taxes	1,300.0	1,850.0	1,966.0	1,214.0	1,380.0
Net income (excluding E&D)	1,300.0	1,850.0	1,966.0	1,214.0	1,380.0

(continued)

EXHIBIT 11 Financial Data for Selected Companies *(continued)*

Discontinued operations	0.0	0.0	0.0	0.0	0.0
Accounting change	0.0	0.0	0.0	0.0	0.0
Net income (including E&D)	1,300.0	1,850.0	1,966.0	1,214.0	1,380.0
Primary EPS excluding E&D	0.63	0.91	0.97	0.67	0.87
Primary EPS including E&D	0.63	0.91	0.97	0.67	0.87
Dividends per common share	0.00	0.20	0.17	0.14	0.12
Shares to calculate primary EPS (millions of shares)	2,056.0	2,037.0	2,021.0	1,827.0	1,590.0

Source: OneSource Information Services.

Yahoo! Inc.
Annual Income Statement
(Millions of U.S. Dollars)

			31 December		
	1999	*1998*	*1997*	*1996*	*1995*
Sales—core business	588.6	245.1	84.1	21.5	1.4
Total sales	588.6	245.1	84.1	21.5	1.4
Cost of goods sold	101.8	52.2	19.9	4.7	0.2
SG&A	251.2	148.9	71.3	22.0	1.8
Depreciation	13.8	2.6	0.0	0.0	0.0
Research & development	67.5	33.9	16.7	5.7	0.3
Unusual income/expense	87.5	21.2	25.1	0.0	0.0
Total expenses	521.9	258.8	133.0	32.4	2.3
Interest net, nonoperating	37.7	18.8	4.8	4.0	0.1
Other—net	–2.5	0.1	0.7	0.5	0.0
Pretax income	101.9	5.2	–43.4	–6.4	–0.8
Income taxes	40.8	17.8	0.0	0.0	0.0
Income after taxes	61.1	–12.7	–43.4	–6.4	–0.8
Preferred dividends	0.0	–1.4	0.0	0.0	0.0
Net income (including E&D)	61.1	–14.1	–43.4	–6.4	–0.8
Primary EPS excluding E&D	0.12	–0.03	–0.11	–0.02	–0.00
Primary EPS including E&D	0.12	–0.03	–0.11	–0.02	–0.00
Dividends per common share	0.00	0.00	0.00	0.00	0.00
Shares to calculate primary EPS (millions of shares)	515.9	440.0	391.5	314.6	218.5

Source: OneSource Information Services.

STANFORD
GRADUATE SCHOOL OF BUSINESS

WEBVAN: THE NEW AND IMPROVED MILKMAN

"He who does not mind his belly will hardly mind anything else." —*Samuel Johnson (1709–1784)*

While food is a basic necessity, consumer-friendly, ubiquitous food delivery on a large scale is a difficult problem. No supermarket company has successfully built a truly nationwide grocery operation in the United States, and consumers find grocery shopping almost as unpleasant and time-consuming as cleaning. Complex logistics, physical constraints, and regional differences have foiled attempts to solve the problem.

Technological advances have given life to online grocers. A group of San Francisco entrepreneurs founded the first online grocer, Grocery Express, in 1981. It offered home delivery of grocery products via Prodigy[1] (in addition to phone and fax orders) to shoppers in the Bay Area. At its peak, Grocery Express had 5,000 customers, but logistical challenges and the inability to build to scale eventually doomed it. Peapod, the leading online grocer for most of the 1990s, followed a different business model that was hailed by the *Harvard Business Review* as "a testament to the power of learning relationships."[2] After years of mounting losses, however, Peapod was rescued from bankruptcy by bricks-and-mortar supermarket chain Royal Ahold in March 2000. Another highly touted online grocery service, Streamline, also lost money until it shut down in November 2000. Priceline's WebHouse Club, which promised to extend Priceline's "name your own price" model to groceries, shut down in October 2000.

Webvan, founded by Louis Borders (founder of bookstore chain Borders Group), set out to build a nationwide infrastructure to solve the logistics problem. Webvan put together a sophisticated distribution and information system, optimized from the ground up for e-commerce. After launching its San Francisco Bay Area service in June 1999, Webvan went public on November 5, 1999 at an offering price of $15 a share. The stock has since declined to less than a dollar per share.

By Haim Mendelson, Graduate School of Business, Stanford University, Stanford, CA 94305-5015. Revised March 2001. Please send comments to haim@stanford.edu.

[1] Prodigy was an online service that allowed users to connect to information sources and services through a simple user interface.

[2] "Do You Want to Keep Your Customers Forever? How Peapod Is Customizing the Virtual Supermarket," *Harvard Business Review*, March/April 1995.

Business Week listed online groceries as one of the "great flawed business models" of the year 2000, calling it "The Toilet Paper Model...in which items such as toilet paper and Häagen-Dazs were purchased over the Internet, then packaged and delivered to the front doors of millions of Americans. No middlemen, no problem—right? But there was a problem. With grocery margins as thin as 2% and things like packaging and delivery so expensive, it could cost the companies as much as $40 an order, and they struggled to make money. What's more, they realized that the warehouses they set out to deal with weren't technologically up to snuff, so they built their own. They also didn't factor in tomato-squeezers—those persnickety customers who insisted on actually seeing and touching produce and other perishables."[3]

Is the online grocery business model doomed? Can Webvan deliver?

INDUSTRY OVERVIEW

The U.S. market for food retailing was $484 billion in 2000.[4] Of about equal size were complementary markets including home meal replacements, gourmet and specialty foods, pharmacies, health and beauty aids, books, music, and video. On average, U.S. households visited a supermarket 2.3 times a week and spent about $87. In 1999, supermarkets accounted for 77% of grocery sales and numbered about a quarter of all grocery stores.[5] The industry was highly concentrated (Exhibit 1 shows the top ten food retailers in the United States in 1999).

In the early twentieth century, there were no supermarkets, shopping was highly personalized, and people bought groceries from multiple retailers which delivered food to their customers. Following the Great Depression, food retailing was dominated by supermarkets, which aggregated different food products and provided efficient self-service that largely replaced home delivery.[6] Supermarkets served as "physical portals," providing convenient one-stop shopping at lower prices. The supermarkets implemented an efficient supply chain, with vendors or distributors supplying products to their distribution centers in bulk. Local stores would replenish their inventories in large quantities—in multiple cases or pallets that vendors delivered to the back of the store and then placed in the appropriate aisle. The resulting economies of scale and scope enabled supermarkets to charge lower prices, and competition drove net profit margins to about 1%. (Exhibit 2 shows the cost breakdown of a traditional supermarket.)

In the 1990s, some segments of grocery shoppers valued home delivery. An Andersen Consulting study[7] identified six categories of grocery shoppers:

- *Shopping avoiders*, who dislike shopping;
- *Necessity users*, who have limited ability to go to stores;
- *New technologists*, who are young and like technology;

[3] "Dot-Com Business Models from Mars," *Business Week*, September 4, 2000.

[4] Source: The Food Institute.

[5] Sources: Food Marketing Institute; Hoover's.

[6] *Encyclopedia of American Industries*, Gale Research, New York, 1994.

[7] *Early Learnings from the Consumer Direct Cooperative*, Andersen Consulting, January 1998.

- *Time starved*, who are price insensitive and need more free time;
- *Responsibles*, who have free time and gain self-worth from shopping; and
- *Traditional shoppers*, who are older, dislike technology, and enjoy shopping.

The Andersen study found that every group except traditional shoppers was willing to buy groceries online, and most of the groups showed strong interest. It predicted that 15–20 million U.S. households would buy groceries online by 2007 (compared to about 250,000 in 1999).

According to the Andersen study, the online grocery opportunity was driven by the desire of consumers, particularly dual-income families, to save time. Half of the people with full-time jobs shopped on weekends. After factoring the time required to drive, park, and unload packages, at least one member of a household spent about 3 hours a week grocery shopping—an unpleasant chore by most accounts. No wonder over 60% of consumers disliked grocery shopping, and many were open to online grocery shopping and home delivery.[8] Webvan sought to capitalize on this opportunity, hoping to become the milkman of the twenty-first century.

WEBVAN

Webvan launched operations in the San Francisco Bay Area in June 1999. It planned to construct up to 26 fulfillment centers around the country within the following two years at a total cost of about a billion dollars. In May 2000, Webvan launched its Atlanta operations and it expanded to Chicago in August 2000. In June 2000, a major competitor, HomeGrocer.com, agreed to merge with Webvan. By the end of 2000, Webvan served 10 markets.

Webvan designed state-of-the-art automated warehouses that could serve an entire metropolitan market within a radius of 50 miles. Each distribution center (DC) had an area of 336,000 square feet and could handle 8,000 orders per day and 50,000 stock keeping units[9] (SKUs) at full capacity. Webvan expected each DC to bring in $300 million in revenue by 2003. (For a review of Webvan's financial and operating data, see Exhibits 3a and b).

In the fourth quarter of 2000, Webvan was operating at a run rate of 2,250 orders per day in Los Angeles and 2,160 in San Francisco. Besides groceries, Webvan delivered books, CDs, health and beauty supplies, small electronics, flowers, office supplies, and some clothes, and it offered film development services. In the fourth quarter of 2000, 34% of Webvan customers in the San Francisco Bay Area added general merchandise products to their grocery orders, up from 26% in the third quarter of 2000. In January 2001, Webvan opened on its Web site a cobranded pet store with Petsmart.com.

Webvan created an automated process that was designed to manage all aspects of the online grocery business, from order taking to delivery. Webvan implemented an

[8] *ibid.*

[9] An SKU (stock keeping unit) is the identifier of a unique product.

integrated information technology (IT) infrastructure, with different areas of operation sharing data through a central database. Many tasks, such as delivery scheduling, route planning, purchasing, and billing were automated and integrated.

Shopping at Webvan[10]

Webvan's Webstore was a personalized, user-friendly Web site that let users navigate and purchase from a wide selection of items. Each DC had a custom Webstore based on a common platform. The Webstore had the "look and feel" of a traditional shopping experience, and it allowed shoppers to browse through different grocery departments, search directly to reach a desired product by name, or select items from personal shopping lists. Customers could enter a special category called "My Personal Market" containing only products they ordered before, as well as lists with the customer's most frequently purchased items sorted according to how often the customer purchased them. Once customers found an item they wanted, they could add it to the shopping cart or save it to a shopping list. Once customers completed their selections, they went to a "checkout" screen where they paid by credit card.

Customers scheduled deliveries by selecting a one-hour time window from a grid of available windows between 6 A.M. and 10 P.M. Webvan's systems ensured that the groceries a customer ordered would be available and that they could be delivered within the window selected by the customer (until December 2000, the time window was 30 minutes).[11] Customers could place orders 24 hours a day, 7 days a week, 1–7 days ahead of the delivery day. Delivery was free for orders over $75 and cost $4.95 for orders under $75 (until November 2000, the minimum order size qualifying for free delivery was $50). Customers had to be at home to accept delivery of perishable or frozen items. Nonperishable items could be delivered when the customer was not at home.

Webvan offered customer service by e-mail and an online "chat" system that connected customers and customer service representatives, in addition to an FAQ page with answers to commonly asked questions. Webvan planned a 12-hour average response time to e-mail. Customers could contact customer service representatives via a toll-free telephone number.

A centralized database recorded all customer data. As it collected more customer data, Webvan could further customize the shopping experience by periodically targeting discounts and promotions to individual customers.

Distribution Centers

Webvan's DCs were highly automated hubs for receiving, storing, and distributing products. They used proprietary systems to handle volumes equivalent to 18 supermarkets at lower labor and real estate costs. The Webvan DC was a mammoth 336,000 square

[10] The information in this and the subsequent four sections are based primarily on Webvan's public filings.

[11] Before they merged, Webvan had a 30-minute time window, and HomeGrocer had a 90-minute time window. Following the merger, the combined company moved to a uniform 60-minute time window.

foot facility, featuring 4½ miles of conveyor belts, with a $3 million dollar investment in electrical wiring and temperature-sensitive rooms.

Webvan's systems were fully integrated from order to fulfillment. Webvan invested more than 50 person-years in developing proprietary inventory management, warehouse management, route management, and materials handling systems. The systems tracked inventory and freshness levels and automatically initiated replenishment and other transactions. An electronic data interchange (EDI) network, which connected Webvan with its key vendors, was used to place orders. As of June 2000, Webvan purchased through 50 distributors and directly from 300 vendors.

The system assigned each order to one or more boxes, or "totes," that traveled over conveyor belts to pickers, who received electronic delivery instructions. The system issued instructions to the various mechanized areas in the DC to ensure fulfillment of the order. Once workers assembled the products constituting an order into totes and moved them to a loading area, they were packed onto refrigerated trucks that took them from the DC to a delivery station.

To store goods at their optimal temperatures, the computer-controlled facility had separate ambient temperature, refrigerated, and frozen areas. Webvan had special temperature-controlled rooms for meat, seafood, produce, and deli items, which were fulfilled manually. The DC also had a food preparation area, where chefs prepared ready-to-eat dishes. Orders were transmitted to terminals in these rooms, and employees could prepare the order as soon as they received it.

To fulfill dry goods orders, the totes and the products were transported to a picking station where the pickers were located. Thus, rather than have the picker move around the DC, the system automatically moved both the tote and the products within the picker's reach. The goods traveled to the picking station on proprietary carousels, similar to those used by dry cleaners. At the end of each carousel was a picking station with a picker, located next to the conveyor belt. The Webvan system rotated the carousel to bring the desired products in front of the picker. Then, the system pinpointed the products using a laser beam, with an electronic panel located next to the carousel showing the quantity to be picked. The picker took the items from the carousel, and another electronic panel on the conveyor belt indicated which totes would receive which individual products.

Thanks to its automated systems, Webvan anticipated employing one-third the number of employees required to operate the equivalent of 18 traditional supermarkets. Webvan could also manage many SKUs: as of June 2000, Webvan sold about 35,000 SKUs, up from 15,000 when it began operations. This selection exceeded most grocery stores, offering 350 types of cheese, 700 different wine labels, and over 300 varieties of fresh fruits and vegetables. The DC could manage up to 50,000 SKUs.

Delivery Operations

Webvan used a hub-and-spoke delivery model, similar to those used by FedEx and UPS. Air-conditioned trucks transported multiple orders from the DC (the "hub") to the Webvan station (the "spoke") closest to a customer's residence. The stations (about 9,000 square feet each) were located within 50 miles of the DC and usually within 10 miles of the customer's residence. Webvan typically leased 12–15 stations for each market it served. From the local station, smaller air-conditioned vans with the "Webvan.com" logo transported the deliveries to customers. Webvan's hub-and-spoke approach helped ensure timely delivery and efficiency. In 1999, 92% of deliveries were on time. The system minimized manual handling: Webvan manually handled produce and other grocery products an average of 8 times compared to an average of 14 times for a traditional supermarket.

To ensure quality, delivery personnel were Webvan employees trained to be friendly, helpful, and professional and to refuse tips. They used a wireless mobile device, similar to a Palm Pilot, to communicate with Webvan's systems. Delivery personnel had the authority to credit customer accounts and accept unwanted goods, updating Webvan's systems through their wireless devices. In 2000, Webvan expanded its service to deliver prepared foods, beverages, and cleaning and office supplies to businesses under its Webvan@work program. In the fourth quarter of 2000, this program accounted for 15% of Webvan's San Francisco Bay Area sales, with an average order size of $130.

Inventory

Supermarkets must carry inventories both at warehouses and in their retail outlets. The regional Webvan warehouse could handle the volume of 18 supermarkets while carrying the inventory of around 5—with a larger product selection. Webvan averaged 18.1 inventory turns for the year 2000.

Technology

Technology development and support were central to Webvan's operation. Webvan's senior vice president of platforms reported to the CEO and was responsible for business processes, technology development, technology deployment, and technology operations. Webvan implemented a centralized IT architecture, with the same platform serving the different markets, while allowing for market-specific features. Webvan outsourced most of its network operation functions, allowing its technologists to focus on core activities. Rather than maintain its own hardware, Webvan hosted its Web and database servers at AboveNet Communications.

COMPETITION

The online grocery market attracted players with different business models. The main ones are described below.

Peapod

Founded in 1989 in Evanston, Illinois, Peapod was the first major online grocer. It was a "virtual supermarket" that did not own warehouses. Instead, it established partnerships with leading supermarket chains in major metropolitan areas such as Jewel-Osco in Chicago and Safeway in Northern California. After customers placed orders using the company's software, Peapod's "personal shoppers" walked through the aisles of local grocery stores, hand-picked the requested items, often paid for them at the checkout, and delivered them to customers. This strategy allowed Peapod to take advantage of the existing supermarket infrastructure and quickly move into new markets, increasing sales volume with a small capital investment.

Under this model, Peapod had to forego its own margins, so that it could pay the supermarket margins and stay competitive. Peapod discovered the hard way that it needed a better operating model. After years of mounting losses (see Exhibit 4), Peapod decided in 1998 to build its own warehouses. As of August 2000, the company provided home deliveries in nine metropolitan markets to about 135,000 customers.

Peapod accepted orders 24 hours a day. It delivered seven days a week, from morning to evening, and customers could choose delivery times from time slots that were allocated on a first come, first served basis. A customer had to order at least one day before the desired delivery date and at most two weeks in advance. Peapod delivered the groceries in temperature-controlled trucks to the customer's door. Tipping was optional. Delivery fees varied by region and by customer type (residential or commercial).

Peapod operated at a loss since its inception (see Exhibit 5). In March 2000, its CEO resigned for health reasons, and the company was running out of cash. A Dutch-based grocer, Royal Ahold, then agreed to invest $73 million for a 51% share of the company. Although Peapod remained a stand-alone company, it was able to leverage Ahold's supermarket management expertise.

Streamline

Streamline, Inc., founded in 1993 in Westwood, Mass., tested the viability of home delivery until 1995. In October 1996 it opened its first consumer resource center (CRC), a 56,000 square-foot warehouse with 10,000 SKUs, and provided regular home deliveries of groceries and other goods and services in the Boston suburbs, learning along the way. As its founder and CEO Tim DeMello put it: "You have to get your business model absolutely perfect before you do a full-scale launch into the market, because if you succeed on the Web, you succeed big. And you can't change a tire on a car that's moving at 80 miles per hour. The way you grow a company is to make it work for one customer. Then you make it work for 10 customers. Then for 100, and then for 1,000. Today we understand our customers. We understand their needs. Now we're ready for a national rollout."[12]

Streamline filled customer orders out of its own warehouse, purchasing groceries direct from manufacturers and importers. It stored goods in a CRC that had three temperature areas—frozen, refrigerated, and ambient—and was optimized for picking and packing. Most of Streamline's CRCs used shoppers to fill orders by hand-picking each item. Wrist computers instructed them where to go and what to pick. When the picked product was placed in a tote, a scanner attached to the shopper's finger compared its barcode to the order to reduce errors. Between 7 A.M. and 9 A.M. each morning, orders were consolidated and loaded onto refrigerated trucks. Streamline took orders through-

[12] "Streamline Delivers the Goods," *FastCompany*, August 1998.

out the week, and customers could order until 11:00 P.M. the night before the assigned delivery day. A delivery truck averaged 6–7 stops an hour.

When customers signed up for Streamline's service, a start-up team visited them at home and set up the 30" × 30" × 65" Streamline Box, which consisted of a full-size refrigerator and special shelves for dry cleaning. The box was usually placed in the customer's garage, and the team installed a keypad access system to ensure security. Streamline assigned customers a day of the week for delivery and always made deliveries on the assigned day. Customers did not need to be home to receive the order. The driver entered the password on the numeric keypad; went into the customer's garage; picked up packages, clothes to be cleaned, and returns from the previous week's shopping; and left the delivery in the customer's Streamline Box.

Streamline also offered other convenience services like dry cleaning, UPS package pickup, video rentals, film processing, and shoe repairs. It also sold specialty products including seafood and meats, deli products, freshly baked goods, prepared meals, and flowers.

Streamline charged a flat monthly fee of $30, plus the cost of groceries and services. There was no setup charge, no charge for the Streamline Box and keypad access system, no minimum order, and no tipping. Specials, promotions, and new products were regularly featured online.

By May 2000, Streamline had a presence in four metropolitan markets: Boston, Chicago, Washington, D.C., and northern New Jersey. In each market, the company opened up a CRC that could serve within a 15–20 mile radius. However, Streamline ran out of cash and had to shut down in November 2000. Exhibit 6 summarizes its financial and operational data up to its demise.

HomeGrocer.com

HomeGrocer.com started in Seattle, expanded in 1999 to three more markets, and was planning rollouts in 24 additional markets. In each market, HomeGrocer built its own warehouse stocking 15,000 items. These included fresh produce, dairy, meat, seafood, packaged goods, specialty foods, gourmet meals, and flowers. HomeGrocer's business model was similar to that of Webvan, but with less automation.

Like Webvan, HomeGrocer stocked its own warehouses, managed by an integrated system that linked its front-end Web site to the DCs, and delivered directly to customers' homes. It spent $100 million on trucks that were equipped with three temperature zones (ambient, refrigerated, and frozen) to accommodate different food items. It hired its own drivers, who brought the groceries into the customer's kitchen within a 90-minute delivery window that the customer had specified.

Orders of more than $75 were delivered free, and customers placing their first order received a free sample bag of fruits and vegetables that was designed to demonstrate the high quality of HomeGrocer's produce. Produce accounted for 15%–17% of HomeGrocer's 1999 sales.

In May 1999, Seattle-based Amazon.com invested $42.5 million in HomeGrocer for a 35% stake in the company. Jeff Bezos, CEO of Amazon, said that HomeGrocer had "a fanatical eye for customer experience. Their shoppers pick out better produce than I could for myself. The delivery people refuse to be tipped. The company really has an unusual attention to detail."[13] In June 2000, Webvan merged with HomeGrocer.com in a stock-for-stock transaction valued at approximately $550 million.

NetGrocer.com

Founded in 1995, privately held NetGrocer was the only online supermarket offering home delivery to customers anywhere in the contiguous United States Shoppers could buy over 5,000 nonperishable groceries, drugs, and general merchandise online. NetGrocer shipped merchandise from a central 135,000 square-foot warehouse in North Brunswick, N.J. by FedEx. It charged for delivery based on the dollar amount of the order. For example, the delivery charge was $5.99 for orders under $60 and $6.99 for orders between $60 and $100. Same-day delivery and perishable items were not available. Netgrocer outsourced its warehousing, picking, and packing operations. It priced its products at or below traditional supermarket prices, resulting in losses.

WebHouse Club

WebHouse Club was an enterprise of Walker Digital, the think tank of Priceline's founder Jay Walker. It allowed Club members to search out highly discounted grocery items (up to 50% discount), telling customers in New York, New Jersey, and Connecticut where to buy their groceries for less. Members of the WebHouse Club could shop online for the lowest prices on items from 140 grocery categories and brands of their choice. They specified the grocery items that they were seeking, the price they were willing to pay, and the top two brands that they preferred for each item. As on Priceline.com, they then entered their credit card number and authorized the WebHouse Club to purchase the items at the prices they had specified. The WebHouse Club determined whether the items were available at the specified price and created a prepaid grocery list that members would then print out and take to the participating grocery store along with their WebHouse Club Card. The WebHouse Club did not deliver groceries. Instead, it sought to reduce the consumer's grocery bill while leveraging the physical infrastructure of the participating supermarkets.

Membership in the WebHouse Club was free to consumers. The discounts were to be financed by the participating supermarkets and manufacturers, but initial financing came from the WebHouse Club itself. The Club had more than 7,000 participating supermarkets, and it distributed over one million cards. It spent over a million dollars a day and ran out of cash by October, 2000, when it closed because it could not raise needed capital.

[13] HomeGrocer.com Press Release, 5/18/99.

EXHIBIT 1 Top 10 U.S. Food Retailers, 1999

Company	*U.S. Headquarters*	*U.S. Sales ($M)*	*U.S. Stores*
1. The Kroger Co.	Cincinnati, Ohio	$45,481	3,062
2. Albertson's, Inc.	Boise, Idaho	36,772	1,647
3. Safeway, Inc.	Pleasanton, California	28,860	1,493
4. Ahold USA, Inc.	Atlanta, Georgia	21,300	1,033
5. Costco Companies, Inc.	Issaquah, Washington	17,572	302
6. Wal-Mart Supercenters	Bentonville, Arkansas	12,800	564
7. Winn-Dixie Stores, Inc.	Jacksonville, Florida	13,617	1,180
8. Publix Super Markets, Inc.	Lakeland, Florida	12,100	586
9. Delhaize America	Salisbury, North Carolina	10,879	1,276
10. Great Atlantic & Pacific Tea Co.	Montvale, New Jersey	10,179	796

Source: Compiled from the Food Marketing Institute.

EXHIBIT 2 Cost Breakdown and Operating Metrics at Traditional Supermarket (1999)

Sales	100.0%
Cost of goods sold	70.5
Gross margin	29.5
Breakout of gross margin:	
Store	21.5
Warehouse/depot	2.5
Delivery	1.0
Marketing	1.5
Management overhead	0.9
Operating profit	2.1
Depreciation, taxes	1.1
Net profit	1.0
Average store size	44,843 sq. ft.
Weekly sales	$334,479
Average transaction size	$23
Inventory turns	16

Source: Author interviews, Food Marketing Institute.

EXHIBIT 3a Webvan Quarterly Income Statement and Operating Data, Q1 1999–Q2 2000 ($ in thousands)

	Q1 99	*Q2 99*	*Q3 99*	*Q4 99*	*Q1 00*	*Q2 00*
Total sales	$12	$383	$3,841	$9,069	$16,269	$28,300
Sequential growth %	0%	3092%	903%	136%	79%	74%
Cost of goods sold	$9	$410	$3,491	$7,379	$12,138	$20,307
Gross profit	$3	($27)	$350	$1,690	$4,131	$7,993
Gross margin	25%	–7%	9%	19%	25%	28%
Operating expenses						
Sales & marketing	$432	$1,907	$4,330	$5,077	$8,359	$9,907
Development & engineering	$3,260	$3,048	$4,330	$4,599	$5,523	$5,465
General & administrative	$6,733	$16,224	$49,083	$20,366	$38,993	$57,890
Amortization of deferred compensation	$1,767	$2,186	$9,590	$22,977	$17,720	$16,774
Total operating expenses	$12,192	$23,365	$67,333	$53,019	$70,595	$90,036
Interest income (expense)	$499	($52)	$2,216	$6,661	$8,649	$7,678
Pretax income (loss)	($11,690)	($23,444)	($64,767)	($44,668)	($57,815)	($74,365)
Income taxes	$0	$0	$0	$0	$0	$0
Other non-cash charges	$169	$3,868	$27,088	$491	$0	$0
Net income reported (incl. deferred comp.)	($11,859)	($27,312)	($91,855)	($45,159)	($57,815)	($74,365)

Operating data	*Q1 99*	*Q2 99*	*Q3 99*	*Q4 99*	*Q1 00*	*Q2 00*
Distribution centers			Oakland	Oakland	Oakland	Oakland, Atlanta
Number of new customers (000s)			22	25	40	73
Total number of customers (000s)			22	47	87	160
Orders per quarter (000s)			52.96	111.54	180.11	310.99
Repeat business percentage*			65%	75%	78%	76%
Customer acquisition cost			$197	$203	$209	$136
Inventory turns			N/A**	20.0	25.0	26.1
DC operating expense	$3,200	$6,800	$10,600	$11,300	$20,600	$34,600

* The repeat business percentage is the ratio of repeat orders to total orders, presented in percentage.

** Webvan's annual inventory turnover rate for 1999 was 4.9.

EXHIBIT 3b Webvan Pro-Forma Quarterly Income Statement and Operating Data, 2000 (Consolidated with HomeGrocer, $ in thousands)

	Q1 00	*Q2 00*	*Q3 00*	*Q4 00*
Gross sales	$38,351	$87,394	$59,470	
Discounts and allowances	($1,505)	($5,143)	($3,100)	
Net sales	$36,846	$82,251	$56,370	$84,191
Cost of goods sold	$29,655	$61,026	$42,619	$61,283
Gross profit	$7,191	$21,225	$13,751	$22,908
Gross margin	19.5%	25.8%	24.4%	27.2%
Operating expenses				
Sales & marketing	$12,741	$23,993	$23,178	$19,225
Development & engineering	$7,403	$9,329	$7,215	$6,352
General & administrative	$73,604	$114,825	$101,728	$110,582
Total operating expenses	$93,748	$148,147	$132,121	$136,159
Interest income (expense)	$9,651	$6,688	$11,048	$4,134
Proforma net (loss)	($76,906)	($120,234)	($107,322)	($109,117)
Operating data	*Q1 00*	*Q2 00*	*Q3 00*	*Q4 00*
Distribution centers			8	9
New customers (000s)	133	158	186	116
Total customers (000s)	180	338	524	640
Est. cust. acquisition cost	$96	$152	$125	$166
Repeat order ratio			75%	86%
Average order size			$103	$112
Of that, general merchandise				$7

Source: Webvan financial reports; Q3 2000 and Q4 2000 analyst calls.

EXHIBIT 4 Additional Webvan Operational Data and Analysis Assumptions

Distribution Center and Stations:

DC size: 336,000 sq. ft.
Annual DC rent per sq. ft: $4.00/sq. ft.
Annual DC equipment depreciation: $7 million
Stations ("spokes") per DC ("hub"): 12
Station size: 9,000 sq. ft. per station
Annual station rent per sq. ft: $5.00/sq. ft.
Annual station equipment depreciation: $30,000 per station
Annual maintenance: $900,000
Annual utilities: $200,000
Annual cost for DC salaried employees: $3.6 million

*Additional Assumptions:**

Picker hourly wage (includes taxes and benefits): $17.50
Driver hourly wage (includes taxes and benefits): $22.00
Perishable items/order: 15
Grocery items/order: 23
Perishable item picks/min: 1.2
Grocery item picks/min: 4.0
Delivery hours/day: 16
Delivery days/week: 7
Annual cost/van (excl. drivers): $35,650 per van
Annual trucking costs (incl. drivers): $105,000 per truck
Number of trucks: 16 (current estimate), 25 (at full capacity)
Deliveries/hr: 3 (current), 4 (target)
Credit card charges: 1.5% of sales

*Sources: DLJ, Bear Stearns, Webvan Web site.

EXHIBIT 5 Peapod Income Statement and Operating Data, 1993–2000

	1993	*1994*	*1995*	*1996*	*1997*	*1998*	*1999*	*Q1 00*	*Q2 00*	*Q3 00*
Total sales	$3,705	$8,346	$15,943	$27,642	$56,943	$69,265	$73,134	$24,914	$22,732	$21,794
Cost of goods sold	(2,893)	(6,745)	(12,731)	(20,485)	(40,823)	(53,903)	(55,585)	19,216	17,574	17,293
Gross profit	812	1,601	3,212	7,157	16,120	15,362	17,549	5,698	5,158	4,501
Operating expenses:										
Fulfillment operations				(6,889)	(14,469)	(16,715)	(23,580)	(8,931)	(7,796)	(7,919)
General and administrative				(3,785)	(5,935)	(8,029)	(9,788)	(2,039)	(2,150)	(2,768)
Marketing and advertising				(4,739)	(7,726)	(7,545)	(7,168)	(1,340)	(1,087)	(1,428)
System development and maintenance				(1,124)	(1,696)	(3,386)	(3,543)	(1,189)	(1,469)	(1,490)
Depreciation and amortization				(651)	(1,234)	(3,264)	(2,222)	(664)	(737)	(942)
Pre-opening costs						(481)	(898)			
Nonrecurring expenses								(4,118)	(1,490)	
Total operating expenses	(2,463)	(5,918)	(9,796)	(17,178)	(31,060)	(39,420)	(47,199)	(18,281)	(14,729)	(14,548)
Operating loss	(1,651)	(4,317)	(6,584)	(10,031)	(14,940)	(24,058)	(29,650)	(12,583)	(9,571)	(10,047)
Other income (expense):										
Investment income				537	2,044	2,683	1,384	(103)	16	776
Interest expense				(72)	(83)	(190)	(187)	(56)	(218)	(525)
Net loss	(1,676)	(4,347)	(6,592)	(9,566)	(12,979)	(21,565)	(28,453)	(12,742)	(10,389)	(9,796)

Operating data	*1993*	*1994*	*1995*	*1996*	*1997*	*1998*	*1999*	*Q1 00*	*Q2 00*	*Q3 00*
Number of customers	3,000	7,900	12,500	33,300	71,500	94,800	111,900	129,800	135,700	119,300*
Number of orders	28,600	70,300	124,100	201,100	396,600	494,700	571,300	205,500	183,700	179,300
Average order size		$96	$103	$109	$110	$115	$123	$111	$115	N/A
Households in service area	1,083,000	1,917,000	2,204,200	3,581,000	6,488,000	6,629,000	8,476,100	8,586,000	8,731,000	8,731,000

* Customer counts do not include customers in three Texas markets and Columbus, Ohio, which ceased operations in September 2000.

EXHIBIT 6 Streamline Quarterly Income Statements and Operating Data, 1998–2000 ($ in thousands)

	Q1 98	*Q2 98*	*Q3 98*	*Q4 98*	*Q1 99*	*Q2 99*	*Q3 99*	*Q4 99*	*Q1 00*	*Q2 00**
Total sales	$1,202	$1,654	$1,672	$2,418	$2,987	$3,631	$3,624	5,138	8,461	8,859
Net product & services revenues	1,072	1,401	1,409	2,144	2,568	3,119	3,007	4,468	7,906	8,091
Subscription fees	77	94	105	116	187	234	272	325	276	408
Advertising fees	53	159	158	158	232	278	345	345	279	360
Gross profit	306	448	508	692	966	1,179	1,081	1,531	2,552	2,869
Gross margin	25%	27%	30%	29%	32%	32%	30%	30%	30%	32%
Operating expenses										
Cost of goods sold	896	1,206	1,164	1,726	2,021	2,452	2,543	3,607	5,909	5,990
Fulfillment center operations	946	1,009	946	1,112	1,385	1,852	2,741	3,058	4,720	5,714
Sales & marketing	285	328	376	490	615	843	1,137	2,391	3,402	3,535
Tech. systems & development	636	664	637	1,065	829	975	1,004	958	1,579	2,031
General & administrative	963	951	884	1,099	1,506	1,553	2,007	2,556	4,611	2,980
Total operating expenses	3,726	4,158	4,007	5,492	6,356	7,675	9,432	12,570	20,221	20,250
Loss from operations	(2,524)	(2,504)	(2,335)	(3,074)	(3,369)	(4,044)	(5,808)	(7,432)	(11,760)	(11,391)
Other income	(40)	(209)	(205)	124	107	(5)	480	574	38	(57)
Net loss	(2,493)	(2,646)	(3,284)	(2,950)	(3,262)	(4,049)	(5,328)	(6,858)	(11,722)	(11,448)
Operating data	*Q1 98*	*Q2 98*	*Q3 98*	*Q4 98*	*Q1 99*	*Q2 99*	*Q3 99*	*Q4 99*	*Q1 00*	*Q2 00*
Number of DCs	1	1	1	1	1	1	1	2	3	4
Number of customers				2,000	2,600	3,000	3,700	4,500	11,000	11,500
Number of orders (000s)			15	20	23	29	32	44	73	74
Average order size			$96.00	$109.00	$112.00	$108.00	$93.00	$102.00	$108.00	$110.00

*Last quarter reported before Streamline was shut down in November 2000.

ONLINE AUCTIONS

Prior to the Internet, auctions were the domain of specialists. Consumers rarely participated in them, and when they did it was usually for fun or charity. Auctions were more common in business settings, although even then their role was confined. The advent of online auctions changed all that. By the end of 2000, just five years after the initial launch of eBay, the number of Web sites that offered auctions had skyrocketed. By some estimates over a trillion dollars worth of transactions would be exchanged in online auctions that year.

Consumers had taken to the online auction format with a zeal that astonished observers. eBay alone boasted 19 million registered users at the end of 2000. Many traded casually, as much for fun as profit, but for many others trading online had become an occupation as they turned online trading into a small business. Along the way, online auctions transformed the market for consumer durables as one person's discarded item, languishing in an attic or garage, became another's cherished possession.

Although businesses took longer than consumers to embrace online auctions, they took root there as well and their eventual impact was predicted to be even greater than consumer auctions. This growth represented both the substitution of Internet-mediated auctions for auctions that had been conducted another way and the increasing use of auctions to mediate exchange.

This case first describes various forms and purposes of auctions. It then surveys the remarkable development of consumer-to-consumer (C2C), business-to-consumer (B2C), and business-to-business (B2B) online auctions, and profiles companies that specialize in each of those market segments.

Professor Garth Saloner significantly updated and revised this case with the assistance of Geoffrey Adamson. The original case, Online Auctions in 1999, was prepared by Research Associates Katie Gray and Trae Neist under the supervision of Professor Garth Saloner and Professor A. Michael Spence as the basis for class discussion rather than to illustrate either effective or ineffective handling of an administrative situation. Margot Sutherland, Executive Director, Center for Electronic Business and Commerce, Stanford Graduate School of Business, managed the development of this case.

AUCTION HISTORY AND BACKGROUND

The burgeoning of electronic auctions made possible by the Internet did not indicate a revolutionary pricing model: auctions existed long before the Internet, computers, or even writing. Indeed auctions and bargaining, which both involved varying the price of a product or service to close a deal, were the earliest forms of trade. Fixed pricing, rather than variable pricing, was the newcomer, having arisen with mass merchandizing when department stores set fixed prices so that their clerks could not offer discounts to their friends and relatives. Historians have found evidence of auctions in the earliest human societies, and Mesopotamian traders had developed sophisticated auctions by 8000 B.C.[1]

By the time the Internet emerged, auctions were used in many settings. A key difference among these settings was how bidders valued the item being auctioned. The amount a bidder was willing to pay was often subjective. For example, different bidders were willing to pay different amounts for a fine bottle of wine that they intended to consume themselves (rather than to keep for later resale) or for a painting they would hang on their wall. This was the *private values* case. In other instances, however, the item for sale had an objective value—for example the right to drill for oil beneath a particular tract of land—and all bidders would share a *common value* (if they knew what it was). Of course, even in that case different bidders might be willing to pay different amounts because they had different information about the item and therefore different estimates of its common value.

The form of auctions also varied. One important distinction was whether the auction was *open* or *sealed bid.* In an open auction, bidders knew previous bidders' bids and could make their own bids in light of this information. The most familiar form of this was the *open outcry* or *English auction* in which bidders called out successively higher bids. In sealed bid auctions, each bidder submitted a single bid, and the winner was the one who bid the highest. In that setting bidders did not know what others were bidding and usually not even how many other bids would be tendered.

Bidding strategy varied depending on whether the values were common or private and whether the auction was open or sealed bid. For example, in an open auction with private values, an optimal strategy was simply to keep bidding up to one's private value. To stop bidding earlier could leave value on the table; to go higher would be to pay more than the item was worth to the bidder. When all bidders behaved in this way, the winning bidder would have to pay only the valuation of the second-highest bidder, which was the price at which the auction would end. Thus the winning bidder would pay less than his private valuation, gaining surplus from the auction. How much less depended on the number of bidders and how much their private values varied (the winning bidder was generally better off the fewer the bidders and the greater the variation in valuations).

In a sealed bid auction, if the item was sold to the highest bid, an individual who bid his true value would receive no surplus. Bidders would therefore try to estimate how much they would have to bid if they did in fact have the highest valuation in order

[1] Denise Schmandt-Besserat, "Oneness, Twoness, Threeness," *The Sciences* 27 (1987), Reprinted in F. Swetz (ed.) *From Five Fingers to Infinity*, Open Court, 1994.

to outbid the second-highest bidder. If they succeeded, the outcome would be the same as in an open auction. However, to avoid the complication of having to estimate what others were likely to bid, some sealed bid auctions specified that the item would be sold not for the highest bid (a so-called *first-price* auction), but that the item would be sold to the highest bidder for the amount that the second-highest bidder bid (a *second-price* auction). The second-price sealed bid auction was more commonly called a *Vickrey* auction after the economist William Vickrey who invented it. In a Vickrey auction bidders could bid their true valuation, because they would win only if the final bid were no higher than the amount they were willing to pay, and they would have to pay only what the second-highest bidder bid. In the private values case, a first-price open auction and second-price sealed bid auction were therefore equivalent.

Bidders' strategies were generally different in the common values case. In an open common values auction, if each bidder bid up to his own estimate of the common value, the one with the highest estimate would generally win. If the estimates were distributed around the true common value, the winner would likely pay too much and suffer the "winner's curse." To compensate for this effect, bidders would generally reduce the amount they were willing to pay.

The potential winner's curse also meant that open and sealed bid auctions were not equivalent in the common values case. If bidders did not know the valuations of rival bidders (as in a sealed bid auction), they would compensate to avoid a winner's curse. In contrast, any information a bidder learned about rivals' valuations would tend to make him or her less conservative. Thus, in common value situations, bids tended to be higher in open than sealed bid auctions because bidders could revise their estimates based on the number of other bidders and how much they bid. It was no surprise, therefore, that most online auctions, which contained some common values component, were open.

Auctions also sometimes included a minimum bid, a minimum bid increment, a reserve price (below which the seller would not sell the item), and a rule for ending the auction. In many auctions the reserve price was secret and exceeded the minimum bid at which the auction began. This sometimes resulted in the item not being sold. Nonetheless setting a reserve price could induce higher bids. Early empirical analysis of online auctions seemed to indicate that reserve price auctions did indeed garner higher prices for high priced items but that sellers often used a higher minimum bid and no reserve price for lower priced items.[2]

Sealed bid auctions typically ended at a predetermined date and time. Live open auctions typically ended when the auctioneer was satisfied that no further bids were forthcoming. Many online open auctions had a predetermined ending time. This raised difficulties because bidders had trouble getting new bids in when they were outbid in the closing minutes. Moreover, in online auctions higher bids were often received late in the auction as bidders tried to pick off low-priced items (a practice called "sniping"). To deter sniping, some auctions were automatically extended if a bid came in in the last few minutes. However, the fixed ending time enabled bidders to bid without revealing

[2] See Pat Bajari and Ali Hortacsu, "Winner's Curse, Reserve Prices and Endogenous Entry: Empirical Insights from eBay Auctions," Stanford Economics Department, mimeo, 2000.

their bids to many other bidders. If other bidders recognized the bidder as an expert, they might bid even more, driving up the price and disadvantaging the expert.

Some auctions used proxy bidding to ensure that bidders were not outbid even when they would have been willing to bid higher. In these auctions the bidder could enter the maximum amount she was willing to bid, and whenever she was outbid, the computer (or in an offline auction, her agent) automatically increased her bid by the minimum amount necessary to again make her the high bidder (as long as the bid did not exceed her stated maximum). In principle this meant that a bidder could state what she was willing to pay and not check the auction again. In practice, however, if some element of common values existed, a bidder would be informed by the bids of others and might be willing to bid more depending on how the auction unfolded.

Because early bids could affect how much later bidders were willing to bid, sellers sometimes had an incentive to bid in their own auctions under a different name (a practice called "shill" bidding). While the seller risked having to buy his own item and thereby squandering the opportunity to sell it and having to pay transactions fees, the potential to raise the price was sometimes worth the risk. Besides, the seller could always post the item for sale again, with better information about what price he could expect the item to fetch. This practice was harder in B2B settings because bidders typically had to go through a qualification process. It was easier in C2C settings because the Internet enabled sellers to hide behind multiple identities. The most significant deterrent to shill bidding on the Internet was the threat of being denied trading privileges in the future.

In C2C auctions the seller typically sold one item at a time. However, in B2C and B2B auctions most sellers had several of the same item to sell at the same time. For those cases *Dutch auctions* were used. Buyers bid on both quantity and price, and the bidders with the highest bid got the requested quantity of items at the lowest winning bid. Typically, multiple bidders won items in a Dutch auction.

The typical auction setting discussed so far involves a single seller and multiple buyers. In other cases a single buyer wished to induce competition among multiple potential sellers. This was a common situation for a firm looking for a supplier or contractor. In that case sellers bid the *lowest* price for which they were willing to provide the good or service. Auctions in which the roles of buyers and sellers were reversed in this way were termed *reverse auctions.*

CONSUMER-TO-CONSUMER AUCTIONS

In August 2000, in addition to eBay, more than 415 sites offered C2C auctions,[3] including all the major portal sites (Yahoo!, Excite, Lycos), other major e-commerce players (Amazon.com), and dozens of newly formed companies.[4] Both the replacement of offline activities and new transactions fueled the enormous growth in online auctions. Before the advent of online auctions, sellers used live auctions, classified advertising, garage sales, flea markets, consignment stores, and retail outlets (e.g., antique stores, comic

[3] AuctionWatch.com.

[4] According to AuctionRover.

book stores) to sell an item if it was of sufficient value. Companies that enabled buyer and seller to meet acted as brokers and made their money either through listing fees (e.g., classifieds) or transaction fees (e.g., consignment). Individuals could also broker their own transactions and pay for display space and/or advertising fees. If an item was not of sufficient value or no acceptable venue for matching buyer and seller existed, the seller simply could not sell the item.

The mechanics of online auctions were simple. To post an item for sale on a C2C site, the seller entered information such as the name of the item, a description, and the location of the seller. Most sellers also posted a picture of the item for sale. Once the item was entered, the seller typically chose the category in which he or she wanted to list the item (e.g., computers, Beanie Babies, etc.). Depending on the number of listings on the site, categories were either very general or further divided into subcategories to facilitate searches by potential buyers. Some sites allowed sellers to feature their item in highly trafficked areas of the site for an additional fee. Depending on the complexity of the back-end software used to run the auction site, sellers also had other options, such as the number of days they wanted to list their item, accepted payment and shipping methods, the quantity of items for sale, the minimum accepted bid, and the reserve price.

Buyers could, browse and make purchases on an auction site for free. On most sites, buyers could browse through all listings, search for particular items, or click through categories to find items that the site listed. Typically, buyers could view current high bids on items and sort available items by several criteria, including time remaining in the auction, high bid, and number of bids. Most sites required buyers to register before they could submit a bid. Once registered, the buyer could place a bid, contact the seller, and, on many sites, request updates when other buyers placed new bids on that item.

Once the auction closed, the site notified the highest bidder and the seller about the closing price on the auction by e-mail. On most C2C auction sites, the buyer and seller then had to complete the transaction. Typically, one party e-mailed the other to arrange payment and shipping. An escrow service could hold valuable items until payment was completed.

Three major types of sites comprised the C2C auction market: general interest, special interest, and auction portals. General interest sites included eBay, Yahoo! Auctions, Amazon.com Auctions, Excite Auctions, Auction Universe, Up4Sale, and dozens of others. Items sold on general interest sites spanned many categories, yet collectibles (Beanie Babies, coins, etc.) were dominant. Most auction sites fit into the general-interest category. At the end of 2000, eBay was the category killer in the C2C auction market. According to AuctionWatch.com, eBay had a 60% share of listings, Yahoo! had 28%, and Amazon.com had 6%.[5]

Special interest sites focused on auctions for niche markets, such as computers (CNET Auctions), comic books (ComicExchange.Net), show business memorabilia (Showbizmart.com), wine (winebid.com), cigars (cigarbid.com), stamps (Stampauction.com), or beanie babies (Beanie Nation). Most special interest sites had difficulty attracting a critical mass of buyers and sellers and typically ranked low on two important

[5] See Robert Hall, *Digital Dealing*, Stanford University, mimeo, 2000.

auction site metrics: number of items up for bid and percentage of items with bids (Exhibit 1). By the end of 2000, many of them had broadened their approaches (e.g., Beanie Nation had become Collecting Nation selling Pokemón cards, dolls, and other categories besides Beanie Babies). Those that remained specialized often had fewer listings of their specialized item than eBay had. For example on a representative day in December 2000, ComicExchange boasted around 2,500 listings, whereas eBay had more than 11,000 "comics" listings.

Auction portals such as Auction Watch, BiddersEdge, and AuctionRover were a potential threat to the leading general interest and specialized C2C auction sites. Auction portals sought to aggregate the listings from multiple individual sites, giving buyers access to the listings on many sites at once and potentially giving sellers a wider audience than a single site would give them. The auction portals were considered a particular threat to the leading sites because they benefited most from the liquidity they had managed to create on their own sites. However, by the end of 2000, the auction portals had not shaken eBay's market lead.

Sellers paid brokers for auction services in three main ways: listing fees, transaction fees, and fees for extra value-added options. Not all C2C sites charged all types of fees. The top three C2C sites' fees were structured as in Table 1.

TABLE 1 C2C Fees

Site	*Listing Fee*	*Transaction Fee*	*Extra Options*
eBay	$0.25–$2.00 Special: Real Estate: $50	5% of first $25 2.5% of $25–$1000 1.25% of >$1000 Special: Vehicles: $25 flat Real estate: None	Bold ($2.00) Featured in category ($19.95) Featured on home page ($99.95) Gift icon ($1.00) Gallery ($0.25) Featured gallery ($19.95) Highlight ($5.00)
Yahoo!	Free	Free	Featured (sellers bid—highest bid is featured at top of list)
Amazon.com	$0.10 Special: $39.99 fixed monthly "merchant" fee for up to 5,000 listings	5% of first $25 2.5% of $25–$1000 1.25% of >$1000	Bold ($2.00) Featured in category (from 5 cents/day)

Compiled from company Web sites, December 6, 2000.

C2C auction sites reported revenues from the following sources: sellers' fees, 70%; advertisements, 27%; product revenue, 23%; other, 10%; and buyer fees 3%.[6] Sellers' fees could be further broken down as follows: percentage of sale, 90%; slotting fees, 38%; per item flat rate, 19%; and add-on services, 19%.

COMPANY PROFILE: eBAY

eBay began in 1995 as AuctionWeb, a site that Pierre Omidyar launched to find an outlet for his girlfriend's Pez dispensers. In March 1996, the site, which had attracted 4,400 subscribers, began to charge a small listing and success fee. By January 1997, AuctionWeb had $2.5 million in monthly transactions and revenues of $165,000.

In September 1997, the site was reengineered and relaunched as eBay. The number of registered users it attracted astonished observers (Exhibit 2). Analysts attributed it to overall market growth, eBay's first-mover position, critical mass of buyers and sellers, strong community on the site, and high switching costs.[7] By the end of 2000, eBay was the most popular shopping site on the Web with 8 million items auctioned at any one time. eBay attracted 2.1 million unique visitors a day, and its users spent an average of 120 minutes a month on eBay, for a total of four million page views.

eBay's impressive growth enabled the company to raise significant funding in the public markets. In September 1998, eBay raised $63 million in an initial public offering. A secondary offering in April 1999 raised more than $1.1 billion. Remarkably for an e-commerce company, eBay reported profit within a year of founding and boasted margins in excess of 75% (Exhibit 3).

eBay provided a forum to buy and sell personal items in more than 4,500 categories. As subcategories grew, eBay would split them off into new ones. Buyers could search the entire database for items that might be arrayed across several categories. Both English and Dutch auction formats were available, and auctions could last 3, 5, 7, or 10 days. Most auction listings included a photograph of the item being sold as well as a description and payment and shipping terms. Buyers could view the bid history (showing the sequence of bidding, but not proxy bids). Buyers and sellers could communicate through e-mail during the auction and had to do so afterward to consummate the transaction. (eBay did not take possession of the good, but did offer escrow services.)

After an item was sold, buyers and sellers could leave "feedback" for one another consisting of a "positive," "neutral," or "negative" rating and a one-line summary, such as "Fast & friendly transaction. Highly recommended eBay user. AAA+++!!! Thanks!" The site listed both the feedback received and a summary rating (number of positive comments minus the number of negative comments) next to each trader's name (or the pseudonym used for trading) whenever he or she bid or sold an item. The site put different colored stars next to the names of traders who accumulated net ratings of various levels (e.g., a yellow star for a net rating of 10).

[6] The Forrester Report, "Consumers Catch Auction Fever," by Evie Black Dykema, March 1999.

[7] Switching costs included the time and effort involved in uploading information on items up for auction and building a reputation on a new site.

By the end of 2000, some traders had net ratings of more than 1,000, especially on the sell side of a transaction. eBay was subject to the 80/20 rule: 20% of the traders accounted for about 80% of the trades, in part because many businesses had been spawned using eBay as the trading platform. Some professionals did nothing but sell (and sometimes buy and sell) on eBay. To formalize this role, eBay established a PowerSellers program that designated sellers who sustained monthly sales of $2,000, $10,000, or $25,000 as Bronze, Silver, or Gold PowerSellers. They received such benefits as a distinguishing logo, e-mail support, customer phone support, or even a dedicated account manager.

Traders cherished their reputations as measured by their ratings and frequently reminded trading partners to enter feedback for them. Buyers were wary of sellers without an established reputation, and sellers often announced that they would not sell to bidders who had several "negative" comments. Some observers believed that the feedback mechanism was crucial to eBay's success and that it explained why buyers were willing to send cashier's checks in the mail to virtual strangers in the hope and belief that the product (of advertised quality) would be shipped in return. eBay itself put a lot of emphasis on the idea that the eBay traders formed a "community" based on trust and respect.

While access to the identity of the other party during and after the auction and to their respective reputations helped increase each party's comfort levels with the other, it also enabled sellers to circumvent the system in a reserve price auction when the item offered for auction did not sell. The seller could e-mail the highest bidder and offer to sell the product at that price (or a price that the buyer and seller negotiated). This was especially a problem for items with high reserve prices. Sellers who were planning to circumvent the transactions fees could set a high reserve to ensure a failed auction. To discourage reserve prices, eBay began to implement an additional fee to place a reserve on an auction (50 cents for a reserve less than $25, and $1.00 above that).

In April 1999, the purchase of Butterfield & Butterfield, a bricks-and-mortar auction house, enabled eBay to tap into a dealer network and authentication services and to move into higher ticket items. In June, the company launched local auction sites for several major U.S. cities to encourage sellers to list higher ticket items, such as automobiles, that were hard to transport and best sold locally.

In 1999 a new battleground emerged. Buyers found it inconvenient to send money orders or cashier's checks or to wait for personal checks to clear, and many would not send cash through the mail (especially for high-priced items). PayPal.com came to the rescue offering a service that enabled users to pay through an online service by crediting or debiting credit cards. PayPal took some of the risk out of the transaction by enabling consumers who used its service to purchase through eBay and failed to receive the item to receive up to $200 from PayPal (in addition to a maximum $200 from eBay's insurance policy through Lloyd's of London). The service was free to the buyer. The seller paid 25 cents plus 1.9% of the transaction amount. PayPal spread rapidly, in part because of an offer of $5 for signing up for the service and another $5 for any buyer that was referred to PayPal.

eBay responded in May 1999 by purchasing Billpoint for $170 million and offering a competitive service. Billpoint charged a flat fee of 35 cents for transactions of less than $15, and an additional 1.75% to 2.5% per transaction (for "merchant" and "standard" accounts respectively). Still, according to PayPal's statistics, in November 2000 50% of eBay's sellers accepted PayPal while only 12%–13% accepted Billpoint, and analysts were questioning whether the investment would pay off.[8]

In June 2000, eBay purchased Half.com for $241 million in stock. Half.com provided a site to sell used books, movies, music, and games. For these items, many different sellers sell the same item, for example a particular book, although sometimes in different condition. Half.com listed all the sellers of an item in one page view, so that buyers could see the condition of the item and the prices that sellers were asking. So, for example, Half.com listed 84 copies of Bonnie Raitt's "Nick of Time" on December 4, 2000. Thirty-one were rated "like new" and carried prices of $2.99 to $8.47. Most of the highest priced items were described as "brand new, sealed." Among the others there was a group for sale at $5.25 and there were 11 for sale by different sellers for $6.78. The maximum listed price was just under half the retail price. Half.com only listed items under half the retail price on the front screen (thus the name).

Buyers simply chose what to buy and from whom, and then, as with eBay's auctions, the buyer and seller consummated the transaction via e-mail. There was no auction component. On the other hand, since the sellers were arrayed next to one another and could easily adjust their prices, price competition tended to drive the prices toward market clearing. Half.com charged a transaction fee of 15%.

During 2000, eBay continued to expand internationally. It was already the market leader in other English-speaking countries such as Australia (1.5 million daily listings), Canada (150,000 daily listings), and the United Kingdom (more than 100,000 daily listings)[9] and had local sites in Japan, Germany, and France. Nonetheless, by December 2000 eBay's market capitalization had shrunk by two-thirds to around $8.6 billion from its high eight months earlier.

BUSINESS-TO-CONSUMER AUCTIONS

B2C auctions enabled merchants to offer products directly to consumers using auction pricing models. Like C2C auctions, B2C auction sites had proliferated several years prior to 2000. A large fraction (75%) of B2C auctions in 1999 involved computer hardware.

Three main types of sites dominated B2C auctions. First, *third-party auction destination sites*, such as Egghead.com/Onsale and *u*Bid, offered new and refurbished branded products for auction. The third-party auction site usually purchased products from the manufacturer at fixed prices and offered them at auction to consumers, pocketing the difference between their costs and the sales price. Second, brand-name manufacturers offered items through *proprietary auction sites* that had three main goals: liquidating of inventory, assessing demand, and promotion. Third, *auction hubs*, such as FairMarket, enabled commercial liquidators, wholesalers, and dealers to offer products directly to consumers or other dealers.

[8] *San Jose Mercury News*, November 27, 2000, p. E1.

[9] AuctionWatch.com, December 4, 2000.

Because many small businesses offered products through C2C sites such as eBay, there was significant crossover between C2C and B2C auctions. For buyers, bidding for items in a B2C auction was like bidding in a C2C auction, with the following differences:

- *Limited sellers*. The B2C site offered items for auction either directly or through a limited network of suppliers. Individuals could not post items for sale.
- *Control of inventory*. B2C auctions typically took control of inventory from manufacturers, suppliers, or retailers. Auctioneers either paid a fixed upfront fee for inventory or accepted items on consignment.
- *Dutch auctions* were more prevalent because multiple units of the same item were often offered for sale.

Unlike C2C auction sites, which derived revenues from listing and transaction fees, B2C sites earned revenue primarily through consumers' purchase of goods. The typical B2C site purchased auction items at a fixed price from a manufacturer and pocketed the spread between their costs and the final sale price of the items. Typical gross margins ranged from 3%–6%. B2C sites were more likely than C2C sites to replace offline models, primarily retail outlets or traditional e-tailers.

Analysts predicted that because of the diversification of products sold on B2C sites, revenues from B2C auctions would surpass those of C2C auctions by 2003.[10] They also predicted that the selection of products offered through B2C auctions would increase, with the percentage of B2C auctions in the computer category declining to 27% by 2003.

In 2000, the market for B2C auctions was consolidating: Onsale merged with Egghead.com in November. Other individual sites offering auctions, including Excite, MSN, Lycos, Dell, and CompUSA had formed a loose partnership through the FairMarket network, increasing the number of buyers and sellers in each site's auctions.

COMPANY PROFILE: *u*BID

Creative Computers founded *u*Bid in April 1997 to facilitate the movement of excess and refurbished inventory online.[11] *u*Bid's auctions offered consumers and small businesses a wide range of excess, close-out, and refurbished brand name products in 12 categories that typically sold for much less than retail prices. The categories covered included computers, consumer electronics, home and leisure, and sports and recreation products. At the end of 2000, a typical daily auction featured 12,000 items. Among those for whom *u*Bid operated online auctions were Sony, IBM, and Hewlett-Packard. The company's real-time commerce system relied on live-action bidding where customers browsed a changing inventory of products.[12]

[10] The Forrester Report, "Consumers Catch Auction Fever," by Evie Black Dykema, March 1999.
[11] The company was incorporated in September 1997 and became listed on the NASDAQ National Market through an initial public offering on December 4, 1998. On June 7, 1999, Creative Computers distributed its 80% stake in *u*Bid to its stockholders.
[12] Merrill Lynch, "*u*Bid: Best Value on the Net," September 27, 1999.

From the beginning, *u*Bid experienced exceptional growth. In 1998 sales grew from $200,000 in the first month of operation to $10 million for December. *u*Bid generated revenues of $48.2 million in its first full year of operations and $204.9 million in 1999. The number of registered users and items auctioned also grew rapidly. By the end of 2000, *u*Bid had more than 1.5 million registered users and had auctioned off more than 2.5 million items (at a rate that was 42% higher in December 2000 than it had been in April). The company said that it had 5 million (not unique) visitors per month and was ranked the second most visited Internet auction site from April to October 2000. Most of *u*Bid's revenues came from computer sales. Analysts estimated gross margins for 1999 to be 9%, up from 8.2% in 1998 (Exhibits 4 and 5).

CMGI acquired *u*Bid in early 2000 in a stock deal worth $407 million. Following the announcement, CMGI's shares fell $4.81 to $115.69. By early December 2000, CMGI's stock price had plummeted to less than $10. Since the acquisition, *u*Bid had entered into agreements with several of CMGI's network companies. For example, it created a cobranded auction channel on AltaVista Shopping.com and integrated Yesmail services into its registration process.

At the end of 2000, *u*Bid launched a C2C auction site, Consumer Exchange, to leverage its consumer traffic on the buy side of the market as well as its listing and payment services.

BUSINESS-TO-BUSINESS AUCTIONS

B2B auctions were pervasive long before the Internet in a diverse range of settings. Drilling rights for oil and logging rights for timber were typically sold by auction. The U.S. Treasury sold billions of dollars of bills, notes, and bonds each week by auction, and the U.S. government had auctioned off radio spectrum in the 1990s. Wholesale used car markets were also typically sold at auction as were various idle assets and excess inventory. In addition, large construction projects, government procurement projects, urban transportation projects, and other large purchases were often sold using reverse auction.

In part because an offline auction structure in B2B already existed, the online B2B auction market developed more slowly than the C2C and B2C markets. Nonetheless by 2000, online B2B auctions were proliferating and were being adopted in a wide variety of circumstances. The first B2B markets generally had one or more of the following features: large, fragmented markets; markets with channel or trading inefficiencies; and seasonal, time sensitive, or short life cycle products that resulted in excess inventory.

Some online auctions were used to automate existing offline auctions (for example, DoveBid was a traditional auction house selling capital assets that moved into online auctions). Others were introduced into markets that had no established auction outlet. Consequently the range of applications was diverse. In financial markets auctions were becoming common, for example, by MuniAuction.com to sell municipal bond issues (auctions lasted only 30 minutes with most bidding occurring near the end of the auction, essentially turning them into sealed bid auctions) and by WR Hambrecht and Co. to sell corporate bonds (OpenBook) and IPO shares (Open IPO).

Online auctions were also blossoming in the sale of excess inventory, including end-of-life or out-of-season products. Disposing of excess inventory was difficult for manufacturers. Factory outlet stores, resellers (retailers who mainly sold excess goods), and liquidators were possible channels but none was particularly attractive: outlet stores had high overhead for low margin items and liquidators and resellers typically engaged in tough-nosed negotiating that resulted in large discounts. B2B auctions could remove these intermediaries, resulting in better prices for buyers and sellers. Auctions provided a structured, competitive selling process that helped move inventory at the best possible prices. Businesses could save from 2%–25%.[13]

Reverse auctions were another area of great activity. However, many procurement decisions could not simply be reduced to price. The identity and reputation of the supplier mattered, and some qualitative assessment was typically required. Especially for direct purchases (those used in manufacturing as opposed to support services), parts were often idiosyncratic to a particular buyer and an investigation was necessary to ensure that the supplier was qualified to produce them. Moreover delivery schedules, payment terms, machinery upgrades, technical support, and so on, needed to be specified. These factors affected the total cost of acquiring the part.

Buyers also often recognized that the deal had to be profitable for the supplier to provide an incentive for repeat transactions and to enable the supplier to recoup buyer-specific investments (such as the set up to produce a particular buyer's parts) and were leery of auction designs that would wring all supplier profit out of the transaction. Accordingly, B2B procurement sites usually were not straightforward reverse auctions but mimicked a setting where the buyer would issue a request for quotation (RFQ) followed by an offer, counteroffer, and perhaps further give-and-take, and then final acceptance. Other sites (for example, PerfectMarket.com) attempted to further automate this process.

A sustained auction site required a steady stream of product. As in B2C and C2C models, the most important factor in B2B auctions was liquidity—the presence of sellers to post merchandise and buyers to bid on the auctions. Sites that gained critical mass early in individual industries were likely to grow. Although large companies who continually had excess inventory might have a private auction site, most companies used a third-party auction site selling related surplus. Most proprietary sites were only open to existing customers and sought to promote a business relationship between the company and its buyers.

In 1999 most sites believed they could charge fees in the 5%–25% range, depending on the perceived value added. However, as 2000 wore on, many sites had lowered their fees to less than 1%. The risk that participants would circumvent the system after they identified an acceptable trading partner was an even bigger problem in B2B auctions than C2C auctions because even with low percentages fees were significant given the value of goods traded. B2B players used several techniques to discourage this behavior, including providing significant value-added services to encourage trading partners to transact within the system and maintaining anonymity until transactions were com-

[13] Freemarkets, Inc., *The Red Herring*, IPO Calendar.

plete, although many sites found it difficult to maintain anonymity through the close of the transaction given the importance of brand and seller reputation.

COMPANY PROFILE: FreeMarkets

Procuring industrial parts was one of the least efficient and costliest processes in manufacturing. Worldwide, manufactures spent 35 cents for every dollar in sales on purchasing industrial parts. They bought these parts on negotiated contracts that typically ran three or more years. In 1999 FreeMarkets.com launched an online auction that attempted to standardize every item in the RFQ. Suppliers who participated in FreeMarkets' auctions agreed not only to supply a particular part, but also to do so on the same schedule, with the same payment terms, inventory arrangements, and so on as everyone else. FreeMarkets.com created transparency and standardized the nonstandard elements of industrial parts purchasing, offering a shrink-wrapped product whose optimal price was then discovered through auction.

To achieve this standardization, FreeMarkets worked with its buyers to select bidders to participate in each auction, specify needs in detail, and tailor the bidding process to the situation. This was essentially a consulting service and FreeMarkets billed for it as such. Indeed most of FreeMarkets' revenue came from such fees, although it also sometimes earned performance-based incentive payments. Because the potential bidders were lined up ahead of time, the auctions were typically short (10–30 minutes), but would be extended if a bid came in in the final minute. Even with the standardization that FreeMarkets imposed on the process, the lowest bid would not necessarily win because the buyer could consider other factors.

FreeMarkets' clients were often large global firms and included Heinz, BP Amoco, Emerson-Electric, Bechtel, and SmithKline Beecham. In 1999, FreeMarkets auctions resulted in purchases of $2.7 billion. (Analysts estimated the market for industrial parts to be $5 trillion.) Clients claimed that they often saved 40% or more of offline costs.[14] A challenge that FreeMarkets faced was that, convinced of the savings, some clients started auction services of their own, including GM, which partnered with Commerce One to create TradeXchange, which Ford and DaimlerChrysler joined in February, 2000.

COMPANY PROFILE: TradeOut.com

TradeOut.com, founded in August 1998, was the world's first B2B Internet marketplace focusing on large companies' excess inventory. It launched its site in June 1999 and in four months had 7,500 customers and had auctioned $22 million worth of products. eBay took an equity stake in TradeOut in October 1999, and as part of that agreement Meg Whitman, eBay's CEO, joined TradeOut's board of directors.

By late 2000, TradeOut believed that it was the leading global online marketplace for business surplus, covering more than 100 categories, including automotive, computers, consumer electronics, consumer goods, industrial equipment, medical equip-

[14] United Technologies Corp. paid $42 million for circuit boards in 1998 which at offline prices would have cost $74 million. *Fortune*, March 20, 2000.

ment, and office furniture. The company facilitated some large auctions. For example, in November 2000, it sold a $13 million Siemens Westinghouse gas turbine generator to the City of Chanute, Kansas, and in September 2000, it auctioned off more than 300 light- and medium-duty vehicles valued at $3.9 million for Penske Trucks during a special nine-day promotion. Its customers ranged from Fortune 500 industrial companies to mid-sized wholesale distributors.

The company's founder, Brin McCagg believed that attacking inefficiencies in the system was the heart of the business:

> *Up until now, getting rid of that surplus has been a tremendously inefficient process. Our goal is to drive the inefficiencies out of the system and create a business-to-business eBay.*[15] . . . *We want to be the primary marketplace for all companies to sell excess inventory, idle assets, and outdated products. We'll achieve this by providing liquidity in what is traditionally not a liquid market.*[16]

Sellers paid a $10 listing fee per unit. However, the company made most of its money through a 5% commission fee on sales. TradeOut also offered consulting services to assist in the posting and marketing of items in excess of $25,000 and had strategic partners for related services including financing, appraisal, testing, escrow, transportation, and logistics.

EXHIBIT 1 Comparison of Top B2C Auction Sites in 1999

Auction site	*Number of items up for bid*	*Percent with bids*
eBay[17]	2,500,000	Not specified ("significant number")
Yahoo! Auctions	500,000	Not specified ("strong")
Amazon.com Auctions	100,000	5 (in books category)
Excite Auctions[18]	72,700	13.6
Auctions.com	45,000	10
Up4Sale[19]	32,000	5.1
Lycos Auctions[20]	25,000	8.1

(continued)

[15] Mel Duvall, *Inter@ctive Week*, "Liquidators Get Boost from Web Auctions," November 1, 1999.

[16] Jackie Cohen, *The Industry Standard*, "Taking Care of Business," September 3, 1999.

[17] Reviewed 8/16/99.

[18] Reviewed 10/20/99.

[19] Reviewed 10/16/99.

[20] Reviewed 9/29/99.

EXHIBIT 1 Comparison of Top B2C Auction Sites in 1999 *(continued)*

Auction site	*Number of items up for bid*	*Percent with bids*
Collecting Nation[21]	8,500	Varied widely by category (0–59)
edeal[22]	10,000	<5
ComicExchange.net[23]	2,500	1.4

Compiled from AuctionWatch.com

EXHIBIT 2 Growth in Registered Users 1996–2000 at eBay

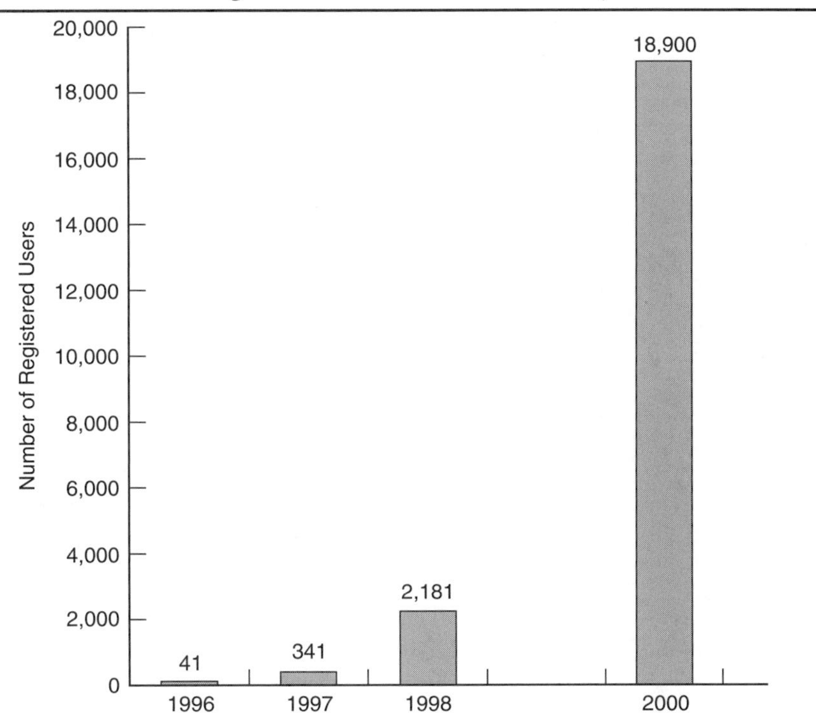

[21] Reviewed 9/1/99.
[22] Reviewed 11/3/99.
[23] Reviewed 10/13/99.

EXHIBIT 3 eBay 1996–1999 Selected Financial Data

	Year Ended December 31			
	1996	*1997*	*1998*	*1999*
Statement of operations data	*(In thousands, except per share data)*			
Net revenues	$32,051	$41,370	$86,129	$224,724
Gross profit	25,248	32,966	70,035	167,136
Sales and marketing expenses	13,139	15,618	35,976	95,956
Product development expenses	28	831	4,640	23,785
General and administrative expenses	5,661	6,534	15,849	43,055
Amortization of acquired intangibles expenses			805	1,145
Merger-related expenses				4,359
Income from operations	6,420	9,983	12,765	(1,164)
Net income	3,338	8,032	12,062	20,213
Net income per share—basic	0.39	0.29	0.14	0.10
Weighted average shares—basic	8,490	24,428	52,064	108,235
Net income per share—diluted	0.07	0.08	0.06	0.08
Weighted average shares—diluted	45,060	84,775	116,759	135,910

	As of December 31	
	1998	*1999*
Balance sheet data	*(In thousands)*	
Cash, cash equivalents	$37,285	$219,679
Short-term investments	40,401	181,086
Working capital	72,934	371,009
Total assets	149,536	963,942
Total stockholders' equity	100,538	852,467

Source: 1999 eBay Annual Report.

EXHIBIT 4 *u*Bid Inc. Statement of Operations 1998, 1999

		Three Months Ended September 30		
	1999	*1998*	*1999*	*1998*
		(In thousands, except share data)		
Net revenues	$55,123	$15,299	$135,03	$24,125
Cost of revenues	49,560	14,046	122,522	22,192
Gross profit	5,563	1,253	12,508	1,933
Operating expenses:				
Sales and marketing	4,878	796	11,484	1,353
Technology and development	1,160	289	2,735	694
General and administrative	4,279	1,188	10,152	2,707
Stock-based compensation	939	—	2,758	—
Total operating expense	11,256	2,273	27,129	4,754
Loss from operations	(5,693)	(1,020)	(14,621)	(2,821)
Interest income	246	—	796	—
Interest expense to creative	(67)	(72)	(204)	(159)
Net interest income (expense)	179	(72)	592	(159)
Loss before income taxes	(5,514)	(1,092)	(14,029)	(2,980)
Provision for income taxes	—	—	—	—
Net loss	(5,514)	(1,092)	(14,029)	(2,980)
Basic and diluted net loss per share	(0.60)	(0.15)	(1.53)	(0.41)
Shares used to compute basic and diluted net loss per share	9,213,278	7,329,883	9,169,258	7,329,883

Source: *u*Bid Inc—10-Q—quarterly report. Date filed: 11/15/1999.

EXHIBIT 5 *u*Bid Inc. Balance Sheet 1998, 1999

Assets	*September 30, 1999 (unaudited)*	*December 31, 1998 (In thousands, except share data)*
Current assets:		
Cash	$61,516	$26,053
Accounts receivable	1,373	623
Merchandise inventories	14,668	7,235
Prepaid expenses and other assets	1,665	195
Total current assets	79,222	34,106
Fixed assets, net	2,699	519
Total assets	81,921	34,625
Liabilities and Stockholders' Equity		
Current liabilities:		
Accounts payable	$16,981	$9,013
Accrued expenses and other current liabilities	5,619	2,371
Due to creative	391	1,277
Total current liabilities	22,991	12,661
Note payable to the creative		3,331
Stockholders' equity (deficit):		
Preferred stock; $.001 par value; 5,000,000 shares authorized; no shares issued or outstanding	—	—
common stock; $.001 par value; 20,000,000 shares authorized; 11,487,581 and 9,146,833 shares issued and outstanding as of September 30, 1999 and December 31, 1998, respectively	4	2
Additional paid-in-capital	85,373	37,138
Deferred compensation expense	(5,267)	(8,025)
Accumulated deficit	(24,511)	(10,482)
Total stockholders' equity	55,599	18,633
Total liabilities and stockholders' equity	81,921	34,625

E-MARKETS 2000

Ultimately, all businesses will buy on a marketplace, sell on a marketplace, host a marketplace, or be marginalized by a marketplace. —Ariba White Paper on B2B Marketplaces in the New Economy

They're testing the bounds of hyperbole on this one . . . most mega-exchanges are years away from their true promise. . . . —Red Herring[1]

E-markets are generating more questions than transactions right now. —ComputerWorld[2]

INTRODUCTION

The Underlying Problems

Consumers and businesses have used markets for millennia to exchange goods and services. Over the centuries, new technologies have enabled these markets to increase their depth, efficiency, and geographic reach: paper enabled records to be kept and prices to be publicly displayed; the railroads enabled the widespread distribution of high weight, low value goods; and the telephone and telegraph allowed instantaneous verbal communication. Despite these and many other advances, during the final years of the twentieth century, industries still faced three significant market-related problems:[3]

Research Associate Christopher Thomas prepared this case under the supervision of Professors Robert Burgelman and Garth Saloner as the basis for class discussion rather than to illustrate either effective or ineffective handling of an administrative situation.

[1] "Revenge of the Bricks," *Red Herring*, August 2000.
[2] "Reality Check for E-Markets," *ComputerWorld*, June 5, 2000.
[3] "The B2B Internet Report: Collaborative Commerce," Morgan Stanley Dean Witter, April 2000.

- Commerce was fragmented, often by geography, creating inefficient markets and uninformed buyers and sellers. Lack of information prevented buyers and suppliers from exploring new trading relationships.
- Value chains[4] had large amounts of excess inventory because of an inability to see and plan for the right mix and volume of sales, forcing producers to build inventory to cover all probable scenarios. Markets were not transparent enough with respect to current information on prices, product availability, product alternatives, and trading partner alternatives.[5]
- Most complex, information-intensive interactions between businesses were performed manually. This was labor intensive, inefficient, expensive, and often prevented the right decision maker from getting the right information at the right time. Most internal planning methodologies were also difficult to integrate with the actions of trading partners.[6]

Building Information Systems to Enhance Transparency

At the end of the twentieth century and the beginning of the twenty-first a new set of tools was introduced that could restructure markets to address the market-related problems. During the 1990s, manufacturers and service companies had cultivated partnerships with key external suppliers. Faced with the pressures of globalization, shorter time-to-market, and demands for customized products, manufacturers had to optimize business processes across both internal units and trading partners. Supply chain management (SCM), the use of powerful computer analytical tools, and advanced business techniques to optimize the delivery of goods and services had become necessary to survive; "No one can dispute that supply change initiatives are key these days to business strategies . . . driving change in many industry markets."[7] However, extending internal data management efforts, often based on enterprise resource planning (ERP) systems, to external SCM collaboration proved difficult. A gap existed between sharing information internally and with trading partners. By 1999, only 50% of large businesses had exposed even one internal computer system to customers or suppliers.

Until the proliferation of Internet technologies, companies had relied on the telephone, fax, e-mail, or electronic data interchange (EDI) systems to share this value chain data. Although point-to-point EDI systems, introduced in the late 1960s and standardized in the 1980s, automated data exchange processes, they were expensive and took a long time to implement. Most EDI networks therefore excluded small and technically unsophisticated trading partners, even though value chains often comprised thou-

[4] This case will use the term "value chain" in the same context as the more commonly utilized "supply chain."

[5] "Information Sharing in a Supply Chain," Stanford Research Paper No. 1549, Hau Lee and Seungjin Whang.

[6] In this case, the word "product" includes goods and services; "buyers and suppliers" means not only manufacturers and end-customers, but all intermediaries along the value chain, such as subcontractors, distributors, resellers, etc. Most companies are both buyers and suppliers.

[7] "Future State: Emerging Scenarios in Vertical Markets," GartnerGroup, April 17, 2000.

sands of these companies, which conducted millions of conversations simultaneously (see Exhibit 1 for an overview of the aerospace value chain).[8] By 2000, however, companies were realizing that new Internet tools could allow them to connect more easily to external systems and develop interenterprise collaboration and integration tools. Ninety percent of CEOs expected to expose more internal systems in the next two years, and 40% expected the number to increase fivefold.[9]

E-Markets into the "Information Breach"

The Internet, combined with online procurement tools, market-making systems, an installed base of ERP systems, and business process optimization (BPO) packages, enabled the adoption of business-to-business electronic commerce (B2B e-commerce) methods that promised to increase the transparency of marketplace operations and efficiency and to allow greater interfirm integration, leading to collaborative commerce.

B2B, first evident in Web storefronts and extranets, was an extension of the cumulative information technology investments of the 1990s. During that decade, companies focused on managing and conforming the vast array of internal computer systems that powered their operations. ERP penetration, an important building block for e-commerce, was well over 50% in the Fortune 500.[10] The collection, analysis, and dissemination of information internally had become central to managing firm operations. Many companies had formed the base for "digital nervous systems" that enabled real-time internal communication as each production/sales event warranted. Internet-based transactions utilized and extended this infrastructure. B2B e-commerce had reached $215 billion in 1999 and was projected to reach $5.7 trillion by 2004.[11] A major, emerging component of B2B e-commerce was electronic markets (Figure 1).

E-markets provided an electronic, Internet-based commerce arena for a group of buyers and suppliers within an industry, geographic region, or affinity group. The key concepts were aggregation and intermediation; formerly point-to-point, one-on-one transactions would be brought into a multiple party environment. These new entities provided the technical infrastructure for communicating timely market data. E-markets also added simple order matching, more complicated online market making, content aggregation, value chain collaboration, collaborative product design, personalization, and value-added services, such as fulfillment and credit processing, and promised to let companies trade items that had never before benefited from a liquid market, such as intellectual property rights and unused telecommunications bandwidth—"any technology that can be translated simplistically . . . to a shrink-wrapped license could potentially be . . . transacted electronically."[12]

[8] "B2B Supply Chains Solutions in Manufacturing: Poised for Proliferation," GartnerGroup, May 22, 2000.

[9] Forrester Research, December 1999.

[10] Casewriter research.

[11] "B2B Commerce Forecast: $5.7 Trillion by 2004," AMR Research, April 2000. There are numerous other projections of total B2B e-commerce transactions in the next 3–5 years.

[12] "Through Integration, a Virtual Exchange for Intellectual Property Is Born," *Wall Street and Technology*, August 2000.

FIGURE 1 The Evolution from ERP to E-Markets[13]

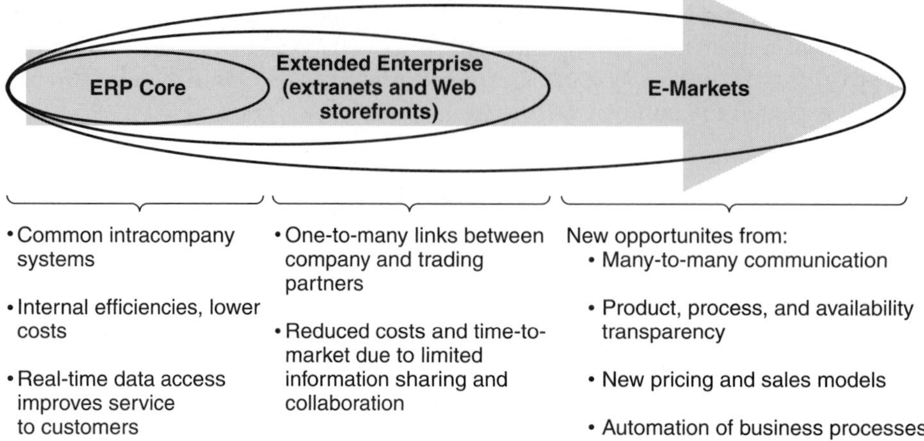
ERP Core
Extended Enterprise (extranets and Web storefronts)
E-Markets
• Common intracompany systems
• Internal efficiencies, lower costs
• Real-time data access improves service to customers
• One-to-many links between company and trading partners
• Reduced costs and time-to-market due to limited information sharing and collaboration
New opportunites from:
• Many-to-many communication
• Product, process, and availability transparency
• New pricing and sales models
• Automation of business processes
• Enhanced data exchange leading to collaboration

Research analysts predicted that between 40% and 60% of B2B e-commerce would take place on e-markets by 2004, totaling between $1.5 and $3 trillion in total transaction value.[14]

Product Design Collaboration

Corporations were also trying to move nontransactional product development efforts online. Many companies were making significant investments in online design collaboration and design for manufacturability applications.[15] In fact, many believed that the greatest benefits to B2B and tightly integrated systems would be reduced design costs, reduced time-to-market, and reduced production costs through design-for-manufacturability. Many e-markets offered nontransaction-based product design and technical collaboration features. This research case, which concentrates on the transaction and value chain integration aspects of e-markets, will only cover these efforts briefly.

[13] Adapted from research performed by Intel Corporation, May 2000.

[14] AMR Research, Forrester Research, GartnerGroup, and Morgan Stanley Dean Witter. Total transaction value included multiple sales. The *Economist* predicted that the global gross value of all goods bought and sold in 2004 will be $105 trillion.

[15] "The e-Business Marketplace: The Future of Competition," Aberdeen Group White Paper, April 2000.

A FRAMEWORK FOR E-MARKETS

On a functional basis, there were three main types of e-markets, segmented by their primary service offering and transaction capabilities (Figure 2).[16]

Efficient Commerce Hub (E-Hub)

These trading networks automated existing transaction flow to make it more efficient. Analysts compared them to "an extranet with aggregation." E-hubs did not attempt to radically reshape existing value chain relationships and pricing models by offering online market making.[17] The transaction relationship could be 1:1, many suppliers dealing independently with one buyer, or many buyers transacting independently with one supplier (Figure 3).

E-hubs attempted to eliminate or minimize underlying transaction inefficiencies, such as error-prone manual processes, paper-based supplier catalogs, inefficient direct or phone-based sales staff, and general dearth of information in the supply chain. They could perform online, automated requisition routing and approval, order matching, fulfillment, settlement, and content management. E-hubs addressed product and

FIGURE 2 A Functional Categorization of E-Markets[18]

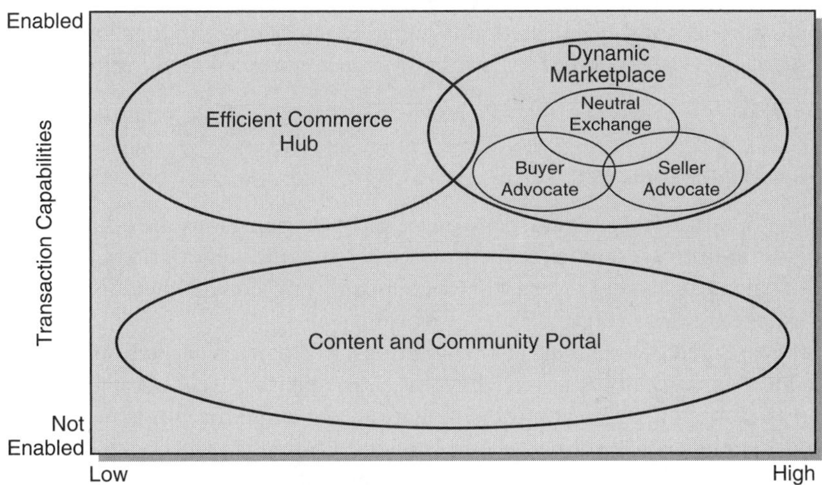

[16] "The E-Market Maker Revolution," GartnerGroup, September 27, 1999. There are numerous other taxonomies, such as Kaplan's and Sawhney's in "E-Hubs: The New B2B Marketplaces," *Harvard Business Review*, May/June 2000.

[17] "Working Models of B2B: Business Information Exchanges," Alexis Gutzman, June 20, 2000.

[18] Adapted from "The E-Market Maker Revolution," GartnerGroup, September 27, 1999.

FIGURE 3 Examples of E-Hubs[19]

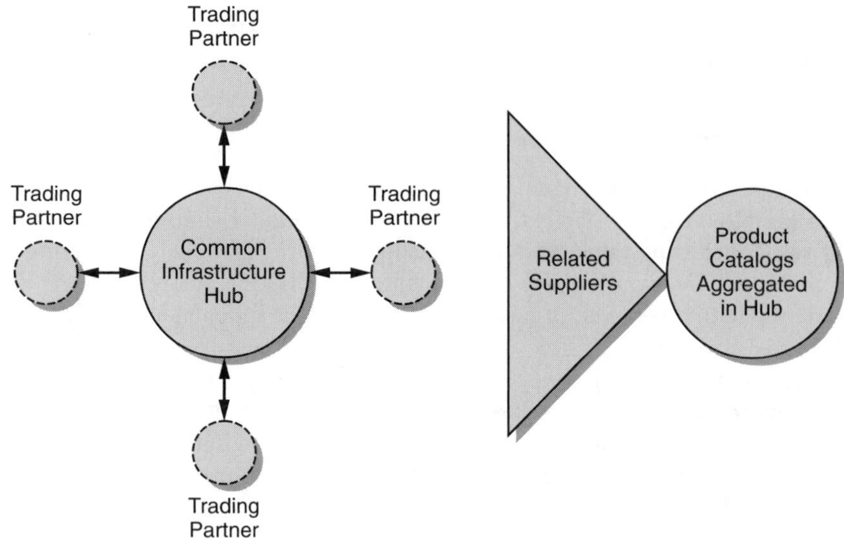

availability transparency and enabled value chain collaboration, but did not offer sourcing alternatives or pricing transparency.

If necessary, e-hubs aggregated and digitized suppliers' catalogs and added links to value-added services, such as logistics and credit, and provided limited integration to a trading partner's back-end system.

Dynamic Marketplaces

These types of e-markets pursued many of the same efficiencies as the e-hubs, yet moved the terms of the transaction, such as product pricing and negotiations, into the marketplace. Dynamic exchanges were what most people envisioned when discussing online exchanges or e-markets (Figure 4).

They employed several market-making mechanisms such as auctions, reverse auctions, request for proposal/quote (RFP/RFQ), or bid-ask exchanges. Dynamic marketplaces attempted to use active intermediation to change the fundamental means by which firms bought and sold goods and services. Online market making might mean more than just price matching: "Price is not the only dimension a B2B trader cares about; size, quality, or delivery considerations, for instance, may dominate. Buyers and sellers will demand value across multiple dimensions."[20] These e-markets were either tilted toward a supplier, a buyer, or a neutral third party. For example, a buyer-focused

[19] Adapted from Xuma.com Web site, http://xuma.com/exchangex/index.html.

[20] Ganesh Mani, CEO of Powerloom.com, as quoted in "The Market Effect," Line56.com, October 10, 2000.

FIGURE 4 A Dynamic Marketplace[21]

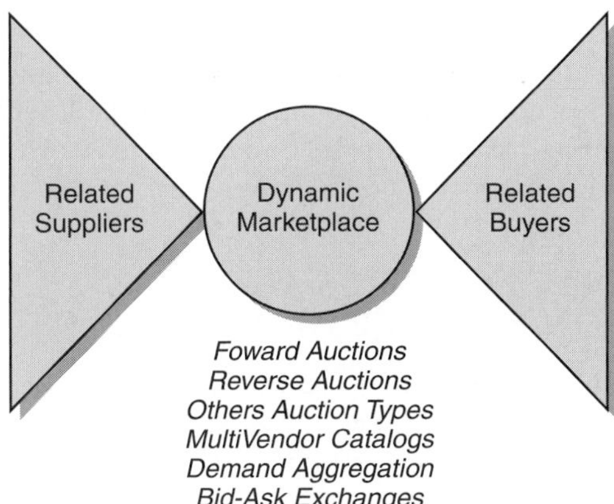

exchange could aggregate buyer product demands in a certain industry to increase customer bargaining power (Exhibits 3–5 depict the three types of exchanges).

The auction process had been receiving the most interest from analysts and industry participants. Firms had used auctions to sell spare, used, perishable, and end-of-life cycle products, but not on a wide basis. Independent companies, such as FreeMarkets and TradeOut, introduced auctions as a stand-alone solution to offloading excess and used inventory. However, auctions were becoming simply one part of larger e-market application offerings. Nearly all new consortia or independent e-markets included auctions as core functionality in their broader e-market offering. Online auctions were still in their infancy: "Today's B2B auctions amount to little more than testing grounds . . . procurement managers are merely dabbling in them."[22] Only 10% of surveyed purchasing managers planned to pursue auctions as a core sourcing strategy.[23]

Many products did not merit real-time trading activity: "Visions of every product up for bid in live trading auctions aren't realistic . . . we won't all be making markets in pencils or Snickers bars soon. We actually have to get some work done at some point."[24]

Content and Community Portal

Many e-markets did not initially offer transaction capabilities; rather, they focused on the sharing of information for community-building and interenterprise collaboration. These were also effective for the product development collaboration discussed previously because the content could include CAD/CAM drawings, specification sheets, bulletin boards, discussion rooms, buyer/supplier lists, and more.

[21] Adapted from Xuma.com Web site, http://xuma.com/exchangex/index.html.
[22] "Auction Bridge," Jennifer deJong, Line56.com, September 2000.
[23] *Purchasing Magazine*, November 1999.
[24] "The B2B Internet Report: Collaborative Commerce," Morgan Stanley Dean Witter, April 2000.

Public versus Private E-Markets

E-markets attempted to be all-inclusive, seeking the largest number of relevant buyers and sellers. This increased both the participants' choice among trading partners and market liquidity, a key component of building markets. Other markets were exclusive, excluding any trading partner that the e-market maker or the major customers/suppliers did not approve.[25]

INDUSTRY CHARACTERISTICS AND THEIR IMPACT ON E-MARKETS

By the middle of 2000, e-market activity had touched nearly every industry in some way. E-markets in a particular industry evolved according to how transactions were currently conducted and the inefficiencies and opportunities in the current processes.

Concentration and Competition Within the Industry

A key industry characteristic that would determine e-market characteristics was the concentration of power in the industry.

Industries were generally supplier dominated, buyer dominated, or fragmented.[26] Analysts determined that nearly half of the worlds' industries were fragmented (such as food services and life sciences), one-third were buyer dominated (such as automobiles and aircraft manufacturing), and less than 20% were supplier dominated (such as plastics and transportation).[27] Successful companies in a concentrated industry probably did not want to radically change market dynamics; those very market characteristics had allowed them to develop their current edge.

The existing industry participants in a concentrated market (either buyers or suppliers) had significant market power. They brought the most important asset to any market: trading liquidity, something "no exchange can live without." The major players' trading liquidity was an important source of leverage, and an e-market could not develop in their industry without their input. This fact prompted leading companies in major industry verticals to join consortia to build e-markets for their industry (to be discussed later).

Market concentration would also greatly affect who retained the greatest amount of value from an e-market; some analysts predicted that the party (buyers or sellers) with the greatest leverage would get 60%–70% of the benefits.[28]

Fragmented industries, often geographically dispersed, offered a different path for introducing e-markets.[29] In these markets, even the top trading partners lacked the market share to form a powerful coalition and create the "rules" for making transactions. Thus, suppliers and buyers faced high search costs for trading partners and below-optimal

[25] "Understanding e-Markets," Jeffrey Brooks and Susan Cantrell, Andersen Consulting, April 14, 2000.

[26] Suppliers and buyers could include channel intermediaries such as distributors and brokers.

[27] "Guide to Industry Consortia, Volume 1.0," Lehman Brothers, May 24, 2000.

[28] "The B2B Internet Report: Collaborative Commerce," Morgan Stanley Dean Witter, April 2000.

[29] "Industry Trading Communities (B2B Exchanges)," GartnerGroup, June 26, 2000.

product selection. An e-market could become the means through which these far-flung trading partners communicated, reducing costs and inefficiencies.

The benefits of e-markets in fragmented industries could be elusive. Many suppliers and buyers had to join the e-market just to create enough trading liquidity for an efficient market and to justify the cost of market membership, creating an acute "chicken and egg" problem.[30]

The level of competition would also affect the evolution of e-markets. If the dominant players in an industry, as Ventro CEO David Perry put it, "stuck together,"[31] they could generate an e-market to their liking. However, even if a group of buyers had the combined clout to shape the e-market landscape in their vertical market, they might not be able to cooperate effectively to do it. Certain industries had been characterized by strong and unfriendly competition, where long-term competitors had been fighting tooth-and-nail for years. They might find it difficult, if not impossible, to build an e-market.

However, other industries had more benign oligopolistic or monopsonistic competition, in which companies had avoided intense battles. An e-market's increased transparency could augment these oligopolistic industry structures by encouraging more collusion because the firms would more easily detect "cheating" on an explicit or implicit agreement.

Benefits to Value Chain Integration and Collaboration

Cyclical industries such as semiconductor and aerospace manufacturing faced, at varying times, supply constraints or excess capacity. Both were expensive because marginal profits were high and capital investments enormous (a new semiconductor wafer fabrication plant could cost $2 billion[32]). Capacity management was therefore extremely important. Business planners needed product availability, lead time, and inventory information from partners up and down the value chain. Because e-markets facilitated this information sharing, these industries may be among the first to adopt them. Integration was also important if the industry value chain was fragmented.

Many industries also had high inventory carrying costs. For example, the value of an Intel microprocessor dropped 90% in six months, making inventory expensive;[33] any information sharing that reduced inventory levels/holding period would generate tremendous value. In other industries, such as telecommunications and commercial air travel, the products (bandwidth and airline seats) were perishable, implying the need for dynamic pricing to sell unused capacity.[34]

Product characteristics also affected their suitability for e-markets in other ways. Creating e-markets for highly customized or engineered products that had only a few buyers and suppliers would generate less value than one for a commodity product with

[30] David Perry, CEO of Ventro in a speech at Online Exchanges Conference 2000, June 2000.

[31] "B2B E-Commerce: Where the New Economy Meets the Old Economy," Ventro White Paper, 2000.

[32] Intel Sales and Marketing Conference, July 2000.

[33] Interview with Jim Erickson, Intel Corporation, July 2000.

[34] "The e-Business Marketplace: The Future of Competition," Aberdeen Group White Paper, April 2000.

many buyers and suppliers who might have transacted with each other in the past; "highly engineered or custom products simply don't have enough buyers and sellers to create a market, since they aren't standard."[35]

Entrenched Procurement Techniques

Companies had employed many processes to buy and sell products, depending on the importance of the product, and the volume and urgency of the purchase. Open sourcing purchases usually took place in the spot market and were often made ad hoc outside the purchasing department. Purchase orders and specialized relationships were generally for repeat buys, recurring purchases with multiple supplier relationships. Strategic partnerships were for program buys with long-term contracts and volume agreements; they were the largest dollar volume of transactions.

However, the greatest number of transaction relationships was based on standard purchase orders, with little open sourcing or collaborative partnering. Analysts expected e-markets to greatly reduce the number of traditional supplier relationships by making open sourcing more efficient with aggregation of content and supplier discovery techniques and making specialized/strategic relationships more attractive and feasible through product, process, and availability transparency (Figure 5).

FIGURE 5 Use of Different Procurement Techniques[36]

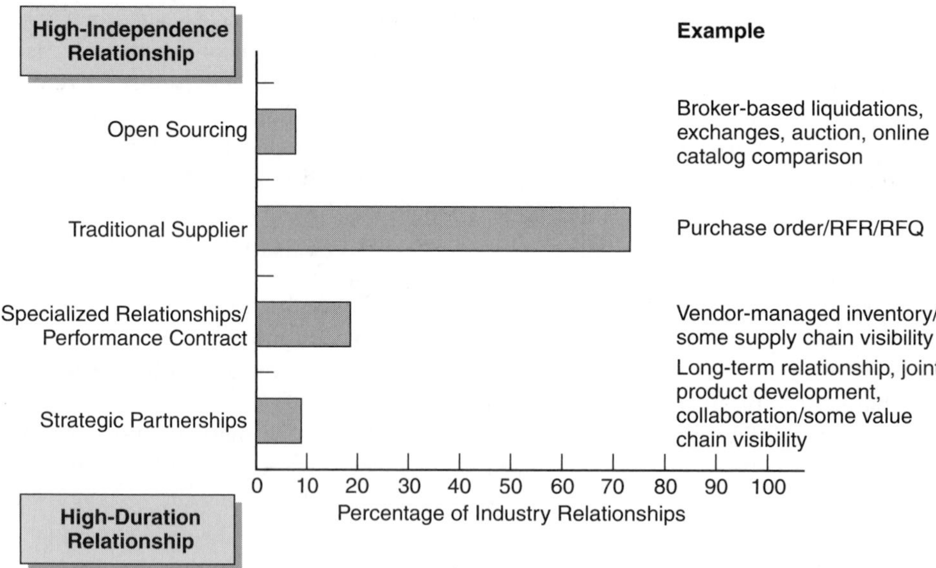

[35] "The B2B Internet Report: Collaborative Commerce," Morgan Stanley Dean Witter, April 2000.

[36] Adapted from "The E-Market Maker Revolution," GartnerGroup, September 27, 1999.

Most e-markets only facilitated spot buys, using price and availability as the key purchasing decisions.[37] This was suitable only for a small percentage of total sourcing decisions; to penetrate procurement further, e-markets would have to become much more functional.

PRODUCT CHARACTERISTICS AND THEIR IMPACT ON E-MARKETS

The total estimated procurement cost of all companies greater than $500 million in revenues globally was about $10 trillion. Firms spent roughly 65% of this on direct materials for products for resale, such as manufacturing raw material; the rest was indirect spending, including administrative supplies and operating inputs.[38]

Direct and indirect procurement were radically different processes in organizations. Corporations had automated direct procurement (generally through dedicated EDI links) more than indirect procurement, because direct materials orders were larger and buyers managed them more closely. Other direct materials tended to be commodities and were available from many suppliers, so buyers were less concerned with managing their procurement process.[39] Direct materials procurement was unique to each vertical industry value chain. Therefore, a vertical e-market that focused on a specific industry, such as electronic components, energy, or chemicals (or, increasingly, subsets of those industries like personal computer manufacturing or specialized chemicals) tended to service direct materials. Vertical e-markets claimed that their significant domain expertise made their operations optimal for their industry.

Indirect materials, which included both products and services, did not go into products for resale. These materials included administrative supplies; maintenance, repair, and operations (MRO) products, project management; IT services; human resource services; etc. Indirect transactions tended to be smaller in dollar volume, and firms performed them far more often than direct purchases. An estimated 80% of all corporate sourcing transactions were indirect.[40] Purchasing indirect products was seldom a core competence of the buying organization, and administrative costs per dollar of materials purchased were high. Indirect purchasing processes tended to be similar across industries.[41] Horizontal marketplaces used this similarity to serve many vertical industries to try to build greater liquidity and scale.[42] Horizontal e-markets would also often provide commodity-based direct materials that many different industries used.

To deal successfully with physical goods, the technical structure of the e-market had to be linked to the enormous physical infrastructure of procuring, processing, holding, and distributing the goods. In addition, in many industries, goods manufacturers had already outsourced many marketing and order and inventory management functions to distributors. Therefore, many e-markets were competing with existing

[37] "Key Components of a Marketplace," Ventro White Paper, 2000.

[38] "The Technology Primer," Morgan Stanley Dean Witter, May 2000.

[39] "Triggering the B2B Electronic Commerce Explosion," GartnerGroup, January 31, 2000.

[40] "SAP and the Online Procurement Market," May 2000.

[41] "Business-to-Business Infrastructure Practices," Jupiter Communications, June 26, 2000.

[42] "Understanding e-Markets," Jeffrey Brooks and Susan Cantrell, Andersen Consulting, April 14, 2000.

distributors to help companies make the value chain more efficient; many distributors were making e-commerce efforts and investments themselves.

In the services industries, middlemen, such as brokers and distributors, usually did not perform physical services and therefore provided less value to buyers and suppliers. Most services were also perishable. These differences mandated entirely different offerings and business models for goods e-markets versus service e-markets.

THE ECONOMIC IMPACT OF E-MARKETS

> *Although it is recognized that a supply chain that makes decisions based on global information would clearly dominate one with disjoint decisions by separate and independent entities in the supply chain, a well-coordinated supply chain has not been easy to achieve. —Hau Lee and Seungjin Whang*[43]

Adopting e-markets could have two major effects: it could increase the total profits available to the entire industry by reducing unnecessary costs or inefficiencies; and it could change the share of total industry profits that the different market participants acquired. The tools e-markets offered, how they managed transactions, and the nature of their business rules would both increase the size of the pie and change the each player's slice.

Increasing the Size of Industry Profits

More efficient and automated transactions reduced procurement costs and minimized ordering errors that resulted in suboptimal decision making. Better information would enable buyers and suppliers to use new decision support tools to build transparency into the supply chain, decrease administrative and logistics costs, increase capital asset intensity, increase inventory turns, and improve manufacturing and procurement processes (see Exhibit 6).

There had been numerous analyses by research analysts and investment houses on the potential cost savings from e-markets. Morgan Stanley Dean Witter estimated the total potential cost savings on procurement administrative costs to be nearly half a trillion dollars. GartnerGroup evaluated several industries and determined that using B2B e-commerce methods, not simply e-markets, could reduce total value chain management costs from 12%–15% of revenues (industry average) to 3%–5% of revenues, a total savings of over a trillion dollars (see Exhibit 7). Bear Stearns projected the savings to be about 25% of current supply chain management costs,[44] while IDC projected a total of $480 billion.[45]

[43] "Information Sharing in a Supply Chain," Stanford Research Paper No. 1549, Hau Lee and Seungjin Whang.

[44] "Revenge of the Bricks," *Red Herring*, August 2000.

[45] "B2B Marketplaces in the New Economy," Ariba White Paper, May 2000.

Changing the Relative Split of Profits in an Industry

E-markets also promised to change the balance of power within industries. Suppliers or customers that had benefited from asymmetric information might see that advantage reduced: "Spreads are going to disappear in our very efficient market."[46] Existing intermediaries or distributors might have to compete with new, online entrants. E-markets such as FreeMarkets had already aggregated demand, where companies came together to make a consortium bid, in the computer equipment and services industry.[47] This practice altered established levels of negotiating power by increasing buyers' leverage.

Some believed that the e-market makers, those who set up and ran the e-markets, would garner a large share of these profits: "In return for delivering incredible value, market makers stand poised to reap substantial rewards by sharing in the returns achieved by buyers and suppliers."[48] "Arms dealers," or those who provided the software and hardware infrastructure of e-markets, may also have been poised to take some of this value (see Exhibit 8).[49]

THE BUILDING BLOCKS FOR E-MARKETS

E-markets required a diverse set of participants: buyers, suppliers, e-market makers, and service companies that provided integration, infrastructure, and associated services. These categories were not mutually exclusive; for example, many suppliers and buyers had set up e-markets, and early e-market makers had licensed their technical platforms to other e-markets.

The E-Market Makers

• ***First Movers.*** An e-market maker, an organization that developed and managed an e-market, was a new entrant in the B2B landscape. The first players, such as FreeMarkets, VerticalNet, and Grainger.com began in 1995 and 1996 as independent companies, or as "bolt-ons" to existing distributors and middlemen.[50] This small trickle of companies had become a river in 1999, as many start-up companies and traditional middlemen attempted to gain first-mover advantage by setting up shop in various vertical and horizontal markets. By January 2000, 20 e-markets had gone public, with a total market capitalization in excess of $100 billion.[51] From January 1999 to the middle

[46] Dr. Andrew S. Grove as quoted in [47] "A Special Report: Inflection Point: Andrew Grove Talks About How E-Commerce Will Change Just About Everything," *Wall Street Journal*, April 17, 2000.
[47] "FreeMarkets Customers Join Together to Save Millions Through Consortium Bid," Press Release, August 29, 2000.
[48] "B2B Marketplaces in the New Economy," Ariba White Paper, May 2000.
[49] "The B2B Internet Report: Collaborative Commerce," Morgan Stanley Dean Witter, April 2000.
[50] "B2B Marketplaces in the New Economy," Ariba White Paper, May 2000 and casewriter research.
[51] Broadview Associates, January 2000.

of 2000, the number of e-markets jumped twelve-fold to nearly 1,000.[52] About 600 of those exchanges were venture capital backed.[53] Most of them initially based their differentiation on technological prowess and first mover advantage, often considered a key for gaining trading liquidity.

Some of these e-markets were horizontally focused, such as MRO.com (for MRO transactions) and FreeMarkets (for the reverse auction of excess industrial parts); others attacked vertical markets; and some, like Internet Capital Group and VerticalNet, attempted to enter many vertical market segments.[54] Many e-market makers had tried to move market making that had previously been done offline onto the Internet, while others focused on products that had not been traded before (e.g., excess bandwidth and excess space in residential moving vans).

High market valuations for those first to go public and a belief that "an early-mover advantage could be easily parlayed into a critical mass of buyers and sellers that would lock the early e-market into a dominant position via the network effect" led to a land rush mentality.[55] B2B e-commerce was the hottest investment sector for both private and public investors (in Q1 2000, venture capitalists backed more business-focused e-commerce companies than consumer-focused e-commerce companies for the first time[56]). However, these first movers generally had "meager transaction volume and equally meager revenues."[57] First-mover advantage may not have been the edge it was thought to be: "Unfortunately for most of the early movers, however, early entrance failed to produce the desired result."[58]

• ***The Entry of the Consortia.*** The first quarter of 2000 radically changed the e-market maker landscape. Large, traditional companies began to join with each other in consortia to create focused vertical markets to compete with the start-up e-markets. During the first four months of the year, an estimated average of two press releases per day trumpeted an e-market joint venture between competitors in a specific industry vertical.[59] Some of the major consortia were Covisint (automotive manufacturers), ehitex.com (electronic components), e2open.com (electronic components), Transora (processed food), Forest Express (paper products), Pantellos (energy), and Exostar (aerospace manufacturers). These efforts were well financed, with total equity contributions per e-market of $200 million or more.

[52] "Developmental Phases of the B2B e-Market Space," Jeffrey Brooks and Susan Cantrell, Andersen Consulting, June 1, 2000. Estimates varied among analysts as to the total number of e-markets, often differing on definitional characteristics.
[53] Line56.com, September 2000.
[54] Internet Capital Group is a holding companies that owned numerous e-market makers in several vertical markets.
[55] "Developmental Phases of the B2B e-Market Space," Jeffrey Brooks and Susan Cantrell, Andersen Consulting, June 1, 2000.
[56] PriceWaterhouseCoopers Money Tree Survey, July 2000.
[57] "Beyond the Exchange: The Future of B2B," *Harvard Business Review*, November/December 2000.
[58] "Developmental Phases of the B2B e-Market Space," Jeffrey Brooks and Susan Cantrell, Andersen Consulting, June 1, 2000.
[59] Comment at Online Exchanges 2000 Conference, June 2000.

Firms created these consortia for three main reasons: to generate the value chain efficiencies described previously, to earn operating profits from managing the e-markets, and to generate financial gains for corporate shareholders through initial public offerings. There were rumors that the main push for these agreements came, not from the purchasing and sales departments, but from corporate finance groups with an ear on Wall Street.[60] "Some of the [consortia] frenzy is related to market-cap envy."[61]

As one aerospace executive involved in a consortia exchange put it, "There's basically two value propositions: one, cost savings and supply integration. And two, that's what we call icing on the cake. That's us putting in the money, getting this up and running, and charging our suppliers and ourselves fees for using the exchange. But the reason we call it icing on the cake is that we're not sure what this company is going to be worth; we only know what it *might* be worth."[62] These consortia were being set up as independent companies with separate facilities and management teams that could eventually be taken public separately from the member companies. However, Wall Street was not impressed; the share prices of consortia members "haven't moved on these announcements."[63]

However, the entry of consortia in the second quarter of 2000 did radically change the valuation of independent e-markets (and many other B2B companies), which had been highly valued based on high expectations for future, not current, earnings. The financial markets believed these new consortia would severely limit future profit opportunities. By May 2000, VerticalNet's market capitalization dropped approximately 75% and Ventro's fell an astounding 93%. E-market maker stocks continued to slump throughout 2000; by November the market value of ICG, an investor in many e-market makers in several verticals, was down 95%.

The entry of these consortia and stock price pressure imperiled existing independent e-markets. To succeed, they had to attract liquidity, the very thing that these large industry players possessed. Independent e-markets had been leveraging their high market valuations by offering equity stakes to large, established companies in return for transaction volume; these relationships were generally not exclusive.[64] This was becoming increasingly difficult. Independent e-markets also had a difficult public relations position; they had initially criticized the new industry-led e-markets, questioning whether they would get off the ground. This was risky; as one analyst said, "Yeah, that's a good idea: criticize the companies you need to make your own marketplace liquid."[65]

Consortia e-markets had other inherent advantages: other trading partners could sign up more quickly because they has less uncertainty about which e-market would win, and the participants could avoid redundant infrastructure costs if they pooled their efforts and avoided investing in several independent, competing efforts.[66]

[60] "Revenge of the Bricks," *Red Herring*, August 2000.

[61] "The B2B Internet Report: Collaborative Commerce," Morgan Stanley Dean Witter, April 2000.

[62] "How the Top Guns Are Doing It," *Red Herring*, August 2000.

[63] "The B2B Internet Report: Collaborative Commerce," Morgan Stanley Dean Witter, April 2000.

[64] *ibid.*

[65] Pierre Mitchell, AMR research analyst, as quoted in *Crain's*, June 19, 2000.

[66] "The B2B Internet Report: Collaborative Commerce," Morgan Stanley Dean Witter, April 2000.

However, industry consortia also faced significant challenges. While the press releases had been filled with hyperbole of cost savings and total market sizes (see Exhibit 9), large companies had only gingerly been experimenting with this new transaction mechanism. Most industry-led consortia had little more than a press release and a memorandum of understanding, let alone definitive partnership agreements or completed transactions.[67] Late in 2000, in response to supplier pressure, many buyer-led consortia began to change the focus of their efforts from market making (auctions, etc.) to reducing procurement costs.[68]

A key problem was governance; industry consortia were new companies that long-term industry competitors with little history of cooperation and collaboration had set up. They often included 20 or more trading partners, making cooperation difficult. The CEO of Ventro said, "The single biggest problem is that joint ventures are hard, joint ventures are twice as hard, and joint ventures with many players who've been competitors for 80 years are nearly impossible."[69]

There were also issues of neutrality; how could potential participants be convinced that the e-market "rules" would not be tilted toward the consortia owners? But then again, was this potential conflict of interest any different from when e-market infrastructure player Commerce One offered 20% of its equity to General Motors in warrants, or when Ventro offered equity stakes to its market participants?[70] Finally, an industry often had more than one consortium, with no clear direction as to how the two markets would interact. For example, two large industry-led consortia were announced in both the retail and the energy markets within a few weeks of each other.

When this case was written, "not a single one of the . . . B2B exchanges had reached even 1% of the overall trading volume" of its industry.[71] Less than 15% of e-markets had even completed a transaction.[72] Many analysts projected that the number of e-markets would increase upward of 10,000, and then consolidate rapidly as some won and others lost. Some predicted that, by 2004, four or five "mega-exchanges" would control most e-market activity. Others thought that a slew of specialists (trade originators, speculators, and sell-order swappers) similar to those in financial markets would support these large exchanges. Still others said that each vertical industry would have 2–3 markets, leaving a total of 50–100 survivors. Finally, a different group forecasted a flood of micromarkets with liquidity in small, specialized product lines linked to large, global technical infrastructures.[73]

• ***E-Market Revenue Models.*** Most e-markets generated (or were attempting to generate) multiple revenue streams.

[67] "Revenge of the Bricks," *Red Herring*, August 2000.

[68] "Beyond the Exchange: The Future of B2B," *Harvard Business Review*, November-December 2000.

[69] "Revenge of the Bricks," *Red Herring*, August 2000.

[70] "Beyond the Neutrality Debate," Line56.com, August 14, 2000.

[71] "Container Case: B2B Exchanges," *The Economist*, October 21, 2000.

[72] "E-doption of E-Commerce," Line56.com, November 2000.

[73] "The B2B Internet Report: Collaborative Commerce," Morgan Stanley Dean Witter, April 2000, and "Beyond the Exchange: The Future of B2B," *Harvard Business Review*, November/December 2000.

- Transaction fees: flat fees or a percentage of the value (a few basis points up to 15%) of sales that the e-market generated
- Product markup fees: for products purchased at a volume discount from the seller and then resold to buyers
- Subscription fees: access fees for monthly or annual usage, often scaling as the trading partner added functionality
- Savings share: a performance-based fee that reflected savings the e-market participant accrued
- "Value-added services," such as escrow, credit, logistics, quality assurance, etc.
- Miscellaneous other service revenues such as sales lead generation, data mining, advertising, software sales, professional services, or systems integration[74]

Some analysts predicted early that between 10%–25% of the added value an e-market generated could accrue to the e-market maker.[75] Others thought this overly optimistic and argued that large-scale order matching would offer limited profit or shareholder value; they pointed to the example of the most liquid, high-volume market in the world, "There is a reason that the NYSE, the mother of all trading exchanges . . . supports $7.3 trillion and 169 billion shares in trading volume but only generates $101 million in income annually. Order matching is inherently a low-margin business."[76] Value-added services would be needed to generate significant profits to make the market more "sticky," increasing or maintaining liquidity. E-market makers often pointed to their value-added services, such as logistics, credit, escrow, and other functions, as a key source of differentiation. Many of these were similar to those traditional distributors offered.

E-Market Infrastructure

> *The technology infrastructure required for a net market is evolving rapidly because the requirements are changing as buyers and sellers become more sophisticated. . . . The Internet provides the highway, but software is a key engine.* —*Charles Phillips, Morgan Stanley Dean Witter*[77]

• ***Building the Central Hub/Marketplace.*** One of the first e-market makers, Ventro, spent $10 million and 18 months building its first exchange site in the mid-1990s. Most of the first e-markets have to develop their own software infrastructure (often with the help of consulting firms). Since then, both the time and the finances required

[74] "Winning E-Marketplace Strategies," GartnerGroup analyst Leah Knight, May 8, 2000.

[75] *ibid.*

[76] "The B2B Internet Report: Collaborative Commerce," Morgan Stanley Dean Witter, April 2000.

[77] *ibid.*

to build an e-market have dropped dramatically. By mid-2000, basic exchange Web sites could be up and running in less than a month, with a total setup cost of about $1 million.[78]

The key technical building blocks for the central infrastructure of an e-market were as follows:[79]

- Application platform: standard e-commerce platform for static and dynamic Web pages, caching engine, content creation and management, load balancing, etc.
- Buy-side commerce server (hosted at central market and trading partner): a workflow engine with electronic procurement rules for a single buying organization, reports on procurement history, and order management
- Sell-side commerce server (hosted at central market and trading partner): provided transaction processing and order status information, created purchase orders, enabled payment processing, merchandising and other seller functions, and provided systems integration to business services such as shipping or credit
- Market-making transaction engine: order matching across multiple buyers and sellers (in multiple formats such as exchanges, auctions, etc.), aggregation of electronic catalogs from multiple suppliers
- Catalog/content management: Tools that created, updated, and maintained electronic catalogs and other forms of searchable and pertinent content
- Community management: provided discussion groups, bulletin boards, news feeds and other pertinent community features

The hub also needed databases for product information warehousing and transaction logs; security and authentication features; and transport, presentation, and routing (TPR) capabilities to communicate reliably with e-market participants (Figure 6).

Two of the strongest infrastructure providers were alliances. IBM, Ariba, and i2 Technologies, a leader in supply chain management software, had formed an alliance to offer B2B systems and software in March 2000; it became e-market focused in September 2000.[80] A strong competitor was the Commerce One/SAP alliance that wedded an e-market builder with the leading ERP provider. Oracle was also offering one-stop shopping for nearly all ERP, supply chain, and e-market needs. Major players offered central hub architecture and buy-side and sell-side applications hosted at the trading partners. While other firms had moved into this market more quickly, the ERP vendors' large installed bases made them competitive; an organization may want

[78] Conversations with Jamie Lerner, CTO of Xuma.com, June 2000.

[79] Numerous sources: Xuma.com homepage, "Commerce One Market Site Portal Solution 3.0" White Paper, 2000, and "The B2B Internet Report: Collaborative Commerce," Morgan Stanley Dean Witter, April 2000.

[80] Advertisement in *Wall Street Journal*, September 7, 2000.

FIGURE 6 Representative Prototype of the Central E-Market Infrastructure[81]

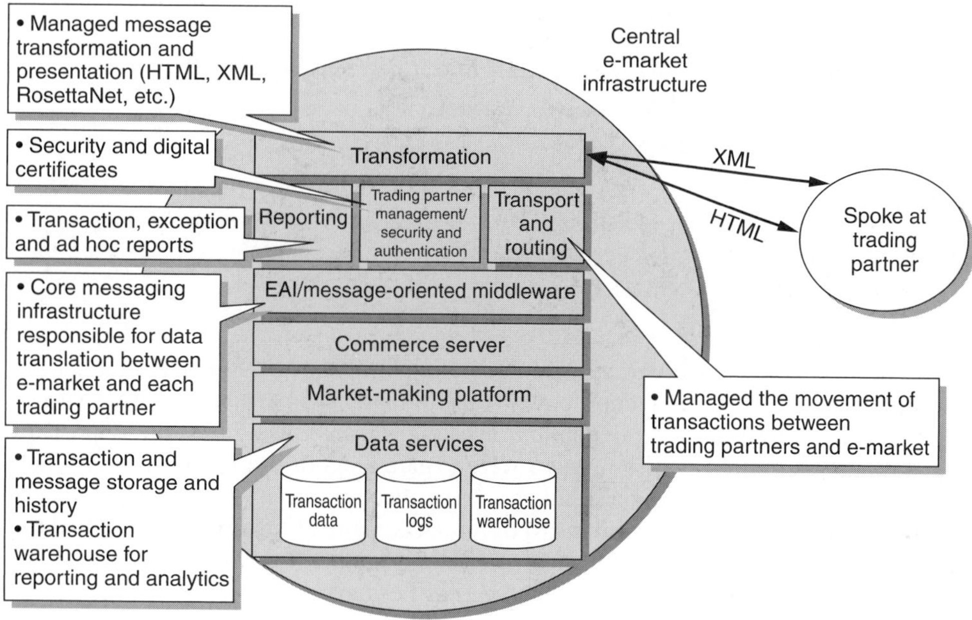

"to keep its systems as much as possible on a single platform."[82] The environment was extremely competitive: "There's no single dominant player yet, much to the dismay of any single vendor claiming that it is."[83]

An important complementary offering was BPO functionality (also called SCM solutions), software that allowed companies or trading partners to make better operating decisions based on the increased information the e-market offered. Leaders in this field were i2 Technologies, Manugistics, Numetrix, and Logility, with the major ERP vendors such as SAP working to improve the SCM functionality in their ERP modules. Many providers also offered a wide variety of niche technical services. These included Web site content management, catalog management, personalization, and channel relationship management modules. Many firms offered specialized, point solutions, such as Moai Technologies with auction market making and Clarus with buy-side procurement (see Exhibit 10 for a list of major providers).

Infrastructure providers were also designing the business structure of e-markets and running exchanges themselves. For example, Commerce One helped to create the Global Trading Web Council, a group of multinational corporations attempting to build

[81] Adapted from analysis performed by PriceWaterhouseCoopers for Intel Corporation, June 2000.
[82] "Businesses Seek to Cut Weak Link from Supply Chains..." *InformationWeek*, March 6, 2000.
[83] "Building an Exchange Machine," Line56.com, October 1, 2000.

a network of e-markets.[84] Oracle had created the Oracle Global Exchange Network to link together multiple e-markets.[85]

- ***Application Integration Between the E-Market and the Trading Partners***

Building the hub is easy, it's the spokes that are hard.
—Jamie Lerner, CTO of Xuma.com Corporation

Until the back-end integration issues are solved, corporate buyers and sellers are left wondering what the real value of B2B e-commerce is.
—Phillip Merrick, CEO of WebMethods Corporation

Early e-markets were initially peripheral to core value chain transactions of trading partners and offered little or no technology integration with the participants' internal systems: "Only 5 to 10 of 600 independent exchanges have any significant support for supply chain integration."[86] If e-markets were to gain a significant proportion of strategic procurement spending, they would have to connect information contained in back-end ERP and manufacturing systems to other participants. One executive dubbed the fact that after e-markets brought a buyer and seller together, transactions were still finished by phone or fax, as "the dirty little secret of e-markets."[87]

E-markets needed both machine-to-person (browser-based) and machine-to-machine connections, which were the most difficult to create. Most large companies had ERP packages that contained the pricing, product, and availability information that e-markets needed. Enterprise application integration (EAI), first used when two internal systems needed to exchange data without human interaction,[88] was rapidly being transformed into interenterprise application integration: "Today, undoubtedly, the lion's share is e-business integration."[89] New entrants, such as Extricity, Vitria, and WebMethods had taken a first-mover advantage. But large, traditional systems integrators like IBM and BEA, as well as other infrastructure providers such as Microsoft, had begun to provide application integration. The major ERP vendors were also pursuing this market.

More important than information systems integration was business process integration; that is, for two trading partners to fully automate a transaction, they had to conform their respective business actions and then systematize those activities into software.

Process integration challenges were considerable: most business processes were not yet fully automated within companies, limiting any attempt at external integration. Many

[84] "Battle to the Bitter End," *Business 2.0*, July 25, 2000
[85] "The e-Business Marketplace: The Future of Competition," Aberdeen Group White Paper, April 2000.
[86] "The Paradox of RosettaNet," Line56.com, September 2000.
[87] Phillip Merrick of WebMethods, quoted in Line56.com, July 31, 2000.
[88] NC.focus White Paper on EAI, 1999.
[89] GartnerGroup analyst Roy Schulte, as quoted by ebizQ.net.

companies did not have an IT infrastructure or used simple accounting software. Moreover, trading partners had optimized business processes and data management for firm profitability and had to deviate from that optimization to integrate their processes with others. Finally, application integration costs were also highly variable and differed on a company-by-company basis (some analysts gave a range of \$1–\$6 million[90]).

• ***Hub-to-hub Integration***

Much like ATM networks, B2B markets are developing as islands.
—Charles Phillips, Morgan Stanley Dean Witter[91]

With the proliferation of both vertical and horizontal e-markets, many with varying levels of specialization, it was becoming clear that these markets had also to connect to one another. Trading partners could become frustrated at attempting to join and then integrate with 2–3 vertical e-markets as well as several horizontal markets for indirect procurement. This problem became more acute if there were many micromarkets.

Technically, it was easiest to link e-markets that the same infrastructure provider designed (e.g., Oracle or Commerce One), allowing these companies to leverage their installed base. Disparate markets from several vendors could also be linked together. i2 Technologies had designed a specific product, TradeMatrix, to sit between e-markets and act as a gateway between them. Waybid was attempting to list merchandise across several e-markets to enhance liquidity.[92] The business rules of such linkages were not yet standard and were negotiated on a market-by-market basis.[93]

E-Business Standards

Companies recognize that unless standards implementation occurs, B2B becomes nothing more than a lot of hype. —Jennifer Hamilton, CEO of RosettaNet[94]

Integration of applications and processes across multiple trading partners and/or e-markets required industry-wide standards.[95]

• ***XML.*** E-markets needed a common, universal means to describe products, processes, trading partners, and other data types. A new tool, extensible markup language (XML) used various "tags" to define the types of data in an electronic document, such as price, invoice number, trading partner, and so forth. It was rapidly becoming the communications standard for data interchange in B2B e-commerce. However, XML only provided a method for defining the data types, not the actual data types or application

90 "Business-to-Business Infrastructure Practices," Jupiter Communications, June 26, 2000.
91 "The B2B Internet Report: Collaborative Commerce," Morgan Stanley Dean Witter, April 2000.
92 "Forget B2B. Think E2E," *Red Herring*, August 2000.
93 *ibid.*
94 "The Paradox of RosettaNet," Line56.com, September 2000.
95 "Understanding e-Markets," Jeffrey Brooks and Susan Cantrell, Andersen Consulting, April 14, 2000.

responses.[96] This was left to two players: standards bodies, who created de jure norms, and e-market software vendors, who created de facto standards through the proliferation of their applications. The vendors, specifically Ariba and Commerce One, moved first in this field with XML variants based on their own e-market applications. However, influential standards bodies and industry consortia soon moved in, with OASIS, OpenApplications Group, RosettaNet, and ebXML (an OASIS/UN joint venture) being representatives of the more than 400 e-business standards bodies, most representing a specific interest or industry.[97] By mid-2000, there were over one hundred different dialects of XML, most so different they were "unusable by partners, suppliers, and customers."[98] Each one had the backing of different constituencies with different motives. Since companies expected to interface with several e-markets across different industries, they would have to adopt the XML data types each one used.[99]

Many industry analysts agreed "universal" XML standards would emerge eventually, but that these would vary by industry because each vertical had different information-sharing needs. Standards bodies understood the need for standards alignment and knew that the lack of clear rules was confusing the marketplace.

• ***Process Conformance.*** To truly automate business interactions, more than standardized data had to be interchanged. The entire transaction process had to be broken down into discrete parts, optimized for the business purpose, and then conformed between trading partners. The first substantial organization to realize this was RosettaNet, a consortium of industry heavyweights in the information technology, electronic components, and semiconductor supply chains, formed in 1998. RosettaNet defined XML data types like other bodies, but it was also developing partner interface processes (PIPs) that set the rules for the actual methods by which trading partners would conduct a transaction (or part of a transaction). It went beyond simple data sharing and was intended to standardize the "what" and "how" of trading partner actions in a transactions. It was slow going, both for the development of PIPs and for the firms adopting them. Most other industries had not yet begun to develop process conformance; in fact, they were approaching RosettaNet about adopting its standards methodology for their specific vertical.

ROADBLOCKS TO E-MARKETS ADOPTION

Despite the projections of enormous trading volume, many things could slow the movement of transaction volume to e-markets.

[96] Stanford Graduate School of Business case study, "SAP and the Online Procurement Market," May 2000.
[97] "The Paradox of RosettaNet," Line56.com, September 2000.
[98] "X Marks the Spot Where No One Can Agree," Tyler McDaniel for Line56.com, July 31, 2000.
[99] "The Paradox of RosettaNet," Line56.com, September 2000.

- Large purchases in many industries were already negotiated under long-term contracts (up to 90% of the monetary value of all transactions[100]), reducing the opportunity for new market-making mechanisms.
- Product and process complexity could make transactions difficult to standardize, systematize, and code into software.
- Buyers and sellers were delaying making e-market decisions to preserve their options.
- Supplier reluctance to join e-markets due to concerns about commoditization.
- System and process integration hindered by sunk cost in other data-sharing links.
- Ineffective efforts to set standards.
- Slow consolidation of competing e-markets.
- Regulatory concerns.

Some of these were particularly important. Many suppliers believed that price, availability, and process transparency tilted the competitive fulcrum toward buyers:

> *Let's see, you want me to put all my products and prices online so my customers can beat me about the head and shoulders. Then I can commoditize myself even more to take my razor-thin margins down to microscopic levels. Finally, I get to pay transaction fees for this privilege. . . . What am I missing?*[101]

Research analysts agreed: "If we had to pick a single party as the largest net beneficiary on an aggregate basis across all industries, we'd have to go with buyers."[102] However, both supplier and buyer participation was necessary for an exchange to be liquid, so any e-market that was inherently too favorable to one side or the other "will likely hit a brick wall of resistance."

Moreover, many companies associated e-markets with auctions and feared that auctions would commoditize their products and reduce margins. Most companies preferred to "buy from an auction, but would never want to sell into one."

Many intercompany electronic transactions continued to be processed using point-to-point EDI; companies had invested heavily in the system and had optimized internal and external processes to use it. Most surveyed executives intended to keep EDI as a significant component of their external communication strategy.[103]

[100] "Container Case: B2B Exchanges," *The Economist*, October 21, 2000.

[101] Anonymous source in "The B2B Internet Report: Collaborative Commerce," Morgan Stanley Dean Witter, April 2000.

[102] "The B2B Internet Report: Collaborative Commerce," Morgan Stanley Dean Witter, April 2000.

[103] "B2B Supply Chains Proliferate in Manufacturing, GartnerGroup, May 2000.

Slow standards alignment could also hinder adoption of e-markets. It took 15 years from the first usage of EDI to widespread use due to disagreements on standards. The financial services industry alone currently has five XML "standards," hindering B2B adoption in that vertical.[104]

Finally, several e-markets, often with overlapping membership and functionality, serviced many industry verticals. Without consolidation, adoption could slow considerably, as uncertainty among trading partners and the costs of attaching to multiple e-markets caused confusion and indecision. In the high-tech electronic components industry in mid-2000, over 50% of key participants were members of more than one e-market, and over 25% had no e-market involvement at all.[105] Membership was also not exclusive; Lucent Technologies, an early member of a high-tech consortia e-market, still planned several separate e-commerce efforts, such as its own private, sell-side hub.[106]

- ***Antitrust Intervention***

> *An increasing number of regulators and firms in the industries being transformed are starting to worry that . . . rather than opening markets to greater competition, B2B exchanges could become powerful monopolistic tools.* —*The Economist, June 17, 2000*

American or European antitrust regulators could also slow or limit the adoption of e-markets. E-markets create opportunities for competitors to share information and processes, a situation that was ripe for illegal, anticompetitive practices, including explicit price collusion or supply aggregation. The powerful network effects of e-markets may have also led to a "winner-take-all" endgame, forcing trading partners to join an exchange to stay in business.

In response to these concerns, the Federal Trade Commission (FTC) investigated three major consortia e-markets in the automotive and aerospace markets.[107] It also convened a two-day workshop on e-markets in June 2000, in which it stated that e-markets would violate the law if they become cartels.[108] European antitrust regulators were also monitoring e-market development. Analysts expected antitrust friction: "The exchanges are going to go as far as they can go until someone slaps their wrists."[109]

CONCLUSION

The promise of e-markets seemed enormous; yet the challenges to attaining those benefits were also large. The Internet communication mechanism and the creation of XML did not magically enable all businesses to effortlessly share error-free, timely, and appropriate data with each other. Early e-markets had many participants, each with its own

[104] Interview with GartnerGroup analyst Susan Cournoyer, August 2000.
[105] PriceWaterhouseCoopers analysis performed by Intel Corporation, June 2000.
[106] Press release, "Lucent Technologies Joins the e2open.com Global e-Marketplace," July 18, 2000.
[107] The FTC approved the Covisint e-market in September 2000.
[108] "FTC Keeps an Eye on B2B Online Markets," *Computerworld*, July 20, 2000.
[109] Lara Abrams of the Aberdeen Group as quoted in "Exchanges Under Scrutiny," *InfoWorld*, July 10, 2000.

agenda; managing these differences would be difficult. Enormous information systems integration and business process conformance would need to be completed by both the e-markets and trading partners. Despite this, large corporations, venture capitalists, entrepreneurs, and the financial markets had placed huge bets on an uncertain and dynamic future. Two opposing views sum up that future:

- "These newly formed B2B exchanges never had sustainable business models from the start. The truth is there may be nothing fundamentally new about Newcos [e-market consortia] at all. Corporations have been trying to make their supply chains more efficient since Eli Whitney jiggered up the cotton gin. The newest trading exchanges, theoretically a quantum leap in the ways of doing business, may actually be nothing more that just a further evolution."[110]
- "B2B marketplaces are redefining how businesses interact with each other. Inevitably, all businesses will be affected by this revolution. The important question that all companies must answer is: 'How?'"[111]

EXHIBIT 1 Aerospace Manufacturing Value Chain[112]

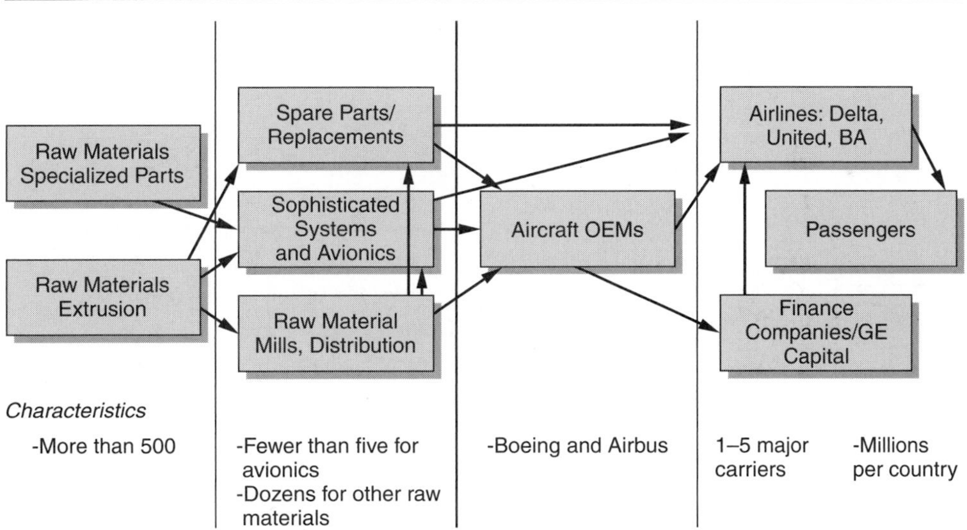

[110] "Revenge of the Bricks," *Red Herring*, August 2000.
[111] "B2B Marketplaces in the New Economy," Ariba White Paper, May 2000.
[112] Adapted from "E-Commerce in the Aerospace Vertical," by Leeds, Leeds, Neist, and Thomas, 2000.

EXHIBIT 2 The Transition of Data Sharing Techniques from EDI to E-Markets[113]

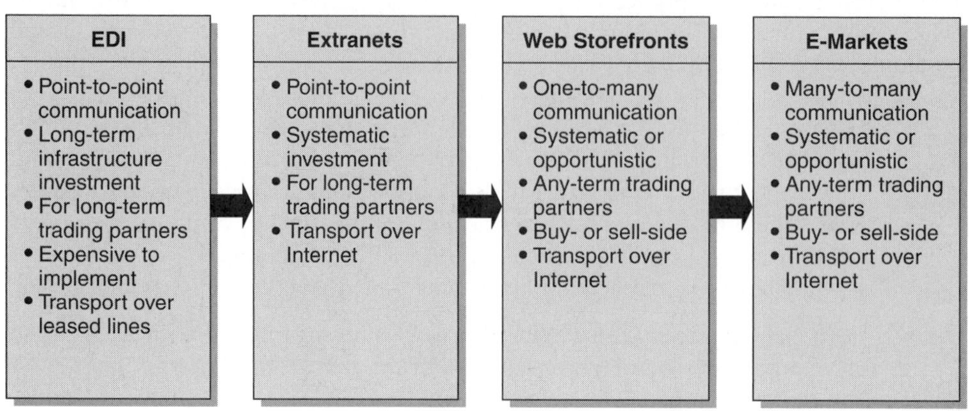

EXHIBIT 3 Buyer-Dominated Dynamic Marketplace[114]

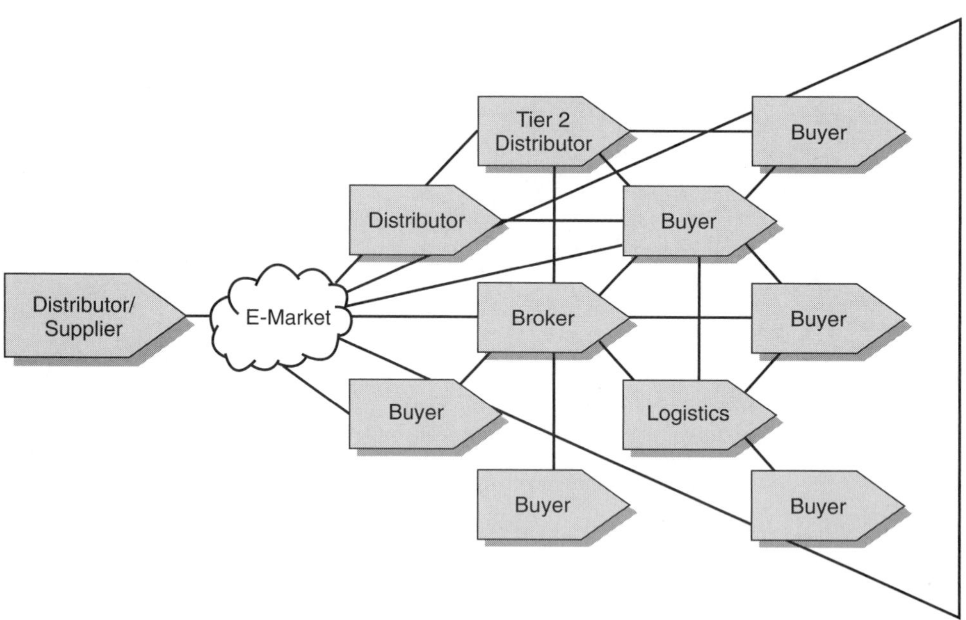

[113] Adapted from "The E-Market Maker Revolution," GartnerGroup, September 27, 1999.
[114] *ibid.*

EXHIBIT 4 Supplier-Dominated Dynamic Marketplace[115]

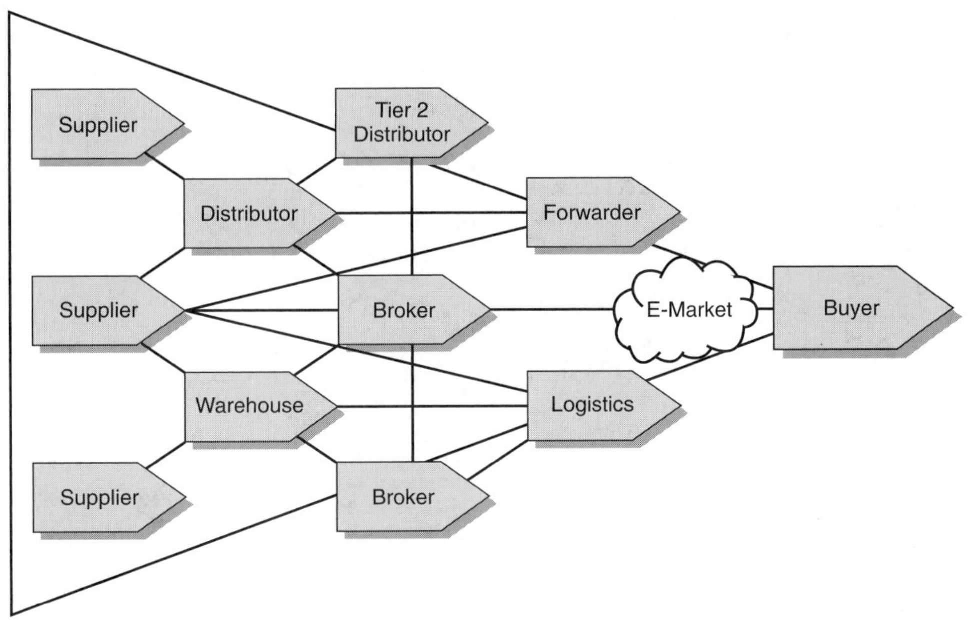

EXHIBIT 5 Neutral Dynamic Marketplace[116]

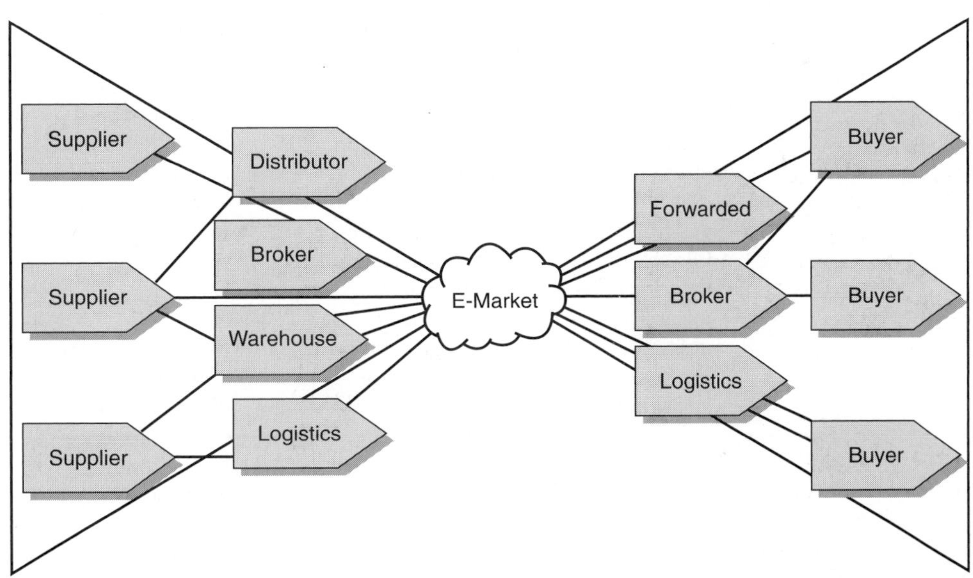

[115] *ibid.*
[116] *ibid.*

EXHIBIT 6 Ways in Which E-Markets Could Increase Total Industry Profits

Category	*E-Market Offering*	*Impact on Buyer*	*Impact on Supplier*
Transaction processing, automation and management	• Systematization and coding of transaction rules so that more business processes can be performed by machines over the Internet, rather than by humans using the phone, fax, and paper	• Reduced procurement administrative costs (savings of up to 90%) due to lower level of "human touch" on orders, reducing chances for errors and labor expense • Elimination of redundant orders • Enforcement of corporate procurement policies and the control of "mavericks"	• Lower level of human touch on sales, reducing chances for errors and labor expense • Reduced order and customer management costs
Value chain visibility and collaboration	• Product, process and availability transparency • Enhanced discovery and choices of buyers and seller • Removing layers of value chain intermediaries, such as brokers and resellers, that block data dissemination • Global, rather than local, optimization of business processes based on joint decision making	• Reduced inventory levels due to more accurate matching of production to supplier inputs • Reduced production lead time due to more efficient sourcing techniques • Reduced barriers to switching between suppliers • Business process optimization using decision support tools • Reduction in power and importance of nonvalue add intermediaries (and rents paid to them)	• Reduced inventory levels due to more accurate matching of production to customer orders • Greater asset intensity and better returns on capital investment due to more accurate forecasting • Reduced barriers to switching between customers • Business process optimization using decision support tools • Reduction in power and importance of nonvalue add intermediaries (and rents paid to them)

(continued)

EXHIBIT 6 *(continued)*

Category	*E-Market Offering*	*Impact on Buyer*	*Impact on Supplier*
Content/community functions	• Sharing of industry best practices, knowledge management, and benchmarking • Industry news and reports • Product information and reviews • Discussion forums	• Better information for better decision making	• Better information for better decision making

EXHIBIT 7 Potential Savings from Usage of E-Markets[117]

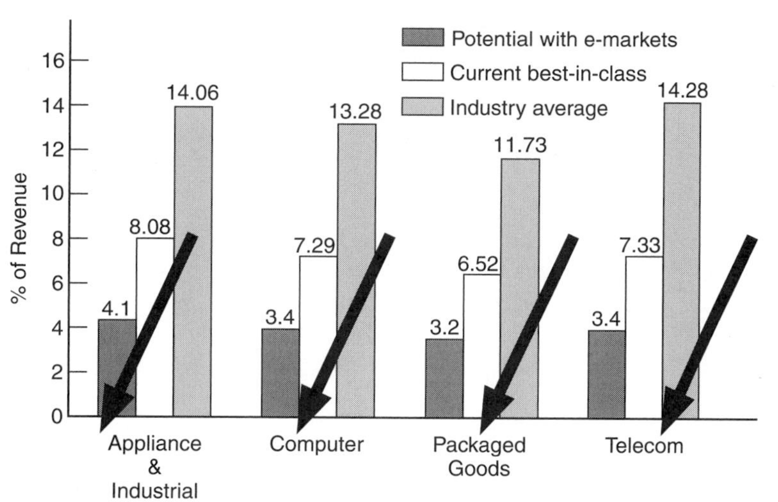

Total value chain management cost was the sum of the following costs: order management, material acquisition, and inventory carrying, as well as value chain finance, planning, and information systems costs.

[117] GartnerGroup research as shared with Intel Corporation, July 2000.

EXHIBIT 8 Ways in Which E-Markets Could Change the Relative Split of Industry Profits

Category	*E-Market Offering*	*Impact on Buyer*	*Impact on Supplier*
Pricing transparency and efficiency	• Alternative transaction mechanisms such as auctions, reverse auctions, bid-ask exchanges, and electronic catalog aggregation • Increasing the number of diverse buyers and sellers • Removing or reducing the power of value chain intermediaries such as brokers and resellers • Real-time price discovery and collection of historical price data • Revenue management techniques such as yield management	• Access to broader number of suppliers, reducing barriers to switching • Potential lower prices due to greater supplier choice and easier comparison shopping	• Access to broader number of buyers, reducing barriers to switching • Better information for negotiations • Potential buyer focus on price due to lower barriers to supplier change
Demand aggregation	• Buyers combine together to push for better pricing and terms from suppliers	• Lower purchase prices due to increased relative power	• Lower selling prices due to decreased relative power

EXHIBIT 9 Press Release, Aerospace Consortia E-Market

BAE Systems, Boeing, Lockheed Martin, and Raytheon to Create B2B Exchange for the Aerospace and Defense Industry

Global Trading Exchange to Be Powered by Commerce One and Microsoft
3/28/00 6:00 P.M. PST
NEW YORK, March 28, 2000

An aerospace and defense industry group including The BAE SYSTEMS, The Boeing Company (NYSE: BA), Lockheed Martin Corporation (NYSE: LMT), Raytheon (NYSE: RTNA, RTNB) and B2B e-commerce solutions leader Commerce One (NASDQ: CMRC) today announced the creation of an independent enterprise that will develop an Internet trading exchange for the global aerospace and defense industry. This open aerospace and defense exchange, based on the Commerce One MarketSite Portal Solution, powered by Microsoft, will be a secure, electronic marketplace where buyers and sellers around the world can conduct business.

The global aerospace and defense industry has commercial and military sales of more than $400 billion. Currently, the four lead participants in this new venture do business worldwide with more than 37,000 suppliers, hundreds of airlines, and national governments globally, all of who will be invited to join the Web-based marketplace. Boeing buys $38 billion annually in goods and services, while Lockheed Martin purchases $13 billion, BAE SYSTEMS spends $11 billion, and Raytheon spends $9 billion for a total combined procurement of $71 billion.

"This trading exchange can deliver enormous buy and sell side efficiencies to our industry," said Phil Condit, Boeing chairman and chief executive officer. "By using a single e-marketplace, all of us manufacturers, suppliers, airline and government customers, and service providers can significantly lower transaction costs and deliver more value."

Vance Coffman, chairman and CEO of Lockheed Martin, said, "This global trading exchange will transform commerce for the aerospace and defense industry on a worldwide basis. It's a catalyst that will set the industry standard for business-to-business e-commerce while driving its increased use of. It also should help us address a major priority of our government customers by reducing acquisition process costs and further aligning the industry with the Department of Defense Integrated Digital Environment Initiative."

According to Sir Richard Evans, chairman of BAE SYSTEMS, "Our industry has always been identified with innovation and the exploitation of innovative ideas. I believe this Exchange to be a good example of that foresight. It embraces established concepts but develops them, capturing the essence of future global trading by bringing together the principals of our industry to serve the market in a truly integrated, global, context."

Raytheon chairman and chief executive officer Dan Burnham said, "We are excited about the potential of this innovative, e-commerce trading exchange. By bringing the supply chain management expertise of the industry's leaders to a single, online marketplace, we will put customers, suppliers, and employees a mouse click away from achieving greater productivity, efficiency, and cost savings."

Mark Hoffman, chairman and CEO of Commerce One, said, "These visionary companies have recognized the dramatic positive impact e-commerce can have on the aerospace and defense industry. This new enterprise will establish the 'mega exchange' for the industry. Our recognized leadership in e-commerce technology solutions built on Microsoft technology combined with the worldwide presence and domain knowledge of BAE SYSTEMS, Boeing, Lockheed Martin, and Raytheon will add a major new e-marketplace to the Commerce One Global Trading Web, the world's largest business-to-business trading community."

"A successful marketplace brings together a critical mass of buyers and sellers of all sizes," said Steve Ballmer, CEO of Microsoft. "We are delighted that Microsoft's Windows 2000 and our extensive Internet services will be the technology employed to create that critical mass in this new aerospace and defense marketplace. We have a proven track record of building marketplaces with Internet leaders like Commerce One, and are proud to be partnering with them again on this exciting project."

The five companies have signed a memorandum of understanding (MOU) to form the new venture. The parties expect to sign a binding agreement soon, and will form a new company that will own and operate the exchange. The Web-based trading exchange is aiming for a launch by mid-year.

Under the terms of the MOU, the founding partners have agreed initially to take equal ownership stakes in the new entity. Adjustments to this allocation will be based on each founding partner's flow of its e-commerce through the exchange over the first three years. Twenty percent of the equity has been set aside for other industry participants and employees of the new venture. Commerce One will have a five percent equity position.

Condit said the new exchange is a logical extension of Boeing's leadership in aerospace e-commerce and evidence of its plan to pursue new-frontier opportunities in the networked economy. "Our PART Page, established in 1996, was the first Web-based ordering system for after-market commercial airplane parts," he said. "In 1999, we generated more than $400 million in online sales and the site was used by more than 250 airlines and about 675 other companies. We'll migrate our industry-leading operation to this new trading exchange," Condit added.

Working with its government customers, Lockheed Martin has pioneered the early implementation of e-commerce solutions, according to Coffman. "Now, we and the other participants in this trading exchange will help provide a common and consistent platform to expand e-commerce across the aerospace and defense industry at large," Coffman said.

EXHIBIT 10 Major Providers of E-Market Technical Infrastructure[118]

B2B E-Procurement (Buy-Side)

Ariba
Commerce One
Oracle
Clarus
Metiom
RightWorks

Market-Making Software

Ariba
Open Site Technology
Calico (Connect acquisition)
Commerce One
Moai Technologies
FairMarket, Inc.

Sell-Side Commerce Servers

BroadVision
IBM
Microsoft
InterWorld
Sun/Netscape
Oracle
SAP
Intershop

Channel Relationship Management

Asera
Channelwave
Click Commerce
Entigo
Marketsoft
Webridge
Comergent

Catalog/Content Software and Services

TPN Register
Aspect Development (I2)
SAQQARA
Mercado
Profile Systems
Requisite Technology
Reed Technology
Commerce One (Mergent Systems)

Personalization

Broadvision
NetPerceptions
Vignette
Documentum

Product Configuration/Interactive Selling

Calico
FirePond
On-Link (Siebel)
Selectica
Trilogy

Web Site Content Management

Interwoven
Vignette
Documentum
Broadvision (Interleaf acquisition)

Supply Chain/Business Process Optimization

i2
Manugistics
J. D. Edwards

118 "The B2B Internet Report: Collaborative Commerce," Morgan Stanley Dean Witter, April 2000. Reproduced with permission.

STANFORD
GRADUATE SCHOOL OF BUSINESS

PRICING AND BRANDING ON THE INTERNET

It's a great time to be a consumer. You have more power than you could possibly imagine. —*Kate Delhagen, Forrester Research*[1]

In Internet retailing, abundant information, reduced transaction costs, and unlimited "shelf space" promise to increase the consumer's purchasing power. Online buyers expect the Web to be an around-the-clock fire sale, with the next bargain just a click away. This "getting a deal" culture is pervasive among Internet shoppers. According to a recent survey, more than half of online shoppers expect a 20%–30% discount from the standard retail price when buying an item that would normally be priced between $30 and $500.[2] "If you're a consumer and you're thinking about any kind of researched purchase, you're leaving thousands of dollars on the table if you don't at least look online," says Kate Delhagen, an online retail analyst with Forrester Research.

Low consumer search costs, the financial markets' tolerance for aggressive spending on customer acquisition, and the Internet's lower entry and operational costs cause many to expect that competition will intensify. Prices will decline and brand loyalty will be threatened as both Internet start-ups and traditional retailers try to acquire and retain customers. At the limit, intense competition and perfectly informed consumers will drive prices down to marginal cost.

Research Associate Kostas Sgoutas, MBA 2000, prepared this case under the supervision of Professor Garth Saloner and Professor A. Michael Spence as the basis for class discussion rather than to illustrate either effective or ineffective handling of an administrative situation. Margot Sutherland, Executive Director, Center for Electronic Business and Commerce, Graduate School of Business managed the development of the case. Research support by the Boston Consulting Group is gratefully acknowledged.

[1] David Bank, "A Site-Eat-Site World," *Wall Street Journal*, July 12, 1999, p. R8.
[2] Bob Tedeschi, "Using Discounts to Build a Client Base," http://www.nytimes.com, May 31, 1999.

Empirical evidence on the impact of the Internet on pricing and branding has been mixed. MIT's Sloan School of Management studied pricing for books and CDs. On the one hand, the results showed that Internet prices average 9%–16% less than conventional channel prices.[3] On the other hand, however, price dispersion on the Internet may suggest that search costs are not minimal or that factors other than price influence consumers' decisions. The same study by MIT concluded, "...there are substantial and systematic differences in prices across retailers on the Internet. Prices posted on the Internet differ by an average of 33% for books and 25% for CDs [Exhibit 1]. At the same time, the dispersion of prices weighted by retailer popularity reveals that Internet markets are highly concentrated, but the retailers with the lowest prices do not receive the most sales."[4] Bizrate.com's survey of online buyers also suggests that product price is the attribute least correlated with a repeat online purchase. Instead, customer service, fulfillment, and trust appear to be more important drivers of online loyalty.

The issue of brand evolution is as controversial as pricing. Some experts argue that brands will be even more important in the online world. Their view of increased brand significance is an ally to the Internet efforts of established "brick and mortar" brands. Others believe that increased information will make brands, at least the way they are defined today, less important in the face of increased information availability. John Hagel and Marc Singer, for example, argue that product-centric brands are a proxy for imperfect information and limited shelf space.[5] As the Internet lifts these constraints, information-centric brands that focus on understanding and satisfying consumer needs will replace them. The Internet will therefore give rise to new types of intermediaries, companies that advocate consumers' needs and facilitate transactions by efficiently matching buyers and sellers. Intelligent agents are one example of such intermediaries.

Intermediaries and other retailers are experimenting with different efforts to grow: regular auctions, reverse auctions, group buying, aggressive marketing campaigns, and price leadership, for example. Which models will be sustainable as more products are sold on the Internet and more people go online is unclear.

AMAZON.COM

Amazon.com has grown from a small online bookseller in 1995 into the Internet's most powerful merchant. Few doubt that Amazon.com has accelerated, if not caused, the rapid adoption of the Internet as a medium of commerce. Besides books, Amazon offers videos, music, auctions, gifts, electronic greeting cards, consumer electronics, toys, software, video games, and home improvement and gift ideas. In September 1999 Amazon introduced zShops, a storefront-hosting product. Amazon has also invested in other e-commerce merchants such as Drugstore.com, HomeGrocer.com, and Pets.com. In the third quarter of 1999, revenue rose to $355.8 million from $153.6 million, for the corresponding quarter of 1998, and Amazon's registered user base exceeded 13 million.

[3] Erik Brynjolfsson and Michael D. Smith, "Frictionless Commerce? A Comparison of Internet and Conventional Retailers," http://ccs.mit.edu/erik, May 1999.

[4] *ibid.*

[5] John Hagel III and Marc Singer, *Net Worth* (Boston: Harvard Business School Press, 1999).

More than 70% of sales were to repeat users. This repeat purchase rate was nearly double the industry average (Exhibit 2).

So far, no one has duplicated Amazon's success. According to Amazon CEO Jeff Bezos, "The most important thing we have that's hard to duplicate is our culture of customer obsession. It pervades customer service, logistics, software, and marketing. Companies' cultures are impossible to copy. They're like little starter pieces of sourdough. Either you've got them or you don't. Once a company has a culture, it's like quick-drying cement. You can't just send someone to a customer-focus class for six weeks and expect results."[6] Bezos also explained why this culture of customer obsession is vital in the online environment: "Customer, customer, customer. I think everything falls out of that. It's especially true online, because the balance of power shifts away from the company and toward the customer. Customers have a bigger voice online. If we make a customer unhappy, they can tell thousands of people. Likewise, if you make a customer happy, they can also tell thousands of people. With that kind of a megaphone in the hands of every individual consumer, you had better be a customer-centric company."[7]

Bezos argues that personalization through extensive interaction with customers will drive loyalty to Amazon. "It's just like in traditional retail. If a small-town merchant knew your tastes, he could tell you if something interesting came in and he suspected you might want it. That was very valuable. If there was another merchant who opened up next door and didn't have five years of experience with you, then you wouldn't have as good a shopping experience there, just because the person didn't know you as well."[8] Personalization at Amazon.com is still relatively unsophisticated. In addition to past purchases and searches, variables in its personalization algorithms include demographics and purchase patterns in different product categories and across similar customer groups. The ultimate objective is to give each customer his or her own, unique storefront.

Amazon has been relatively successful in translating its customer focus and aggressive marketing spending (approximately 22 cents per dollar of revenue) into a strong consumer brand. In a Harris Interactive poll, online customers cited Amazon's brand twice as often as Barnes & Noble. "It's not that there is no meaning behind Amazon.com, it's that there are multiple meanings to people," says Christopher Ireland, Principal of Cheskin Research.[9] "To you it might be the biggest bookstore, to me it may be the best place to sample music or to sell antiques. It's not the traditional way to communicate a brand." No traditional retailer enjoys this constant evolution and dynamic definition of Amazon's brand. Traditional retailers think long and hard before changing anything for fear of eroding brand value. According to Nick Shore, a cofounder of brand agency NickandPaul, "Amazon is saying, 'We're not a book brand, we're a convenience brand with books, music, auctions, video.' They are locking into a higher need state, we'll see more of that, and it's part Internet-fueled. They realize their competitive set is not just other bookstores. They can go anywhere."[10]

[6] George Anders, "The View from the Top," *Wall Street Journal*, July 12, 1999, p. R52.

[7] James Daly, "Running Scared," *Business 2.0*, April 1999, p. 66.

[8] George Anders, "The View from the Top," *Wall Street Journal*, July 12, 1999, p. R52.

[9] Becky Ebenkamp, "We're All Brands Around Here," http://www.brandweek.com, June 21, 1999.

[10] *ibid.*

As Exhibit 1 shows, Amazon.com has been able to leverage its brand recognition and consumer trust to extract a premium over most of its competitors. Three of the eight online book retailers in the MIT study have lower prices, on average, than Amazon.com.[11] The lowest priced retailer, Books.com, has prices that average $1.60 less than Amazon's prices and are lower than Amazon's price 99% of the time. Yet Books.com has only about 2% of the online book market versus Amazon's more than 80%. A recent McKinsey & Co. survey found that 80% of online shoppers do not compare prices before buying. "It is very counterintuitive, but so far the trend among customers has been not to compare prices," said John Hagel, who leads the e-commerce practice for McKinsey. "Customers tend to settle quickly on one site in a given category. Once people learn how to get around a site and have a positive experience, they tend to go back"[12] According to Hagel, that's partly because most popular items now selling on the Web are low-ticket goods like books and CDs, that do not reward for price comparison. Moreover, price-comparison technology is still unsophisticated.[13]

While Amazon currently can afford to charge a premium, change is in the offing. A recent *Wall Street Journal* article discussed how Amazon executives have watched in dismay as online shoppers used Amazon's site's easy-to-use format, in-depth reviews, and expert recommendations, and then made purchases at sites such as Buy.com at even lower prices.[14]

Despite soaring revenues, strong brand recognition, and evidence of premium extraction, losses for Amazon have also been widening. The third quarter loss in 1999 grew to $197 million from $45.2 million a year earlier, though Amazon expects its books division to be profitable in the fourth quarter of 1999. Analysts expect Amazon to begin breaking down overall performance by division to show profitability for its more mature businesses. This may make investors feel more comfortable about the long-term prospects of Amazon's stock. Yet on October 31, 1999 Amazon's stock traded at $70.60, nearly 40% lower than the company's high of $110.60 in the previous 52 weeks.

Bezos does not seem concerned. When discussing a short period of profitability in late 1995, Bezos said that any reasonable management team should have been punished for that: "I believe that if we're investing in something and it works, then we should invest more. Profitability is important to us, but it's long-term profitability that's important, not short-term profitability. I don't want to leave anyone with the impression that we don't care about it. But if what you're trying to optimize for is long-term success, then that causes you to make different decisions in the short term. It would be a mistake to optimize for profitability in the short term, because that would mean you weren't investing aggressively in the things that were working and the things that we really, really believe in."[15]

Amazon has pursued an aggressive growth strategy. "We hope to offer hundreds of additional market opportunities in the next few years," said Bezos. But increased

[11] Erik Brynjolfsson and Michael D. Smith, "Frictionless Commerce? A Comparison of Internet and Conventional Retailers," http://ccs.mit.edu/erik, May 1999.

[12] Bob Tedeschi, "Using Discounts to Build a Client Base," http://www.nytimes.com, May 31, 1999.

[13] *ibid.*

[14] David Bank, "A Site-Eat-Site World," *Wall Street Journal*, July 12, 1999, p. R8.

[15] James Daly, "Running Scared," *Business 2.0*, April 1999, p. 66.

spending to promote the Web site, investing in other companies, expanding distribution capacity, and adding new products have widened Amazon's losses. Amazon's horizontal expansion has raised mixed reactions. "They're trying to broaden the franchise to be preemptive and be the one-stop e-commerce shop—and that costs money," Bill McVail, analyst at Turner Investment Partner, told Bloomberg. "But if e-commerce continues to grow the way we believe it will, Amazon is going to benefit."[16] For Barry Par, director of Internet and e-commerce at International Data Corporation, Amazon has to expand. "The market is demanding it. Amazon's market cap wouldn't make any sense if they were only selling books."[17] Yet, analysts warn that Amazon risks major losses if it dilutes its brand identity by spreading itself too thin as it expands. "Amazon moves into music and videos and gifts and other things, [yet] they have to make sure they are still specialists at books," said Jupiter's Michael May. "Otherwise, they are likely to lose the customers who were primarily and largely attracted to their book business. Amazon will find Barnesandnoble.com and Borders.com willing competitors."[18]

David Cooperstein of Forrester Research identified three additional challenges that could potentially damage Amazon's customer-centric brand as it expands.[19] First, customer service will become woefully complex and require more customer service time as Amazon starts selling more complex products such as DVDs and VCRs. Second, as customers use one-click shopping across categories, Amazon will need to efficiently link seven distribution centers to ensure a single delivery and a seamless customer experience. Finally, Amazon will need to create rigorous product reviews for items such as consumer electronics to remain the leader in product information richness.

As Amazon expands horizontally, it finds itself in the ironic position of investing heavily in brick-and-mortar warehouses. Yet despite some analysts' recommendations, it has not yet revealed an offline consumer strategy. Editors of *Red Herring* magazine encouraged Jeff Bezos to get "real." "An Internet-only business model leaves Amazon.com mired in the past as traditional retailing continues to evolve. Retailers must interact with customers through any channel those customers desire, whether online, face-to-face, through the mail, or over the phone, and they must accept multiple forms of payment—cash, credit, check, debit card, and various forms of electronic payment systems. Not only are retail systems changing, but so are the products themselves. Already, electronic books that hold content downloaded from the Internet are available. Bookstores could be transformed into veritable jukeboxes of CD-ROMs that contain thousands of titles. The books themselves could be printed and bound, on demand, for consumers. An Internet-only business could not exploit these opportunities."[20]

Wal-Mart's expected relaunch of its commerce site prompted the analysts' recommendations for an offline strategy. "Lacking an offline presence," Cooperstein says, "Amazon and other pure-plays will have a hard time reaching the majority of American shoppers who are not online. Meanwhile, Wal-Mart has the opportunity to cross-

[16] Tim Clark, "Amazon Shares Ink on Earnings News," CNET News.com, July 22, 1999.

[17] S. Junnarkar and T. Wolverton, "Specialty e-Tailers Risk Dilution in Growth," CNET News.com, July 12, 1999.

[18] *ibid.*

[19] David M. Cooperstein. "Amazon.com Attacks Wal-Mart," *The Forrester Brief*, July 13, 1999.

[20] *Red Herring* Editors, "Open Letter: Get Real," *Red Herring*, September 1999, p. 114.

market its nearly ubiquitous stores with its Web site."[21] Clay Ryder of Zona Research agrees: "If Wal-Mart starts selling everything it has in the stores online, it could become the premier online retailer."[22]

Bezos believes that offline and online environments need to be optimized differently. "If you are going to build a company that supports a chain of 1,000 stores, you need an extremely hierarchical culture. You need the store environments to be identical. The last thing you want is creativity on the part of a store manager—who is trying to set his own prices or change the signage and decor. That's a disaster. So the successful companies have avoided having creativity at that level. That's antithetical with developing an Internet company from the ground up for speed of response. With 1,000 stores, you don't want speed of response. If you make mistakes, it's expensive. But on the Internet, you can change the look of your Web site, and if people don't like it, you can change it back in a day. You really do want to optimize differently for the two different environments."[23]

Auctions are an interesting area of Amazon expansion. While Bezos believes in the efficiency of non-negotiable, fixed prices for commodity products, he thinks that auction pricing is suitable for unique items or for items where the price changes rapidly. But he also believes that auctions will be an important part of Amazon's future because the "referral business" as Bezos calls it, will permit Amazon to sell products it doesn't need to stock. "If our goal is to have the earth's biggest selection," he says, "you have to realize that you can't carry and sell directly all those items yourself. It's impractical."[24]

Lauren Cooks Levitan, an analyst at BancBoston Robertson Stephens, says Amazon wants to become the first "e-tail portal, which means standing in the middle of every transaction on the Web." The company plans to accrue "fat margins in the form of lead fees" from commerce sites linked to Amazon.[25] To grow through a referral model, Amazon has acquired Junglee, a price comparison engine, and Alexa, which is well known for its browser integrated technology that generates a dynamic list of related Web sites while users surf the Web. These acquisitions helped Amazon launch zBubbles and zShops. zBubbles provides both consumer product reviews and information on where to find the best prices. The company's entry into the market for cross-site price comparisons is a response to intelligent agents such as mySimon that threaten Amazon's brand building efforts. With zShops, Amazon's storefront hosting product, small and large merchants can sell their products on Amazon.com. In exchange, Amazon receives a small fee and a cut from transactions. Merchants will gain access to Amazon's 13 million users, and Amazon will gather information on the buying habits of consumers.

BARNES & NOBLE

The bricks-and-mortar bookseller Barnes & Noble launched Barnesandnoble.com in May 1997 as its Internet arm. Two years later, Barnesandnoble.com was spun off, with

[21] Troy Wolverton, "Look Out Amazon, Wal-Mart's Coming," CNET News.com, July 12, 1999.
[22] *ibid.*
[23] George Anders, "The View from the Top," *Wall Street Journal*, July 12, 1999, p. R52.
[24] *The Industry Standard* Editors, "Taking on Wal-Mart," *The Industry Standard*, June 28, 1999.
[25] *ibid.*

Barnes & Noble and the international media corporation Bertelsmann each owning approximately 40% of the company. The company went public in May 1999, raising $421.6 million, the largest Internet IPO at the time. Priced at $18 per share, the stock traded as high as $26.63 before retreating more recently to its offering price. On October 30, 1999 Barnesandnoble.com's market cap of $529.3 million was 50 times lower than Amazon's.[26]

Media Metrix ranked Barnesandnoble.com as the fourth largest e-commerce site in June 1999. Barnesandnoble.com sells books, magazines, CDs, videos, and software and opened an online music store in July 1999. Ben Boyd, a company spokesman, said that it plans to focus on products that can be digitized. "We understand the bandwidth of our brand and we won't go beyond that," Boyd said. "We're not going to sell pet food."[27]

Revenues for the third quarter of 1999 were $49.1 million compared to $15.6 million for the same quarter in 1998. Barnesandnoble.com posted a $21.9 million loss compared with $18.6 million a year earlier. Customer accounts increased to over 2.9 million. During the quarter, repeat customer orders increased to more than 63% of orders. "All of our key metrics exceeded expectations, illustrating the growing momentum of our business," said Barnesandnoble.com chief executive Jonathan Buckley following their second quarter announcements.[28]

Other business leaders and e-commerce analysts share Buckley's optimism for the successful adoption of the Internet by established brands. Lou Gerstner, IBM's CEO, described the new dot-com companies as "fireflies before the storm—all stirred up, throwing off sparks." But he continued, "The storm that's arriving—the real disturbance in the force—is when the thousands and thousands of institutions that exist today seize the power of this global computing and communications infrastructure and use it to transform themselves. That's the real revolution."[29]

Brand recognition is arguably the most powerful competitive advantage that traditional retailers such as Barnesandnoble.com have against their Internet-only competitors. While e-commerce has made huge strides in recent years, online consumers are still oblivious to most online brands. According to a Harris Interactive poll, 40% of online consumers cannot name an online retailer in 12 of 13 categories.[30] As traditional retailers expand online and the Internet population's demographics come closer to the national average, the long-term prospects for Internet-only retailers come into question. In their letter to Jeff Bezos, *Red Herring*'s editors said: "Look no further than your chief competitor, Barnes & Noble, to see just how valuable a real-world brand can be. During the past two years, the very period you were meant to be 'disinterme-

[26] In late 1999 a patent dispute case about one-click shopping strained the relationship between Amazon.com and Barnesandnoble.com. In December 1999, a federal district judge in Seattle granted Amazon.com a preliminary injunction, barring Barnesandnoble.com from using a one-click system for online orders.

[27] S. Junnarkar and T. Wolverton, "Specialty e-Tailers Risk Dilution in Growth," CNET News.com, July 12, 1999.

[28] Sandeep Junnarkar, "Barnesandnoble.com Revenues Soar," CNET News.com, July 22, 1999.

[29] Economist Survey: Business and the Internet, "The Real Revolution," *The Economist*, June 26, 1999.

[30] Kim Girard, "Online Consumers Oblivious to Most Net Brands," CNET News.com, June 24, 1999.

diating' offline business, Barnes & Noble's annual revenues topped $3 billion, and its net income rose 73.7% to $92.4 million. And Barnesandnoble.com, the company's online venture, will only help the company's brand, inventory, distribution systems, and physical presence."[31]

The trust a strong brand inspires increases in the online environment. In addition to trusting that retailers will deliver the promised service or product, Internet users are also concerned about their privacy and security. As Internet retailers know more than ever about consumer behavior through both information that consumers volunteer and tracking with cookies, online users want to make sure that retailers do not misuse the information collected about them. Whether traditional brands will enjoy a "trust" advantage over Internet-only companies remains unclear.

Barnes & Noble was reluctant to expand in the online environment. It formed Barnesandnoble.com more than two years after Amazon.com started selling books. The huge negative implications of a possible misstep partly explain this delay. "Its very difficult for these companies to think of spending an inordinate amount of money on a cyberstrategy that will ultimately reduce their margins," argues Jerry Kaplan, CEO of Onsale.com. "Forced to choose between doing nothing while some Internet entrepreneur eats their lunch and committing hundreds of millions of dollars to online retailing with little anticipated return, traditional retailers face some difficult decisions."[32] In the past, these constraints led traditional retailers to use the Internet to defend their market share from third-party cannibalization. Jupiter Communications found that only 6% of online sales in 1999 were incremental and therefore noncannibalizing.

However, some traditional retailers are now viewing the Internet as an opportunity rather than a threat. They now see it as a logical extension of a storefront's physical presence, one that complements existing customer relationships, business processes, and distribution systems.[33] "Branding is a tremendous advantage," says Scott Silverman, director of Internet retailing at the National Retail Federation, "and cross-promoting it over the Internet and in physical stores will open up new selling opportunities." Melissa Bane, an analyst with the Yankee Group, agrees: "Some of the smarter ones are starting to realize that it's their game to lose. They already have the customers, and now they can use the Internet in their stores as a tool to expand their share of customers."[34]

Borders.com, one of Barnesandnoble.com's key competitors, is attempting to integrate its physical presence with the online environment. Borders has rolled out Internet kiosks in its bookstores. The company launched a pilot project in the fall of 1999 that linked the kiosks to its Web site, so that customers could check a database of some 3 million titles and then custom order titles through a store clerk. "Our strategy is to be the most integrated provider in our industry," says Borders Online president Rick Vanzura. Forrester's Cooperstein says, "It's better to leverage an asset than to ignore

[31] *Red Herring* Editors, "Open Letter: Get Real," *Red Herring*, September 1999, p. 114.

[32] Brian E. Taptich, "Less Than Zero Margins," *Red Herring*, March 1999.

[33] Blaise Zerega, "Getting Virtual," *Red Herring*, September 1999, p. 124.

[34] Bob Tedeschi, "Conventional Retailers Use Web to Improve Service," http://www.nytimes.com, August 16, 1999.

it." He believes that unlike Borders, Barnesandnoble.com has done little to tie itself to the brick-and-mortar stores its Barnes & Noble parent owns.[35] For instance, the two have different pricing and product return policies. The Barnesandnoble.com Web site says, "We can offer lower prices online because we do not incur the high costs associated with operating retail stores" and states that "purchases from Barnesandnoble.com cannot be returned to Barnes & Noble retail stores."

Unlike Barnesandnoble.com, Charles Schwab decided to absorb short-term losses to integrate the Internet with its offline presence. David S. Pottruck, its co-chief executive, noted that when the company merged its online and offline divisions in 1998 and lowered the charge for offline clients from roughly $65 a trade to $30 (to match the online fee), it cost it between $125 million and $150 million.

Also controversial was Barnes & Nobles's spin-off of the Internet division, with Bertelsmann owning approximately 40%. Bill Gurley, a partner at the venture capital firm Benchmark Capital, said, "The idea of a successful major retailer giving away 50% of its control of a division that is complementary to its core business sends exactly the wrong message to the Street. Should the correct message be, 'We believe in this business so much that we're going to give away 50% of the upside to somebody else'? Or would Barnes & Noble have been better off if CEO Leonardo Riggio had stood up on stage and said, 'We believe in the Internet so much that we need you to come with us. We're going to lose money for a while, but we must invest and grow this part of our business, because it's going to be very important.'"[36] With critics questioning their strategy, executives at Barnes & Noble and Barnesandnoble.com need to decide to integrate the Internet division with the powerful parent brand.

BUY.COM

Scott Blum founded Buy.com in 1996 as Buycomp.com. The company's roots are in online computer hardware sales, but in November 1998, armed with $60 million in funding, Blum acquired Speedserve, an online retailer of books and videos, from Ingram Entertainment and quickly began to expand his company's offerings. Just before the 1998 holiday season, the company changed its name to Buy.com and grabbed attention by guaranteeing the Web's lowest prices on everything its family of Web sites sold, including software, games, music, and videos in addition to books and computer hardware.

Softbank, an investor in nearly 100 Internet companies, including Yahoo! and E-Trade, founded the company. John Sculley, Apple Computer's former CEO, and Don Kendall, PepsiCo's founder and onetime CEO, sit on Buy.com's board. Buy.com posted $120 million of revenue in 1998, its first full year of sales, beating Compaq Computer's 15-year-old record for a company in its first year. About 30% of Buy.com's customers come from the consumer market, about 40% from small businesses, and the rest from large companies and the government.[37] Revenue for the third quarter of 1999 more

[35] Troy Wolverton, "Borders Sets Up a Net Hybrid Strategy," CNET News.com, July 26, 1999.

[36] Alex Gove, "In Play," *Red Herring* "Going Public," 1999, p. 64.

[37] Mark Halper, "Zero Hero," *Business 2.0*, April 1999, p. 58.

than quadrupled to almost $160 million from about $35 million a year earlier. In October 1999, the company filed for its IPO.

Buy.com guarantees to beat the prices of its top three competitors in each product category by 10%—even if that means selling the item at or below cost. This requires Buy.com to use a Web crawler to scan the Web daily for prices. For the nine months that ended September 30, 1999, Buy.com said its cost of goods sold was $401.2 million, exceeding net revenue of $397.6 million for the same period.[38] Buy.com CEO Greg Hawkins says he plans to make money by advertising and selling services like installation and maintenance for its higher-end products, such as computers. Already, he says, Buy.com is making some money on shipping fees and by selling many of its diverse range of products above wholesale prices. "We clearly use some visible products as a means to acquire customers," he says, though "most of our products are priced above cost."[39] Blum is calling his plan "optometry economics." Believing customers will never again be so cheap to acquire, Blum plans to make money by attracting tens of millions of eyeballs to the Buy.com site and then using those numbers to lure deep-pocketed advertisers searching for an online audience. Blum bets that "the world's lowest prices" will attract so many shoppers willing to at least look at Buy.com that he can sell his ad space at a huge premium to large, consumer-products companies.[40] Blum says, "Whatever it takes. The Internet doesn't have a lot of room to finish third. Our business model is to win."[41]

Many industry leaders think that Buy.com is on to something that will not go away soon. Benchmark Capital partner Bill Gurley says, "The lowest prices on the Web: that's a damn good marketing message. It sticks in your head."[42] "Buy.com may not be profitable for a while," says Forrester analyst Kate Delhagen, "but I expect it will do lots of business for a long time to come. This is a land-grab opportunity. The priority is not making money, but building brand and a huge customer database. Internet retailers will continue to practice extraordinary price gouging."[43] J. Neil Weintraut, the venture capitalist from 21st Century Internet Venture Partners, is even more enthusiastic: "Products are content! Companies use products to attract a critical mass of customers and make profits through a smorgasbord of collateral revenue streams!"[44]

Buy.com's reliance on advertising revenue has raised some skepticism, however. First, the saturation of the medium and the decline in response rates are pushing ad prices down. Second, Buy.com's demographic primarily consists of bottom feeders who only care about price and is thus less attractive to advertisers.

The Buy.com model also misses the issue of consumer price sensitivity. On big-ticket items such as computer hardware, Buy.com might have an advantage. But "when you're looking for a book on Amazon.com, you're just not that price sensitive," says Genni Combes, an analyst at Hambrecht & Quist in San Francisco. "Who's going to

[38] "Buy.com Files for IPO," *Bloomberg News*, October 27, 1999.

[39] Lisa Bransten, "The Bottom Line" *Wall Street Journal*, July 12, 1999, p. R10.

[40] Mark Halper, "Zero Hero," *Business 2.0*, April 1999, p. 58.

[41] David Bank, "A Site-Eat-Site World," *Wall Street Journal*, July 12, 1999, p. R10.

[42] Alex Gove, "In Play," *Red Herring* "Going Public," 1999, p. 64.

[43] Brian E. Taptich, "Less Than Zero Margins," *Red Herring*, March 1999.

[44] *ibid*.

say, 'Oh my god, I saved 50 cents on the new [John] Irving novel'?" Yet Buy.com's approach resonates quite well with the current "get a deal" culture of the Web. Its executives believe that as higher-ticket item sales increase, and online users' income levels come closer to the nationwide averages, Buy.com's model will win a significant segment of online buyers. "There's always going to be customers who look for price, and there's always going to be customers who look for service, just like some people shop at Saks and some shop at Wal-Mart," said Eli Katz, president of e-commerce for Fragrance Counter and Cosmetics Counter. "That will hold true on the Web as well."[45]

Brand loyalty is also a question mark for Buy.com. "It's a brilliant concept," says Buy.com board member and former Apple Computer CEO John Sculley. "The way to look at it is not as selling below cost, but as building a branded franchise as the low-price leader."[46] Lauren Cooks Levitan, an analyst at BancBoston Robertson Stephens in San Francisco, questions the consumer loyalty associated with this brand message. "These guys are setting themselves up to be price leaders, and so that's all their customers are going to care about," she says. "As they raise prices, those customers will leave."[47] Other analysts argue that Buy.com can forge unique consumer relationships by leveraging its enormous database, which closely tracks consumers' buying habits, to sell higher-margin targeted merchandise to its most active and loyal customers.

Another threat to the Buy.com brand is its poor reputation for order processing, order fulfillment, and customer service. A running joke claimed the best way to receive a quick shipment from Buy.com was to cancel an order, which would prompt it to rush the product out the door to collect payment. Customers have been outraged when Buy.com posted prices for much less than cost, and then rescinded the price for units not in stock.[48] Glitches in the execution of the company's "virtual strategy" may account for these problems. Softbank, for instance, runs two customer support call centers for Buy.com, while Ingram Micro is its exclusive distributor in the computer business. Buy.com takes ownership, but never possession, of the product it sells: it buys the product from Ingram and sells it to the end consumer. Blum says this arrangement is superior to Amazon.com's. "Our model is better than Jeff Bezos'. We have 85 employees, he has 2,100. We don't have warehousing, he has warehousing. We don't have inventory, he has inventory. His worst nightmare is he has to write off the value of inventory when he cuts price. Jeff Bezos has a business model that will never turn a profit."[49]

MobShop

Consumer power will rise up. If 1,000 prospective buyers of Toyota Camrys knew of one another's existence, they'd have enormous potential clout. The Web makes it easy. Look for a boom in team buying and cyber-fleet sales. —*Forbes Magazine, April 1999*

[45] *ibid.*
[46] Mark Halper, "Zero Hero," *Business 2.0*, April 1999, p. 58.
[47] David Bank, "A Site-Eat-Site World," *Wall Street Journal*, July 12, 1999, p. R8.
[48] Mark Halper, "Zero Hero," *Business 2.0*, April 1999, p. 58.
[49] *ibid.*

MobShop (formerly Accompany.com) is an Internet-based network that leverages the power of the Internet to aggregate demand for products and services to pool consumers' purchasing power. Once consumers decide which product to purchase, they join that product's Buy-Cycle™. A graph that is continually updated to reflect the current number of buyers and the current price per unit of the product visually represents the Buy-Cycle. Each Buy-Cycle is separated into volume-tiers. As the number of buyers "fills" each tier, the price drops by the next increment. Exhibits 3 and 4 describe MobShop's dynamic demand aggregation model in more detail and provide an early example of the user interface (prior to the name change).

The company was founded in 1998 and raised $3.65 million during its first institutional round of equity financing. "The Internet, with its just-in-time demand fulfillment capabilities, is transferring power from the supplier to the buyer. Unlike auction commerce sites that pit buyer against buyer, or conventional retail sites where individual customers derive no value from each others' purchases, MobShop's buyer advocacy model encourages customers and suppliers to work together to extract the greatest value possible from volume sales."[50]

"We feel that [MobShop] will fundamentally change the way buyers and sellers do business on the Internet, shifting the balance of power from seller to buyer through aggregation, access, and advocacy. We feel that a customer is truly empowered when marketed to one-to-one, yet able to transact many-to-one," said Jim Rose, CEO and cofounder. "Through our buyer-driven approach, we will redefine commerce, bringing people together from across the neighborhood, city, or nation to derive true value from the Web."[51]

MobShop is selling products for other e-tailers such as chipshot.com, GolfDiscount.com, Electronics.net, Roxy, Shades.com, Superbuild, Reel.com, and Fogdog Sports. According to the company, participating suppliers can reach an exponential number of customers without incurring additional incremental acquisition costs. Suppliers gain incremental revenue and profitability opportunities by dealing with larger purchasing parties. "[MobShop's] innovative real-time demand coordination network will enable us to generate aggregate sales at a minimal marginal cost while attracting those fragmented consumers who traditionally are more difficult and expensive to reach," said Nick Mehta, vice president of marketing at chipshot.com.[52] "Sites are spending $40 to $60 per customer," CEO Rose says. "We say, why not take a $50 piece of software, get 20 buyers together and cut the price by 10%? So instead of paying $40 to $60 for a customer, they're spending just $5."[53]

MobShop never takes possession of a product. Instead, suppliers agree to hold a certain amount of inventory for the duration of a sale and then collect between 2% and 6% of the sale.[54] By contrast, MobShop's primary competitor, Mercata.com, is essentially becoming a retailer by keeping in-house all fulfillment and customer-related

[50] "Accompany, Inc. to Revolutionize Commerce; Buyers Come Together for Best Value," http://www.accompany.com.

[51] *ibid.*

[52] "Accompany, Inc. to Gather Steam," http://www.accompany.com.

[53] Penelope Patsuris, "Group Buying: The More the Merrier," Forbes.com, August 6, 1999.

[54] *ibid.*

functions. MobShop is not trying to become a destination site on the Web. Instead, it is selling its technology to other sites such as Excite@Home, which are privately branding it. Sites can hence increase the loyalty and stickiness of their site by expanding the purchasing power of their members. From MobShop's perspective, Rose argues, "The more access points we have online, the more consumers we have access to."[55] Demand is aggregated across all sites and not site-by-site. "There are only going to be a few dominant players in this space who can get enough volume on the front end," says Rose, referring to the chicken-and-egg problem faced by all intermediaries. Jupiter analyst Mike May says, "The problem is you need lots of suppliers to add value and attract consumers, and at the same time you need lots of consumers in order for suppliers to get involved."[56]

Jim Rose is betting that a certain set of consumers will wait a few extra days to get a $1,000 PC for $925 from CompUSA with its service package included, and forgo getting it at that price immediately from Buy.com without the service.[57] "What we didn't anticipate was that people would wait three days to get 50 cents to a dollar off a $20 Palm Pilot cover," he says. "But they're doing it." While the typical look-to-buy ratio on the Web is 1%, Rose claims the ratio on his site is five to eight times higher. He attributes this bump in part to the site's interactivity implemented through the "click and tell a friend" feature that lets users participating in a sale e-mail others who may be interested about it. "Human beings are far more effective at identifying others who are in the market for a product than any direct marketing program ever will be," says Rose. If a friend has mentioned he or she is in the market for a Palm Pilot, why not drop that person a line? "Also, people are far more inclined to trust someone their friends are already involved with," he adds.[58] As Jim Rose tries to aggregate buyers, develop partnerships with suppliers, and compete with companies like Mercata.com, he also has to consider that a player with an established brand and traffic, such as Amazon.com or eBay, might invade his niche.

PRICELINE.COM

Priceline.com, with its patented "name your price" model, enables brand-flexible consumers to save on goods and services. Priceline.com consumers provide price requests to participating sellers, who can fill as much of that guaranteed demand as they wish at price points the buyers determine.[59] Priceline.com is currently applying its "demand-collection system" to three distinct product categories: a travel service that offers leisure airline tickets and hotel rooms; a personal finance service that offers home mortgages, refinancing, and home equity loans; and an automotive service that offers new cars on a test basis in the New York and Tampa metro areas. On November 8, 1999 Priceline announced that it would offer international and domestic long-distance telephone service in 2000.

[55] *ibid.*
[56] *ibid.*
[57] *ibid.*
[58] *ibid.*
[59] "Priceline.com Reports Second Quarter 1999 Financial Results," http://www.Priceline.com, July 1999.

Revenues increased to $152.2 million for the third quarter that ended September 30, 1999, a 36% increase over the second quarter and a 1,654% increase over the same period in 1998. The company's net loss for the third quarter 1999 was $102.2 million, from $19.8 million a year earlier. On October 31, 1999, Priceline's stock was down 64% from its highest value of $165. The company went public in March 1999. Over 2.9 million unique customers have used Priceline's travel, home finance, and automotive services. "This dramatic growth in the business further substantiates the appeal of the Priceline.com concept among consumers and brand-name companies across a number of industries," said Priceline.com Chairman and CEO Richard S. Braddock. "By giving consumers the ability to leverage their brand flexibility for savings and giving businesses a new way to move inventory without disrupting retail sales channels, Priceline.com offers a powerful new form of commerce that works."[60]

"Just six months ago, Priceline.com was selling an average of 5,000 to 7,000 tickets a week. Today, we sell six times that amount, or approximately 40,000 tickets a week. At peak times, we receive a ticket request every second. Demand continues to increase strongly and we believe even a more significant portion of reasonable ticket requests can be satisfied with more inventory," says Braddock.[61] Priceline takes a bid from a consumer and compares it against the inventory its suppliers offer. In 1998, only about 7% of the guaranteed offers from consumers actually resulted in a sale. Priceline gets to keep the difference between the bid and the offer whenever a sale occurs. To grow however, Priceline has been accepting bids on tickets where it is losing money. According to the company's prospectus, "Priceline.com has chosen to sell a substantial number of tickets below its cost in order to increase airline and adaptive marketing revenues, build a record of successful transactions and enhance the Priceline.com brand."

Like any intermediary, Priceline.com has to balance the interests of suppliers and consumers, so that it can continue to grow. For example, with the company's leisure airline ticket service, travelers agree to fly on any major airline willing to accept their price. The airline releases fully confirmed seats on flights where it has empty seats that depart between 6:00 A.M. and 10:00 P.M. Flights may be nonstop or include at most one connection each way. Tickets purchased through the service are nonchangeable and nonrefundable, and consumers cannot earn frequent flyer miles. Once an airline accepts a consumer's price, the consumer's credit card is automatically charged. The consumer cannot reject or change the offer or specify the time of day or the airline.

Some industry observers believe that this relatively unfriendly consumer product is appropriate for the targeted price-sensitive demographic. The Priceline "name-your-price" process is also a wonderful mechanism of price and latent demand discovery that can be leveraged in many one-to-one marketing opportunities. Others argue that because Priceline, with an unproven business model and no aggregated consumer base, had little leverage vis-a-vis its inventory suppliers when it first negotiated its inventory deals, it could not negotiate for a more consumer friendly service. Finally, some industry experts argue that by making the product so unfriendly, Priceline took a huge market opportunity—the 30% of all airline seats that largely go unsold—and narrowed it down

[60] *ibid.*
[61] *ibid.*

to a small customer niche with unattractive demographics. "Excluding students and perhaps some time-insensitive retirees or part-time employees, there are not that many people with so much time on their hands. It does not take a rocket scientist to figure out that if I want to spend the weekend with my family, Priceline seats are going to be available on Friday morning and not in the afternoon when everybody else is also returning home." Also, an extremely price-sensitive consumer demographic and a relatively "unsatisfying" consumer experience makes brand loyalty questionable.

Suppliers' fear of cannibalization and of putting downward pressure on prices affects the form of the consumer product. According to Braddock, suppliers are benefiting from incremental sales. "Airlines and hotels fill seats and rooms that would otherwise go empty and can do so without disrupting their retail pricing structure," he says.[62] Brad Jones, a Brentwood Venture Capital principal, believes that an inherent conflict between the interests of suppliers and Priceline could limit the company's growth potential. "If it had the potential to be incredibly successful and absorb a high percentage of sales for airlines, etc., the vendors would just sell tickets directly to squeeze them out."[63] This upper limit to its growth may have caused Priceline to pursue horizontal growth by expanding into hotel rooms and financial and automotive services.

The term "reverse auction" refers to auction sites that give consumers control of the bidding and purchasing processes. Many in the industry began using the term to describe Priceline.com's method of letting consumers name their own price.[64] Priceline's growth has helped trigger many start-ups that attempt to implement demand driven, nonfixed pricing systems. Exhibit 5 outlines two of the alternative approaches in the reverse auction space. Despite these competitors, Priceline still enjoys a first mover advantage in the dynamic pricing space. Documents filed with the Securities and Exchange Commission (SEC) indicate that Priceline might license its patented "name-your-price" method to a "consumer-to-consumer transaction business" controlled by Jay Walker, Priceline's founder and vice chairman.[65] Buyers could make conditional purchase offers to acquire used goods, such as stereos, from other consumers. eBay's profitability and stock market valuation indicate the attraction of the auction market. Forrester Research expects the person-to-person auction market to grow from $2.3 billion in 1999 to $6.4 billion by 2003. The other growth opportunity under consideration would enable consumers to use the Internet to name the price they are willing to pay for retail merchandise. The consumer-to-consumer and retail merchandise ideas fit with Priceline's strategy of expanding its model horizontally to other areas of e-commerce.

[62] "Priceline.com Delivers Savings for Flexible Travelers in Side-by-side Price Comparison," http://www.Priceline.com, May 28 1999.

[63] Edward Silver, "Net IPO Investors Think Like Venture Capitalists, Given Firms' Youth," http://www.latimes.com, August 9, 1999.

[64] Microsoft's introduction of a similar price-matching product for hotel reservations (Hotel Price Matcher) has challenged Priceline's patent on its Internet-based price-matching model. Priceline filed a patent infringement suit against Microsoft in October 1999.

[65] "Priceline May Offer Auctions Among Consumers," *Bloomberg News*, July 30, 1999.

Priceline would license the Priceline.com brand and the name-your-price concept to two new companies owned by Walker Digital, which is also controlled by Jay Walker, and might also invest in them. Walker expects to "devote a considerable portion of his time" to developing and implementing the consumer-to-consumer and retail merchandise Internet businesses. "Priceline is a company about big ideas," Walker says. "The long-term legacy of Priceline will depend on whether or not we can successfully introduce the first new pricing system in probably 500 years."[66]

mySimon.com

Michael Yang and Yeogirl Yun founded mySimon.com in April 1998 to empower consumers to find the best prices for any product on the Web. The company's background section explains:

> *The mySimon shopping service evolved from the proprietary Virtual Learning Agent (VLA) technology, created by cofounder Yeogirl Yun. VLA is a highly scalable information retrieval system that uses the power of next-generation intelligent agent and advanced parallel search technologies to automatically comb Web merchants' sites in real time. Search results offer instant product comparison based on price, availability, and merchant information. With one click, users link to the merchant's "buy" page for easy purchasing. mySimon's Internet e-commerce hub is the largest comparison shopping site on the Web, with over 1,000 merchants in categories such as Computers, Books & Music, Electronics, Fashion, Flowers, Sporting Goods, Toys, and many more. A one-stop, unbiased resource for smart shopping, mySimon helps shoppers find the best values on millions of products, saving visitors time and money. mySimon distributes its shopping service selectively to key third-party Web sites to achieve additional reach. In addition to the growing number of products to shop for at mySimon, the team is constantly expanding the breadth of its product categories and continuing its development of innovative features that will further simplify and enhance the Web shopping experience.*[67]

mySimon, which received $21 million in its fourth round of financing, competes in a space that has seen significant consolidation. Excite acquired NetBot and its Jango technology, Amazon.com bought Junglee, and Inktomi bought C2B Technologies. In January 2000, CNET announced its plans to acquire mySimon for approximately $708 million in stock. The combined entity will have 250 product categories and more than 2,600 merchants and advertisers. The acquisition enables CNET to quickly expand its online buying guides, product reviews, and shopping services far beyond the computer and consumer electronics markets. The sites will, at least initially, remain separate and maintain their individual brands. mySimon CEO, Josh Goldman, said that the CNET acquisition option gave the company the fastest way to integrate content such as product

[66] *The Industry Standard* Editors, "Idea Man," *The Industry Standard*, June 28,1999.

[67] http://www.mysimon.com.

reviews and consumer feedback to its site. "It's all about speed," he said, "and we want to integrate rich media with comparison shopping to create more shareholder value."[68]

mySimon's original strategy was to charge a commission of 2%–5% of each sale made to a buyer who accessed the merchant site through a mySimon search. "Our model is to become like MasterCard or Visa—they take a transaction fee every time," said mySimon cofounder Michael Yang. Allowing merchants to place their logo or messages next to shopping bot results would generate more revenue. However, merchants don't need to do so to be searched. Yang compares the sponsorship model to the *Yellow Pages*. "You can pay for an ad there, but you still get listed even if you don't," he says.[69] In practice, the sponsorship model proved more viable than the commission-based one. Retailers were more willing to pay to get preferential placement on the mySimon site than to give up 2%–5% of their revenues every time mySimon referred an eventual buyer to their site.

mySimon is also pursuing a strategy of cobranding its service with portals and other sites to aggregate consumers and expand its reach. "The market is certainly there," said Aberdeen Group analyst Mark Peabody. "The whole price comparison shopping space is very attractive to the user. Cobranding with major portal sites and specialty portal sites is an interesting model. Portals can now look at heading out into a market that doesn't force you to get in bed with an Amazon."[70]

Merchants are willing to be "comparison-shopped" because the Web traffic they get is motivated to buy.[71] "They want the traffic, and it's high conversion traffic," says Kirstin Hoefer, product manger of the Jango agent technology at Excite. Nicole Vanderbilt of Jupiter is less excited about the value of the traffic originating at sites like mySimon. "It's a fine line between love and hate. Retailers never like to be side by side with their competitors," she says.[72] Most retailers want to build brands by having consumers come directly to their site. But no retailer can ignore the intelligent agent sites that have aggregated consumers.

While intelligent agents such as mySimon cannot for practical reasons search the entire Web, they come closest to bringing "perfect information" to the online buyer. Yet, the role of price comparison engines in the evolution of e-commerce is uncertain. Forrester Research estimates that price comparison engines will work for 30% of value-focused buyers who shop around, accounting for 22% of all online shoppers in 2003.[73] While mySimon executives believe that price comparison will become popular as higher-ticket item sales increase and intelligent agents become more sophisticated, others are skeptical. "It's been said that agents would change the dynamics of Internet commerce, and that certainly hasn't happened yet," said Julia Pickar, an analyst at Zona Research, Inc. "They're making some waves with the most price-sensitive shoppers, but they're not for everybody."[74] Clinton Wilder, a senior writer at *InformationWeek*, argues that

[68] Penelope Patsuris, "MySimon says," Forbes.com, January 20, 2000.

[69] Clinton Wilder, "Agents Go Price Shopping," http://www.techWeb.com, December 7, 1998.

[70] Paul Festa, "MySimon to Launch Pricing Site," CNET News.com, October 26, 1998.

[71] Clinton Wilder, "Agents Go Price Shopping," http://www.techWeb.com, December 7, 1998.

[72] *ibid.*

[73] Seema Williams, "Shopping Engines Threaten Online Retailers," http://www.forrester.com, June 16, 1999.

[74] Clinton Wilder, "Agents Go Price Shopping," http://www.techWeb.com, December 7, 1998.

Web commerce is evolving into a marketplace that's more like the real world than many would have expected. "Surprisingly, branding and marketing matter a lot more on the Web than technology does. Moreover, customer loyalty has prevented rampant commoditization of products. Price matters, but not to the exclusion of consumer concerns like brand trust and service."[75]

According to Paul Gaffney, VP of commercial sales at Office Depot, Inc., the intelligent agent concept can only be applied to easily definable consumer commodities. "But even then, what's the legitimacy of the lowest-price merchant? In some cases, agents actually work against 'perfect information' because price is just one part of that." This concern has led to the emergence of second-generation intelligent agents, sites that provide more than pure pricing information. For example: Bizrate.com aggregates merchant-specific, consumer-generated feedback about all aspects of online shopping,[76] epinions.com aggregates product reviews, and comparenet.com compares product features for different models.

Whatever the future of price comparison engines may be, one of mySimon's most important assets is the wealth of consumer behavior data it can track. mySimon can analyze consumer searches and the subsequent referrals to merchant sites to specific consumer behavior. Information-rich consumer profiles combined with the trust earned by being independent and unbiased can put mySimon in an advantageous position between consumers and retailers. John Hagel and Marc Singer argue in their book *Net Worth* that these intermediaries, "infomediaries" the authors call them, can leverage their position to launch value-added services. (See Exhibit 6.) Infomediaries can use information to attract more buyers and sellers and learn more about their business transactions to create a virtuous circle.[77]

Ironically, the Internet's most distinctive business model is a new kind of intermediary. "Only a couple of years ago, enthusiasts were predicting widespread 'disintermediation' when Internet commerce took hold. On the friction-free Web, suppliers would be able to reach their customers direct without having to bother with greedy middlemen. Now intermediaries are suddenly fashionable again. Instead of 'disintermediation,' the new buzzword is 'reintermediation.'"[78] How mySimon and CNET will evolve their business model to capitalize on the opportunities created by their position between consumers and retailers remains to be seen.

PRICING AND BRANDING ON THE INTERNET: CLOSING THOUGHTS

"In five years' time, all companies will be Internet companies, or they won't be companies at all," says Intel's chairman Andy Grove.[79] Few people doubt that the Internet is changing business and commerce. Despite its phenomenally fast evolution, however,

[75] *ibid.*

[76] Including price, on-time delivery, site navigation, privacy, etc.

[77] Economist Survey: Business and the Internet, "The Rise of the Infomediary," *The Economist*, June 26, 1999.

[78] *ibid.*

[79] Economist Survey: Business and the Internet, "The Net Imperative," *The Economist*, June 26, 1999.

it is still in its infancy. Which business and pricing models will prove to be sustainable in a rapidly growing environment where the types of products sold on the Internet proliferate and an increasingly segmented population goes online remains unclear.

EXHIBIT 1 Book Wars[80]

The total price at selected sites for a basket of 10 best-selling books and 10 miscellaneous titles.

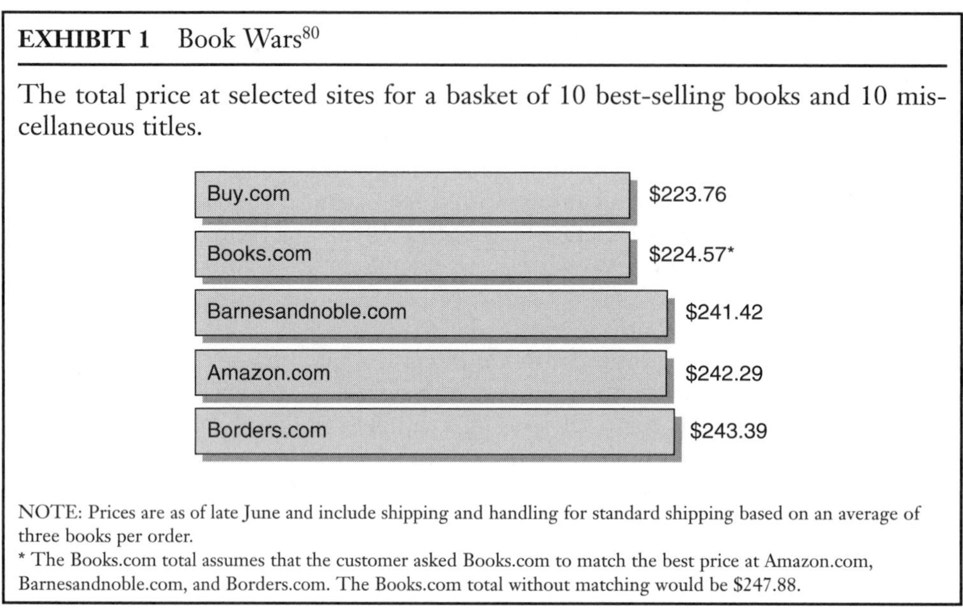

NOTE: Prices are as of late June and include shipping and handling for standard shipping based on an average of three books per order.
* The Books.com total assumes that the customer asked Books.com to match the best price at Amazon.com, Barnesandnoble.com, and Borders.com. The Books.com total without matching would be $247.88.

[80] Reprinted with permission from Erik Brynjolfsson and Michael D. Smith, "Frictionless Commerce? A Comparison of Internet and Conventional Retailers," http://ccs.mit.edu/erik, May 1999.

EXHIBIT 2 Consumer Loyalty by Vertical (1998)[81]

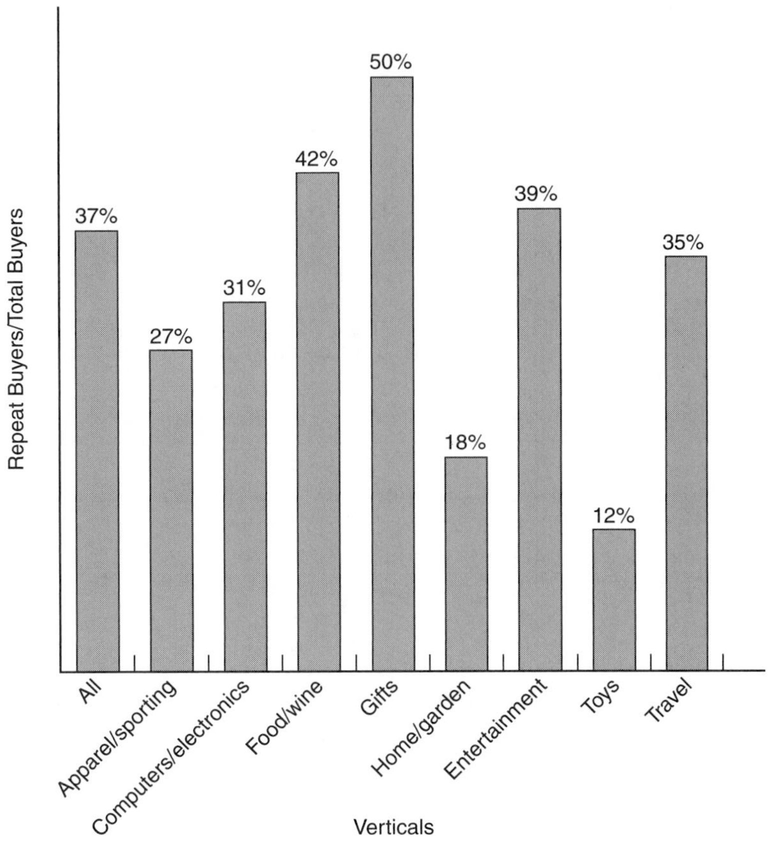

[81] Reprinted with permission from Shop.org/BCG, "The State of Online Retailing 2.0," July 1999.

EXHIBIT 3 The MobShop Buy-Cycle™ [82]

- Customers access MobShop's service directly or through a partner site.
- Upon deciding which product to purchase, customers join that product's Buy-Cycle. A Buy-Cycle is the period of time during which an item is open for buyers to join the purchasing process. The Buy-Cycle is updated in real time; the more people who join, the more the price continues to drop.
- MobShop will aggregate each customer's demand using its patent-pending demand coordination engine, which enables individual buyers to transact as a group. Customers will be billed at the Buy-Cycle's close, usually at a price significantly lower than when they joined.
- The more people who join a Buy-Cycle, the greater value each participant receives. To that end, each customer is encouraged to refer friends and family to MobShop through its Click and Tell e-mail program.

[82] http://www.accompany.com.

EXHIBIT 4 Example of the MobShop User Interface (Before Company Name Change)

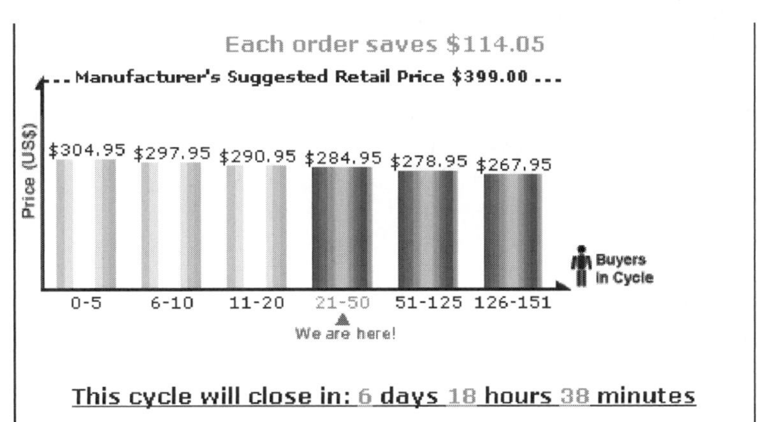

Reproduced with permission from MobShop Inc.

EXHIBIT 5 Alternative Reverse Auction Models

NexTag

The NexTag service lets buyers negotiate price with name-brand sellers of computer products. According to the company, NexTag's speedy way to purchase keeps the consumer in control of the transaction at all times. Unlike Priceline.com's service, the user has the comfort of knowing the agreed-to price before committing a credit card. Sellers can dynamically accept, decline, or counter-offer bids with bundles, complementary products, or different prices. NexTag chief executive, Purnendu Ojha, said that his service "enables sellers to compete for buyers," resulting in better prices for buyers and lower selling costs for sellers. While Ojha acknowledges that Priceline.com has done a lot of legwork in explaining the new purchase process to the market, he takes a shot at Priceline.com's strategy of not allowing any type of negotiation between buyer and seller: "We do not believe deals can be made until both sides agree on price," Ojha said.[83]

Respond.com

Respond.com is another start-up attempting to give consumers more flexibility and control during the buying process. At the company's Web site, you simply type in a description of what you want, the price you're willing to pay, and your deadline. Respond.com then contacts its network of merchants without revealing the user's identity. If any of Respond.com's participating merchants accepts, you get what you seek at the price you want. Sellers pay a listing fee for each category they are in. In the future, Respond.com is contemplating charging a nominal fee for each response to a prospective customer's e-mail. There are no transaction or user fees for the service. "Transaction fees would limit their scalability," says Jupiter Communications analyst Michael May. "What's attractive about their model is that it integrates well with consumer behavioral patterns on the Web, but unlike Priceline.com there's no commitment on behalf of the buyer. As their network grows, however, there is an increased likelihood that each bid will result in a purchase."[84]

[83] Tim Clark, "New Service Targets Priceline," CNET News.com, August 7, 1999.

[84] Charles Dubow, "The Reverse eBay," Forbes.com, August 4, 1999.

EXHIBIT 6 The Infomediary Business Model

According to John Hagel and Marc Singer's book *Net Worth*, infomediaries can leverage their consumer profiles and position of trust to introduce consumer services that include:

- **Targeted/permission marketing** where the consumer agrees (opts-in) to be contacted for targeted promotions or other direct marketing opportunities in exchange for providing some level of personal information to the infomediary.
- **Agent services** where the consumer makes a request about a service (e.g., insurance, travel, etc.) or a product (e.g., a hard-to-find item). The infomediary then contacts a network of suppliers attempting to satisfy the consumer's request.
- **Group buying** where the infomediary aggregates consumer demand to provide consumers with volume savings (similar to the MobShop model).
- **Market Research** where the infomediary provides vendors with targeted marketing research services.

The infomediary collects a "connection" fee from each transaction it facilitates. According to the McKinsey & Co projections, infomediary revenues start at $13 million in year one and increase to $4.9 billion in year 10. These revenue-generating services are coupled with privacy and filtering services that are aimed to protect consumers from unsolicited marketing (spam).

GAP.COM

This is about being clicks and mortar—letting customers access the Gap brands, whether in the store or online. —*Ron Beegle, E-VP, Gap Inc. Direct*

An industry renowned for its resistance to change considered Gap, Inc., headquartered in San Francisco and one of the first bricks-and-mortar retailers to venture online, an e-commerce pioneer. Long before other apparel companies were even considering venturing into cyberspace, Gap began developing its online strategy, re-examining its infrastructure, and shoring up key areas that would support its e-venture. While Gap recognized the opportunity the Web offered to leverage customers' familiarity and loyalty to its brand, maintaining the value of the brand was Gap's biggest concern as it developed its online strategy. Gap launched its first Web site, which was purely informational, in December 1996. In November 1997, however, Gap opened an online store at www.gap.com, and in 1998, GapKids and BabyGap went online, followed in 1999 by BananaRepublic.com and oldnavy.com.

Staying ahead of industry trends had long been a key to Gap's success; the company had reinvented itself several times, introducing new brands, innovating merchandising, and becoming synonymous with high-value, casual style. While it had seen downturns, Gap had largely escaped the typical vagaries and cycles of the fashion apparel industry, and had consistently grown faster than the industry itself. In the first years of Gap's online expansion, analysts estimated that it generated more apparel sales on the Web than any other apparel retailer. (Exhibit 1 provides Gap financials.)

Research Associates Katherine McIntyre and Ezra Perlman prepared this case under the supervision of Professor Garth Saloner and Professor A. Michael Spence as the basis for class discussion rather than to illustrate either effective or ineffective handling of an administrative situation. Margot Sutherland, Executive Director, Center for Electronic Business and Commerce, Stanford Graduate School of Business managed the development of the case.

COMPANY BACKGROUND

In 1969, Don Fisher, a 41-year-old real estate developer, and his wife Doris opened the first Gap store in San Francisco. The company took its name from the "generation gap" and targeted the late-teen customer. Fisher sought to build his brand around a single product—Levi's jeans—which he offered in more styles and sizes than consumers could get elsewhere. The Levi's strategy was an early hit, and the Fishers expanded—by the end of 1970, there were six Gap stores. Six years later, with 204 units, Gap went public.

In 1974, after the margins on Levi's began to erode because an FTC regulation allowed retailers to discount Levi's products, Gap introduced private-label lines to pull it out of price-based competition with larger retailers. Private-label clothing lines gave Gap control over the entire supply chain; it owned or oversaw product development from concept to customer and could control its prices, which enabled it to compete on product and brand image rather than price.

In 1983, when there were 566 Gap stores, Millard (Mickey) Drexler joined the company as president of Gap Stores. Drexler came to Gap from Ann Taylor, an upscale women's mass retailer, where he had built a reputation for establishing large consumer brands. Drexler improved Gap's margins, promoted growth, and redefined its image. Among his early initiatives was consolidating the multiple private-label lines into a Gap brand. He also extended Gap's reach by acquiring Banana Republic in 1983 and opening the first GapKids store in 1986. In 1987, Gap opened its first international store in London. In 1989, GapKids launched the BabyGap line of infant and toddler clothing. In 1991, Gap stopped selling Levi's (which represented less than 2% of sales at the time) and moved to only private-label products. Under Drexler's leadership, Gap launched innovative advertising initiatives, including the well-known and creative campaign "Who Wore Khakis." In 1994, Gap introduced the Old Navy brand. Drexler sought to reposition Gap as a global brand, rather than just a retailer.[1]

With its multiple brands, Gap sought to segment the market; each brand represented a unique image and catered to a distinct demographic. Casual, basic styles were aimed at the middle market. Although Gap's sweet spot was the college-age customer (more female than male), it also targeted teens and 25- to 35-year-olds. Banana Republic offered more stylized products to an older, more affluent consumer. Old Navy targeted families, and offered fashionable, value-oriented clothing to the bargain-minded consumer.

In April 2000, the Gap, Inc. divisions had 3,145 stores, and Gap, Inc. accounted for approximately 5% of all apparel dollars spent in the United States.[2] (Exhibit 2). Although same-store sales growth slowed at Gap flagship stores in 1999, as a result, some analysts believed, of Old Navy's success, most analysts were confident that Gap's aggressive plans for new stores, the successful Old Navy format, and Drexler's consistent ability to reinvent Gap would continue the company's historical success. Thirty years after entering the retailing industry, Gap had an established, prominent position

[1] Nina Munk, "Gap Gets It," *Fortune*, August 3, 1998.

[2] Tradeline, June 25, 1999.

in the specialized retail apparel industry and consistently achieved among the highest margins in the industry.

COMPANY STRUCTURE

Gap's internal structure supported the company's goal of specific identities for each of its clothing-brand lines (Gap, Banana Republic, and Old Navy). Each brand was a subsidiary/division of Gap, Inc. and had complete control of its product through a vertically integrated corporate structure. In 1991, Gap also established an international unit, which was a channel-based division, not a brand division.

ONLINE APPAREL SALES IN 1999

Although, by the end of 1999, online apparel sales had not grown as quickly as online sales of books or CDs, they were rising steadily. As in other consumer markets, traditional retailers were trying to tap into this burgeoning market and protect their existing customer bases from online-only retailers. Estimates for 1998 online apparel sales ranged from \$330 million[3] to \$460 million,[4] and expectations for 1999 sales ranged from \$642 million[5] to \$1.4 billion.[6] Longer-term projections also varied. Forrester predicted that online sales would be \$20 billion by 2003[7] (7% of total apparel sales) and Jupiter expected 6% penetration by 2006. Despite these different estimates, the Web was clearly important for apparel retailers. Moreover, analysts predicted that most Web sales would not be incremental gains, but would represent consumers moving their existing purchases to the Web. Jupiter Communications estimated that only 6.5% of online commerce sales in 2002 would be incremental sales.[8] While analysts expected e-commerce to shift rather than expand overall sales, individual companies hoped that effective Web initiatives would attract new customers and steal market share from competitors.

In addition to potentially gaining market share, retailers believed that the Internet could let them solidify their brands, improve customer relationships, serve markets that could not support a store, and cut costs. Bricks-and-mortar companies could use the Web to cut costs in several ways. The typical bricks-and-mortar department store could use the Internet as a distribution channel to reduce costs in selling and support services, service and operations, and property and equipment. (See Figure 1.)

Although the Internet might lower cost for pure-play retailers, bricks-and-mortar retailers with online stores appeared to have advantages over pure-plays. Retailers could sell more if they reached consumers through multiple channels—50% of consumers

[3] Valerie Seckler, "A Warning to Stores: Get Online or Risk Loss of Share to Net," *Women's Wear Daily*, August 4, 1999, p. 1.
[4] Louise Lee, "'Clicks and Mortar' at Gap.com," *Business Week*, October 18, 1999.
[5] Mercedes Cardona, "Apparel Makers Add E-Commerce," *Advertising Age*, March 29, 1999, p. 38.
[6] Louise Lee, "'Clicks and Mortar' at Gap.com," *Business Week*, October 18, 1999.
[7] John Sterlicchi, "The Gap Promotes Web Commerce with Fashion News, Reminders, Discounts," *Knight Ridder Tribune Business News*, July 14, 1999.
[8] Jupiter Communications, Channel Shift Study, June 1999.

who bought from the same company online and in stores spent more than when they shopped only at stores.[9] Surveys indicated that many online users were afraid to make a purchase on the Web. These fears were allayed when offline brands went online, because consumers already trusted these brands.[10] Moreover, offline retailers could allay these fears, whereas Internet-only competitors could not.

FOR EVERY GENERATION, THERE'S A GAP

Given the compelling opportunities that online apparel sales offered, the Internet was a natural extension of Gap's efforts to control an increasing share of the consumer's apparel dollars. In e-commerce Gap used the same strategy that had worked for it offline—establishing new markets, focusing on stylish, value-driven product offerings, and controlling value drivers in-house.

Gap began to consider the appropriate e-commerce initiative in 1996. Gap introduced its individual brands' Web sites over time: Gap.com was introduced with e-commerce capabilities in 1997; the other brands followed over the next two years. By early 2000 only oldnavy.com was not e-commerce functional. It was expected to be in operation later that year.

FIGURE 1 Assessment of Typical Expenses of a Bricks-and-Mortar Department Store[11]

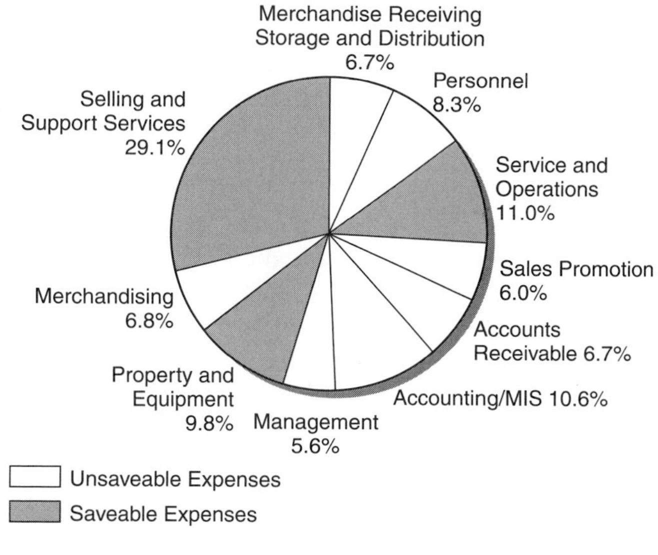

[9] Louise Lee, "'Clicks and Mortar' at Gap.com," *Business Week*, October 18, 1999.

[10] Valerie Seckler, "Buying in Cyberspace: Price May No Longer Be Enough of a Spur," *Women's Wear Daily*, April 14, 1999.

[11] Reproduced with permission from Jupiter Research, a Jupiter Media Metrix company, June 1999.

Gap only launched a Web property when it had brought all of the key business drivers in-house. The launch of the Old Navy Web site exemplified Gap's primary concern to protect the core brand. For Old Navy, Gap did not launch a commerce-enabled site until after the 1999 holiday season because Gap wanted to ensure that the Old Navy Web site met its high standards. Analysts believed this was an example of how Web initiatives took a back seat within traditional companies when the expected return on investment in bricks-and-mortar was higher.[12] International was another case in point: a worldwide rollout of Gap Online was not expected until the end of 2000 when Gap would have distribution facilities to support the online initiative.[13]

Gap designed each brand's Web site to look and feel like the brand's retail locations. The online stores offered customers more sizes and products than most retail locations did. The Web site also offered products that were available only in select retail locations (e.g., GapBody). Prices were comparable to bricks-and-mortar stores (though without sales tax), and customers could return products to bricks-and-mortar locations.

Gap Web sites integrated technology to enhance the customer experience—for example, customers could easily compare sizes for different cuts and styles, there were multiple navigation schemes, and wish lists and other tools to record their preferences. This technology gave Gap extensive customer data, including where customers lived, when they accessed the site, the length of their visit, frequency of purchases, products selected, and dollars spent—data that Gap had never been able to get through its bricks-and-mortar locations.

PROMOTING GAP.COM

Gap geared promotions for its Web sites, both online and off, to drive customer registration and collect e-mail addresses. As incentives it often offered discounts and contests. Displays by cash registers at Gap and Banana Republic promoted the online store and periodically ran promotions that allowed customers to register by filling out a form at one of its stores or through a Web kiosk. Gap used this contact information to send customized e-mails to registered users promoting new arrivals, specials, and other promotional events, as well as offering a birthday and gift reminder service. The e-mail promotions drove a significant percentage of online sales.

Out of its 1998 advertising budget of $400 million[14] (4.4% of total sales), Gap spent approximately $3 million on Gap.com[15] ads on the Web, and many offline Gap promotions included the gap.com URL to drive further awareness. In addition to leveraging the formidable offline Gap marketing power, the company began pursuing distribution partnerships with major Web brands. In 1999, Gap aggressively stepped up Web partnership efforts: in August, a three-year anchor placement deal was signed

[12] *Advertising Age*, September 6, 1999, p. 26. While Gap representatives denied the rumors, there had been talk on Wall Street that Gap could spin off its Direct, Old Navy, or Banana Republic units.

[13] John Sterlicchi, "The Gap Promotes Web Commerce with Fashion News, Reminders, Discounts," *Knight Ridder Tribune Business News*, July 14, 1999.

[14] *Women's Wear Daily*, February 26, 1999.

[15] *Women's Wear Daily*, October 29, 1998.

with AOL to promote the Gap brands; in November, a joint marketing promotion was initiated between Gap.com and eToys, as well as a partnership with CD Now.

CLICKS AND MORTAR

Gap executives echoed analyst expectations that apparel was a product uniquely positioned to benefit from a multichannel strategy. Gap saw its bricks-and-mortar stores not as an impediment, as many Internet pure-plays liked to assert, but as a key asset that it could leverage to give consumers a complete shopping experience. Consumers benefited in several ways when an established bricks-and-mortar retailer pursued a multichannel strategy.

- *Return policy:* Whereas with Internet pure-plays customers had to mail back products that didn't fit, they could return products to any Gap store if they bought through Gap online.
- *Alterations:* Consumers could bring anything they bought at the Banana Republic Web site or catalog to any Banana Republic store for free alterations (just as if they had purchased it there).
- *Trusted brand:* Customers were more comfortable buying online because of Gap's well-established brand and reputation. Traditional merchants' customer retention rates were also 10 to 20 percentage points higher than those of online-only competitors.[16]
- *Pre-shopping:* Many customers liked to do product research on the Web and then buy at a bricks-and-mortar store.
- *In-store promotions:* Gap used several strategies to leverage its stores to drive Web site traffic, including Gap's "surf.shop.click" posters and Web lounges in New York, Chicago, San Francisco, Los Angeles, and Aspen.

SUPPORTING THE NEW CHANNEL

Initially, the online unit was set up as a subunit of the Gap division, but in third quarter 1998, the company made the decision to break out a new division, Gap, Inc. Direct. Its responsibilities included the online properties for Gap, Banana Republic, and Old Navy and the new catalog business that began with the return of the Banana Republic catalog in fall 1999 and was to be followed with catalogs for Old Navy and Gap. Ron Beegle, E-VP of Gap, Inc. Direct, headed the unit in the spring of 2000. Analysts estimated that in the first 24 months, a traditional bricks-and-mortar retailer's Web initiative could easily cost more than $30 million.[17]

[16] "A Man of Words Remains Partial to One: Loyalty," *New York Times*, December 29, 1999, p C6.
[17] BCG, "Winning on the Net: Can Bricks-and-Mortar Retailers Succeed on the Internet," August 1999.

Since Gap's existing distribution system was optimized to ship large quantities of merchandise to retail locations, it had to develop a pick, pack, and ship operation to ship individual items directly to customers. Gap initially set up the online distribution operations within existing distribution centers, but, shortly after the launch of the Gap Web site, it established distinct warehouses for the online unit.

Gap also needed to develop customer support operations. Before the Internet, Gap had dealt with customers exclusively in its retail channels, and it handled customer problems in stores. To support its online unit, Gap launched its first 800 number and staffed a full-scale call center with Gap, Inc. personnel.

HUMAN RESOURCES

Attracting the best information technology (IT) workers was difficult at all organizational levels. The fierce competition for top IT workers was in evidence when Gap hired its new CIO, Ken Harris, from Nike in mid-1999. The new appointment prompted a noncompete lawsuit.[18]

As the corporate unit drove promotions into the bricks-and-mortar channels, store personnel were asked to promote the Web site to their customers. For most of these workers, who constituted the vast majority of the Gap's 190,000 employees, compensation was not tied to store sales; instead, store management often created incentives through in-store employee contests. Store managers' bonuses were tied to sales objectives that district and regional managers set. Online sales were not yet significant enough to make store managers worry that the online channel was a competitor to their stores—a competitor that Gap asked them to promote daily in their stores.

RESULTS

While Gap did not break out online sales from overall brand sales, analysts estimated that Gap.com sales for the year ending September 1, 1999 fell between $80 million and $100 million.[19] These figures were a significant jump from the $20 million that analysts estimated Gap sold online in 1998.[20] Based on overall industry sales estimates targeting online apparel sales for 1999 to be between $640 million and $1.4 billion, Gap.com captured between 7% and 15% of that total, in addition to the already formidable 5% of offline sales that Gap controlled.

Industry observers wondered whether Gap's online strategy would be a source of sustainable competitive advantage. In some ways, Gap seemed particularly well positioned to pursue a clicks-and-mortar strategy. For example, while many apparel retailers were concerned about high product return from their online operations, Gap claimed that returns on its online sales were approximately the same as for store purchases.[21]

[18] Jennifer Mateyaschuk, "The New CIOs," *Information Week*, August 16, 1999, p. 18.

[19] Louise Lee, "'Clicks and Mortar' at Gap.com," *Business Week*, October 18, 1999. Estimated online sales for JCPenney.com over the same period were $60–$80 million, $55–$75 million for Eddiebauer.com, $40–$60 million for JCrew.com, and $25–$40 million for Victoriasecret.com.

[20] *ibid.*

[21] *ibid.*

Most people knew their size for Gap clothes, and the casual clothes that Gap sold were less size sensitive than higher-end brands. Moreover, Gap owned its retail outlets and felt that it could manage conflict between its online and offline channels. Would this give Gap an advantage over manufacturers who did not have captive downstream channels?

EXHIBIT 1 Gap, Inc. 1999 Quarterly and Annual Financial Statements

Quarterly Figures: (GPS)

Income Statement Summary	*Oct 99*	*Jul 99*	*May 99*	*Jan 99*
	US$ (000)	US	US	US
	(9-MOS)	(6-MOS)	(3-MOS)	(YEAR)
Total revenues	7,776,459	4,731,073,000	2,277,734,000	9,054,462,000
Cost of sales	4,518,798	2,777,700,000	1,334,155,000	2,403,365,000
Other expenses	2,106,088	1,308,446,000	615,149,000	0
Loss provision	0	0	0	0
Interest expense	18,366	7,809,000	4,638,000	13,617,000
Income pretax	1,133,207	637,118,000	323,792,000	1,319,262,000
Income tax	419,991	238,919,000	121,422,000	494,723,000
Income continuing	713,216	398,199,000	202,370,000	824,539,000
Discontinued	0	0	0	0
Extraordinary	0	0	0	0
Changes	0	0	0	0
Net income	713,216	398,199,000	202,370,000	824,539,000
EPS primary	$d;	$d;	$d;	1
EPS diluted	$0.79	$0.44	$0.22	$1.37

Source: 1998 Gap Annual Report.

(continued)

EXHIBIT 1 *(continued)*

Annual Figures: (GPS)

Income Statement Summary	*Jan 99*	*Jan 98*	*Feb 97*	*Feb 96*
	US$	US	US	US
	(YEAR)	(YEAR)	(YEAR)	(YEAR)
Total revenues	9,054,462,000	6,507,825	5,284,381	4,395,253
Cost of sales	2,403,365,000	1,635,017	1,270,138	1,004,396
Other expenses	0	–2,975	–19,450	–15,797
Loss provision	0	0	0	0
Interest expense	13,617,000	0	0	0
Income pretax	1,319,262,000	854,242	748,527	585,199
Income tax	494,723,000	320,341	295,668	231,160
Income continuing	824,539,000	533,901	452,859	354,039
Discontinued	0	0	0	0
Extraordinary	0	0	0	0
Changes	0	0	0	0
Net income	824,539,000	533,901	452,859	354,039
EPS diluted	$1.37	$1.30	$1.58	$2.46

Source: 1998 Gap Annual Report.

EXHIBIT 2 Gap, Inc. Store Growth

	Net New Stores Year Ending April 29, 2000(a)	*Total Stores April 29, 2000*
GAP		
Gap Domestic	279	1,812
Gap International	107	433
Banana Republic	59	354
Old Navy	126	546
Total	571	3,145

	1998	*1997*	*1996*	*1995*	*1994*	*1993*	*1992*	*1991*	*1990*
Number of stores opened	318	298	203	225	172	108	117	139	152
Number of stores expanded	135	98	42	55	82	130	94	79	56
Number of stores open at year end	2,428	2,130	1,854	1,680	1,508	1,370	1,307	1,216	1,092
Net increase in number of stores	14%	15%	10%	11%	10%	5%	7%	11%	14%
Comparable store sales growth	17%	16%	5%	0%	1%	1%	5%	13%	14%

Source: Gap, Inc. 1998 Annual Report and Q1 2000 Report

NIKE—CHANNEL CONFLICT

As 1999 drew to a close, Mary Kate Buckley, general manager of nike.com, knew her division was at a crossroads. Over the last year, nike.com had rolled out an ambitious e-commerce initiative, signed an exclusive deal with Fogdog Sports that allowed Nike products to be sold by a pure Internet company for the first time, and had grown from 12 to 150 employees. But nike.com faced critical decisions in the coming months. Specifically, it needed to plan its own direct-to-consumer sales strategy and its policies for other vendors online sales of Nike products.

COMPANY HISTORY, STRATEGY, AND STRUCTURE

BRS, the company that would evolve into Nike, was founded in 1964 by Phil Knight to make high-performance athletic shoes for the U.S. market. Knight, a Stanford MBA and middle-distance runner at the University of Oregon, recognized that inexpensive, well-made Japanese imports could fill an unmet need for quality athletic footwear. Knight started selling these imported shoes directly to runners at track meets in his spare time, and Nike was born.

Over the following 35 years, Nike grew from a part-time job for Phil Knight into the world's dominant athletic footwear and apparel company by following a consistent and logical strategy: to capitalize on the importance of sports in people's lives and to be identified with competition and victory in consumers' minds (the company is named for the Greek goddess of victory).

Research Associates Katherine McIntyre and Ezra Perlman prepared this case under the supervision of Professors Garth Saloner and A. Michael Spence as the basis for class discussion rather than to illustrate either effective or ineffective handling of an administrative situation. Margot Sutherland, Executive Director, Center for Electronic Business and Commerce, Stanford Graduate School of Business, managed the development of this case.

Located on a bucolic campus in Beaverton, Oregon, Nike stood out as atypical for a large apparel company. Its culture was famous for internal collegiality and outward competitiveness, a tribute to Phil Knight's influence. Knight had held close control of the company since its founding and had ruled with a mix of closely allied senior managers.

The company's brand management efforts focused on endorsing the best possible athletes and making the famous Nike swoosh emblem ubiquitous. The roster of athletes who wore and promoted Nike products read like a multisport hall of fame, including mega-stars such as Michael Jordan, Tiger Woods, Mia Hamm, and Ken Griffey, Jr.

Nike went to tremendous lengths to promote its brand and image across the world. It typically spent over 11% of revenues on advertising, sports marketing, and promotional spending, or nearly one billion dollars in fiscal year 1999 (Exhibit 1). Nike's advertising included controversial campaigns that stressed winning above all else. Other campaigns were downright whimsical, such as ads showing basketball encounters between humans and loveable cartoon creatures.

Nike was highly centralized and focused. Management concentrated on core corporate functions, such as brand building and supply chain management, while a dedicated sales force sold Nike products to retailers or, in a few countries, to distributors.

NIKE VALUE CHAIN

Manufacturers/Suppliers

Consistent with its original strategy, Nike outsourced most of its footwear manufacturing to low-cost Asian or South American manufacturers. By 1999, the primary locations for Nike production were Indonesia, Vietnam, Korea, and China. Managing its global supply chain was a core strategic advantage for Nike, and its operations ensured smooth integration with contract manufacturing.

The company worked with hundreds of manufacturing partners to develop long-term, trusting relationships. Manufacturing partners did not necessarily provide the cheapest production, but most of them delivered consistent, timely shipped goods that met Nike's high standards. The partners invested to manufacture new designs or features, knowing that production levels would offset the investment.

Nike generated its own new product ideas and managed the design process in-house. Once a design was perfected, a manufacturer would begin the eight-month cycle of developing volume production capabilities in all the relevant sizes. Once production was online, Nike could expect manufacturers to fulfill orders within 90 days, plus 30 days for shipping by sea freight.

Product Life Cycle

Getting a new athletic shoe model on a store shelf could take 15 to 18 months from initial planning to final product distribution. Volumes were determined long before shoes arrived at consumer outlets, requiring careful forecasting from Nike and its merchants. A typical new Nike shoe had a market life of three to six months from introduction to depletion of inventories. Because the product life was so much shorter than the production cycle, Nike could not adjust production runs to meet unexpected consumer demand. As a result, Nike did not try to match supply of any given shoe model with demand, preferring instead to set conservative production targets and then begin designing the next generation model.

A typical Nike factory produced between 2,000 and 3,000 pairs of shoes a day, implying a three-month production run for a line that would sell 200,000 shoes. It was difficult for Nike to make money on smaller production runs, although it did produce specialty shoes at lower volumes.

Retail Sales Channel

Nike sold its products through a large in-house sales force in different types of stores—multi-sport general athletic department stores, specialty athletic department store retailers, and general-purpose shoe stores. Despite the company's origins selling shoes straight to track runners from the back of Phil Knight's car, Nike had not been very interested in direct-to-consumer sales. The company lacked a catalog or mail-order business and had only a few stores of its own, called NikeTowns, that were more a marketing and brand-building effort than a source of sales.

Athletic footwear and apparel was a fragmented retail market (Exhibits 2 and 3). The top ten sporting goods retailers represented 14% of total U.S. sales. Because these retailers were so small, they had been slow to use sophisticated technology to track purchases and inventory, leading to frequent stockouts and misallocations of inventories. Nike had suffered from imperfect information about retailers' inventory levels and wanted to improve inventory monitoring.

Nike's 40% market share in U.S. athletic footwear gave it influence with the merchants who carried its products. The company encouraged advance planning from its retail partners—nearly 90% of its orders from retailers were for deliveries nine months out. As a result, Nike could plan manufacturing and distribution far in advance to meet its guaranteed future sales. Nike could also negotiate favorable contract terms with its retailers, including displays, inventories, and other details that influenced consumers.

The company distributed most of its own products from its factories to retail stores or distribution centers through a complex process: a retailer's monthly order of 300,000 pairs of shoes could involve shipping over 50 different models to 100 different locations. In the late 1990s, Nike invested over one billion dollars in large regional distribution centers to replace its smaller centers. Nike also gave discounts to retailers who managed their own distribution from the Nike factory, thus avoiding the need to go through a Nike distribution center. Nike tried to keep inventories to a minimum and managed more than five inventory turns a year.

Direct Sales Channels

In 1999, Nike owned and operated 13 NikeTown superstores, most of them in high-traffic, upscale shopping neighborhoods. The first NikeTown store opened in Portland, Oregon in 1990. Its designer described it as a cross between the Smithsonian, Disney World, and Ralph Lauren. While the store sold a broad range of Nike footwear and apparel (at full retail price), its layout and merchandise also made it a showcase of Nike products.

Nike followed the Portland store with a 70,000-square-foot operation located in downtown Chicago that quickly became the city's largest tourist attraction; 7,500 visitors a day flocked to see the two-story mural of Michael Jordan and try Nike shoes out on the store's miniature basketball court.

The NikeTown stores were not run to be independently profitable, or even to be major selling channels for Nike products. Instead, they were showcases for Nike's newest or most innovative product lines, an opportunity to strengthen ties with consumers, and an extraordinary brand advertising opportunity. They also carried hard-to-find products or specialty items not available from typical retailers and souvenir items, such as the Michael Jordan paraphernalia sold at the Chicago store. Initially, retailers feared that they would lose sales to NikeTown stores, but they were reassured as the company's intentions became clearer. Some within Nike felt that the efforts to appease retailers' concerns about competing directly with Nike had prevented the NikeTown stores from realizing their full potential.

Nike also operated 53 outlet locations to liquidate overstocked or outdated inventory. This channel let Nike control price and quality while disposing of excess inventory without ceding too much control by relying on other liquidation channels.

THE SPORTING GOODS E-COMMERCE LANDSCAPE

The online market for sporting goods in 1999 was chaotic. Various competitors were eager to join the Internet frenzy—traditional sporting goods retailers, manufacturers that wanted to sell direct to consumers, and start-up companies wanted to exploit the Internet. Global Sports, Inc. (GSI), an Internet start-up with an innovative outsourcing-based business model, complicated the picture.

Traditional Retailers

Virtually every significant sporting goods retailer had established a Web presence by late 1999. Retailers, such as Foot Locker and Copeland's Sports, had their own Web businesses, typically offering a full range of products at prices similar to what was charged in their stores. These real-world retailers leveraged their existing brands and operational capabilities to offer extensive shopping experiences. Footlocker.com, for example, offered over 14,000 products from 150 different manufacturers at prices equal to or lower than in-store prices. It also offered in-store returns of online purchases.

In 1999, 6 of the 20 largest sporting good retailers, including The Athlete's Foot and The Sports Authority, signed deals with the Internet division of GSI to manage their Web sites and their complete e-commerce operations. GSI would handle the design, order fulfillment, processing, shipping, and business development of the retailers' Internet businesses. The participating retailers simply chose their product lines and pricing strategy, and generated Web customers. By developing a common sporting goods e-commerce infrastructure for its multiple retail partners, GSI claimed to lower the costs associated with e-commerce. Each retailer collaborated with GSI in decisions related to its brand presentation, Web site, and e-commerce operations.

Nike's Direct Competitors

Nike's competitors, the other leading athletic footwear and apparel manufacturers, faced similar dilemmas and problems related to their own e-commerce strategies. Because these competitors were smaller and less powerful than Nike, they relied even more on their traditional retail partners for sales. These companies had little or no experience selling directly to consumers and entered into e-commerce differently.

By late 1999, Nike's major competitors (Adidas, Converse, Reebok, and New Balance) had established Web sites with detailed product information, store locators, and editorial content about athletes or events. Each competitor, however, took a slightly different approach to the strategy and operation of its e-commerce capabilities. Converse neither sold its products online nor offered information about how to acquire them online. Adidas and Reebok each offered limited product lines at full retail prices to their Internet customers. New Balance adopted a hybrid approach, allowing customers to select any of its current products and then directing them to the Web sites of its affiliated retailers (both real-world and Internet-only) that carried those products.

Nike's competitors were more willing than Nike to allow retailers to sell their products over the Internet. They also exerted less control over the retail experience than Nike and gave more flexibility to their Internet retail partners. Reebok allowed both online only and bricks-and-mortars retailers to offer their full product lines (often at a discount) on their Web sites. New Balance was slightly more protective of both product offerings and pricing, but unlike Nike did not exclude Internet retailers from entire product lines. Adidas was the only major competitor who had taken a similar position to Nike, severely restricting sale of product online.

Pure Online Start-ups

As in other consumer segments, sporting goods attracted a number of Internet entrepreneurs seeking to take advantage of the new technology to exploit the inefficient cost structure of traditional retailers. These Internet endeavors included full-range retailers (such as Fogdog.com) and specialized niche players (such as Lucy.com for women's sports or Chipshot.com for custom-made golf clubs). Many sports media concerns were also eager to leverage their viewer base into e-commerce customers. ESPN.com, a division of Walt Disney Corporation, and SportsLine.com (partially owned by CBS) each had avid followings among sports fans due to the content they had leveraged from their media conglomerate owners. Each of those companies were pushing to convert their Web site viewers into purchasers.

NIKE'S INTERNET STRATEGY

Other Internet Sellers (Non-Nike)

As new online retailers opened and traditional retailers launched their own Internet initiatives, merchants bombarded Nike with requests to sell its products online. Initially, the company was extremely hesitant, worrying that careless Internet retailers would dilute the Nike brand value.

"We saw a lot of online retailers who were not putting the right emphasis on product presentation," explained Mary Kate Buckley. "Our bricks-and-mortar partners offer a convenient location where customers can feel the product quality and try products on. . . . We were concerned that over time if everyone is selling the same thing online, the only difference would be price."[1]

Nike's traditional retail partners wanted to expand into online sales, but Nike moved cautiously, allowing its largest retail partners to sell its products on their Web sites if they maintained the same standards the stores enforced. Foot Locker and Copeland Sports (through its Shopsports.com division) each started selling Nike products, but Copeland quickly learned that Nike meant what it said. In the summer of 1999, Nike stopped selling to Shopsports.com because "they were not meeting our marketing standards."[2] Although Nike soon resumed sales to Shopsports.com, it had made its point. By the end of 1999, Nike had approved 10 of its bricks-and-mortar retail partners to sell Nike products over the Internet. It doubted, however, that those retailers could deliver acceptable service levels and monitored their performances carefully.

Some Internet sellers acquired Nike products from other retailers' overstocks and other unofficial channels. Once these goods had passed from the hands of Nike-authorized retailers, Nike could no longer affect how they were marketed or priced. Because Nike handled its own international distribution and liquidated inventory through its own outlets, it saw less of these after-market resales than other manufacturers. Nike also strictly enforced sales agreements with retailers and policed the Web for offenders.

Fogdog Deal

In September 1999, Nike signed a deal with Internet sporting goods retailer Fogdog Sports that allowed Fogdog to sell the entire Nike product line on its Web site. It gave Fogdog exclusive access (among Internet-only sellers) to the Nike product line for six months in return for warrants to buy up to 12% of Fogdog's shares at a pre-IPO valuation.

Fogdog Sports was founded in early 1998 (as SportSite.com) to sell athletic gear directly to consumers over the Internet. The company was the evolution of a Web design

[1] "Nike, Long Wary of E-Marketers, Links Up with Fogdog." *New York Times*, September 27, 1999.

[2] Conversation with Mary Kate Buckley, VP, Nike, January 7, 2000.

and e-commerce company that three graduates of Stanford University started in 1994. In 1998 VenRock Associates and Draper Fisher Jurvetson gave it venture capital financing. In September of 1999, after negotiations with Nike had begun, Fogdog hired Tim Joyce, formerly VP of global sales at Nike, as its new president.

After repeatedly rebuffing Fogdog, Nike was finally attracted to Fogdog's reputation and its pricing policy of respecting manufacturers' recommended minimum prices. Fogdog was able to point to three years of consistently executing its pricing policy. Its ownership stake gave Nike an incentive to make the deal work. It agreed to treat Fogdog like any other major account, giving it preferred prices, joint promotions, and information sharing. Nike also gave Fogdog other special considerations, such as product images for display on the Fogdog.com Web site, product and sales data, and unusual return privileges.[3]

Nike also agreed not to sell to other virtual retailers for at least six months, including those sites Global Sports, Inc. managed. This promise angered some of Nike's most important bricks-and-mortar partners, such as The Athlete's Foot, which relied on Nike for 40% of its footwear sales. As Michael Rubin, the CEO of GSI, commented: "Our six partners are all among Nike's top 20 accounts. Nike needs to support them, and they need to be on the Internet in order to survive in the twenty-first century."[4]

Nike.com

Nike launched the nike.com Web site in August 1996 to provide information and entertaining content to its customers. The site had no e-commerce capabilities; instead, it reflected a typical Nike approach to brand building. Different sports received their own separate pages, with tips and advice from Nike athletes, news and updates on sports events, and detailed product information, including design inspirations and athlete endorsements. Despite the lack of e-commerce and no efforts to drive traffic to the site through advertising expenditures, nike.com logged 14 million visitors in 1998.

At first, Nike approached the Internet with caution. A plan to sell posters on the Nike Web site was considered for nearly a year before being launched during the Christmas 1998 season. Over the next year, however, Nike's Web site strategy evolved substantially. In February 1999, Nike launched a test to sell its high-end Alpha Project line of footwear and apparel. It also redesigned the Web site to provide a store locator and more detailed product information.

In June 1999, Nike relaunched a completely overhauled and redesigned Web site, with expanded e-commerce functionality. Nike made hundreds of its most popular products available for purchase, all at full retail prices. For the first time, the company's senior management seemed to understand the revolutionary importance of the Internet. Phil Knight admitted that "online commerce is a partial return to our original roots

[3] Conversation with Mary Kate Buckley, VP, Nike, January 7, 2000.

[4] "Nike, Long Wary of E-Marketers, Links Up with Fogdog," *New York Times*, September 27, 1999.

of selling products at track meets from the trunks of our cars—rekindling the direct relationship between Nike and its consumers."[5]

Despite the push into e-commerce, much of Nike's Web site focus remained on brand-building and inspirational content. Nike added profiles on its athletes, new information on future product development, and innovative technologies. Many of the Web functions were so advanced that consumers could not use them without downloading plug-ins. "I wouldn't say we're on the bleeding edge of design technology, but I will say we're on the bruised edge," said nike.com's creative director, Bob Lambie.[6]

MANAGING NIKE.COM

Operational Concerns

Running a successful e-commerce business required operational capabilities that Nike lacked. Because Nike had no experience with remote order fulfillment, it could not pick, pack and ship orders, track delivery, or handle customer service. Rather than building each of those capabilities from scratch, Nike outsourced them to United Parcel Service (UPS) which provided warehousing, shipping, and a call center with 500 dedicated customer service operators. Entrusting its brand identity to another company was uncharacteristic, but Nike believed it was preferable to doing an inferior job inhouse and would enable it to learn and gather data.

To satisfy its e-commerce customers, Nike needed vital new skills in Web design, systems infrastructure, and other related information technology (IT) areas. The company outsourced many of these needs and relied on proven market leaders like Inter-World Corporation for its enterprise commerce software and Red Sky Interactive for Web site design and production.

Strategic Concerns

The dedication to direct e-commerce over the nike.com Web site raised strategic concerns for Nike and its partners. Traditional retailers of Nike products, always concerned about being cannibalized by direct sales, were more worried than ever before as they were denied the opportunity to compete head-to-head with Nike for Internet customers. Nike knew it would have to strike a difficult balance to reassure its traditional retailers while expanding its own direct sales efforts. Nike hoped maintaining full retail pricing on its site would alleviate traditional retailers' concerns over unfair competition. "We are hoping that our Web site will expand the pie, not take market share away from retailers,"[7] explained Mary Kate Buckley. Nevertheless, Nike understood that the real opportunity for nike.com lay in defining a new, more profitable channel for selling shoes and other goods to consumers. "We want to be cognizant of channel conflict," said Buckley, "not apologize for it."[8]

[5] PR Newswire, June 22, 1999.
[6] *ibid.*
[7] "Nike Swooshes into Internet Retailing," *Financial Post*, June 24, 1999, p. C4.
[8] Conversation with Mary Kate Buckley, VP, Nike, January 7, 2000.

Nike was also concerned about the experience of its e-commerce customers. Nike had never had significant direct contact with consumers and needed to make the shopping experience consistent with the Nike brand. For "touch and feel" products like athletic shoes, Nike would have to find creative ways to satisfy customers' desire to know how the products looked and fit. It was hard to see how Nike could fulfill that need without continuing support from its bricks-and-mortar partners.

As Nike considered further expansion into e-commerce, it had to rethink its approach to all of its core functions. Manufacturing standards would have to change if Nike was to ship goods directly to consumers who had to rely on consistent sizing for sight-unseen purchases. Nike needed to learn manufacturing planning and inventory management to satisfy uncertain consumer demand rather than predetermined retailer orders. By customizing marketing, the Web made Nike rethink its approach to selecting athletes. It could now use athletes with smaller but intensely loyal fan bases. Direct-to-consumer sales also allowed prices to be more flexible and forced Nike to better understand price sensitivity across narrow bands of consumers.

Organizational Issues

The rapid growth and extraordinary potential of nike.com created difficult organizational dilemmas. The initial stages of Nike's e-commerce launch were conducted in stealth mode by a small team that reported directly to the president of the company. Decisions were made quickly and often secretly, in contrast to Nike's culture of candor and consensus. The media eagerly reported any new developments and speculated on what the future held for nike.com.

Once it became clear that nike.com would play an integral role in the future of the company, it became a vastly larger and more visible department. Nevertheless, it retained an aura of distinction within the company. At a time of disciplined spending within Nike, the online division had an enviable budget. When nike.com began reporting directly to Phil Knight in the summer of 1999, its stature within the company and in the media increased. Despite rapid headcount growth and a preference for internal candidates, nike.com could not satisfy the ever-growing roster of internal applicants.

As other Nike departments began to realize nike.com's importance, they became involved in its strategic decisions. The sales department helped to ensure that online sales policies were consistent with Nike's fundamental standards and policies. The manufacturing department collaborated on plans to produce customized shoes for specific online customers based on individual preferences. The marketing department assessed how to modify real-world advertising for the online world.

New Opportunities

Nike's e-commerce operations presented opportunities that were not available to Nike under its old wholesaling model. For the first time, Nike could directly collect considerable data about both customer demographics, and shopping habits—price sensitivity, purchase frequency, and product bundling. This information enabled Nike to market new goods or services to exactly the right customers, increasing the effectiveness of its marketing.

Perhaps the most important new opportunity to Nike was the ability to capture the enormous mark-ups between wholesale and retail prices for its goods (see Exhibit 4 for a breakdown of the value chain). Throughout its history Nike had managed its value chain successfully while only participating in the central and core functions. By not manufacturing or selling in-house, Nike had grown dramatically while remaining profitable. Encroaching into the new territory of direct sales presented Nike with an opportunity to capture more of the value chain than ever before.

THE FUTURE

Nike understood throughout 1999 that it had to learn how to do business over the Internet. Mary Kate Buckley explained Nike's Internet philosophy in June 1999: "The new site is really just the next stage in a grand experiment. . . . More than anything, our work over the last six months has proven that the future of Internet presence for a global brand like Nike will be in a constant state of incubation."[9] Buckley also understood that nike.com had to define a new, more profitable way to sell products to its loyal consumers. She began to think about what Nike should do in the year 2000.

EXHIBIT 1 Nike Financial Results (in millions), 1997–1999

Year Ended May 31	*1999*	*1998*	*1997*
Revenues	$8,776	$9,553	$9,186
Costs and expenses:			
Costs of sales	5,493	6,065	5,503
Selling and administrative	2,426	2,623	2,303
Interest expense	44	60	52
Other income/expense, net	21	21	32
Restructuring charge, net	45	130	—
Total expenses	8,031	8,900	7,891
Income before income taxes	746	653	1,295
Income taxes	295	253	499
Net income	$451	$400	$795

Source: Nike Annual Reports.

[9] PR Newswire, June 22, 1999.

EXHIBIT 2 U.S. Athletic Footwear Retail Outlet Market Share

	1993	*1994*	*1995*	*1996*	*1997*	*1998*
Discount stores	14.0%	15.9%	16.2%	14.7%	14.8%	14.4%
Athletic shoe stores	21.9%	19.5%	18.9%	20.0%	19.4%	19.9%
General shoe stores	11.8%	10.7%	9.7%	9.8%	9.2%	8.8%
Sporting goods stores	12.9%	12.7%	12.5%	12.6%	13.2%	13.2%
Department stores	22.0%	22.8%	22.3%	22.2%	21.5%	21.5%

Reproduced with permission from SGMA Athletic Footwear Market Index by NPD.

EXHIBIT 3 Projected Footwear and Apparel Sales, 1998–2003

(SBN)	*1998*	*1999*	*2000*	*2001*	*2002*	*2003*
Footwear	0.05	0.1	0.2	0.3	0.6	1.2
Apparel and accessories	0.4	0.8	1.4	2.4	4.1	6.7
Total	0.5	0.9	1.6	2.8	4.7	7.8

Source: Jupiter Research, September 2000.

EXHIBIT 4 Value Chain for $100 Pair of Nike Shoes

Material cost	$15.67
Direct labor cost	$2.59
Administration and overhead	$4.56
Factory profit margin	$1.90
Net factory price	*$24.71*
Shipping, customs, and finance charges	$3.88
Net landed price	*$28.59*
Warehousing and distribution	$0.76
Royalties	$0.38
Net quality costs	$0.27
Direct ship allowance	$0.21
Research and development	$0.23
Other costs of sale	$0.17
Total COGS	*$30.62*
Sales discounts	$4.61
SG&A	$8.29
Corporate overhead	$1.75
Interest expense	$0.21
Income taxes	$2.56
Total Nike cost	*$48.03*

(continued)

EXHIBIT 4 *(continued)*

Nike net profit	$4.00
Gross wholesale price	*$52.03*
Retail costs and profit	*$47.97*
Retail sales price	*$100.00*

Source: Nike documents.

STANFORD
GRADUATE SCHOOL OF BUSINESS

DISINTERMEDIATION IN THE U.S. AUTO INDUSTRY

In a very short period of time, the last stupid customer is going to walk through our dealership doors. —*Richard W. Everett, Chrysler Corporation, December 1997*[1]

Though still in its infancy, the retailing of vehicles over the Internet had emerged as a significant trend by 2000, fueled by the rapid rise of independent online buying services (OBSs) such as Autobytel.com. OBSs initially referred leads to traditional car dealers, who then closed the sale. But some OBSs were taking more control of the transaction—by providing financing and insurance, extended-warranty coverage, even delivery of the vehicle to the buyer—thus pushing the traditional dealer into a fulfillment role with little or no customer contact. Several hybrid "clicks-and-mortar" ventures had also combined an online sales channel with a physical distribution network. Other Internet businesses included online lenders, used-car sellers, and automotive-services providers. Though online players accounted for only a tiny fraction of the overall market, they were vying for a larger share of the trillion-dollar U.S. auto industry.

Meanwhile, auto makers were beefing up their own e-commerce efforts—some even laying the groundwork for Internet direct sales to consumers. Both GM and Ford—the country's number-one and number-two car makers—established e-commerce units in 1999, and Toyota (the number-one Japanese nameplate) created its Office of the Web. The auto makers gave these units broad-ranging mandates to ratchet up the compa-

---

Case Writer Eric Martí prepared this case under the supervision of Professor Garth Saloner and Professor A. Michael Spence as the basis for class discussion rather than to illustrate either effective or ineffective handling of an administrative situation. The Boston Consulting Group and McKinsey & Company provided research assistance. Margot Sutherland, Executive Director, Center for Electronic Business and Commerce, Stanford Graduate School of Business managed the development of the case.

[1] "Haggling in Cyberspace Transforms Car Sales," Rebecca Blumenstein, *Wall Street Journal*, 12/30/97, p. B1.

nies' Internet strategies, touching on all areas from supply chain management to retail distribution. A sense both of opportunity and alarm motivated these moves. For manufacturers, the Internet provided a powerful means to interact directly with car buyers and owners, a role that historically only dealers had played. At the same time, manufacturers feared ceding the customer relationship either to independent OBSs or to clicks-and-mortar cyber dealers who had no allegiance to any single manufacturer.

In 1999 an estimated 2.7% of car sales originated over the Internet (most via referrals to established car dealers), versus 1.1% the year before. Analysts at market research firm J. D. Power and Associates expected that number to hit 5% in 2000.[2] AutoNation alone, the country's largest car retailer, estimated that it had online sales of about one billion dollars in 1999. J. D. Power also reported that in 1999, 40% of car buyers used the Internet to shop for their vehicle (primarily to gather product and price information), up from 25% in 1998 and 17% in 1997.[3] The firm expected that figure to reach 66% in 2001.[4] By 2003, Forrester Research predicted the Internet would influence 8 million new-car purchases, with 470,000 cars sold entirely over the Internet from start to end of transaction.[5]

Few auto executives or analysts foresaw the online channel entirely eliminating traditional dealers. Substantial impediments stood in the way, including a host of state "franchise laws" that protected traditional dealerships from retail competition by manufacturers and OBSs. Dealers were also not standing still: 79% operated their own Web sites in 1999, up from just 21% in 1995.[6] And some aggressively pursued online sales. Everyone agreed that the Internet had unleashed powerful forces on auto retailing, but no one was sure how the industry would evolve.

U.S. AUTO MANUFACTURING INDUSTRY BACKGROUND

In 1999, foreign and domestic auto makers sold nearly 17 million new cars and light trucks in the United States (up from 15.54 million units in 1998), generating estimated retail sales of more than $400 billion—a record year for the industry (see Table 1).

The automotive industry also included used-vehicle sales (more than 40 million changed hands each year, producing revenues of $350 billion in 1998); financing ($440 billion in outstanding loans); service, parts, and accessories ($156 billion); insurance premiums ($136 billion); new-car advertising ($12 billion); and used-vehicle classified advertising ($19 billion).[7]

[2] "The eStats Report: eRetail," *eMarketer*, Vol. II, 9/99, p. 161; "Racing for a Slice of a $350 Billion Pie, Online Auto-Sales Sites Retool," Fara Warner, *Wall Street Journal*, 1/24/00, p. B1.

[3] "New-Vehicle Buyers Take Control of Negotiation Process," J. D. Power and Associates, press release, 7/27/99.

[4] "The eAuto Report," Jordan Hymowitz and Justin Hughes, Robertson Stephens, 1/11/00, p. 14.

[5] "New-Car Buying Races Online," J. L. McQuivey, K. Delhagen, and C. Ardito, Forrester Research, 1/99, p. 10.

[6] "The eAuto Report," Jordan Hymowitz and Justin Hughes, Robertson Stephens, 1/11/00, p. 31.

[7] "AutoWeb.com, Inc.," S. C. Franco and T. M. Klein, US Bancorp Piper Jaffray, 4/19/99, p. 1.

TABLE 1 U.S. Passenger-vehicle Unit Sales and Retail Value, 1990–1999[8]

Year	*Passenger cars*	*Light trucks*	*Total vehicles*	*Retail value ($B)*
1990	9,300,200	4,557,500	13,857,700	220.34
1991	8,174,700	4,135,300	12,310,000	197.58
1992	8,213,100	4,647,400	12,860,500	219.91
1993	8,517,900	5,378,100	13,896,000	252.91
1994	8,990,500	6,068,100	15,058,600	289.13
1995	8,635,000	6,093,100	14,728,100	301.19
1996	8,526,800	6,570,400	15,097,200	330.63
1997	8,272,100	6,858,100	15,130,200	342.70
1998	8,137,400	7,404,500	15,541,900	366.79
1999	8,699,362	8,258,374	16,958,670	401.00*

*estimate

AUTOMOTIVE MANUFACTURING: INDUSTRY STRUCTURE

Six companies dominated the manufacture of passenger vehicles in the United States—three domestic (GM, Ford, DaimlerChrysler[9]) and three Japanese (Toyota, Honda, and Nissan, all of which produced many of the cars sold in the United States in North American assembly plants). Collectively, these six accounted for 87% of all new vehicles sold. Non-U.S. firms divided the remaining share (see Table 2).

TABLE 2 U.S. Car and Light-truck Unit Sales by Manufacturer (Percentage of Total Units Sold), 1995–1999[10]

Manufacturer	*1999*	*1998*	*1997*	*1996*	*1995*
General Motors	29.2	29.4	31.3	31.4	32.9
Ford	23.8	24.8	25.2	25.5	25.8
Chrysler	15.6	16.1	15.2	16.2	14.7
Toyota	8.7	8.8	8.1	7.7	7.4
Honda	6.4	6.5	6.2	5.6	5.4
Nissan	4.0	4.0	4.8	5.0	5.2
Volkswagen	1.9	1.7	1.1	1.1	0.7
Other imports	10.6	8.6	8.0	7.6	7.9
Total units sold	16,958,670	15,541,900	15,130,200	15,097,200	14,728,000

[8] National Automobile Dealers Association, *Automotive Executive*, 8/99, p. 41; *Wall Street Journal*, 1/6/00.

[9] In 1998, Chrysler merged with German car maker Daimler-Benz to form the transoceanic Daimler-Chrysler. In 1999, the Chrysler division sold 2.64 million units in the United States versus 189,437 units for the Daimler-Benz (i.e., Mercedes) division.

[10] National Automobile Dealers Association, *Automotive Executive*, 8/99, p. 41; *Wall Street Journal*, 1/6/00.

The top six manufacturers, as well as most other major producers, operated globally. For example, GM, the world's largest auto manufacturer with worldwide production of 7.56 million units in 1998, derived 31% of its revenues from non-U.S. markets; Ford, 30%. Many manufacturers had production facilities around the world, and some owned (or had significant stakes in) foreign car makers. Ford, for example, owned British car makers Jaguar and Aston Martin, and in 1999 acquired the passenger-car business of Sweden's Volvo. It also had a 33% interest in Japanese manufacturer Mazda. GM owned Vauxhall (U.K.), Opel (Germany), and Saab (Sweden), and had stakes in Japan's Isuzu (49%) and Subaru (20%).

Automobile manufacturing was both capital- and labor-intensive. Manufacturers' major costs were direct materials and labor: cost of sales averaged about 75% for the industry. Materials accounted for 45% of the retail price of an automobile; labor, 25%.[11] Car makers also invested significant sums in constructing and maintaining of factories and on R&D. After deducting these expenses—plus those for marketing, sales, and general administration—auto makers averaged a pretax net margin of about 6.5% (1994–1998). However, the industry was cyclical and car makers often posted losses during economic downturns.

Car makers focused most of their resources on three primary functions: design, engineering, and manufacturing. Automotive design addressed both the aesthetic styling and the functionality of the vehicle—e.g., trunk size, interior space, and dashboard layout—to appeal to targeted groups of consumers. Engineering concentrated on vehicle performance and handling, involving engine power, steering, electronics systems, emissions control, fuel efficiency, and so on. Manufacturing entailed the entire range of production, from fabrication of components to final assembly of vehicles. The manufacturing labor force was largely unionized.

DESIGN AND MANUFACTURE

The design and manufacture of an automobile was a lengthy and expensive process. It took car makers 18–36 months (and up to $1 billion) to design and develop a new vehicle before it could go into production. Auto manufacturing required a complex supply chain and production infrastructure. Thousands of companies from a broad array of industries—steel, rubber, plastic, glass, electronics, oil, and chemicals, among others—supplied inputs to car makers. The typical vehicle comprised several thousand individual components. For example, DiamlerChrysler's Neon (a small-car model) had 1,900 parts, while the BMW Z3 roadster (assembled at BMW's plant in Greer, S.C.) contained more than 3,000 parts.[12]

Though manufacturers outsourced an increasing share of their operations, they still produced many vehicle inputs. Prior to the spin-off of its parts-manufacturing unit Delphi Automotive Systems in May 1999, GM made 70% of the components used in its cars. Ford produced 50% of its parts (much of it through its Visteon Automotive

[11] "Are You Tough Enough to Manage Your Channels?" C. B. Bucklin, S. P. DeFalco, J. R. DeVincentis, and J. P. Levis III, *McKinsey Quarterly*, 1996, No. 1, p. 106.

[12] "Neon Helps Cut Costs," Paul Gargaro, *Chicago Sun-Times*, 3/7/99, p. 54; "Area BMW Maker Builds Sport Activity Vehicle," C. F. Smith, *Knight Ridder Tribune Business News*, 8/17/99.

Products division), and DaimlerChrysler fabricated 25% of its components.[13] Manufacturers viewed certain highly engineered inputs—primarily engines and transmissions (the so-called powertrain)—as "strategic content" that differentiated their products and usually did not outsource their manufacture.

Production Planning

Automobile assembly plants were designed to batch produce vehicles in large numbers. Plants had one or more assembly lines, each set up to produce a particular model of vehicle with a range of optional features. Given the many options available—exterior color and trim; interior materials and color; engine size and features; roof and wheel treatments; sound systems; and so on—any given car had thousands of possible permutations. For example, DaimlerChrysler's Neon (model year 2000) came in 2,800 variations—down from 51,000 variations for the 1999 model.[14] To limit the number of permutations, manufacturers generally required consumers to choose from predefined option packages. (This was not as significant an issue for Japanese manufacturers, particularly the so-called transplants that had North American assembly plants: they limited options and variations far more than U.S. makers.)

In addition to the huge capital expenditures to build plants, union contracts obliged manufacturers to pay assembly workers full-time wages even if production rates dropped. To keep the unit cost of production profitable, plant utilization rates had to be high. Moreover, changing a plant's setup to produce a different vehicle was costly and time consuming. Manufacturers generally limited changeovers to once a year, to accommodate production of the next model-year vehicles.

Production runs required 30–60 days advance planning so auto makers set production rates to keep 60 days of supply in inventory. Quantities for production runs were based on a number of variables, including the stock and custom orders dealers submitted. Stock orders accounted for 80%–85% of dealers' total orders: American consumers generally purchased their cars from those available in a dealer's inventory—only 15%–20% of buyers custom-ordered cars from the manufacturer. Market researchers attributed this pattern to the American car-buyer's preference to compromise on specific features rather than wait 30–60 days for delivery of a custom-ordered vehicle.[15]

Capacity-utilization requirements also dictated a minimum rate of production at each plant. Manufacturers based the total production capacity for any one model on past sales and forecasted demand. These estimates had to be made well before actual production: they were typically based on research that was a year old when the vehicles reached the dealer showrooms. Manufacturer predictions of demand were frequently off by as much as 30%–60%, causing oversupplies of many models and shortages of others.[16]

[13] *WEFA Industrial Monitor 1999–2000*, P. Trumbull and F. R. Price, eds., 1999, p. 20.17.

[14] "DaimlerChrysler Keeping Small Cars Simple," David Phillips, *Gannett News Service*, 3/8/99.

[15] By contrast, European car distribution was more "pull" oriented: consumers typically did not buy from a dealer's inventory; instead, they ordered cars and waited months for delivery. European car dealerships generally stocked few vehicles, which were available primarily for customers to test drive.

[16] "GM Rolling Out New Supply Chain Monitoring System," John Couretas, *Crain's Cleveland Business*, 10/18/99, p. 35.

Distribution and Marketing: The Franchised Dealership Channel

Manufacturers distributed their products through a network of franchised dealers. The franchise was a formal legal agreement entitling the dealer to operate a factory-authorized sales and service outlet for a specific brand of automobile in a defined geographic area. The franchise included many requirements, such as minimum sales levels and service capabilities. Only franchised dealers could purchase inventory direct from the manufacturer.

Dealers kept about 60 days of supply in stock. In 1998, for example, dealers' supply averaged 63 days for domestic and 54 days for imported vehicles.[17] (Inventory levels varied among manufacturers. For example, GM dealers as a group averaged 69 days of supply in inventory in 1998, compared with just 34 days of supply for Toyota dealers.[18]) The combined average inventory of new cars—dealer and manufacturer—equaled approximately $125 billion (retail sales value).[19]

Dealers submitted stock orders to manufacturers 1–2 months ahead of delivery, based on a "turn and earn" system: dealers were allotted one new vehicle for each one they sold. However, manufacturers typically could not fulfill orders precisely due to shortages on popular models and oversupplies on less popular ones. So, while rationing the supply of fast-selling cars and trucks, manufacturers also had to provide incentives for dealers to move excess inventory.

Car makers supported their dealers through extensive advertising and promotional campaigns. As a whole, auto makers led all other industries in spending on broadcast, print, and billboard advertising in the United States, with total expenditures of $7.43 billion in 1998.[20] GM alone spent $2.94 billion on advertising, or about $643 per passenger vehicle it sold that year.[21] Car makers also spent an average of $2,000 per vehicle in rebates and other incentives to both consumers and dealers, costing the industry more than $30 billion.[22]

Manufacturers conducted continuous and exhaustive market research to identify and track consumer preferences and trends, and they designed each model to target a specific consumer segment. While many preferences were tied to car buyers' age, gender, and income, consumers also exhibited pronounced differences in vehicle choice based on region, marital status, occupation, and other factors. Consumer tastes and priorities also tended to shift over time. For example, a 1998 Roper survey found that 61% of consumers considered ease of maintenance and repair "most important" in choosing a car, up from only 46% in 1993; those who demanded that the car be American-made declined by 7%.[23] These complex dynamics meant that manufacturers were frequently surprised by market response to their products.

[17] *Automotive Executive*, National Automobile Dealers Association, 8/99, p. 40.

[18] *Ward's Automotive Yearbook 1999*.

[19] Total industry inventory value computed from data for retail and wholesale sales of new cars.

[20] *Automotive News*, *1999 Market Data Book*, p. 96.

[21] "Total Measured U.S. Ad Spending by Category & Media in 1998," *Advertising Age*, 9/27/99, p. S1.

[22] "Order Disorder: The Gap Between What Customers Want and What Factories Build Remains Huge," *Automotive News*, 10/11/99.

[23] "Consumers Keep the Upper Hand," Jon Berry, *American Demographics*, 9/98, p. 20.

On average, distribution costs accounted for approximately 30% of the retail sales price of a vehicle. About half of these costs were manufacturer-related: expenditures on advertising, promotion (including cash rebates and low-interest loans), transportation, and handling. The other half was dealer-related: inventory financing and insurance, advertising, payroll and sales commissions, general overhead (rent, salaries, etc.), and profit.

THE AUTO RETAILING INDUSTRY

In early 1999, approximately 15,000 dealer principals—most of which were sole proprietors—owned 22,076 franchised dealerships in the United States. Collectively, they controlled nearly 47,000 franchises (many dealerships operated more than one franchise). The top six manufacturers accounted for 88% of the total (see Table 3). More than 23,000 independent dealers served the used-vehicle market.

History and Evolution of the Dealership Channel

Car makers had employed dealerships to sell their vehicles to consumers since the advent of the mass-market automobile early in the twentieth century. Because auto manufacturing was capital- and resource-intensive, car makers tended to build a relatively small number of high-capacity factories, generally located near sources of key supplies (i.e., iron and steel). To reach consumers, however, manufacturers required an extensive distribution network with outlets across the country, not only to sell cars but also to service them: this was critical in the early auto industry, when automobiles broke down more frequently.

TABLE 3 Number of Dealerships and Franchises by Manufacturer[24]

Manufacturer	*Number of dealerships*	*Number of franchises*	*Passenger vehicles sold in 1999*	*Average vehicles sold per dealership*
General Motors	8,118	16,904	4,947,359	609.4
Ford	4,834	8,228	4,028,662	833.4
DaimlerChrysler[25]	4,484	11,567	2,638,561	588.4
Toyota	716	1,195	1,475,441	2,060.7
Honda	676	995	1,076,893	1,593.0
Nissan	554	1,075	677,212	1,222.4
Total, all manufacturers	22,076	46,882	16,958,670	768.2

[24] Sources: *Automotive News, 1999 Market Data Book*; *Wall Street Journal*, 1/6/00. Figures for DaimlerChrysler do not include Mercedes-Benz data. Dealership figures for Japanese manufacturers count only those that handled the designated make of car; franchise figures are all-inclusive. All figures are as of 1/1/99.

[25] Includes data only for Chrysler division.

Rather than tie up their own capital and administrative resources in these retail and service operations, car makers offered dealership franchises to independent businesspeople. Not only did this arrangement leverage the capital of private investors, but local dealers had better knowledge of the markets they served and could more accurately forecast demand.

For the first half of the century, most Americans resided in small towns and rural areas and consequently, the number of dealerships proliferated to serve these many local markets. By 1949, new-car dealers peaked at 49,123. As the U.S. population began to concentrate in cities and outlying suburbs, car dealerships in marginal markets closed or merged with others; the number of new-car dealerships had declined to about 22,100 in 1999.

Though the dealership model had served manufacturers well for decades, car makers (and many dealers themselves) were seeing major problems with it. For manufacturers, one problem was the sheer number of dealerships in their retail network. Though the number had declined since the 1950s, U.S. manufacturers believed they still had too many dealers. (Foreign manufacturers that entered the U.S. market more recently did not inherit a legacy of an overcrowded retail network.) Manufacturers believed that they could save significant distribution costs by shipping vehicles in higher quantities to fewer, but larger, dealers. The oversupply of dealers also contributed to the rampant price competition in auto retailing: many dealers competed against other dealers selling the same makes and models, rather than against other manufacturers' dealers. This dynamic suppressed dealer profits and contributed to the high-pressure sales tactics typical of the industry—which tainted customers' views of both dealers and manufacturers.

Dealer Revenues, Costs, and Profits

Franchised car dealers derived revenues from several sources: sales of new and used cars (including revenues from financing, insurance, and service contracts) and parts and service. Sales of new vehicles (including revenues from financing, insurance, and service contracts sold along with the vehicle) accounted for 59.4% of the average dealership's revenues in 1998 (down from 62.9% in 1988), but they contributed just 29% of total profit. Many dealerships also derived significant income from fleet sales and volume sales to companies and public agencies that maintained fleets of automobiles primarily for employee use.

In 1998, the average dealership sold about 600 new vehicles at an average retail sales price of $23,600. The average gross margins on new-vehicle sales was 6.5% of the retail price. In addition to the markup (if any) over invoice, dealers' margin on new-car sales came from several sources:

- Dealer "holdback": this was an amount, usually about 2%–3% of dealer invoice, that many manufacturers paid to dealers when they sold a vehicle;
- Manufacturer incentives (for sales of models that manufacturers were promoting);

- Fees paid by lenders and insurers for referring financing and insurance (F&I) business to them (for example, dealers got fees for arranging loans from the manufacturer's captive credit operation, e.g., GM Acceptance Corp.); and
- Fees from selling manufacturer-sponsored, dealer-sponsored, or third-party service contracts (so-called extended warranties). These contracts were lucrative: on average, consumers paid $1,000 for an extended warranty, but collected just $250.[26]

See Table 4 for the revenue and cost structure of the average dealer.

Though dealers' gross margins on new-vehicle sales had improved slightly in the late 1990s due to strong demand, they had generally declined over the previous dozen years (from more than 8% in 1988). Analysts attributed much of this margin erosion to one key factor: starting in the mid-1980s, consumers had access to detailed information about dealers' costs—first from publications such as *Consumer Reports* and *Edmund's New Car Prices*, and later from Web sites that published dealer-invoice data for new cars. With this information, consumers could negotiate more effectively. Haggling with dealers over price used to proceed by working down from the manufacturer's suggested retail price (MSRP), which reflected a generous dealer markup. But increasingly consumers insisted on dealer cost as the starting point, and many buyers knew what dealers would accept over the dealer invoice as a final price. Online forums, such as the "Town Hall" discussion section on Edmund's Web site (www.edmunds.com),

TABLE 4 Revenue and Cost Data for Average U.S. Franchised Dealership[27]

Item	*1998 ($ 000)*	*% of sales*
New-vehicle sales	14,086	59.4
Used-vehicle sales	6,782	28.6
Parts and service	2,845	12.0
Total sales	23,713	
Cost of goods sold	20,583	86.8
Operating Expenses		
Payroll	1,755	7.4
Advertising	2,371	1.0
Rent and equivalent	2,371	1.0
Floor-plan interest	119	0.5
Other (admin., insurance, supplies, etc.)	4,742	2.0
Net income	308	1.3

[26] "Promises, Promises," J. Edgerton, *Money*, 2/1/99, p. 173.

[27] "Auto Retailing—1999 Outlook," L. K. Mullins, D. Reidel, and A. Sutphin, Salomon Smith Barney, 4/29/99.

enabled consumers to exchange information about the prices they had paid on specific vehicles. According to J. D. Power and Associates, car buyers who used the Internet to get dealer-invoice information saved an average of $1,000 per sale over buyers who lacked this information.[28]

By contrast, for the average dealership, used vehicles (including revenues from financing, insurance, and service contracts sold along with the vehicle) generated 28.6% of sales in 1998 (up from 22.8% in 1988) and contributed 44.2% of total profits. The average gross margin on used-vehicle sales was 10.8%. Franchised dealers sold 19.3 million used vehicles in 1998, about half of the estimated 41 million that changed hands that year. Sales by private parties and nonfranchised used-car dealers accounted for the balance.

Service and parts generated 12% of franchised dealers' sales in 1998 (down from 14.3% in 1988). But with a gross margin of 44%, dealers' service and parts business contributed more than 25% of total profits. This business, however, was under pressure from a growing number of competitors. In addition to the many independent service stations, dealers faced increasing competition from regional and national service franchises that focused on a specific service (e.g., oil change, muffler installation, tires, body repair, tune-ups, transmission repair) and from chains of auto-parts specialty stores. As a result, dealers' share of the service and parts market was falling.

A major component of dealers' profit on sales of vehicles (both new and used) was the fee income from referring F&I business to lenders and insurers. While these fees constituted a small percentage of overall sales (typically from 1% to 6%, averaging about 3%), they had gross margins of 75% or more. When broken out separately from other sources of profit, F&I contributed 32.9% of the average dealer's net income in 1999—the single largest source of profits (see Table 5).

TABLE 5 Contribution to Dealer Profit by Activity (% of Net Income)[29]

Year	*New-vehicle sales*	*Used-vehicle sales*	*Finance & insurance*[30]	*Service & parts*
1990	17.5%	24.8%	27.6%	30.1%
1991	17.6	26.2	29.0	27.2
1992	18.0	27.3	28.7	26.0
1993	19.1	29.2	28.3	23.4
1994	19.1	29.3	27.8	23.8
1995	20.8	29.1	26.4	23.7
1996	20.2	26.9	28.0	24.8
1997	19.6	24.9	30.1	25.5
1998	18.6	23.5	32.1	25.8
1999	18.5	22.0	32.9	26.7

[28] "The Great American Car Chase," *Yahoo! Internet Life*, Sean Kelly, 3/1/99.

[29] "The eAuto Report," Jordan Hymowitz and Justin Hughes, Robertson Stephens, 1/11/00, p. 11.

[30] Figures represent finance and insurance profits from both new and used vehicles.

Sales commissions accounted for 25% of payroll expense: dealers paid salespeople an average of $355 per car sold (or more than $435,000 a year for the average dealer). "Floor-plan interest" was the amount dealers paid to finance the purchase of their inventory: manufacturers typically extended dealers credit and charged interest on the loans. Dealers also had to carry insurance on their inventory. Variable carrying costs of inventory ranged from $20–$80 per vehicle per day.

Consolidation of Auto Retailing

The U.S. car dealership industry had experienced significant consolidation as the number of franchised car dealers had fallen steadily since 1950. However, small dealerships—those selling fewer than 400 cars per year—accounted for most of the decline. The number of larger dealerships was rising, and the top 5% of dealer principals accounted for 31% of all new-vehicle sales in 1998 (see Table 6).[31]

Four key factors were accelerating consolidation of the industry. First, manufacturers were issuing few new franchises. Second, many marginal dealers were going out of business—either through voluntary liquidation or bankruptcy—or selling out to other dealer principals. In particular dealerships in rural areas were closing due to declining populations.

Third, the capital-resource requirements to operate a dealership were escalating: to compete with larger players, dealers had to offer customers wider selection, which increased inventory costs. In addition, as vehicles became technologically more complex, dealers' service departments had to invest in expensive diagnostic and repair equipment, stock more parts, and extend their hours to compete against the auto-parts and convenience service chains.

Fourth, aggressive consolidators had recently emerged, several of which (e.g., AutoNation, United Auto Group, Sonic Automotive) had raised money in the public markets to fund their drives. All of the major publicly traded consolidators had commenced operations or become public since 1996 (see Table 7).

TABLE 6 Number of U.S. Franchise Dealers by Annual New-Vehicle Unit Sales[32]

Annual new-unit sales	*1999*	*1989*	*1979*
0–149	4,256	6,725	11,500
150–399	6,160	8,275	9,200
400–749	6,160	4,775	3,700
750+	5,824	5,225	4,100

[31] "Automotive Manufacturers Need to Recognize Two Distinct Classes of Retailers," J. D. Power and Associates, press release, 12/9/98.

[32] *Automotive Executive*, National Automobile Dealers Association, 8/99, p. 37.

TABLE 7 Public Auto Dealerships—Sales ($ Millions) and Franchises Owned, 1997–1998[33]

Dealership	*New vehicles retailed, 1998*[34]	*Sales, 1998*	*Franchises, 1998*	*Sales, 1997*	*Franchises, 1997*
AutoNation, Inc.	286,179	15,221.0	361	10,355.6	266
United Auto Group, Inc.	77,403	3,343.1	103	2,600.0	118
Group 1 Automotive	39,822	2,400.0	83	1,600.0	58
Sonic Automotive	37,674	2,800.0	111	1,680.0	39
CarMax Group	N/A	1,470.0	17	874.2	4
Lithia Motors	17,708	1,240.0	77	620.0	50
Cross-Continent Auto[35]	14,551	689.9	10	569.2	10
Hometown Auto Retailers	N/A	313.0	12	240.2	12
Major Automotive Group	N/A	182.9	7	144.0	5

The entrepreneurs behind these companies were attempting to leverage both economies of scale and concentrated market power to produce superior returns. While their efforts had met with mixed results, they were bringing dramatic change to an industry whose essential structure had evolved very little since its inception nearly a century before.

Manufacturers generally regarded the publicly traded dealer concerns as a threat, but they welcomed certain aspects of dealership consolidation. Ford and GM had long been concerned about the bloated number of dealers in their channel, which added to distribution costs and contributed to intrabrand price competition. Indeed, both companies had attempted to reduce dealer numbers by buying franchises (where permitted by state law), consolidating them, and operating them as factory-owned stores. Dealers, however, resisted those efforts. In September 1999, for example, GM terminated a plan to buy up to 10% of GM dealerships nationwide after dealers opposed it. Ford slowed down a similar effort.

Car makers worried that large dealership groups, which operated multibrand stores, could erode the manufacturers' brands and usurp the customer relationship. AutoNation, for example, carried brands of every major auto maker. Why then, manufacturers asked, would AutoNation care if a customer bought a Ford, a Chevy, or a Dodge? Moreover, as large operators amassed market share, they could increase their bargaining power with manufacturers.

THE CAR-BUYING EXPERIENCE

Industry observers generally agreed that the auto industry's push-oriented system of production and distribution (by which manufacturers pumped product into the

[33] *Automotive News 1999 Market Data Book*; *1998 Market Data Book*; *1997 Market Data Book*; company reports.

[34] Figures do not include fleet sales.

[35] AutoNation acquired Cross-Continent in February 1999.

distribution channel based on imperfect measures of demand), coupled with an oversupply of dealers, created the high-pressure sales environment car buyers loathed. While high-demand vehicles sold quickly, less-popular models required more sales and promotional effort. Because dealers had to pay interest and insurance on vehicles each day they remained on the lot, they wanted to move their inventory as quickly as possible. Dealers often motivated their salespeople to sell lower-demand vehicles by offering higher commissions on those sales.

Wishing to maximize their profit per vehicle, dealers sought to extract the highest price a customer would pay. Dealers knew that individual car buyers differed in their price sensitivity, in their knowledge about dealers' willingness to reduce prices, and in their ability to negotiate. Hence, dealerships stressed strong sales and negotiation skills. This situation created the uncomfortable sales environment that typified most dealerships.

Consumer surveys corroborated the many anecdotal accounts of poor car-buying experiences. A 1999 Gallup Poll, for example, asked people to rank the honesty of various professions: car dealers scored lowest.[36] Gallup also found that only 42% of consumers had a "positive experience" buying a new car.[37] And car dealerships were the subjects of more complaints to Better Business Bureaus than any other industry.[38] Women reported more dissatisfaction with car buying than men. Moreover only 7.3% of all new-car salespeople were women. (A notable exception was Saturn, which targeted women buyers and had about a 25% female sales force.[39])

Dealers' poor customer loyalty reflected consumers' distaste for the car-buying experience. While manufacturers enjoyed moderate rates of customer loyalty—averaging 56.9% repeat business for the industry overall[40]—dealers saw only 20% of their customers return to buy a car.[41] Dealers fared somewhat better on service: as the manufacturers' exclusive providers of authorized service, dealers as a whole captured virtually all warranty-covered business. But in-warranty cars accounted for only 20%–25% of the 205 million vehicles on U.S. roads (the median age of which was about 8 years); dealers had only 15% of the market for nonwarranty service.[42] Overall, the average dealership saw less than 50% of its buyers ever return, whether for service or to purchase another vehicle.[43]

As the quality and reliability of automobiles tended to reach parity across all makes in a category, manufacturers' comparative advantage on these dimensions decreased. Instead, dealer-related factors became the primary drivers of customer loyalty: a 1997

[36] "Auto Dealers See Delicate Balance in Online Quotes," J. Gaw, *Los Angeles Times*, 8/16/99, p. C1.

[37] "U.S. Auto Dealers Hope ESOPs Yield Happy Workers, Buyers," Andrea Puchalsky, Dow Jones News Service, 8/13/99.

[38] "Used Car Superstores," *Encyclopedia of Emerging Industries*, Gale Research, 1999 (published by OneSource Information Services, Inc.).

[39] "Why So Few?" Tom Incantapulo, *Newsday*, 1/31/99, p. F08.

[40] "Ford Wins Most Categories in Polk Loyalty Study," *Automotive News*, 12/15/97, p. 10.

[41] "Car Retailing Needs a Tune-Up," R. S. Sisodia and J. N. Sheth, *Wall Street Journal*, 12/20/99, p. A26.

[42] *Automotive News, 1999 Market Data Book*, p. 60; "Car Retailing Needs a Tune-Up," R. S. Sisodia and J. N. Sheth, *Wall Street Journal*, 12/20/99, p. A26; author's estimates.

[43] "Auto Retailing—1999 Outlook," L. K. Mullins, D. Reidel, and A. Sutphin, Salomon Smith Barney, 4/29/99.

study by R. L. Polk found that the single most important variable determining customer loyalty was "attitude of sales staff."[44] Manufacturers had long recognized that dealer sales tactics turned consumers sour on car buying. Haggling over purchase terms—price, trade-in value, financing, and insurance—caused consumers the most anxiety. But auto makers also realized that in a distribution system overcrowded with retail outlets, intrabrand price competition was inevitable. When GM created its Saturn division, which started selling cars in the early 1990s, the company addressed this problem head on.

ONE-PRICE SELLING: THE SATURN EXPERIMENT

GM set up the Saturn dealership franchises to cover broad market areas. It also recruited dealers who could operate a network of adjacent dealerships, so that each dealer principal controlled a larger market area than the typical GM dealer. Limiting the number of franchises and enlarging their scope helped reduce pressure on dealers to compete on price. Moreover, GM recruited dealers who believed in the Saturn approach to customer relations, which included no-haggle pricing, a complete absence of sales pressure altogether, and an emphasis on customer service. Saturn dealers set their own compensation and incentive schemes, which tended to reward employees based on group efforts, customer satisfaction, and overall performance of the dealership rather than individual sales results.

Though the Saturn division was not a stellar financial performer for GM, Saturn dealers enjoyed higher margins and customer satisfaction than the average dealer. Nevertheless, less than 5% of franchised dealers nationwide operated one-price stores in 1999.[45] Many dealers believed that customers preferred to negotiate price: one study found that 62% of consumers preferred negotiation and only 35% favored a system that offered the same price among all dealers.[46] Still, many dealers expressed interest in moving to no-haggle pricing, but they could not do so without widespread adoption among their competitors. When a group of Ford dealerships were consolidated in the Tulsa, Oklahoma area and adopted a one-price system, they lost market share to other Ford dealers in outlying areas who undercut them on price. Consumers were willing to travel further to get a lower price.

ONLINE BUYING SERVICES

Since March 1995, when Autobytel.com became the first independent OBS, many more sites had emerged, and different business models had evolved. All of these players were attempting to exploit consumer distaste for traditional offline car buying and to shift bargaining power to the buyer by giving consumers information and easy access to more

[44] "Changing Channels in the Automotive Industry," E. R. Hirsh, L. F. Rodewig, P. Soliman, and S. B. Wheeler, *Strategy & Business*, First Quarter 1999, p. 44.

[45] "Motor City Dealers Haggle Over the One-Price, No-Dicker Approach to Auto Sales," D. W. Nauss, *Los Angeles Times*, 2/25/99, p. W2.

[46] *ibid.*

dealers. In the past, other entrepreneurs had seen the same opportunity—but they did not have the power of the Internet available to them.

PRECURSORS: BROKERS AND BUYING AGENTS

Prior to the advent of Autobytel.com and its OBS brethren in the mid-1990s, a small industry of intermediaries, mainly brokers and buying agents, catered to car buyers who used them for two reasons: to get better prices and to avoid negotiating with a dealer.

Brokers

In states where they were permitted, brokers acted as an intermediary between the franchised car dealer and the consumer. Consumers would engage a broker to find a specific desired car and negotiate its purchase. The dealer, rather than the consumer, paid the broker's commission. Often, the broker took legal title to the vehicle and resold it the consumer. Brokers advertised that they could get consumers lower prices on vehicles through their market knowledge and negotiating expertise and anecdotal evidence supported this.

Buying Agents

Buying agents charged the consumer a fee (usually a flat fee) to provide services similar to those of a broker. The agent located the desired vehicle and negotiated price and terms with the dealer on the buyer's behalf, but the consumer concluded the transaction directly with the dealer. Like brokers, buying agents also claimed that they could negotiate better terms for the consumer.

Both brokers and buying agents were generally small businesses serving local markets, though a few operated nationally with offices in several cities. They conducted business with both consumers and dealers primarily by phone and fax. Their ability to locate vehicles and negotiate terms depended largely on their knowledge of the local dealer market, including dealer inventories. According to J. D. Power and Associates, 11% of new-vehicle buyers in the recent past used sources such as brokers and buying agents to shop for a vehicle.[47]

OBS MODELS

Online car-buying services took one of five general forms, though some offered a combination.

- Referral service
- Classified listings
- Auction and reverse auction

[47] J. D. Power and Associates, press release, 8/20/97.

- Broker
- Direct sales (auto "e-tailers")

Referral Service

Autobytel.com, established in 1995, pioneered the online car-shopping business with the referral service approach. Many players were offering different variants of the model, but the central feature was a referral system: registered dealers received leads from the OBS and paid it a fee—a flat fee, or a per-lead or per-transaction fee, or some combination of the two. Consumers could shop the site and specify which vehicle they wanted. They could then submit a "purchase request" to a registered dealer, who would phone or e-mail the customer with a price quote. Dealers generally had exclusive rights to leads (for the brand of vehicle they retailed) in a defined market area. (However, AutoWeb.com users could get quotes from two competitive dealers in an area.) To complete the transaction, the buyer would go to the dealership, where further haggling sometimes took place (over trade-in terms, for example). Both Autobytel.com and AutoWeb.com went public in early 1999; by January 2000, both stocks had lost about 75% of their value.

Many dealers were signing up with OBSs: in 1999, Autobytel.com alone had signed up more than 3,000 dealers (up from 1,800 at the beginning of 1998), and 28% of all dealer principals used OBSs, nearly triple the number in 1998.[48] Among high-volume dealers, 58% had registered with OBSs.[49] The buying services gave dealers an increasingly important source of leads: in the fourth quarter of 1999, Autobytel sent its dealers more than 600,000 purchase requests (up from 342,000 in the first quarter of 1998),[50] and it reported that its dealers closed 28% of those leads.[51] (On average, dealers using OBSs received 37 leads a month from the referral services and converted about 15% of them to sales.[52])

In a move that alarmed participating dealers, however, many OBSs were expanding their services beyond referrals to include F&I—key profit areas for dealers. OBSs saw F&I as an obvious way to diversify their revenue base: 94% of new-car buyers financed their purchase. An increasing number of traditional lenders were also offering online loan services, and a few services—such as Giggo.com—operated only through the Internet channel. OBSs referred financing business both to online and offline providers, in which some OBSs had equity interests.

[48] "Sharp Increase in Dealer Demand for Independent Online Buying Services," J. D. Power and Associates, press release, 3/25/99.

[49] "Car Chase," Robert McGarvey, *Upside*, 12/99.

[50] "Autobytel.com, Inc.," S. G. Andrikopoulos and J. J. Patel, Duetsche Banc Alex. Brown, 10/28/99.

[51] "CEO Interview—Autobytel.com, Inc.," *Wall Street Transcript*, 11/99.

[52] "The Driver's Seat: New Web Sites Give Consumers a Powerful Tool in Their Search for a New Car," John Dodge, *Wall Street Journal*, 7/12/99, p. R40.

Classified Listing Services

Rather than charge for leads, this type of service provided online classified space for dealers and others to post vehicles for sale. Shoppers could search listings for price, model, location, and so on. Ads included links to the dealer sites, and transactions were completed offline. Classified listing services were essentially an online version of the automotive classifieds found in publications. Yahoo! and other portals and specialty classifieds sites maintained an extensive classifieds section for cars (new and used).

Auctions and Reverse Auctions

Several sites offered online auctions for new cars, whereby consumers could bid on listed vehicles. The online car buying scene also included reverse auctions: Priceline.com, the Internet's largest reverse auction site for consumer commerce, added autos to its product offerings in 1999. In a reverse auction, the prospective buyer listed the vehicle desired, along with a price he or she was willing to pay. Dealers who could meet or beat the posted price contacted the shopper to bid for the sale.

Online Brokers

Many of the auto brokers who operated offline in the pre-Internet days now had an online presence. But the real news in this category was CarsDirect.com, a start-up backed by renowned Internet innovator Bill Gross of idealab! (an incubator of Internet businesses) and funded by Dell Computer founder Michael Dell, among other investors. CarsDirect.com transacted business directly with the buyer, rather than referring leads to a dealer. Shoppers specified the vehicle they wanted, and CarsDirect.com quoted a low price: according to the company, its prices were in the bottom tenth percentile of market prices for any given model. To grow its customer base, CarsDirect.com even sold some cars at a loss. "I'm prepared to spend $80 million building our brand over the next two years," said CarsDirect.com founder and CEO Scott Painter, who viewed such losses as the cost of customer acquisition.[53]

Buyers could also transact financing and insurance for the vehicle through the CarsDirect.com site. It even offered its own financing service via CD One Financial (a venture with Bank One in which CarsDirect.com held a controlling interest). CarsDirect.com had contracts with some 1,700 dealers nationwide: it located the vehicle at a participating dealer and arranged for the purchase, insulating the buyer from interaction with the dealer. Buyers went to the dealer only to sign the final papers—with no further negotiations—and pick up the vehicle. In states where it was permitted, customers could have the papers and vehicle delivered via flatbed truck to their home or office instead. (One key challenge facing this model was what to do with trade-ins: 57% of new-car buyers owned a vehicle that they wished to trade in with their purchase.[54] CarsDirect.com did not accept trade-ins.)

[53] "Car Chase," Robert McGarvey, *Upside*, 12/99, p. 160.

[54] "The eAuto Report," Jordan Hymowitz and Justin Hughes, Robertson Stephens, 1/11/00.

Direct Sales

Though many dealers had entered the online car-selling business by settir own Web sites and signing with a referral service, few had pursued pure online sales (in contrast to relying on referral- or broker-based intermediaries). But in late 1999, action was heating up in this area. AutoNation, for example, the country's largest auto retailer with 1998 sales of $13.5 billion, had launched an Internet store called AutoNationDirect.com. The company estimated that its online sales in 1999 totaled $1 billion. By 2003, it expected 33% of its sales to come over the Web. The Web's ability to expand the effective size of their market was especially attractive to dealers: traditionally, dealers sold 90% of their cars to customers who lived or worked within 10 miles of the dealership.[55] Online sales, however, brought in customers from farther away: 61% of AutoNationDirect.com's customers came from more than 10 miles away, versus only 9% of the megadealer's offline customers.[56]

Several new ventures had also emerged to sell cars directly online, including two start-ups with impressive credentials: Greenlight.com and carOrder.com. Greenlight.com launched its service in January 2000 backed by Asbury Automotive Group (the country's third-largest car retailer) and Kleiner Perkins Caufield & Byers, a prominent Silicon Valley venture-capital firm. Amazon.com had also taken a 5% stake in the start-up and signed a promotional agreement to introduce Greenlight.com to Amazon's 16 million customers. Greenlight.com operated a clicks-and-mortar hybrid model: it partnered with traditional dealers—who provided inventory, fulfillment, and after-sale support and service—but it handled the sales transaction online, with a no-haggle approach. Greenlight.com thus served as a seller's agent, with a customer interface that insulated the buyer from the dealer throughout the sales process.

CarOrder.com also proposed a clicks-and-mortar model, but it intended to build its network from the ground up, rather than partner with traditional dealers. It planned to buy 100 franchises in outlying metro areas and convert them into holding depots for transferring inventory quickly between manufacturer and customer. In September 1999, CarOrder.com received $100 million from parent company Trilogy Software to fund the franchise acquisitions. CarOrder.com sought to undercut traditional dealers' prices by avoiding the high costs of inventory and showroom overhead. And because all sales would be transacted over the Internet at no-haggle prices, CarOrder.com would not pay sales commissions. CarOrder.com's founders believed that their business model could reduce the average retail price of a car by nearly $1,300 from that of a traditional dealer (see Table 8). To date, CarOrder.com had not purchased any franchises. Instead, it was operating much like CarsDirect.com, essentially brokering sales between traditional dealers and consumers.

Other Auto-Related Internet Services

Besides the OBSs, a crop of Internet-based auto-related services also was emerging to attack various links in the dealer value chain. Sites such as those operated by Kelley

[55] *The eStats Report: eRetail*, eMarketer, Vol. II, 9/99.
[56] "The eAuto Report," Jordan Hymowitz and Justin Hughes, Robertson Stephens, 1/11/00, p. 32.

TABLE 8 Cost Data for Average U.S. Franchised Dealership vs. CarOrder.com[57]

Cost item	*Dealer cost per car*	*CarOrder.com cost per car*
Advertising	$340	$100
General and administrative	194	100
Inventory	312	20
Rent	326	20
Sales commission	355	0
Total costs per car	1,527	240

Blue Book, Edmund's, IntelliChoice, and Consumer Reports—which provided reviews, price data, trade-in values, and other information—had become leading destinations for car shoppers. Other entrants offered online auto loans and automotive services. For example, CarStation.com (founded in late 1998) focused on providing an e-commerce solution for the collision-repair industry: it enabled businesses and customers to manage the collision-repair process via the Internet. It provided a suite of online marketplace and information services for various segments of the repair industry, such as repair shops, suppliers, and insurers. For example, via its RepairStation service, which car owners accessed via the site's ConsumerStation channel, repair shops could market their services to consumers. This channel enabled consumers to learn about the repair process, schedule repairs, and monitor work in process. Consumers could also purchase parts and accessories through CarStation's electronic catalogs.

MANUFACTURERS' INTERNET INITIATIVES

Manufacturers were attempting to leverage Internet technology in four primary areas. First, they were moving their indirect procurement and supply chain operations to the Internet. In November 1999, for example, both GM and Ford announced initiatives to create rival online marketplaces that would connect each firm's entire base of both direct and indirect suppliers. GM and Ford each spent more than $80 billion annually on purchases. By handling the purchases over the Internet, both companies expected to dramatically cut costs and speed up operations. GM and Ford also invited other car makers, such as Toyota and Honda, to join their purchasing networks.

Second, auto makers were integrating Internet services into vehicles. GM and Ford, for instance, had announced plans to equip some of their models with Web and e-mail access. By subscribing to a monthly service, drivers could use the car's built-in smartphone wireless device to connect to the Web or read and send e-mail. (More futuristic plans called for vehicles' mechanical components to be connected to the Internet,

[57] Source: "A Car Dealer by Any Other Name," Scott Woolley, *Forbes*, 11/29/99; CarOrder.com costs are company estimates.

enabling them to automatically send and receive information about performance and service needs directly to and from the manufacturer or service provider.)

Third, car makers were creating or extending Internet-based systems to tie together their entire sales, marketing, and distribution systems (including dealership operations). At GM, for example, this meant consolidating dozens of databases.

Fourth, manufacturers were boosting their efforts to attract online customers. Several manufacturer Web sites, for example, emulated the OBSs and enabled shoppers to initiate a purchase online by referring requests to dealers. At the GMBuyPower.com site, shoppers could compare side-by-side the features and prices (MSRPs) of GM versus competitor models. About 80% of GM's dealers participated on the GMBuyPower.com site: a shopper could determine if a dealer held a specified model in stock and could then request a "best price" offer. Ford was even experimenting with providing an "e-price" for its online customers, which in contrast to a MSRP was closer to the actual "street price" dealers were offering in the shopper's area. Ford dealers opposed this.

Car makers also tried to access more online customers by signing comarketing agreements with major online players. In January 2000, GM and Ford signed extensive comarketing agreements with, respectively, America Online and Yahoo! Ford was also laying the groundwork for an online build-to-order system. It had taken a 25% stake in Microsoft's CarPoint.com, the software company's online buying service, and the two companies planned to enable shoppers to configure a vehicle online. The system would search in real time for the specified vehicle, first in dealer inventory, then manufacturer inventory (including work-in-progress on the assembly line); if the right car was not found there, an order could be placed online to build it. It would then be delivered to the consumer via a Ford franchise dealer.

But manufacturer sites faced major challenges both to get customers to initiate purchases online and to create online build-to-order capability. While many consumers visited manufacturer sites to get the latest product information—for example, online traffic monitor Media Metrix reported that Ford.com had 954,000 unique users in November 1999, versus 573,000 for Autobytel.com[58]—few consumers used manufacturer sites to buy a car (see Table 9).

TABLE 9 Sources of Internet-generated Leads[59]

Source of lead	*Percentage of all online leads originating from this source*
Manufacturer Web site	4
Dealer Web site	2
OBS or other third-party site	94

[58] "The eAuto Report," Jordan Hymowitz and Justin Hughes, Robertson Stephens, 1/11/00, p. 15.
[59] "Internet Showrooms," *New York Times*, 3/28/99.

Moreover, industry observers agreed that if an online build-to-order system were to succeed, manufacturers would have to deliver a custom-ordered car within a reasonable time, probably less than a week. Even if the specific desired vehicle existed within the manufacturer-dealer inventory, car makers lacked the information systems to give them a global view of the entire pipeline, including their entire dealer networks—though they were trying to create such systems as part of their Internet initiatives. Further, manufacturers required weeks to deliver custom-ordered cars that did not exist in inventory (see Table 10).

The actual assembly of the vehicle took only a small part of the overall cycle time: many vehicles could be assembled in a single shift, and most were assembled in just two to three shifts. Total person-hours required to assemble a car ranged from 18 to 76, but most North American plants did the job in fewer than 30 person-hours.[60] Setup and special handling, plus transportation, accounted for most of the time required. Reducing the order-to-delivery cycle was a major objective for manufacturers: for example, GM's goal was 10 days. Cutting the order-to-delivery cycle would increase customer satisfaction—the customers would get the car they wanted rather than have to choose one from dealer inventory—and reduce inventory levels. One expert estimated that a 50% reduction in inventory could lower a car's price by 10%–15%.[61]

REGULATORY OBSTACLES TO MANUFACTURER-DIRECT SALES

Even if car makers had been intent on selling vehicles directly to consumers—bypassing both dealers and the OBSs—laws in most states prevented them from doing so. In nearly every state, "franchise" laws kept manufacturers from operating dealerships—either explicitly (as in about half the states) or through various requirements that produced the same result. Some states even outlawed car brokers: in Texas, for example, no party that did not have a dealer's license could take a cut of a transaction, even if the purchase was done through a licensed dealer. Hence, Autobytel.com was allowed to operate in Texas (because it charged dealers a fee that wasn't

TABLE 10 Order-to-Delivery Times for Selected Manufacturers[62]

Manufacturer	*Average number of days required to deliver custom-ordered vehicle*
Toyota	20–30
Chrysler	32
Ford	38
GM	54

[60] *The Harbour Report 1999: North America*, Harbour and Associates, Inc, 1999, p. 59.

[61] "Dell Points the Way," John Couretas, *Automotive News*, 5/24/99, p. 3.

[62] "Made to Measure," Jerry Edgerton, *Money*, 12/99, p. 287 (data for Ford, Chrysler, and GM); figure for Toyota is author's estimate.

tied to a sales transaction), but CarsDirect.com and CarOrder.com were not, because they acted as unlicensed intermediaries (that is, they bought cars from dealers and resold them to consumers).

GM and Ford, too, had run up against Texan franchise laws in 1999 when they tried to sell used vehicles directly to consumers in the Houston area online. In Ford's case, the company operated a Web site that listed used vehicles from the car maker's inventory of expired leases. However, a franchised Ford dealer, who received a commission on the transaction, handled every purchase. The site had been running for more than a year when Texas regulators shut it down in November 1999 because they claimed the unlicensed site was acting as a dealer. "If you put a car up on a site, and describe the car and put up a price," claimed a Texan official, "it doesn't make a difference who actually consummates the paperwork."[63] Ford sought an injunction in federal court to overturn the shutdown order, and a hearing was scheduled for January 2000.

GM's plight was similar to Ford's, with one key difference: GM had sought to get a license to launch an online store but Texan authorities rejected it. The auto maker wanted to use the Houston metro area to pilot-test a Web site, called GM DriverSite, to sell pre-owned GM vehicles directly to consumers. Only after GM transferred ownership of the online store to a licensed GM dealer in September could the site launch. Both Ford and GM were victims of a law passed in early 1999 that extended the state's prohibition against manufacturers "acting in the capacity of a dealer" to sell used as well as new cars.

At the state and local level, dealers generally held strong influence over lawmakers. Car dealerships were an important economic segment in many locales. They generated 20% of state sales tax revenues and 3% of all state revenues—and dealerships were also a significant source of jobs.[64] Moreover, both individually and through their regional associations, dealers supported politicians who promoted legislation favorable to their interests (e.g., laws that blocked manufacturers from moving into auto retailing). At least one Internet firm, CarOrder.com, was lobbying to change state regulations to permit Internet companies to act as dealers. To date, however, dealers have the advantage in regulatory influence. Indeed, several states—including Nevada, North Carolina, Virginia, and Georgia—had further restricted manufacturers from entering the dealership business.

THE FUTURE OF THE DEALERSHIP CHANNEL

While manufacturers recognized the liabilities of the dealership channel, they also realized its necessity. Brian Kelley, head of Ford's e-commerce unit, suggested a thought experiment:

> *If Ford's 6,000 dealers were suddenly wiped out tomorrow, what would we do? Well, we'd have lots of unhappy customers. We'd have to go out and build service*

[63] "Ford Asks Court to Upend Texas Ruling Banning It from Used-Car Sales on Web," Sholnn Freeman, *Wall Street Journal*, 12/7/99, p. B10.
[64] "Car Chase," Robert McGarvey, *Upside*, 12/99, pp. 156–164.

> *centers to provide maintenance service and parts. We'd also have to put up showrooms around the country. It begins to look a bit familiar. How many would we have? It's hard to say exactly, but we'd probably have something like half the number of showrooms and twice the number of service centers. Consumers are willing to drive farther to buy a car, since it's an infrequent purchase, but they want the convenience of a near-by service center.*[65]

Other manufacturers shared Kelley's view that dealers were not going away. Except for Korean auto maker Daewoo, all manufacturers emphasized that they did not plan to bypass their dealers by selling direct to consumers over the Internet. But most auto executives agreed that the way dealers operated was going to change dramatically. At e-GM, General Motors' e-commerce group formed in August 1999, an "e-dealer council" was forging a new model of the dealership role. Rick Lee, general manager of e-GM, North America, noted that under this new model, the manufacturer and dealer would share much more of the customer relationship than they previously had. Moreover, he noted, the dealer's economic model would be more dependent on "subscription revenues" attached to services delivered through the customer's ownership of the vehicle. "This represents enormous change from where we are now," he observed. "We better be creative in how we change that mindset."[66]

[65] Interview with Brian Kelley, January 2000.
[66] Interview with Rick Lee, January 2000.

E-COMMERCE BUILDING BLOCKS

We assume that every great idea has six to ten venture players or management teams that are trying to build it. Because of this, companies needed to get to market quickly, with lots of exposure, to succeed today. There is no room for mistakes.
—Steve Ledger, eCompanies[1]

At the end of the 1990s, approximately 1,000 start-up companies in global Internet and electronic commerce (e-commerce) markets received funding each fiscal quarter.[2] Most of these companies were created with little more than a business concept and founding team. Turning ideas into successful companies required many resources: funding, business strategy development, human resources, technology, real estate, finance and accounting, as well as the basics—office supplies and space. Many e-commerce entrepreneurs relied on venture capital, angel financing, or similar external funds to gain access to these resources and develop at Internet speed, rather than internal "bootstrapping." This case provides an overview of major service providers to e-commerce companies, the relationships and partnerships they offered, and the costs and benefits of accessing these services in early 2000.

Research Associates Christopher Thomas and Elizabeth Urban, both MBA 2000, prepared this case under the supervision of Professor Garth Saloner as the basis for class discussion rather than to illustrate either effective or ineffective handling of an administrative situation. Margot Sutherland, Executive Director, Center for Electronic Business and Commerce, Stanford Graduate School of Business managed the development of this case.

[1] Steve Ledger, eCompanies, as quoted in "Venture Funding is Reinvented," *Red Herring*, December 1999, p. 188.
[2] Peter D. Henig, "And Now EcoNets," *Red Herring*, February 2000, p. 98.

BUILDING BLOCKS

Providers of building blocks to e-commerce companies fell into five major types: Internet holding companies,* venture capitalists (VCs), strategy consultants, Web professional services firms, and Internet data services. Figure 1 lists the resources and services these firms offered.

In the late 1990s, the market for these services was changing rapidly, and the boundaries between service providers were increasingly blurred. Traditional providers of financial resources, such as venture capitalists, had been forced to provide a far broader set of offerings to compete in a world where "cash is a commodity."[3] Draper Fisher Jurvetson and General Atlantic Partners, both premier venture capitalists, had financed incubators.[4] iXL and Scient, Web professional services firms, were also managing venture funds. Chemdex, a CMGI venture company, had renamed itself Ventro and was attempting to leverage its expertise by developing e-commerce platforms for other companies.[5] Web hosting companies, such as Exodus and Intel, were providing "second generation" hosting services, such as Web site development (usually in collaboration with third parties).[6] The shifts in the marketplace made it difficult for entrepreneurs to select service providers that offered the skills and resources their firms needed, at the right price.

A shortage of resources to select from exacerbated the difficulty of selecting services. The explosive growth in e-commerce had filled to capacity the dockets of Web development firms: 45% of e-commerce companies had outsourced a significant portion of Web site design to professional design firms or interactive agencies.[7] An estimated 96% of all Web operations were also understaffed.[8] The industry's performance problems were well known. Pat Ortman, a partner at Empty Street Productions, benefited from companies' dissatisfaction: "We're getting a lot of calls from clients who are desperately unhappy with the service they get from the mega-Web companies like iXL and USWeb."

Start-ups were under intense pressure to overcome these problems and move from concept to reality quickly. Managerial and investor greed, fueled by the longest bull

* The term "Internet holding company" describes an entity that provided capital, contacts, and services to a portfolio of Internet companies in exchange for a significant portion of their equity. Other terms for these types of organizations included "EcoNets," "economic networks, keiretsu, ekeiretsu, and zaibatsu."

[3] Brad Garlinghouse, CMGI @Ventures general partner, as quoted in Bruce D. Temkin with Jeremy Sharrard, "The Rise of B2B eKeiretsus," *The Forrester Brief*, December 30, 1999.

[4] Bradley Spirrison, "Draper Fisher Funds Cambridge Incubator," *Venture Capital Journal*, February 1, 2000. George Moriarty, "E-finance World Gets Its First VC Accelerator Firm," *Investment Dealers Digest*, February 14, 2000.

[5] http://www.ventro.com

[6] Kwon, McCarron, Thomas, Vidalakis, and Yoon, "Intel Online Services," November 1999.

[7] Abhi Chaki, "Co-Managed Hosting," Jupiter Communications, March 1998, p. 12. Cormac Foster, "Web Site Scaling: Preparing for the Traffic Onslaught." Jupiter Communications, May 1999, p. 3. Ken Allard, "Web Site Infrastructure: Key Challenges in Planning, Investing, and Implementation," Jupiter Communications, July 1998, p. 1.

[8] Cormac Foster, "Web Site Scaling: Preparing for the Traffic Onslaught," Jupiter Communications, May 1999, p. 2.

FIGURE 1 Service Providers to E-Commerce Companies

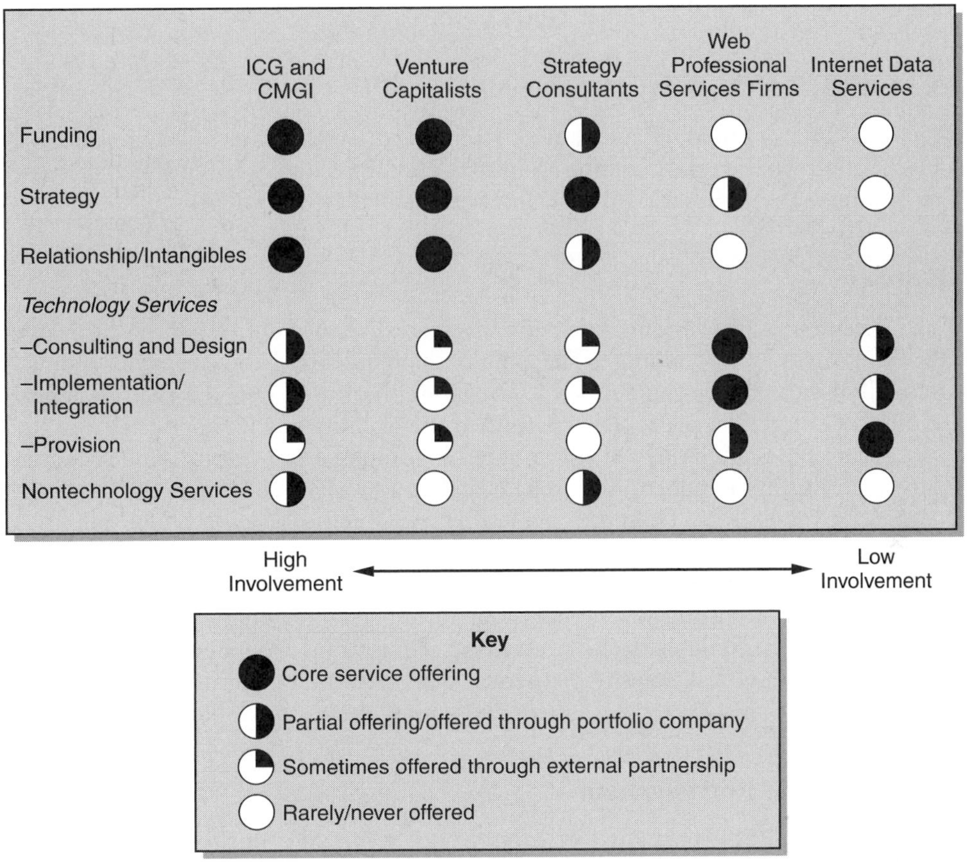

	ICG and CMGI	Venture Capitalists	Strategy Consultants	Web Professional Services Firms	Internet Data Services
Funding	●	●	◑	○	○
Strategy	●	●	●	◑	○
Relationship/Intangibles	●	●	◑	○	○
Technology Services					
–Consulting and Design	◑	◔	◔	●	◑
–Implementation/ Integration	◑	◔	◔	●	◑
–Provision	◔	◔	○	◑	●
Nontechnology Services	◑	○	◑	○	○

High Involvement ←→ Low Involvement

Key

● Core service offering

◑ Partial offering/offered through portfolio company

◔ Sometimes offered through external partnership

○ Rarely/never offered

market in history, spurred the quest for speed.[9] Financial markets, however, were volatile, and no one knew how long the bull market would last. Still, the initial public offering (IPO) market was buoyant and supported the capitalization of companies that were younger, smaller, and, surprisingly, less profitable than ever (Exhibit 1). Entrepreneurs and investors realized that a shorter time to IPO meant a shorter time to the end of the post-IPO "lock-up period" in which management and other large shareholders had to hold their shares: management and investors wanted to get money sooner rather than later.

In the rush to build new ventures, entrepreneurs wanted solutions that would answer their immediate needs without constraining the future development of their companies. Many choices would impact the direction, culture, and competencies of their firms over the long haul. We discuss next the Internet holding companies, venture capitalists (VCs), strategy consultants, Web professional services firms, and Internet data

[9] E. S. Browning, "Nasdaq Falls 7.06%, into 'Bear' Territory," *Wall Street Journal*, April 13, 2000, p. C1.

services that e-commerce entrepreneurs needed to evaluate to provide services to move their companies forward.

INTERNET HOLDING COMPANIES

The term "Internet holding company" encompassed a wide range of business models. This section reviews traits common to Internet holding companies and then discusses two prominent examples: CMGI and Internet Capital Group (ICG).

Overview

The ultimate goal of a holding company was to realize the value from the companies in which it invested by building or developing them quickly, they were either acquired or could raise capital through an IPO. The strength of the capital markets in general and the IPO market in particular determined the viability of the model.

Internet holding companies not only took advantage of buoyant capital markets to unleash value in their portfolio companies; they also harnessed the market's strength to go public themselves. These companies often claimed that going public amounted to "the democratization of venture capital" because it opened access to such investments to everyone, rather than just the super-wealthy.[10] However, going public also gave the holding company several potential advantages. The market provided a currency that the firm could use to make strategic acquisitions, attract talent, and encourage complementary businesses to cooperate. The investment community also helped fuel the "hype" that attracted executives and companies to the holding company.[†]

Benefits to the Entrepreneur

Holding companies purportedly sped growth and, eventually, time to exit for new ventures by providing them with immediate access to customers, technology, and partnerships. For instance, at the time of its IPO, Engage, a CMGI company that profiled Internet users' surfing and purchasing behavior, had CMGI-affiliate Lycos as a primary contributor of profile data. Holding companies also facilitated information exchange among their portfolio companies. This exchange either increased the rapidity with which a company scaled the learning curve or prevented a company from making costly or time-consuming mistakes.

Holding companies also reduced the search time for services. Their head office or their portfolio companies/affiliates provided services such as real estate, human resources/recruiting, Web hosting/network infrastructure, finance and accounting, legal, business strategy and development, and sales and marketing/public relations. For exam-

[10] Jim Evans, "Incubator, Hatch Thyself," *The Standard*, February 14, 2000.

[†] The ability of a holding company to go public was regulated by law. According to the Investment Company Act of 1940, any firm whose portfolio contained more than 40% of its assets in nonownership positions had to be classified as a mutual fund. As such, the company must operate under stricter reporting guidelines and regulations than if it were not so classified. CMGI and ICG employed innovative methods in structuring their businesses in recognition of these legal constraints.

ple, within two weeks of CMGI's purchase of a 50% stake in Raging Bull, an online investor chat room, Raging Bull had moved its headquarters to CMGI headquarters, contracted for technical support with NaviSite, a CMGI company, and begun to collect revenue by selling ad space on its site through Adsmart, another CMGI company.

A key structural advantage of holding companies was membership in a network. Companies could use the combined size/power of the network during negotiations with suppliers and partners. For instance, CMGI often negotiated group deals with vendors and then offered its portfolio companies the option of taking part. The aggregate clout of the holding company was also often a plus when the portfolio companies needed to arrange for prominent space at trade shows such as Internet World. Another advantage was increased ammunition with which to fight or negotiate with competitors. For instance, when CMGI bought AltaVista in the summer of 1999, it bought a company that was the biggest customer of DoubleClick, a direct competitor to several CMGI portfolio companies. CMGI publicized its willingness to use its new position to its portfolio companies: "CMGI is one of DoubleClick's biggest customers and is now threatening to pull the plug on the business."[11]

Costs to the Entrepreneur

Perhaps the most important cost to the entrepreneur of involvement with a holding company was the equity, from 20% to a controlling stake that holding companies demanded. But dilution was not the sole concern. Entrepreneurs questioned whether they would be able to retain control over their businesses. Many entrepreneurs became entrepreneurs in the first place precisely because they wanted to control their own business. The control issue had several dimensions. One was the fear that holding companies, in their rush to take a company public, would force-fit the company into a "vanilla" business model. Another controversial area was the perceived pressure to use or partner with other portfolio companies; holding companies often supplied customers, partners, technology platforms, and even top executives. Jerry Colonna, former partner in CMGI's first Internet venture fund, commented: "There's inherent conflict built into the structure of CMGI"[12] Finally, the question of control became more thorny when holding companies began to retain substantial ownership stakes in their portfolio companies, even after they had gone public.[‡]

Even if there were no "adult supervision," some entrepreneurs recoiled at being part of a conglomerate in a business environment that revered the small and nimble competitor. There were personal reputations to consider. Keith Benjamin of Highland Capital Partners quipped, "It's kind of like a Groucho Marx thing, any entrepreneur that needs to be incubated is not an entrepreneur I'd like to back."[13]

[11] Cintra Scott, "CMGI, DoubleClick Go Chest to Chest," *SmartMoney.com*, October 1, 1999.

[12] Paul C. Judge, "One Big Happy Family—But For How Long?" *Business Week*, October 25, 1999, p. 148.

[‡] The Investment Company Act of 1940, which deemed investments of more than 50% to be "controlling" and therefore helped prevent a company from being classified as a mutual fund, motivated this tendency.

[13] Peter D. Henig, "And Now EcoNets," *Red Herring*, February 2000, p. 102.

Entrepreneurs and analysts had raised other concerns about holding companies: that they lacked expertise in the areas in which they were investing and that their ever expanding, ever more complex networks raised the potential for conflict of interest. ICG's acquisition of RightWorks, a business-to-business (B2B) software player that competed with Tradeum, a B2B software company with similar focus that one of ICG's portfolio companies had just purchased, substantiated the latter concern. Finally, some analysts were concerned that publicly traded Internet holding companies could be outright frauds. Scott Lundstrom of AMR Research observed:

> *If it doesn't pan out that these companies are worth what they're valued at, people may look at [CMGI's David Wetherell] as a con artist. He'd be in good company, but in ten years we could be writing books about massive group delusion. And he'd be a chapter in that book.*[14]

Internet Holding Companies and Internet Incubators

There were crucial distinctions between Internet holding companies and Internet incubators (also called venture catalysts, venture construction companies, and accelerators). Holding companies invested in companies ranging from early-stage to those already public, while incubators generally invested only in early-stage companies. Because companies were in an earlier stage when they chose an incubator partner, the choice of that partner was especially important. Indeed, the incubator often helped create the business idea and execution plan.

Incubators generally demanded equity stakes of approximately 50%, while holding companies' stakes ranged from smaller, minority blocks to outright acquisition. Incubators usually colocated all the companies in which they invested in one facility. While this proximity increased the interactions among these portfolio companies and with the incubator itself, it could diminish originality in the start-up firms' business concepts and models: "It's such a cookie cutter approach, and all ideas aren't created equal."[15] In contrast, holding companies generally allowed their acquisitions to stay where they were or locate in a business-appropriate site. Holding companies typically only moved portfolio companies into headquarters if there were an acute real estate need and/or the company was majority owned. Finally, although a few incubators, such as Idealab and Divine Interventures, had filed to go public in the spring of 2000, this was the exception rather than the rule; the two most prominent holding companies, CMGI and ICG, were public companies. (Exhibit 2 lists several Internet incubators.)

The two most prominent examples of Internet holding companies were CMGI and ICG (Exhibits 3 and 4 describe these two companies). These firms generated investor and media attention because of their stock market success and the "visionary" quality

[14] Aaron Zitner, "Riding the Creature: CMGI's Wetherell Saw Net's Wild Potential and Tamed It," *Boston Globe*, February 7, 2000, p. D1.

[15] Jim Evans, "Incubator, Hatch Thyself," *The Standard*, February 14, 2000.

of their leaders, and attracted many "me-too" followers. Vinod Khosla, of Kleiner Perkins Caulfield & Byers (KP), said,

> *Everybody is looking at CMGI and ICG and saying, "I can do that too." But they [the followers] don't have the expertise . . . that's helpful to the entrepreneurs. It's a money grab, which is distasteful and a disservice. There's a real mercenary attitude out there right now.*[16]

CMGI

> *[CMGI] is in the business of creating and managing the largest, most diverse network of Internet companies in the world. . . . CMGI's business model . . . consists of a network of diverse yet interconnected companies all holding leadership positions, or the promise of leadership, in Internet-related businesses.*[17] —*CMGI Web site*

> *The new economy demands a flexible aggressive model based on investment, development, and M&A. That is what we have.*[18] —*David Wetherell, CEO of CMGI, during a chat with investors on Raging Bull*

CMGI was structured as two distinct business units. One was CMGI's operating group, which consisted of CMGI's majority- or wholly-owned companies. This group generally bought second-tier Internet properties and attempted to quickly turn them around, spinning them out to the public markets at substantially higher multiples than their purchase price. Typically, CMGI took controlling stakes in or acquired outright companies that fit its major areas of strategic thrust (e.g., CMGI's push into Internet advertising led it to acquire AdForce and Flycast Communications in the fall of 1999). The second business unit was @Ventures, CMGI's venture capital arm, founded in 1995, which generally took minority stakes in companies.[§] @Ventures generally functioned like any other venture capital firm. When this case was written, CMGI directly operated 17 Internet companies and, since 1995, had made more than 50 additional investments in Internet companies through @Ventures. CMGI's run rate was approximately one acquisition and three @Ventures investments per month.[**]

CMGI began as a direct marketing company based in Andover, Massachusetts. Originally called the College Marketing Group, it was founded in 1968 to sell mailing lists of college professors to textbook publishers. In 1986, David Wetherell was hired to run CMG, but almost bankrupted it when he acquired a troubled direct marketing

[16] *ibid.*

[17] http://www.cmgi.com

[18] John Hechinger, "Shareholder Scoreboard, Best 5-Year Performer: CMGI," *Wall Street Journal*, February 24, 2000, p. R4.

[§] There were exceptions. For instance, @Ventures was the investment vehicle through which CMGI originally took its 80% stake in Lycos.

[**] This dual business unit structure could, in a market downturn, allow the operating arm of CMGI to acquire underperforming @Ventures investments.

company. Fortunately, as CMG's founder, Glenn Matthews, described, "Dave managed to charm the bank," shielding CMG from bankruptcy.[19] Wetherell changed the name of the company to CMG Information Services, led the company to IPO in 1994, and invested $2 million in BookLink Technologies, an early browsing technology company. Later in 1994, AOL acquired BookLink from CMG Information Services in a stock transaction eventually worth more than $70 million. CMG Information Services officially became CMGI in 1998. As of spring 2000, Wetherell remained CMGI's CEO.

While much was written about Wetherell's vision, he was, at core, a deal maker; Wetherell spent up to two-thirds of his time at CMGI deal making. As he described, "I'm more of a facilitator and catalyst. I'm better at getting things started than completing them. I think of good ideas, recognize good ideas, but there are few things on the technical side that I'm capable of doing."[20]

CMGI's investments focused on building a network of Internet companies with "critical mass." Its portfolio companies fell into four categories: advertising/marketing, content and community, e-commerce, and enabling technologies (Exhibit 5). The categories evolved to adapt to market dynamics. On the CMGI Web site, "The CMGI Network" page emphasized the strength of the firm's business model as well as the types and even identities of its portfolio companies. CMGI claimed that its operating companies formed a "virtuous circle," with each company providing products and services for several other CMGI companies, both in the operating and @Ventures groups.

CMGI had been aggressive about acquiring companies that could benefit its existing portfolio companies. In 1999 alone, CMGI made 22 acquisitions using its then highly valued stock; many of these businesses complemented one or more of CMGI's existing companies. Said Wetherell, "We're looking for synergies. If a company needs a capability and we don't have it at CMGI, we'll go out and buy it."[21] While deals between CMGI companies were negotiated at arm's length (for example, when Flycast and Adsmart were folded into Engage, each retained its own banker), CMGI provided its operating company executives with CMGI shares as an incentive to cooperate with each other. It also ran regularly scheduled "summits" that brought together CEOs or business development/technology/marketing people across the various CMGI companies. CMGI avoided investing in companies that competed directly with one another.[22]

The CMGI corporate office provided centralized services, such as human resources, accounting, and legal, for its portfolio companies. It also offered strategic guidance. However, CMGI's central office staff was small; as of spring 2000, CMGI still listed only 10 individuals as part of "CMGI Corporate."

For operating group companies, executives within CMGI corporate headquarters were compensated via base salary plus stock options. However, for @Ventures investments, these same executives received 20.0% to 22.5% of the profits (most senior CMGI executives, including Wetherell, held positions with both business units). CMGI exec-

[19] Paul C. Judge, "One Big Happy Family—But For How Long?" *Business Week*, October 25, 1999, p. 148.
[20] Victoria Griffith and Andrew Hill, "CMGI's Venture Catalyst in Search of Synergy," *The Financial Times*, April 18, 2000.
[21] *ibid.*
[22] *ibid.*

utives therefore benefited more handsomely from deals in CMGI's venture capital arm than from operating company investments. As Gregory Avis, a venture capitalist and former CMGI director commented, "If you see an opportunity, is it an @Ventures deal or a CMGI deal?"[23] For instance, in August 1999, CMGI owned an 18% stake in Lycos through @Ventures, and CMGI's operating group was contemplating an outright bid for the company (the deal fell through). If the deal had gone through, the @Ventures partners (the sellers) would have wanted the highest price for Lycos while CMGI (the buyer) would have wanted the lowest.

Internet Capital Group

> *Internet Capital Group is an Internet holding company actively engaged in business-to-business e-commerce through a network of partner companies. It provides operational assistance, capital support, expertise, and a strategic network of business relationships intended to maximize the long-term market potential of its more than 30 business-to-business e-commerce partner companies.* —*ICG Web site*

> *Its goal is nothing short of world domination: to own a big piece of every leading online exchange that its founders predict will emerge in each of the 50 most lucrative sectors of the B2B economy, ranging from health care to cattle ranching.*[24]
> —*The Economist*

Internet Capital Group (ICG) aimed to become "a GE built for the twenty-first century" and hoped to apply similar learning and management techniques across a wide range of vertical industries.[25] ICG invested predominantly in a specific type of B2B company (market makers), betting that as much as 70% of what made an exchange successful was common to all exchanges.[26] ICG approached its investments from the top down, first identifying 50 priority markets, and then attempting to own at least one-third of the "number one player" in each of those markets.[27] ICG thus prioritized by first picking the right industry, and then choosing a promising company within it, hoping eventually to spin that company out in the public markets for much more than the purchase price. "We add 80% of our value after we invest in a company,"[28] claimed Todd Hewlins, director of strategy.

Walter W. Buckley III and Kenneth A. Fox founded ICG in 1996 as an "operating holding" company for Internet B2B ventures. They believed that "the Internet will be pervasive and create a demand for efficiency that will have a dramatic impact on

[23] "At a Web Highflier, an Unusual Pay Bonanza," *Wall Street Journal*, August 8, 1999, p. B1.

[24] "The A to Z of B2B," *The Economist*, April 1, 2000, p. 61.

[25] Bruce D. Temkin with Jeremy Sharrard, "The Rise of B2B eKeiretsus," *The Forrester Brief*, December 30, 1999.

[26] "The A to Z of B2B," *The Economist*, April 1, 2000, p. 61.

[27] Michael Rubinkam, "Internet Capital Group Flush with Cash After Second Offering," *Associated Press*, December 17, 1999.

[28] "The A to Z of B2B," *The Economist*, April 1, 2000, p. 61.

the way we do business,"[29] and that "B2B represents the greatest market opportunity on the Internet."[30] The founders had worked together at Safeguard Scientifics, a Philadelphia-based technology-investing firm, before starting ICG. One of ICG's first liquidity events came in April 1998, when it sold Matchlogic to Excite for stock worth $89 million. In the spring of 2000, Managing Director Fox was 29 years old and CEO Buckley was 39.

ICG was structured as a single entity; it did not have separate business units for operating companies versus passive investments. In late 1999, ICG also created an internal group called eColony to create new companies from scratch.

Of ICG's 65 partner firms, 20 were focused on Internet infrastructure, and the rest were market makers (Exhibit 6).[31] Market makers brought buyers and sellers together to transact online, with "vertical" market makers focused on a single industry (e.g., the automotive supply chain) and "horizontal" market makers focused on selling goods across many vertical industry groups (e.g., selling office supplies to auto manufacturers, aircraft manufacturers, etc.). ICG's infrastructure companies fell into three categories: strategic consulting/systems integrators, software providers, and outsourced service providers. ICG planned to make about three-quarters of its investments in B2B market makers.[32] Fox commented: "Our focus and our sweet spot are market makers."[33]

ICG's approach to choosing the markets—and, therefore, the market makers—in which it invested was disciplined. It targeted industries according to their level of inefficiency, online and offline competition, profit potential, and leverageable information sources (product catalogs, trade journals, etc.). Target company identification criteria included potential for industry leadership, management quality, level of ICG ownership, and "network synergy"[34] (Exhibit 7). For each of its companies, ICG recruited management teams with experience in the relevant vertical industry. To overcome the "chicken and egg" dilemma of attracting both buyers and suppliers to new marketplaces, ICG sometimes partnered with large incumbents (e.g., DuPont for its B2B chemical exchange).

ICG provided extensive resources to its partners via its head office, strategic partners, and advisory board. A team of 29 experts in areas ranging from deal making to human resources comprised ICG's head office. ICG's separate recruiting and human resources staff, run by Rick Devine, formerly of Heidrick & Struggles, was an in-house 30-person executive search unit that partner companies could use to fill out their senior management teams. ICG also emphasized its ability to leverage the expertise of its strategic partner companies on behalf of its investments.[††] For instance, for expert advice, it could call on Comcast for e-commerce and distribution, Compaq for distribution,

[29] http://www.internetcapital.com/history.htm

[30] *ibid.*

[31] Dinah Wisenberg Brin, "Internet Capital's Offering Dubbed 'Largest Internet Offering,'" *Dow Jones Business News*, December 16, 1999.

[32] Eric Upin and Carey Jennings, "Internet Capital Group," Robertson Stevens, January 11, 2000.

[33] Dinah Wisenberg Brin, "Internet Capital's Offering Dubbed 'Largest Internet Offering,'" *Dow Jones Business News*, December 16, 1999.

[34] http://www.internetcapital.com/aboutourpartners.htm

[††] As of late 1999, Comcast had 9.9% ICG ownership, Compaq 4.0%, GE Capital 2.9%, and Safeguard Scientifics 14.4%.

and GE Capital for supply chain. ICG also had a deep and diverse management team and advisory board. Management ranks included senior hires from Microsoft, McKinsey & Co., Amazon, Baan, and Japan's Softbank. Gary Wendt, former head of GE Capital, sat on ICG's advisory board, along with present and former executives from Cisco, Merrill Lynch, Coca-Cola, Exodus Communications, MasterCard, and IBM.[35]

ICG's Web site promoted the firm's "Strategic Network" in describing the formal and informal mechanisms through which it attempted to promote innovation and collaboration among its partner companies (Exhibit 8). In addition to sponsoring an annual ICG conference for its companies, ICG periodically held smaller seminars focused on specific business issues. The company managed and channeled the flow of ideas: "The collaboration of ICG's Partner Companies is the result of the company's role as the hub of the network. . . . ICG encourages and regulates the information flow among Partner Companies."[36]

Criticisms of the ICG model centered on the risk associated with its B2B focus. This was a competitive market with over 1,700 exchanges; industry leaders like the Big Three auto companies were leading the charge.[37] These giants threatened independent firms like ICG. For example, in the plastic resin market, the General Electric-sponsored B2B marketplace GEPolymerland.com had processed over $100 million in transactions in 1999, while ICG-incubated PlasticsNet.com had sold only $445,000 in the first nine months of that year.[38]

VENTURE CAPITALISTS

Venture capital (VC), a form of private equity investing,[‡‡] grew from a small investment pool in the 1960s and early 1970s to a mainstream asset class that was a viable and significant part of institutional and corporate investment portfolios. Venture capital firms were pools of capital, typically organized as limited partnerships that invested in companies that represented the opportunity for a risky yet high rate of return. Over 50% of investments in venture capital/private equity came from institutional public and private pension funds; the balance came from endowments, foundations, insurance companies, banks, and individuals.[39]

In the early days, individuals were the archetypal venture investors. While individual investment did not disappear, the modern firm emerged as the dominant venture investment vehicle. However, during the late 1990s, individuals again became a

[35] "The A to Z of B2B," *The Economist*, April 1, 2000, p. 61.

[36] http://www.internetcapital.com/strategicnetwork.htm

[37] Robert L. Simison, Fara Warner, and Gregory L. White, "Big Three Car Makers Plan Net Exchange," *Wall Street Journal*, February 28, 2000, p. A3.

[38] Julia Angwin, "Online Exchanges Also Suffer from a Glut of Players," *Wall Street Journal*, April 7, 2000, p. B1.

‡‡ The term "private equity investors," as opposed to public market investors, generally described focused investment firms that took substantial or controlling stakes in private companies and assets. The key types of private equity investors were venture capital, leveraged buyout, real estate, mezzanine, private debt, and some hedge funds.

[39] NVCA Web site, http://www.nvca.org/, "What Is Venture Capital?"

potent part of the early-stage start-up venture life cycle. "Angel investors" would often mentor a company and provide needed capital and expertise.

Not all venture capitalists invested solely in start-ups. A venture capitalist may have invested before there was a real product or company (so-called seed investing), or may have provided capital to start up a company in its first or second stages of development (known as early-stage investing). The venture capitalist could have provided needed financing to help a company grow beyond critical mass to become more successful (expansion stage financing) or focused on "later stage investing" by providing financing to help a company bridge to a stock offering or a merger with another company. Venture capitalists generally took significant or controlling stakes in their portfolio firms and had significant ownership rights.

A key benefit of having a top-tier venture capitalist invest in a new company was the relationships and credibility that it could bring. Experienced and successful venture capitalists, such as Benchmark Capital, Sequoia Capital, and General Atlantic Partners, could marshal large networks in the technology and financial industries in the start-up's cause. "What's really important is not the money, but what's attached to it, like brainpower and contacts," said Soon-Chart Yu, a successful entrepreneur and founder of Gazoontite.[40]

High financial returns for venture capital firms during the second half of the 1990s (Exhibit 9) led to a stampede of investments into both established venture capital firms and a plethora of new competitors. Exhibit 10 demonstrates the tremendous amount of funds venture capitalists raised in the late 1990s, much of which was invested in seed and early-stage start-up companies (Exhibit 11). By 2000, some of the largest venture capital investors were not traditional VCs, but established technology companies such as Intel, Cisco Systems, Oracle, and Andersen Consulting; corporations put $7.8 billion into start-up companies in 1999, a 35-fold increase over 1995.[41] In fact, 20% of the Fortune 1000 had some form of corporate venture arm in early 2000 (as opposed to 1% just two years earlier).[42] Corporate investors brought competitive assets that traditional VCs may have lacked: operating insights into technology and markets, as well as proprietary access to channels, customers, and intellectual property for the start-up company. Many large technology companies viewed venture capital investments as an alternate form of R&D; they hoped to acquire the best technologies they funded. Finally, traditional buyout funds, such as KKR, Texas Pacific Group, and The Blackstone Group, had expanded their former investment focus, purchasing established businesses, to include more venture activities. Silver Lake Partners and Francisco Partners had raised multibillion dollar funds to concentrate solely on technology transactions.

Venture capitalists were being forced to adapt to the new scale and speed of their industry. The enormous increase in venture capital fund sizes meant that firms were no longer interested in providing the small tranches of investment capital that a start-up needed; instead they wanted to put capital to work in $20–$50 million pieces.[43] Most of these venture capital firms were performing many more transactions without them-

[40] Tom Stein, "Who Wants to Be a Venture Capitalist," *Red Herring*, May 2000, p. 128.

[41] Jonathan Rabinovitz, "Venture Capital, Inc.," *Industry Standard*, April 17, 2000.

[42] Tom Stein, "Who Wants to Be a Venture Capitalist," *Red Herring*, May 2000, p. 126.

[43] Peter Rojas, "Venture Funding Is Reinvented," *Red Herring*, May 1999, p. 188.

selves adding significant human resources. Just as venture capitalists were underscoring the need to differentiate themselves via improved services and a more "personal touch" with regard to their portfolio companies, the partners at such firms were sitting on more boards and evaluating more transactions than ever before. Pitch Johnson, one of the first venture capitalists and an investor in notable successes Amgen and Octel, stated:

> *The amount of help you get from your VC investor is not the same as it used to be . . . guys run too many board meetings; they haven't got time, and they're under terrible pressure to take their portfolio companies public.*[44]

Prior to the long bull market in the 1990s, venture capital funds raised in "good" years had fared worse than those raised in bear markets or less favorable investing environments: "History tells you that the funds raised now will underperform."[45] The consensus was that many venture capitalists were trend followers, which could make raising funds easy if the entrepreneur's start-up were in a "hot" sector, but difficult if it were not. In the words of Vinod Khosla, a legendary venture capitalist at KP, "Does the VC industry fall prey to the herd instinct? Yes, absolutely."[46]

TRADITIONAL STRATEGY CONSULTANTS

Top-tier strategy consulting firms had traditionally been magnets for young, ambitious professionals. However, the incredible success of young Internet entrepreneurs had reduced the relative attractiveness of the industry. At some leading business schools, the number of new graduates entering consulting firms had dropped by 25% in the second half of the 1990s and "all the firms [were] affected, especially premium firms like McKinsey, Bain, and BCG."[47]

Other trends threatened the way these successful firms had traditionally done business. Pure-play Web consultants had begun to invade their "turf"—the provision of long-term, relationship-based strategic advice—through the creation of strategy arms to complement their technical and design expertise (and these competitors often had high public market valuations that attracted the strategy consultants' personnel). Many of the consulting firms' traditional clients were also focusing on incorporating the Internet and a Web presence into their operations. The major strategy firms responded by creating e-commerce practices and enabling young associates and partners to share in equity market upside by investing firm capital in start-up companies, allowing their professionals to take temporary executive management positions in start-up companies, taking equity rather than fees for services, and even by creating incubators that

[44] Anthony and Michael Perkins, *The Internet Bubble*, (New York: Harper Business) 2000, p. 54.

[45] Brad Koenig, head of the technology banking practice at Goldman Sachs, as quoted in Anthony and Michael Perkins' *The Internet Bubble*, (New York: Harper Business) 2000, p. 64.

[46] Speech at Stanford University, April 12, 2000.

[47] Konstantin Richter and Stephanie Grumer, "Turnaround Artist: European Consultants Lose MBAs at an Alarming Rate," *Wall Street Journal Europe*, November 12, 1999, p. 1.

turned business concepts into established companies. In the spring of 2000, whether these efforts would increase staff retention was unclear.

Strategy consultants offered start-up companies a straightforward value proposition. They provided the most focus, experience, and credibility in building sustainable and effective business strategies; they had an extensive external network and deep industry expertise from their client relationships; and they were flexible in taking cash or equity for their services.

- ***Bain & Co.*** Bain moved into the start-up market earlier than others, having set up a venture capital group in 1995 that had earned on average 50% annual returns since its inception.[48] Bain's technology and e-commerce practices provided about 35% of total firm revenues in 1999.[49] In late 1999, the company established bainlab, an Internet incubator that offered strategy consulting as well as business services, information technology (IT) consulting, public relations, marketing, Web design (all through partnerships), and up to $10 million in seed funding for minority equity stakes in start-up clients.[50] Bain also announced in April 2000 that in partnership with investment firms KP and Texas Pacific Group, it was forming eVolution Global Partners, a London-based "accelerator" to help non-U.S. firms move to the Internet.[51]

- ***Boston Consulting Group (BCG).*** BCG made early, limited forays into creating and developing e-commerce businesses, such as when it took an equity stake in and aided Whirlpool and Hearst to create brandwise.com, a consumer-based home appliances Web site. BCG was also a long-time key contributor to the premier consumer e-commerce research and industry group, Shop.org. In November 1999, BCG formed Web Labs, a major initiative in e-commerce, to research, develop, and prototype innovative interactive solutions and Web sites, and in close collaboration with BCG strategy and e-commerce consulting teams, conceptualize, define, and test e-commerce ideas. BCG had also funded or announced plans to fund Internet incubators in Silicon Valley, India, and China.[52]

- ***McKinsey & Co.*** In mid-1998, McKinsey began to take equity stakes in emerging companies and owned between 5% and 20% stakes in more than 100 technology start-ups when this case was written.[53] Its e-commerce practice was thriving, with over 300

[48] David Leonhart, "Consultants Are Putting a New Price on Advice," *New York Times*, January 18, 2000, p. 2.
[49] Beth Healy, "Bain Promotes Donahoe," *Boston Globe*, February 22, 2000, p. D6.
[50] Konstantin Richter and Stephanie Grumer, "Turnaround Artist: European Consultants Lose MBAs at an Alarming Rate," *Wall Street Journal Europe*, November 12, 1999, p. 1.
[51] Beth Healy, "Bain Joins Kleiner Perkins in Overseas E-commerce Venture," *Boston Globe*, April 7, 2000, p. C3.
[52] "New WebLab to Provide Rapid Prototyping of E-Commerce Concepts," BCG Press Release, November 4, 1999. "BCG to Launch e-commerce Incubator in China," Reuters English News Service, March 21, 2000. Bradley Spirrison, "Draper Fisher Funds Cambridge Incubator," *Venture Capital Journal*, Februrary 1, 2000.
[53] Mark Walsh, "McKinsey Ups Ante: Consulting Firm to Offer Pay Raises, Share of Profits to Retain Talent as Internet Start-ups Beckon," *Crain's New York Business*, March 13, 2000, p. 1.

consulting projects slated for 2000. McKinsey was building 10 "accelerators" in Europe and North America that would provide relatively standard incubator services for both start-ups and Internet efforts of established corporations. As of February 2000, the firm had moved or planned to move nearly 500 employees into its e-commerce practice and these accelerators.[54] McKinsey was also going to advise General Atlantic Partners and Capital Z Partners, two investment firms, on their $300 million joint venture to develop new e-finance companies.[55]

WEB PROFESSIONAL SERVICES FIRMS

E-commerce upset traditional ways of doing business in nearly all industrial and consumer markets. As both established companies and new players attempted to build and execute winning business strategies on the Internet, they created an opportunity for outside service providers to offer strategic, creative, and technical advice and integrate existing business and information systems with new, Internet-based technologies. Many start-up companies used these service firms to develop a Web presence more quickly or to add competencies they lacked in-house. These service providers had many names: Web developers, system innovators, e-consultants, e-business service providers, e-commerce integrators, and more. We use the term "Web professional services firms" to describe players that offered strategic, technical, and creative advice to e-commerce companies. The market was large and growing: in 1999, North American revenues were $10 billion and growing 50% annually. By 2003, the market for Web professional services was projected to be $65 billion.[56]

The Web professional services industry was in its third stage of evolution. The first generation of companies comprised primarily Web site builders, such as online advertising agencies, whose personnel understood the World Wide Web (WWW) and hypertext markup language (HTML). Second generation service providers added traditional systems integrations skills, often in an ad hoc manner. These firms built attractive Web sites and integrated them with transaction systems. The third generation, still in its formative stages in early 2000, combined business and strategic skills with these technical abilities and was attempting to provide both online and offline expertise.[57] For many clients, the Internet was no longer simply another sales channel or advertising medium. It was changing traditional business processes as well as creating new ways for firms, suppliers, and customers to interact. These service firms were trying to help their clients understand and react to these changes.

The array of companies attempting to provide these services was stunning: traditional client/server systems integration companies such as Cambridge Technology Partners and Sapient; the Big 5 consulting firms such as Andersen Consulting and KPMG; the service arms of system architecture vendors such as IBM, EDS, and Oracle; the interactive online advertising agencies like Agency.com and Organic Online;

[54] Peter D. Henig, "And Now EcoNets," *Red Herring*, February 2000, p. 99.

[55] Mark Walsh, "McKinsey Ups Ante: Consulting Firm to Offer Pay Raises, Share of Profits to Retain Talent as Internet Start-ups Beckon," *Crain's New York Business*, March 13, 2000, p. 1.

[56] Christina Overby, "Sizing eCommerce Services," *The Forrester Report*, October 1999.

[57] Scient White Paper, "Systems Innovation: Driving the eBusiness Revolution," 1999.

Web application developers like Proxicom, USWeb (which merged with Whittman-Hart into MarchFirst in 2000); and even the Web hosting companies such as Exodus (discussed in the next section); and over ten thousand small niche Web services firms.[58]

In this section, the discussion is focused on pure-play, online services firms created in the 1990s to deal with the Internet and e-commerce. However, much of the material, especially that concerning the service offerings, applies to any type of provider in the industry.

Service Offerings

The market for Web services could be segmented along two main dimensions. The first was whether the firm offered one or a combination of strategic, creative, or technical advice and implementation. The second was whether the provider focused on the front- or back-end of the online operations.

Building Web sites and integrating them with a transaction system was costly; building a basic transactional user interface and a rudimentary back-end system cost an average of $500,000.[59] Building an online business site with a top-tier developer ran between $3 million and $7 million.[60] A state-of-the-art site could cost $15 million.[61]

Table 1 describes some of the activities that service providers offered along these two dimensions. The list is not complete because each client engagement was unique and the boundaries separating these groupings were not definitive. Exhibit 12 provides an overview of the major pure-play Web professional service providers.

Front-end providers helped clients create, design, and architect Web sites and associated user interactions. The major competitors in this space were basic Web site design firms, the "Internet" units of traditional advertising agencies like Ogilvy and Mather, and interactive agencies such as Agency.com, Organic Online, and Razorfish. In a comprehensive engagement, the front-end firm would help the client determine a Web site's goals, branding strategy, target market, transaction requirements, and other fundamental underpinnings of the site design. Then the provider would design and create the interface, technical architecture, and navigation scheme. Subsequently, it would create the graphics, write the copy, and code the applications, culminating in testing of the site prior to launch. These activities needed to be coordinated with internal or outsourced systems integration teams and external data service providers, such as Web hosters. The front-end service provider would then help launch the site in coordination with other marketing and public relations efforts and may also have helped in ongoing content management and site updates.[62]

Back-end providers helped an e-commerce company create the transactions systems and other tools to support e-commerce activities and integrate these systems with existing enterprise resource planning (ERP), ordering, returns processing, accounts

[58] Dana Tower, "Interactive Architects Recast," *The Forrester Report*, March 1998.

[59] *NetMarketing Guide to Web Pricing* as quoted in "Hiring for a Large-Scale Interactive Development Project," Agency.com White Paper, 1999.

[60] Rick Barker and Michael Sippey, "When to Outsource," *Business 2.0*, March 2000.

[61] J. C. Bradford & Co., *Diamond Technology Partners*, June 30, 1999.

[62] "Hiring for a Large-Scale Interactive Development Project," Agency.com White Paper, 1999.

receivable, and customer information systems. They also developed middleware and custom application program interfaces (APIs) to make incompatible systems communicate with each other. As the market matured, these back-end providers could purchase pre-packaged commerce packages, APIs, and component platforms for better-defined and standardized client needs, rather than build custom systems.[63]

TABLE 1 Web Services

	Strategy and marketing	*Creative and design*	*Technical*
Front-end	• "General" Internet strategy • Corporate and product branding • Channel synchronization • Marketing communication • Customer service • 1:1 customer relationship management • Advertising analysis • ROI and other "return" calculations	• User interface design • Information content choice/creation • Brand graphics creation/integration • Content management templates • Frames optimization • Human factors, usability and other market testing • Linking form to transaction objectives	• Coding and scripting in HTML, Java, XML, etc. • Content catalog management • Implementation of advertising and marketing rules • Interface personalization algorithms • Web site updates
Back-end	• Process reinvention and change management to incorporate Internet innovations • Development of end-to-end commerce processes—transactions, inventory checks, delivery tracking • Development of processes that capitalize on customer and dealer extranets/hubs • Global integration	• Not applicable	• Legacy systems integration • Commerce and Web server deployment • Linking company systems to those of customers and suppliers for dynamic trading systems • Business application and middleware deployment • Real-time transaction processing

(continued)

[63] Christina Overby, "Sizing eCommerce Services," *The Forrester Report*, October 1999.

TABLE 1 *(continued)*

	Strategy and marketing	*Creative and design*	*Technical*
Market size (1999)[64]	$1.3 billion	$2.7 billion	$6.6 billion
Market size (2003 est.)[65]	$21 billion	$12 billion	$32 billion

The evolution of the services industry was pushing service providers to focus on consumer marketing or business process expertise (roughly equivalent to building business-to-consumer (B2C) or B2B e-commerce functionality). The former group, which included iXL, Agency.com, Strategic Interactive Group, and Razorfish, had creative strengths, could develop brand communication and promotion, build personalized content, and manage consumer transactions. The latter group, which understood business trading processes, customer and supplier extranet interfaces, payment certification, inventory management, and how to manage the supply chain, included Proxicom, most of USWeb's operations, and others.[66]

New vendors also provided and managed the entire back-end operations for e-commerce companies. Loudcloud, a start-up company run by Netscape founder Marc Andreessen, packaged all the technology needed to run a Web site, from servers to database software, and sold the package to companies for a monthly fee.[67] The client picked its options from a "menu" of configurations (based on type of content, number of users, transaction abilities, etc.). Loudcloud then leased the cages and rack space at a Web hoster, procured all hardware, software, switches, and so on, got the systems up and running, developed proprietary "opsware" that systematized the operations, and then scaled and monitored the system.[68] Electron Economy, run by a founder of USWeb, went one step further by attempting to assemble and integrate the entire logistical and information systems aspect of its clients' e-commerce operations, from the pressing of the buy button to the delivery of packages to the customer's home.[69] While both companies got substantial press coverage, it remained to be seen if they would be able to develop successfully the back-end operations of their clients.

Growing Pains, Acquisitions, and Quality Control

Many of these firms were publicly held (or attempting to go public), unlike the traditional partnership models of strategy consultants and the Big 5. Public markets enabled

[64] *ibid.*

[65] *ibid.*

[66] Dana Tower, "Interactive Architects Recast," *The Forrester Report*, March 1998.

[67] Steve Hamm, "Marc Andreessen: A Pioneer Once More," *Business Week Online*, February 28, 2000.

[68] Carol Pickering, "Ahead in the Clouds," *Business 2.0*, March 2000.

[69] Penelope Patsuris, "Electron Economy: The McKinsey of the 21st Century?" *Forbes*, October 22, 1999.

firms to access expansion and consolidation capital, but the ups and downs of the market could adversely affect employee compensation. Earnings of consulting firms had always been volatile (a tendency public market investors disliked), and activities that slowed growth rates (regardless of whether they were necessary for customer satisfaction) could hammer stock prices.[70] When Cambridge Technology Partners experienced problems with its earnings and management in 1999, its stock dropped nearly 90% from its high (and remained there through early 2000). The low stock price damaged the firm's ability to keep talent in a tight labor market.[71]

Most Web professional services firms also focused their efforts on becoming full-service entities and expanded their offerings to provide a range of strategic, creative, and technical services on both front- and back-end projects. In the words of one client, "Being prepared to offer the total package of creative, marketing, application development and integration—either inclusively or through partnerships—will become even more important."[72] USWeb (an established front-end player) merged with Whittman-Hart (known for its back-end expertise) to provide end-to-end services to clients.[73] Viant teamed with Cognizant, a large India-based systems integrator, to provide the same services.[74] However, most market analysts doubted that any provider could offer the best end-to-end solution; the CIO of Fujitsu PC stated that "Internet solution providers come in different flavors. At this point, there is no group that does everything well."[75]

Growth through acquisitions and partnerships (USWeb and iXL were each built from over 40 acquisitions in three years[76]) had caused problems. While former USWeb CEO Robert Shaw claimed that acquisition integration had been easy and had "gone off without a hitch,"[77] many felt that these firms were too busy and immature to integrate so many disparate pieces smoothly. There were culture clashes. Christina Ross of Forrester Research wrote about the MarchFirst merger that, "USWeb/CKS has a reputation as a hip new integrator with smart, flashy people . . . by contrast, Whittman-Hart has a slow-and-steady flavor and a pragmatic style. Uniting the two will bring significant challenges in terms of . . . an equal blending of the two cultures."[78] The corporate upheaval also made employees nervous: "The minute one of these deals gets published, headhunters are all over the place."[79]

[70] "Sacrificial Offerings," *Management Consultant International*, February 11, 2000.

[71] "E-Business Winners and Losers: Services," *UPSIDE Today*, February 16, 2000.

[72] Elizabeth Gardner, "Demanding Clients Are Driving Innovation," *Internet World*, November 1, 1999, p. 56.

[73] David Jastrow, "USWeb/CKS Want to MarchFirst," *Computer Reseller News*, March 27, 2000, p. 96.

[74] Larry Greenemeier, "E-Services Teams Offer Integration—Providers Join Forces to Help Businesses Link Front and Back-End Systems," *InformationWeek*, February 21, 2000.

[75] Gregory Dalton, "Smaller Is Better—Small Web Consulting Firms Offer Speed, Flexibility, and a Complete Internet Focus," *InformationWeek*, April 26, 1999, p. 121.

[76] Eryn Brown, "The E-Consultants: They Used to Be Those Geeks Who Designed Your Web Pages. Now They're Web Strategists Running $100 Million Consulting Firms," *Fortune*, April 12, 1999, p. 116.

[77] *ibid.*

[78] Christina Ross, "USWeb/CKS and Whitman-Hart Merger: Mismatched and Misguided," *The Forrester Report*, December 21, 1999.

[79] Kelly Rodriques, CEO of Novo Interactive, as quoted in "Demanding Clients Are Driving Innovation," *Internet World*, November 1, 1999, p. 55.

Industry turmoil, volatile financial markets, and high demand for Web-savvy consultants fueled employee turnover. Annual turnover rates of more than 25%, along with missed deadlines and poor quality control, generated customer dissatisfaction.[80] Nearly one in three client executives had fired a Web design firm for poor work.[81] Managing knowledge transfer, a key component of any consulting and implementation project, had also been difficult for these fast-growing firms. They had immature mechanisms for ensuring that when an engagement ended, the client could perform the necessary steps to attain or maintain success.[82] Many competitors, such as US Interactive, recognized this and took steps (such as developing extranets with project- and knowledge-management capabilities) to ensure smoother transitions.[83]

Finally, start-up companies had difficulty hiring consultants because most providers had a backlog of work.[84] As Scott Dunlap, VP of product management at Loudcloud, remarked about Viant, Scient, and USWeb, "You need a couple million to even get their attention."[85]

INTERNET DATA SERVICES: WEB AND APPLICATION HOSTING

At the beginning of the Internet era, most firms purchased (or developed in-house) and maintained proprietary hardware and software systems to connect the company to the global Internet. This relegated the WWW to the domain of the Fortune 1000 companies or start-up Internet companies. Less technologically capable firms were initially left behind because they could not "get connected." The explosion in the number of Internet users, content, and applications increased both the demands on the hardware and software that held the Internet together and the scale and complexity of firms' internal Internet infrastructures and greatly taxed information systems and personnel. Moreover, developing and maintaining an internal and external Internet presence became mission-critical for both established and start-up e-commerce companies.

Internet data service (IDS) providers offered a way for Internet-based enterprises to cost-effectively outsource Internet access, hosting, and network services. These Internet technology facilitators provided the physical hardware, software, and services that connected the firm's mission-critical IT systems with the Internet. The various technical layers of the IDS industry included network connectivity, content distribution, data center facilities, and managed and application services.

Data center facilities and managed services were the key components of Web hosting, the most prominent area of IDS. Web hosting involved the outsourcing of customer Web site physical server and data storage requirements, the monitoring and

[80] Elizabeth Gardner, "Demanding Clients Are Driving Innovation," *Internet World*, November 1, 1999, p. 55.

[81] *ibid.*

[82] Ken Allard, "Professional Services for the Web," Jupiter Communications, November 1998, p. 13.

[83] Fawn Fitter, "Arming Goliath," *Knowledge Management*, February 2000.

[84] Elizabeth Gardner, "Demanding Clients Are Driving Innovation," *Internet World*, November 1, 1999, p. 55.

[85] Recruiting event at Stanford University, February 2000.

maintenance of equipment, high-speed connectivity to the Internet, and technical support. Essentially, Web hosting provided the platform that managed and gave reliable Internet access to the applications and systems developed either internally by the firm or by the professional services firms discussed in the previous section.

The Web hosting customer benefited from significant economies of scale and scope—the majority of the one-time hardware costs and recurring support services expenses were shared among many users (Exhibit 13). Outsourced Web operations cost 70%–80% less than Web sites that were maintained and hosted in-house (Exhibit 14).[86]

If the Web site was administered internally, the managerial burden of continuously upgrading Internet operations to incorporate the best available technology also had to be considered. When Internet hardware and operations were kept in-house, start-up companies risked focusing on operations outside the firm's core competencies at the risk of missing technological trends and network efficiency improvements, and/or implementing an ineffective network connectivity strategy. An effective IDS provider was focused on adapting to the speed of change of the Internet, constantly improving its service offerings to utilize "best-of-breed" technologies and keeping customers on the cutting edge. In a survey just before this case was written, over 60% of online firms had already outsourced hosting to an external provider.[87]

Competition in the rapidly evolving IDS industry was intense. The many new entrants had strategies and different positioning within the value chain. Competitors included telecommunications companies such as AT&T and Qwest that had moved toward providing data services for their voice customers, focused and established Web hosting companies such as Exodus Communications and Digex, mainstream hardware component suppliers and assemblers like Intel and Dell, applications solutions providers (ASPs), and even professional service firms such as MarchFirst. (See Exhibit 15 for an overview of the major Internet data services providers.)

EVALUATING THE OPTIONS

To move at Internet speed, entrepreneurs had to choose from among a wide array of service providers, investors, and consultants. Their options ranged from joining an Internet holding company and being provided with a wide array of prepackaged services, to selectively using specialist providers with a heavy dose of "do-it-yourself."

In early 2000, while many entrepreneurs struggled with these choices, the service market was rapidly evolving. Internet holding companies CMGI and ICG saw their combined market value drop by 70% between the NASDAQ peak in early March 2000 and its trough on April 14; venture capitalists contended with stiff competition and an increase in the pace of investment; strategy consultants fought to retain their staff and relevance in the digital age; and pure-play Web professional services firms fared almost as badly in the market as the Internet holding companies. Faced with this tumultuous

[86] The Internet Data Services Report, Morgan Stanley Dean Witter, August 11, 1999.

[87] "Hosting: Build Management Expertise Internally; Outsource Infrastructure Needs," Jupiter Communications, April, 1999.

landscape, entrepreneurs had to assess their immediate needs with an eye to the impact that choices made today would have on their company's future shape.

> *You're kidding, right? A couple of kids fresh out of Harvard Business School sketch up a plan for an Internet services company (gee, there are only, what, thousands of those) and raise $100 million? It all seems like a bad dream.* —*Upside Today: E-Business Winners and Losers: Services (in discussing the start-up consultancy Zefer Enterprise)*

EXHIBIT 1 Hot Internet IPO Market Provides Exit Mechanism

Selected Statistics for 1999	
Portion of total IPOs that were Internet related	50%
Average Internet IPO return*	233%
Average aftermarket return for investors in Internet IPO†	86%
Portion of total IPOs founded less than 5 years ago	57%
Portion of total IPOs without earnings	73%
—Percentage of these IPOs that were Internet related	63%
Portion of IPOs with less than $5M in sales	20%
—Percentage of these IPOs that were Internet related	85%
Portion of IPOs with less than $1M in sales	7%
—Percentage of these IPOs that were Internet related	76%

* Total return if stock bought at IPO price on day of IPO and held until end of 1999.
† Total return if stock bought at end of first day of trading and held until end of 1999.

EXHIBIT 2 Internet Incubators Provide Range of Services for Portfolio Companies

Internet incubatory	*Status*	*Services offered**								*Notable portfolio companies*	*Market value ($ billion)*†
		RE	*HR*	*W*	*F*	*$*	*L*	*BD*	*SM*		
Hotbank‡	Public	✓	✓	✓	✓	✓	✓	✓	✓	TheStreet.com, Launch Media, USWeb/CKS	N/A
Safeguard Scientific	Public		✓			✓	✓	✓	✓	Internet Capital Group, US Interactive	4.2
Acacia Research	Public	✓	✓	✓	✓	✓	✓	✓	✓	MerkWerks, Soundbreak.com, Soundview Technologies	0.3
Net Value Holdings	Public		✓		✓	✓		✓	✓	Asia CD, AssetExchange.com	0.1
Idealab	Private§	✓	✓	✓	✓	✓	✓	✓	✓	GoTo.com, eToys, NetZero	N/A
Divine InterVentures	Private**	✓	✓	✓	✓	✓	✓	✓	✓	Neolorma, SHO Research, Whiplash	N/A
Cambridge Incubator	Private	✓	✓	✓	✓	✓	✓	✓	✓	Etineraries, Veritas Medicine, BrandStamp	N/A
eCompanies	Private	✓	✓	✓	✓	✓		✓	✓	Business.com, eMemories.com	N/A
Techfarm	Private	✓	✓	✓	✓	✓	✓	✓	✓	Cobalt Networks, Resonate, NetMind	N/A
Redleaf Venture Management	Private	✓	✓	✓	✓	✓	✓	✓	✓	Bitlocker, NetGravity, Startups.com	N/A

Compiled by case writer from *Red Herring* and finance.yahoo.com.

* Key: RE (real estate), HR (human resources/executive placement), W (Web hosting, network infrastructure), F (finance and accounting), $ (funding), L (legal), BD (business strategy and development), SM (sales and marketing).

† As of April 20, 2000.

‡ A division of publicly traded Softbank.

§ Has filed for an initial public offering.

** Has filed for an initial public offering.

EXHIBIT 3 CMGI vs. ICG

	CMGI	*ICG*
Market value (4/20/00)	• $16.144 billion	• $11.562 billion
Structure	• 2 business units: operating group and venture arm, @Ventures	• Single company
Reputed competitive advantage	• Ability to add substantial value to second tier Internet companies through network	• Replicable expertise in building market makers • Managerial "stars"
Stock market performance	• IPO in January, 1994 • Best 5-year performer (1995–2000); CAGR of 213.1%* • Recently, market cap down almost 65% from January peak of $46B	• IPO in August, 1999 • Best-performing share of 1999 (27-fold increase) • Recently, market cap down almost 80% from January peak of $56 billion
Companies		
Number invested in	• 17 operating companies;† 50+ @Ventures investments‡	• 65: 20 infrastructure, 45 B2B market makers§
Average stake (%)	• Unknown	• 36%**
Number that have gone public	• 8	• 5
Number acquired	• 11	• Unknown
Leadership	• Founder and CEO David Wetherell	• Cofounders: Ken Fox and Walter Buckley • Deep bench
Investment focus	• Many different kinds of companies that create "network" of properties • Within this, focus on categories that evolve over time	• B2B market makers (vertical and horizontal) • Internet infrastructure

(continued)

* John Hechinger, "Best 5-Year Performer," *Wall Street Journal*, February 24, 2000, p. R4.

† This includes the pending acquisition of *u*Bid.com but also assumes that Engage has already acquired Adsmart.

‡ http://www.ventures.com

§ http://www.internetcapital.com

** Julia Angwin, "Online Exchanges Also Suffer from a Glut of Players," *Wall Street Journal*, April 7, 2000, p. B1.

EXHIBIT 3 *(continued)*

	CMGI	*ICG*
Acquisition approach	• Operating group tends to pay larger premiums for established players. • @Ventures makes earlier stage investments.	• Generally invests in earlier stage companies. • New unit called Ecolony created to start companies from scratch.
Resources/services offered	• Funding, real estate, human resources, Web hosting, finance and accounting, legal, business and strategy development, and sales and marketing services • Primary resources: corporate, @Ventures partners, portfolio companies	• Funding, real estate, human resources, Web hosting, finance and accounting, legal, business and strategy development, and sales and marketing services • Primary resources: corporate, portfolio companies, advisory board, strategic shareholders
Financing	• Funded through share sales and private equity placements • No secondary offering to date	• Funded through initial and secondary offering • Also through private placements by strategic shareholders

Source: Case writer synthesis of publicly available documents and research materials.

EXHIBIT 4 CMGI and ICG Stock Price History

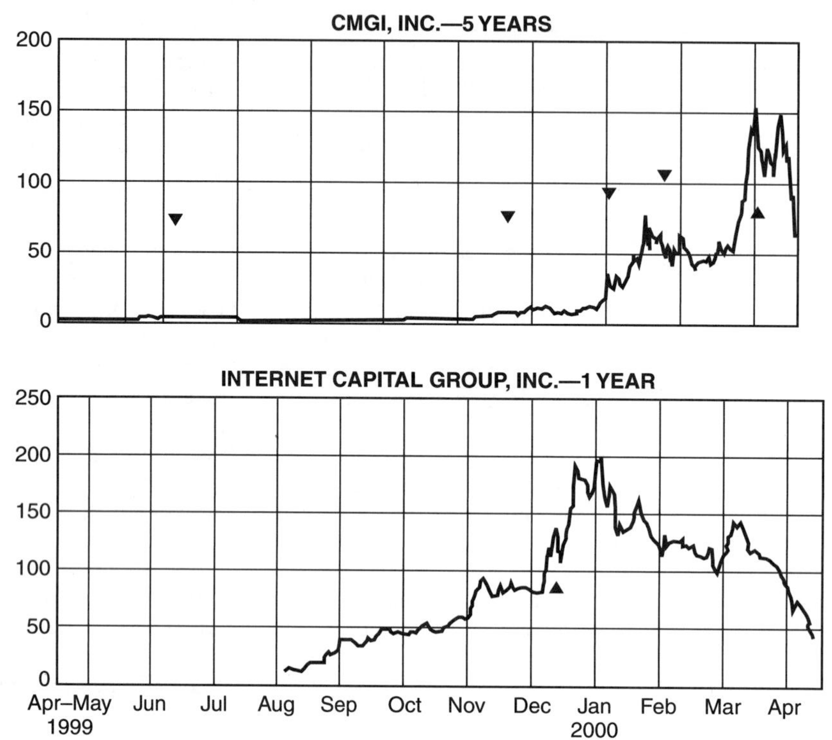

Source: Netscape Netcenter. Reproduced with permission from CSI.

EXHIBIT 5 Snapshot of CMGI Portfolio Companies

Type of company	*Marketing / advertising*	*E-commerce*	*Content and community*	*Enabling technology*
CMGI	CMGI marketing/ advertising companies deliver services, including profiling, advertising sales, ad serving, and measurement.	CMGI e-commerce companies include both business-to-consumer and business-to-business players, with an historical emphasis on business-to-consumer.	Historically, CMGI helped build Lycos and Geocites. Today, CMGI is focused on personalization, customization, multimedia, and self-publishing, among others. It has also recently purchased AltaVista.	CMGI's Enabling Technology Companies provide strategies, designs, and technologies to help companies build robust technicalogical and scalable platforms.
Operating Companies	1stUp.com AdForce Adsmart Engage Flycast Communications YesMail.com	AltaVista SalesLink *u*Bid.com	AltaVista iCAST MyWay.com	IclickCharge 1stUp.com Activate CMGI Solutions Engage Equilibrium NaviSite NaviPath SalesLink Tribal Voice
@Ventures Investments	Vicinity	BizBuyer.com fooodbuy.com GoFish.com KnowledgeFirst NextOffice.com Ventro CarParts.com EXP.com NextMonet.com WebCT Auction Watch.com Boatscape.com buyersedge.com CraftShop.com Furniture.com Half.com Mondera.com MotherNature.com NextPlanetOver.com PlanetOutdoors.com Productopia Snapfish	KnowledgeFirst KOZ.com Oncology.com ThingWorld.com Lycos FindLaw WebCT Asimba.com Domania eCircles.com Egroups.com Gamers.com Hotlinks Silknet Software MyFamily.com Spotlife	Critical Path idapts OneCore.com Radiate Speech Machines Vcommerce Vicinity Virtual link Spotlife Viso blaxxun interactive

Compiled by case writer from http://www.cmgi.com/network/index.html, April 8, 2000.
Note: Some companies are listed in multiple categories because they serve more than one function.

EXHIBIT 6 Snapshot of ICG Portfolio Companies

Market Makers

Market-makers may operate in particular industries ("vertical"), such as chemicals, food, or auto parts, or may sell goods and services across multiple industries ("horizontal").

Horizontal Market Makers				*Vertical Market Makers*			
Company	*Industry*	*ICG ownership*	*Partner since*	*Company*	*Industry*	*ICG ownership*	*Partner since*
assetTrade.com	Used capital equipment	26%	1999	CyberCrop.com, Inc.	Agricultural market	75%	1999
eMarketWorld, Inc.	Special event services	42%	1999	Animated Images	Apparel	50%	1999
NetVendor, Inc.	Industrial goods	26%	1999	InvestorForce.com	Asset management	46%	1999
e-Credit	Financial services	33%	2000	Autovia	Auto parts	15%	1998
Onvia.com, Inc.	Small business services	20%	1999	e-Chemicals, Inc.	Chemicals	35%	1998
ICG Commerce, Inc.	Sourcing	60%	1999	BidCom, Inc.	Construction	24%	1999
Residential Delivery Services (RDS)	Logistics/delivery services	38%	1999	RetailExchange.com	Consumer goods	30%	1999
VerticalNet, Inc.	Industrial services	36%	1996	Simplexis	Education	56%	2000
VerticalNet Europe	European industrial services	11%	2000	iParts	Electronic components	85%	1999
Logistics.com	Transportation	36%	2000	Eu-supply.com	European construction	28.5%	2000
eColony	U.S. incubation	20%	2000	eMetra	European metals	45%	2000
Vivant! Corporation	Personnel services	23%	1998	EumediX	European hospital supplies	31.5%	2000
				FOL Networks	European agriculture	30%	2000
				Internet Commerce Systems, Inc.	Food	43%	1999
				USgift.com	Gift, garden, and home decor	35%	1999
				Internet Healthcare Group	Healthcare and insurance	34%	1999
				EmployeeLife.com	Insurance and healthcare	52%	1999
				FreeBorders	International trade	46%	2000
				CourtLink	Legal	19%	1999
				JusticeLink	Legal	37%	1999

(continued)

Compiled by case writer from www.internetcapital.com/partnercompanies.htm, April 8, 2000.

EXHIBIT 6 *(continued)*

Market Makers

Horizontal Market Makers				*Vertical Market Makers*			
Company	*Industry*	*ICG ownership*	*Partner since*	*Company*	*Industry*	*ICG ownership*	*Partner since*
				eMerge Interactive, Inc.	Livestock	28%	1999
				TALPX Inc.	Lumber and panel	30%	2000
				Deja.com, Inc.	Media	29%	1997
				BuyMedia.com	Media	32%	2000
				CentriMed	Medical devices	47%	2000
				StarCite, Inc.	Meetings and events	43%	1999
				Metalsite.com	Metals	44%	1999
				PaperExchange	Paper	27%	1999
				CommerX, Inc.	Plastics	42%	1998
				Collabria	Printing	12%	1999
				Computerjobs.com, Inc.	Technology employment	33%	1998
				Arbinet Communications	Telecommunications	16%	1999
				Universal Access	Telecommunications	26%	1999

(continued)

Compiled by case writer from http://www.internetcapital.com/partnercompanies.htm, April 8, 2000.

EXHIBIT 6 *(continued)*

Enabling Service Providers

Enabling service providers sell software and services to businesses engaged in e-commerce. Many businesses need assistance designing business practices to take advantage of the Internet and in building and managing the technological infrastructure needed to support B2B commerce. ICG places enabling service providers into one of three categories: consulting and systems integration, software providers, and outsourced service providers.

Strategic Consulting and Systems Integration			*Software Providers*			*Outsourced Service Providers*		
Company	*ICG ownership*	*Partner since*	*Company*	*ICG ownership*	*Partner since*	*Company*	*ICG ownership*	*Partner since*
Benchmarking Partners, Inc.	13%	1996	Blackboard, Inc.	30%	1998	Breakaway Solutions, Inc.	49%	1999
Context Integration	18%	1997	ClearCommerce	15%	1997	CommerceQuest, Inc.	29%	1998
US Interactive	3%	1996	Entegrity Solutions	12%	1996	Jamcracker, Inc.	24%	1999
			ServiceSoft Technologies, Inc.	6%	1998	LinkShare Corporation	34%	1998
			Syncra Systems, Inc.	35%	1998	PrivaSeek, Inc.	16%	1998
			Tradex Technologies, Inc.	10%	1999	SageMaker, Inc.	27%	1998
						iSKY	31%	1996
						TeamOn.com	36%	2000
						traffic.com	20%	1999
						United Messaging, Inc.	41%	1999
						RightWorks	51%	2000

Compiled by case writer from http://www.internetcapital.com/partnercompanies.htm, April 8, 2000.

EXHIBIT 7 Industry and Company Selection Criteria

Internet Capital Group Web Site: http://www.internetcapital.com
Reproduced with permission from Internet Capital Group.

History
About our Partners
List of Partner Companies
Partner Company Table
Contact Information
Directions

About Our Partners

ICG's expertise in the B2B e-commerce market allows it to build or identify companies that are positioned to succeed. It then applies a disciplined analysis that capitalizes on this competitive advantage. When ICG evaluates whether to build a new company or acquire an interest in an existing company, it weighs the following industry and partnership company factors:

Industry Criteria

- **Inefficiency.** ICG considers whether the industry suffers from inefficiencies that may be alleviated through e-commerce. Also under consideration is the relative amount of inefficiency, as more inefficient industries present greater profit potential.
- **Competition.** ICG evaluates the amount of competition that a potential Partner Company faces from traditional and e-commerce business.
- **Market Maker Profit Potential.** When evaluating market makers ICG considers the number and dollar value of transactions in the industry. In the multi-billion dollar industries that ICG targets, offering even incremental efficiency improvements presents significant profit potential.
- **Centralized Information Sources.** When evaluating market makers, ICG considers whether the industry has product catalogs, trade journals and other centralized sources of information regarding prices, customers and other factors. The availability of such information makes it easier for market makers to facilitate transactions. ICG generally avoids industries where such information is not available.
- **Enabling Service Provider Profit Potential.** When evaluating enabling service providers, we examine the size of the market opportunity, the profit potential in serving the target market and whether the enabling service provider can provide assistance to ICG's market maker companies.

Partnership Company Criteria

- **Industry Leader.** ICG partners with a company only if its management team believes that this company has the products and skills to become the leader in its industry.
- **Management Quality.** ICG assesses the overall quality and industry expertise of a potential partner company's management.
- **Significant Ownership.** It is considered whether ICG will be able to obtain a significant position in the company and exert influence over the company.
- **Network Synergy** ICG considers the degree to which a potential Partner Company may contribute to, and benefit from, network and operational resources.

HOME | INVESTOR RELATIONS | ABOUT US | NEWS
B2B E-Commerce | Competitive Advantage | Strategic Network

EXHIBIT 8

Internet Capital Group Web Site: http://www.internetcapital.com
Reproduced with permission from Internet Capital Group.

Strategic Network

- PARTNER COMPANIES
- ADVISORY BOARD
- STRATEGIC SHAREHOLDERS

Strategic Network

One of the principal goals of our network is to promote innovation and collaboration among our Partner Companies,which has resulted in shared knowledge and business contacts among our Partner Companies and the formation of numerous strategic alliances.

We promote collaboration formally by hosting regularly scheduled seminars relating to Partner Company operational and business issues. At these seminars, the executives of Partner Companies share their experiences with each other, our Management Team and the Advisory Board. For example, at a recent seminar, thirteen chief executive officers of our market maker and enabling service provider Partner Companies gathered to discuss e-commerce strategies and business models. On an informal basis, we promote collaboration by making introductions and recommending Partner Companies to each other.

A recent example of collaboration among our Partner Companies include:

- VerticalNet and e-Chemicals are collaborating to provide customer leads for e-Chemicals. This relationship enables VerticalNet to provide a greater breadth of services to its customers in the chemicals business and provides more buyers for the products distributed by e-Chemicals.

The collaboration of ICG's Partner Companies is the result of the company's role as the hub of its network. Through the network, ICG identifies prospective alliances, makes introductions, assists in strategic planning and monitors the ongoing relationships among its Partner Companies. ICG encourages and regulates the information flow among Partner Companies.

The collaboration of ICG's Partner Companies is the result of the company's role as the hub of its network. Through the network, ICG identifies prospective alliances, makes introductions, assists in strategic planning and monitors the ongoing relationships among its Partner Companies. ICG encourages and regulates the information flow among Partner Companies.

HOME | INVESTOR RELATIONS | ABOUT US | NEWS
B2B E-Commerce | Competitive Advantage | Strategic Network

EXHIBIT 9 Venture Capital Returns (Based on Year Fund Was Raised)

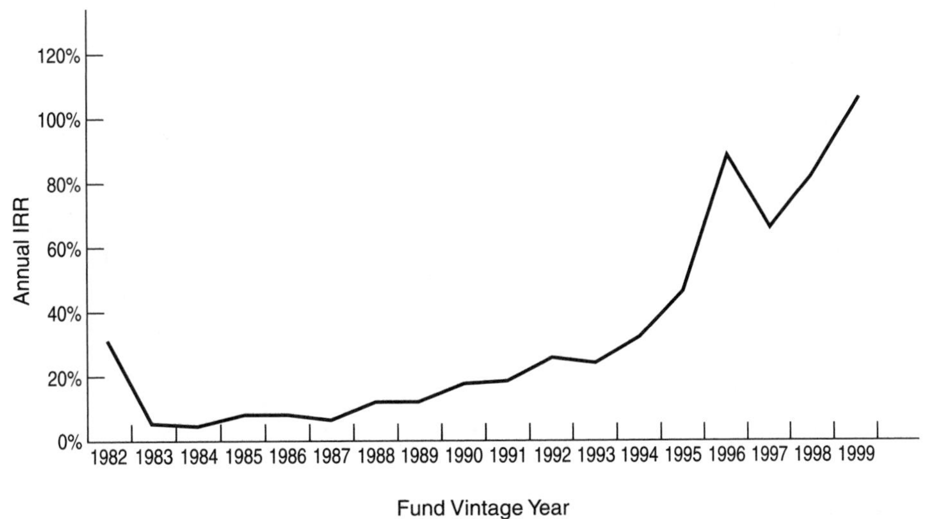

Reproduced with permission from VentureEconomics.

EXHIBIT 10 Marked Increase in Investment Flows to Venture Capital Funds

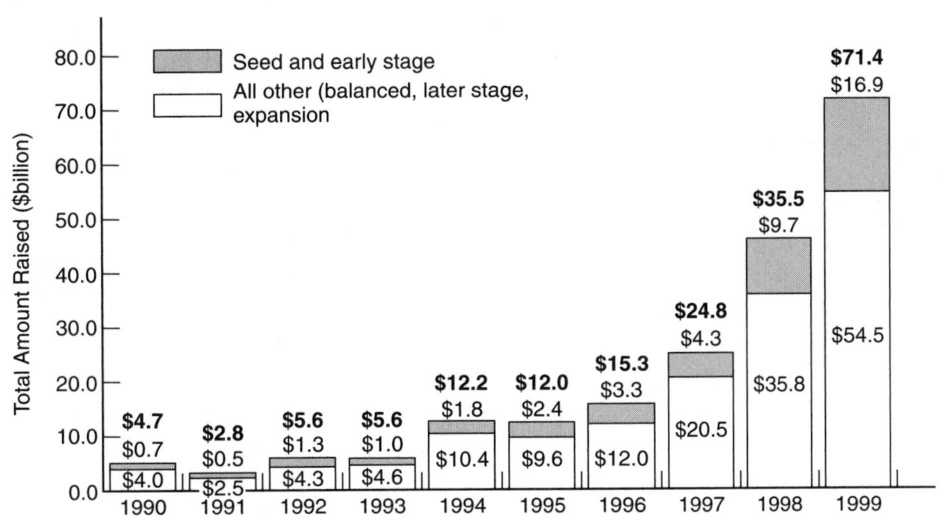

Reproduced with permission from VentureEconomics.

EXHIBIT 11 Venture Capital Investments in Seed and Early Stage Companies

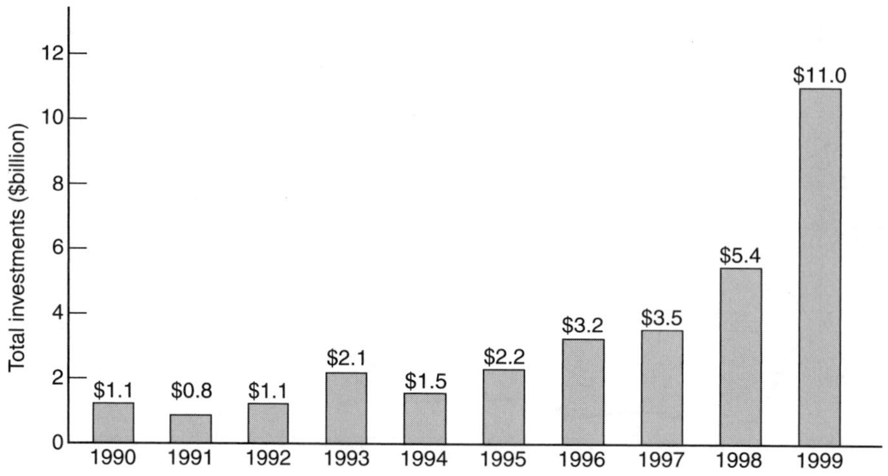

Reproduced with permission from VentureEconomics.

EXHIBIT 12 An Overview of the Major Web Professional Services Firms

Company	*Market value*	*Revenues*	*Employees*	*Major areas of competence and other key facts*
Agency.com	$622 million	$88 million	1,100	• Strong creative skills, with less experience in strategy consulting and organizational design • One of the few pure Web designers to have successfully moved to broader strategic consulting and marketing assignments • Had acquired companies for technical integration skills, but often teams with client's IS department • Many established Fortune 500 clients
Cambridge Technology Partners	$729 million	$628 million	4,200	• Former client/server integrator that had some difficulty moving into the electronic commerce space

(continued)

EXHIBIT 12 *(continued)*

Company	*Market value*	*Revenues*	*Employees*	*Major areas of competence and other key facts*
				• Low stock price and other turbulence led to staff defections
Diamond Technology Partners	$1.4 billion	$125 million	433	• Strong strategic background, with an attempt to increase implementation skills in response to customer demands • Generally product/solution (hardware, software, implementation) agnostic • Had taken equity in several clients
iXL Enterprises	$1.3 billion	$218 million	2,100	• A roll-up of dozens of smaller firms, it was having difficulty establishing a common culture and retaining staff • Client list was primarily large corporations • Typical engagements from $250,000 to $1 million • Both U.S. and European operations • Focused on providing complete back- and front-end solutions
Loudcloud	Private	N/A	N/A	• Packaged all the technology that is needed to run a Web site, from servers to database software, and sold the package as a service to companies for a monthly fee • Focused on start-ups and established clients
MarchFirst	$3.5 billion	$780 million	8,900	• The combination of front-end player USWeb and back-end integrator • Whittman-Hart was attempting to provide end-to-end solutions for its clients

(continued)

EXHIBIT 12 *(continued)*

Company	*Market value*	*Revenues*	*Employees*	*Major areas of competence and other key facts*
				• USWeb had a techno-centric culture and was not seen as particularly strong at brand strategy • Combined company expected 80% of its revenue from medium-sized and large businesses, with 20% from start-ups
Organic Online	Private	N/A	125	• Background in online branding and site development; little back-end experience • Strong telecommunications client base • Avoided acquisitions and preferred to grow by adding people • Lower turnover than industry average
Pandesic	Private	N/A	300	• Joint venture of Intel and SAP • Focused on providing the system architecture and the technology to implement a firm's Internet strategy (technology services on both the front- and back-end) • Back-end integration with SAP R/3 considered a strong point • Strong business process and supply chain management knowledge—analysts said they were better at developing business-to-business applications

(continued)

EXHIBIT 12 *(continued)*

Company	*Market value*	*Revenues*	*Employees*	*Major areas of competence and other key facts*
Proxicom	$1.8 billion	$83 million	692	• Attempted to provide full range of services: strategic, design, and technology on both the front- and back-end • Traditional strength in site architecture, systems integration, and technical skills; was lacking in design and branding experience • Global 1,000 customer base
Razorfish	$1.8 billion	$170 million	1,355	• Advertising background; began as a design shop; purchased technology consultant i-Cube to bolster technical skills • Promoted its ability to integrate front- and back-end systems, but it had little experience and often depended on the client's technical/IS team • Focused on financial services, media, and telecommunications • Clients were both start-ups and established companies
Sapient	$3.9 billion	$276 million	2,100	• Formerly a client/server development shop, it moved into the design areas with acquisitions of Studio Archetype and Adjacency; analysts praised its transition to the Internet • Strong technical skills, especially integration and site architecture

(continued)

EXHIBIT 12 *(continued)*

Company	*Market value*	*Revenues*	*Employees*	*Major areas of competence and other key facts*
Scient	$3.0 billion	$120 million	874	• Reputation for completing projects on-budget and on-time • 85% Fortune 500 revenue/ 15% start-up revenue • Helped develop core Internet strategies for both start-up and established clients • Back-end expertise: architects, designs, and delivers systems • Powerful brand and strong customer base • Revenues are 60% Global 1,000 and 40% start-up • Average project size of $2–$3 million
US Interactive	Private	N/A	N/A	• Front-end marketing, strategic and design focus • Global 1,000 customer base
Viant	$1.1 billion	$61 million	405	• Front-end strategic, marketing and system architecture expertise • Little or no systems integration experience • Mix of large and small clients • Partnerships with large hardware and infrastructure providers • Incubated clients in its office (the client team worked in the Viant offices during development)

Source: Case writer's synthesis of research reports, business press articles, and other published sources.
Notes: Market values as of April 20, 2000. Annual revenues and employees from latest published figures at time of case. For those companies whose year-end is not December, revenues are latest year-to-date revenues annualized. The employee figures for Diamond Technology Partners include only professional staff.

EXHIBIT 13 The Economies of Scale in the Internet Data Services Business

Cost category	*Rationale*	*Benefits of scale*
Hardware	• Improved utilization through load balancing and 24 × 7 usage • Increased company purchasing power • Allowed for faster upgrades of new technology	Very high
Communications costs	• Improved pricing due to high volume • Better service and support from telecommunications companies	High
Human resources	• Attracted higher quality talent • Assembled complete skill set for multiproduct offering	High
Pricing	• Could negotiate better contracts due to established presence and brand name • More stable cost structure resulted in more accurate market pricing	Medium
Software	• Volume pricing in purchases	Low

Reproduced with permission from McKinsey & Co.

EXHIBIT 14 The Cost Benefits to a Customer of Outsourcing Web Site Hosting

Item/Service	*Approximate cost*
One-Time Start-up Costs	
Web server hardware (Web server NT)	$9,000
Web server software	10,000
T-1 connection	2,500
Network hardware	4,500
Battery back-up	1,000
Firewalls and back-up	15,500
Total one-time costs	$42,500
Recurring Costs/Year	
T-1 connection	$24,000
Tape back-up and storage	7,200
Web master, technical, and other 24 × 7 support	100,000
Total recurring costs	$131,200
Total first year costs	$173,700
High-end outsourced site (annual)	$25,000

Source: NaviSite Corp.

EXHIBIT 15 Major Providers of Internet Data Services

	Telcos			ISP		Hosting Companies					Integrators
	Qwest	AT&T	GTE/ Global	UUNET	Con-centric	Above Net	Exodus	DIGEX	Digital Island	Verio/ Navisite	IBM/ EDS
Application solutions	○	◐	○	○	◐	○	○	◐	○	●	●
Managed hardware	◐	◐	◐	◐	○	○	◐	◐	◐	●	◐
Content distribution network	○	○	○	○	○	○	○	○	◐	○	○
Data center facilities	●	●	●	◐	●	●	●	●	●	◐	◐
Backbone network	●	●	●	●	●	◐	○	○	○	○	○
Main customer segment (S/M/L)	S/M/L	S/M	M/L	M/L	S/M	M/L	M/L	S/M/L	M/L	SM	L

● Core business domain

◐ Noncore/new domain

○ Extended domain

Source: Kwon, McCarron, Thomas, Vidalakis, and Yoon, "Intel Online Services," November, 1999. Reproduced with permission.

KAREN BROWN

In July 1999, Karen Brown was at her desk contemplating whether to accept a proposal from a major online travel site. This site would expose her name and content to millions of users, but putting all her content on the Web for free would cannibalize her book business. As more people turned to the Web for travel information and to book flights and hotels, and as other travel publishers placed their content on the Web, Karen decided that she needed to use the Web to maintain and build her business. She had already invested $30,000 in her own Web site, but most visitors already knew about Karen Brown's Guides. She needed to attract new customers and wanted to improve her margins by selling more books directly through her site. Whatever she decided to do she had to maintain the integrity and quality of her content.

KAREN BROWN'S GUIDES

Karen Brown's Guides were high-quality travel guides for the affluent, discriminating traveler. They offered an intimate and personal account of selected inns and bed and breakfasts (B&Bs) in Western Europe and California (Exhibit 1). One-quarter of each guide was devoted to easy-to-follow itineraries for specific areas of each country that included historic sites and scenic driving routes (Exhibit 2). Each book also had general logistical information and instructions about how to book rooms. Several guides offered an overview of the country's history.

Karen's Guides had a unique personal touch. She had been called "a pioneer and still leader in this category of high-quality small inns and B&Bs"[1] and had a loyal following. Most of the people who purchased Karen's guides were experienced upscale travelers who had the time to plan every detail of their vacations. They were not

---

Research Associate Kasey Craig, MBA 2000, prepared this case under the supervision of Professor Garth Saloner and Professor A. Michael Spence as the basis for class discussion rather than to illustrate either effective or ineffective handling of an administrative situation. Margot Sutherland, Executive Director, Center for Electronic Business and Commerce, Stanford Graduate School of Business managed the development of this case.

[1] *Gourmet* magazine, as quoted on the back of Karen Brown's 1999 guides.

particularly price sensitive and found it valuable to carry her books with them on their trips. Most customers purchased Karen's Guides in a bookstore along with other books and sometimes a map. These additional books provided practical, "get-around-town" information that Karen's guides lacked. Her customers used her books to plan which parts of a country they might visit and where to stay. While some of Karen's existing and potential customers might have used the Web to find information, they were unlikely to use the Web as a replacement for her books.

KAREN BROWN'S BACKGROUND

Karen grew up in the San Francisco Bay area. Her mother, Clare, ran a travel agency and recognized a need for a guide to inns and countryside routes in Europe and she suggested that Karen write one. Karen agreed and thought that writing a travel book would be a great way to spend some time in France. When a small publishing company reneged on a deal to publish her book, Karen secured a loan by promising to sell her books door to door and published it herself. In 1977, she printed 10,000 copies of her French travel guide and shipped them from her college dorm room. She shipped 200 copies to top editors to review her book. When a professor learned that Karen had been able to sell all her books with little marketing, he convinced her to expand her coverage and increase the number of titles. Karen published her second book, on Great Britain, in 1980, and her third, on Switzerland, which her mother helped her research, in 1984. Another researcher, June, joined the team in 1985. One of the three covered each country and visited all the inns in it every year for up-to-date, annual editions. By 1999, they were covering 10 countries and California with 13 titles.

NEW CHALLENGES

In 1998, Karen sold over 135,000 books, which generated over $1 million in revenue and $300,000 in net income. Most books sold for $18.95 retail, on which Karen made a profit of $2.82 (Exhibit 3). Until 1994, Karen's book sales had increased at about 10% per year. From that point on, however, sales showed only minimal growth. Karen felt pressure to expand but did not know in which direction to grow. Adding more countries and states within the United States would require human resources that she lacked. Partnering with another reviewer of B&Bs would require putting her name on material with which she was not personally familiar.

Karen struggled with the tradeoff between going to the mass market with licensing and distribution deals and protecting the authenticity and integrity of Karen Brown's Guides in which she took pride. She had spent over 20 years building a reputation and was reluctant to relinquish control of her content and publishing. She rejected offers to license her content and name or to purchase Karen Brown publications. Karen acknowledged that to grow her business, she might need to give up some control, but she wanted to remain a critical part of any change in her business over the next few years. She had done little mass marketing and relied largely on word-of-mouth advertising from her loyal customers. She considered ways to increase her name recognition: allowing inn guides to use her name ("Recommended by Karen Brown"), creating a television series, and increasing her presence on the Internet. A television pilot series was being considered, an option that had great appeal to Karen.

To complicate the options, channels for book sales were shifting in the late 1990s. Small mom-and-pop stores had been Karen's bread and butter for years, hand-selling and personally recommending the Karen Brown's Guides. The advent of superstores like Barnes & Noble and Amazon.com gave rise to new marketing challenges. Salespeople at the larger stores were less familiar with Karen's books and rarely noticed when the store ran out of a title. To expand distribution, Karen had negotiated a five-year distribution deal with Random House Publishing because it had greater leverage with the chains. Random House agreed to distribute her books and pay her 62% of wholesale sales.

Over the course of the previous year, Karen had built a Web site at http://www.karenbrown.com, where she offered visitors a taste of what they could find in her books. Users could go into a specific country guide to find a listing and brief description of accommodations and a sample itinerary. To avoid alienating smaller stores, Karen encouraged her site visitors to visit their local bookstore instead of buying books directly through her (a more profitable alternative). She was still uncertain how to market the site and how much free content to give away to the consumer. She listed about one-quarter of the information that could be found in her books, but did not provide the unique full country itineraries. Karen worried that offering all her content on the Web would discourage book sales.

TRENDS IN TRADITIONAL MEDIA PUBLISHING

How to use the Web also challenged traditional publishers of magazines and newspapers. Publishers had to decide whether to charge for their content or give it away. With nearly half of online consumers saying that they would not pay for content, the revenue prospects for online publications were slim.[2] While some publishers had developed a model to make money from their online business, most were seeing no return from their sites.

The proliferation of free content on the Web fueled consumer perception that online content should be available for free. In 1999, over 90% of the most trafficked sites did not charge for content.[3] The *New York Times* had initially toyed with charging international users; in 1998, however, it decided that "leveraging registration data for targeted advertising by global companies—while growing the overall base—was a more profitable course of action."[4] Rather than requiring payment, the *New York Times* required users to register to have access to its Web content. Requiring payment had a much more negative impact on traffic than registration. Moreover, because most on-demand content and monthly subscription fees were likely to be under five dollars, publishers were further discouraged from charging for content. Credit card transactions in this range were usually a net loss for merchants.

The sites that were successful in charging for content provided highly differentiated content and offered users greater functionality online than through print media

[2] Sinnreich, "Paid Content: Maximizing Limited Opportunity with Net Value," Jupiter Communications, August 1999.

[3] *ibid.*

[4] *ibid.*

via such features as access to past publications; interaction with writers, editors, and other readers; greater search capabilities; and increased customization. *Consumer Reports* was one of the few traditional publishers that had created a successful online model. As the strongest brand in the consumer product testing space, *Consumer Reports*' unique content attracted customers. It boasted a subscriber base of 310,000 in August 1999 and claimed to attract nearly 1,000 new subscribers per day.[5] Consumers who paid a monthly subscription fee had access to the *Consumer Reports* buying guides, both current and past.

While few publishers operated profitable Web sites, most continued to investigate how to use the Web for fear of losing their core business to other publishers. Because of the significant constraints to charging for content online, most publishers decided to give most of their content away, even though they feared that this would adversely affect sales of print publications. However, Forrester Research found that while some people canceled their print subscriptions because the same publication was available online, the Internet was more likely to drive consumers to purchase print versions rather than to replace them.[6] People could not pick up and take online versions of magazines and newspapers with them elsewhere. However in the future, as people became more comfortable with using the Web as their primary source of information, free, up-to-date online content might wean readers from print publications.

TRENDS IN TRADITIONAL BOOK PUBLISHING

Shifts in technology were forcing traditional book publishers to change both the way they distributed content and their relationships to authors. Despite the proliferation of and attention given to online book retailers and the growth of book clubs, book sales were expected to grow only slightly over the next five years.[7] New technologies were causing the book market to become increasingly fragmented.

In the late 1990s, book sales over the Web exploded. Online bookselling was the fastest growing channel of distribution for books as the growth of superstores fell to the low single digits. Amazon.com was the leading online retailer, with sales of $610 million in 1998, and was growing rapidly. Other traditional superstores were growing their online business, but Barnesandnoble.com's book sales were still only one-tenth that of Amazon's. Some studies suggested that Internet book sales would grow to over 25% of total sales by 2005.[8] Buying books online was easy and convenient, especially when consumers knew what topic they were interested in. Online bookselling also reached a new set of customers. Traditional bookstores hoped to draw customers who wanted to browse and enjoy the social aspect of book buying. Industry experts debated whether, over time, the Internet would attract new book buyers or cannibalize sales from other channels.

[5] *ibid.*

[6] Shepard, et al., "Do Wired Readers Abandon Print?" *The Forrester Brief*, December 4, 1998.

[7] Shatzkin, Mike, *Publishers Weekly*, May 24, 1999.

[8] *ibid.*

ELECTRONIC BOOK PUBLISHING

Traditionally, the relationships among authors, editors, and publishers drove the book publishing business. However, the advent of affordable technologies, such as the e-book (a handheld hardware device to which book content could be instantly downloaded from the Internet) and print-on-demand technology, could change publishers' core business processes. While these new technologies had not yet had a major impact on the industry, they raised questions about the future role of the publisher.

The Internet allowed publishers to focus on their core competencies—creating content and marketing—and take advantage of emerging technologies in printing and distribution. Because word-of-mouth and recommendations influenced consumers' purchases, the Internet was forcing publishing houses to develop a clear brand identity to become known as the destination for information and recommendations for certain genres of books. The Internet also created new marketing techniques to generate excitement. Some publishers, such as Harvard Business School Press, provided electronic promotion kits that included the table of contents, the book cover, and interviews with the author. Publishers of fiction often e-mailed chapters of an upcoming book to readers to generate interest. They also set up online chats with authors, created links to authors' Web sites, and utilized direct marketing to newsgroups formed around a particular subject.

Because the Internet enabled publishers to forgo bricks-and-mortar retail outlets, they could conceivably bypass the middleman and sell direct to consumers. Publishers were undecided about how much they wanted to engage in e-commerce. Simon & Schuster and Random House had terminated their e-commerce businesses, while e-commerce was a key part of Time, Inc.'s strategy.[9] Large publishing houses would also have to contend with the democratization of publishing—the Internet enabled small, niche publishers to place their product on equal footing with the largest houses.

How publishers would price and maintain copyright integrity while partnering with outside parties to utilize new technologies and deliver content remained uncertain. The industry had not settled on a standard for protecting authors' royalty payments or whether content arrangements would be published under licensing or distribution agreements. Nor had a pricing structure between the publisher and the outside technology provider been agreed on. One other outstanding question pertained to the ultimate price to the consumer of content purchased through these new technologies. The new technologies decreased publishers' overhead, inventory, and distribution costs; what portion of these savings would publishers pass on to consumers?

TRAVEL PUBLISHERS AND THE WEB

Although most traditional publishers were planning to charge for their content over the Web, travel publishers were giving much of their content away because they viewed the Web as a way to promote sales of their books. All major content providers were investigating their online options: from selling books on their site, to partnering with large travel agencies, to licensing content to a wide range of partners. Rough Guides

[9] Zeitchik, Steven, *Publishers Weekly*, January 4, 1999.

and Moon Travel Guidebooks enjoyed success from placing their content on the Web. Rough Guides' sales jumped from 825,000 to 1.5 million books over two years, and Moon's *Road Trip USA* become its best selling title after a Web roll-out of the content.

Moon Travel Guidebooks

Moon Travel Guidebooks, of Chico, California, was preparing to launch a cobranded Web service with a major travel company that would combine all of Moon's content with their partner's online ticketing and hotel/tour booking capability. Moon would have its content prominently displayed and receive a percentage of the revenue from trips booked through the site.

Moon was not concerned about placing its books online; in the new Web site, each Moon guidebook would be saved in multiple smaller files that the database architecture could call up. Moon believed it would be so hard and time consuming for users to download and print out an entire book that they would continue to buy the real thing. This approach had worked with *Road Trip USA*, which had been posted in segments as it was being written. Overall, traffic on Moon's site had more than doubled during the previous year. As a result, Moon was willing to license its content to travel sites or related services. Typically, Moon did not charge its partners for use of the content, nor did partners ever pay to place Moon's content on another site. However, Moon retained ownership of its content, including any formatting or technical changes that the partner made to it.

The Lonely Planet

The Lonely Planet, perhaps the best-known, low-budget travel guidebooks, had an extensive Web presence and licensed its content to both Yahoo! and Travelocity. For each of the Lonely Planet's books, a Web companion included snippets from the original text. However, none of the online Lonely Planet guides included the all-important reviews and contact information for hotels, hostels, and restaurants. In essence, the online content was a marketing device, and at the bottom of every page was a link to the Lonely Planet online store, where users could order every guidebook with the click of the mouse. The Lonely Planet Web site also offered excerpts from travelogues and stories, and extensive photo libraries. It aimed to create a sense of community through chat forums. Lonely Planet devoted parts of its site to health issues and breaking news from around the world to increase the site's stickiness.

Fodor's

In mid-1999, Fodor's had the most extensive travel Web site. Beyond providing summaries of its travel guides, Fodor's online strived to be a one-stop shop for travelers' every need. A resource center on the site dispensed advice on everything from first aid to language issues; a forum allowed travelers to post observations and solicit advice from other travelers. Like most other travel publishers, Fodor's did not post all of its content on its site. However, a searchable database of its content, called miniguides, surpassed those of its rivals and allowed visitors to custom-tailor concise guides to 110 locations worldwide—guides that included hotel and restaurant information. Like other publishers, Fodor's also did not sell books on its site, referring visitors first to local and then to online retailers. Preview Travel served as the booking engine on the Fodor's site, promoted Fodor's heavily on its own site, and used the Fodor's miniguides for most of its destination content. Fodor's reach also extended beyond Preview's. Some of Preview's partners not only used Preview as the booking engine but also carried the same Fodor's content. Fodor's name was prominently displayed on all its content wherever it appeared.

THE GROWTH OF ONLINE TRAVEL

According to Forrester Research, consumers were adapting to online travel faster than to any other online retail sector.[10] Online airline and hotel bookings were expected to grow 57% annually over the next five years. While only 0.5%–3.0% of travel was currently booked online, that number was expected to grow to total approximately 10%–12% of airline and hotel bookings by 2003. Bookings were the revenue-generating aspect of travel on the Web, but these numbers did not even begin to take into account the millions of users who used the Web for information and then booked over the phone. Most major airline and hotel companies allowed consumers to book reservations online. Even smaller properties were getting online.

The travel aggregators, namely, Travelocity, Expedia, and Preview Travel, received the most traffic and booked the most reservations online.[11] These sites offered consumers similar services but different information. The online travel industry understood that improved content was the best way to increase both the percentage of bookings and user loyalty. Content helped the site satisfy consumers' travel needs and made them more comfortable making a purchase.

Travel sites looked to many sources to provide quality content. Often, the editorial staff would write part of the content and license the rest from other providers. Many sites offered cobranded content on their own site and also passed people on to other sites through links. Whereas earlier, a travel site might have paid a content provider, now a content provider had to pay the travel site to display its content and thus gain the content provider access to millions of potential customers. This was especially true when a travel site offered a link to another Web site.

Recognizing that travel was a growing source of revenue on the Internet, the major portals developed relationships with the travel aggregators. While some portals merely passed the consumer through to the travel Web site, others used only the booking engine and provided their own travel content. Portals considered travel as a high priority because they were constantly looking to attract new customers.

For online information on inns and B&Bs, many sites gave consumers a list of linked sites. The most frequently, and often most prominently, listed link for small hotels and

[10] McQuivey et. al., "Leisure Travel's Booking Boom," *The Forrester Report*, September 1998.

[11] In October 1999, Travelocity announced plans to acquire Preview Travel, but the deal had not been completed when this case was written.

inns was the B&B Channel (http://www.bedandbreakfast.com), which allowed users to find information and book reservations with B&Bs around the world. The B&B Channel was the most direct potential competitor to Karen Brown. It was part of Inns and Outs, a company that provided information on more than 20,000 B&Bs and inns; however, its information outside the United States was limited. Of all the Web sites that provided information on inns and B&Bs, the B&B Channel had the largest presence on the Web and had agreements with Travelocity, Expedia, AOL, Yahoo!, and others. However, the B&B Channel was often hard to find and was only one of many links listed.

DECISION TIME

Karen Brown thought hard about where she wanted her business to be in five years. She had researched how the Web was affecting traditional publishers and how travel publishers were using it. She recognized that she might be left behind as more people migrated to the Web and as travel-related sites established relationships with content providers.

To grow her business without increasing her resources, she had to attract new buyers to her existing books and increase profits. Because Karen's profit margin on a book sold directly was six times that of her margin on a book sold through a store, she was determined to sell more books directly through her Web site. But to sell more books on her site and overall, Karen had to find a way to attract new customers. She concluded that the Web was an effective tool to market herself and build brand recognition.

Karen decided to make several changes to improve her existing site and to become part of the Yahoo! shopping network. By paying Yahoo! $300 per month, Karen could sell her books and itineraries on her site without having to invest in the infrastructure to support e-commerce transactions. Essentially, when a Karen Brown user decided to buy a book on her site, that user was sent into a portion of Yahoo! Shopping that Karen could customize to look like the Karen Brown site. Yahoo! performed the back-end functions, processed the transaction, and e-mailed the shipment information to Karen. Because Yahoo! sent users looking for "inns," "itineraries," and Michelin maps to Karen Brown's Yahoo! store, more users were sent to Karen's site through Yahoo! than through any other site. As a complement to her books, Karen partnered with Michelin to sell maps on her site. She considered packaging Michelin maps with her books as a supplement to the books' artistic renderings of driving routes.

Other improvements on the Web site included hotel news, tips of the day, property of the month, postcards from the road, and romantic inns and recipes. To create a community on her site, Karen set up a "reader's forum" to allow readers to share experiences from Karen Brown accommodations. She also provided links to AutoEurope and other travel services.

Karen believed that the Internet would attract new customers to her books. She thought that licensing her content to a high-traffic, travel-related site could expose millions of people to her books and name. Karen's unique content would fill a niche that no other player served at the time. She might be able to persuade a major site to cobrand her content. Building interesting travel content was a priority for both travel sites and portals. Initially, Karen believed that she would need to license all of her content to the partnering company to make her content appealing. While she hesitated to give it *all* away, she felt that licensing the whole package might be the only way that a partner would find her content unique and useful. She thought that expanding her presence on the Web might increase her brand recognition and sell enough new books to outweigh any cannibalization of existing book sales.

FINDING A PARTNER

Karen decided to target high-volume travel-related sites. She did some research and spent some time on the Web before deciding to contact Expedia, Travelocity, Preview Travel, Yahoo! Travel, Excite Travel, and AOL. She contacted everyone she knew in order to find a personal contact within these companies. When she didn't have a contact name, she worked her way through the company until she found someone who knew something about travel-related content. She never heard back from some people. She called others several times before she got any kind of response. She sent copies of her books along with some company information to people who expressed interest. One portal ultimately decided that while travel was an important part of their business, they just weren't ready to start building up that part of their site. Another portal's initial excitement fizzled after a few weeks. One travel site expressed interest in having Karen write a few feature articles but was not interested in acquiring all of her content. Finally, Karen struck gold when one of the major online travel sites, which we shall call "MOTS" to maintain anonymity, expressed sincere interest in placing the Karen Brown content on its site. Karen had some initial conversations with a MOTS representative in business development. She explained her reasons for wanting to license her content and convinced the site that her unique content filled a niche that no other player currently served. They threw out a few ideas for how the licensing agreement might be structured, but nothing was put in writing.

With over eight million registered members and more than three million unique visitors in August 1999, MOTS could expose Karen's content to millions of potential travelers. Moreover, MOTS's users were similar to Karen's existing book buyers—affluent, mostly female, leisure travelers. The site also had strong relationships with major portals that used MOTS's booking engine and content. In looking to create a more complete experience for users, MOTS believed that Karen's content provided a unique editorial voice and covered properties that previously were not listed anywhere on the site.

As Karen got closer to a deal with MOTS, she was forced to decide what was essential and what she could be flexible on. Karen had to consider the following questions:

- How much control over her content was she willing to give up?
- How long a contract was she willing to sign?
- What presence on the travel site would make giving up her content worthwhile?
- How much content was she willing to give away for free?

- Should she set up a link to her own site or license her content to the travel site?
- Should she expect to generate revenue from the arrangement?
- How much would she pay to expose her content to millions of people on the Web?
- What alternatives did she have?

THE PROPOSAL

After having several conversations with Karen, MOTS presented her with a proposal (Exhibit 4). Unfortunately, it wasn't exactly what Karen had in mind. She thought that she might be able to change some of the terms but wasn't sure how to prioritize the various issues.

EXHIBIT 1 Example Hotel Description

MALLORCA–Deia LA RESIDENCIA Map: 7a

La Residencia, perched high in the hills with views to the sea yet just steps from the quaint village of Deia, is a faultless hideaway. This gem of a hotel, nestled in 34 acres, is imaginatively created from two 17th-century farmhouses built of the golden-tan stone of the region. In keeping with its past, the decor is elegantly simple with white walls accented by beautiful antiques and bouquets of fresh flowers. Even the reception is exceptional. Check-in is handled quietly and without fuss at an antique desk. Nearby are intimate lounges and bars where guests can sit quietly with friends as if in a private home. However, most guests "live" outdoors—the hotel has its own private club by the sea, serviced by a shuttle bus. For those who don't want to leave the property, the manicured gardens offer an exquisite retreat, with secluded shady nooks where guests can relax with only the fragrance of flowers and the song of birds for company. The hotel is built on a hillside with two swimming pools tucked onto terraces. Adjacent to the lower pool is a bar where guests can order lunch or have dinner if they want to dine casually. For those who want to dine elegantly, in the room where the olives were pressed, there is a gourmet restaurant, El Olivo, which holds a Michelin star for excellence. The bedrooms are all fabulously furnished. The suites are stunning, but even the standard doubles (such as number 9, overlooking the garden) are outstanding.

LA RESIDENCIA
07179 Deia, Mallorca
Balearic Islands, Spain
Tel: (971) 63.90.11, Fax: (971) 63.93.70
www.karenbrown.com/spaininns/laresidencia.html
*65 rooms, Double: Pts 36,100–47,400**
**IVA not included, breakfast included*
Open all year, Credit cards: all major
Restaurant open daily, pools
27 km N of Palma de Mallorca
Michelin Map 443, Region: Balearic Islands

Source: *Karen Brown's SPAIN: Charming Inns & Itineraries* (1999). Reproduced with permission.

EXHIBIT 2 Example Partial Itinerary

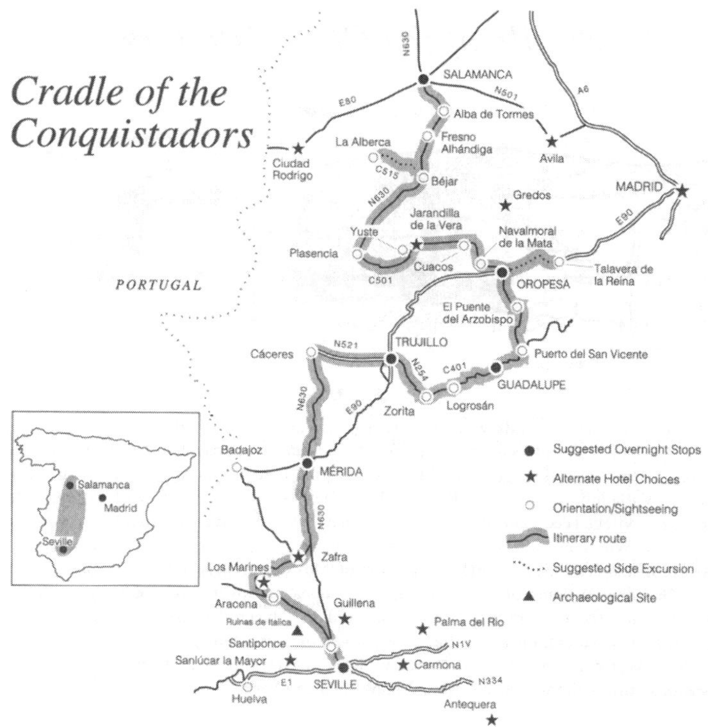

Cradle of the Conquistadors

Guadalupe

Most of this itinerary finds you in Extremadura—an area of Spain less frequented by tourists, which is part of its appeal. The name *Extremadura* originated during the Reconquest period and translates as "land beyond the river Duero" (which runs across the country from Soria to Valladolid to Zamora). Historically somewhat at the periphery of national life,

(continued)

Source: *Karen Brown's SPAIN: Charming Inns & Itineraries* (1999). Reproduced with permission.

EXHIBIT 2 *(continued)*

and less privileged economically, the area was rich in young men eager to seek their fortunes in the New World, as the name of this itinerary suggests. Some famous Extremadurans you may recognize are Hernán Cortés, conqueror of Mexico; Francisco Pizarro, conqueror of Peru; Orellano, explorer of the Amazon; and Balboa, discoverer of the Pacific Ocean. Indeed, since the explorations were sponsored by Queen Isabella of Castile, which included Extremadura, only Castilians were given the opportunity to make the journey to the New World during the 16th century. The area is still resplendent with fine old mansions built with the treasures found in Mexico and Peru.

Typical cuisine of Extremadura includes one of our favorite Spanish specialties: raw-cured ham (*jamón serrano*), as well as lamb stew (*caldereta de cordero*), fried breadcrumbs with bacon (*migas*), and numerous game dishes such as pheasant (*faisán*) and partridge (*perdiz*). The major local wine is a simple white called Almendralejo.

The last destination brings you into Old Castile and the enchanting medieval university city of Salamanca.

ORIGINATING CITY SEVILLE

It is never easy to leave Seville, Spain's most romantic city, but, if you fall under its spell, you will be back. However, Spain offers many additional enchantments and much more of it remains to be seen, so set your sights north. Note: for more in-depth suggestions on sightseeing in Seville, see our chapter titled *Seville Highlights*, pages 157–162.

DESTINATION I MÉRIDA

Leave Seville heading west across the bridge and turn north toward Mérida. After about 24 kilometers look for N433 which takes you northwest to the little hill town of Aracena, a popular escape from the heat of the Andalusian summer. The **Sierra de Aracena**, the western part of the Sierra Morena, is known for copper and pyrite production, as well as the justifiably famous and delicious *jamón serrano*, which must be sampled—especially if you are a prosciutto-lover. It is a ubiquitous and favorite *tapa* throughout the country, and you will have more than likely seen the hams hanging from the ceiling of many a Spanish bar. (Enjoy it while you are here, but do not try to take any home with you, as you will not be allowed through US customs with it.)

About halfway between Seville and Aracena is the dazzling white town of **Castillo de las Guardas** nestled against a green mountainside. As the drive approaches the pretty town of **Aracena**, the air gets cooler, the earth redder, and the hills are covered with cork trees. Aracena is tiered up a hillside, dramatically crowned with the 13th-century church of the Knights Templar and the 12th-century ruins of a Moorish fort with a beautiful brick mosque tower. Directly beneath the castle, within the hill itself, is the **Gruta de las Maravillas** (Cave of Marvels), hollowed out by underground rivers and an amazing sight to behold. Limpid pools and rivers and an underground lake reflect magnificent and multicolored stalactites and stalagmites. The guided visit takes about 45 minutes, but you may have to wait for a group to form for the tour: if so, wile away the time in the quaint shops around the entrance to the cave that offer a surprisingly good-quality selection of regional ceramic ware.

Continue west on N433 for 16 kilometers and turn right on N435 to **Zafra**. Zafra preserves one of the most impressive fortified palaces in the region, now the **Parador de Safra** (see the hotel listing), on one of the prettiest little plazas in the area. Actually the former palace of the Duke of Feria, it was the residence of Hernán Cortés just before he embarked for the New World. Its conversion to a parador has not spoiled it in the least,

(continued)

Source: *Karen Brown's SPAIN: Charming Inns & Itineraries* (1999). Reproduced with permission.

EXHIBIT 2 *(continued)*

and it's worth a short visit to see the fabulous chapel and the other faithfully restored public rooms. Leave Zafra on N435 and you have quite a fast drive to today's destination—**Mérida**, caretaker of the richest Roman remains in Spain.

You find Roman antiquities among those decorating your next hotel suggestion, the **Parador Vía de La Plata**, elegantly installed in an old convent that was built on the site of a Roman temple at the top of town. It has also seen duty as a hospital for the plague victims of 1729, and briefly as a jail. The combination of authentic Roman, Arabic, and Spanish architectural features (most discovered on the site) within the hotel make it unique, indeed, and interesting to explore. The parador fronts onto a plaza where it is practically impossible to park, but you will gratefully discover that the hotel has provided parking in back, next to its pretty Mudéjar gardens, as well as an underground parking garage.

Parador Vía de La Plata, Mérida

Founded in 25 B.C., the Roman town of Emerita Augusta, now Mérida, was so well situated at the junction of major Roman roads that it was soon made the capital of Lusitania. Outstanding Roman remains dot the city: bridges, temples, a racecourse, two aqueducts, an arena, and a theater—all attesting to Mérida's historical importance under Roman occupation. If your time is limited, you must not miss the **Roman Arena** (built in the 1st century B.C. with a seating capacity of 14,000) and next to it, the **Roman Theater** (built by Agrippa in the 1st century B.C. with a seating capacity of over 5,000). The astounding theater alone, with its double-columned stage, is worth a detour to Mérida. (If you are here in late June or early July, check at the hotel to see if the Classical Theater Festival is offering live performances.) Just across the road from the arena and theater is a stunning modern museum that you must not miss, **Museo Nacional de Arte Romano**. In this spectacular brick-vaulted, sky-lit building many Roman artifacts and panels of mosaics are displayed. Be sure to also see the **Casa Romana del Anfiteatro** (1st century A.D. with mosaics and water pipes) and the **Alcazaba** at the city end of the Roman bridge (built by the Moors in the 9th century). If your time and archaeological knowledge are limited, you might want to arrange for a guide who can take you to all the interesting places more efficiently than you can do it on your own. Inquire at your hotel, the Teatro Romano, or the tourist office for information. A few blocks southeast of the parador, you find the **Plaza de España**, Mérida's main center of

(continued)

Source: *Karen Brown's SPAIN: Charming Inns & Itineraries* (1999). Reproduced with permission.

EXHIBIT 2 *(continued)*

activity. It is a wonderful place to sit with a drink at one of the outdoor cafés and watch the world go by.

Mérida, Roman Theater

EXHIBIT 3 Breakdown of Karen Brown's Costs

	Bookstore sales	*Direct sales*
Retail price to consumer	$18.95	$18.95
Wholesale cost to bookstore[1]	9.48	—
Fee to Random House[2]	2.65	—
Research costs	2.50	2.50
Printing costs	1.50	1.50
Other[3]		1.50
Profit per book	2.82	13.45

[1] On average, distributor sells book to retailer for 50% of retail price.
[2] Karen pays Random House 28% of the wholesale cost to bookstores.
[3] Includes costs of picking and packing.
Source: Karen Brown's Guides.

EXHIBIT 4 Proposal from Major Online Travel Site (MOTS) to License Karen Brown Content

Karen Brown will grant MOTS a perpetual worldwide fully paid license to the Karen Brown books published in the next three years. In addition, MOTS will have the right to renew the agreement on the same terms for an additional three years. MOTS will place all or part of the Karen Brown content (at its discretion) on the MOTS Web site (and/or its distribution partners' Web sites). In addition, MOTS may, at its discretion:

(i) intersperse Karen Brown content with other MOTS and/or third-party content (so long as Karen Brown gets proper attribution for its content);

(ii) translate all or part of the content into foreign languages and place it on MOTS affiliated Web sites;

(iii) e-mail portions of such content to its users and/or enable its users to create printed miniguides;

(iv) correct any mistakes in the Karen Brown content, abridge any part of the Karen Brown content so long as the overall tone is maintained, and (with Karen Brown's consent which will not be unreasonably withheld) otherwise alter the Karen Brown content.

MOTS will give proper attribution to the Karen Brown content (i.e., identify it as having been written by Karen Brown).

This license will be exclusive except that:

(i) Karen Brown may license the content to one general-purpose portal Web site, but only if the Web pages on which Karen Brown content appears: (a) encourage readers to book their travel through MOTS and prominently link to MOTS's various services (subject to MOTS's approval), and (b) such Web pages do not promote or advertise any other travel booking service and do not have any other travel-booking-related links, and

(ii) Karen Brown may develop its own Web site so long as MOTS is the exclusive travel booking service promoted, advertised, or linked to from the Karen Brown Web site.

Neither party shall pay the other party under this agreement. Each party will keep all revenues from sales of advertising on the Web pages it serves. Karen Brown represents that the establishments listed in the Karen Brown books do not and will not pay compensation to Karen Brown. Karen Brown represents (and will indemnify MOTS) that the Karen Brown content and this agreement do not infringe or violate any rights of any other party.

Starting with the year 2000 books, Karen Brown will print on the front cover of each book the MOTS URL (and if applicable, the MOTS AOL keyword) where the

(continued)

EXHIBIT 4 *(continued)*

Karen Brown content can be found online. In addition, Karen Brown will use the inside front cover of each book to promote MOTS as its recommended site for online travel planning and booking (details to be discussed). Karen Brown will also describe and recommend MOTS's services, Web site, and AOL keyword in the introductory passages of each book. Karen Brown will also include a MOTS color promotional page in each book [see the 1999 and 2000 Fodor's gold guides for an example of this]. Other online travel companies will not be mentioned in the Karen Brown books.

Within four months, Karen Brown will deliver its content to MOTS in a database format and structure to be determined by MOTS. Subsequent years' content will be similarly delivered at least two months prior to publication of the printed books. Karen Brown will also deliver to MOTS multiple copies of each book each year (for internal use and to be given away as special promotions).

Karen Brown will present and recommend MOTS's services in its television show (details to be discussed). MOTS will be granted a nonexclusive license to broadcast this show on the Internet.

The parties will issue a joint press release announcing their agreement.

MOTS would also like to discuss other ways of promoting the Karen Brown content on its site. Possibilities to be included on MOTS's Web site (and/or its distribution partners' Web sites) include:

(i) creating a Karen Brown question and answer column;

(ii) holding chat sessions with Karen Brown; and/or

(iii) including other Karen Brown editorial content such as a romantic travel column.

Source: Karen Brown's Guides.

BROKER.COM

The future of our industry will be based on open architecture with increased choice—all based on client empowerment. In fact, that is the model we are building at Merrill Lynch. And I think we will see aggregation and consolidation driven by the complementary forces of client empowerment, the Internet, and open architecture. In this period of aggregation, firms that deliver the right bundles of best-in-class products and services will be the big winners. —John "Launny" Steffens, vice chairman and executive vice president U.S. Private Client Group, Merrill Lynch, May 1999

Merrill Lynch's about-face was dramatic. Less than a year earlier, in July 1998, Steffens had reportedly espoused the opposite view: "The do-it-yourself model of investing, centered on Internet trading . . . is a serious threat to Americans' financial health." Over the course of the year, Merrill learned instead that investors' desires to make their own financial decisions online could become a threat to Merrill's future health.[1]

The sudden growth in the popularity of online trading explained Merrill's about-face. Between 1996 and 1999, online trading's share of U.S. individual investor trades grew from 8% to 48%, and in 1999, investors began to demand it from full-service brokers. Although popular with investors, the Internet challenged the established brokerages. Full-service brokers such as Merrill Lynch, Morgan Stanley Dean Witter, and PaineWebber had not developed their long-established business models and processes with online trading in mind. Pure online brokers such as Datek and E*Trade, however,

---

Haim Mendelson, Daricha Techopitayakul, and Philip Meza prepared this case under the supervision of Haim Mendelson as the basis for class discussion rather than to illustrate either effective or ineffective handling of an administrative situation. The development of this case was managed by Margot Sutherland, Executive Director, Center for Electronic Business and Commerce, Stanford Graduate School of Business. Send comments by e-mail to Haim Mendelson, haim@stanford.edu.

[1] Charles Gasparino and Rebecca Buckman, "Facing Internet Threat, Merrill to Offer Trading Online for Low Fees," *Wall Street Journal*, June 1, 1999.

had designed their entire business models around the Internet, and discount brokers like Schwab were accustomed to exploiting low-cost channels. Nevertheless, all brokers competed in a fast-changing environment, buffeted by technological and regulatory change, and all were working to incorporate the functionality of the Internet into their businesses.

IMPACT OF THE INTERNET ON THE BROKERAGE INDUSTRY

The speed at which the Internet transformed the brokerage industry surprised everyone. Since 1997, the number of trades executed on the Internet had grown at a compound annual rate of over 111%, accounting for about a sixth of the market by 1999 (Exhibit 1). The share of U.S. retail commission revenues garnered from online trading increased from 2.2% in 1996 to almost 10% by 1999, even though online trading commissions were far less than full-service commissions. Internet technology, based on open standards and scaleable computing power, had decreased both the fixed and variable costs of the brokerage business and lowered barriers to entry for the industry. New online brokerages, unhampered by the legacy systems of traditional firms, sprang up and offered fees that were less than one-tenth of those charged by full-service brokers.

Discount brokers, whose primary source of revenue was transaction services, keenly felt the impact of the new entrants. Discounters had come into being 20 years earlier on May 1, 1975, when the U.S. Securities and Exchange Commission deregulated brokerage commissions. May Day, as the industry called the watershed event, had enabled discounters to put price pressure on full-service firms in the 1970s, which caused a massive shake-out in the industry.[2] In the mid-1990s, the tables were turned against the discounters. Lombard and E*Trade, which began operations in 1992 and 1995 respectively, targeted the discount brokers' customer base of investors interested in fast, cheap trades. A price war resulted: E*Trade reduced its prices seven times between 1993 and 1996, before settling down at $14.95 per trade. From early 1996 through the end of 1997, the average commission charged by online brokers decreased by two-thirds from $53 to about $18.50 per trade.

Online brokers also used the Internet to bridge the gap between the value propositions of discount and full-service brokers. While full-service brokers had provided advice based on institutional research and analysis, and discount brokers had offered stock quotes and cheap trades, online brokers could now offer investors access to a wide range of information sources (including information from independent nonbrokerage firms), and investors could form their own investment strategies and trade at prices lower than even discounters could offer.

By mid-1999, when Merrill Lynch announced its low-cost online offering, Merrill Lynch Direct—priced at $29.95 per trade to match the commissions charged by

[2] After May Day, brokerage industry prices fell by 50% and industry profitability fell by 40%. Within a few months, more than 150 brokerages merged or closed shop. The price of seats on the New York Stock Exchange, which had sold in 1969 for $500,000, plummeted to $35,000, the lowest price since 1895. However, the brokerage industry adapted to the change, and by the end of 1999, the price of a New York Stock Exchange seat had rebounded to about $2 million.

online brokerage leader Charles Schwab—the brokerage industry had reached a crossroads. Industry players recognized the potential of the Internet and its profound effect on the customer-broker relationship. Merrill's new strategy challenged Schwab—and the entire brokerage industry—yet Merrill's stock dropped 10% on the news, largely because of the commission discounting pressure associated with online trading: Merrill Lynch Direct was estimated to cost $1 billion in lost equity commissions.[3] Merrill's stock price drop signaled that to fight the competition, traditional firms would need to implement full-scale changes in the way they conducted business. Indeed, by the end of 1999, full-service brokers implemented online offerings that were closer to those of the discount brokers than to their traditional full-service offerings (Exhibit 2).

BROKERAGE INDUSTRY DEVELOPMENTS: 1970–2000

Before May Day, the exchanges fixed brokerage commissions and investors traded through full-service brokerages, which bundled three basic services: information, investment selection, and trade execution (Exhibit 3). Brokerages provided clients with investment research, market news, and stock quotes. Brokerages also provided clients with research reports they compiled on companies and advice, including buy and sell recommendations and strategies for asset allocation. Finally, brokerages bought and sold shares for their clients through the stock exchanges or from their own inventory.[4] For this bundle of services, brokerages charged clients a hefty commission on each trade.

On May 1, 1975, brokerage commissions were deregulated. One result was the emergence of discount brokers, who charged a fraction of the commission full-service brokers charged for executing investors' orders to trade. For the reduced transaction price, clients forfeited tips and advice from a personal broker and used their own research and asset allocation strategies to trade. To drive down costs, discounters exploited technology. For example, many discount brokerages created call centers and took orders over the phone. By offering to provide services that individuals could not do for themselves—price quotes and trade execution—discounters began to unbundle the product offering of full-service brokers, a process that was expanded in the 1990s.

By the end of the 1990s, Internet-based players had unbundled the entire value chain of the brokerage industry. Investors could obtain investment research for 2–5 basis points (bp),[5] asset allocation advice for 1–10 bp, and quotes and trade execution for 2–5 bp. The cost of online players' services compared favorably to the 60–80 bp full-service brokerage firms charged for bundled services (Exhibit 4). The Internet's ability to drive down the costs of information collection and dissemination, combined with the service void discount brokerages left, allowed new firms to unbundle full-service offerings and put more pressure on the business model of traditional brokers. When investors compared the low price offerings of online brokers to full-service alternatives, it was clear that the full-service brokers had recovered from the shock of May

[3] Leah Nathans Spiro, "Merrill's E-Battle," *Business Week*, November 15, 1999.

[4] When a brokerage was also a market maker in a security, it typically sold shares of that security to clients from its own inventory or bought shares from its clients and placed them in its own inventory. The full-service brokerages also sold their customers proprietary products, such as mutual funds.

[5] A basis point is 1/100 of a percent (100 bp = 1%).

Day: full-service retail markups were again substantial, exceeding even the markup on restaurant wine. However, it was unclear how full-service brokerages would meet the challenges of online competition as it continued to gain momentum.

INVESTMENT GROWTH

In the 1990s, a new breed of customers, the baby-boomers, born between 1946 and 1964, were poised to receive the largest intergenerational wealth transfer in history. Conservative estimates projected that between 1990 and 2040, baby-boomers would receive \$5 trillion in bequests.[6] Serving the baby-boomers, who insisted on both high quality and low price, was a major challenge.

In addition to the boomers, the number of affluent investors was growing in the United States. In 1995, total liquid household assets amounted to \$11.9 trillion, of which households with at least \$500,000 in investable assets held about \$6.4 trillion. Total U.S. liquid household assets had grown to \$18.2 trillion by 1999, and households with at least \$500,000 in investable assets held more than \$12 trillion. These trends were expected to continue into the future, along with the asset growth of the baby-boom generation.

CHARACTERISTICS OF ONLINE AND OFFLINE INVESTORS

The growth in the online brokerage industry had come primarily from young, educated, and technology-savvy investors. The average age of online investors was 39, and an estimated 44% of them had completed more than four years of college. Offline investors averaged 52 years, and only 36% had completed more than four years of college. Seventy-eight percent of online investors used personal computers at work, in contrast to only 43% of investors who traded through traditional brokers.[7]

Almost a third of all online traders had six-figure salaries, and almost half had salaries in the \$50,000–\$100,000 range. Close to one-fifth of online traders held at least a half-million dollars in securities.[8] Online investors also tended to be price conscious and self-directed. Full-service brokers were surprised to learn that many affluent investors withdrew assets from their full-service brokers to invest online. A Merrill Lynch client from Austin, Texas with a 20-year relationship with the firm told Steffens in 1999 that he used a separate online account for his frequent trades—and that Merrill Lynch was one of the stocks he traded in that account.[9]

Forrester Research classified investors (Exhibit 5) based on their inclination to trade ("active" vs. "buy and hold") and wealth ("affluent" vs. "moderate wealth") and analyzed their demographic and trading characteristics (Exhibit 6). Early adopters, mostly from the "active" category, spurred the early growth of online brokerages. To continue

[6] "The Newly Wealthy," *The VIP Forum*, July 2, 1999.

[7] Forrester Research and Salomon Smith Barney, as cited in *The Online Brokers*, Salomon Smith Barney Equity Research, October 25, 1999.

[8] Forrester Research, as cited in "In the Mirror. Who's Trading OnLine," *Wall Street Journal*, September 8, 1998.

[9] Charles Gasparino and Rebecca Buckman, "Facing Internet Threat, Merrill to Offer Trading Online for Low Fees," *Wall Street Journal*, June 1, 1999.

to grow, brokerage firms had to appeal to mainstream investors, who accounted for 87% of investing households in the United States.

Besides offering the right services to mainstream investors, brokerages also had to offer the right price structures to attract customers. Different types of investors varied in their price sensitivities and investment styles. *Self-directed* investors (about 15% of investors) wanted to make their own decisions and opted for low-cost, do-it-yourself providers. *Opinion-seeking* investors (about half of all investors) made their own decisions but sought some information and advice; these investors preferred bundled execution and advice. *Fully-dependent* investors (about a third of investors) preferred relationship-oriented providers, who would become their financial guardians. Self-directed investors tended to be the most price sensitive. Even among high net worth individuals, 64% of self-directed investors were "extremely/very" price sensitive, compared to 44% for opinion-seeking, and 25% for fully-dependent investors.[10]

In 1999, Wall Street began to offer investors a range of ways to trade online along with varying degrees of contact and involvement with an actual broker, instead of only offering one or the other. Wall Street proceeded with trepidation, however. Analysts estimated that online trading could take an initial 20%–50% off the average broker's compensation.

BROKERS AND ADVICE

Traditionally, investment advice was offered by commission-based brokers, the bread-and-butter of full-service brokerages, or by Registered Investment Advisors (RIAs). Unlike commission-based brokers, RIAs charged an hourly fee or a fee based on assets under management. The Internet changed the dynamics of the industry, providing a novel delivery mechanism for information and investment advice and facilitating low-cost transactions—and altering the context in which commission-based brokers and RIAs offered their services.

Commission-based Brokers

Brokers were a powerful force in all full-service brokerage firms: they induced customers to trade and thus pay commissions. Brokers promoted their firms' proprietary—and profitable—products and received a large fraction of the proceeds as compensation. Top producers were highly sought after because they brought their firm substantial commission and fee revenues and gathered millions of dollars in assets. In 1999, the average broker earned $175,000, making brokers one of the most highly paid professions in the United States[11] (Exhibit 7).

In the late 1990s, as full-service brokerages grappled with the challenges and opportunities the Internet created, they had to rethink the role of brokers. Broker compensation was a particularly sensitive issue. In 1995, the Securities and Exchange Commission

[10] *VIP Forum* Buyer Value Study.

[11] These numbers are averages for NYSE member firms, and were taken from the Securities Industry Association.

recommended that securities firms change how they paid brokers to lessen the conflict of interest between brokers, who were motivated to move the firm's proprietary products, and customers, who wanted their money invested in the best product on the market. A blue-ribbon panel called the Tully Commission urged brokerages to spurn upfront signing bonuses, sales contests, and incentives to push proprietary products, such as in-house mutual funds. The commission, chaired by Daniel Tully, then Merrill Lynch's CEO, warned that these practices could pose conflicts and harm investors. The industry agreed to follow the commission's recommendations, but progress was slow.

In 1986, Merrill Lynch introduced a compensation system that rewarded its brokers for accumulating customer assets, opening margin accounts, and making larger trades, while cutting compensation when brokers made small trades or offered customers commission discounts. In the 1990s, full-service brokerages continued to shift their broker compensation structures from a pure commission base to a mixed model (Exhibit 8). Yet, most traditional brokerages had not settled on alternative business models, and compensation structures changed slowly.

Later in the decade, overcapacity began to surface in the industry. In 1999, retail brokerage executives estimated that 25% of brokers were redundant, and analysts believed that technology would replace labor in the industry's cost structure at an accelerating rate. Yet, the long-running bull market had raised broker compensation to an all time high (Exhibit 7).

Registered Investment Advisors

RIAs had been around since the Registered Investment Advisors Act of 1940. However, independent financial advisory services only became significant in the late 1990s. In 1992, the entire RIA industry had only $120 billion under management, compared to $151 billion of assets under professional management at Merrill Lynch alone.[12] By September 1999, RIAs managed more than $700 billion in assets—a compound annual growth rate of about 25%.[13]

Unlike commission-based brokers, RIAs charged an hourly fee or a fee based on assets under management. They did not work for, nor were affiliated with, any brokerage institution or organization selling investment products. They ran their own firms (sole proprietorships to multipartner firms) and prided themselves on their objectivity. Fee-only planning removed commission-based incentives and aligned the goals of the planner and the client to maintain or grow total assets. Most RIAs charged an annual fee of 100–200 bp on the size of the portfolio they managed. RIAs benefited from investor concerns about the conflicts of interest between brokers and investors under the commission-based model that dominated the brokerage industry.

[12] In the same year, Merrill Lynch had $463 billion in U.S. private client assets.

[13] "The Future of the Financial Advisory Business and the Delivery of Advice to the Semi-Advisor," *Undiscovered Managers*, September 1999.

THE INTERNET

By the late 1990s, the tidal wave of online trading had transformed the brokerage industry, challenging both discount and full-service brokerages. A variety of Internet-based services emerged to fill the information voids left between the discount and full-service offerings. Pure online brokers, as well as discount broker Charles Schwab, were already a long way down the learning curve on the use of technology to meet their customers' needs. Full-service brokers Merrill Lynch, Morgan Stanley Dean Witter, and PaineWebber had to decide how to respond to the threats and opportunities the Internet presented. The following synopses describe these brokerages' journeys into cyberspace. Exhibit 2 compares their online capabilities as of year-end 1999.

The Discounter Charles Schwab & Company

Charles Schwab, a Stanford M.B.A., founded Charles Schwab & Company in 1971 in California. The company quickly established itself as an innovator. A defining moment came with the 1975 May Day, when Schwab took advantage of the new opportunities deregulation offered. Schwab would not provide advice on which securities to buy and when to sell as the full-service brokerage firms did. Instead, it gave self-directed investors low-cost access to securities transactions.

From the late 1980s to the early 1990s, before the commercial use of the Internet, Schwab used technology to increase efficiency and quality and expand its services. Schwab's innovations harnessed technology to the solution of business problems. As Schwab's president and co-CEO David Pottruck put it, "We are a technology company in the brokerage business." Schwab introduced TeleBroker, a fully automated telephone system that allowed customers to retrieve real-time stock quotes and place orders. Schwab also leveraged its back-office operations with SchwabLink, a service to provide fee-based financial advisors with back-office custodial services and the capability for RIAs to plug into Schwab's computers to trade. The RIA market became an important source of revenue for Schwab. By 2000, Schwab had 5,900 affiliated RIAs, who controlled about 30% of Schwab's assets, up from zero in 1987. Merrill Lynch viewed these RIAs as a "virtual salesforce" for Schwab: "We don't compete with the discounters. We do compete with Schwab. They have essentially built a Merrill Lynch by proxy."[14]

Schwab introduced the Mutual Fund OneSource program in 1992, enabling customers to purchase no-load mutual funds without paying commissions. The vast majority of OneSource assets were in non-Schwab funds, except the SchwabFunds money market, the only money market fund offered to OneSource customers. Funds were ranked and presented to Schwab customers based on objective characteristics (e.g., sector, investment style, or management fees) and performance. Customers could use their Schwab account to buy or sell more than 1,100 mutual funds from about 200 third-party fund families without paying any fees, and the transactions were integrated into their Schwab account statements and reports. Schwab serviced these accounts, aggregating all OneSource trades into a single daily transaction that was communicated

[14] Arthur Urciuoli, SVP for Retail Marketing, Merrill Lynch, as cited in *Institutional Investor*, April 1996.

electronically to the participating funds. Schwab charged fund providers a 25–35 bp fee for listing the fund in OneSource and providing shareholder services.

• ***Schwab and the Internet.***[15] In 1995, Schwab recognized the increasing importance of the online channel. It put together a team to develop a new software-based online trading product called e.Schwab, which enabled investors to trade by dialing a toll-free number. The separate development unit reported directly to David Pottruck, Schwab's co-CEO and evolved over time into a separate Electronic Brokerage Enterprise. Priced at $39.95 for up to 1,000 shares, e.Schwab was piloted in December 1995 and rolled out nationally in January 1996. Customers had to open a separate e.Schwab account and could use only a PC keyboard to trade, with no human contact. E.Schwab customers were allowed one free customer service phone call per month and had to pay for additional calls. Further, e.Schwab customers could not receive service at a Schwab branch.

As e.Schwab was being launched, Charles Schwab challenged his Electronic Brokerage team to devise a Web trading product by Valentine's Day 1996. By the end of February 1996, the Electronic Brokerage group had a prototype to show Schwab, and the company went live with Web trading on March 31, 1996. Initially, customers could only check balances, buy and sell stocks, and get real-time stock quotes. Nonetheless, customer response to Web-trading was enthusiastic. Schwab aimed to have 25,000 Web trading accounts by the end of 1996; it realized that goal in the first two weeks of operation, even though Schwab did not advertise the service and most customers only learned of it by word-of-mouth.

Schwab quickly dropped the price of Web trading to $29.95, but kept the restrictions of the e.Schwab account. "We were trying to offer a technical product that didn't have all the rest of the services that Schwab had to offer but could offer a lower price," recalled David Pottruck. When it became clear that the dual pricing structure confused and irritated Schwab's customers, who had to choose between service and price, Schwab altered its strategy. Pottruck explained:

> *[Initially] we made our customers choose—if you wanted Internet service at the Internet price you go over there. If you want the full array of services Schwab has to offer, you can't have that kind of pricing. That was a mistake. . . . The key to our success is how we melded the Internet into the middle of who we are and what we try to do for our customers.*

Starting January 15, 1998, Schwab offered Web trading for everyone at $29.95 for up to 1,000 shares. Rather than try to prevent cannibalization, estimated to cost the company $125 million a year in lost revenues, Schwab pushed all of its customers to its Web site (http://www.schwab.com/). This was a phenomenal success: by the end of

[15] This account is based on S. Dewan and H. Mendelson, *Schwab.com*, Standard Business School case, Stanford University.

1999, Schwab had 3.3 million active online accounts holding assets of $349 billion, and 73% of Schwab's trades were conducted through online channels.

While most Schwab's trades originated on the Web, the company maintained a strong presence across multiple delivery channels—functionality that Schwab's customers highly valued. Customers' ability to select a channel, whether they were placing a trade or seeking information, was core to Schwab's value proposition. Schwab customers could trade through Schwab's branch offices, through representatives at call centers, via automated telephone services, over the Internet, and over wireless devices. Schwab sought to take advantage of synergies between the Internet and its traditional channels. For example, Schwab planned to hold over 13,600 online investing seminars in 2000 in its branches for those not comfortable with Internet technology.

Schwab revamped its branches, replacing the teller-like counters with desks and private conference areas for meetings with customers. Telephone calls to the branches were directed to the national call centers, where a representative or a machine would provide the requested service. This allowed branch reps to spend more time helping investors on topics like financial planning and mutual fund selection. Schwab encouraged reps to develop a field of expertise, such as retirement planning or insurance. Schwab's brokers earned a salary and were not motivated through commissions on trades. Like most Schwab employees, brokers were eligible for cash bonuses and stock options based on how their individual group and the firm as a whole performed. Their salaries and bonuses were around $50,000–$70,000.

To enhance its advisory capability, in January 2000 Schwab acquired U.S. Trust, which offered trust, estate planning, and private banking services to wealthy clients. In February 2000, Schwab also acquired CyberCorp, a fast-growing brokerage with specialized electronic trading technology for active traders. CyberCorp's order routing technology allowed customers direct-access trading to the main stock markets and Electronic Communications Networks (ECNs). As CyberCorp's CEO Philip Berber explained, "Rather than create our own ECN, CyberCorp created a link to all ECNs and market makers to allow us to search for the best price at the volume that the trader wants." Further, Schwab reduced the commissions charged to active traders using a graduated scale that declined to $14.95 for customers making more than 60 trades in a quarter.

Schwab offered differentiated services according to customer assets and trades. Customers who had $100,000 of assets with Schwab or executed at least 12 trades a year qualified for Signature Service, which included free access to additional research. Signature Gold Service was available for customers who had at least $500,000 of assets with Schwab; Signature Platinum Services for customers with $1,000,000 of assets with the company; and Signature Pinnacle Services for customers with $7,500,000 of assets with Schwab. Dedicated account teams offered one-on-one customized services to clients in the Platinum and Pinnacle tiers.

By the end of 1999, Schwab provided securities brokerage and related financial services to 6.6 million active customer accounts. The company had 340 branch offices in 47 states, Puerto Rico, the United Kingdom, and the Virgin Islands. Schwab had 18,100 employees and was 40% employee owned. It boasted customer assets of $725 billion. In 1999 alone, Schwab had attracted $80.8 billion in net new customer assets and opened 1.5 million new accounts (see Exhibit 9 for Schwab's income statement).

FULL-SERVICE BROKERAGES

The following sections discuss full-service brokerages Merrill Lynch, Morgan Stanley Dean Witter, and PaineWebber. Exhibit 10 compares client assets for the three brokerages and Charles Schwab, and Exhibit 11 compares services that the full-service brokers offered online.

Merrill Lynch & Co., Inc.

Charles Merrill, a Wall Street bond salesman, opened an underwriting firm in 1914, and six months later, Edmund Lynch joined him as a partner. In the 1920s, the firm offered personal service to small individual investors. During the Great Depression, the firm sold its retail business to E. A. Pierce, Wall Street's largest brokerage. Merrill rejoined the business in 1940, with a clear vision: by applying mass marketing techniques to retail brokerage, the firm will "bring Wall Street to Main Street." Merrill's ideas were an instant success. By the 1950s, Merrill Lynch was the largest brokerage house on Wall Street, and by the 1960s, it was grossing almost four times as much as its biggest competitor. During the 1960s, the firm grew its offerings to include government securities, real estate financing, asset management, and consulting. In 1971, Merrill Lynch went public.

Merrill has long had a strong sales organization and a record of product innovation. During the 1970s, it built up investment banking, insurance, and foreign operations. In 1977, Merrill invented the Cash Management Account (CMA), which combined a money market checking account and a debit card (later extended to a credit card) with a brokerage account that held stocks and bonds.[16] The minimum balance required to open a CMA was $20,000, and the money-market checking account paid more interest than banks did, but it was not federally insured.[17] Merrill Lynch spent four years introducing CMA; 95% of Merrill branches offered it by November 1981. The CMA, a package that handled a person's entire financial life, was one of the most successful retail financial products of all time and led to tremendous growth for Merrill Lynch. CMA Money Trust[18] assets grew from $3 billion to $10 billion in 1981 alone, making it the second largest money market mutual fund. The number of CMA customers exceeded half a million by the end of 1981. In 1982, Merrill put together its vision for the 1990s in a document entitled "All Things to Some People." Merrill Lynch would focus on the "total financial relationship" with its clients, requiring that their "Account Executives must become highly skilled financial planners and advisers—not just product pushers."[19] In 1984, Merrill's retail Account Executives were renamed Financial Consultants.

[16] For example, customers could use the card to borrow against their investments.

[17] Under the Glass-Steagall Act, enacted after the Great Depression, brokerages could not offer banking services. The Act erected a wall between banking institutions (where the federal government insured the deposits) and securities firms (where the customer's money was at risk). It was repealed in 1999.

[18] CMA Money Trust was the money market mutual fund in which CMA credit balances were invested. Merrill added two other money market funds to CMA in 1981.

[19] That is, retail brokers.

During the 1980s, Merrill Lynch's underwriting business also exploded, making it a global leader in new offerings. By the beginning of the 1990s, Merrill became the undisputed 500-pound gorilla of the brokerage industry. It had few close rivals and had been on the vanguard of technology and product development for 20 years. By 1999, Merrill Lynch was the leading brokerage, with 15,000 brokers serving over 5 million accounts in 800 offices across the United States. See Exhibit 12 for Merrill's income statement.

In the 1990s, Merrill became a member of several non-U.S. stock exchanges, and in 1995 it acquired Smith New Court, which provided global equity and research capabilities. Two years later, Merrill acquired Mercury Asset Management, adding to the firm's global and institutional investment management expertise. Through alliances and acquisitions, Merrill also established its presence in Japan, Canada, South Africa, Spain, Italy, Australia, and other parts of the Asia-Pacific region. By 1998, Merrill was present in 43 countries.

As a full investment bank, Merrill gave its brokerage customers an inside track on the stock and bond offerings it underwrote. The brokerage had over 800 respected analysts on staff, producing research reports for Merrill clients.

Merrill was accustomed to leading its competitors—until December 28, 1998, when the market capitalization of Schwab, which Merrill had dismissed as merely a "discounter," surpassed that of Merrill Lynch. The news shook Merrill's management.

• ***Merrill and the Internet.*** Although Merrill Lynch was slow to embrace online brokerage, it had deployed various related technologies in the mid-1990s. In 1996, the company started rolling out Trusted Global Advisor (TGA), an $840 million, five-year initiative to upgrade its retail brokerage unit, the U.S. Private Client Group. TGA was an intranet designed to support brokers with flexible, intelligent replacements to its legacy terminal applications. TGA's capabilities included financial and portfolio modeling, news, market data, analysis, research, e-mail, fax, and multimedia tools. The system integrated market data, client information (including "household views" of client activities), and research from hundreds of legacy databases. Brokers could view research reports and historical data side by side with external databases and news sources, enabling them to plan, help clients, and manage money more effectively. The TGA rollout started in March 1996, and it was fully deployed in all Merrill Lynch U.S. branch offices by 1998.

In November 1996 Merrill launched Merrill Lynch OnLine, which allowed clients to view multiple accounts, examine their portfolio positions, and browse statements and research reports. When Launny Steffens proudly showed it to an outspoken Silicon Valley business leader, his reaction was: "Launny, your site sucks. Your research is just about the best out there, but you keep it hidden away, reserved for current clients. Why isn't it free?"

On November 2, 1998, Merrill Lynch launched AskMerrill, making its entire database of corporate research available free through a new Web site for a four-month trial period. According to Steffens, AskMerrill was designed to showcase the company's research; the value of the Web site would be "even further enhanced when a Financial Consultant can provide the context in how that research should be used." Merrill Lynch used this free research offer to acquire new customers. By early January 1999, out of 90,000 AskMerrill registered users, more than 2,000 became new Merrill brokerage clients.[20]

Senior Merrill Lynch management were skeptical of online brokerage, publicly stating that online trading encouraged customers to speculate—to the dismay of even their nearest and dearest. After Steffen's July 1998 warning against the "do-it-yourself model of investing," his son, a Merrill broker in North Carolina, called and asked his father to "get his act together."[21] Eventually, online trading proved too compelling for Merrill Lynch to resist. In February 1999, Merrill Lynch acquired D. E. Soft, a technology unit of D. E. Shaw[22] that had developed an online trading system. On the day of the announcement, Merrill's stock rose four points. The following month, Merrill debuted an online trading service for roughly 1% of its clients with at least $100,000 in fee-based accounts.

On June 1, 1999, Merrill announced its plan to augment its traditional offerings with an online trading service, either through a fee-based or a discount-commissioned account (Exhibit 11). "Merrill realizes they have to compete. It's easier to maintain relationships than it is to draw customers back after that customer has left," observed an analyst at Tower Group, financial technology consultants.[23] In July 1999, Merrill began offering Unlimited Advantage, which charged a 0.2%–1% annual flat fee starting at $1,500 and provided full service, including unlimited trading—online or offline. By the end of 1999, Unlimited Advantage had attracted $70 billion,[24] of which $9 billion were new to the firm. It launched Merrill Lynch Direct, a discount online trading service featuring $29.95 trades, in December 1999. By June 2000, Merrill Lynch Direct had attracted $2.7 billion in client assets. The array of services allowed clients to choose their preferred level of advice (with a Financial Consultant, self-directed, or delegated), access (person-to-person, online, or by phone), and pricing (a la carte or as a percentage of assets). By the end of 1999, Merrill Lynch had 721,000 online accounts, and 22% of its U.S. Private Client assets were online.

• ***Transition and Future.*** Incorporating online services had been difficult and had required the right timing. Chief executive David H. Komansky and chief strategist Jerome P. Kenny, who both started at Merrill Lynch as brokers, had argued that the firm needed to wait until its brokers accepted the new reality of the online world. After the rollout, Merrill estimated that if it had initiated online trading earlier, 75% of the brokers would not have supported it. Merrill would have risked losing both its brokers and the assets they managed.

[20] *Wall Street Journal*, January 6, 1999.

[21] Charles Gasparino and Rebecca Buckman, "Facing Internet Threat, Merrill to Offer Trading Online for Low Fees," *Wall Street Journal*, June 1, 1999.

[22] D. E. Shaw was a private securities and investment firm specializing in the intersection of technology and finance. David E. Shaw founded the firm after receiving a Ph.D. from the Stanford Computer Science Department.

[23] Ed Kountz quoted in *The Star-Ledger*, June 2, 1999.

[24] According to Merrill Lynch, Unlimited Advantage assets grew 20 times faster than Merrill's earlier fee-based offerings.

With more than 14,000 commissioned brokers, Merrill had faced a more difficult transition to a new compensation model than Schwab did with its 7,000 salaried brokers. Steffens, who led the transition, explained the new strategy to brokers. He reminded brokers how, in the 1960s, GM assumed that consumers would not buy inexpensive Japanese cars and continued to produce only big expensive vehicles. The result: GM had to close 50 to 100 plants and fire 20,000 employees. "I didn't want us to be in the same position. Telling these clients to go to someone else is not a good idea."[25] The new strategy also put Merrill Lynch's earnings at risk. While retail commissions constituted only 10%–15% of Merrill's earnings, the company estimated that Merrill Lynch Direct could cost $1 billion in equity commissions. Kenny, however, believed that increases in client assets would more than offset the loss.

To meet the challenge, Merrill started to restructure its entire business—from research through brokerage to asset management. Kenny said, "We concluded that the firm has to be converted to an Internet-based firm." Komansky put it differently: "We will take the capabilities of Web technology and use it wherever we can to improve our business life." Through 2000, Merrill aggressively rolled out a banking extension to the CMA account, where assets are swapped into a federally insured bank instead of a money market fund—while still paying attractive money market rates. In April 2000, Merrill announced a joint venture with global banking giant HSBC to provide Internet-based banking and investment services outside the United States. As Merrill Lynch CEO David Komansky put it, the new company, headquartered in London, would be "the first global online banking and investment services company, reaching an online active investor market that is expected to grow to 50 million households across Europe, Asia Pacific, and Latin America in the next decade." In May 2000, Merrill's Private Client Group (its retail brokerage arm) was reorganized, and the unit's customer-focused businesses were combined into a Client Relationship Group, with channel-specific units reporting to the new group. Both the Private Client Group and the Client Relationship Group were headed by executives who had never been brokers themselves. The rationale for the change was that "the unit needed to be more effective in segmenting its client base by offering tiered services across different channels."[26]

To implement its strategy, Merrill formed partnerships with companies such as Microsoft, Multex, Medialink.com, Standard & Poor, Intuit, and Works.com to provide marketing, content, and e-commerce services. It also entered the media business with the launch of its Global Investor Network (GIN), an in-house video news service. GIN hired broadcast journalists to anchor news reports, cover business segments, and broadcast Merrill's morning call, where analysts talked about the upcoming day—a meeting that used to be open only to institutional investors. Without any promotion, GIN garnered 7,000 hits a day by late 1999.

To build customer loyalty, Merrill also offered an extensive array of e-commerce services. Companies such as Barnes & Noble, eToys, Reel.com, and Cooking.com signed up to sell products through Merrill's portal. The company offered Merrill Visa Signature

[25] "Merrill's E-Battle," *Business Week*, November 15, 1999.

[26] Merrill Taps Another Nonbroker to Help Run Brokerage Business," *Dow Jones Newswires*, May 26, 2000.

cards, which—along with the CMA—provided a convenient payment system for its clients. Komansky explained:

> *We are trying to build relationships. We are trying to attract clients to capture as many of their assets and as many of their commercial transactions as possible. Not necessarily to earn a profit on these. We are trying to create a financial portal, and you have to have things to attract them. When somebody wants to go to Amazon.com or any other portal, we are competing.*[27]

By the end of 1999, Merrill offered more than four million products in its e-commerce offering and had issued 500,000 Visa Signature cards whose owners spent $6.6 billion.

Merrill Lynch's institutional business faced an even more competitive environment.[28] At year-end 1998, 26% of institutional equity trading was executed electronically and it was expected to reach 44% by the end of 2000. Merrill Lynch bought a stake in the Archipelago ECN and participated in multidealer systems such as Securities.Hub, a marketplace linking dealers and institutional clients for securities offering, trading, and information sharing. As of year-end 1999, Merrill was also developing an institutional portal that would enable corporate treasurers to do most of their business with Merrill at one Web site with one password.

• ***Merrill's Broker Force.*** In 1999, Merrill Lynch had 15,000 brokers—the largest U.S. broker force. An average broker at Merrill generated $410,000 in annual commissions and maintained $84.5 million in assets. Merrill was the first full-service brokerage to change its broker organization fundamentally in response to the Internet and other industry forces. In early 1999, brokers began to receive bonuses mainly for asset gathering from high net worth households into a defined set of products and services. Merrill designed its compensation plan "to provide a greater degree of alignment" between broker pay and the firm's strategy to meet client needs. "There's no such thing as a straight transaction," said a recruiter about Merrill's plan. "Everything is tied together and production is almost irrelevant."[29]

Under Merrill's plan, brokers received a 25% payout on the amounts they produced; additional amounts were deferred until brokers reached specified production goals or years of service. Brokers could also earn an annual bonus based on net new growth in accounts with a minimum of $250,000 in combined assets and credit products. The bonus increased if the account grew to $1 million (and increased even more for $2.5 million), or if the client invested in a defined set of products.

Whereas Merrill Lynch's compensation plan credited brokers for asset gathering and commissions in the firm's online accounts, it expected the new pricing structure

[27] "The Winds of Change Are Upon Us," *Business Week*, November 15, 1999.
[28] At the end of 1999, 48% of assets under management at Merrill Lynch were institutional (52% were retail).
[29] "Broker Compensation Ups and Downs," Pamela Savage Fobat, *Registered Representative*, February 1999.

to reduce the payout to those brokers who were paid chiefly on commissions. To ease the transition, Merrill gave brokers gap payments, in cash and deferred compensation, through the first half of 2001. The firm planned to increase the number of its brokers to 20,000 by 2002. However, between June 1999 and March 2000, Merrill lost more brokers than ever before. Many of those who left were the established, commission-producing brokers whose clients had larger asset bases. Christos Cotsakos, E*Trade's CEO, described Merrill's situation: "This isn't about E*Trade saying, 'Boot your broker.' This is Merrill booting their own brokers."

Morgan Stanley Dean Witter Discover & Co.

Morgan Stanley Dean Witter Discover (MSDW) was the product of the 1997 merger of the white shoe Morgan Stanley and its scrappier competitor, Dean Witter Discover. The latter was itself the product of a merger between broker Dean Witter and Discover, the financial services company that offered the Discover credit card. By late 1999, MSDW was offering financial services and products ranging from traditional brokerage and asset management to mortgage loans and insurance. (Exhibit 13 shows the firm's income statement.)

Dean Witter was an early mover in online brokerage. In 1996, it acquired Lombard Brokerage, Inc., a San Francisco-based Internet securities transaction firm. Lombard was founded in 1992 as a discount brokerage that offered trading over the phone. In August 1995, Lombard enabled its customers to place orders over the Internet through its own Web site. By the time of its acquisition by Dean Witter, Lombard had $30 million in annual revenue and 45,000 accounts. It charged $14.95 for electronic trading.[30] The company won Barron's "Best Online Broker" awards in 1996 and 1997.

Dean Witter kept Lombard at arms-length from its full-service brokerage. In June 1997, soon after the merger of Morgan Stanley and Dean Witter, MSDW renamed Lombard "Discover Brokerage Direct" (DBD).

• ***Sibling Rivalry.*** Dean Witter kept its Internet brokerage operation separate from its core business. Dean Witter's 9,000 retail brokers were concerned about the Lombard acquisition, but the firm's executives insisted that its brokers had nothing to fear from the new entity, which would be "totally separate and distinct" from Dean Witter's brokerage business. "Lombard reaches customers we don't reach in our traditional securities business," said Philip Purcell, Dean Witter's chairman and CEO. The company said that according to its extensive research, self-directed customers who used the Internet for securities transactions comprised a separate market segment, distinct from the full-service brokerage clientele. Full-service brokers hoped that new techno-savvy investors would turn to traditional brokerage once their asset levels increased.

Until 1999, the brokerage had done little to publicize its online trading unit and had no plans to link MSDW's full-service accounts with Discount Brokerage Direct. DBD did not use the Morgan Stanley or Dean Witter names, because management believed online brokerages appealed to a demographic group that had more in common

[30] For up to 5,000 shares.

with Discover cardholders than with full-service brokerage customers. "Using the Morgan Stanley Dean Witter name for the discount service could be viewed as diminishing the value of your brokers and of that brand," explained Scott Appleby, who followed online brokers for ABN Amro, Inc. "It's much more difficult if I'm a broker and I'm providing this value-added service, and I turn around and my client can get a trade for $16 from the same company."

The TV commercials of online brokerages like E*Trade, Ameritrade and Datek played to their clientele's attitudes and often ridiculed traditional brokers. In contrast, DBD's TV campaigns focused on the ability of the man on the street to make quick profits, without alluding to the contrast between traditional and online brokerage. "I don't think we would ever do that, for obvious reasons," said John Yost, a founding partner of Black Rocket, the San Francisco ad agency that Discover used.

After the acquisition, DBD began to lose ground to E*Trade, despite Lombard's reputation for having a more reliable Web site and trading engine. Industry experts said that DBD's uneasy coexistence in the same organization with an army of full-service brokers who made their living charging hundreds of dollars per trade had constrained its growth.

This uneasiness was reflected in the way DBD customers received access to two of MSDW's most prized possessions, Morgan Stanley research reports and IPOs. Morgan Stanley was a recognized Internet economy leader; its analysts, including Mary Meeker, were influential in the online world; and it was a lead underwriter in many of the Internet's top IPOs such as Netscape, Priceline.com, and Akamai Technologies. DBD began offering its clients stock research in summer 1998 in response to competition from other online brokerage firms. But DBD charged clients an extra $4.95 a month for information on one company and $34.95 a month for 40 companies (full-service clients got the reports free). The DBD research reports were edited versions called "Discover Brokerage Equity Research"; only footnotes revealed that Morgan Stanley analysts had prepared the reports. Moreover, the DBD Web site section on research said only that the reports came from "a leading research institution." Thomas O'Connell, president and CEO of DBD, explained that the firm did not want to upset the Dean Witter brokers by making their research seem like a cheap commodity. "We don't want to do something to make life hard for them."

As an underwriter of IPOs, Morgan Stanley had curried favor with the Internet community, which had produced some of the most impressive stock debuts in recent years. Morgan Stanley handed over IPO shares of Ziff-Davis and Priceline.com for resale to online underwriters E*Trade and Wit Capital Group, Inc., while denying those same shares to its own online customers at DBD. In late April 1999, with E*Trade and Wit having their own IPO programs, Morgan Stanley finally announced plans to give DBD customers with at least $100,000 in assets limited access to IPOs.

• ***Transition and Future.*** By July 1999, MSDW decided to change its approach. DBD's O'Connell explained:

> *We learned that customers of online brokerages are the same people as the customers of full-service firms. We also learned that the concept of online brokerage as*

> *a distinct business from broker-based business really isn't true. It's just a different perspective. The Internet allows the customer to control the data . . . the broker's value is in the advice, not handling the transaction or the data.*

Company officials conceded that the sibling forms were competing for the same business.

On October 20, 1999, MSDW unveiled its new service platform, iChoice, which included a fee-based account and a self-directed account with online trading in addition to the traditional full-service account (Exhibit 11). DBD was rechristened Morgan Stanley Dean Witter Online, offering $29.95 online trading. DBD customers were given a grace period on their lower fee ($14.95 for market orders up to 5,000 shares) before they had to switch to the new, more expensive platform. The fee-based account, Enhanced Choice, offered advice and unlimited trading with a minimum annual fee of $1,000. The fees varied depending on size of assets, type of investments, and level of service required. While the posted fees were higher than at other brokerages (30bp to 2.25%), brokers negotiated the actual fees with individual clients. As one broker put it, "Here they give you flexibility to price the client where you were pricing them before."

Morgan Stanley Dean Witter Online was up and running one day after its announcement. MSDW's stock surged 16% on the news, compared to the 14% price plunge after Merrill announced its cyber trading plan in June 1999.

MSDW's management was pleased with the asset and customer growth in the iChoice accounts. MSDW had a record quarter after it implemented iChoice, with 70%–80% of new asset flows into iChoice coming from relationships new to the firm. Moreover, existing clients who switched to the fee-based Enhanced Choice account became more profitable for MSDW than they had been under the commission-based structure.

• ***MSDW's Broker Force.*** By the end of 1999, MSDW had a broker force of over 12,000, second only to Merrill Lynch. MSDW brokers generated an average of $325,000 in commissions, with assets per broker of $43 million. When MSDW rolled out iChoice, the average traditional Dean Witter commission was about $175.

When it rolled out the iChoice program in October 1999, MSDW was sensitive to its brokers' concerns. Fees on the Enhanced Choice account were higher than those Merrill charged, so MSDW brokers might not lose as much income. Also, MSDW brokers received a $3 cut of each $29.95 online trade if they opened the account or if the customer let them monitor it. Brokers had input into the development of the iChoice strategy, and most of them understood that MSDW had to adapt to the competitive environment. As the Internet came to be seen as a mainstream medium for investing rather than a discount outlet, brokers became more willing to offer online trading as part of their full-service menu. MSDW officials said brokers wanted to add more Internet services and weren't antagonistic about the new online program. When company president John Mack first toured Dean Witter branch offices in 1997, he observed, "There [were] real questions, fear, anger" about the Internet. "Now, when I go into the branches, the question is, when are we going to be online?"

In the late 1990s, MSDW expanded its army of U.S. brokers more than twice as fast as Merrill Lynch. The number of MSDW brokers jumped 28% between 1995 and 1999, and was expected to reach 18,000 by 2005. [31]

James Higgins, president of MSDW's brokerage operation, considered the notion that the "broker is obsolete" hogwash. When customers' assets hit about $100,000, "over 80% of them look for some guidance in terms of financial advice." Higgins also stated, "We are not targeting any one competitor . . . but we are not going to take a back seat to any of our peer competitors, or the e-brokers or the discounters."[32]

PaineWebber Group, Inc.

PaineWebber Group, founded in 1879, was one of the largest and best-known full-service securities firms in the United States. By 1999, it was the nation's fourth-largest brokerage. Its primary mission was to serve the investment and capital needs of individual and institutional clients through its broker-dealer subsidiary.

In the early 1990s, PaineWebber made several choices that defied conventional wisdom. While other financial giants began offering everything from investment banking to insurance, PaineWebber stayed small. Its 1999 net revenues of $5.3 billion were only 10% larger than MSDW's profits of $4.8 billion. PaineWebber also remained focused on the domestic market (95% of 1999 net revenues were from the U.S.) and retail segment (76% of 1999 net revenues came from individual investors) (Exhibit 14).

PaineWebber targeted the high-end market. Donald Marron, its CEO since 1980, said: "Our strategy has been to be in the center of the flow of household assets from the more affluent segment of the population," defined as customers with $100,000 in income or $500,000 in net worth, excluding their primary residence. This segment was expanding at 9% a year. In 1998, the "affluent segment" owned 56% of the $18 trillion in investable assets in the United States. According to PaineWebber's director of retail marketing, United States. investable assets would increase to $28.8 trillion by 2003, and the "affluent segment" would own more than three-quarters of them.

PaineWebber's strategy was successful. The firm built client assets that grew at an annual compound rate of 24% from 1994 to 1999, and by the end of 1999, it had gathered $423 billion (Exhibit 10). PaineWebber's broker force was an integral part of the firm's success. PaineWebber brokers brought in average revenue of over $400,000, one of the highest averages in the industry. Its securities trading and investment banking divisions were small. PaineWebber's stream of fees plus interest earnings covered all of its fixed expenses, so that commissions, investment banking fees, and other revenues could fatten the bottom line. Between 1997 and 1999, commissions were 36%–38% of net revenues. Much of PaineWebber's success came from the rapid accumulation of fee-bearing assets. At the end of 1999, 40% of PaineWebber's client assets were fee

[31] In the 12 months ending February 29, 2000, the number of brokers increased by 1,619.

[32] *Wall Street Journal*, November 24, 1999.

based, with 28% of them in "wrap" accounts, in which investors paid a fixed annual fee for all investment services, thereby generating recurring revenue.

Research was another PaineWebber strength. PaineWebber consistently ranked in the top 10 of *Institutional Investor*'s All America Research Team. According to the *Wall Street Journal*'s July 1999 quarterly study of the performance of stocks that 15 major brokerages recommended, PaineWebber had the best performance over a five-year period, with returns nearly double those of Merrill Lynch and MSDW.

In July 2000, UBS AG, the world's largest private bank, acquired PaineWebber for $10.25 billion—almost 50% above its pre-announcement value. The takeover, which left PaineWebber's management structure intact, combined the international reach of UBS's commercial and investment banking businesses with PaineWebber's U.S. retail-brokerage operations while sustaining the company's mutual emphasis on high net worth clients.

• ***The Internet.*** PaineWebber used the Internet to communicate with its clients. In early 1997, PaineWebber introduced its online client service, PaineWebber Edge, which provided detailed account tracking, research, and broker interaction. By the end of 1999, Edge served 176,000 households with assets of $140 billion, a third of the assets PaineWebber controlled.

In 1999, PaineWebber rolled out InsightOne, an asset-based fee account that offered clients unlimited online trading and a channel to all the firm's technology and services. Clients needed to have $100,000 in their accounts and pay fees, negotiated with their brokers, of 0.75%–2% of assets with a minimum annual fee of $1,500 (Exhibit 11). InsightOne was part of a bundled service with pricing schedules negotiated up front. Service schedules were custom designed and priced according to the level of service and attention the client desired. InsightOne drew $1.7 billion in assets in its first six weeks. To the firm's surprise, the most eager adopters of the new online platform were its wealthiest clients—those with an average of $800,000 in assets and aged in their 50s. Unlike Merrill Lynch and MSDW, PaineWebber opted not to offer discounted self-directed trading.

PaineWebber also used the Internet to penetrate what it called the "emerging affluent" market—high-income individuals under age 40 who were building (rather than preserving) wealth. About a quarter of these individuals' wealth was in 401(k) and stock benefits plans, and most of them traded online and did not want a broker's advice. To tap this market, PaineWebber provided employers like Cisco, Dell, General Electric, and Aetna employee benefit plans to manage 401(k) retirement plans and company stock options. PaineWebber put together an Employee Services Portal offering online tools, stock quotes, PaineWebber content, and alerts. Employees could also access an automated voice response system or salaried customer service representatives. PaineWebber used the service to create a relationship with these employees, to mine data about their investment behavior, and to use the resulting profiles to "hand them off" to a broker when they were ready to become regular PaineWebber customers.[33] PaineWebber

[33] By February 2000, 139,000 employees were sponsored into these accounts. Their unexercised stock options were worth about $37 billion at that time.

hoped that this service would give it an entrée into the ranks of the newly paper rich when they "graduated" to become advice-seeking affluent. PaineWebber expected to have a million employees enrolled in this program by the end of 2000.

• ***PaineWebber's Broker Force.*** By the end of 1999, PaineWebber's broker force had reached 7,500, almost a 40% increase in five years. PaineWebber brokers were among the most productive financial advisors in the industry, with an average retail production per broker exceeding $400,000 and assets per broker of over 60 million.

The Internet changed PaineWebber. Its president Joe Grano tried to change the company from an army of commission-based brokers to an organization of asset gatherers and advice givers. Grano said, "The only thing that changes a culture is pain and agony. And reading in the newspaper every day about the imminent extinction of the old-time broker has caused plenty of motivational pain."[34]

CEO Marron stated that the firm had been trying to transform its brokers from order takers into asset gatherers, then into asset allocators and in some cases, asset managers. Through the stages, the brokers' business became steadier, more lucrative, and better aligned with clients' needs. In the late 1990s, PaineWebber adjusted how it paid its brokers to reward them for gathering and retaining assets and for increasing the firm's share of the customer's wallet.

In 1999, PaineWebber offered its brokers both a carrot and a stick to promote asset gathering. Brokers could earn back an across-the-board 1% payout cut for the year, plus another 1%, if they surpassed new asset hurdles. The cash bonus depended on the net new assets brokers brought in,[35] the current asset level they managed, and the broker's years of service. Brokers who started the year with at least $150 million in assets earned the minimum 25 bp bonus by bringing in at least $6 million in net new assets. It took $15 million in net new assets to earn back the 1% payout cut and $27 million to max out at 2%.[36] Brokers who started the year with less than $150 million in assets faced a complicated bonus formula based on a percentage of their 1998 assets and a minimum net asset hurdle based on length of service.

Some PaineWebber brokers liked the firm's emphasis on rewarding assets, but not how it structured the reward. "Asset targets are nice to have," said one broker, "but for bigger producers they're giving us a lot to gather in one year and still maintain current business. I think the firm will find it's unrealistic." Another broker found the new bonus structure discouraging: "The way the firm is doing it is so convoluted. It's confusing to have more than one way of getting paid on assets. It's not motivational."

Like Merrill Lynch, PaineWebber also had new incentives to place client assets in fee-based products. Gone was the bonus on assets under control. Brokers would only get a bonus on assets in PaineWebber's fee-based products and services, such as central asset accounts, wrap accounts, trust accounts, and IRAs. However, to prevent brokers from defecting following PaineWebber's acquisition by UBS, the company put together a retention plan paying top-producing brokers 35% of their trailing 12 months

[34] "Street Smarts: PaineWebber's Strategy of Courting the Rich May Pay Handsomely," *Barron's*, November 22, 1999.

[35] The assets had to be new to the firm and could not include dividends, interest, or market appreciation.

[36] The bonus was capped at $40,000.

of commissions annual production in restricted stock, plus stock options; lower-producing brokers received a lower percentage of the amounts they produced.

EPILOGUE

One of the celebrated effects of the Internet was putting the customer in charge. As Merrill's brokerage chief Launny Steffens put it:

> *In everything we do, two principles of the digital age should be kept in mind: clients are smart and the world is transparent. . . . A total financial relationship is not about trying to control clients or push proprietary products—that is a failed proposition in a world of transparency and smart investors. Instead, it is about adding real value for clients by delivering the right set of products and services to simplify their lives and help them make better financial decisions.*[37]

This threatened the traditional broker. Indeed, unlike RIAs, who used the Internet extensively and largely believed that it aided their business, only 38% of full-service brokers believed the Internet helped their business, and their use of the Internet was sparse (Exhibit 15).

Yet, even at the dawn of the twenty-first century, full-service brokerages spared no expense to compete for proven brokers. When PaineWebber set out to recruit a top-producing team of four Merrill Lynch brokers in Michigan, it flew them to New York first class, and over dinner at the Waldorf-Astoria Hotel, PaineWebber's brokerage chief made them an offer they couldn't refuse: a signing bonus of $5.25 million, plus $2 million more if they brought more customers to PaineWebber.[38]

Intense competitive pressures to gather client assets led full-service brokerages like PaineWebber, Salomon Smith Barney, Prudential Securities, and Merrill Lynch to increase upfront signing bonuses and give brokers other perks. Brokerages continued to provide incentives to sell in-house products, and Morgan Stanley Dean Witter brokers said they were under constant pressure to sell the firm's proprietary mutual funds.[39]

The Tully Commission's recommendations to ban such practices in order to align brokers' incentives with their clients' were so disregarded that the industry's self-regulatory body, the National Association for Securities Dealers, proposed new rules to enforce them. Full-service brokerages cited competitive pressures and the flow of investor dollars to online trading firms as reasons for ignoring the recommendations, and some firms said they never formally agreed to adopt them.[40]

The *Wall Street Journal* described a recent dinner honoring Mr. Tully. Speaker after speaker praised his contributions to the industry, culminating in the Tully Commission. James Higgins, who headed Dean Witter's brokerage unit, "graciously thanked

[37] Speech at the Securities Industry Association's meeting, Boca Raton, Florida, November 1999.

[38] *Wall Street Journal*, March 28, 2000.

[39] *ibid.*

[40] *ibid.*

Mr. Tully for his years of service to the industry, including his crowning achievement, the Tully Commission Report. Then, pointing to Merrill's brokerage chief, Mr. Steffens, he said to hearty laughter from the crowd: "By the way, Launny, if you have a minute, you should read the Tully Report."[41] Higgins and Steffens declined requests to comment on the incident.

EXHIBIT 1

(a) Average Number of Daily Online Equity Trades in the United States

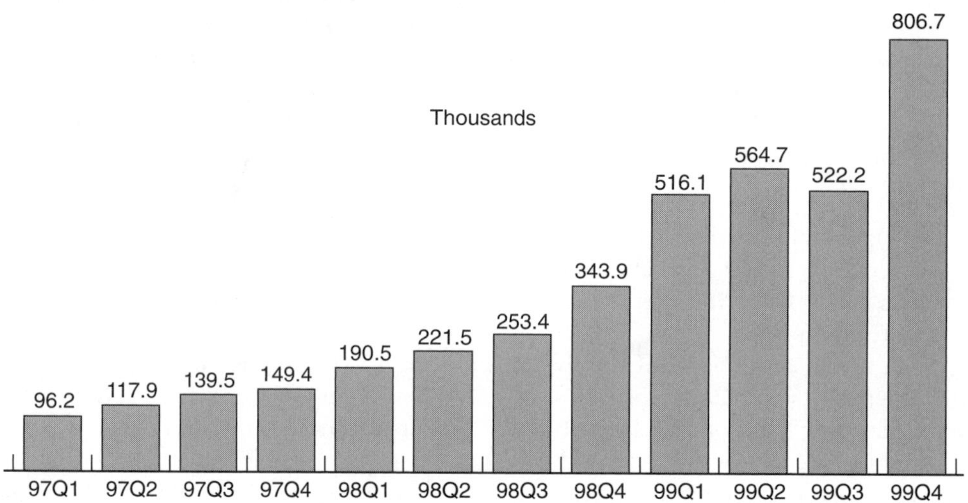

(b) Share of Online Trading in U.S. Individual Investor Trades

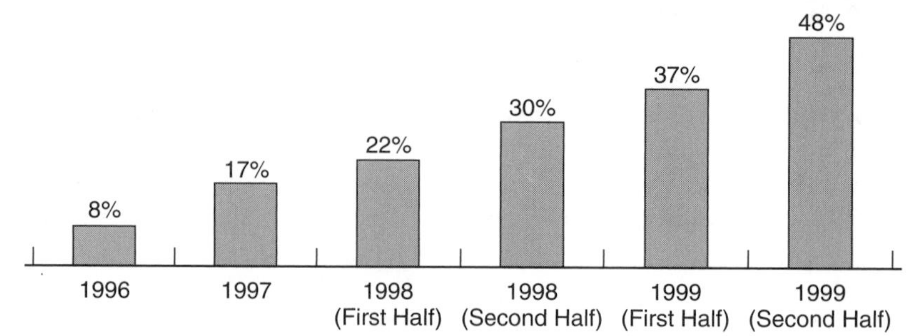

Source: Compiled from U.S. Bancorp Piper Jaffrey reports.

[41] *ibid.*

EXHIBIT 2 U.S. Online Brokerage Functionality Comparison (Discounted Accounts for Full-service Brokers)

	Stock Commission (1,000 shares)			*Banking Services*				
Company Name	*Market*	*Limit*	*Number of Mutual Funds Offered*	*Check Writing*	*ATM/ Debit Card*	*Online Bill Payment*	*Institutional Research*	*IPOs*
Datek	$9.99	$9.99	7,000	X	–	–	–	–
E*Trade*	14.95	19.95	5,000	X	–	–	BancBoston RS	E*Offering
Charles Schwab*	29.95	29.95	1,650	X	X	X	CSFB, Hambrecht & Quist	CSFB, Hambrecht & Quist, Schwab
Merrill Lynch	29.95	29.95	2,500	X	X	X	Merrill Lynch	Merrill Lynch
Morgan Stanley Dean Witter (Discover Brokerage Direct)	29.95 (14.95)	29.95 (19.95)	5,000	X	–	X	MSDW	MSDW
PaineWebber	N/A	N/A	N/A	X	X	–	PaineWebber	PaineWebber

Numbers as of the end of 1999.
Online commission price for Morgan Stanley Dean Witter is effective October 1999.
Online commission price for Merrill Lynch is effective December 1999.
Compiled from company Web sites, Morgan Stanley Dean Witter Research, *Wall Street Journal*
*Discount provided for active traders.

EXHIBIT 3 Brokerage Business Models Before May Day (1975)

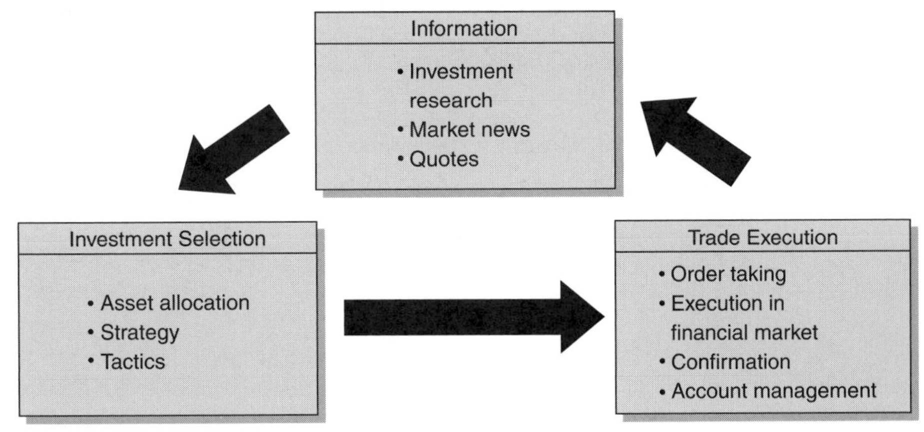

Source: Dewan and Mendelson.

EXHIBIT 4

(a) Average Fees for Unbundled (Internet) Brokerage Offering Versus Traditional Brokerage Accounts

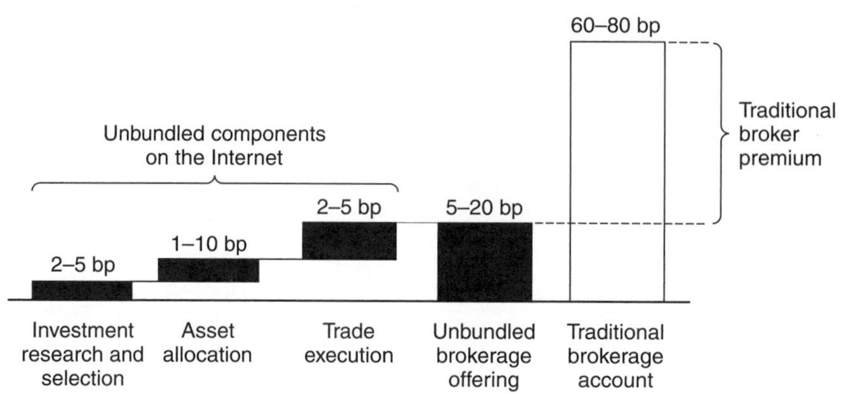

(b) Unbundling of Stock Brokerage Product Offering

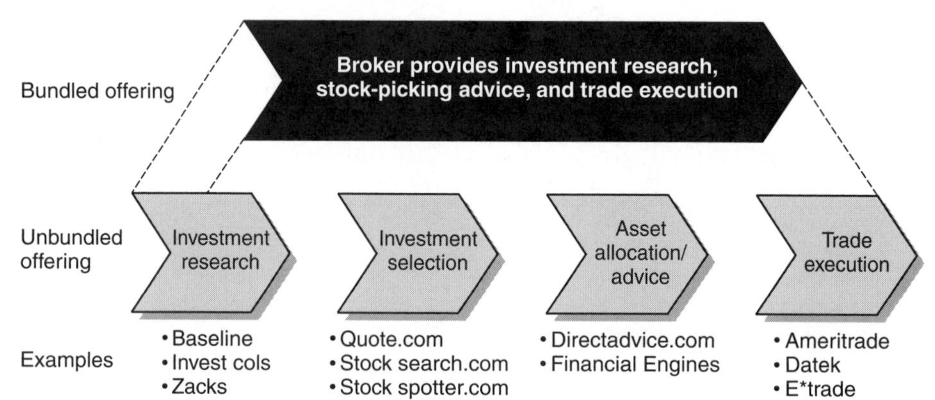

Reproduced with permission from the Corporate Executive Board, VIP Forum Program, Corporate Executive Board. "The Final Frontier: the Opportunities and Challenges of Internet Delivery," p. 16, 1999, Washington, D.C.

EXHIBIT 5

Forrester Research segmented investors into four distinct types in its Technographics (TM) research.[42]

• ***Active affluent (AA).*** These young, middle-aged investors possessed the highest household income and net worth. They were well-educated and took investing seriously. Most would analyze their investments and rely on information from traditional sources, such as financial magazines and TV. Of the AA, 73% were online, and they tended to integrate the Web into their existing research processes. Most AA were self-directed and risk-tolerant, but some were opinion seeking. Although many strongly preferred to transact online, most still used the phone to trade.

• ***Active moderate-wealth (AMW)—"get rich quick."*** These young, moderate-to-high-income, well-educated investors grew up with the Internet. Being young, AMW investors had a lower net worth, were risk tolerant, used fewer sources of information and were strongly self-directed. They found advice from financial advisors less valuable than other segments—and could not afford it. More than other groups, AMW used software and the Web to track their investments, and they were the most frequent traders. Forrester Research characterized this segment as "get rich quick."

• ***Buy-and-hold affluent (BHA).*** The oldest investors had built their hefty net worth over decades of savings. BHA were the most risk-averse and the least self-directed segment. Electronic media played a negligible role in how BHA invested. They relied on paper statements and calls to their brokers. Most BHA investors were fully dependent and considered advisor recommendations critical for their investments. Despite their six-figure portfolios, this group traded infrequently. Once they did, they preferred in-person transactions, either face-to-face or with a live agent on the phone.

• ***Buy-and-hold moderate-wealth (BHMW).*** The true mass market, BHMW were average, middle-class American families and accounted for nearly half of all investors. They described themselves as least sophisticated and adhered to a get-rich-slowly strategy. Most BHMW were opinion-seeking, but they had to settle with being self-directed, largely because they could not afford professional advice. They made investment choices based on a few simple criteria and ignored daily market fluctuations. Thus, the Web and other real-time information sources played a minor role in their investments. BHMW traded less than once a year on average, and they mostly owned mutual funds. A few transacted online, but most preferred to make their transactions in person—face-to-face or on the phone.

---

[42] "Which Investors Matter Online?" Forrester Research, Inc., November 1999. Forrester called the four categories aggressive affluent, get rich quick, portfolio cruise control, and retirement by the book. Technographics is a registered trademark of Forrester Research, Inc.

EXHIBIT 6 Segmentation of U.S. Investors

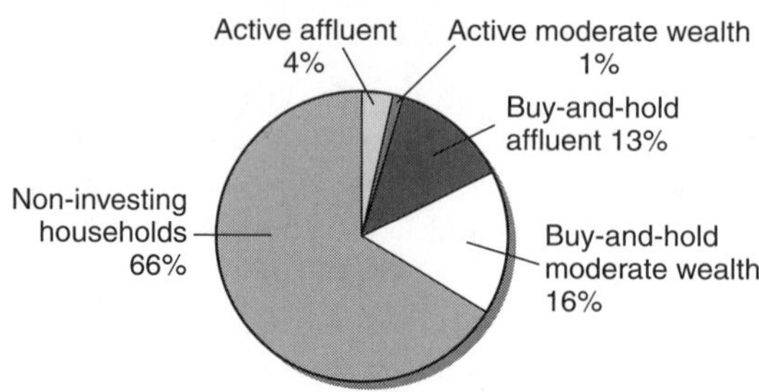

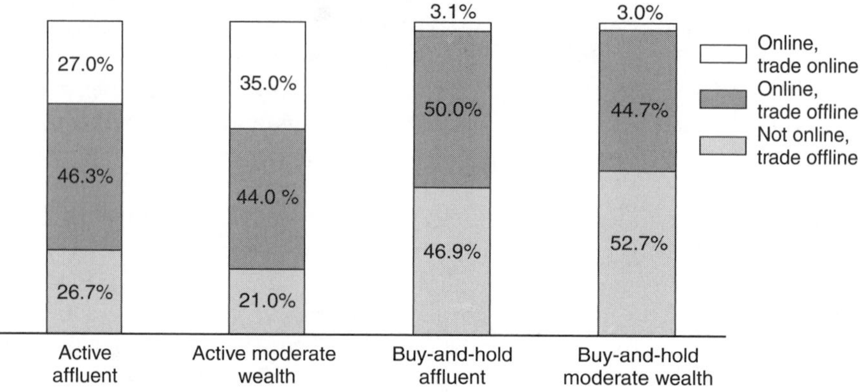

Profiles of Investor Segments

	Active affluent	Active moderate-wealth	Buy-and-hold affluent	Buy-and-hold moderate-wealth	Non-investing households
Mean age	48.5	37.4	52.0	44.0	47.0
Mean household income	$76,000	$56,000	$64,000	$46,000	$37,000
Mean net worth	$432,000	$48,000	$365,000	$54,000	$85,000
Mean stock assets	$186,000	$21,000	$70,000	$11,000	–
Percent male	71.7%	75.0%	55.5%	52.7%	48.4%
Mean trades per year	10.28	10.85	1.50	0.93	N/A
Percent online	73.3%	79.0%	53.1%	47.7%	29.4%

Source: Forrester Research, Inc., 1999.

EXHIBIT 7 Average Full-service Brokers' Annual Compensation, 1990–1999

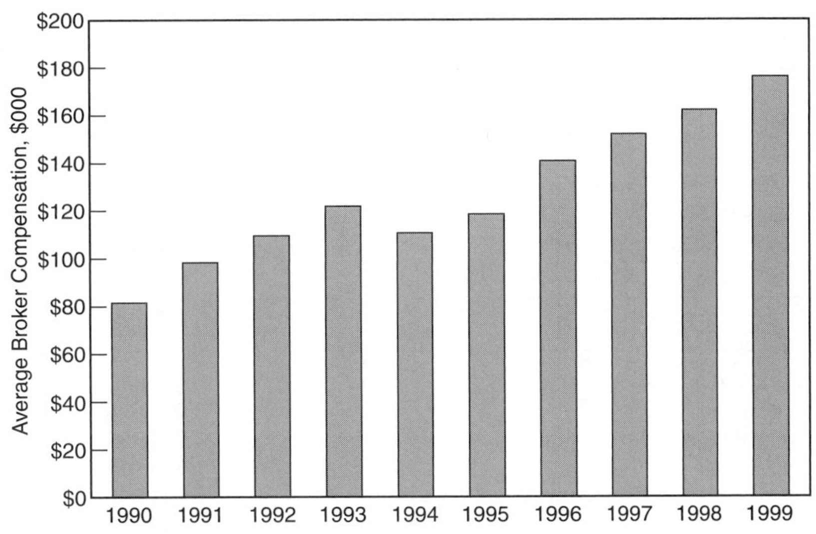

Compiled from: SIA and *Wall Street Journal.*

EXHIBIT 8 A Full-service Brokers' Compensation Structure in 1995 and 1997

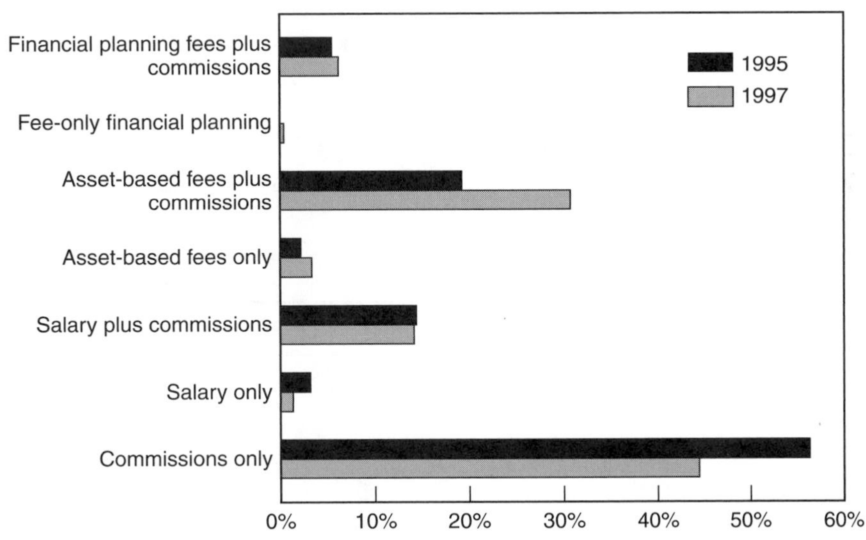

Compiled from results of *Registered Representative* surveys of full-service brokers' compensation structures. The chart shows the percentage of brokers subject to each of the listed compensation structures in 1995 and 1997.

EXHIBIT 9 Charles Schwab Corporation Consolidated Statements of Income (In Thousands, Except Per Share Amounts)

Year Ended December 31	*1999*	*1998*
Revenues		
Commissions	$1,863,306	$1,309,383
Mutual fund service fees	750,141	559,241
Interest revenue, net of interest expense of $768,403 in 1999 $651,881 in 1998	702,677	475,617
Principal transactions	500,496	286,754
Other	128,202	105,226
Total	3,944,822	2,736,221
Expenses excluding interest		
Compensation and benefits	1,624,526	1,162,823
Occupancy and equipment	266,382	200,951
Communications	265,914	206,139
Advertising and market development	241,895	154,981
Depreciation and amortization	156,678	138,477
Professional services	151,081	87,504
Commissions, clearance, and floor brokerage	96,012	82,981
Other	171,095	125,821
Total	2,973,583	2,159,677
Income before taxes on income	971,239	576,544
Taxes on income	382,362	228,082
Net income	$588,877	$348,462
Weighted-average common shares outstanding—diluted	843,090	823,005
*Earnings per share**		
Basic	$0.73	$0.44
Diluted	$0.70	$0.42
*Dividends declared per common share**	$0.0560	$0.0540

*All periods have been restated for the July 1999 two-for-one common stock split.
Source: Company reports.

EXHIBIT 10 Client Assets for Merrill Lynch, Morgan Stanley Dean Witter, PaineWebber, and Charles Schwab: 1990–1999

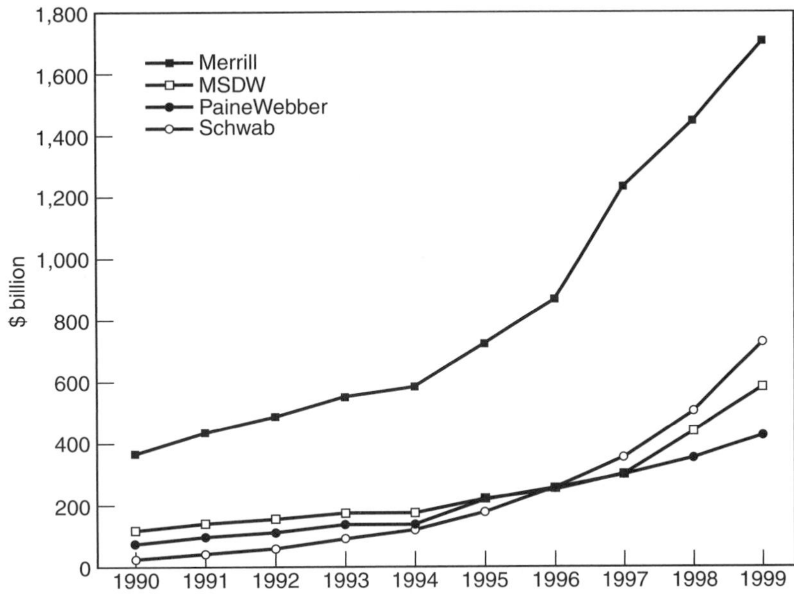

Compiled from: Merrill Lynch, Morgan Stanley Dean Witter, PaineWebber, and Charles Schwab annual reports; Morgan Stanley Dean Witter U.S. Investment Research, October 12, 1999. Morgan Stanley Dean Witter's client assets over the 1990–1997 period are from Dean Witter.

EXHIBIT 11 Online Accounts of Full-service Brokerages

	Merrill Lynch	*Morgan Stanley Dean Witter*	*PaineWebber*
Fee-based account	Unlimited Advantage	Enhanced Choice	InsightOne
Minimum account size	$100,000	$50,000	$100,000
Minimum annual fee	$1,500	$1,000	$1,500
Fees	20–100 bp	30–225 bp	75–200 bp
Discount online account	Merrill Lynch Direct	MSDW Online	
Minimum account size	$20,000	$2,000	
Commission per trade	$29.95	$29.95 (electronic trade) $39.95 (customer service trade)	

EXHIBIT 12 Merrill Lynch & Co., Inc. Preliminary Unaudited Earnings Summary

	For the Year Ended	
(In millions, except per-share amounts)	*December 31 1999*	*December 25 1998*
Net Revenues		
Commissions	$6,334	$5,799
Principal transactions	4,361	2,651
Investment banking	3,614	3,264
Asset management and portfolio services fees	4,753	4,202
Other	720	623
Subtotal	19,782	16,539
Interest and dividends	15,097	18,035
Interest expense	13,010	17,027
Net interest profit	2,087	1,008
Total net revenues	21,869	17,547
Noninterest expenses		
Compensation and benefits	11,153	9,199
Communications and technology	2,038	1,749
Occupancy and related depreciation	941	867
Advertising and market development	779	688
Brokerage, clearing, and exchange fees	678	683
Professional fees	567	552
Goodwill amortization	227	226
Provision for costs related to staff reductions	—	430
Other	1,408	1,057
Total noninterest expenses	17,791	15,451
Earnings before income taxes and dividends on preferred securities issued by subsidiaries	4,078	2,096
Income tax expense	1,265	713
Dividends on preferred securities issued by subsidiaries	195	124
Net earnings	$2,168	$1,259
Preferred stock dividends	$38	$39
Net earnings applicable to common stockholders	$2,580	$1,220
Earnings per common share		
Basic	$7.00	$3.43
Diluted	6.17	3.00

Note: Certain prior period amounts have been restated to conform to the current period presentation.
Source: Company reports.

(continued)

EXHIBIT 12 *(continued)*

(in millions, except per share amounts)	*For the Year Ended* December 31 1999	December 25 1998
Average shares		
Basic	368.7	355.6
Diluted	418.1	406.3
*Cash basis**		
Net earnings	$2,845	$1,485
Earnings per common share—basic	7.61	4.07
Earnings per common share—diluted	6.71	3.56

*Cash basis excludes goodwill amortization.
Note: Certain prior period amounts have been restated to conform to the current period presentation.
Source: Company reports.

EXHIBIT 13 Morgan Stanley Dean Witter (Consolidated Statements of Income)

Fiscal year (dollars in millions, except share and per share data)	*1999*	*1998*
Revenues		
Investment banking	$4,523	$3,340
Principal transactions:		
Trading	5,983	3,283
Investments	725	89
Commissions	2,921	2,321
Fees:		
Asset management, distribution, and administration	3,170	2,889
Merchant and cardmember	1,492	1,647
Servicing	1,194	928
Interest and dividends	13,755	16,436
Other	165	198
Total revenues	33,928	31,131
Interest expense	11,390	13,514
Provision for consumer loan losses	529	1,173
Net revenues	22,009	16,444
Noninterest expenses:		
Compensation and benefits	8,398	6,636
Occupancy and equipment	643	583
Brokerage, clearing, and exchange fees	485	552
Information processing and communications	1,325	1,140
Marketing and business development	1,679	1,411
Professional services	836	677
Other	915	745
Merger-related expenses	0	0
Total noninterest expenses	14,281	11,744

Source: Company reports.

(continued)

EXHIBIT 13 *(continued)*

Fiscal year (dollars in millions, except share and per share data)	*1999*	*1998*
Gain on sale of businesses	0	685
Income before income taxes and cumulative effect of accounting change	7,728	5,385
Provision for income taxes	2,937	1,992
Income before cumulative effect of accounting change	4,791	3,393
Cumulative effect of accounting change	0	(117)
Net income	$4,791	$3,276
Preferred stock dividend requirements	$44	$55
Earnings applicable to common shares[1]	$4,747	$3,221
Earnings per common share[2]		
Basic before cumulative effect of accounting change	$4.33	$2.90
Cumulative effect of accounting change	0.00	(0.10)
Basic	$4.33	$2.80
Diluted before cumulative effect of accounting change	$4.10	$2.76
Cumulative effect of accounting change	0.00	(0.09)
Diluted	$4.10	$2.67
Average common shares outstanding[2]		
Basic	1,096,789,720	1,151,645,450
Diluted	1,159,500,670	1,212,588,130

[1] Amounts shown are used to calculate basic earnings per common share.
[2] Amounts have been retroactively adjusted to give effect for a two-for-one common stock split, effected in the form of a 100% stock dividend, which became effective on January 26, 2000.
Source: Company reports.

EXHIBIT 14 PaineWebber Group Inc. Consolidated Statements of Income (In thousands except share and per share amounts) (Unaudited)

	For the year ended December 31	
	1999	*1998*
Revenues		
Commissions	$1,948,959	$1,641,283
Principal transactions	1,110,080	868,807
Asset management	911,099	713,570
Investment banking	558,224	530,972
Interest	3,123,440	3,352,708
Other	170,951	142,242
Total revenues	7,822,753	7,249,582
Interest expense	2,532,578	2,844,468

Source: Company reports.

(continued)

EXHIBIT 14 PaineWebber Group Inc. Consolidated Statements of Income (In thousands except share and per share amounts) (Unaudited)

	For the year ended December 31	
	1999	*1998*
Net revenues	5,290,175	4,405,114
Noninterest expenses		
Compensation and benefits	3,049,568	2,601,364
Office and equipment	352,712	301,845
Communications	168,071	154,272
Business development	122,678	103,287
Brokerage, clearing, and exchange fees	95,211	97,430
Professional services	136,758	123,265
Other expenses	330,375	308,644
Total noninterest expenses	4,255,373	3,690,107
Income before income taxes and minority interest	1,034,802	715,007
Provision for income taxes	373,959	249,208
Income before minority interest	660,843	465,799
Minority interest	32,244	32,244
Net income	628,599	433,555
Dividend on redeemable preferred stock	22,802	23,647
Unamortized discount charged to equity on redemption of preferred stock	59,883	0
Net income applicable to common shares	$545,914	$409,908
*Earnings per share**		
Basic	$3.77	$2.91
Diluted	$3.56	$2.72
Weighted average common shares		
Basic	144,931,000	140,864,000
Diluted	153,214,000	150,611,000

* Reflects the effect of the unamortized discount of $59.9 million charged to equity resulting from the redemption of preferred stock.

Source: Company reports.

EXHIBIT 15 Survey of U.S. Financial Advisors, 1999: Independent Advisors (RIAs) vs. Full-service Brokers

(a) Question: "Does the Internet Aid or Threaten Your Business?"

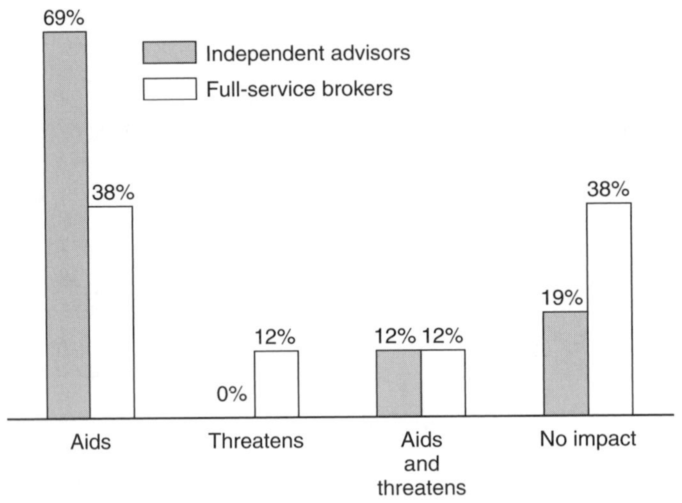

(b) Question: "What Do You Use the Internet For?"

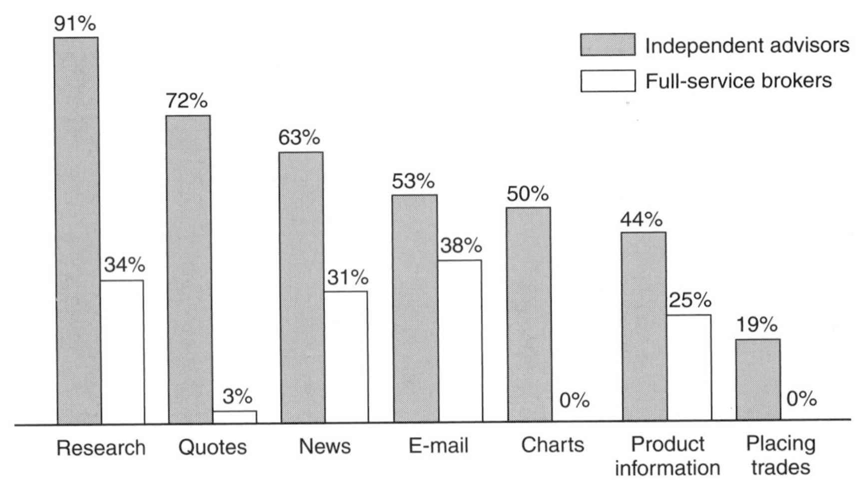

Source: "Arming Captive Advisors," Forrester Research, Inc., July 1999.

BABYCENTER

One of the reasons that I think we have done well at BabyCenter is that we tell our employees that we're not an Internet company . . . we're a service company for new and expectant parents. We think really hard about what that very specific audience wants and how we can deliver services to them in a new way. —*Matt Glickman, CEO and cofounder of BabyCenter*

In April 1999, Matt Glickman, CEO and cofounder of BabyCenter, had a lot on his mind. BabyCenter, an online provider of content, community, and commerce for new and expectant parents, was facing new competitors. (See Exhibit 1 for BabyCenter's home page.) Pure-play online baby companies kept popping up, and traditional retailers like Toys"R"Us (parent company of Babies"R"Us) were talking about building stronger Web presences. Glickman wondered how many online companies the U.S. market could support and which would succeed. Glickman was also seeking to expand internationally. To maintain BabyCenter as the leading source of information and products for new and expectant parents, Glickman believed that the company had to expand internationally, although the executive team had not reached a consensus about which markets to enter at which times.

With these strategic issues on his mind, Glickman was surprised when a mutual investor in BabyCenter and eToys approached him with an unexpected proposition—for eToys to acquire BabyCenter. (See Exhibit 2 for eToys' home page.) eToys, an online children's product retailer, had been both an advertiser on BabyCenter.com and a competitor. The BabyCenter founders had always spurned acquisition offers. In fact, Glickman and cofounder and president, Mark Selcow, were in the middle of successful

---

Research Associates Tyee Harpster and Meredith Unruh prepared this case under the supervision of Professor Garth Saloner and Professor A. Michael Spence as the basis for class discussion rather than to illustrate either effective or ineffective handling of an administrative situation. Margot Sutherland, Executive Director, Center for Electronic Business and Commerce, Stanford Graduate School of Business managed the development of this. Research support provided by The Boston Consulting Group is gratefully acknowledged

discussions with major players in the Internet and traditional media markets—companies like Yahoo!, AOL, Amazon, NBC, CBS, and Disney—about investing in BabyCenter to maintain its momentum and prepare for a public offering. The eToys offer surprised Glickman because eToys had filed to go public and was supposed to start its IPO road show in a few weeks. Glickman had to reflect—would combining forces with eToys help or hurt BabyCenter dominate the baby content, commerce, and community markets?

BEGINNING OF A START-UP

In October 1996, just two and a half years before the eToys offer, Glickman and his Stanford Graduate School of Business (GSB) classmate, Selcow, both age 27, left their corporate jobs to start BabyCenter. Glickman had been working as Group Product Manager for Quicken at Intuit, Selcow as Product Manager at the biotechnology firm, Amgen. They had planned to start a company together since they met at the GSB, but they wanted to get management experience at established firms first. The BabyCenter idea came out of one of Glickman's brainstorming sessions at Intuit.

> *We were always talking at work about how to use the Internet. At Intuit, we were focused a lot on how you help people through a life event. The Internet is really good at bringing everything together and we were particularly focused on the buying-a-house life event because there are so many financial implications. But I just thought ahead. Also, my wife and I were starting to plan a family and so the personal and professional realization came together that the life event of having a baby is the biggest, most important, most fun life event and one that we can be really successful with because it is a big, fragmented market, people are relatively price insensitive, and they have tons of questions.*

The partners left their jobs in October 1996 and decided to give themselves nine months to raise money for the BabyCenter concept before moving on to another idea. They raised their first round of financing in just four months—an $800,000 seed round led by Broderbund Software's online venture fund. In September 1997, a venture round of $2.5 million followed, then $10 million more in October 1998.

In November 1997, one year after the company was founded, BabyCenter.com was launched with headquarters in San Francisco and 25 employees. Its mission was "to build the most complete resource on the Internet for new and expectant parents—a resource that would improve parents' confidence and make their lives easier." The site was exclusively content and community until October 1998 when the online store launched.

Market

• ***Size.*** BabyCenter addressed a significant market opportunity. About four million babies are born each year in the United States, and American parents spend an average of $7,100 in their baby's first year.[1] In 1998, the U.S. baby products market for newborns to age 2 was $18 billion ($5.6 billion for apparel; $5.5 billion for baby care; $3.5 billion for nursery and furniture; $1.0 billion for toys; $2.3 billion for food).[2]

• ***Demographics.*** The Internet was a natural place to address the baby market. In late 1998, 83% of people who used the Internet were gathering information; 43% were specifically looking for health information. Women represented 46% of Internet users and were the fastest growing group of Internet users. Women were also an attractive demographic to target because they accounted for 70% of all retail sales. Seventy percent of Internet access also occurred at home, where new parents usually spent most of their time immediately after the birth of a child.[3]

The convenience of the Internet was especially important for busy new parents. Most mothers returned to work after having their babies, which increased their need for timesaving opportunities. In 1998, 53% of new mothers were in the labor force both before delivering their babies and a year after delivery. New parents were also better connected to the Internet than the average population—35% of new parents were online versus an average of only 25% across the general population.[4] Many new parents were hungry for discreet information sources because they were often geographically separated from their families and secretive during early pregnancy.

BabyCenter.com

Content

Since BabyCenter's goal was to provide guidance to new and expectant parents, Glickman and Selcow's first priority was to build an editorial team. To ensure quality, they selected medical experts, including obstetricians and pediatricians, to act as advisors and contributors to the site, writing and verifying content. They also hired experienced staff from magazines such as *Parenting*, *Parents*, and *Health*. Glickman commented, "We originally thought that we would aggregate content, but we got some early guidance that the company would be built on the relationships that we establish with people and that we needed to develop our content to really control the quality. It's a much more expensive decision and much more difficult to implement, but we made the choice to do it and it proved to be a good move." They also focused the content exclusively on the market segment from preconception to toddlers—up to age 2. This focus allowed the company to address topics from fertility to labor to child care to financial planning for the baby's education. BabyCenter offered original expert content, rather than user-generated or community content (although the site had community features). When eToys made its offer in April 1999, BabyCenter was the largest information source for

[1] Peter Sinton, "E-Tailing's Rising Stars," *San Francisco Chronicle*, January 27, 1999.

[2] BabyCenter Media Kit, April 1999.

[3] *ibid.*

[4] *ibid.*

expectant and new parents on the Internet with 15 million page views, 560,000 unique users, 180,000 registered users, and 1 million e-mails generated each month.[5]

Personalization was a key component of BabyCenter's content strategy because parents had different concerns at the various stages of pregnancy and their babies' development. BabyCenter addressed the need for tailored content at its launch by offering personal pages and weekly e-mails based on stage of development. (See Exhibit 3 for an example of a personal page.) The site also offered interactive tools to help parents plan and make decisions, such as a baby name finder, an immunization scheduler, and a calculator to work out how much to save for a child's college education.[6]

To earn revenue from its content, BabyCenter instituted a sponsorship program. It targeted companies with well-known brands, such as Johnson & Johnson, Charles Schwab, General Motors, and Procter & Gamble, to sponsor sections of the site that related to their products. Some observers criticized BabyCenter for creating relationships that could interfere with its objectivity, but advertising was a significant source of revenue for BabyCenter. The company charged a premium because of its targeted audience.

Community

Through market research, Glickman and Selcow learned that new and expectant parents were not only hungry for expert advice, they were also eager to talk to other people going through the same experiences. To provide a community forum, the site launched with bulletin boards to which hundreds of users wrote in with comments such as:

> *Thank you very much. I feel like your Web site saved my life (OK, maybe I am being a bit dramatic—it's the hormones), but really, until today I was feeling very alone in my pregnancy. My husband is amazing but can't understand what I'm going through. I was having a bit of a problem with my weight gain thus far, but after using your chat room and posting my concerns on the bulletin boards, I have talked to a lot of women who feel the same way as me. It is so nice to know that I am not alone. I plan to visit your site daily and tell everyone I know about it. You are doing more than you will ever know for me and I am sure tons of other women.*[7]

By 1999, BabyCenter had dozens of bulletin boards and regular live chat sessions with hosts to facilitate discussions.

[5] *ibid.*
[6] *ibid.*
[7] BabyCenter Web site.

Commerce

In October 1998, BabyCenter.com added an online store to its site. By then, BabyCenter had 55 employees. The site had won its first Webby Award, was getting approximately 10 million page views per month, and was generating about 400,000 e-mail newsletters per month.[8] After considering whether to partner with retailers or go it alone, BabyCenter's founders decided to become a full-fledged retailer—opening a warehouse, hiring merchants, taking on inventory, and handling fulfillment. Glickman felt that the opportunity for adding commerce to BabyCenter's existing site was unique given the market landscape.

> *There were information providers—doctors, books, and magazines—and there were retailers who sell products. But no one put the two together. If you think about it from the consumer perspective, they don't segregate like that. If you sat in on a focus group of moms they would very quickly weave between information concerns and products. Our approach was going against conventional wisdom in many ways. People asked "How can you sell product and have your information be unbiased and objective?" We are proving that consumers seem okay with that.*

BabyCenter's store leveraged the site's content to provide detailed product guides and reviews. For example, BabyCenter's interactive personal shopper asks customers 10 key questions about what features they want in a product, such as price, weight, size, and color, and can make recommendations based on customer's answers. To learn how to provide the best service and content about products, BabyCenter contracted with Lullaby Lane, an independent San Francisco-based baby store chain, to serve as a consultant. BabyCenter also offered product buying guides that consumers could consider before making a final purchase. Customers could find parents' product recommendations for certain products in the customer comment screens and in bulletin boards and could consult feature articles, such as a shopping checklist for preparing for baby, and a database that contained information product recalls. The store also provided gift services, such as gift wrapping, gift certificates, and gift guides, which recommended products based on a child's age. BabyCenter planned to launch a gift registry by the end of 1999. (Exhibit 4 contains financial data on BabyCenter and eToys.)

The BabyCenter store launched with 2,000 baby products and supplies and maternity items.[9] By the time eToys approached BabyCenter the number of SKUs available through BabyCenter had increased to 3,500 and included "everything you would ever need as a pregnant woman or parent."[10] The product mix included diapers, pacifiers, strollers, cribs, high chairs, linens, toys, and maternity and baby clothes. BabyCenter was also considering carrying private label items.

Customer service was a top priority. BabyCenter was organized to respond to e-mails, telephone calls, and faxes. Glickman summarized:

[8] BabyCenter Press Release, Jan 25, 1999.

[9] Renee M. Kruger, "Baby On Board," *Discount Merchandiser*, March 1999.

[10] *ibid.*

We expect Internet commerce to do very well in this market because convenience is so important. New parents are typically starved for time and they need an easy way to purchase baby gear, supplies, and gifts. Plus, if you're pregnant or bringing along a baby, it's harder to get around in the physical world. We're open 24 hours a day, 7 days a week, and we're accessible from anywhere in the world, including the comfort of home when the baby is napping.[11]

By April 1999, online retail sales represented about 1% of total U.S. retail sales. While Glickman expected BabyCenter to steal share from traditional retailers, he also believed that online retailers would grow the market.

Granted, our channel will probably take a little bit of share from the independents and a little bit of share from the giants, but we're not going to kill them, we're going to sit alongside them. I actually see the baby market expanding—that's what Amazon did for books, and we have an even better opportunity. Having a baby is such an intense time in people's lives that if we could just reach them with more information about products that can help them, I think that we will all sell more products overall and really grow this market.[12]

Consumer Health Interactive Division

In the same month, October 1998, that BabyCenter's online store launched, the company also launched a new custom publishing division called Consumer Health Interactive (CHI). CHI provided another outlet to leverage BabyCenter's content by serving as a resource for health plans that wanted to use the Internet for marketing and branding. CHI services included market research and editorial content development often in the form of weekly prenatal and pediatric e-mail newsletters, Web sites, and print products that BabyCenter cobranded with healthcare companies, such as Blue Shield of California and Oxford Health Plans.

Marketing and Advertising

BabyCenter's marketing strategy was initially focused on public relations and online advertising. The company received newspaper, magazine, and TV coverage. It also distributed marketing information that doctors could give to new and expectant parents in key markets. By April 1999, BabyCenter was advertising offline as well, mostly in parenting magazines, and was providing content to portals such as Excite, Netscape, Infoseek, and Go. However, it was not featured prominently in the Yahoo! or Lycos directory nor did it have banner ads for key words, such as baby, on those sites.

[11] *ibid.*
[12] *ibid.*

Technology

Technology accounted for most of BabyCenter's spending in its first year. The company's strategy was to build the tools that were core to its business advantage and to buy or outsource the rest. BabyCenter bought standard components like the application server, Web server, and chat software. It ran the site on Sun Solaris, a UNIX application and colocated Web servers at Exodus. The development team built a unique authoring system and content presentation system that targeted users by stage of pregnancy or age of baby and an e-mail system to support the targeting. The BabyCenter team customized the commerce software in the ATG's Dynamo application server to support unique features like gift registries.

U.S. Competition

BabyCenter faced several different types of competitors as summarized in Table 1. In the online space alone, more than 100 sites focused on the baby content and commerce markets. (See Exhibits 5, 6, and 7 for comparisons between competitors. See Exhibit 8 for Media Metrix data on several competitors.) Glickman commented: "Since parenting is a fun time, many would-be entrepreneurs are enthusiastic about selling some idea or product on the Internet—a lot of small sites have popped up run mostly out of people's homes. But it's very expensive to build an infrastructure, do the proper marketing, and maintain a true baby e-commerce business."[13] By April 1999, no major acquisitions or mergers had occurred between online baby content and commerce companies. However, some content sites were forming alliances with the commerce sites, placing them as links on their sites. For example, BabyNet.com, a site focused on content, had links to baby retailers and manufacturers on its site, including Babies"R"Us, BabyExpress.com, and Graco. Many offline competitors were also in the baby content and commerce markets, including books, magazines, doctors, friends, and family for information and catalogs, and national chains and local retailers for products. In April 1999, Glickman was most concerned with iVillage and Babies"R"Us.

TABLE 1 Competitors

Focus of Competitor	*Examples*	*Detail*
Online baby content	ParentSoup (part of iVillage.com), Family.com, Yahoo.com	Exhibits 5, 6, 7
Online baby retail	iBaby.com (part of iVillage.com), BabyBag.com, Wal-Mart.com	Exhibits 5, 6, 7
Offline baby content	*Parenting* magazine	
Offline baby retail	Babies"R"Us, Wal-Mart, Target, BabyGap	

[13] *ibid.*

• ***iVillage Sites: ParentSoup, ParentsPlace, iBaby/iMaternity.*** By April 1999, iVillage.com was the most visited women's online portal. The site consisted of 14 channels organized by topic addressing the interests of women aged 25 to 54. Channels included: family, health, work, money, food, relationships, shopping, travel, pets, and astrology. iVillage's channels related to BabyCenter's market were ParentSoup, ParentsPlace, and iBaby/iMaternity. (Exhibit 9 shows their home pages.) Eighty-two percent of its approximately 6 million visitors per month were women. iVillage had about 2 million members and averaged about 102 million page views over the quarter ending June 30, 1999. iVillage went public in March 1999. On April 15, 1999 the company had a market capitalization of about $2.5 billion. AOL owned approximately 8% of iVillage while NBC owned about 6%.[14]

• ***ParentSoup.*** iVillage described ParentSoup as "a parent site providing users with a branded online community where parents share parenting solutions, talk with experts, and find answers and support."[15] ParentSoup's audience ranged from couples beginning to plan their families to parents of teenagers. To allow for personalized use the site was organized by stage of parenting (pre-pregnancy, expecting parents, parents of babies, parents of toddlers, etc.). Like BabyCenter, ParentSoup sent e-mail newsletters tailored to the stage of children's development. The site offered many of the same features as BabyCenter including expert advice and community centers. (See Exhibit 10 for a comparison of site features.)

• ***ParentsPlace.*** ParentsPlace was "a parenting community center site that includes, on AOL and the Web, approximately 700 bulletin boards and approximately 80 weekly chats in addition to information regarding childhood disease."[16] Like ParentSoup, ParentsPlace's audience ranged from couples beginning to plan their families to parents of teenagers. iVillage acquired ParentsPlace in December 1996. Unlike ParentSoup, ParentsPlace was "created by two stay-at-home parents who believe parents are the best resource for other parents"—a more grassroots approach. ParentsPlace also sent e-mail newsletters tailored to children's development stage. The difference between ParentSoup and ParentsPlace's service and information offerings was unclear on the iVillage home page as well as within the individual sites.

• ***iBaby/iMaternity.*** iBaby Inc. was a wholly owned subsidiary of iVillage consisting of iBaby, the online store for baby products, and iMaternity, the associated online store for maternity products. The two were linked—if you were on iBaby, iMaternity was present as a tab you could click on and vice versa. iVillage acquired iBaby in 1998 and iMaternity in the spring of 1999. Although iBaby/iMaternity was a separate channel from iVillage's baby content channels, it was advertised on ParentSoup and ParentsPlace. The online store offered over 5,000 products from over 400 manufacturers for children under age 3. iVillage contracted with Kid's Warehouse, iVillage's former joint ven-

[14] iVillage S-1 Registration Statement, August 17, 1999.
[15] *ibid.*
[16] *ibid.*

ture partner in iBaby, to handle the inventory and fulfillment for iBaby. The contract was scheduled to terminate on November 1, 1999 when iBaby would perform its own inventory and fulfillment functions. A separate company handled the fulfillment for iMaternity. iBaby had approximately 50 employees in April 1999. The site offered content and services including buying guides, gift registries, gift finders and checklists, instructions (e.g., how to install a car seat), baby shower ideas, product recalls, and pregnancy tools. iBaby linked to iVillage through the iBaby homepage. However, users could only link to ParentSoup or ParentsPlace from iBaby/iMaternity by clicking on unbranded content/tool options, which linked out to either ParentSoup or ParentsPlace. iBaby had distribution agreements with AOL, Yahoo!, and Snap.

• ***Babies"R"Us.*** Babies"R"Us, a division of Toys"R"Us, was another serious competitor. The chain included 118 stores around the United States and was the leader in its category. These superstores were typically 38,000 to 42,000 square feet and carried a wide array of products for newborns to preschoolers, including furniture; car seats; strollers; clothing; toys; and feeding, health and beauty, and baby care supplies. The stores also offered an in-store baby registry service. Although the company's Web site contained only a store locator and some marketing information, there was always the threat that it would launch a full-scale e-commerce site like Toys"R"Us, which was talking about increasing its online offerings. In fiscal year 1998 (ending January 30, 1999), Babies"R"Us comparable store sales were up almost 20%. It was the shining star for Toys"R"Us, which announced plans to open 20 more Babies"R"Us stores in 1999.[17] Toys"R"Us had $11.2 billion in sales in fiscal year 1998, of which Babies"R"Us and Kids"R"Us (for older children) accounted for $1.6 billion. On April 15, 1999 Toys"R"Us market capitalization was $4.8 billion. (See Exhibit 11 for Babies"R"Us' homepage.)

BabyCenter INTERNATIONAL

By April 1999, BabyCenter faced new opportunities and challenges internationally. To maintain its perceived presence as the leading resource and retail site for expectant and new parents on the Internet it could no longer focus only on the U.S. market. While rates for PC penetration, online penetration, and e-commerce were higher in the United States than abroad, the real potential for future growth in this market lay in other developed countries that were coming up the Internet curve. Glickman knew that BabyCenter needed to evaluate the international marketplace, assess the key markets where its limited resources would produce immediate success, and develop a strategy for future growth. Failure on any of these fronts threatened to undo much of the company's progress.

Mission

From the outset, management encapsulated its mission for international expansion in three principles. The first was to expand BabyCenter, so that it would be identified as

[17] Toys"R"Us Annual Report, April 28, 1999.

a powerful global brand. Local markets demanded commerce and content that reflected their specific needs and desires. A successful rollout could stall if the local markets perceived the site and offerings as just a conduit of information and products from the United States. With the movement of Europe to the European Community (EC) model and e-base firms just starting up in Asia, Glickman believed that BabyCenter could become the brand of choice for parents around the world. The second principle was to balance near-term risk and long-term value creation. A critical error or misstep in the beginning could result in a permanent handicap while excess caution could allow the larger and local players time to blunt BabyCenter's challenge. Speed was a key but dangerous ally. The third principle was to minimize the impact of expansion on the financial and physical resources of BabyCenter USA. The firm's new international groups needed to be able to subsist from locally generated revenue while still staying within the orbit of the BabyCenter guidelines. Too much focus on meeting the bottom line risked alienating key elements of the customer base while a wrong choice of partner could mean financial and organizational suicide.

Approach

Like most other e-focused firms, BabyCenter faced a familiar set of challenges in considering its opportunities for international expansion. Fellow e-centric firms, such as Yahoo!, E*Trade, and Real Networks had each decided that expansion into international markets was the key at a similar point in their growth. However, despite the same core issue, each firm had exhibited a unique strategy that met with varying success. These strategies and their related risks fell into three separate approaches: fully licensing technology to a domestic player, funding and operating a wholly owned subsidiary, or creating a joint venture (Exhibit 12).

• ***Licensing.*** Those who saw speed as the primary concern often chose to license out the core technology and brand to a local group that could provide the immediate presence and resources to make a powerful entrance. This was often cost effective and successful, but if the wrong partner were chosen it could jeopardize both a firm's current operations and revenues and its long-term image and reputation. Nowhere was this concern greater than in the online space where a single misstep could create negative consumer perceptions that could require months or even years to undo.

• ***Subsidiary.*** Firms with both deep pockets and experienced employees often set up their own subsidiary operations to exercise the maximum control. A matrix model that focused on responsibility at both the regional and product levels, allowed the parent organization to constantly monitor and direct actions abroad. This model minimized risk but was prohibitively expensive and often led to "decision gridlock" that endangered the firm. With so many individuals involved in every key evaluation, the firm could miss important opportunities and lose market share.

• ***Joint Venture.*** The joint venture option (JV) offered the firm a middle ground between the full financial commitment of owning a subsidiary and the lack of influence that licensing created. Time to market and brand risk were similarly positioned between the other two structures. Envisioned as a way to maximize management skill at headquarters in conjunction with local administration, the JV applied to many firms. To date, however, online firms had had only limited success with this model because battles between participants over strategic direction and control often led to delays and missed market opportunities. Both partners also often saved their best employees for critical projects closer to their core operations instead of contributing them to the JV. BabyCenter's unique content/commerce model and sensitive consumer base made the choice of a JV more critical and difficult.

Competition: The Bricks-and-Mortar Firms

Small firms that were primarily family owned, inefficient, and often without effective distribution crowded the traditional bricks-and-mortar space in many countries outside the United States. Product designs were frequently outdated and sometimes dangerous. Prices were high, but so was demand for imported products (primarily from American manufacturers). The potential for increased sales due to pent-up demand was enormous. On the surface, this sector appeared to offer the "low-hanging" fruit that BabyCenter was after. Nonetheless the international market and its players could not be treated lightly. Consumer buying patterns still favored the traditional model, and most of these firms knew their markets and the needs of their customers. A mother was much more likely to buy a stroller from the shop that had sold one to her mother and whose owner she saw every day than she was to buy from a firm that she had only just heard of. To garner even 5% of a specific country's revenue in this space would take considerable local expertise and a push to educate the local public about the merits of both the firm and the Internet itself. Nevertheless, BabyCenter had the chance to gain a huge lead in its race to become the preeminent worldwide retail brand among new parents.

Competition: The Online Firms

The online space for the international market was wide open. The Internet had enjoyed the lion's share of its growth within the United States, which gave BabyCenter a definite advantage in leading the race to win online consumers in new markets. The knowledge and experience gained from its original launching offered BabyCenter the chance to take a leading position almost immediately. The Internet offerings of local players were often little more than a scanned photo and description of a product. The option for an e-commerce transaction was rare and purchases often required bank transfers or a money order before the merchandise would be shipped. Furthermore, these online players were often only retail and mail order firms with no experience or understanding of e-commerce. Every market had one or two competitors with the potential to challenge online, but as of early 1999, these challenges were in a fledging stage at best (Exhibits 13, 14, and 15). The biggest challenges were local regulatory environments and the very size of the potential market. Attitudes and opinions toward the Internet varied by country, and a firm could be frozen out of a national market if lawmakers saw it as a threat to a segment of their national economics. In addition, many international markets were small compared to the U.S. market. In some international markets, the user base in 1999 might not justify launching a site.

Location

BabyCenter identified three geographic regions as "e-zones." These consisted of a German e-zone (Germany, Austria, Switzerland, and Benelux), a U.K. e-zone (U.K., Ireland, and Scandinavia), and an Asian e-zone (Japan, China, Taiwan, and Australia). Key criteria included Internet usage, e-commerce penetration rates, population size, baby-specific spending levels, and per capita income. BabyCenter also considered ease of marketing, distribution, availability and quality of content partners, and the ability to leverage its existing strengths. E-toy's potential acquisition of the firm (at the time) and that company's international market strategy complicated the choice of international markets.

• ***German E-zone.*** The cultural characteristics of the German e-zone posed many problems for BabyCenter. Regulations of the German e-zone were among the most severe in the EC. Many of the products that faced little scrutiny under U.S. laws would have to be tested and checked against much higher standards before they could be sold in this region. As a result, delays and additional costs to manufacturers could drive the price of an offering out of the consumer's range. Parents in this e-zone also rated product quality and safety as top priorities. Design was a key factor in purchasing decisions, and some proven brands and products led sales for decades. Because content was unknown in these marketplaces, BabyCenter would need to partner with an established magazine or group of authors to make an impact. Despite these difficulties, the German e-zone offered the best combination of e-commerce penetration and established core baby product market. Research indicated that BabyCenter would face the smallest hurdles to establishing noticeable Internet based sales in this region.

• ***U.K. E-zone.*** Similarities in both consumer preferences and usage patterns between the U.S. and the U.K. e-zone pushed this region to the head of the line for the launch location. Despite differences in styles of presentation and interface with the e-consumer, so much potential for cross-transfer of both content and product existed in this e-zone that BabyCenter would be hard pressed to go elsewhere given the market and competitive pressures that were arising in this sector. Many of the top-selling products in the pre- and postnatal care sector were the same for the United States and the United Kingdom, and content offerings in the form of magazines and media were similar. Nevertheless, pursuing this market had risks. First was the risk that BabyCenter would be unable to penetrate other e-zones if became bogged down in the U.K. e-zone. Germany and Asia, which had greater long-term potential, could be lost and never regained. Consumers and competition in these e-zones could also paint or perceive BabyCenter as "Anglo-centric" and use this image to retard the firm's potential to grow outside the United States and the United Kingdom. Finally, the potential revenue of the U.K. market was smaller than that of the other e-zones.

• ***Asian E-zone.*** Unlike both the German and U.K. e-zones, the Asian e-zone appeared to be primarily about future potential and the opportunity to be the first to market with a product that might be 4–5 years ahead of any equivalent local offering. While the existing user base in the Asian e-zone was equivalent in numbers to the German and U.K. e-zones, the growth rates in all critical areas were far greater. The problems however, were equally great. BabyCenter had little expertise or understanding about what Asian consumers desired or about their needs for information and products. While imported products were often priced at a premium and considered prestigious, more than 85% of sales were of products made domestically, with materials and designs noticeably different from those of imports. Tapping into this group of consumers would be an unprecedented challenge. Developing effective content would also require a strong commitment of resources and expertise.

eTOYS

While Glickman had intended to take BabyCenter public in the near future, eToys forced him to consider how eToys' market position, strategy, technology, and culture would complement BabyCenter.

Company Background

At the same time that Glickman and Selcow were starting BabyCenter in 1996, Edward Lenk, who had been vice president of strategic planning at Disney after graduating from Harvard Business School was starting eToys in southern California. Like BabyCenter, eToys' Web site launched a year after the company was founded, in October 1997. eToys was the first Internet player in its category.

Market

The U.S. retail toy market was $30 billion in 1998.[18] Jupiter Communications reported that the U.S. online toy market was $52 million in 1998 and expected to grow to over $1 billion by 2003. The entire worldwide toy market was approximately $68 billion in 1998. (See Exhibit 16 for more information on the worldwide toy market.) eToys also had potential to address the markets for children's apparel, books, sporting goods, and back-to-school and party supplies, which constituted another $35 billion in 1999. Some analysts expected at least 10% of children's retail sales market to migrate to online in the near future.[19]

[18] Shop.org, Boston Consulting Group, 1998.
[19] Jamie Kiggen, "eToys Inc.," DLJ, June 14, 1999.

Strategy

eToys' goal was to become one of the world's leading retailers of children's products. To reach that goal, eToys had formulated a strategy that included the following elements:

1. Focus on online retailing of children's products.
2. Increase net sales by expanding product offering within existing categories, adding more of children's products, and new shopping services; expanding internationally; and acquiring complementary businesses, products, and technologies.
3. Encourage repeat purchases by direct marketing to existing customers and improving personalization and customer services.
4. Build strong brand recognition by marketing both online and offline.
5. Maintain technology focus and expertise in dealing with customers, vendors, and internal distribution and operations.[20]
6. Glickman estimated that eToys was about a year ahead of BabyCenter in terms of technology. eToys also operated a 60,000 square-foot distribution facility in Commerce, California.

Web Site

In April 1999, eToys sold children's products including toys, video games, software, videos, and music. The company provided its 365,000 customers with a choice of over 9,500 SKUs representing more than 750 brands. eToys had net sales of $24 million in 1998 (95% in the fourth quarter) and a net loss of $16.5 million.[21] (Exhibit 4 contains more financial data.) eToys offered extensive product choice among well-known and specialty brands, detailed product information, and shopping services. With its slogan "We bring the toy store to you," eToys was committed to making shopping for toys as easy as possible offering content, reviews, and services, such as gift search and reminder services. (Exhibit 2 shows eToys home page.)

Marketing and Advertising

When eToys launched in 1997, it paid AOL $3.1 million to become an anchor tenant on AOL's sites for 26 months. AOL would prominently promote and advertise eToys on a nonexclusive basis in online areas AOL controlled.[22] By February 1999, eToys had affiliate agreements with 5,000 other Web sites, such as USA Today and Ameritech, giving them 25% of each sales dollar when they steered a new customer to

[20] eToys Prospectus, May 20, 1999.
[21] *ibid.*
[22] *ibid.*

eToys.[23] eToys also had deals with Children's Television Network and Moms Online to feature eToys as the preferred online toy retailer. eToys had marketing relationships with Yahoo!, Microsoft, Excite, Lycos, and Infoseek. eToys had a print advertising campaign in publications, such as *Parenting*, *Parents*, and *Child* and did radio and TV advertising. The TV campaigns were separate copromotions with Visa and Intel.

Competition

By April 1999, eToys competed with different types of players both on- and offline. eToys was the leader in the online toy market with approximately 46% share in 1998. However, the online market was still less than 2% of total U.S. toy retail sales that year. Table 2 provides a description of some of eToys' competitors in April 1999. The toy industry was concentrated: the top five retailers had 54% (Table 3) of the market in 1998, and the top two manufacturers had 50% of the wholesale market.[24]

• ***Wal-Mart.*** Wal-Mart was the largest retailer in the world with over 1,800 discount stores, 550 supercenters, and 450 Sam's Clubs by April 1999. Wal-Mart overtook Toys"R"Us as the number-one retailer of toys in the United States in 1998. Toys accounted for about 5% of Wal-Mart's $138 billion sales in fiscal year 1998 (ended January 1999). The company offered about 200 toys through its Web site in the spring of 1999. Wal-Mart's market capitalization was about $435 billion on April 15, 1999.

TABLE 2 eToys' Competitors

Type of Competitor	*Examples*	*Offline*	*Online*
Store-based toy retailers	Toys"R"Us, FAO Schwarz, Zany Brainy, Noodle Kidoodle	✓	✓
Mass market retailers	Wal-Mart, Target, Kmart	✓	✓
Specialty retailers	Disney Stores, Warner Bros.	✓	✓
Manufacturers of children's products	Mattel, Hasbro		✓
Catalog retailers	Toys"R"Us and FAO Schwarz had mail and Internet catalogs	✓	✓
Online toy retailers	BrainPlay.com, RedRocket.com, ToySmart.com		✓
Online retailers with toys	Amazon.com		✓
Internet portal with shopping channels for children's products	Yahoo!, AOL, Excite		✓

[23] Patricia Sellers, "Inside the First E-Christmas" *Fortune*, February 1, 1999.
[24] Shop.org, Boston Consulting Group, 1998.

TABLE 3 Top Five U.S. Toy Retailers in 1998[25]

Company	*Toy Sales (billions)*	*Market Share*
Wal-Mart (discount stores only)	$4.7	23%
Toys"R"Us (U.S. stores only)	4.6	22
Kmart	2.2	10
Target	1.9	9
KB Toys	1.3	6
Top five total sales	14.7	70

• ***Toys"R"Us.*** Toys"R"Us was the largest toy-only retailer in 1998 operating 1,156 traditional toy stores, 212 Kids"R"Us stores, 118 Babies"R"Us stores, and 2 mail-order catalogs. Toys"R"Us began selling online in June 1998. By April 1999, the company offered about 2,000 products from over 200 vendors through its Web site and catalogs.[26]

POTENTIAL ACQUISITION

Glickman knew that eToys might help BabyCenter to grow, but the companies were different. Some of the key points of comparison are listed in Table 4. (Exhibit 4 contains more financial data.)

Decision Time

Lenk wanted the BabyCenter acquisition to happen. After the mutual investor contacted BabyCenter and received the usual answer, "We will certainly consider it, but we are not for sale," Lenk requested a personal meeting with Glickman and Selcow. The BabyCenter founders decided to talk to him although they did not need to do the deal for the capital it would bring. BabyCenter had not touched a penny of the $10 million venture round it had raised in the autumn of 1998. Plus, the founders were in the midst of raising another round from strategic investors to prepare for their own public offering. As Glickman thought about the deal, he considered the state of his company. The online space was growing, competitors were popping up in the United States and internationally, and alliances were beginning to form. Glickman believed that BabyCenter could survive on its own, but he wondered if it might need a bigger partner to reach its full potential, and if so, was eToys the right one? Perhaps one of the other Internet or traditional medial players like Amazon, Yahoo!, or NBC might be a better fit for BabyCenter.

[25] Mitch Bartlett, "eToys Inc.," Dain Rauscher Wessel, June 14, 1999.
[26] *ibid.*

TABLE 4 Comparison of BabyCenter and eToys

	BabyCenter	*eToys*
Location	San Francisco, Calif.	Santa Monica, Calif.
Number of employees	105	306
Annual revenue	$4.8 million	$30.0 million
Gross profit	$3.8 million	$ 5.7 million
Gross profit margin	79% (includes only five months of commerce, analysts expected this to drop to about 55%)	19%
Sources of revenue	Product sales, advertising, sponsorships, fees from CHI	Product sales
Number of users*	690,000	1,163,000
Average minutes spent per usage month*	12.6	7.2
Average order size+	$75	$52
Projected acquisition cost per customer+	$40	$35
Year 1 frequency of purchases per customer+	2.7×	3.0×
Year 4 frequency of purchases per customer+	1.1×	2.0×

Data from fiscal year 1998 (ended March 3, 1999) unless otherwise noted. eToys Prospectus, May 20, 1999.
* Media Metrix Data, May 1999.
+Estimates from Mitch Bartlett, "eToys Inc.," Dain Rauscher Wessel, June 14, 1999.

EXHIBIT 1 BabyCenter.com Homepage (April 1999)

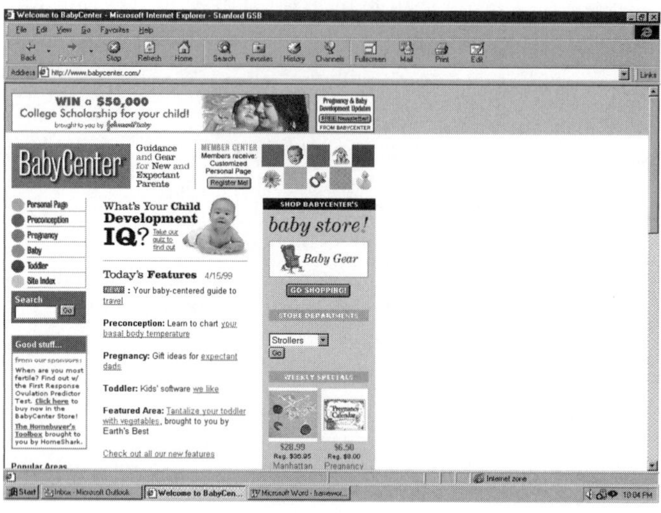

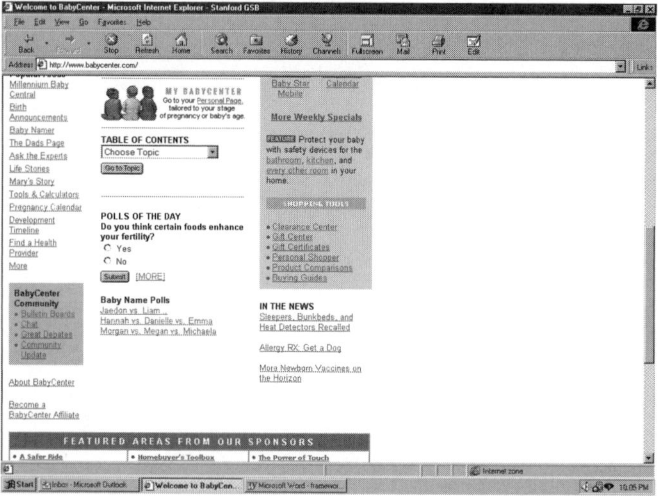

EXHIBIT 2 eToys.com Homepage (February 2000)

EXHIBIT 3 BabyCenter Personal Page (February 2000)

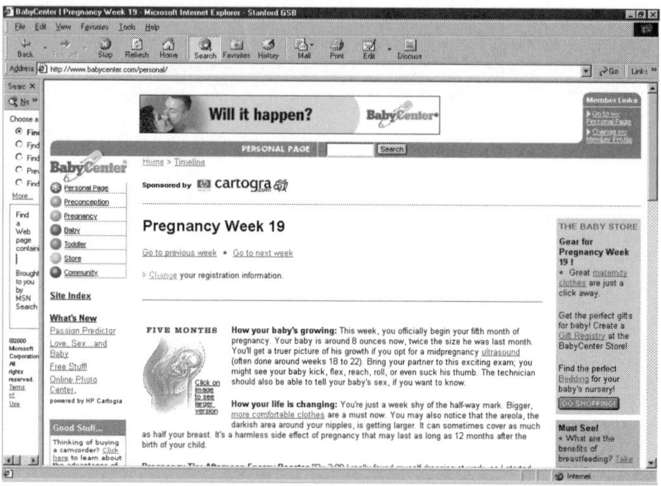

EXHIBIT 4a Financial Data for BabyCenter and eToys

(In thousands)	*Fiscal Year Ended March 31*		
	1998 eToys	*1999 eToys*	*1999 Pro Forma eToys + BabyCenter Merged*
Statement of Operations Data			
Net sales	$687	$29,959	$34,727
Cost of sales	568	24,246	25,227
Gross profit	119	5,713	9,500
Operating expenses			
Marketing and sales	1,290	20,719	23,180
Product development	421	3,608	7,360
General and administrative	678	10,166	16,405
Goodwill amortization	—	319	36,455
Total operating expenses	2,389	34,812	83,400
Operating loss	(2,270)	(29,099)	(73,900)
Interest income (expense), net	3	542	798

Source: eToys Prospectus May 20, 1999.

(continued)

EXHIBIT 4a *(continued)*

(In thousands)	*Fiscal Year Ended March 31*		
	1998 eToys	*1999 eToys*	*1999 Pro Forma eToys + BabyCenter Merged*
Statement of Operations Data			
Loss before income taxes	$(2,267)	$(28,557)	$(73,102)
Provision for income taxes	1	1	1
Net loss	(2,268)	(28,558)	(73,103)
Balance Sheet			
Cash and cash equivalents	$1,552	$20,173	$29,173
Working capital	1,456	21,821	29,643
Total assets	2,927	30,966	222,639
Long-term capital lease obligations, less current portions	—	477	1,041

Source: eToys Prospectus May 20, 1999.

EXHIBIT 4b eToys Quarterly Results of Operations

	Dec. 31, 1997	*March 31, 1998*	*June 30, 1998*	*Sept. 30, 1998*	*Dec. 31, 1998*	*March 31, 1999*
Statement of Operations Data						
Net sales	$530	$157	$381	$608	$22,910	$6,059
Cost of sales	438	130	311	496	18,201	5,238
Gross profit	92	27	70	112	4,709	821
Operating expenses						
Marketing and sales	444	658	1,370	2,372	10,611	6,365
Product development	145	215	404	697	905	1,602
General and administrative	234	312	462	703	3,180	6,140
Total operating expenses	823	1,185	2,236	3,772	14,696	14,107
Operating loss	(731)	(1,158)	(2,166)	(3,660)	(9,987)	(13,286)
Interest income (expense), net	–15	18	5	277	166	104
Provision for income taxes	0	1	0	0	1	0
Net loss	(746)	(1,141)	(2,161)	(3,383)	(9,822)	(13,182)

Note: Quarterly data does not include BabyCenter.
Source: eToys Prospectus May 20, 1999.

(continued)

EXHIBIT 4b *(continued)*

	Dec. 31, 1997	*March 31, 1998*	*June 30, 1998*	*Sept. 30, 1998*	*Dec. 31, 1998*	*March 31, 1999*
As a Percentage of Net Sales						
Net sales	100%	100%	100%	100%	100%	100%
Cost of sales	83	83	82	82	79	86
Gross profit	17	17	18	18	21	14
Operating expenses						
Marketing and sales	84	419	360	390	46	105
Product development	27	137	106	115	4	26
General and administrative	44	199	121	116	14	101
Total operating expenses	155	755	587	620	64	233
Operating loss	(138)	(738)	(569)	(602)	(44)	(219)
Interest income (expense), net	(3)	11	1	46	1	2
Provision for income taxes	0	1	0	0	0	0
Net loss	(141)	(727)	(567)	(556)	(43)	(218)

Note: Quarterly data does not include BabyCenter.
Source: eToys Prospectus May 20, 1999.

EXHIBIT 5 Major U.S. Online Players in Baby Content and Commerce Markets (April 1999)

Category Focus	*Description*	*Content*	*Community*	*Commerce*	*Number*	*Examples*	*Comments*
Content	Baby-focused comprehensive sites	✓	✓	✓	1	BabyCenter.com	Content, community, and baby and maternity commerce on one integrated site
	Baby-focused pure content sites	✓	✓		70+	Parenttime.com, AmericanBaby.com, BabyNet.com, ParenthoodWeb.com	Some are the online sites of magazines like *Parenttime* and *American Baby*. Others are developed by moms and dads. Some link out to various online stores or manufacturers.
	Family and women's portals with baby/family channels	✓	✓	✓*	3	iVillage.com, Women.com, Family.com, OxygenMedia.com	Portals with different channels focused on baby or parenting. Shopping and content are located on different sites within the portal family.
	Health portals	✓			10	OnHealth.com	Sites with broad range of health information including pregnancy and baby.

(continued)

EXHIBIT 5 *(continued)*

Category Focus	*Description*	*Content*	*Community*	*Commerce*	*Number*	*Examples*	*Comments*
Content	Portals	✓		✓	6	Excite.com, Yahoo.com, Go.com	Some sites have a baby or family channel with basic aggregated content, others simply link out to other sites. Separate shopping channels.
	Baby-care manufacturers				10	Pampers.com, Evenflo.com	Mostly marketing sites. Few have content. None sell product.
Commerce	Baby products			✓	30+	BabyBag.com, BabyFurniture.com, BabyCatalog.com	Wide variety of depth. Some focus on higher ticket items like furniture, strollers, etc. Some offer maternity items. A few offer limited content such asproduct recommendations.
	Baby superstores				1	Babies“R”Us.com	A marketing site for a 118-store chain.
Mass merchandise	Retailers			✓	3	Wal-Mart.com, Kmart.com	Have baby product and toy aisles among broad product offering. Some are linked to content.

(continued)

EXHIBIT 5 *(continued)*

Category Focus	*Description*	*Content*	*Community*	*Commerce*	*Number*	*Examples*	*Comments*
Specialty commerce	Toy stores			✓	10+	eToys.com, Toys"R"Us.com	Several have an offline presence and were expanding outside of toys.
	Baby clothing stores			✓	100+	BabyGap.com, ChildrensPlace.com	Many have an offline presence.
	Maternity clothing stores			✓	20+	iMaternity.com	Offer selection of maternity clothes.
	Bookstores			✓	100+	Amazon.com, Barnesandnoble.com	Many have an offline presence.
	Drugstores	✓		✓	5+	Drugstore.com, Planetrx.com	Good selection of baby health and care products. Some have content.

* As part of separate sites.
Source: Case writer and The Boston Consulting Group.

EXHIBIT 6 U.S. Online Players in Baby Markets by Category (April 1999)

	Contents/community focus	*Both on one site*	*Commerce focus*
Baby only	BabySoon.com ePregnancy.com StorkNet.com StorkSite.com (Women.com) WholeNineMonths.com (Women.com)	BabyCenter.com	BabyBag.com BabyCatalog.com BabyFurniture.com BabyGap.com iBaby.com/iMaternity.com (iVillage.com)
Baby and children	ParentSoup.com (iVillage.com) ParentsPlace.com (iVillage.com) MomsOnline.com (OxygenMedia) Parenttime.com ParenthoodWeb.com iParenting.com		BabyStyle.com eToys.com ChildrensPlace.com
Broad	OnHealth.com	Excite.com Yahoo.com Snap.com Planetrx.com	Wal-Mart.com Kmart.com Drugstore.com Amazon.com

Source: Case writer.

EXHIBIT 7 Perceptual Map—Content vs. Commerce of U.S. Online Players in Baby Markets (April 1999)

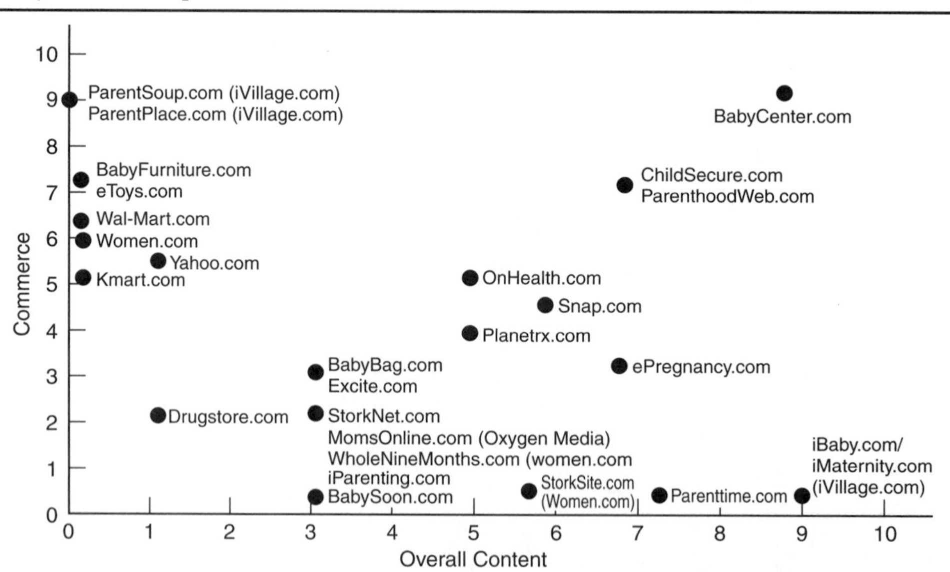

EXHIBIT 8 Media Metrix Data (May 1999)

	Reach and Frequency								
Site	*Digital Media Reach %*			*Digital Media Unique Visitors (000)*			*Average Usage Days per Visitor*		
	Home/ Work	*Home*	*Work*	*Home/ Work*	*Home*	*Work*	*Home/ Work*	*Home*	*Work*
WWW/Online	100.0	100.0	100.0	64,751	60,296	22,073	13.9	11.6	13.1
Web sites	100.0	100.0	100.0	64,751	60,926	22,073	13.9	11.6	13.1
BabyCenter.com	1.1	0.7	1.3	690	435	286	1.7	1.7	1.6
eToys.com	1.8	1.5	1.2	1,163	939	275	1.3	1.2	1.6
iVillage: The Women's Network	5.9	4.1	6.4	3,822	2,509	1,415	2.0	1.9	2.1
Women.com sites	3.1	2.1	3.7	1,984	1,301	815	1.7	1.5	1.8
AOL Network— Proprietary & WWW	71.4	67.8	64.7	46,243	41,301	14,286	9.4	8.6	7.2
AOL Web sites	62.3	56.3	59.3	40,364	34,331	13,093	5.5	4.7	5.1
Microsoft sites	50.0	45.1	54.9	32,389	27,454	12,118	6.5	5.6	5.7
Yahoo! sites	48.3	41.9	53.2	31,299	25,537	11,751	6.0	4.9	6.0
Lycos	46.3	38.7	43.2	29,963	23,570	9,531	3.2	3.0	2.8
Go Network	32.2	26.0	34.7	20,864	15,846	7,664	3.5	3.1	3.4
GeoCites	30.8	25.7	27.0	19,965	15,687	5,953	2.7	2.6	2.3
Netscape	28.6	22.5	35.8	18,537	13,681	7,907	5.8	4.9	5.6
Excite Network, The	26.6	21.7	27.8	17,192	13,211	6,147	4.2	3.9	3.7
Amazon.com	16.7	12.7	17.8	10,831	7,740	3,919	2.0	1.8	2.0
eBay	12.8	10.9	13.0	8,262	6,624	2,868	5.2	5.1	4.3
Drugstore.com	1.4	0.9	1.6	910	565	345	1.4	1.3	1.5

Source: Media Metrix, Inc.

EXHIBIT 9 iVillage.com Baby-Related Web Sites (April 1999)

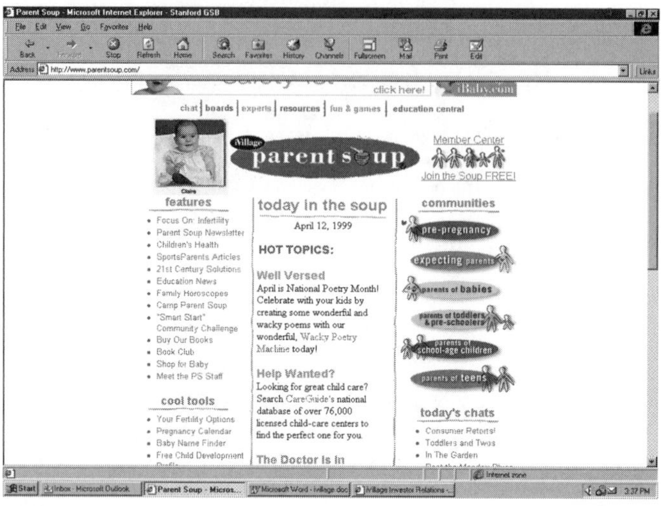

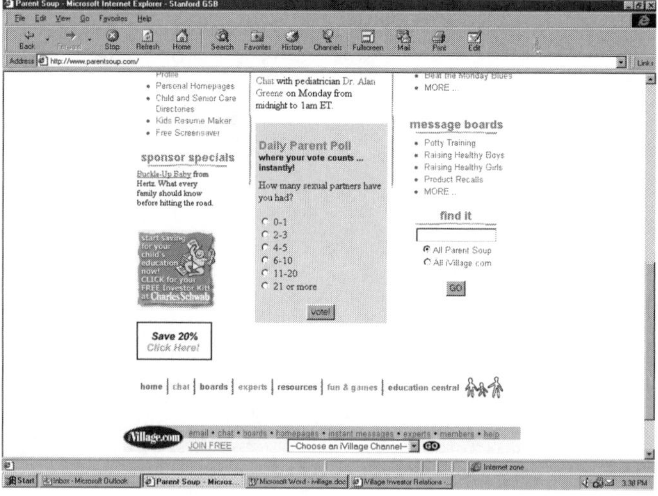

EXHIBIT 9 *(continued)*

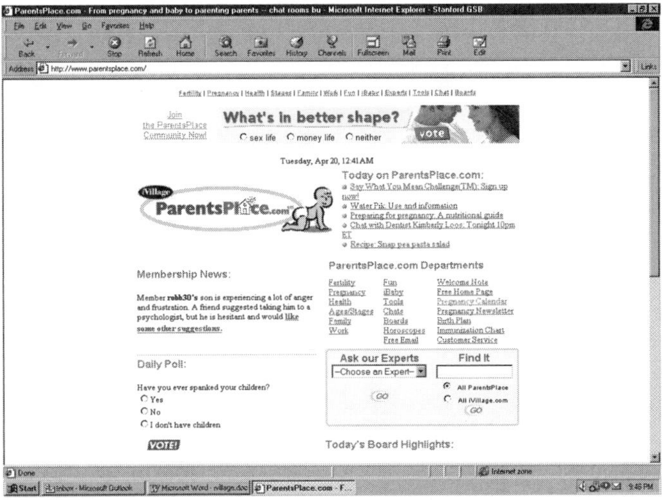

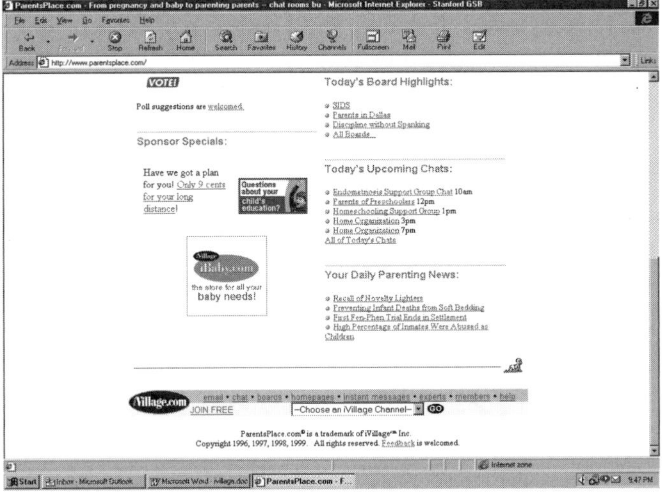

EXHIBIT 9 *(continued)*

EXHIBIT 10 BabyCenter vs. iVillage Feature Comparison (April 1999)

Features	BabyCenter	iVillage's ParentSoup	iVillage's ParentsPlace	iVillage's iBaby/iMaternity
Hard medical	excellent	none	excellent	none
Care and parenting	excellent	excellent	excellent	none
Ask the experts	excellent	good	good	none
Baby namer	excellent	very good	very good	none
Chat/message	excellent	excellent	excellent	none
Product info	excellent	none	none	excellent
Recall	excellent	excellent	good	excellent
Store	excellent	none	none	excellent
Fun for mom	fair	excellent	excellent	none
Entertainment for kids	none	good	excellent	none
Future planning tools	very good	very good	none	none
Local resources	fair	good	none	none

Legend: excellent, very good, good, fair, none

EXHIBIT 11 Babies"R"Us Homepage (February 2000)

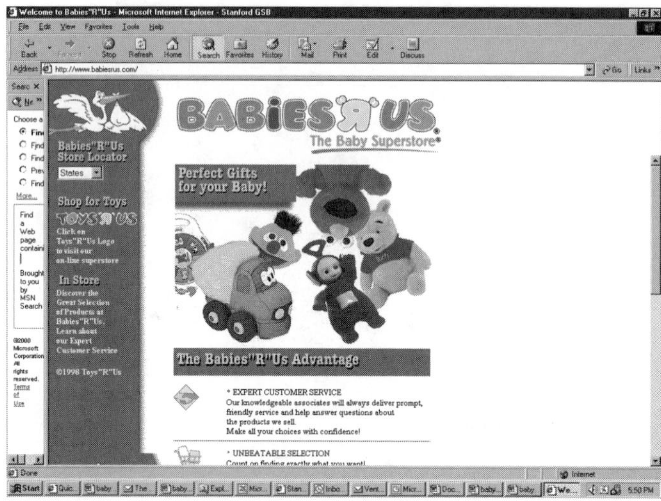

Reproduced with permission from Babies"R"Us/Toys"R"Us.

EXHIBIT 12 International Operating Structure—Key Decision Criteria

	BabyCenter Perspective	*Owned Subsidiary*	*Joint Venture*	*License*
Financial risk	High	High	Medium	Low
Brand risk	High	Low	Medium	High
Time to market	High	Low	Medium	High
Impact on U.S. operations	High	High	Medium	Low
Control over operations	Medium	High	Medium	Low
Need for management	Low	High	Medium	Low

Source: Case writer.

EXHIBIT 13 U.K. E-zone

Country/Name/URL	*Company Background*	*Business Model*	*Content*	*Community*	*Commerce*	*Overall Threat*
United Kingdom						
Mothercare www.mothercare.co.uk	Leading U.K.-based international catalog and B&M retailer of infant products. 340 stores in the U.K. and another 100 throughout the world.	1. Allows consumer to order catalog and provides information on how to order products. 2. Allows PDF download of content but very slow/limited. 3. Provides physical store finder database (ZIP code).	Yes, limited	No	No	High: Requires e-commerce build-out to truly maximize threat
Babies“R”Us—U.K. www.babiesrus.co.uk	U.S.-based, international B&M retailer.	E-commerce focused but with limited content. Includes store search directory and online registry.	Yes, very limited	Yes	Yes	High: Strong brand and existing distribution infrastructure
Tots 2 Teens www.tots2teens.co.uk	U.K. fashion retailer focusing on children’s clothing.	E-commerce retailer. Focused on clothing for infants and babies. Search by price and category.	No	No	Yes	Medium: Expansion of product selection and content
Babyworld www.babyworld.co.uk www.babyworld.com	U.K.-based Web site for expectant and new parents.	In-house experts for buying advice and product recommendations. Limited e-commerce functionality.	Yes	Yes	No	Medium: Needs to build brand and e-commerce capability

Source: Case writer.

EXHIBIT 14 Asian E-zone

Country/Name/URL	*Company Background*	*Business Model*	*Content*	*Community*	*Commerce*	*Overall Threat*
Taiwan						
BabyHQ.com www.babyhq.com.tw	Retailer of infant products. Three physical stores selling baby products such as toys, cradles, car seats, clothes, and feeding equipments.	No e-commerce capabilities. Site exists to provide information/advertisement for physical store.	Minimal—suggestions for mothers on number of items to buy.	No	No	Low
Heartland						
www.geocities.com/Heartland/Pointe/6326/	Heartland is a Taiwan-based retailer of infant products: car seats, strollers, cradles, toys, baby feeding equipment. Note: Sponsored by geocities.	Web site exists to provide information on products carried by company. Provides some content to draw eyeballs.	Has baby health advice such as allergies to protein, immunization, bathing procedures.	No	No	Medium
Singapore						
Tollyjoy www.tollyjoy.com.sg	Tollyjoy is a manufacturer of infant products.	Site exists to provide product information only. Does not provide pricing information.	Has product information.	No	No	Low

(continued)

EXHIBIT 14 *(continued)*

Country/Name/URL	*Company Background*	*Business Model*	*Content*	*Community*	*Commerce*	*Overall Threat*
Anton & Tan						
http://web.singnet.com.sg/~antint/index.htm	Anton & Tan is a retailer of infant products.	Site exists to provide information on NUK products only.	Has product information on NUK.	No	No	Low
China						
Lovebaby.com www.lovebaby.com	Ai Bao Bao	Site exists to provide information and links to hospitals and retailers of baby products. Has great content: information ranging from rules of getting married in China to detailed pregnancy symptoms to infant care.	Great content	Has a discussion board	No	Low

(continued)

EXHIBIT 14 *(continued)*

Country/Name/ URL	*Company Background*	*Business Model*	*Content*	*Community*	*Commerce*	*Overall Threat*	*Comments*
Japan							
Aprica www.aprica.co.jp	Manufacturer of car seats, strollers, etc. Excellent reputation within the Japanese market space for design and quality.	Web site exists to provide information such as lists of retailers; repair locations; and detailed explanation of product. Product search based on age. Another means to order from catalog.	Good information on their products. Advice on suitability, etc.	Some attempt. Comments and letters from visitors to site and users of product. Not very well tied in with consumer.	No	Low	Factories in Japan, China, Taiwan. Other branches in Italy, U.S., and Korea.
Milky Age www.milkyage.com	Leading children's product mail catalog firm.	Site exists to provide product information and the ability to order a catalog online.	Has product information and descriptions.	No	No	Low to medium	Good reputation. Potential for entry into commerce space.

(continued)

EXHIBIT 14 *(continued)*

Country/Name/ URL	*Company Background*	*Business Model*	*Content*	*Community*	*Commerce*	*Overall Threat*	*Comments*
Mikihouse www.mikihouse.co.jp	The leading domestic retailer of toys in Japan.	Online commerce but secondary to information on products and ground locations of stores.	Product offerings	No	Yes	Medium to high	Large name brand and resource base. Only site that allows use of credit.

Source: Case writer.

EXHIBIT 15 German E-zone

Country/Name/URL	*Company Background*	*Business Model*	*Content*	*Community*	*Commerce*	*Overall Threat*
Germany						
BabyProfi Markt www.babyprofi.de	Retailer of infant products. Physical presence in five German cities. Commercial part of Web site not active yet.	E-commerce to support physical network in sales and advertising.	Only provides links to content/advice pages across the German Web.	No	Yes	Medium
Pitti Plasch www.pitti-platsch.de	Straight to the point commerce. Potentially an extension of physical presence.	Easy to use, pictures—no content. Pure capitalism.	No	No	Yes	Medium
Klapperstorch Online www.klapperstorch-online.de	Similar in feel to BabyCenter—just in its “infant” stages. Site will support e-commerce.	Collects e-mail addresses to start database on information dissemination.	Emphasis on content even though currently fairly thin.	No	Not active yet—plans are made explicit.	Medium-high
Baby Online www.babyonline.de	Commercial site in the beginning stages.	Hard core commerce, variety of merchandise. “Everything for the baby.”	Minimal	No	Yes	Medium-high

Source: Case writer.

EXHIBIT 16 Worldwide Toy Market

Worldwide Toy Market
(Billions of U.S. dollars)

	1996	*1998*
North America	23.4	27.6
Asia	16.8	18
Europe	16	16.9
Latin and South America	2.6	2.8
Oceania	1.3	1.4
Middle East	1.0	1.0
Total	61.1	67.7

Toy Expenditure per Child (1997)	
North America	$340.51
Middle East	252.02
Europe	144.25
Latin and South America	16.03
Asia	13.85
Africa	1.54
World average	$128.03

Distribution Channels (1997)
Percentage of Total

	Toy Chains	*General Merchandise*	*Toy, Hobby, Game Retailers*	*Department Stores*	*Other*	*Total*
North America	23	42	7	3	25	100
Europe	28	32	9	10	21	100
Asia	23	26	31	10	10	100
Latin and South America	16	41	20	17	6	100

Source: The Boston Consulting Group. Reproduced with permission.

HP E-SERVICES.SOLUTIONS

The concept behind e-services is there's a particular task, asset, or capability that you want to gain access to, that now can be made available to you over the Net, because it's now being created as an Internet service. —*Linda Lazor, Director of Operations, ESS, Hewlett-Packard*

How does any large company reinvent itself? Can a company with a past have a future? I mean that's basically the question that we're posing because a lot of people claim that anyone who has a past does not have a future in this world. —*Nick Earle, President, ESS, Hewlett-Packard*

In April 2000, Nick Earle sat in his cubicle in the Hewlett-Packard (HP) campus in Cupertino, California. He wore a wireless telephone headset that allowed him to wander about his team's open cubes as he fielded calls from potential business partners. Earle, age 42, was president and chief evangelist of the 90-person E-Services.Solutions (ESS) group, which had grown out of a task force he had put together more than a year earlier. Asked to create an Internet marketing strategy, he and several other "frustrated radicals" created a plan that led to the ESS group. ESS now held the mandate to develop an Internet strategy and framework for HP.

Earle's team faced tough challenges. They had pulled together some great technologies and products within HP and secured partnerships with other companies, new and old, but could they create a sustainable strategy? Could they act fast enough and reinvent HP for the new economy? Or would they be a forgotten experiment? Earle pondered these questions as he took a call from CEO Carly Fiorina. She asked him to meet with her to discuss the ESS strategy and its new compensation program.

Research Associates Michelle Moore and Cara Snyder, both MBA 2000, prepared this case under the supervision of Professor Garth Saloner as the basis for class discussion rather than to illustrate either effective or ineffective handling of an administrative situation. Margot Sutherland, Executive Director, Center for Electronic Business and Commerce, Stanford Graduate School of Business managed this case.

THE HP CONTEXT

Hewlett-Packard Company

HP was a leading manufacturer of computer products, including printers, servers, workstations, and personal computers. In 1999, HP generated revenue of $42.4 billion and net income of $3.1 billion.[1] Most of the revenue was split between printing and imaging ($19 billion) and computing systems ($18 billion); the remainder came from information technology (IT) services ($6 billion). HP was the world's second largest producer of computers after IBM. Since 1995, HP's revenues and net income had grown at compound annual growth rates of 14% and 12%, respectively (Exhibit 1). It had over 80,000 employees worldwide. However, HP also had a strong local presence in Silicon Valley. Known as Silicon Valley's first "start-up," HP was also the largest employer in the Bay Area in 1999.

The HP Legacy

In 1939 Bill Hewlett and Dave Packard, two Stanford electrical engineers, founded their company in a one-car garage at 367 Addison Avenue in Palo Alto.[2] Their goal was to invent something useful. If the product wasn't useful, it simply didn't leave the garage. In the post World War II era, HP's workforce created many electrical instruments and consumer electronic products, including oscilloscopes, signal generators, and electronic calculators. The company also created its own unique way of doing business: "The HP Way."

The evolution of the HP Way began early. Hewlett and Packard wanted a decentralized management style. Successful product lines became their own divisions. In 1957 Hewlett and Packard met with their key managers to formalize a set of corporate objectives, which, along with underlying corporate values that shaped how the objectives would be met, remained the foundation for "The HP Way." Original practices such as Management By Wandering Around, Management By Objectives, and the Open Door Policy inspired later additions, including Open Communication and Total Quality Control (Exhibit 2).

The HP Way created a unifying corporate culture within a decentralized company. It stressed trust, openness, consensus, and an egalitarian culture. It also resulted in a loyal workforce. Still, HP was known for being very conservative. Decentralization bred turf battles that disrupted growth. A focus on products instead of customer needs diverted resources from growth areas. While decentralization and the HP Way had promised growth when HP was smaller, some of its elements made it difficult to run a $40 billion company.

[1] Restated to reflect the spinout of Agilent Technologies, HP's test and measurement business.

[2] In 1989 the Addison Avenue garage became a California Historical Landmark and "the birthplace of Silicon Valley."

Recent History

Dave Hewlett and Bill Packard led HP until John Young became president in 1977 and CEO in 1978. Under his watch, HP became a major player in the computer industry, producing a range of computers from desktop machines to powerful minicomputers. HP also embarked on its successful dominance of the printer market, with the launch of inkjet and laser printers that connect to personal computers.

Young managed the business until 1992, when Lew Platt, another insider, succeeded him. Platt was known as a soft-spoken, modest executive who regularly flew coach class on business trips and drove the standard Ford Taurus company car. "There isn't an arrogant bone in his body," said U.S. Representative Anna Eshoo, who represented Palo Alto, California, home of HP's headquarters. Ron Gonzales, the mayor of San Jose and a former HP executive, recalled, "What comes to mind when I think of Lew is him going to the cafeteria and grabbing a tray like everyone else did, and then sitting down at a table with employees and just talking with them."

Under his leadership, HP's sales grew from $16 billion to $47 billion in 1998.[3] Yet the company failed to meet Wall Street's expectations. Since 1995 HP's revenue growth rates had declined—from 24%, to 12%, to 11%. By 1998 its stock price hadn't budged from the $70 range in 18 months (Exhibit 3). HP had cited weakness in Asian markets and price competition in hardware as explanations for the softness, but analysts questioned whether HP had a viable long-term strategy, particularly in the Internet space. As Platt told a reporter, "It was a difficult time. We were being heavily criticized, and probably rightfully so, for having missed the Internet market."

By late 1998, Platt realized that HP needed change. First, he proposed to spinout HP's test and measurement business, which had over $7 billion in annual revenue. Platt later told *Fortune*:

> *HP was beginning to have some of the characteristics of a large company—complexity, breadth, a loss of accountability. . . . [This] just caused us to be not quite as focused as we should have been. I spent a few hours a week on the measurement business. I didn't have a single competitor in the computer business who spent a second a week on such things. We often watered down our message to be sure it included everything we're doing. More focused management time and energy, more focused messages, and greater visibility of the pieces would lead to a better outcome.*[4]

By December 1998 HP's board had approved the spin-off. The new company, Agilent Technologies, went public in the fall of 1999.

Next, Platt reconsidered HP's core strategy. Because of HP's decentralized style, no one division owned strategy. Platt hoped to create *one* organization to drive a strategy for hardware, software, and services. In particular, he wanted an Internet strategy. In October 1998, Platt put HP's corporate software and support division and corporate systems division under one roof. The next month, he chose Ann Livermore to run

[3] Includes $7.6 billion of revenue for the test and measurement business, Agilent Technologies.

[4] Lew Platt and Eric Nee, "Lew Platt: Why I Dismembered HP," *Fortune*, March 29, 1999.

this new Enterprise Computing Solutions Organization (ECSO), a unit with $15 billion in revenues and 44,000 employees.

Livermore, age 41, had been with HP for 18 years. She chose Nick Earle for her chief marketing officer. Born in Liverpool, England, Earle had joined HP in 1982 and spent his first 14 years in the field in Europe. He had been with HP's worldwide marketing unit since 1996.

Livermore put Earle in charge of developing a marketing strategy for the enterprise group. HP's competitors, Sun Microsystems and IBM, had launched high-profile Internet marketing campaigns, and Sun had a leadership role in the industry, using the tagline "We put the dot in dot com." Livermore gave Earle until the end of January 1999 to devise a branding plan and encouraged him to think outside of the HP box and take risks: "I really wanted Nick to be a renegade. I told him unless I got three complaints a week about him, he wasn't doing his job."[5]

THE EMERGENCE OF E-SERVICES.SOLUTIONS

Earle assembled a task force of ten "revolutionaries," five from within HP and five from outside it. The HP people came from different functional areas and had varying skill levels, but shared a frustration with HP's slow progress in the Internet. The outsiders recognized an opportunity to recreate an IT icon. A key early hire was Allison Johnson; then at Netscape, she had been the chief architect of IBM's e-business branding campaign. The team locked itself in a room for 30 days to tackle the problem. Earle commented:

> *We had a room which is just in that corner [in the middle of the upper floor in Building 44], and we blacked out the windows, we put a lock on the door, basically to keep people out. There are no locks on any doors anywhere in HP but the front doors, and we locked the doors. You couldn't come in to see what was going on.*

In the first week, the group concluded that the root of the problem was a marketing weakness. HP was already in the Internet space but hadn't communicated it well. The solution was simple: tell the marketing department to market the fact that HP's OpenView software managed 70% of Web sites and HP's security software handled Web transactions for over 120 financial institutions. The group cited proof of HP's presence in the Internet economy until someone shouted:

> *Stop! What the hell are you doing? Who are we trying to convince? All we're trying to do is convince ourselves really. And, so what? Let's say we advertise it. So what? We're still no better an Internet company than Sun, because there is no such thing as a second mover advantage, and it's really scary. There is no second mover advantage.*

[5] Kathryn Dennis, "Inventing a New HP Way," *MC Technology Marketing Intelligence*, January 1, 2000.

Forming a Vision

The group admitted that this was more than a marketing problem. They stepped back and considered the evolution of the Internet. They talked about "waves," with the first being the client-server wave, which prepared the world for the Internet by deploying a networked PC infrastructure. HP had ridden the client-server wave but had not positioned itself to catch the next wave (Exhibit 4).

The second wave—the one breaking in 1999—was about the Internet and the audience on it. While other players were nearing the crest of that wave, HP was not even thinking about it. However, the group reasoned, that wave couldn't last: it wasn't creating real value, and only venture capitalists and advertisers were making any money. The goal was to identify a third wave and leapfrog the competition.

In fact, the group believed a third wave was about to break. They envisaged the following: the world would be mobile appliance-centric not PC-centric; software would evolve to a pay-for-use model; and all products would be more valuable when "wrapped" in services. In fact, products would become services when delivered over the Web, that is, applications, computing power, and storage would all be rented online. The world was heading toward electronically delivered services or "e-services." Whereas the last wave was about searching, buying, and selling on the Internet—a sort of Chapter One of the Internet—the third wave would take the Internet to Chapter Two.

Chapter Two would be about e-services, transactions, and the partnerships that provided them. E-services would include one-stop brokered search engine requests, where the Web worked for the consumer, for example, gathering the best deals from airlines, hotels, and rental car companies for a vacation to Hawaii. E-services would also include getting applications, extra computing power, or extra computer storage as services "on tap" over the Net on a per usage basis. HP's role would be to market its infrastructure, services, and appliances as e-services with a network of partners.

Announcing the Vision

By February 2, 1999, Earle and his team had articulated a rough story and now had to communicate it internally. Earle remembered:

> *The question is what do you do with it? Do you walk it around HP and try to persuade everybody, which I could, or do you do something insane which is tell the world? Of course, we did the latter. So what happened was the next day there was a NationsBank Montgomery Securities conference in San Francisco. . . . At the last minute I had to replace our CFO, so I did the speech . . . and said this is what HP is going to do, etc. Somebody said how much money are you going to spend on launching this? I said $100 million. Of course, I didn't have it yet, but I just said it.*

The *Wall Street Journal* reported that Earle announced "a major branding campaign touting its new Internet strategy."[6] The paper added that he "declined to discuss details but said the first of several events would happen shortly." When the *Journal* called Platt for comment, he called "this Nick Earle" for an explanation. It became clear that Earle had bypassed HP's traditional decision processes, but Earle hedged, "Well, it's only a marketing strategy." Looking back, Earle reflected on his motives: "HP was like a herd of 46,000 wildebeest. Everyone knows we're there, but we were just meandering around. I wanted to cause a stampede—and then figure out where we're going."[7] Fortunately for Earle, Livermore provided "air cover" for his group. Fortunately for HP, its stock price closed up $4. Livermore approved Earle's $100 million marketing campaign and a $1 billion budget for acquisitions and equity investments to support the e-services strategy.

Transition at the Top of HP

In March 1999, HP announced the formation of an e-services unit. In May 1999, HP announced the rollout of a new vision, new technologies, and new buzzwords for what its executives called "Internet Chapter 2." At a June analyst's meeting, Platt introduced and Earle presented the e-services strategy (Exhibit 5).

However, the e-services vision was not HP's main focus at this time. In March 1999, Platt announced that he was leaving as CEO. He also went outside HP for his successor—the first time HP had ever done so. In the summer of 1999 he was instrumental in hiring Carleton "Carly" S. Fiorina.

Fiorina was the former president of the $20 billion sales and service division of Lucent Technologies, a leading telecommunications equipment provider formed from the systems and technology units that were formerly a part of AT&T Corp. Her former boss, Richard McGinn, CEO of Lucent, called her "wicked smart." HP's need to refocus on its customers needs played to Fiorina's marketing and sales strengths; she had become known as a super-saleswoman, winning over customers for Lucent in 43 countries. Plus, with HP spinning off its non-core businesses, her experience in leading Lucent's record-setting IPO would help her spinout Agilent in the fall of 1999. As she told *Fortune*, "I have an ability to grow businesses, and the experience I had with the AT&T-Lucent split, and what opportunities a split like that represents for both companies are very relevant for HP."[8]

Fiorina also offered HP the charisma and energy to take charge. She added star power to an IT company, at a time when other companies' senior executives—Scott McNealy, CEO of Sun Microsystems; Larry Ellison, CEO of Oracle Corporation; and Michael Dell, CEO of Dell Computer Corporation—were becoming business icons. Her charisma contrasted Platt's understated style. Whereas he drove the Ford Taurus

[6] "Ad Notes...," *Wall Street Journal*, February 5, 1999.

[7] "HP's Carly Fiorina: The Boss," *Business Week Online*, August 2, 1999.

[8] Sue Zesiger, "Fortune Cover Girl Storms the Valley," *Fortune*, August 16, 1999.

issued to HP's senior managers and flew on commercial flights, Fiorina insisted on driving her Audi A8 and immediately bought a Gulfstream jet for her business trips.

E-Services Legitimized

In Fiorina's first week at HP, Earle called her office to see if she would like him to present the ECSO e-services plan to her, but was told "no." Earle and his group wondered whether they should start calling back some of the headhunters they had ignored. The put-off was intentional, however, as Fiorina was spending her first six weeks at HP traveling the world to meet key HP customers. In October 1999, Fiorina unofficially recognized Earle as chief strategist for the Internet and put him in charge of expanding the ECSO plan into an e-services framework for the rest of HP. In mid-November, Fiorina made the keynote speech at Comdex, the world's largest IT tradeshow in Las Vegas, and the central focus of her speech was the Internet revolution and how the Net economy would impact business. In late November 1999, Livermore officially announced Earle's group to security analysts: "Nick will lead this function to drive the strategy and business development for e-services across all of Hewlett-Packard."[9] In mid-November 1999, Earle hired key executive talent. By early 2000, ESS had started the ramp-up in its functional ranks.

THE STRATEGY OF ESS

HP was betting that "eventually the whole world will be services that you access through appliances powered by an infrastructure." Earle predicted:

> *You'll have 20 appliances that you use during the course of a day and you'll be accessing the Internet. You won't know it's the Internet; it will be invisible. You'll be accessing services: travel, schedule, book lunch, where's my next appointment, weather, stock, buy, sell, chat. You'll be talking to your watch, and your earring will beep. That's going to be the world.*

The three key "vectors" of the ESS strategy were services, appliances, and infrastructure, and HP was uniquely positioned to deliver them. First, HP was creating services or helping other companies create services. HP Labs, the company's cross-divisional R&D unit, would create technologies to support those services.[10] Second, appliances would proliferate until anything with a microchip would connect to the Web, and HP was the world's third largest appliance company. Third, infrastructure—computers, storage, and software—had to support the "trillions of transactions" and "billions of appliances." HP, as a leading infrastructure provider, was essentially a "big plumber." Earle explained, "The killer segment is where you get infrastructure, services, and appliances all intersecting. The growth is where these three things intersect."

[9] HP Web site, http://www.hp.com/financials/personnel/secanal/1199_sec_livermore_1.html.
[10] Exhibit 6 very briefly describes three HP technologies to enable e-services.

Target Markets

The ESS strategy entailed predicting the winning e-services and figuring out which end market segments would be their lead adopters. They looked for "hot pockets of activity" that would be "launch points" for e-services. In April 2000 this included nine segments.

1. Mobile and wireless
2. Internet data service providers and telecom companies
3. Dot-coms and start-ups
4. Trading communities and business hubs
5. Small- to medium-sized businesses
6. Incubators and VCs
7. Printing e-services
8. Corporate information portals
9. Digital media and publishing and education e-services

The list was not exhaustive: it did not include healthcare, for example. Earle guaranteed the list would change in a month as the markets shook out.

Partnering

In areas where it had an appropriate asset or service in house, HP could directly provide e-service—for example, computing "on tap," storage "on tap," or leveraging HP's installed base of printers as digital mailboxes. For other e-services that HP wanted to deliver it would look for partners. ESS also thought about the stack of services, software, and hardware that enabled a provider to deliver an e-service. The stack included the product or service, the network infrastructure, billing, security, etc. Either HP would provide the enabling technology or partner with someone who could. Building this "keiretsu" or ecosystem of partners would allow HP to provide services or technologies it didn't have in-house and would attract more partners who wanted the plug and play solutions HP was lining up.

Financing

Venture financing would also attract partners. ESS funded equity investments in start-ups and extended "creative" financing to start-ups looking to invest in an HP platform. Bob Pearse was in charge of equity investments. He had a budget of $100 million to make minority investments, typically of about $5 million, with venture capital firms in start-up companies. These investments were strategic bets on new marquee technologies for HP. Joanna Wampler was in charge of allocating up to $500 million in ESS debt financing—providing the leases for equipment. She could extend terms riskier than typical for HP, such as, revenue sharing, convertible debt, or warrants in exchange for equipment. Revenue sharing meant that partners could pay for equipment or services with, for example, 3% of revenues from the e-service. These unconventional deals created great press and interest from customers, but they were thought likely to comprise only 2%–3% of HP's alliances.

HP's Value Proposition to Its Partners

ESS complemented these technology solutions with nontraditional options. Earle explained, "We're the arrowhead organization that can bring any product or solution from anywhere in HP into one solution for the customer."[11]

First, ESS could provide financing. Second, it could market and sell the e-service through the HP marketing organization and sales channels. This meant 6,000 sales representatives and 30,000 channel resellers who could be leveraged to sell a partner's e-service, and it also included Earle's $1 billion marketing budget and being mentioned in Fiorina's speeches. Third, HP offered "membership" in the network it was creating. Fourth, ESS offered consulting and thought leadership. Earle insisted this visioning was "a hell of a door opener." And fifth, ESS offered use of HP's brand name. As Wampler remarked, "You would be amazed at how many start-ups want to partner with HP in order to have our name on their S-1 [the registration statement for going public] as a partner."

The ESS group reasoned that many of their partners would be either start-ups strapped for resources or bricks-and-mortar companies looking for fast one-stop solutions to enter the Internet space. The opportunities to secure an HP platform, to finance HP computers and software in creative ways, to gain marketing and sales support from HP, and to share business risk would both attract and retain such partners. As Earle insisted, "We're not selling computers anymore. When we go to an Internet service provider, I don't say, 'Our box is better than so-and-so's box.' I say, 'Look, I'll build a business with you, and I'll completely share your risk.'"

Measuring Success

HP would also benefit. These partnerships would drive incremental sales of HP hardware, software, and services, which would be the benchmark for measuring ESS's performance. In its first year, ESS wanted to bank $400 million in increased orders fulfilled from the rest of HP but booked through ESS deals. These dollars were meant to be incremental sales that HP would not otherwise have gained. Earle even claimed that his group to date had a 10 to 1 leverage effect on increased sales: $400 million would increase to $4 billion more in sales for HP. For example, if ESS booked a $30 million deal with Ford, that would translate into $300 million in revenue from other customers who heard about the deal and wanted to partner with HP.

Earle insisted that ESS be measured on HP's sales and that sales be booked with HP not ESS to avoid grabbing sales from the HP sales force. He realized that this ran

[11] Dennis.

counter to the accounting system typical of a large organization—which would require matching the ESS budget and people to specific sales. But that would mean, according to Earle:

> *[ESS would] have to pinch orders off the rest of the field. And eventually what happens is the rest of the field kills the group because they say, "I'm not ever going to work with you. Every time I meet you you're going to take bread out of the mouths of my children." So, what we do instead is we say, "No, no, no, you're the sales rep; I will work with you. I will add* lots *of resources; this deal will close more likely because I'm working with you. You now are going to book the whole thing still but it's going to be 10 times bigger. You book it."*

In addition to this "hard" measure, ESS had a "soft" measure that counted the "strategic wins" gained through partnerships and equity investments because these could lead to "the next billion dollar ecosystem." Earl understood that analysts would ignore any gains in equity that did not come from operations. But, ultimately, he wanted ESS to lead HP away from intense price competition in hardware to profits from relationships and services. Thus he considered credit from soft wins to be important.

Deals

By May 1, 2000, ESS had announced alliances with 41 partners (Exhibit 7). Earle struck the first deal with Ariba, a vendor of operating resource management systems to be the exclusive launch partner of Ariba's Ariba.com Network. Bobby Lent, cofounder of Ariba, and Earle talked on a plane from London to San Francisco for five hours; in fact, they got kicked out of first class for the noise they were making. At the end of the flight, Lent decided HP would be the exclusive launch partner. The terms of the deal were surprising. HP promised to give Ariba millions in equipment such as HP 9000 servers, OpenView management software, and hosting services. Plus, HP would help market and sell the service: Earle gave Ariba access to 6,000 sales calls a day, and Earle and other ESS executives mentioned Ariba in their speeches. In exchange, Ariba would pay nothing up front, only a percentage of the memberships fees it charged. Ariba's cofounder Bobby Lent said:

> *About 80 percent of our customer base is using HP hardware. They see how closely aligned HP is with Ariba and how that close relationship is resulting in good stuff for them. Risk is something people want to mitigate. What's clear, if you go with HP and Ariba, they make things work; it's a repeatable event.*[12]

The biggest alliance partnership was with Qwest Communications, a telecommunications service provider with a nationwide, high-capacity fiber optic communications

[12] Dennis.

network. "The real challenge for us was to win over the new apps-on-tap providers," Earle remembered. The Qwest deal got HP into a core e-services market: application service providers (ASPs). Earle recalled the deal cut in May 1999: "We gave Qwest $500 million of servers, software, storage, and consulting. We said to them: 'Here it is, and it's free. But pay us on a percentage of the value you create by using our products.'" The alliance helped Qwest accelerate the launch of its CyberCenters, its bid to play in the hosted application services market. Qwest agreed to make HP its preferred supplier and to incubate its own program for software start-ups seeking an e-services outlet. Earle believed the deal could bring in $1 billion in revenues during the next three years.

In September 1999, HP and Qwest expanded their relationship to include storage. Lew Wilks, President of Qwest's Internet and multimedia markets, commented:

> *What we have created is a partnership model that becomes a template for successful partnering in the industry and, certainly, one that we'll use again and again. The agreement is structured so that both parties have an interest to accelerate both parties' businesses and increase market share aggressively. We have mutual objectives.*[13]

A third strategic alliance with Yahoo! involved the corporate information portal market, connecting companies' employees to external information services that were unique to their job functions. Yahoo! had a leading consumer portal that many individuals were using, but could not integrate its system with a company's intranet, which demanded impeccable security. Linda Lazor, director of operations of ESS, explained the deal in August 1999:

> *The main things Yahoo! wanted from HP were to have access to our enterprise sales force that calls on the Fortune 50 as well as the ability for HP to design the server that sits inside the firewall and provides access through their portal to both the company intranet as well as going outside the firewall to the standard Yahoo! Feeds. . . . So they came to us and said they understand the consumer space, they understand the content feeds, but we can link all that stuff sitting behind the firewall into their screen and we have a sales channel to get to enterprises. They asked why don't we play the lead in putting that part of the program and the product together for them.*

Competitive Positioning

ESS believed they were positioned well versus their main competitors, Sun Microsystems and IBM. Historically, these two firms had been the company's top two rivals.

[13] Dennis.

All large computer manufacturers, they competed heavily to offer the powerful servers that run networks, Internet sites, and corporate databases. HP believed its technology choices, financing, and sales reach were better than Sun's. First, HP could build UNIX, Linux, or Windows NT platforms; Sun essentially offered only UNIX. Second, Sun had no financing itself and instead had a financing deal with GE Capital, which HP believed prevented Sun from extending riskier financing opportunities. In contrast, HP's substantial financing operation—with $6 billion in credit outstanding—was prepared to take risks. Third, Sun lacked a PC business, while HP marketed and sold its products to both enterprises and individuals. If a dot-com were looking for marketing and sales support, no one had better reach than HP.

Earle believed that IBM, having built an extensive consulting practice, needed to sell consulting as the bulk of its "e-business" offering. These consultants could then help customers build and implement an e-business solution in their company. ESS, on the other hand, involved a network of partners that could supply "plug and play" pieces of the stack, so that a new partner did not have to implement a complicated internal plan. "An IBM will never embrace apps-on-tap, for a very simple reason: [installing apps-on-tap] doesn't sell consultants. . . . If I sold you an [e-services] solution, you don't actually implement it inside your company, and you don't need busloads of consultants."[14]

Finally, most of HP's competitors didn't make appliances, while HP did. HP had an extensive product penetration—an installed base of one million printers and 300,000 PCs shipping each month—available to leverage as mail boxes or screen real estate. Lazor explained, "So we can bring into these deals anything from our laser printers to our calculators to our consumer PC franchise in addition to our standard server business."

E-services, however, changed the competitive landscape: it was no longer limited to HP's traditional hardware and software competitors. HP's business definition now included procurement of enabling technologies for "the stack" and Web development and expertise. As Bob Pearse said, "The world was simpler two years ago [in 1998]. It's not clear who our competitors are. The Suns, IBMs, Dells, Compaqs of the world may be our competitors, but the e-commerce strategy consultants and technology solution providers of the world might be as well. They may also be our partners though, too."

THE CULTURE AND OPERATIONS OF ESS

Earle realized that the culture of his group had to be distinct from that of the rest of HP. He recognized an implicit danger in attacking the HP Way, but HP's human resources (HR) policies, incentives, and habits did not suit the speed or attitude of a start-up organization. Yvonne Hunt, the ESS HR manager, was "mortified" to see the dull gray applicant packet that went out to HP job candidates, with its "20-times photocopied sheet" of HP's history in electrical instrumentation. She remembered:

[14] Dennis.

> *So we're selling these people on "come and join the revolution, we're different, creative," and here is this! . . . But it was just indicative. You know those things that maybe happened over the years, now when you stand back and you look at it you go, wow, well what kind of message does that send? And how many other [messages] are around that we're just not even seeing because we've been here for so long?*

Signs posted in HP corridors requested, "Please do not speak in the corridors. People are working." Earle, instead, infused fun and levity:

> *In my cube I have a box of toys, balls, footballs, foam rubber light bulbs, and I wander around doing my phone calls with my wireless headset, and I'm throwing the balls to people, and they're throwing back. I have these low walls so I can throw to these guys 10 cubes down, I mean there are missiles whizzing across the cubes. I'm not trying to be a big kid, but what I am doing though is really trying to get this spirit of fun and motivation. As a result, people will work until 11:00 at night. They work Saturdays and Sundays.*

Although ESS's offices were initially situated in Building 44 on HP's Cupertino campus, Earle planned to move the group off-site by the fall of 2000. As Hunt said, "We want to go somewhere where can be expressive. So if we want to paint the walls green, we can paint the walls green, not having to go through 28 people to be told we can't paint the walls green."

At an early off-site meeting, the ESS group gathered at Palo Alto's Gordon Biersch brewpub. While not unusual for a start-up, this took many former HP employees by surprise. Hunt explained, "For HP, it had always been work, work, work . . . never any play." At this event, to highlight the culture change, Hunt distributed a new colorful book called "The Revolution Starts Here." In it, mantras with pictures urged the group: "First ponder, then dare. Be the catalyst. Exemplify the rules of the garage. Be impatient. Persevere."

The financing teams also made a shift to a culture that encouraged risk and speed. Pearse, now in charge of ESS equity investments and formerly with HP corporate finance, pointed out how HP wanted every financing decision to have a clear business case with heavy analysis. His group didn't have time for business cases, and they took a portfolio approach—something foreign to HP. Wampler, head of debt financing, remembered approving a $10 million line of credit to a start-up in St. Louis that needed computers:

> *Even though these people looked bad on paper, based on how I was used to looking at companies, I knew deep in my heart that they were going to be successful. So I okayed a $10 million line of credit. That was a big epiphany for me. Before it took us several weeks to make a decision on extending credit. Start-ups want to hear that you can act fast. That's the number one term that they are interested in.*

Recruiting

In March 2000, Earle had 90 people in the ESS Group, 20 of them hired from outside HP. Hunt preferred a mix of people from inside and outside HP. While outsiders brought a new perspective, people from other HP divisions could link back to their former groups. Of the 70 people who came over from HP, most had been with the company for five or six years. As Hunt said, "We have a lot of people who are frustrated with HP and the lack of progress in their own little business. . . . In fact I have many people who resign and their managers say [to them], 'Before you leave, just go and talk to Yvonne in e-services because it may be that even though you don't want to stay here you might want to join that group.' So we get people as they're going through the door literally."

Earle wanted to grow the group to 200, but the job had start-up pressures and lifestyle coupled with HP's own incentive structure. Still, ESS, unlike HP, offered people $5,000 as a referral bonus. But why would the best and brightest join HP if they had more attractive options? And headhunters were wooing away key HP employees every day. Earle observed:

> *We're the big sitting ducks right in the middle of the Valley. I mean, here we are with 40,000 people in California. Guess who they call first? Everyone who works for me—if they're not being headhunted, they should be because they're all great people. As a result, my group is an experiment where we've basically said we need a system to retain key people because they're being offered millions to leave.*

Compensation

Beyond senior executives, HP did not offer its employees significant pay-for-performance compensation. There were no cash bonuses. The profit-sharing program was typically only 3%–5% of salary. In addition, most employees on average received 300 to 400 options per year. If you progressed up the corporate ladder, senior managers were entitled to the company car, a Ford Taurus. Finally, raises did little to reward top performers: top performers earned a 7% raise, but poor performers pay rose 3%. Hunt believed a lack of accountability for results had crept in.

Earle and Hunt decided to opt out of the traditional HP pay scheme and structured a compensation plan and culture that rewarded performance but minimized the risk of joining HP. Earle recalled, "Culturally we had to break every rule in the book to do that. . . . We went to meeting after meeting after meeting with the HR community with people saying, 'You can't do this, you can't do this,' and I just kept on saying to the HR manager, 'Do it, do it, do it.'"

In March 2000, they won approval for a new ESS payroll and incentive scheme, separate from the rest of HP. The changes aligned rewards with stock performance and diminished other benefits. Most ESS employees' annual salaries were decreased by 15% (Earle himself took a 25% pay cut), and they were no longer eligible for profit-sharing or for a company car.

In exchange, ESS employees were offered new incentives. First, an annual cash bonus representing 20%–60% of salary was contingent on the group's meeting its incremental sales target. Second, each employee was granted an average of 10 times more stock options. Some options had accelerated vesting based on ESS's and HP's performance.

Earle had high expectations for how employees would perceive the plan: "I thought they'd be dancing in the street because the average employee who works for me can earn $1 million—that's the *average* employee. And we actually had the opposite reaction." People were shocked at the cut in salary:

> *They said, "You've told me I can now earn less money. It's possible for me to earn less money, so I don't like it. You've taken the security away!" And so I responded, "Well, yeah it's not a country club! Welcome to the world of accountability!" And we underestimated—we grossly underestimated—the cultural impact of accountability amongst engineering people. Anyway, we got through that, and we showed them how much money they can earn, and the fact that the stock went up today, that kind of helps. They'll earn a lot of money. And some people won't like it still, and they'll leave, and that's ok.*

Some people had already resigned to pursue dot-com "fever." Hunt also expected to lose others to HP and that this would cause alarm within ESS: "Again, that's something that people are not used to. They're not used to people leaving. Historically, people joined HP for life. Well, you know, this world is different now."

Operations and Integration with the Rest of HP

Earle reported to Livermore who reported to Fiorina. Earle focused on outbound activities, such as meeting with potential partners and the press. He had eight direct reports, including the finance, operations, and HR managers mentioned previously (Exhibit 8). Three general managers tackled the nine target markets, identifying deals and owning the relationships with strategic partners. Twenty percent of new deals came from pursuing new opportunities, 80% from the buzz ESS generated; Earle wanted the balance to swing the other way.

Many of the deals came to ESS from HP's 6,000 field sales representatives. HP reps essentially sold one type of product: computers, PCs, printers, or software. Because ESS sold multiproduct solutions to market segments, Earle had to re-educate sales people and change sales compensation. He explained:

> *The average hardware salesman here basically used to sell a box and get paid for it, but now they sell a service. You've got to fundamentally change your compensation and training model because what you're saying is guess what, the job is no longer to sell a box to the end user. Cultural whoa! Massive! And that you don't do in a month, you don't even do it in six months.*

The massive effort to train sales included Web casting, video, seminars, and speaking events. But target markets could change in a month. Earle admitted, "So it's a real issue for us—scalability—and we're spending a lot of money on training. I don't think we've solved it yet, short of cloning."

While ESS closed deals, other HP divisions, the printer business, for example, delivered the services or products. ESS therefore worked in tandem with people in the other businesses. Maintaining relationships with the rest of HP was essential.

Hunt hired two people to work on HP relationships. Denny Georg was ex-HP Labs, he worked the technology relationships across HP. In April 2000, Rich Raimondi was named COO of ESS to manage the internal work within ESS and back into HP. He had worked in most of the HP businesses and nurtured relationships between them and ESS.

Hunt believed that ESS had to communicate better with the rest of HP. Most communication was through personal relationships. While senior management knew about ESS, lower levels did not. What message to communicate was another challenge. Earle noted: "On the one hand you have to be out there with the customers saying we can do the deals, but we don't want to come across internally as the masters of the universe, the swagger. That is very tough."

LOOKING AHEAD

In April 2000, Earle focused on three goals:

1. Create, own, drive, and get agreement across HP for the Internet strategy. Be the central point for strategy.
2. Be a deal-making machine.
3. Transfer knowledge from ESS. Take the learnings of the group and "throw them over the wall" to the rest of HP.

The great danger he saw was:

> *If we just achieved the first two goals, we'd be wildly successful, and the rest of HP wouldn't change. In many ways our job is to infect the rest of the organization—positively—so that we help them change. Trying to change 100,000 people is an interesting job.*

ESS as Change Agent

In Hunt's opinion, November 1999 through April 2000 comprised Phase 1 of ESS—its design and incubation. Phase 2 would emphasize sharing and learning. She was working to create an HR framework that other HR managers could share. Explaining it repeatedly with no context took time. For example, as Earle and Hunt rolled out the new compensation plan, Fiorina decided it should be a pilot for the rest of HP. Hunt feared the extra demands on her time as other HR managers called her to learn more about it. She expressed the problem: "How much do you incubate what we're trying to do versus how much do you allow the change machine to start taking place?"

Susan Bowick, HP's vice president for HR, who reported directly to Fiorina, was watching the implementation of and response to this new program. Bowick told Earle she wanted to reinvent HP HR using ESS as an example. Earle was spending 20% of his time with the rest of HP sharing what his group was doing. He said, "I spend a lot of my time internally rallying the organization, preaching the vision, defending the group, subtly selling it."

Cultural Change at HP

While ESS was piloting new cultural initiatives for HP, Fiorina was trying to change how HP operates. In December 1999, HP introduced a new advertising campaign and a more contemporary logo featuring only the company initials, underscored by the word "invent." The logo was intended to convey a faster, invigorated, committed HP and remind audiences of HP's roots as a company of inventors that was reinventing itself (Exhibit 9).

Fiorina also returned to HR's roots and developed the "Rules of the Garage" (Figure 1).[15] She tasked a "Rules of the Garage" committee of senior managers to determine what HP's new culture should be. Hunt, who served on the committee, added, "We've all seen the HP Way, all of the literature and books. Well, what is the HP Way for the future?"

Future of ESS

By April 2000, Fiorina was spending more time with Earle and ESS customers. In early April, Earle noted: "I've been with her every day for the last 10 days. And I think what that shows is as this thing gets more momentum, she's giving it more of her time, and it's adding value."

FIGURE 1 Rules of the Garage

Rules of the garage

Believe you can change the world.

Work quickly, keep the tools unlocked, work whenever.

Know when to work alone and when to work together.

Share—tools, ideas. Trust your colleagues.

No politics. No bureaucracy. (These are ridiculous in a garage.)

The customer defines a job well done.

Radical ideas are not bad ideas.

Invent different ways of working.

Make a contribution every day. If it doesn't contribute, it doesn't leave the garage.

Believe that together we can do anything.

Invent.

[15] HP Web site, http://www.hp.com/ghp/features/invent/rules.html, May 1, 2000.

Success would depend on many things: changing the market's perception of HP; executing the deals well; and pulling together resources from inside HP. Hunt noted that while deals created positive energy, the bureaucracy and impediments to "getting things done" in a large organization created a lot of negative energy.

Fiorina's efforts to break down silos across HP would be crucial. Hunt commented:

> *We're having to work through all of the old systems and processes, and we are also part of a large organization which doesn't report into Carly. We report into Ann Livermore's organization, so we have to go through that organization before we get to that next level. So there are extra steps that are in there that are time consuming and frustrating at times.*

The future of ESS was uncertain. When asked about it, Earle answered:

> *First of all, the chances of our existing in this form in a year's time are remote. The honest answer is we don't know, because long-term planning is three months. But if I had to predict, my goal would be that we would be completely obsolete, but I don't think it will ever happen. In other words, if we really are successful—it's like don't give people fish, teach them how to fish—if we are really teaching them how to do Internet deals, then once everyone knows how to do it, why would they need us?*

EXHIBIT 1 HP Revenue History 1995–1999

Hewlett Packard (\$ billions)	*1995*	*1996*	*1997*	*1998*	*1999*	*CAGR*
Net revenue	25.4	31.6	35.5	39.4	42.4	13.6%
Annual growth rate		24.4%	12.2%	11.1%	7.5%	
Net income	2.0	2.1	2.5	2.7	3.1	11.6%
Annual growth rate		5.0%	19.0%	8.0%	14.8%	
Net income as a % of revenue	7.9%	6.6%	7.0%	6.8%	7.3%	

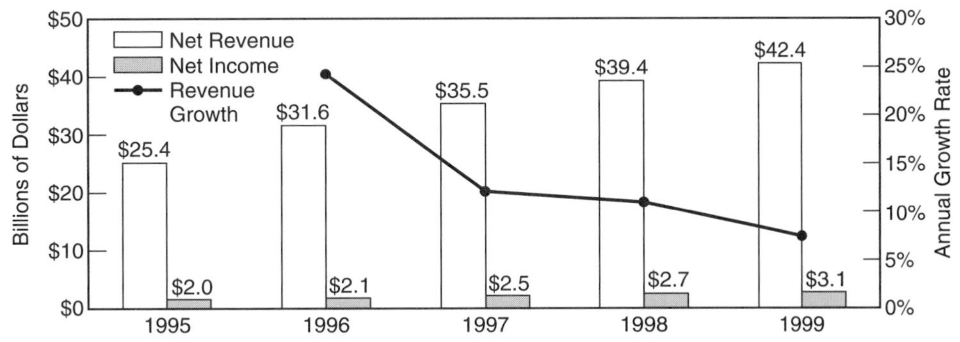

EXHIBIT 2 The HP Way

Some examples of HP Way practices:

• ***Management By Wandering Around (MBWA).*** An informal practice, which involves keeping up to date with individuals and activities through informal or structured communication. Trust and respect for individuals are apparent when MBWA is used to recognize employees' concerns and ideas.

MBWA might look like:

- a manager consistently reserving time to walk through the department or be available for impromptu discussions.
- individuals networking across the organization.
- coffee talks, communication lunches, and hallway conversation.

• ***Management By Objective (MBO).*** Individuals at each level contribute to company goals by developing objectives, which are integrated with their manager's and those of other parts of HP. Flexibility and innovation in recognizing alternative approaches to meeting objectives provide effective means of meeting customer needs.

MBO is reflected in:

- written plans which guide and create accountability throughout the organization.
- coordinated and complementary efforts and cross-organizational integration.
- shared plans and objectives.

• ***Open Door Policy.*** The assurance that no adverse consequences should result from responsibly raising issues with management or personnel. Trust and integrity are important parts of the Open Door Policy.

Open Door may be used:

- to share feelings and frustrations in a constructive manner.
- to gain clearer understanding of alternatives.
- to discuss career options, business conduct, and communication breakdowns.

(continued)

EXHIBIT 2 *(continued)*

• ***Open Communication.*** At the core of our practice of open communication is the belief that when given the right tools, training, and information to do a good job, people will contribute their best.

Open communication leads to:

- strong teamwork between HP people, customers, and others.
- enhanced achievement and contribution.
- customer relationships built on trust and respect.

Source: HP Web site, http://www.hp.com/abouthp/hpway.html, May 1, 2000.

EXHIBIT 3 HP Stock Performance

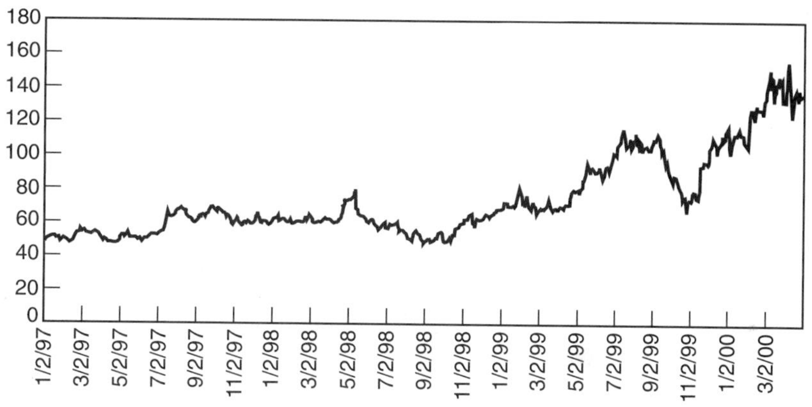

EXHIBIT 4 The "Third Wave"

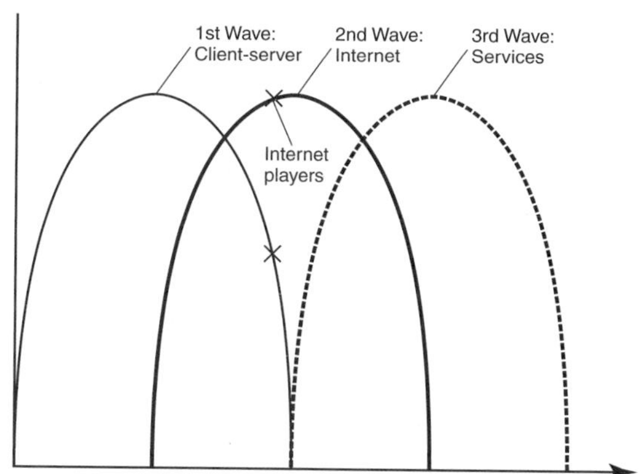

EXHIBIT 5 Excerpts from the June 2, 1999 HP Presentation to Security Analysts

On June 2, 1999, HP hosted its semiannual meeting with security analysts in New York. (A second meeting is held every winter in Palo Alto.) The following are excerpts from Lew Platt's opening comments.

E-SERVICES: A UNIFYING STRATEGY

E-services is an important strategic direction for HP.

We're putting energy and dollars behind it. We're rolling it out in a way that's unique for our company. And employees, partners and customers are rallying around the e-services concept.

It's a logical next step in the Internet story—we call it Chapter 2—and that's what makes it so compelling.

It's also a unifying and inclusive strategy for HP. We see broad opportunities in business-to-business, computing, and consumer services.

Many have asked: Is the e-services strategy here for the long term? Will it stick?

The answer is yes. And yes.

And here's why.

First, the strategy represents a natural evolution for our company. It's part of our DNA.

Joel Birnbaum, HP's former director of HP Labs and now our company's chief scientist, created the vision of computing as a utility almost 20 years ago. He predicted that a whole host of appliances would plug seamlessly into this utility.

In the 1980s, HP committed to open systems and standards-based computing. We were pioneers of RISC technology, drove development of client-server computing, and are today leaders in UNIX technology.

These are the foundations of Internet-based computing and e-services.

Second, our computing-and-imaging businesses are now organized to deliver on the e-services vision.

Third, e-services will benefit all of our businesses. Here's why:

- most of our products, services and solutions can either be an e-service or be part of one;
- PCs, appliances, and imaging products all become the on and off ramps of the net and are part of the e-services world;
- our servers, net software, and services deliver the front end and back end required for supply chain and e-commerce "apps-on-tap" e-services.

All our businesses share the belief that e-services is the next evolutionary step in the Internet story.

(continued)

EXHIBIT 5 *(continued)*

Most important, e-services will greatly benefit our customers and help them use the power of the Net to achieve competitive advantage. And we believe Hewlett-Packard is uniquely positioned to deliver on that vision.

That, ultimately, is why the e-services vision will stick and is here to stay.

Source: HP Web site, http://www.hp.com/financials/textonly/personnel/secanal/0699_sec_platt.html, May 1, 2000.

EXHIBIT 6 HP Enabling Technologies

Below are some new technologies HP was developing to help businesses implement e-services.

- ***E-speak.*** Under development for more than six years, HP Labs designed the e-speak platform as a common services interface for the development, deployment, and intelligent interaction of e-services. Intended to be the universal language of e-services on the Internet, the software allowed all Internet sites to talk to each other to competitively bid to deliver goods and services by performing the functions of discovery, negotiation, mediation, and composition. E-speak enabled an e-service to discover other e-services anywhere on the Internet and link with them on the fly—even if they were built using different technology. In 1999, HP posted the basic software code on the Web and released an open-source version that customers and even competitors will be able to build into their own products.

- ***Chai.*** Chai was a family of software products that enabled a variety of memory-constrained appliances to access e-services and to communicate intelligently with each other. The software used the Java™ programming language and other Web standards.

- ***E-squirt.*** E-squirt allowed small footprint devices with limited user interfaces to participate in rich Web services by interacting with Web-connected appliances. For example, a Palm V could e-squirt a Web page to a printer, a presentation to a projector, or an MP3 file to an Internet Radio.

Sources: HP Web site, http://www.hp.com/e-services/technologies/index.html, May 1, 2000. "HP Pushes E-business," *Los Angeles Times*, March 10, 1999, p. C-3. HP Web site, http://cooltown.hp.com/code.html, May 1, 2000.

EXHIBIT 7 E-Services.Solutions Alliance Partners

The following were ESS partners current as of May 1, 2000.

Alcatel	Intelisys	SIA
Ariba	LPG Innovations	Sonera SmartTrust
BEA Systems	Mimeo.com	Stamps.com
Broadvision	Monterey Design	Telenomics
Comptel	MyContacts	TEN Online
EAI	Newspaper Direct	Tesla Group
Encryptix.com	Oracle	USi
FedEx	Portal	USA Net, Inc.
Getthere.com	Praxisline GmbH	Viador
Helsinki Telephone	printCafe	Xcelera
i2	PSINet	Yahoo!
ImageTag	Qwest	Yomi Media
Impress	Sapient	Zantaz.com
InfoCure	Screaming Media	

Source: HP Web site, http://www.hp.com/e-services/alliances/index.html, May 1, 2000.

EXHIBIT 8 Organization Charts

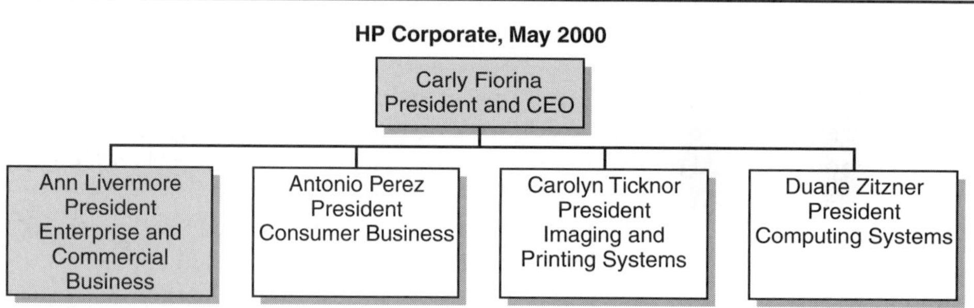

Note: Gray shading highlights HP management mentioned in the case. Chart reflects Fiorina's August 1999 reorganization of HP into four divisions: two focused on customers (business and consumer) and two focused on product technology and production (printers and computers).
Source: Interviews, ESS Executives, March through May, 2000.

EXHIBIT 8 *(continued)*

E-Services.Solutions Organization Chart, May 2000

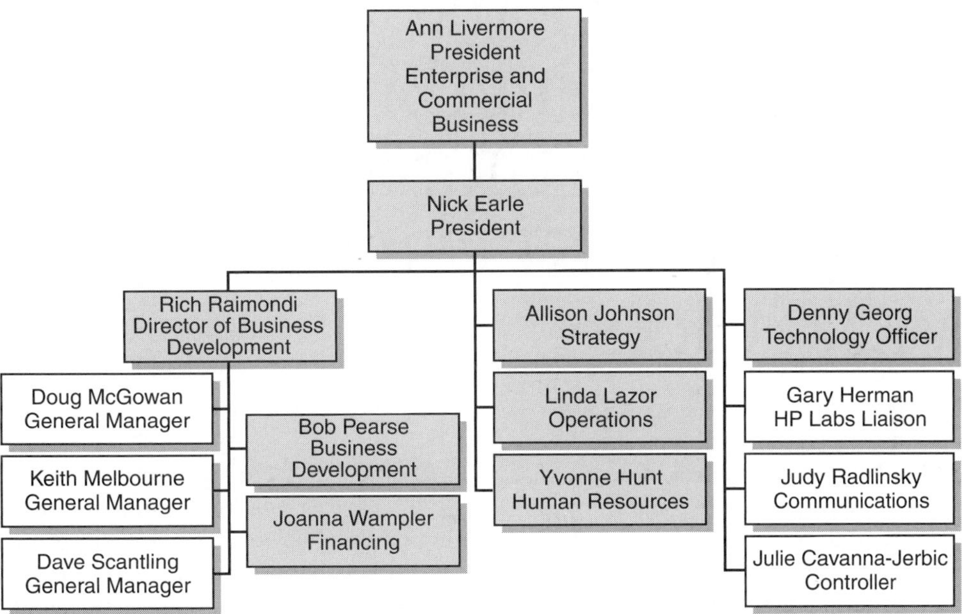

Source: Interviews, ESS Executives, March through May, 2000.

EXHIBIT 9 HP's New Logo

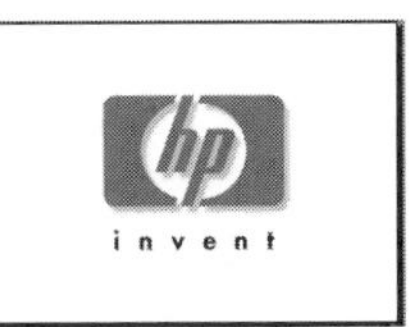

Source: HP Web site, http://www.hp.com/ghp/features/invent/logo.html, May 1, 2000.

CISCO SYSTEMS: A NOVEL APPROACH TO STRUCTURING ENTREPRENEURIAL VENTURES

Mike Volpi, vice president of business development at Cisco Systems, was in his office in San Jose at Cisco's headquarters on June 27, 1997. He was considering strategic questions that he had faced many times since joining Cisco's business development group in 1994. Volpi's colleagues had identified a new networking opportunity in optical routers, and Volpi wondered whether Cisco should develop the product internally or pursue external talent that was more familiar with the technology and market segment. If the external route was the best strategy to get the right product to market on time, should Cisco build its own external venture—or just acquire someone outright?

NETWORKING OPPORTUNITY: PIPELINKS

For the previous two years, Cisco had been preaching about the promise of a multiservice network—a single network that could transport data, voice, and video. Cisco's service provider customers agreed that network convergence would ultimately improve cost effectiveness and allow them to expand their service offerings. However, most ser-

---

Research Associates James McJunkin and Todd Reynders prepared this case under the supervision of Professor Garth Saloner and Professor A. Michael Spence as the basis for class discussion rather than to illustrate either effective or ineffective handling of an administrative situation. Margot Sutherland, Executive Director, Center for Electronic Business and Commerce, Stanford Graduate School of Business managed the development of this case.

vice providers were saddled with huge investments in circuit-based voice networks. This implied a market need for optical (Sonet/SDH) routers that leveraged the existing infrastructure while enabling a transition to multiservice networks: the market needed a product that could simultaneously transport circuit-based traffic and route IP (Internet protocol) traffic.[1]

Discussions with representatives from Cisco's service provider line of business (SPLOB) indicated that developing optical routers internally was not a viable option. A brief search had failed to identify attractive acquisition targets—no player had the people, products, technological innovation, ownership concentration, and location that Cisco wanted. In a fortunate coincidence, however, entrepreneur Amit Shah had approached Cisco with an idea for a Sonet/SDH router that was similar to the product that Cisco envisioned. Shah's company, Pipelinks, was still in the "idea" stage—so an outright acquisition was not yet appropriate. Volpi realized that this situation exhibited similarities to one he had faced a year earlier. When Cisco had created a made-to-order company called Ardent Communications to fill a market void, plenty of mistakes had been made in structuring the venture, but much had been done right. Volpi dug up the Ardent file and contemplated possible strategic and structural improvements that could be made, in the hope that some incarnation of the spin-in model would be an effective way to serve the current market need.

BACKGROUND ON CISCO SYSTEMS, INC.[2]

Leonard Bosack and Sandy Lerner, husband and wife computer scientists at Stanford University who invented a technology to link their disparate computer systems together, founded Cisco Systems in 1984. They developed the first "multiprotocol" router—a specialized microcomputer that allowed two or more networks to "talk" to each other by deciphering, translating, and funneling data between them. Cisco's technology opened up the potential to link the world's disparate computer networks together the way different telephone networks were linked around the world.

Cisco began by offering high-end routers primarily in the LAN (local area network) market. The devices were the traffic cops of cyberspace—they directed network traffic to its final destination via the most efficient, least congested network path. As the global Internet and corporate intranets became more important, so did Cisco. With an early foothold in this rapidly growing industry, Cisco quickly became the leader in the data networking equipment market—the "plumbing" of the Internet. By 1997, Cisco made approximately 80% of the large-scale routers that powered the Internet. Although routers, LAN switches, and wide area network (WAN) switches would remain Cisco's core products, the company's product line included other networking solutions, including Web site management tools, dial-up and other remote access solutions, Internet appliances, and network management software. Despite the breadth of its product offerings, Cisco held the number one or two position in most markets in which it competed.

[1] Sonet/SDH (synchronous optical network/synchronous digital hierarchy) is a protocol for data transmission over fiber optic lines.

[2] Excerpts taken from "Cisco Systems, Inc. Acquisition Integration for Manufacturing," Case number OIT-26, Graduate School of Business, Stanford University and Harvard Business School, revised January 1999.

Cisco's Internetwork Operating System (IOS) software was also becoming the de facto industry standard for delivering network services and enabling networked applications.[3]

Cisco received its initial funding from the venture capital firm Sequoia Capital, who helped to recruit John Morgridge as CEO in 1988. The company went public in February 1990 with a $222 million market value and grew into a multinational corporation with over 10,000 employees in 54 countries. By 1997, revenues had increased over ninety-fold since the IPO, from $69.8 million in fiscal 1990 to $6.4 billion in fiscal 1997 (Exhibit 1). In June 1997, Cisco's market value totaled $46.3 billion.

Two respected CEOs have led the company: John Morgridge and John Chambers. Morgridge shaped the Cisco culture from day one, focusing on customer satisfaction, product quality, and frugality. He once gave a legendary presentation on frugality to the Cisco sales force, after being appalled by reports that salespeople were flying first class on business trips. Equipped with slippers, earplugs, and eye covers, Morgridge displayed how to fly coach and make it seem like first class. John Chambers, who joined Cisco in 1991 and succeeded Morgridge in January 1995, was known for his fair but ultra-competitive nature. Chambers, a former IBM and Wang Laboratories marketing and sales veteran, fostered Cisco's strong customer focus and was credited with continuing Cisco's striking success in the networking industry.

Corporate Strategy

Throughout the 1990s, organizations of all sizes were beginning to recognize the value of their information networks and the Internet as a source of business advantage. As a result, more of Cisco's customers sought end-to-end networking solutions. Building on its expertise in routers, Cisco strove to deliver a wide range of new products, expand its offerings through internal and external efforts, enhance customer support, and increase its presence around the world.

The main element of Cisco's strategy during this expansion phase was to maintain a passionate customer focus and consistently try to exceed customer expectations. To deliver on that goal, Chambers reorganized Cisco to target three key markets: enterprise, service providers, and small/medium business. The new organization enabled Cisco to provide market specific, end-to-end solutions that included integrated software, hardware, and network management and to customize its sales, support, and business programs to each market.

One of the keys to the company's success was the Cisco brand, which was recognized as a leading name in networking. Customers associated the Cisco brand with a secure, reliable, high-performance network. Chambers wanted to enhance and expand the brand, and increased Cisco's marketing to include television, Internet, and print advertising.

[3] Cisco's IOS software was the industry leading internetworking software, like Microsoft Windows for networking. IOS is a platform that delivers network services and enables networked applications. IOS enables interoperability connections between otherwise disparate hardware, and accommodates network growth, change, and new applications. It also contains security features, including access control, authentication, firewall, and encryption.

The ongoing deregulation of telecommunications and technology convergence were driving the trend toward the integration of voice, video, and data networks. Historically, there had been three separate types of networks: phone networks for transmitting voice, computer networks for transmitting data, and broadcast networks for transmitting video—but advances in digitization allowed these forms of communication to be translated into binary computer language. This, in turn, made it possible to transmit voice, data, and video over one network more efficiently and economically than using three disparate networks. As a result, phone companies were beginning to transform their archaic voice networks into unified, multiservice networks.

Chambers believed that this transition to the "New World" of communications would enable Cisco to capture share in the $250 billion telecom equipment market that huge, well-capitalized companies such as Lucent Technologies and Northern Telecom had dominated. These competitors were so large that Chambers instilled a David vs. Goliath mentality within Cisco. While expanding into these new markets, Cisco also strove to maintain its product leadership in each of the market segments it already served. The product leadership strategy involved the innovation of Cisco's engineering teams, complemented by alliances, acquisitions, and minority investments.

Building Shareholder Value Through Acquisitions, Investments, and Alliances

As the networking space became more competitive, and as minimizing time to market became more important, Chambers realized that Cisco could not keep up with the changing market needs solely through internal development. Acquisitions and alliances to gain access to world-class technologies and people became a defining component of Cisco's strategy. This strategy was relatively unique: most high-tech companies considered looking to the outside for technological help a sign of weakness. Chambers commented on the acquisitions and alliances strategy:

> *They are a requirement, given how rapidly customer expectations change. The companies who emerge as industry leaders will be those who understand how to partner and those who understand how to acquire. Customers today are not just looking for pinpoint products, but end-to-end solutions. A horizontal business model always beats a vertical business model. So you've got to be able to provide that horizontal capability in your product line, either through your own R&D, or through acquisitions.*[4]

Although Chambers and Ed Kozel, Cisco's chief technology officer, were a key driving force behind Cisco's business development strategy, many in the industry regarded Mike Volpi as the man responsible for shaping Cisco's legendary business development

[4] "The Art of the Deal," *Business 2.0*, October 1999.

practice.[5] When Volpi joined Cisco in 1994 after graduating from the Stanford Graduate School of Business, Cisco had completed only one acquisition, Crescendo Communications. Two more acquisitions closed soon after Volpi arrived, but he was involved in all subsequent acquisitions.

Before pursuing a new market opportunity, Volpi's group assessed the buy vs. build strategies. If Cisco did not have the technological capability, engineering capacity, or time to develop the product internally, the business development group would often opt to acquire or partner with an external player. Although the acquisitions made headlines, licensing, partnering, and investing were equally important to Cisco's strategy. Cisco was an active minority investor, which gave it insight into new technologies without having to deploy internal development resources. Volpi used a simple chart to assess companies (Figure 1).

The public equity markets were the principal exit strategy for hot high-tech start-ups, but a Cisco acquisition appealed to many networking companies. Cisco was the most effective tech company at identifying, acquiring, and successfully integrating companies into its culture. By June 1997, after the Ardent deal closed, Cisco had acquired 19 companies for an aggregate total of roughly $7 billion (Exhibit 3). Why did Cisco do this better than the competition? "We made every mistake in the book," Volpi stated, "but we learned from these mistakes, and they have helped us in subsequent transactions."

FIGURE 1 Range of Cisco's Business Development Activities

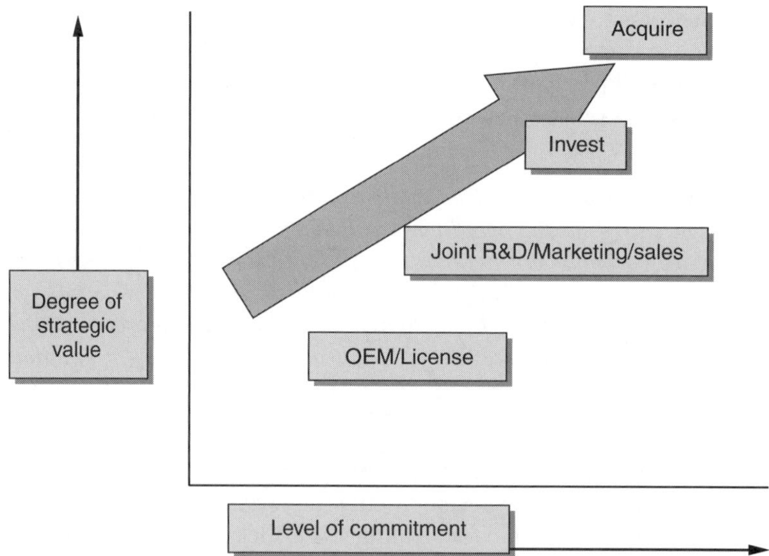

[5] Volpi initially reported to Charles Giancarlo, who joined Cisco through the Kalpana acquisition in 1994, and served as VP of business development until March 1997, when Volpi assumed that title.

Instead of acquiring large, established, public companies, Cisco typically acquired small private companies, for $200 million or less.[6] The smaller acquisitions made integration easier—large, established companies with strong corporate cultures were more difficult to integrate. Chambers also asserted that Cisco did not acquire to gain short-term market share, but to find technology and talent for the future:

> *When we acquire a company, we aren't simply acquiring its current products, we're acquiring the next generation of products through its people. If you pay between $500,000 and $3 million per employee, and all you are doing is buying the current research and current market share, you're making a terrible investment. In the average acquisition, 40%–80% of the top management and key engineers are gone in two years. By those metrics, most acquisitions fail.*[7]

Charles Giancarlo, Cisco's vice president of business development from 1994 to 1997, reiterated the importance of acquiring and retaining key people:

> *When you are buying a company . . . it's obviously not for today's products. That means keeping the people in place who can create that growth. We won't do a deal if a company has "golden parachutes"—accelerated vesting for employees that kicks in once a company is sold. The minute you buy the company, they all get rich. We prefer "golden handcuffs," which are applied with two-year noncompete agreements with key executives and technical personnel at the target companies, and the provision of Cisco stock options that vest over time.*[8]

LOOKING BACK TO 1996: THE MARKET OPPORTUNITY FOR A NEW ACCESS PRODUCT

In 1996, the evolution of network infrastructure was creating business opportunities in virtually every sector of networking. Cisco's unique vantage point allowed it to rapidly identify these new markets. By early 1996, Cisco believed that a need existed for an inexpensive product to carry voice, data, and video traffic from a company's LAN to the WAN.

Cisco identified two principal customer needs. The first was to simplify and improve management of network access equipment. The conventional approach to public network access required cabling disparate hardware components together (such as leased line modems, channel banks, etc.), creating a complex hardware puzzle. Companies incurred high maintenance costs and trouble-shooting nightmares because a different

[6] The $4.6 billion acquisition in April 1996 of StrataCom, which filled Cisco's hole in WAN switching products, stands out as an exception.

[7] "The Art of the Deal," *Business 2.0*, October 1999.

[8] "Cisco's Secret: Entrepreneurs Sell Out, Stay Put," *Inc. Magazine*, March 1997.

management system controlled each component. The second was to optimize use of expensive WAN bandwidth. Despite the industry buzz about high-speed ATM trunks,[9] Cisco believed that these solutions would remain expensive, especially compared to LAN bandwidth where Ethernet technology dominated.[10] Cisco expected high-speed network access solutions, running at T3 (4.5Mbps) or OC-3 (155Mbps), to be confined to niche markets for the foreseeable future. Most customers would choose the slower, more economical T1/E1 (1.5Mbps) link to the WAN.

These factors highlighted a market opportunity for an access solution that aggregated LAN-based data, voice, and video traffic over the low cost T1/E1 ATM trunk. This solution would help service providers:

- Provide an integrated T1/E1 access solution that was cost-effective for wide deployment;
- Contain costs by using a single product in multiple applications;
- Contain upgrade/conversion costs by using a remotely configurable product; and
- Contain support costs by using a product with an interface familiar to both customers and service providers.

This product concept was the genesis of Ardent Communications.

New Venture Strategy

In 1996, Volpi contemplated the traditional buy and build alternatives for the market that Ardent Communications would serve. Building the product in-house had several advantages—notably not having to integrate two different organizations. The multiservice access business unit had been doing similar things on a day-to-day basis, but lacked the human resources to devote to the new project. Diverting resources away from current projects was not feasible. Building the product in-house would take too long—competition from 3Com, Ascend, US Robotics, and Micom made time to market a priority. The business development team concluded that Cisco had neither the time nor the resources to go after the new market on its own.

Buying a company whose products addressed this market was another option. However, Cisco had a clear conception of the market need, but was unable to identify attractive companies that were focused on this space. Volpi's experience suggested that finding the right acquisition target would be difficult—in all cases Cisco would have to spend time and effort modifying the product set and integrating the newly acquired com-

\9 A trunk is an access line that connects remote offices or central sites to the service provider network. Asynchronous transfer mode (ATM) is a data transfer technique where multiple service types, such as voice, video, or data, are conveyed in small, fixed-size cells.

10 In 1996, Ethernet technology penetrated every corner of the Enterprise network with 10BaseT (10Mbps), 100BaseT (100Mbps), and the coming Gigabit Ethernet (1000Mbps).

pany into the Cisco organization. Retaining key employees post-acquisition was also always difficult.

Finding neither the buy nor build alternatives satisfactory, Volpi mused, "Why not custom make a start-up to build exactly the product we want, and then buy them later if they succeed?" This solution would entail creating a new venture as a spin-in from day one—"build to buy." This spin-in model seemed to address three key issues: time-to-market, recruiting top talent, and integration with the relevant Cisco business unit.

However, the Cisco business development team realized that the hybrid nature of the spin-in solution raised difficult trade-offs. What structure would allow the start-up to leverage Cisco's strategic assets without quashing the entrepreneurial feel? How should Cisco structure the venture to minimize the trade-off between the virtues of independence and the need for smooth ex-post integration? Could Cisco personnel coach the new team without stifling creativity? Should Cisco invite other investors to participate in the financing? How large an initial ownership stake should Cisco take in the venture? Incentives would also be a major issue: How could Cisco provide the right incentives for the new venture's management and employees, without upsetting the current Cisco employees who would help integrate the new venture? Eventually, the new venture would have to live within an existing Cisco business unit and rely on Cisco employees for success.

Structuring the Ardent Communications Venture

To develop a potential model for the new venture approach in 1996, Volpi and Kozel had reflected on an earlier deal that Cisco had considered. In the spring of 1996, Wu Fu Chen, a networking entrepreneur, was working with Sequoia Capital and two Cisco employees to launch a new networking company. The idea for this company came from the Cisco employees, who intended to leave their jobs at Cisco to build a solution that they hoped Cisco would want to acquire. The product concept had potential, and the founding team was flush with engineering talent. Wu Fu Chen had cofounded four companies since 1986, including Cascade Communications and Arris Networks. Yet the Cisco business development team declined to invest: Chambers believed that funding Cisco employees to go out and build new networking companies would set a dangerous precedent.

Mike Volpi and Ed Kozel believed that Wu Fu would be an excellent person to recruit as president and CEO of the proposed spin-in venture, which they would call Ardent Communications. Kozel contacted Wu Fu and outlined the Ardent business idea and Cisco's spin-in concept. Volpi later characterized the initial message to Wu Fu as simply, "Make this product and we'll give you lots of money." After a series of discussions, Wu Fu agreed to head up the Ardent venture.

Defining the Ardent 101 Product

In June 1996, Kozel, Volpi, and Wu Fu outlined the basic functional specification for the first Ardent product, tentatively called Ardent 101. For Cisco to buy the new company, Wu Fu and his team needed to develop a traffic aggregation device for data, voice, and video with certain functional requirements (Figure 2). The group also developed milestones that would set expectations for the product timeline (Figure 3).

FIGURE 2 Ardent 101 Functional Requirements

1. Ability to accept data, voice, and video traffic
2. Aggregate up to 2Mbps traffic on the WAN side
3. Support ATM, frame relay, and TDM trunks
4. Support standard office environments
5. Support bridging, IP routing for LAN data traffic
6. Support circuit emulation for voice and video applications
7. Support voice and data compression
8. The target list price for the base configuration is about $5,000; cost of goods target is $800 or lower
9. Will consider support of data encryption
10. Support European requirements (E1)

FIGURE 3 Ardent 101 Milestones

1. Six months after the effective date of the agreement, the company shall have completed the specifications for function, architecture, and design for the product.
2. Twelve months after the effective date of the agreement, the company shall have begun integration of the product.
3. Fifteen months after the effective date of the agreement, the company shall have begun the beta program for the product.
4. Eighteen months after the effective date of the agreement, first customer shipment shall have occurred.

Capital Structure

By June 14, 1996, Cisco and Wu Fu's team had agreed on a preliminary term sheet for the new venture (Exhibit 4). Kozel and Volpi invited Sequoia Capital to participate in the financing to create a more start-up feel. To foster an entrepreneurial environment with strong employee incentives, Cisco gave the founding team and employees a large ownership position—over 55% on a fully diluted basis. Cisco sought an equity stake of only 32% for itself. This was a major departure from the large equity shares other parent companies were requesting in their spin-ins and spin-outs (arguing that their intellectual property, brand name, and other resources entitled them to "free" equity). Sequoia Capital also took a relatively small equity position of 11%. All parties agreed that a balanced board of directors would deliver the right control over the company's direction. Initially, the board would consist of Wu Fu, Ed Kozel, and Sequoia's Mike Goguen.

Unlike most venture deals, the Series A and Series B rounds were negotiated simultaneously, with closing dates less than two months apart. In the A round (July 11 closing) Wu Fu and the other members of the founding team would purchase 3 million shares of Series A Preferred Stock at $0.333 per share. The low share price was analogous to cheap founders' stock in an entrepreneurial venture. Neither Cisco nor Sequoia would participate in the A round. The implied post-money valuation as of July 11 was $2.4 million.

For the B round, the new company decided to issue 11 million shares. On August 30, Ardent received the first cash infusion of the B round, in which Sequoia Capital purchased approximately 2.5 million shares at $1.00 per share. Cisco also made its investment at $1.00 per share, purchasing 7.535 million shares of Series B Preferred Stock on September 20. Seven days later, the founders purchased another one million shares. The remaining equity capitalization consisted of 9.25 million shares of common stock, of which approximately 3 million shares would go to the engineering team as option grants. The implied post-money valuation as of August 30 was $23.3 million. Exhibit 5 describes the rough capitalization table Cisco used.

Retaining Key Employees

Volpi knew that even though Cisco was creating Ardent to produce a specific product, it was the people, not the product, that represented much of Ardent's value. Cisco therefore laid out a four-year vesting period for the options granted to employees—25% would vest after the first year, with the remainder vesting monthly over the next three years. Upon a change in control, like the planned acquisition by Cisco, only Wu Fu Chen's vesting would accelerate (at most one year of vesting would remain, but he was subject to a one-year lock up agreement which kept him from leaving Ardent upon acquisition).

Facilitating the Spin-in: The Put/Call Feature

Cisco needed a legal mechanism that would allow Ardent to cleanly spin-in at some point in the future. The founding team proposed a simple put/call structure that would give Cisco the *option* to purchase the company at a prespecified price, but would also *obligate* Cisco to purchase the company if the new team succeeded in building the product. This was the first time that Cisco had integrated a put/call feature into a strategic investment. John Chambers and Ed Kozel viewed it as an innovative mechanism for developing a made-to-order company. The "Option" section of the term sheet explained the call option:

> *Until the earlier of fifteen (15) months from the closing or one (1) month after the first customer shipment, Cisco shall have the right to acquire either all of the outstanding equity securities of the Company, or all of the Company's assets, in Cisco's*

> *discretion, for a purchase price of $232,500,000, payable either in cash or equity securities of Cisco.*[11]

Since Cisco would also write a put option, the shareholders in the new venture could force it to purchase the company at the prespecified price, as long as the ten specific functional requirements were met. To keep matters simple, the put and call would have the same strike price. The put option read:

> *. . . if First Customer Shipment occurs within (15) months after the functional requirements for the Product are first defined, and in Cisco's reasonable judgment, the product meets the specifications set forth, each of the security holders shall sell its Securities to Cisco, and Cisco shall be obliged to and will purchase such Securities, in accordance with the purchase price and other terms of purchase. . . .*[12]

Cisco believed that although the put/call structure truncated the upside for investors and employees, it mitigated enough risk to make the investment or employment decision attractive from a risk/reward standpoint. The option agreement turned out to be a very effective recruiting instrument. If the product requirements and milestones were met, the 15–20 person engineering team would share a $30 million payout in less than 15 months. The five person founding team would do even better: delivering on the product would allow them to share more than $100 million.

Leveraging Cisco's Assets

• ***IOS.*** The Ardent product would complement Cisco's existing multiservice access products (called the 3800 product family). To facilitate interoperability, Volpi decided to license Cisco's IOS software to Ardent free of charge until Cisco's option to buy the company expired. IOS was to be the architectural foundation for Ardent 101. Ardent would focus on adding the technologies of ATM and frame relay over a T1/E1 connection, circuit emulation for digitized voice over ATM or frame relay, voice compression, and telephony capabilities. These changes were not on the official evolutionary path of IOS, though they were similar to development work being done within Cisco. Many Cisco employees had also created and modified IOS for use in the various products Cisco sold, but not to be sold as a shrink-wrapped software product. The procedures to use and adapt IOS were not well documented, which would present a challenge to the Ardent employees. Under the terms of the licensing deal, Cisco would retain all ownership of IOS, including software Ardent developed to interact directly with IOS.

[11] Excerpt from *Memorandum of Terms for Private Placement of Series A and B Preferred Stock of Ardent Corporation*, June 1996.
[12] *ibid.*

Licensing IOS software to Ardent for free was contentious—it upset Cisco personnel who felt that the company was giving away the crown jewels, the real value-add in Cisco's solutions, and then paying to buy it back.

• ***Engineering talent.*** Ardent would also need engineering help to integrate IOS into its new product. To address this issue, a few Cisco employees were selected to work with the Ardent team throughout the development process. This was not unusual, because Cisco had provided consulting services in the past. Ardent paid the standard fee for these engineering resources, $250,000 per engineer per year. Since this was regarded as a temporary assignment, these people remained employees of Cisco under the same terms as they had before Ardent surfaced.

• ***Testing and certification facilities.*** Cisco also provided testing and certification facilities. Cisco allowed Ardent to use its testing and certification facilities free of charge until the option period expired, after which Ardent would pay a nominal fee.

• ***Business unit expertise.*** A key issue was the extent to which the multiservice access business unit should coach Ardent through the development process and stay informed about what progress had been made. Cisco had similar products in the pipeline, but none overlapped significantly with Ardent 101 as defined in the product requirements document. Volpi and Kozel decided not to involve the business units until after the Ardent product was completed. This approach seemed appropriate because the product specification had already been narrowly defined, minimizing the degrees of freedom and therefore the need for frequent coaching or updates. Hence, Ardent operated in stealth mode through early 1997.

• ***Cisco form factor.*** Both Cisco and Ardent wanted the new product to have the look and feel of the Cisco product line, although the product specification did not require it. Instead of designing a tailored box for Ardent 101, Chen decided to adhere to the existing Cisco product line and required his engineers to adopt the form factor for the Cisco 2500 series. This solution was compact and familiar to Cisco's carrier customers. Squeezing Ardent 101 into the 2500 box would be an engineering and manufacturing challenge, but the Ardent engineers felt confident it could be done.

• ***Accounting issues.*** The Ardent spin-in model had implications for the accounting methods Cisco could employ to account for the venture and complete the spin-in. Many of Cisco's acquisitions had used the pooling-of-interests method. For acquisitions when Cisco paid far more than the assets' book value, the pooling method was preferable.[13] Pooling-of-interests accounting required, among other things, that the acquisition occur in a single transaction where more than 90% of the company was acquired and that no prior control be exerted on the company. Since Cisco took an initial 32% stake in

[13] Net income is generally lower under the purchase method because significant goodwill, an intangible asset which represents the excess of the purchase price over the assets' book value, must be amortized over a defined period.

Ardent, and the call option translated into significant control, pooling was never a possibility—but the venture's strategic value outweighed the accounting effects. Volpi commented, "We certainly look at the accounting impact in our decision process, but I don't think that accounting issues should ever dominate the strategic issues in making decisions."

The accounting for Cisco's investment in Ardent was relatively straightforward. Since Cisco owned more than 20% but less than 50% of the company, generally accepted accounting principles (GAAP) required that Cisco use the equity method of accounting. Hence, the Ardent investment was recorded on Cisco's books at acquisition cost plus its pro-rata share of Ardent's earnings (or losses).

The Ardent Acquisition

In June 1997, Volpi and Kozel discussed whether Cisco should exercise its option to purchase the outstanding shares of Ardent. In many ways, the decision was immaterial, because Chen and his team were likely to meet the acceptance criteria and exercise their put option, obligating Cisco to purchase Ardent. Hence, the key consideration was timing: Should Cisco wait until the end of the option period to spin-in Ardent or do it now? Volpi and Kozel determined that doing the deal sooner rather than later would deliver two principal benefits. First, Cisco could begin to integrate Ardent into the Cisco family, speeding time to market for the Cisco branded solution. Second, purchasing early would avoid confusing the marketplace. Ardent's marketing people had begun to put their own spin on the product, now called "Integress." However, Cisco might want to use a different marketing approach. If Ardent educated the marketplace, Cisco would either have to continue the same marketing program or re-educate potential customers. Historically, re-education had not worked well. In fact, competitors were highlighting Cisco's "inconsistent messages" in their white papers and marketing materials.

On June 24, Cisco announced its intention to acquire Ardent. The press release stated: "Under the terms of the acquisition agreement, shares of Cisco common stock worth approximately $156 million will be exchanged for the outstanding shares and options of Ardent" (Exhibit 6). This was consistent with the agreed upon total acquisition price of $232.5 million because Cisco already owned 32% of the company.

Cisco paid approximately $10 per share. The founders received approximately $102.3 million—more than 100 times their initial investment. Sequoia Capital received $24.6 million, a relatively small sum but still 10 times the money invested in less than 12 months.

Although the Ardent deal had several flaws, Cisco had learned a lot about how to structure future deals from the acquisition. Volpi turned his attention away from the Ardent acquisition and back to the Pipelinks opportunity.

JUNE 1997: VOLPI CONSIDERS THE PIPELINKS OPPORTUNITY

Several of Volpi's colleagues at Cisco had identified the market opportunity for a Sonet/SDH router capable of simultaneously transporting circuit-based traffic and routing IP. Cisco would target the product at many of its service provider customers who were struggling to bring their networks into the "New World" of unified networks, but wanted to make the transition without scrapping their existing circuit-based TDM infrastructure.

One factor was Cisco's expertise in optical routing. In 1997, it was limited. High-speed Sonet/SDH networking solutions were much larger and more expensive (with price points in the hundred thousand to multimillion dollar range) than Cisco's traditional products. Because this was an unfamiliar market for Cisco, Volpi and his team looked externally to pursue the market opportunity, but none of the existing players met Cisco's criteria.

Volpi's team believed, however, that Amit Shah's idea might address this market need. Shah, who had sold his first networking company to Cabletron Systems, a Cisco competitor, realized the increasing need for bandwidth on the access points of the Internet infrastructure—the "metro" space near large population areas. Shah conceived a Sonet/SDH router product similar to the one Cisco envisioned. He called the idea Pipelinks. After a series of discussions, Volpi and Kozel determined that Cisco would like to bring Shah's product to market using the Ardent spin-in model. Shah was intrigued by the idea—it seemed like an effective way to raise funds, recruit the right people, and execute with customers. Once Shah had agreed in principle to structure Pipelinks as a spin-in, Volpi sat down to outline the terms of the deal. As he dug through the license agreements, term sheets, and product requirements in the old Ardent file, Volpi identified several potential improvements and modifications that he would make.

EXHIBIT 1 Cisco Systems Historical Financials

Balance sheet Fiscal year ending July 31	*1990*	*1991*	*1992*	*1993*	*1994*	*1995*	*1996*	*1997*
Annual assets (000s)								
Cash	$35,842	$40,323	$39,955	$27,247	$53,567	$284,388	$279,695	$269,608
Marketable securities	21,102	51,104	116,477	61,738	129,219	279,754	758,489	1,005,977
Receivables	15,874	34,659	61,258	129,109	237,570	421,747	622,859	1,170,401
Inventories	3,701	6,078	9,142	23,500	27,896	81,805	301,188	254,677
Other current assets	1,673	8,797	20,244	26,702	59,425	116,466	197,409	400,603
Total current assets	78,192	140,961	247,076	268,296	507,677	1,184,160	2,159,640	3,101,266
Net prop, plant & equip	4,114	12,665	28,017	48,672	77,449	172,561	331,315	466,352
Invest & adv to subs	—	—	46,866	274,260	457,394	583,871	1,060,758	1,630,390
Deposits & other asset	367	519	1,974	3,985	11,174	51,357	78,519	253,976
Total assets	$82,673	$154,145	$323,933	$595,213	$1,053,694	$1,991,949	$3,630,232	$5,451,984
Annual liabilities (000s)								
Accounts payable	$4,973	$7,743	$16,262	$24,744	$31,708	$59,812	$153,683	$207,178
Accrued expenses	6,290	17,965	46,953	77,492	130,846	257,099	445,776	656,707
Income taxes	1,976	542	15,108	17,796	42,958	71,970	169,894	256,224
Total current liability	13,239	26,250	78,323	120,032	205,512	388,881	769,353	1,120,109
Other long-term liability	123	436	—	—	—	—	—	—
Total liabilities	13,469	26,686	78,323	120,032	205,512	388,881	769,353	1,120,109
Minority interest	—	—	—	—	—	40,792	41,257	42,253
Shareholder equity	69,204	127,459	245,610	475,181	848,182	1,562,276	2,819,622	4,289,622
Total liability & net worth	$82,673	$154,145	$323,933	$595,213	$1,053,694	$1,991,949	$3,630,232	$5,451,984

(continued)

EXHIBIT 1 *(continued)*

Income statement *Fiscal year ending July 31*	*1990*	*1991*	*1992*	*1993*	*1994*	*1995*	*1996*	*1997*
Net sales	$69,776	$183,184	$339,623	$649,035	$1,334,436	$2,232,652	$4,096,007	$6,452,000
Cost of goods	23,957	62,499	111,243	210,528	450,591	742,860	1,409,862	2,243,000
Gross profit	45,819	120,685	228,380	438,507	883,845	1,489,792	2,686,145	4,209,000
R & D expenditures	6,168	12,687	26,745	44,254	106,680	306,575	399,291	1,210,000
Sell gen & admin exp	18,260	41,809	72,248	130,682	276,995	485,254	886,048	1,370,000
Operating income	21,391	66,189	129,387	263,571	500,170	697,963	1,400,806	1,629,000
Nonoperating income	2,088	4,567	6,719	11,557	22,330	40,014	64,019	262,000
Interest expense	—	—	—	—	—	—	—	—
Income before tax	23,479	70,756	136,106	275,128	522,500	739,977	1,464,825	1,891,000
Taxes	9,575	27,567	51,720	103,173	199,519	281,488	551,501	840,000
Net income	$13,904	$43,189	$84,386	$171,955	$322,981	$456,489	$913,324	$1,051,000

Source: Cisco Systems

EXHIBIT 2 Cisco Systems Monthly Stock Price Chart: February 1990–June 1997[14]

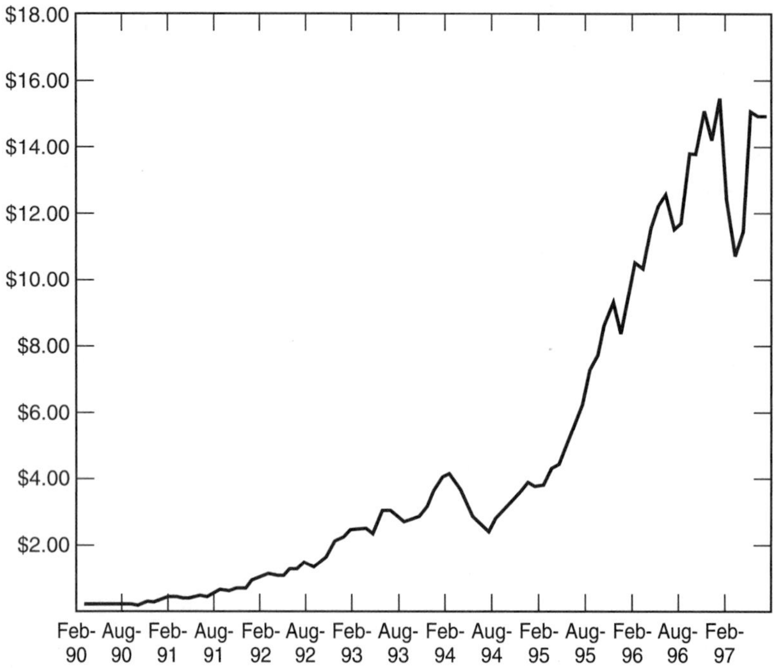

Source: Cisco Systems

EXHIBIT 3 Summary of Cisco's Acquisitions as of June 1997

Company	*Date*	*Purchase Price*	*Description*
Crescendo Communications, Inc.	September 1993	$95 million	High-performance work group CDDI and FDDI switching solutions.
Newport Systems Solutions, Inc.	July 1994	$93 million	Software-based routers for remote network sites of small- to medium-sized networks.
Kalpana, Inc.	October 1994	$240 million	Manufacturer of modular and stackable LAN switching products that extend the usability and data capacity of existing Ethernet LANs.

(continued)

[14] Prices adjusted for all splits since IPO, based on January 25, 2000 stock price.

EXHIBIT 3 *(continued)*

Company	*Date*	*Purchase Price*	*Description*
LightStream Corp.	October 1994	$120 million	Jointly held company formed in 1993 by Bolt Beranek and Newman and UB Networks offers enterprise ATM switching, and workgroup ATM switching, LAN switching and routing.
Combinet, Inc.	August 1995	$132 million	Supplier of ISDN (integrated services digital network) remote-access networking products useful for telecommuting and other networked applications.
Internet Junction, Inc.	September 1995	Not public	Developer of Internet gateway software connecting central and remote office desktop users with the Internet.
Grand Junction, Inc.	September 1995	$400 million	Inventor and leading supplier of Fast Ethernet (100BaseT) and Ethernet desktop switching products.
Network Translation, Inc.	October 1995	Not public	Manufacturer of cost-effective, low-maintenance network address translation and enterprise Internet firewall hardware and software.
TGV Software, Inc.	January 1996	$138 million	Internet software products for connecting disparate computer systems over local-area, enterprise-wide, and global computing networks, including the Internet.

(continued)

EXHIBIT 3 *(continued)*

Company	*Date*	*Purchase Price*	*Description*
StrataCom, Inc.	April 1996	$4.666 million	Leading supplier of ATM and frame relay high-speed WAN switching equipment transporting a wide variety of information, including voice, data, and video.
Telebit Corp.'s MICA Technologies	July 1996	$200 million	Modem ISDN channel aggregation (MICA) technologies will deliver high-density digital modem technology with Cisco's dial-up and access product lines.
Nashoba Networks, Inc.	August 1996	$100 million	Token ring switching technologies for providing users with a wide choice of employing high-performance switched workgroup and backbone Token Ring environments.
Granite Systems	September 1996	$220 million	Standards-based multilayer Gigabit Ethernet switching technologies for developing a wide choice of backbone network technologies.
Netsys Technologies	October 1996	$79 million	Network modeling and design software intended to help common customers base design and plan for networks ideally suited to their unique business requirements.
Metaplex, Inc.	December 1996	Not public	Specialist in network product development in the enterprise marketplace; gives customers the ability to migrate from SNA to IP.

(continued)

EXHIBIT 3 *(continued)*

Company	*Date*	*Purchase Price*	*Description*
Telesend	March 1997	Not public	Specialist in WAN access products; gives telecommunications carriers a more cost-effective way to deliver high-speed data services for Internet and intranet access applications.
Skystone Systems Corp.	June 1997	$102 million	Innovator of high-speed synchronous optical networking/synchronous digital hierarch technology to carry information to high-capacity backbone networks, such as those operated by telecommunications carriers and ISPs.
Global Internet Software Group	June 1997	$40 million	GISG is a pioneer in the Windows NT network security marketplace with its Windows NT Centri Firewall for small- to-medium-size businesses.
Ardent Communications Corp.	June 1997	$156 million	Pioneer in designing combined communications support for compressed voice, LAN, data, and video traffic across frame relay and ATM networks.

Source: Cisco Systems.

EXHIBIT 4 Preliminary Ardent Term Sheet, June 1996

Memorandum of Terms for Private Placement of Series A and Series B Preferred Stock of Ardent Communications Corporation June 14, 1996

Offering Terms	
Issuer:	Ardent Communications Corporation, a California corporation ("the Company")
Securities to be Issued:	3,000,000 shares of Series A Preferred Stock and 11,000,000 shares of Series B Preferred Stock
Price:	$.333 per share of Series A and $1.00 per share of Series B

(continued)

EXHIBIT 4 *(continued)*

Terms of Series A and Series B Preferred Stock

Dividends:	Annual $.03 and $.08 per share dividend, respectively, payable when and if declared by Board; dividends are not cumulative. For any other dividends or distributions, Preferred Stock participates with Common Stock on an as-converted basis.
Liquidation Preference:	First pay cost plus accrued dividends on each share of Preferred Stock. Thereafter Preferred and Common share on as-converted basis, until such time as the Preferred Stock has received an aggregate of two times cost, thereafter all proceeds shall go to the Common Stock. A merger, reorganization, or other transaction in which control of the company is transferred will be treated as if a liquidation.
Conversion:	Convertible into one share of Common Stock (subject to antidilution adjustment) at any time at the option of the holder. Automatically converts into Common Stock upon consummation of underwritten public offering with a price of $5.00 and aggregate proceeds in excess of $7,500,000.
Antidilution Adjustments:	Conversion ratio adjusted on narrow weighted average basis in the event of a dilutive issuance. Proportional adjustments for stock splits and stock dividends.
Voting Rights:	Votes on an as-converted basis, but also has series vote as provided by law and on (i) the creation of any senior or pari passu security, (ii) repurchase of Common Stock except upon termination of employment, (iii) any transaction in which control of the Company is transferred, and (iv) any adverse change to the rights, preferences, and privileges of the Series A or Series B Preferred.

Terms of Preferred Stock Purchase Agreement

Representations and Warranties:	Standard representations and warranties by the Company.
Assignment of Inventions and Confidentiality Agreement:	All employees and consultants shall enter into company's standard form inventions and proprietary information agreement.

Terms of Investor Rights Agreement

Registration Rights:	(a) Beginning earlier than June 28, 2000 or six months after initial registration, two demand registrations upon initiation by holders of at least 30% of outstanding Preferred Stock for aggregate proceeds in excess of $10,000,000. Expenses paid by Company. (b) Unlimited piggyback registration rights subject to pro rata cutback at the underwriter's discretion. Full cutback upon IPO; 30% minimum inclusion thereafter. Expenses paid by Company. Preliminary Ardent Term Sheet, June 1996

(continued)

EXHIBIT 4 *(continued)*

	(c) Unlimited S-3 Registrations of at least $1,000,000 each upon initiation by holders of 20% of the Preferred. Expenses paid by Company.
	Registration rights terminate (i) five years after initial public offering or (ii) when all shares can be sold under Rule 144, whichever occurs first.
	No future registration rights may be granted without consent of a majority of Investors unless subordinate to Investors' rights.
Right of First Refusal:	Cisco Systems shall have the right to purchase all securities issued in subsequent equity financings of the Company, provided the Option, as defined below, has not expired.
Financial Information:	The Investors shall receive standard information rights including audited financial reports, quarterly unaudited financial reports, monthly unaudited financial reports, and annual budget and business plan, as well as standard inspection rights.
Board of Directors:	Board shall consist of four members. Board composition at Closing shall be Wu Fu Chen, Ed Kozel, and Mike Goguen. One other representative will be designated by a majority vote of the Series B Preferred Stock.

Post-Closing Capitalization

Series A Preferred Stock Outstanding	3,000,000	shares	12.9%
Series B Preferred Stock Outstanding	9,000,000	shares	47.3%
Common Stock held by Founders	6,250,000	shares	26.9%
Common Stock Reserved for Employees (However, an additional 3,750,000 shares shall be available for grant after expirationof Option, held by Cisco.)	3,000,000	shares	12.9%
TOTAL:	23,250,000	shares	100.0%

Other Matters

Common Stock Vesting:	Common Stock shall vest as follows: After twelve months of employment, 25% will vest; the remainder will vest monthly over the following 36 months. Repurchase option on unvested shares at cost. No acceleration in the event of a Change of Control, except for Mr. Chen, whose vesting shall accelerate in the event of a Change of Control such that at most one year of vesting shall remain.
Restrictions on Common Stock Transfers:	(a) No transfers allowed prior to vesting.
	(b) Right of first refusal on vested shares until initial public offering.

(continued)

EXHIBIT 4 *(continued)*

	(c) No transfers or sales permitted during lock-up period of up to 180 days required by underwriters in connection with stock offerings by the Company.
Option:	Until the earlier of fifteen (15) months from the Closing or three (3) months after First Customer Shipment, Cisco shall have the right to acquire either all of the outstanding equity securities of the Company, or all of the Company's assets, in Cisco's discretion, for a purchase price of $232,500,000 payable either in cash or equity securities of Cisco.
Closing Conditions:	Closing subject to negotiation of definitive legal documents and completion of legal and financial due diligence by Investors.

Source: Cisco Systems.

EXHIBIT 5 Ardent Capitalization Table

	Preferred A	*Preferred B*	*Common*	*Total*	*Ownership*
Cisco	—	7,535,000	—	7,535,000	32%
Sequoia Capital	—	2,465,000	—	2,465,000	11%
Founders	3,000,000	1,000,000	6,250,000	10,250,000	44%
Engineering team	—	—	3,000,000	3,000,000	13%
Total	3,000,000	11,000,000	9,250,000	23,250,000	100%
Valuation ($/shr)	$0.33	$1.00	$0.001		
Valuation ($)	$2,400,000	$23,250,000	$23,250,000		
Cash inflow	$990,000	$11,000,000	$9,250		
Option to acquire					
Acquisition price	$232,500,000				
Return	*Cash Out*	*Cash In*	*Multiple*		
Cisco	$75,350,000	$7,535,000	10.0		
Venture capital	$24,650,000	$2,465,000	10.0		
Founders (5 employees)	$102,500,000	$1,002,250	102.3		
Engineering team (20 employees)	$30,000,000	$3,000	9,978		
Return (cash in–cash out) per employee					
Founders	$20,299,550				
Engineering team	$1,499,850				
Cisco cost/head	$6,286,000				
Cisco cost	$157,150,000				

(continued)

EXHIBIT 5 *(continued)*

Conditions

- No accelerated vesting for employees or founders, except for Wu Fu Chen
- Commitment from Wu Fu to stay one year postacquisition
- Right to future offerings in the company or direction of those offerings

Source: Cisco Systems.

EXHIBIT 6 Press Release for the Ardent Communications Acquisition

CISCO SYSTEMS TO ACQUIRE ARDENT COMMUNICATIONS CORP.

Further Investment in Data, Voice, and Video Integration for Public and Private Networks

SAN JOSE, Calif., June 24, 1997—Cisco Systems, Inc. today announced it has signed a definitive agreement to acquire privately held Ardent Communications Corp. Previously, Cisco and Sequoia Capital held minority equity stakes in Ardent. San Jose-based Ardent is a pioneer in designing combined communications support for compressed voice, LAN, data, and video traffic across public and private frame relay and ATM networks.

Under the terms of the acquisition agreement, shares of Cisco common stock worth approximately $156 million will be exchanged for the outstanding shares and options of Ardent. In connection with the acquisition, Cisco expects a one-time charge against after-tax earnings of 23 cents per share in the fourth fiscal quarter of 1997. The acquisition is expected to be completed by late July 1997 subject to various closing conditions, including clearance under the Hart-Scott-Rodino Antitrust Improvements Act and Ardent shareholder approval.

Cisco Steps Up Integration Over Frame Relay and ATM Networks

With the continued pace of deregulation of the telecommunications service industry, carriers are increasingly offering services which integrate communication channels of voice, video, and data. As a result, the demand for low-cost, easy-to-use, multiservice access products for new carrier services is rapidly expanding. The acquisition of Ardent will complement Cisco's 3800 series within carrier service offerings for branch offices and remote sites by extending leadership in integration of voice, video, and data. Based on Cisco IOS software, Ardent's low-cost platforms will natively support multiservice traffic and implement voice compression using high performance Digital Signal Processor (DSP) technology. Ardent's early affiliation with Cisco has resulted in a complementary product platform offering superior interoperability with existing Cisco multiservice access and switching product lines.

(continued)

EXHIBIT 6 *(continued)*

About Ardent Communications

Ardent Communications was founded in 1996 by CEO Wu Fu Chen. Mr. Chen has cofounded four other companies since 1986, including Cascade Communications and Arris Networks. Ardent's approximately 40 employees will remain in San Jose and become part of the multiservice access business unit led by vice president and general manager Alex Mendez within Cisco's service provider line of business.

Ardent Communications is on the leading edge of integrated access equipment design. Founded in 1996, Ardent designs, manufacturers, and distributes advanced access products for integrating voice, video, and data on public or private frame relay or ATM networks.

Source: Cisco Systems.

TRADEWEAVE

In May 1999, the board of directors and senior management of QRS were considering the opportunities the Web presented. The Internet seemed to hold the potential to dramatically improve the functioning and structure of demand chains. QRS was well positioned to participate in those trends but which opportunities to pursue was unclear. Moreover, the QRS management team was running flat out in pursuit of its primary objectives—to tightly manage the company's existing businesses and find, execute, and integrate acquisitions that would enhance to its existing businesses. Some established companies were pursuing Internet opportunities through separate dot-coms, sometimes in partnership with venture capitalists. QRS would have to decide whether to emulate them or stretch its existing management structure. One thing was clear: QRS would need to move quickly if it expected to control its own destiny and fend off competitors.

QRS BACKGROUND

Founded in 1985, QRS Corporation aimed to be a leading provider of demand chain management services to suppliers of consumer goods.[1] By 1999, the company had become a leading provider of electronic data interchange (EDI) services to the U.S. retail industry. Reselling IBM's network services, QRS had achieved a 40% market share for EDI services in the soft goods sector (apparel, accessories, and footwear). It had also developed the retail industry's largest and most widely used uniform product code (UPC) catalog. With more than 7,700 customers, including 270 retailers and nearly 7,500 manufacturers and carriers, QRS was an ingrained service provider to the retail industry.

Research Associate David Doctorow (MBA 2000) prepared this case under the supervision of Professor Garth Saloner and Professor A. Michael Spence as the basis for class discussion rather than to illustrate either effective or ineffective handling of an administrative situation. Margot Sutherland, Executive Director, Center for Electronic Commerce and Business, Stanford Graduate School of Business managed the development of this case. Research support provided by The Boston Consulting Group is gratefully acknowledged.

[1] See the Stanford GSB Case, "QRS," EC-3, for a more detailed discussion.

Since its initial public offering in 1993, QRS had generated sales growth of 33% and net income growth of 36% on a compound annual basis. In 1998, sales and net income were $91.9 million and $12.1 million, respectively. Over all but one of the last 10 quarters, QRS had generated quarter-over-quarter sales and earnings growth of at least 20% (Exhibits 1 and 2). This consistency was attractive to institutional investors who had seen QRS's market capitalization, which was $697 million at the end of June 1999, grow 43% on a compound annual basis over the previous three years (Exhibit 3).

The QRS Keystone catalog was the company's flagship product. Developed in 1987, it helped retailers and suppliers improve their purchasing and fulfillment operations: suppliers could upload current UPCs to the database, and retailers could retrieve accurate UPCs for their ordering and inventory management systems. Keystone contained nearly 73 million UPCs as of mid-1999, over 42 million of which were apparel related. The catalog contained significantly more UPCs than any competing product and was more than an order of magnitude larger than the average retailer's UPC portfolio of 1 million.[2] With such a large share of all apparel UPCs, QRS was well positioned to be the market-leading provider of demand chain management services to participants in the apparel goods market, including retailers and vendors.

To cultivate the Keystone installed base, QRS had pursued a hub-and-spoke customer acquisition strategy, focusing its marketing efforts first on senior management at large retailers such as Federated who could understand the value proposition and could define the "terms of trade" with their vendor trading partners. The Keystone catalog cut retailers' costs by automating processes, improving information quality, and tightening monitoring and control. QRS provided secure, reliable, and high quality service. When QRS's "hub" retailers announced that they would only procure products electronically through QRS and mandated trading partners to upload their own product portfolios into the Keystone Catalog, the weaker "spoke" vendors had to join in. QRS captured a portion of the value its system created for hub retailers by charging both hubs and spokes subscription and transaction fees. In the process, QRS developed relationships with executives in the spokes' IT organizations.

Although some large apparel vendors were not yet "hub" customers, QRS was concerned that its continued growth would slacken as the Keystone base matured within the apparel goods market. To further its reach, QRS broadened its customer acquisition efforts to include large vendors, many of which had already become QRS customers through their relationships with large retailers. Most of these vendors could also dictate their terms of trade with smaller retailers.

To stimulate additional revenue, QRS had developed new products within its Inventory Management Services and Logistics Management Services product lines. It had also acquired a few companies, including its service bureaus (SBs) and Retail Data Services (RDS). The SBs, QRS's fastest growing business, helped small vendors convert electronic purchase orders from retailers to hard copy for vendors and converted paper documents from vendors to electronic format for transmission to retailers. RDS was a national market research and data management firm serving the grocery and con-

[2] Source: QRS internal research.

sumer packaged goods markets that collected, verified, and analyzed competitive retail pricing, promotion, and distribution information.

QRS's senior management and board of directors had also begun to consider strategic alternatives that might bolster the company's ability to generate consistent earnings growth. One option was to broaden the scope of the installed base beyond apparel to include other UPC-driven verticals, such as sporting goods,[3] canned foods and grocery, household furnishings, toys, and general merchandise. A second was to create more new product offerings in-house. A third was to acquire more companies that could enhance the QRS product portfolio. The board also considered creating new, organizationally segregated businesses that might enhance and deepen the QRS product offering to provide a more complete solution for the needs of its existing and future customers.

QRS AND THE U.S. APPAREL GOODS SUPPLY CHAIN

Apparel retailing was a $192 billion market in the United States in 1998.[4] Together with general merchandise retailing, which included department store retailers, this represented a retail trade of approximately $500 billion (see Exhibit 4). The top 10 apparel retailers, eight of which were QRS customers in 1998, distributed approximately 50% of apparel retailing dollar volume.[5] The top 50 apparel retailers, 26 of which were QRS customers in 1998, distributed approximately 83% of this dollar volume. Of the remaining thousands of U.S. apparel retailers, a small percentage were QRS customers in 1998. Overall, QRS did business with retailers that represented approximately 57% of the apparel retailing market.[6] General merchandise department stores were the largest channel within this market, approximately 34% of total volume. QRS did business with retailers that represented over 90% of volume in this channel in 1998. QRS management also believed that it controlled roughly 57% of the outsourced demand chain management services market in the apparel goods retailing.

Net profit margins for most retail segments were typically in the low to middle single digits: department and discount stores, for instance, averaged 3.1% over the last five years; grocery stores, 2.2%; home improvement stores, 4.7%; drug stores, 2.6%; and apparel retailers, 6.9%.[7]

In 1998, QRS management believed that approximately 7,000 vendors supplied apparel and general merchandise to retailers.[8] A dominant portion of manufacturers

[3] Roughly 60% of the sporting goods products were apparel related.

[4] Source: The Boston Consulting Group. According to S&P Apparel & Footwear Industry Survey, the 1998 market was actually $180 billion. Estimate based on retail trade dollars, which were roughly two times wholesale cost to retailers at the margin (N.B. wholesale cost to retailers equals vendor revenues, in theory). Includes retail sales by vertically integrated retailers, such as Gap, that manufacture, distribute, and sell their own merchandise through captive channels to end consumers.

[5] These and following figures are case writer estimates.

[6] Source: Tradeweave Opportunity Analysis, August 31, 1999.

[7] Retail profitability data from *Market Guide, Inc.* (published by OneSource Information Services, 8/99).

[8] Some vendors manufactured their own merchandise and distributed it through noncaptive retail channels—these were known as "vendor/manufacturers." Other vendors outsourced the manufacturing of the product that they distributed.

distributed nonbranded merchandise to private label retailers.[9] However, a smaller group of leading vendors, such as Tommy Hilfiger and Levi Strauss, accounted for a large dollar volume and distributed branded merchandise to a more select group of retailers. In certain segments of the apparel industry, branded manufacturers was an especially significant portion of volume, as Table 1 indicates.[10]

In addition, roughly half of vendors produced "basic" merchandise, or "basics," items that remain in style from season to season and year to year, while others produced "fashion" items that were more transitory.[11] Table 2 illustrates this split for a few segments of the apparel industry.[12]

A small proportion of vendors also maintained a direct marketing channel to consumers through outlet stores and/or a Web site. As of 1998, QRS management believed that approximately 2,000 vendors maintained a Web presence, although most did not support e-commerce transactions. QRS management believed that its apparel vendor customer base represented roughly 70% of the total $74 billion 1998 wholesale vendors' volume in the apparel industry[13] and that it also controlled roughly 70% of the

TABLE 1 Branded Vendors by Segment

	Number of Vendors		
	Branded	*Top*	*% Branded of Top Vendors*
Pants	13	16	81
Women's sportswear	26	27	96
Sportswear	13	14	93
Intimate wear	4	5	80

TABLE 2 Fashion Vendors by Segment

	Number of Vendors			
	Basics	*Fashion*	*Top*	*% Basics of Top Vendors*
Pants	13	3	16	81
Women's sportswear	—	27	27	0
Sportswear	9	5	14	64
Intimate wear	5	—	5	100

[9] Based on estimates prepared by QRS indicating that approximately 10% of vendors supply branded merchandise.

[10] Source: QRS internal research.

[11] Note that perishable in the apparel goods context was best described by fashion merchandise that may not be salable in the next selling season, as might be the case for "basic" merchandise.

[12] Source: QRS internal research.

[13] Source: Tradeweave Opportunity Analysis, August 31, 1999. Excludes "wholesale" revenues associated with vertically integrated retailers.

outsourced demand chain management services market in the apparel goods manufacturing vertical.[14] Net profit margins for most vendor segments were typically below 5%.

SURPLUS MERCHANDISE IN APPAREL GOODS RETAILING

One possible Web-based opportunity lay in the surplus merchandise area, which had attracted attention from nascent Web companies. Some retailers considered surplus merchandise any merchandise that was marked down. Others defined surplus as merchandise that was disposed of through outlet stores or liquidation channels, including "jobbers," intermediaries that acquired surplus merchandise to sell it to "resellers," off-price or off-style retailers. Vendors generally considered surplus to be any merchandise that resulted from production overruns, cancelled orders, out of season merchandise, short lots, damaged goods, irregulars, returns, or discontinuations.

Surplus merchandise was a fact of retailing life. In apparel retailing, design, order, and production lead times could be as long as 6–12 weeks, 4 months, and 6–8 weeks, respectively.[15] As a result, early estimates of expected demand, which varied randomly—and sometimes dramatically—from actual demand, determined styles, order, and production quantities. For instance, even unusual weather could cause excesses or shortages, as happened in Vancouver, Canada, when unusually heavy rains during the summer of 1999 unexpectedly and negatively affected swimsuit sales.[16]

For an apparel vendor, who earned a poor margin on average, a production underage was more costly than a production overage. Similarly, for an apparel retailer, failing to stock a specific item that was in demand was more costly than carrying an item that did not sell right away. As a result, both vendors and retailers tended to carry generous safety stocks that they would have to dispose of as quickly and efficiently as possible at the end of a selling season. In 1998, approximately 15% of merchandise that apparel vendors distributed had to be liquidated, implying a vendor-generated surplus merchandise market of $11 billion.[17]

In apparel retailing, where retail buyers were generally responsible for demand forecasting and determining order quantities and pricing, the surplus merchandise problem was especially acute. Buyers for retailers changed positions or left roughly every nine months on average. They were also generally rewarded for sales volume and gross margin performance. As a result, institutional knowledge—which tended to be

[14] Source: QRS internal research.

[15] Source: QRS internal research. Based on discussions with the director of inventory management at Levi Strauss. Although initially placed four months ahead, retailer orders may be revised as frequently as every two weeks based on actual selling. Design lead time estimate varies based on whether fabric and finish are already developed; estimate allows for pattern fits and changes and completion of engineering specifications for a complete size range.

[16] The weather in Vancouver probably also unexpectedly increased demand for waterproof windbreakers, but this likely only partially mitigated the retailers' surplus problem, since they probably had not planned to sell (and therefore did not buy) as many waterproof windbreakers as consumers demanded.

[17] Source: The Boston Consulting Group and Tradeweave research, 1999.

an ancillary objective for retail buyers at best—suffered.[18] As a result, some retailers had given other managers, such as the vice president of finance, the responsibility to dispose of surplus merchandise. In 1998, apparel retailers disposed of 5% of the merchandise they acquired outside of their stores, implying a (narrowly defined[19]) retailer-generated surplus merchandise market of 9 billion wholesale dollars.[20] Together with vendor-generated surplus, this implied a total apparel surplus market of $20 billion in 1998, up from $2.5 billion in 1994 and $5 billion in 1995.[21]

SURPLUS MERCHANDISE DISPOSITION

Both apparel vendors and retailers considered surplus merchandise disposition a time-consuming, inefficient, and painful process. In a space-constrained retail environment, holding and incremental marketing costs for unsold merchandise were severe. Retailers would mark down as much as 45% of their merchandise to prices that were a small fraction of wholesale cost to avoid disposing of the merchandise in some other way.[22] Powerful retailers also negotiated financial returns-to-vendor (RTVs), in which vendors would credit retailers with part of their original disbursement. While these concessions mitigated the retailers' costs, the physical merchandise typically remained with the retailers, who still had to dispose of the surplus. In addition, although many retailers attempted to track merchandise flows by UPC, retail shrinkage and physical handling costs made cataloguing merchandise for sale to jobbers a difficult, manual task. As a result of all these costs, retailers generally recovered only 10–20 cents on the wholesale cost dollar through sales to jobbers. Consequently they only disposed of 5%–10% of surplus merchandise through these channels, on average.

With limited physical space and the threat that surplus disposition would either "train" consumers to wait for off-price merchandise at the end of the season or cause channel conflict, surplus merchandise disposition also troubled vendors.[23] In addition, vendors of branded and fashion merchandise tended to be especially concerned about diluting their brands. Some even shredded their merchandise and sold the remnants as rags. Others developed relationships with jobbers and resellers whom they came to trust over time. A salesperson whose only job it was to sell surplus or the head merchant at vendors' outlet stores generally managed these relationships.

Some companies such as Ross Stores, a large retailer representing approximately 17% of the pure-play large reseller market, with net sales of $2.2 billion in 1998, actively sought to create this trust. Ross maintained a 150-person buying organization that reg-

[18] Estimate of retail buyer turnover based on industry lore and Peter Johnson's personal observations over time. According to Johnson, the buyers transferred between categories, moved between buying and selling, were promoted, left to join another retailer or a vendor, or left retailing altogether.

[19] Narrowly defined because this definition only includes the surplus that is likely to reach liquidation.

[20] Source: The Boston Consulting Group and Tradeweave research, 1999.

[21] Source: *Catalog Age*, 4/26/96.

[22] Source: QRS Corporation press release, 12/1/99.

[23] Certain retailers may be concerned with the same issues with respect to their own private label merchandise.

ularly called on a pre-established list of vendors (Exhibit 5).[24] Other companies, including some large, branded vendors who wished to remain unnamed, worked with only a few jobbers, who in turn sold merchandise in those U.S. and foreign markets that were least likely to create channel conflict.[25]

In 1998, roughly 40%–60% of apparel surplus merchandise (more broadly defined) was disposed of through captive channels, such as outlet stores and Web sites.[26] In addition, 30%–50% was disposed of through large resellers, such as TJ Maxx, Filene's Basement, Ross Stores, and Burlington Coat Factory. The remaining 5%–10% of surplus was disposed of through other intermediaries, including international retailers. Jobbers frequently serviced this portion of the market.

NEW ENTRANTS ON THE SURPLUS MERCHANDISE DISPOSITION SCENE

Recognizing the inefficiencies in the current surplus disposition process, Web-based intermediaries were trying to make surplus merchandise disposition more efficient and effective. While new entrants and potential substitutes were emerging, QRS believed that none of the current players was adequately servicing the apparel goods vertical, the one that it believed it was best positioned to serve. To date, most new entrants had maintained a broader focus on connecting buyers and sellers or on surplus merchandise in general rather than on doing so in the apparel vertical specifically.

Business-to-Business Multivertical Sites

A cursory analysis indicated that at least a dozen business-to-business (B2B) sites provided content, commerce, and community functionality specific to a given vertical (or multiple of them). Only a few seemed to focus on disposing of surplus merchandise. Even fewer were generating significant volume. TradeOut and VerticalNet were among those that were.

TradeOut.com claimed to be "the world's leading online marketplace for buying and selling surplus." It had created an engine for sellers of surplus to post merchandise for sale and for buyers to browse by industry vertical and/or product category. The company had established seven super-categories of listings in over 100 product categories. Although apparel and footwear was one of these categories, fewer than 100 auctions were posted and outstanding as of September 1999.

VerticalNet, a public company with a $1.8 billion market capitalization, claimed to be "the Internet's leading creator and operator of vertical trade communities" by attracting buyers and sellers from around the world with similar professional interests through relevant content, community, and commerce features. It updated daily content, which included white papers that industry leaders wrote, interactive software,

[24] Pure-play large resellers are assumed to include TJX Companies, Ross Stores, Burlington Coat Factory Warehouse, and Filene's Basement. Excludes comparable companies that were subsidiaries of larger holding companies.

[25] Source: Tradeweave internal research. Of these there were purportedly roughly 15 major U.S. ones.

[26] Source: Tradeweave Opportunity Analysis, August 31, 1999.

industry news, product information, directories, classifieds, job listings, and other services. Community tools enabled users to exchange ideas and information. Although not explicitly focused on surplus merchandise and in their infancy stages, commerce features included the ability to transact in an auction. VerticalNet had already created or acquired communities in various evolutionary stages in over 40 different verticals. In 1999 VerticalNet did not cover either apparel or footwear.

QRS believed that other B2B multivertical sites had already or might enter the surplus merchandise disposition market to cover particular niches. For example, Liquidation.com professed to be the leading (and first) B2B liquidation auction. It posted limited number of items for sale as of September 1999—some of which were apparel—but virtually no bids were outstanding.

Business-to-Business Apparel Vertical Sites

Although a number of different players had begun to emerge, none appeared to be building either a functionally robust site or an installed base. Nonetheless, many sought to improve the efficiency of the apparel surplus merchandise market.

Apparelbids.com planned to develop a Web site with three sections: auction, warehouse, and classified advertising. According to the company, "The Auction section will be for machinery and large apparel liquidation . . . the Warehouse section will offer off-price merchandise at a set price on a daily basis that is available for immediate shipment subject to prior sale . . . [and] the Classified Advertising section will provide access to numerous products and services. . . ."

C-Me planned to connect retailers with their vendors via private Internet Sourcing Networks and to host a Virtual Trade Show™, a centralized product showcase that featured vendors' products and allowed buyers to customize searches. It also provided customized Web design and hosting for vendors and was planning to launch a Wholesale Auction Center and a Factory Outlet Mall. Although not 100% focused on B2B activities, this seemed to represent most of the site's focus. How surplus disposition would figure in the site's offering was unclear.

Other apparel-focused sites had appeared on the scene, but had not determined their service offerings yet. These sites included ApparelDistrict and ClothingBids.

Business-to-Consumer Multivertical and Apparel-Focused Sites

Dozens of business-to-consumer (B2C), surplus-focused sites had appeared on the scene, but few had gained traction in apparel surplus. Among those that had or seemingly could were OnSale and BuyClearance, both multivertical sites, and BlueFly, which was focused specifically on apparel goods.

OnSale, which merged with Egghead, had created a single shopping site for new and surplus computers, electronics, sporting goods, and vacations. Unlike Priceline.com, OnSale/Egghead had traditionally taken possession of its inventory, primarily first-run merchandise. However, through its product categories it maintained a substantial presence in surplus auctions. Egghead.com had a market capitalization of approximately $600 million.

BuyClearance, a new online store that was part of the Buy.com family, maintained that it would purchase "high-quality, brand-name merchandise from some of the most popular manufacturers" at volume discount prices (and presumably pass some of the benefit on to consumers). The company obtained its inventory through liquidations, overages, promotions, and discontinuations. BuyClearance also took possession of its inventory. Up to this point, BuyClearance had focused on computer products, home electronics, and technology-related "value bundles."

BlueFly hoped to become "the preeminent Internet retailer of excess and end-of-season apparel, fashion accessories, and home products. To achieve this objective, it had focused its resources on pioneering the direct-to-consumer name brand discount apparel market on the Internet. By December 1998, after only four months in operation, it had shipped over 2,733 orders and hosted 664,000 unique visitors. The site offered approximately 3,400 styles of products from over 90 branded designers. Bluefly's market capitalization was approximately $70 million.

Bricks-and-Mortar Companies Maintaining Outlet and/or Online Presence

Some retailers and vendors had also begun to rely more heavily on liquidating through their own outlet stores and Web sites. As of mid-1999, Lands' End, J.C. Penney, J. Crew, Eddie Bauer, Gap, and REI all disposed of surplus merchandise online.[27] Many other companies maintained their own bricks-and-mortar outlet stores, including Nordstrom, J. Crew, Gap, Nine West, Eddie Bauer, Old Navy, Levi's, and Guess.[28]

TRANSACTION FACILITATOR REVENUE MODELS

Generally, B2B auction transaction facilitators such as Chemdex, Paper Exchange, MetalSite, and NeoForma charged the seller of merchandise a fee calculated as a percentage of the aggregate transaction value. The marginal percentage charged per dollar transacted typically fell at certain predetermined volume levels, so that the average unit cost of a transaction generally fell with incremental volume.[29] In general, this commission fee ranged from 0% (e.g., ClothingBids.com) to 12% (e.g., NeoForma for small transactions). Some sites applied a fixed fee to all transaction levels. Typically, the buyer did not pay a transaction fee.

Many B2B auction transaction facilitators had either implemented, or were considering other revenue models, including but not limited to:

[27] Source: Tradeweave internal research.

[28] Source: QRS internal research.

[29] This is sometimes called an inverse sliding scale. For example, suppose a transaction closes for $100,000. The first $5,000 might be charged at 7%, producing a fee of $350; $5,001 to $25,000 would be charged at 5%, producing a fee of $1,000; $25,001 to $100,000 would be charged at 3%, producing a fee of $2,250. The total fee would be $350 + $1,000 + $2,250 = $3,600.

- Listing fees—upfront and fixed fees per transaction that prospective sellers usually paid whether or not a transaction was consummated
- Hosting fees—fees paid by vendors or retailers who wanted to conduct their own auctions (potentially cobranded with the auction transaction facilitator), but did not want to create their own auction processing engine
- Image scanning fees—fees that prospective sellers of merchandise paid who wanted to outsource the production of a digital picture of the merchandise for sale
- Subscription fees—fees that prospective buyers and/or sellers paid to gain access to an auction market
- Advertising—fees that prospective sellers of merchandise paid in exchange for the chance to stimulate demand for their merchandise; also fees that those who were likely to gain targeted access to the participants in the auction community, such as trade publications or prospective employers, paid

DEMAND CHAIN INEFFICIENCIES

QRS also wondered whether other Web-based opportunities existed to minimize surplus rather than accept it as a fact of life. Surplus only arose because the wrong goods were in the wrong place at the wrong time. A long-time goal of the use of information technology (IT) to improve the operation of demand chains had been to ensure that information was where it needed to be to match production with demand. QRS's mission had been to help retailers and vendors achieve that goal.

Yet much inefficiency remained. For example, buyers typically "went to market" seasonally and then ordered what they thought would sell. Invariably, however, demand would exceed what they had ordered in some lines and fall below it in others. At that point, the retailer either had to deal with the surplus issue or scramble to find substitutes for the items that were in high demand. They currently had no good way to do that.

Going even further back in the purchase cycle, the vendors had to decide what lines to produce with limited knowledge of what the retailers would find appealing. Moreover, no forum for "give-and-take" around product design to meet the requirements of specific retailers existed. When it came time to order, there was also the need for a conversation between retailer and vendor about what assortment (number of items by size, style, color, etc.) to provide. The retailer and vendor typically had different information about what was optimal, and so here too some conversation back and forth was required.

While QRS's inventory management and sales analysis products improved the functioning of the retail demand chain, senior management wondered whether the Internet did not provide additional opportunities. Rather than taking surplus as given and worrying about its efficient disposition, perhaps they could attack the core problems that caused surplus in the first place.

ORGANIZATIONAL AND IMPLEMENTATION ISSUES

If QRS decided to pursue a new Web-based business opportunity in either or both of the surplus disposition or demand chain improvement areas, it would have to face critical organizational issues. Many traditional companies had established separate dot-com structures to pursue new electronic commerce initiatives. They set up a new organization with its own financial and governance structure. In some cases, investments from the company and one or more venture capital firms financed stand-alone enterprises. The management of the stand-alone firm would also typically have an ownership stake (through stock options) in the new venture. In those cases the new venture would have its own board of directors. In other cases, firms pursued the new ventures internally, as a new venture group or product development effort by the existing product development organization.

Whatever organizational structure QRS employed, it had to make certain implementation decisions. Given tremendous time-to-market pressure, a key issue would be how to design, develop, and launch a product quickly. It could retain a Web development firm to do that or use internal QRS resources. QRS also had to decide how to time the opportunity analysis and the product development. The more time spent researching the opportunity, the higher the chance of producing the right product, but the greater the risk of missing the window. QRS could hire a management consulting firm to help with the effort. Most of the leading management consulting firm would consider accepting such an engagement in exchange for stock or stock options rather than their usual fee-for-service basis. QRS would have to make these decisions in short order.

EXHIBIT 1 QRS Corporation Quarterly Revenues

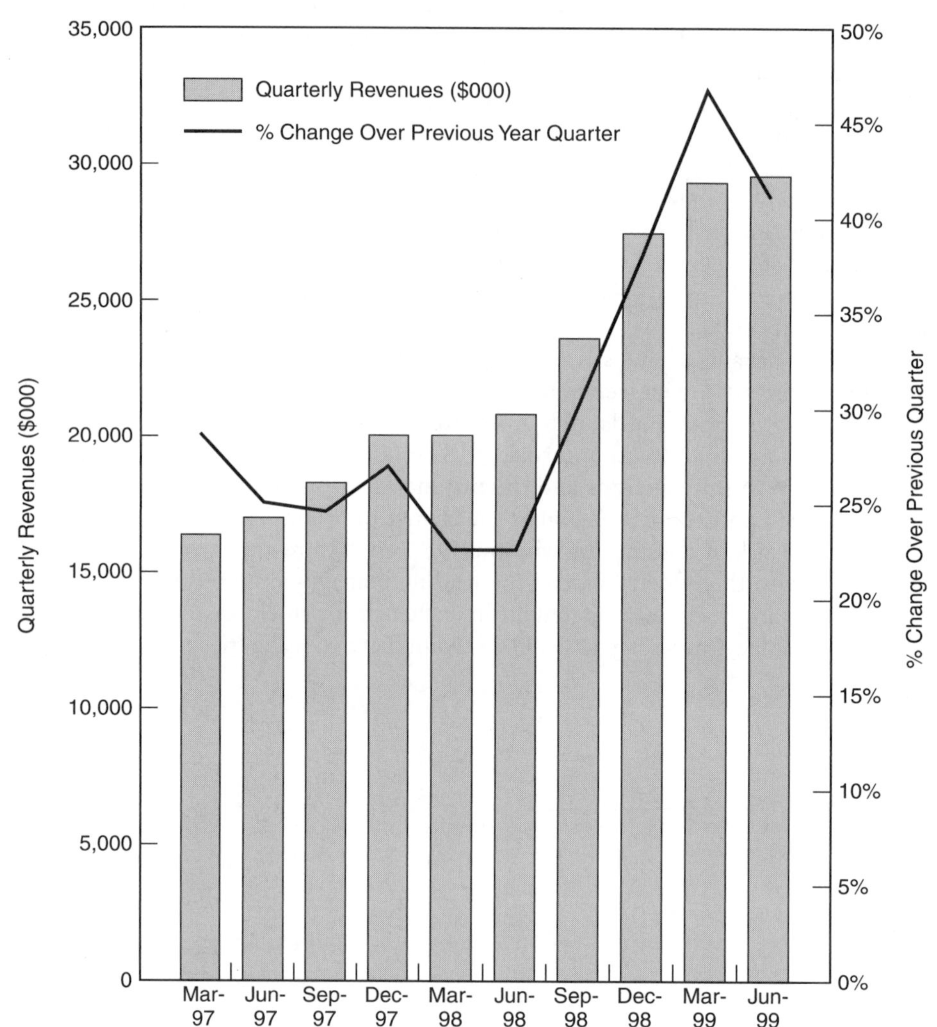

Source: QRS SEC filings.

EXHIBIT 2 QRS Corporation Quarterly Earnings

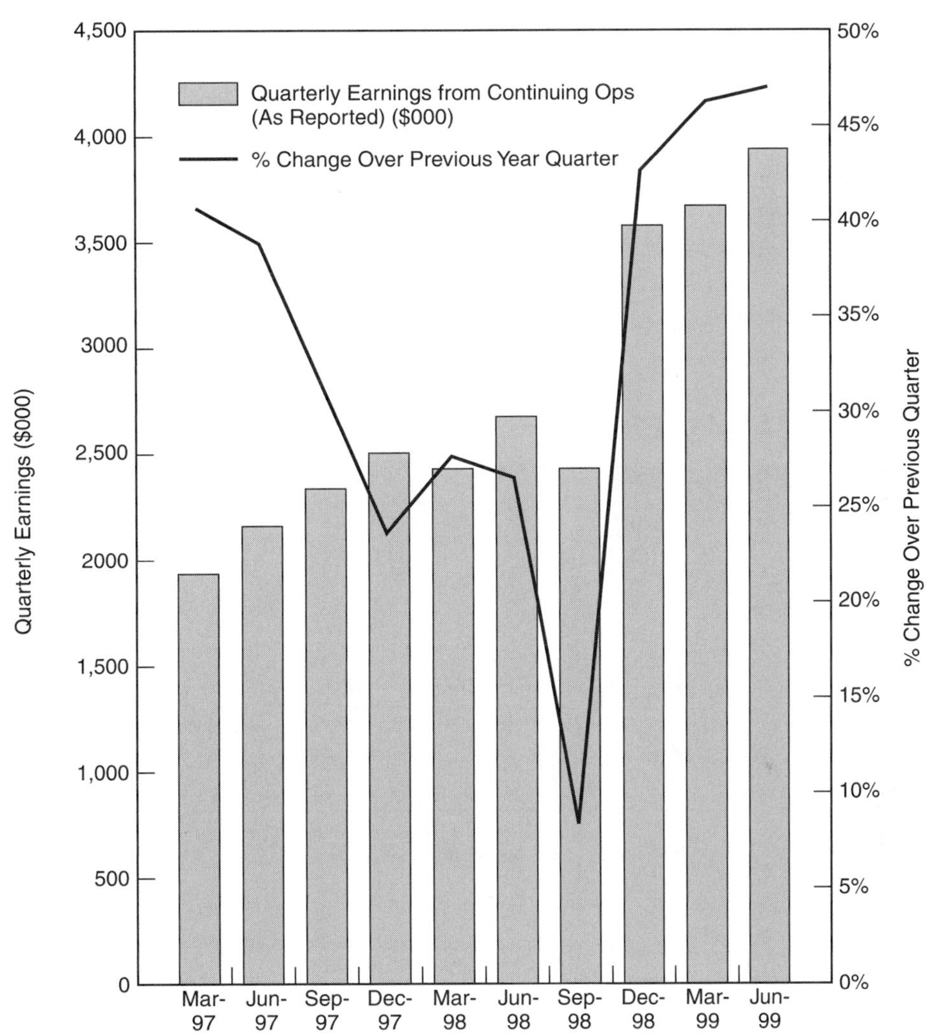

Source: QRS SEC filings.

EXHIBIT 3 QRS Corporation Market Capitalization, by Quarter

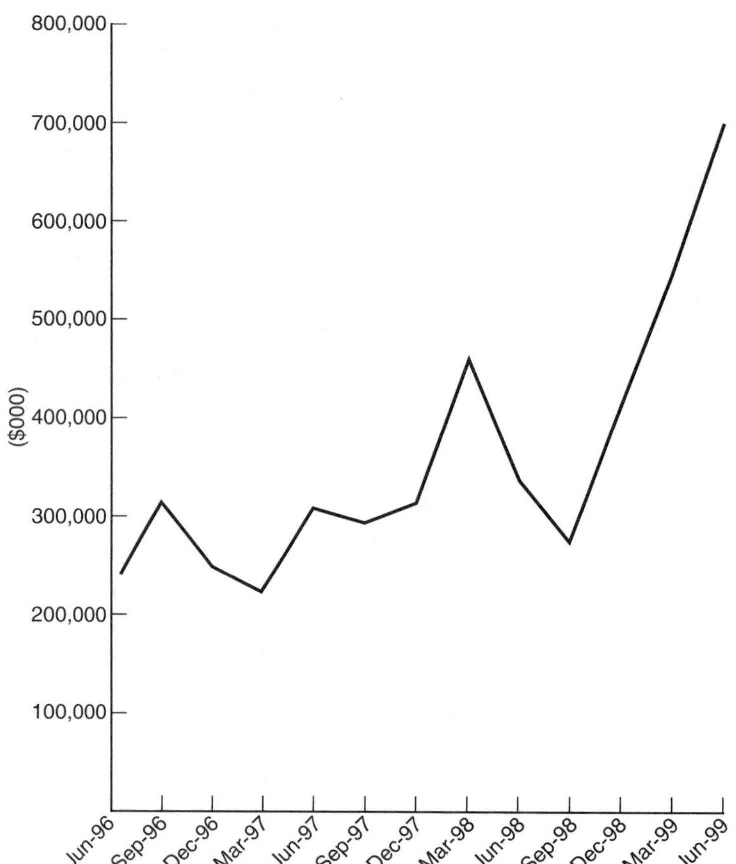

Source: Yahoo!Finance. Reproduced with permission.

EXHIBIT 4 Apparel and General Merchandise Retail Trade

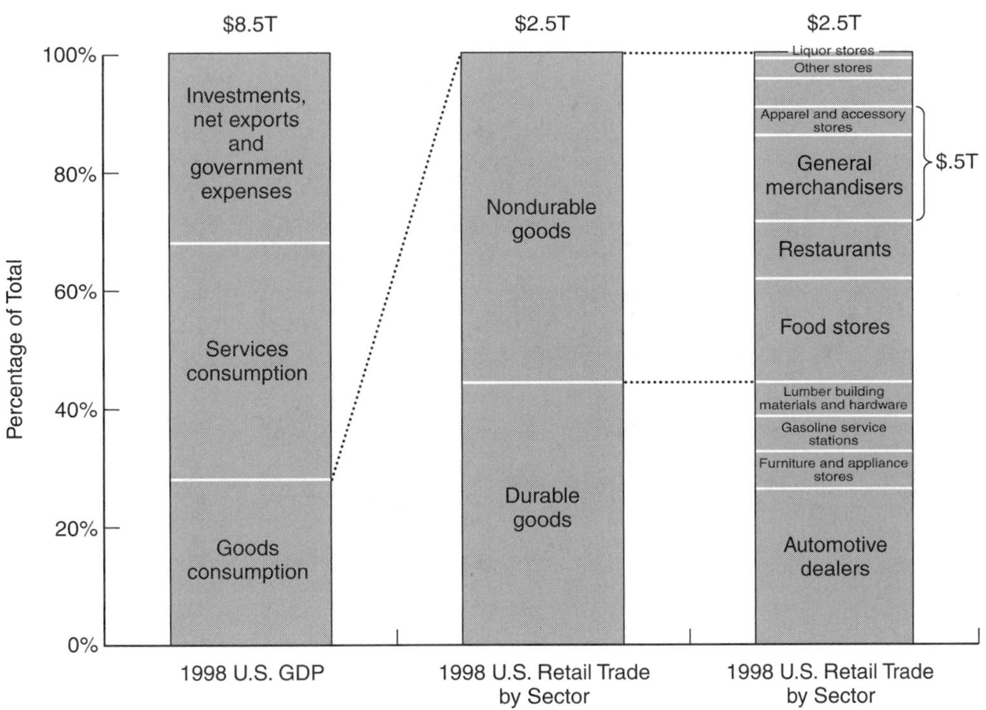

Source: QRS internal research.

EXHIBIT 5 Pure-Play Reseller Market Share Analysis

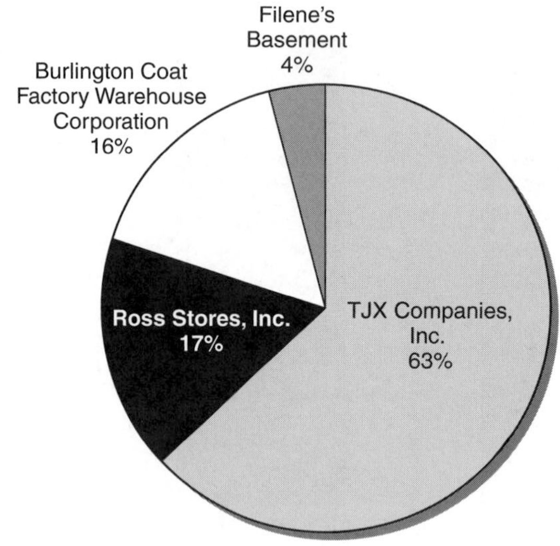

Source: QRS internal research.

STANFORD
GRADUATE SCHOOL OF BUSINESS

DOUBLECLICK AND INTERNET PRIVACY

It is clear from these discussions that I made a mistake by planning to merge names with anonymous user activity across Web sites in the absence of government and industry privacy standards. —*Kevin O'Conner, CEO of DoubleClick, March 2, 2000*

INTRODUCTION

DoubleClick, the industry leader in Internet advertising services, saw its $1.7 billion strategic investment in Abacus Direct dissolve in the face of a privacy firestorm over the merger of the Abacus data on offline purchasing with information gleaned from the browsing of Internet users. DoubleClick tracked Web activity on its DoubleClick Network of 1,500 Web sites and placed banner advertisements on 11,000 sites. The information it collected was identified only by an ID number assigned to a cookie deposited on the user's computer by the banner advertisements. DoubleClick's DART software technology processed the anonymous information to generate user profiles used to tailor advertisements for Web sites. Abacus Direct was the leader in collecting information from catalog purchases and using that data to target advertising and catalog configurations to consumers. Abacus had five-year buying profiles on 88 million households, including name, address, telephone number, credit card numbers, income, and purchases.

DoubleClick recognized that the value of targeted online advertising would be substantially increased if information from consumers' online browsing activities could be linked with their offline purchase activities. Rates for targeted advertising based on anonymous profiling were 50%–100% higher than for untargeted bulk advertising, and rates for targeted ads based on the merged databases would be even higher.

DoubleClick's plans were interrupted in February 2000 when *USA Today* disclosed that it planned to merge its anonymous online data with Abacus Direct's database. A firestorm erupted, and DoubleClick quickly suspended its plan to merge the databases. It then faced the problems of developing a strategy for regaining public confidence and for the collection and use of information going forward.

DOUBLECLICK, INC.

Kevin O'Conner founded DoubleClick in 1996 to serve advertisers on the Internet. By early 2000 DoubleClick had 1,800 employees, 7,000 customers, offices in 30 countries, and a market capitalization of $10 billion. Its revenue for the first quarter of 2000 was $110 million, an increase of 179% over the year-earlier quarter. Its gross profit was $53 million, but heavy marketing expenses resulted in a loss of $18 million. Forrester Research projected that online advertising would increase from $3.3 billion in 1999 to $33 billion in 2004.

Shortly after founding DoubleClick O'Conner stated in an interview that the company would not collect and keep information that identified a person. He said that linking data to names and addresses "would be voluntary on the user's part, and used in strict confidence. We are not going to trick people or match information from other sources."[1] In accord with this policy DoubleClick allowed Internet users to opt out of its data collection system. Its opt-out policy was available on its own Web site at the end of a lengthy legal notice and a description of cookies.

To target advertisements to Internet users' interests, DoubleClick tracked their click-stream data. The technology for tracking click-stream data began with cookies.[2] A cookie is a small text file deposited on a user's hard drive that contains an ID number associated with the computer but not the user. Cookies were a major convenience to many users. They enabled a portal such as Yahoo! to remember a user's password and immediately bring up personalized pages and information. They also allowed advertising and other content to be targeted by ID number. When a user visited a Web site that had deposited a cookie on the user's hard drive, the visit and ID number would be recorded. DoubleClick collected the visit information through its network of Web sites, which included AltaVista and Travelocity. Since the ID number was associated with a computer and DoubleClick had no information on who owned or used the computer, the information remained anonymous. Abacus Online, however, was different.

DOUBLECLICK'S ABACUS ONLINE STRATEGY

DoubleClick's market strategy was to integrate the two databases to offer advertising better tailored to Internet users' actual purchasing behavior as well as their browsing activity. To implement its strategy DoubleClick formed Abacus Online. Participating Web sites identified users by name but were required to post a notice explaining the information to be collected and giving users the opportunity to opt out. Participating users could also choose whether to receive targeted advertisements. DoubleClick was actively recruiting companies and Web sites to join Abacus Online. AltaVista and Travelocity had not yet decided whether to join.

Sites participating in Abacus Online not only allowed click-stream data to be collected, but they also collected personal information when individuals identified themselves to the site; that is, when they made a purchase, completed a survey, or signed up for a drawing. With that personal information the ID number assigned to the cookie

[1] *Forbes*, November 4, 1996.

[2] Information on cookies is available at http://www.cookiecentral.com/faq.

on the computer could be associated with the user. The click-stream data then could be combined with Abacus Direct's database of offline information. DoubleClick operated one such site, Netdeals.com, where users could sign up for drawings for prizes, giving their name, age, and street and e-mail addresses. Users who agreed to receive "valuable offers" were added to its database.

DoubleClick explained its objective: "This is about getting the right ad to the right person at the right time. It's important for users to understand that the only time DoubleClick will actually have personally identifiable information attached to a browser is when the user has volunteered [it] and been given notice and choice."[3] DoubleClick had no intention of selling or disclosing information on individuals' Internet use to any third party. The information would only be used internally to enhance the value of its services to advertisers. DoubleClick also pledged that it would not collect data on medical, financial, or sexual transactions or browsing, or on children's browsing.

DoubleClick argued that the information it planned to collect would benefit consumers because advertisements would be tailored to their interests and purchasing behavior. Just as consumers using Amazon.com received messages about books that might be of interest based on their past purchases, DoubleClick would provide advertisements of interest to the users of a Web site based on the purchasing and browsing behavior of those who visited the site. Similarly, just as a consumer could design a personalized page on a portal such as Yahoo!, DoubleClick would provide personalized information for the consumer. Because advertisements were provided on virtually all the Web sites, a consumer would benefit from receiving advertisements of interest rather than blanket ads.

Kevin O'Conner said, "There are some people on the Internet who want to go back to the old days when there was no advertising and it was government controlled. We believe that [the Internet] is a tremendous thing and that it should be free. That means it is going to be funded by advertising."[4] O'Conner pointed to recent polls indicating that 70% of Internet users understood that the Internet was free because of advertising and that two-thirds of users liked the personalization of information.[5] Broadcast television and radio were also funded by advertisements, and magazines and newspapers were largely funded by ads.

Dana Serman of Lazard Freres predicted, "Over time, people will realize it's not Big Brother who's going to show up at your door in a black ski mask and take your kids away or dig deep into your medical history. This is a situation where you are essentially dropped in a bucket with 40 million people who look and feel a lot like you do to the advertising community."[6]

Lowell Singer of Robertson Stephens observed, "As long as advertisers don't cross the line, they're not going to get a tremendous amount of consumer protest. If they respect the parameters, I think they will continue to grow their targeting capabilities. And I think that's a good thing."[7]

[3] *USA Today*, February 2, 2000.

[4] *The Guardian*, February 25, 2000.

[5] *Wall Street Journal*, March 7, 2000.

[6] *Washington Post*, February 18, 2000.

[7] *San Francisco Chronicle*, January 27, 2000.

INTERNET PRIVACY

The U.S. Constitution does not have an explicit privacy provision, other than the Fourth Amendment's restrictions on searches and seizures by government. A number of court decisions, however, had established certain privacy rights supported by Constitutional interpretation.[8] A right to privacy was also established in a number of state constitutions, including that of California.

Although there was no legislation specifying Internet privacy rights, other legislation reflected the sensitivity of privacy issues. The Privacy Act of 1974 restricted information gathered for one purpose to be used for another purpose or shared with another government agency. For example, the Internal Revenue Service was prohibited from sharing income tax information with other agencies. In 1988 Congress enacted the Video Privacy Protection Act that prohibited video tape service providers from disclosing information about rentals or requests by individuals. The 1994 Driver's License Privacy Protection Act prohibited states from selling driver's license information. The Fair Credit Reporting Act regulated the disclosure of credit application data and credit histories. The Electronic Communications Privacy Act prohibited unauthorized access to e-mail, and other statutes prohibited unauthorized wiretaps. In 1998 Congress passed the Children's Online Privacy Protection Act which prohibits collecting information from children under the age of 13 unless their parents authorize it.[9] In 1999 Congress passed the Financial Services Modernization Act, which limited disclosure of nonpublic personal information to nonaffiliated third parties unless disclosure and opt-out requirements were met.

The Federal Trade Commission (FTC) had jurisdiction over unfair and deceptive practices, and in 1999 the FTC decided not to regulate Internet privacy. One commissioner, however, dissented and advocated immediate action on Internet privacy. The FTC established an Advisory Committee on Online Access and Security.

SELF-REGULATION AND THE ACTIVIST LANDSCAPE

The e-commerce industry had taken steps to better assure security and privacy and to stop theft and fraud on the Internet. Two industry groups, the Online Privacy Alliance and the Electronic Commerce and Consumer Protection Group, advocated continued self-regulation by Internet companies.[10] A number of Internet companies had established TRUSTe to certify the privacy policies of Web sites, and other organizations

[8] See *Griswold v. Connecticut*, 383 U.S. 479 (1965).

[9] The act also restricted children's access to pornography on the Internet, but in June 2000 in a case brought by the American Civil Liberties Union, the Internet Content Coalition, and others, the U.S. Court of Appeals upheld a lower court decision that the law violated the First Amendment to the Constitution. The Internet Content Coalition consists of over 20 publishers with online ventures, including the *New York Times*, MSNBC, and Time, Inc.

[10] The Online Privacy Alliance has 85 corporate and association members. The members of the Electronic Commerce and Consumer Protection Group are AOL, AT&T, Dell, IBM, Microsoft, Network Solutions, Time Warner, and Visa U.S.A.

and companies also provided certification.[11] This self-regulation and the complexities of the privacy issue had led the U.S. government to go slowly in establishing explicit consumer privacy rights for the Internet. Not everyone, however, was satisfied with self-regulation. Marc Rotenberg of the Electronic Privacy Information Center (EPIC) said, "self-regulation is inviting a race to the bottom."

When it acquired Abacus Direct in 1999, DoubleClick was criticized by privacy activists who feared that it would integrate the information it collected online with the personalized information in Abacus Direct's database. Some activists drew analogies to George Orwell's *1984*, and Jason Catlett, head of JunkBusters, a for-profit consulting company, said, "Abacus is now becoming part of a company that will be despised by anyone who values privacy."[12] In response to the criticism, DoubleClick and nine other Internet advertising and online profiling companies formed the Network Advertising Initiative to develop privacy protection guidelines.

JunkBusters and EPIC had earlier created a storm when they revealed that Intel planned to put a serial number on its new Pentium III processor, allowing identification of the computer on which it was installed. EPIC threatened to lead a boycott, and Intel quickly backed down and abandoned its plan. A number of other companies had also had privacy incidents and were forced to change their policies. Lexis-Nexis was forced to abandon its plans to provide personal information to other companies. Similarly, in 1997 America Online (AOL) planned to release its subscribers list to telephone marketers despite an earlier pledge not to do so.[13] Referring to Marc Rotenberg of EPIC, Steve Case, chairman of AOL, said, "The guy can create a privacy uproar at the click of a mouse."[14]

Privacy activists were also suspicious of companies' stated privacy policies. First, policies could be changed at any time. For example, in August 1999 Amazon.com changed its policy and introduced "purchase circles" that used personal data and purchase data to identify publicly the best-selling products by geography, employer, university, or organization. Second, companies could violate their policies and escape detection. For example, in November 1999 RealNetworks was revealed to be collecting information on users' Internet activity without disclosure and in violation of its own privacy policy.[15] The company apologized and stopped the practice.

A basic objection to the collection of click-stream data was that it was invisible to users. Activists argued that average consumers did not know their activity was being

[11] TRUSTe was established in 1996 based on the principles that users have a right to informed consent and that "no single privacy principle is adequate for all situations." TRUSTe grants a site a "trademark" if it meets the tests of (1) adoption and implementation of a privacy policy, (2) notice and disclosure, (3) choice and consent, and (4) data security and quality and access (to personal information). By mid-2000 approximately 2000 Web sites had received TRUSTe approval.

[12] *Forbes*, November 24, 1999.

[13] Swire, Peter P. and Robert E. Litan. 1998. *None of Your Business*. Brookings Institution: Washington, D.C., p. 10. AOL continued to sell its subscribers list but notified its subscribers of the practice.

[14] *Business Week*, May 15, 2000.

[15] Its free RealJukebox allowed users to convert music to a digital format and play it on a personal computer. People downloading the software were required to give their e-mail address and ZIP code and were assigned a globally unique identifier. The software transmitted daily information to RealNetworks on songs downloaded to their PCs. RealNetworks was TRUSTe approved.

tracked let alone how the information was being used. Another objection was that the identifiers of consumers were persistent and that the user did not have a relationship with the company doing the tracking, as when a consumer made a purchase using a credit card.

Some activists opposed the transformation of the Internet from an anonymous environment to one in which individuals were identified and their Internet use monitored. As one commentator put it, "You can escape your surroundings through the Internet, but your actions can easily catch up with you."[16]

THE REACTION TO ABACUS ONLINE

Shortly after Abacus Online was revealed, the Center for Democracy and Technology (CDT) launched a consumer education campaign to alert Internet users.[17] CDT provided an Operation Opt-out Web site allowing consumers to "opt out" of DoubleClick's system and urged them to write letters to DoubleClick protesting its policies. Several thousand letters were also sent to Web sites that participated in the DoubleClick Network.

Jason Catlett of JunkBusters characterized Abacus Online: "Thousands of sites are ratting on you, so as soon as one gives you away, you're exposed on all of them. For four years, [DoubleClick] has said [the services] don't identify you personally, and now they're admitting they are going to identify you."[18] He added, "If you don't like Yahoo!'s privacy policy, you don't have to use its site. But it's very difficult for consumers to avoid DoubleClick because most don't know when it is collecting information."[19] Richard Smith, a privacy advocate, added, "Computers are like elephants: they never forget. And they are watching us all the time."[20] Other critics likened DoubleClick to the computer HAL in the movie *2001* and referred to the company as "Doublecross." Jonathon Shapiro, senior vice president of DoubleClick argued, "We are good actors. We've been leaders in protecting consumer privacy for the past four years, and we think our commitment to providing notice and choice to consumers puts us ahead of the curve."[21]

DoubleClick pointed out that since its founding 50,000 people had opted out of its tracking. Tom Maddox, editor of Privacyplace, argued, "People don't know they have to opt out."[22] David Banisar of Privacy International said, "This is not permission. That is fraudulent on its face."[23] Barry Steinhardt of the American Civil Liberties Union said, "The onus should be on the data collector to get your affirmative consent, in a knowing way. You shouldn't have to bargain for your privacy."[24]

[16] Esther Dyson, *Los Angeles Times*, March 20, 2000.

[17] Members of CDT include America Online, AT&T, Business Software Alliance, Disney WorldWide, Ford Foundation, Markle Foundation, Microsoft, the Newspaper Association of America, the Open Society Institute, and Time Warner.

[18] *USA Today*, January 26, 2000.

[19] *U.S. News & World Report*, March 6, 2000.

[20] *Financial Times*, January 29, 2000.

[21] *Los Angeles Times*, February 3, 2000.

[22] *San Francisco Chronicle*, January 27, 2000.

[23] *USA Today*, January 26, 2000.

[24] *Financial Times*, January 29, 2000.

Privacy advocates argued that consumers should have access to the data collected on them so that they could correct errors and decide whether to continue allowing the data to be collected. They also argued for an opt-in policy under which consumers would have to give their express permission before any information could be collected on them. In June 2000 the Supreme Court let stand a Court of Appeals decision voiding part of a statute that had required local telephone companies to obtain "opt-in" permission before using billing records to try to sell new services to customers. U S WEST had filed the lawsuit so that it could use an "opt-out" policy instead.

PERSONAL ASSURANCE OF INTERNET PRIVACY

Most people seemed willing to give personal information and credit card numbers to catalog companies such as L.L. Bean and Lands' End. Information on credit card transactions was routinely collected, and financial services companies had for many years used data that passed through their systems to target consumers. Moreover, the growth of the Internet and electronic commerce had been very rapid under the self-regulation approach without explicit Internet privacy rights. A Forrester Research poll of 10,000 Internet users revealed that two-thirds were willing to provide personal information, but 90% wanted control over how that information was used.

Users had a growing array of direct means of assuring privacy, including both those taken by ISPs and those taken individually. ISPs adopted privacy policies and published those policies on their Web sites. A growing number had their policies and practices certified by independent companies and organizations, such as TRUSTe, BBBOnline, and SecureAssure. SecureAssure affixed a seal to a Web site that pledged not to sell personal information about a user to a third party without express permission.[25] In contrast, sites with BBBOnline and TRUSTe approval could sell data.

Another means of avoiding online profiling was to block cookies from being deposited on a computer. Cookies could be blocked by simply configuring Internet Explorer (IE) or Netscape Navigator to reject them. On IE go to Tools, Internet Options, Security, and choose high. On Navigator go to Edit, Preferences, Advanced, and select the option.

Economic theory predicted that if there were a demand for Internet privacy the marketplace would supply the means of achieving it. Webroot.com's Windows Washer allowed a user to cleanse certain areas of Windows of cookies. Some companies, including TopClick International, Anonymizer.com, and Zero-Knowledge, provided anonymous surfing of the Internet using technologies that masked a user's identity. Zero-Knowledge's Freedom program gave users digital pseudonyms and routed their surfing through a variety of servers to cloak their activity. Anonymizer acted as an intermediary and encrypted a user's inquiries. Hundreds of remailers removed revealing information from e-mail messages. Earth Proxy Inc. provided free downloadable software intended to inhibit tracking software.

Purchasing items on the Internet, however, required a billing record, which gave sellers information on purchasers. Infomediaries such as PrivaSeek, Inc. offered

[25] The fee charged by SecureAssure ranged from $200 to $2,500 a year.

subscribers downloadable software that allowed them to decide what information was made available when they purchased online. In May 2000 at a weekend privacy retreat organized by the U.S. Chamber of Commerce, Microsoft and a number of other companies displayed technologies to protect consumers. One technology demonstrated by DataTreasury Corporation allowed transactions to be made within its secure system.

In 1998 the World Wide Web Consortium, backed by a group of companies including AOL, AT&T, IBM, and Microsoft, along with the Massachusetts Institute of Technology and universities in France and Japan, formed P3P, the Platform for Privacy Preferences Protection.[26] P3P was unveiled in June 2000, and Microsoft announced that it would incorporate it in its next version of Windows. Both Microsoft and AOL said they would offer it as a plug-in to their browsers. P3P software allowed Internet users to specify the amount of personal data they wanted to divulge to a Web site, and P3P technology notified them when a site requests additional information. The participants in P3P were reported to have been unable to agree on more than a notification procedure. Marc Rotenberg of EPIC referred to P3P as "pretty poor privacy," criticizing it for being an opt-out rather than an opt-in procedure and requiring too much initiative by Internet users. He said, "It is not a technology to protect personal privacy. It's a means to enable the disclosure of personal information."[27] Dr. Horst Joepen, CEO of Webwasher.com, a German software privacy company affiliated with Siemens, characterized P3P as "too little, too late."

GOVERNMENT ACTION

As a result of the privacy concerns raised about Abacus Online, the Center for Democracy and Technology (CDT) filed a complaint with the FTC, which began an inquiry into DoubleClick's data collection and advertising practices.[28] CDT, the Privacy Rights Clearinghouse, Consumer Action, the Gay & Lesbian Alliance Against Defamation, and the American Civil Liberties Union subsequently filed a "Statement of Additional Facts and Grounds for Relief" with the FTC.

In addition to the FTC inquiry the New York State attorney general initiated an informal inquiry. The attorney general of Michigan referred to DoubleClick's plan as "a secret wiretap" and announced that she would file suit against the practice. "The average consumer has no idea that he or she is being spied upon," she said, and the lack of warning constituted "a deceitful practice under our consumer-protection act."[29] She said that DoubleClick's policy was like putting a "bar code" on a consumer's back. A California woman filed a lawsuit alleging that DoubleClick violated her state constitutional right to privacy.

Legislation on Internet privacy had been introduced in Congress by Senators Burns and Wyden, Senator Leahy offered another bill, and Representative Markey introduced

[26] The Center for Democracy and Technology also participated in the project.

[27] *New York Times*, June 22, 2000.

[28] Some Web sites became nervous about participating in the DoubleClick Network. The complaint mentioned Kozmo.com, which quickly announced that it would not release data to DoubleClick unless a user had given express permission.

[29] *Washington Post*, February 17, 2000.

another. A number of members of Congress supported a federal Internet privacy agency. The Clinton administration was also concerned about online privacy but favored self-regulation. The administration backed the P3P technology and installed it on the White House Internet site.

In May 2000 the FTC reversed its position and voted 3–2 to ask Congress for new legislation granting it rule-making authority to regulate privacy on the Internet. The FTC sought required notice of privacy policies, including telling consumers how the data would be used and allowing them to inspect and correct their information. Companies would also be required to implement security measures to prevent unauthorized disclosure. In a statement FTC chairman Robert Pitofsky said, "This is not a report that comes to the conclusion that self-regulation has failed. On the contrary, self-regulation has made considerable progress. But in certain respects it looks as if self-regulation would be more successful if there was some backup legislation."[30] In his dissent commissioner Orson Swindle called the FTC request "breathtakingly broad."

The FTC's survey of Internet sites had revealed that only 41% posted a privacy policy that told users how data was used and only 20% of the major Internet sites had adequate privacy policies. Commissioner Swindle said the survey was "embarrassingly flawed." The Direct Marketing Institute countered with a survey showing that 93% of major Internet sites had privacy policies and most of them told users how their data would be used.

Industry generally supported self-regulation and opposed government regulation, but some companies feared that states would enact their own Internet privacy laws. Internet privacy legislation had already been introduced in 17 states. A number of companies believed that some federal regulation was an acceptable price if it would preempt state regulation. Tod Cohen of eBay said, "We would work with the FTC, Congress and the administration to develop a national standard." Robert Levitan, CEO of Flooz.com, commented, "I would like to think that industry could self-regulate, but I think we all have accepted the fact that there will be some regulation. We're not jumping up and down complaining about regulation. We're just saying, let's do it wisely."[31] Andy Grove, Chairman of Intel, stated, "I would prefer to recognize this trend and get ahead of the possibility that . . . states are going to take matters in their own hands."[32]

THE EUROPEAN UNION PRIVACY DIRECTIVE

Europeans had been concerned with privacy issues for some time, and those concerns had led to regulation of information on credit card use and restrictions on direct marketing. Some countries banned telephone marketing and unsolicited sales attempts by e-mail or fax. Germany and The Netherlands had strong national laws and enforcement agencies governing information. For example, in allowing Citibank (now Citigroup) to provide a credit card, Germany obtained the right to supervise the data Citibank stored on cardholders. Inspectors from the Datenschutz regularly visited

[30] May 22, 2000.
[31] *New York Times*, May 22, 2000.
[32] *National Journal*, June 17, 2000, p. 1924.

Citibank's Sioux City, South Dakota data center to ensure that the data were processed according to German law. Citigroup also had to obtain permission from German employees to send their personnel information to a computer in the United States. An official with the Data Protection Agency of The Netherlands commented, "We are at the beginning of a new information society, and no one really knows the outcome. But privacy and trust are important parts of this society."[33]

In commenting on the difference in perspectives in Europe and the United States, Peter Swire and Robert Litan wrote, "It is roughly accurate to say that America does not have the general presumption that data should be used only for the purpose for which they were collected."[34] A spokesperson for Time Warner in Brussels observed, "In Europe, people don't trust companies, they trust government. In the U.S., it's the opposite way around: Citizens must be protected from actions of the government."[35]

The concern about Internet privacy led to action by the European Union (EU) to harmonize the privacy policies of its member states. The Directive on Data Protection, often referred to as the Privacy Directive, took effect in 1998 and prohibited the processing of personal data unless "the data subject has unambiguously given his consent" or the processing was necessary for the performance of a contract or government order.[36] Data could also be processed if it were in the vital interests of the individual, as in the case of a medical emergency. Individuals also had the right to inspect any personal data maintained and to correct any errors. Furthermore, an individual had to be notified in advance if any personal information were to be transferred to a third party. The Directive sought a "reasonable balance" between the fundamental rights of the data subject, particularly the right to privacy and "the business interest of the data controllers. . . ."[37] To implement and enforce the Directive, each member of the EU established a data protection (privacy) agency, and the privacy commissioners served as a continuing body to monitor the progress on the Directive.

The Directive also protected EU citizens from processors of information in other countries. Article 25 permitted data transfers only if the other country had an "adequate level of protection." Since the United States had no privacy policy to govern the Internet, the processing by U.S. companies of personal information on Europeans outside the EU was problematic.

Critics of the EU Directive argued that it was an unwarranted extraterritorial application of EU law. The National Business Coalition on E-Commerce and Privacy, which included such financial services companies as General Electric, Fidelity, and Aflac, in addition to Home Depot, Deere, and Seagrams, said, "The EU privacy principles that would effectively be imposed on American business . . . far exceed any privacy require-

[33] *New York Times*, October 26, 1998.

[34] Swire and Litan, p. 178.

[35] *Business Week*, November 2, 1998.

[36] Directive 95/46/EC of the European Parliament and Council. A directive is implemented through national laws by each member of the EU. In contrast to a regulation a directive provides some limited flexibility in implementation for EU members.

[37] "Data Protection: Background Information," The European Commission, http://europe.eu.int/comm/internal_market/en/media.

ments that have ever been imposed in the U.S., thus raising a very real question of national sovereignty."[38] The EU responded by stating that it had no interest in "exporting" its laws to other countries, but it also emphasized that it had to protect the privacy of its citizens and would block the transfer of information to countries with inadequate protection. It invited non-EU countries "to express their views." Jim Murray, director of the European Consumers' Organization said, "We want anyone doing business with the EU to respect the rights that we have built up here."[39] The U.S. and EU governments initiated discussions about what U.S. policy would meet the adequacy standard.

While establishing broad privacy rights, the EU Directive failed to address a number of issues. One was whether cookies and other devices could be used in the anonymous tracking of click-stream data. Another was whether companies could internally transfer personnel information from the European Union to their offices in other countries.

DOUBLECLICK'S CHALLENGE

In putting Abacus Online on hold, Kevin O'Conner said, "It is clear from these discussions that I made a mistake by planning to merge names with anonymous user activity across Web sites in the absence of government and industry privacy standards." Kevin Ryan, president of DoubleClick, commented, "I think we could have done a better job of communicating. Because we are the largest and most successful Internet company in our space, we certainly attract more attacks than other people."[40] He observed, "There are always going to be controversies when people start using new technologies. When credit cards were introduced, people wouldn't use them because they were worried that the credit card companies would be tracking them. And when people first started using the Internet, they wouldn't buy anything because they were worried about credit card fraud. But they got over it."[41]

[38] *The Wall Street Journal*, April 6, 2000. The financial services companies were concerned about their ability to use and sell information about customers.

[39] *San Jose Mercury News*, June 5, 2000.

[40] February 18, 2000.

[41] *U.S. News & World Report*, March 6, 2000.

STANFORD
GRADUATE SCHOOL OF BUSINESS

eBAY AND DATABASE PROTECTION

I don't want to sound flip, but when people tell me, "The Internet's like the Wild West," I like to remind them we used to hang cattle rustlers in the Wild West.[1]
—Edward Miller

INTRODUCTION

The popularity of online auctions pioneered by eBay, Inc. led not only to rival Internet auction sites for items ranging from antiques to automobiles and from real estate to time with celebrities, but it also spawned a group of "auction aggregators." Companies such as Bidder's Edge, AuctionRover.com, and ultimatebid.com search Internet auction sites, extract data, and provide it to their users. Bidder's Edge, for example, provided information on auctions in a variety of categories corresponding to those on eBay's front page. A person searching for an ancient coin on Bidder's Edge received information on coins available on eBay, Yahoo!, and Amazon.com. This provided comparative information and convenience to users, but it was based on information developed by eBay and extracted from its site. One of eBay's most important strategic assets was the information it gained from conducting auctions. This information was invaluable for the design of auctions and for identifying service enhancements and other business opportunities, including partnering with other service providers. The aggregators threatened the value of that asset.

eBAY AND ONLINE AUCTIONS

Pierre Omidyar founded AuctionWeb in September 1995 with the business concept of providing an Internet site where person-to-person trading could take place. Buyers and sellers flocked to the site, and AuctionWeb became eBay in September 1997. eBay recruited Meg Whitman, who had been a general manager of Hasbro and president

---

This case was prepared by Professor David P. Baron from public sources and interviews with eBay employees involved in the database protection issue.

[1] *Wall Street Journal*, April 10, 2000.

and CEO of FTD, to serve as president and CEO, and Pierre Omidyar continued as chairman. eBay's growth was spectacular. By mid-2000 eBay had over 15.8 million registered users who traded items in more than 4,320 categories. On any day approximately 4.3 million auctions were active on eBay's site, with 500,000 new items listed every day. Nearly 1.8 million visits were made to its site on an average day, and the average visit was 20 minutes.

An online auction involved listing an item for sale with a closing date and time. The seller provided a description of the item, and most provided pictures. The seller could specify a minimum opening bid, a bid increment, and a reserve price that was not disclosed to bidders, although bidders were told whether the reserve had been met. A bid consisted of an initial bid and a maximum bid, which authorized eBay to increase the bid to the maximum if forced by another bidder. Often, there was a flurry of bidding just before the closing. Transactions between the seller and the high bidder were executed without eBay's involvement. Sellers and buyers were identified by their account names or e-mail addresses, and they earned reputations through feedback from their trading partners. The feedback was summarized and available to buyers and sellers.

eBay's principal asset was its ability to aggregate buyers and sellers on its Web site, for which it charged small fees for listings and sales. eBay strove for a high level of customer satisfaction, and its reputation helped maintain its leadership among the online auction sites that had followed in its footsteps. The company stated, "The key to eBay's success is trust. Trust between the buyers and sellers who make up the eBay community. And trust between the user and eBay, the company." eBay relied on its community to help police its site. "The community is also self-policing, and users frequently form 'neighborhood watch' groups to help guard against misuse or violations of site etiquette." eBay also sought to ensure the privacy of its users. Its privacy policy was TRUSTe approved, and eBay was a founding member of the Online Privacy Association.

eBay's revenue in 1999 was $224.7 million, and its net income was $11 million. The first half of 2000 saw a doubling of revenue from the previous year and consolidated net income increased by nearly 400% to $17.9 million. In 2000 its market capitalization reached $30 billion, reflecting its leading position in the online auction market and its seemingly unlimited potential. In spring 2000, however, its market capitalization fell to $16 billion with the market decline in high tech stocks.

Jupiter Communications forecast that online person-to-person auction revenues would increase fivefold to $15 billion by 2004. eBay's rivals ranged from small niche Web sites to Yahoo! and Amazon.com. eBay, however, was estimated to host nearly 90% of the online auctions in the United States and to have 85% of the market. eBay had expanded into international markets and was a leading online auction site in Canada, Germany, Australia, and the United Kingdom. It planned to expand into France and Italy. In February 2000 eBay entered the Japanese market, where Yahoo! Japan Auctions was the leader.

AUCTION AGGREGATORS AND DATABASE PROTECTION

Bidder's Edge and two dozen other auction aggregators, or "auction portals" as some preferred to be called, searched across auction sites to provide listings and price information for their users. The opportunity for auction aggregators was provided by a 1991 U.S. Supreme Court decision (*Feist Publications, Inc. v. Rural Telephone Service Co.*, 499 U.S., 340), in which the Court held that "facts," even if collected through "sweat and effort," remained in the public domain. Earlier court decisions had held that databases were protected by copyright under the "sweat of the brow" doctrine. This doctrine prevailed despite 1976 amendments to the Copyright Act that required a degree of creativity or originality for compilations of data to be protected by copyright law. In *Feist* the court affirmed the originality and creativity requirement and stated that "all facts—scientific, historical, biographical, and news of the day . . . are part of the public domain available to every person." For example, the telephone white pages cannot be copyrighted because they are simply an alphabetical list of names and numbers, whereas the Yellow Pages can be copyrighted because the information is arranged by category, which has a degree of originality. This ruling gave auction aggregators a legal basis for extracting "facts" from eBay and other online auction sites.

The first auction aggregator appeared in the spring of 1999, and in September eBay declared that the listings on its Internet site were its "property" and prohibited auction aggregators from searching its site. Bidder's Edge stopped its searches and took out a full page ad in the *New York Times* protesting eBay's move. Undaunted, other auction aggregators resumed listing eBay items on their sites, and seeing itself at a competitive disadvantage, Bidder's Edge did also.

eBay attempted to work with the auction aggregators, and offered a license for a small fee and a bounty for each user directed to eBay's site. Five aggregators took licenses, allowing them to query eBay's system as a user would. The license, however, prohibited copying data. eBay entered into negotiations with Bidder's Edge on a license, but little progress was made. As Kevin Pursglove of eBay explained, "This is a clear-cut example of one business trying to get a free ride off eBay's success. What we've been trying to do is reach out to these third parties and establish some appropriate business guidelines." AuctionRover, for example, had agreed to eBay's conditions and had a separate eBay tab on its Web site. Scot Wingo, CEO of AuctionRover, said, "We've taken a more pro-eBay approach. Our competitors have taken a more, if you pardon the vernacular, 'screw eBay!' approach."[2]

Bidder's Edge obtained data from nearly 100 online person-to-person and merchant auction sites, providing users with an overview of available items, comparison information, and tracking services of items available for auction. Items available on eBay, however, accounted for 69% of Bidder's Edge's database. Instead of querying eBay's system to fulfill a user's search request, Bidder's Edge used a robotic program that daily copied approximately 80,000 pages, which were stored on Bidder's Edge's computers and updated recursively. A query by a visitor to Bidder's Edge's Web site was then answered by searching its rather than eBay's database. Since Bidder's Edge searched recursively, the information it provided to its users was necessarily stale and could be inaccurate. Bidder's Edge accounted for between 1.1% and 1.53% of the queries received by eBay and imposed a heavy load on eBay's computers. More importantly, eBay believed

[2] *MSNBC*, November 2, 1999.

that those using Bidder's Edge and other auction aggregators were not receiving the full experience of its Web site and the eBay community.

eBay used a robot exclusion standard and a robots.xtx file that notified those searching its site that robotic searches were prohibited. Compliance was voluntary, and search sites such as Yahoo! and Google respected the standard. Bidder's Edge, however, did not. eBay also had a security unit that detected any unusual number of queries from an IP number and blocked those suspected of violating its policies. Bidder's Edge used proxy servers to avoid eBay's IP blocks.

In addition to eBay there were other Internet service providers that sought to protect their databases. For example, Reed Elsevier PLC and Thomson Corporation provided a comprehensive database of court cases and decisions. Reed Elsevier's Lexis unit was locked in a legal battle with Jurisline.com, whose founders had leased Lexis' 160 CD-ROMs for $2,365, copied them, and provided the data free on its Internet site. Jurisline contended that the data were developed from court records, which were public information and hence could not be copyrighted.

Other Internet service providers were concerned about database protection and access but had quite different interests. Virtually all companies that searched across Internet sites to bring information to users wanted to maintain access to information on Web sites. These companies included America Online, Yahoo!, and other portals and search engines. In addition, shopping bots feared that they would be shut out of the information they used to provide price and other comparisons for consumers.

INTELLECTUAL PROPERTY LAW AND DATABASES

Intellectual property law provided protection for information through patents, trademarks, copyrights, know-how, and trade secrets. The Coalition Against Database Piracy (CADP), however, argued that existing intellectual property laws provided little protection for databases. (Exhibit 1 presents the membership of CAPD and other coalitions.) According to the CADP, "copyright law only protects a database to the extent that it is creative in the selection, arrangement, or coordination of the facts it contains. Copyright law does not shield the database's factual content from thievery. Very few databases meet this 'creativity' requirement because all the things that make a database valuable and user-friendly—its comprehensiveness and its logical order (whether alphabetical in print products or random in electronic products)—are deemed to involve no 'creative' selection, arrangement or coordination."[3]

CADP also argued that the U.S. Antihacking Statute as well as state contract and misappropriation laws provided inadequate protection. Moreover, state laws could vary considerably. The Antihacking Statute has "never been held to apply to a published database at all—no matter what its format. Nor would the statute apply in a situation where a database producer—like eBay—makes information available over the Web without a password or firewall protecting it." State contract law applied only to

[3] CADP Web site, http://www.gooddata.org.

signed agreements. Moreover, "[M]isappropriation is an ill-defined state law doctrine and it does not provide database creators with uniform, nationwide protection."[4]

STRATEGY ALTERNATIVES

One alternative available to eBay was to attempt to establish through the courts intellectual property rights to the data it generated from its auctions. If successful this would allow eBay to block the auction aggregators. The *Feist* decision, however, placed a heavy burden on eBay to demonstrate creativity. Another possibility was to use the Computer Fraud and Abuse Act to claim that the aggregators were committing fraud. If eBay decided to take legal action, it could direct its action against Bidder's Edge or it could name additional auction aggregators as defendants. eBay also had to decide which arguments to use to support any course of action in the courts.

eBay could also seek a preliminary and ultimately a permanent injunction against Bidder's Edge and other auction aggregators. To obtain a preliminary injunction, eBay would have to demonstrate probable success in a trial and convincingly show that the absence of an injunction would cause irreparable injury. Although eBay believed that it would prevail, it recognized that pursuing a court resolution could be both costly and time consuming. Moreover, decisions could be appealed, and in the rapidly changing field of Internet law, legal innovation could thwart what appeared to be the current law. In addition, since eBay was by far the largest online auction site, legal action might attract the attention of federal or state antitrust authorities and possibly raise issues of unfair business practices, the exercise of market power, and the use of the courts to stifle competition.

For several years companies, including Reed Elsevier and other publishers, had backed the "Collections of Information Antipiracy Act" to protect their databases. In 1998 the bill had passed the House of Representatives but the Senate had not acted. Another alternative for eBay was actively to support the bill when it was reintroduced.

The World Intellectual Property Organization (WIPO) also sought stronger protection of intellectual property in light of the *Feist* decision.[5] A treaty negotiated under the auspices of WIPO provided additional protection for creative works and limited protection for online information that could be protected by copyright. Each signatory was to enact legislation to bring its laws into accord with the treaty, and the United States did so in the Digital Millenium Copyright Act of 1998. The Act established liability for online copyright infringement and protected ISPs from liability from material posted on their services, but it did not overturn *Feist*.[6]

eBay could also attempt to use technology to thwart attempts to extract information from its database. A technology fix in the form of a firewall, however, could make its site less convenient for consumers. It could also lead to a technology race as aggregators developed software to overcome the barriers erected by eBay.

[4] CAPD Web site, http://www.gooddata.org.

[5] WIPO was one of 16 specialized agencies of the United Nations system of organizations.

[6] In 2000 a federal court ruled that the Digital Millenium Copyright Act did not protect Napster, which allowed peer-to-peer swapping of digital music files, against copyright infringement lawsuits.

eBAY AND PUBLIC POLICY

As with many high-tech companies eBay had begun to address public issues. In the past two years it had established a Washington office and hired professionals to represent it. It had also established a PAC, the eBay Committee for Responsible Internet Commerce, which had contributed to members of Congress. eBay executives began to make Washington one of their regular stops on the East Coast.

In July 1999 eBay and eight other Internet service providers, Amazon.com, America Online, DoubleClick, Excite@Home, Inktomi, Lycos, theglobe.com, and Yahoo!, formed NetCoalition.com.[7] The coalition's mission statement read, "As the collective public policy voice of the world's leading Internet companies, NetCoalition.com is committed to building user confidence in the Internet through responsible market-driven policies; preserving the open and competitive environment that has allowed the Internet to flourish; and ensuring the continued vitally of the Internet through active dialogue with policymakers." Meg Whitman explained, "We want to be active participants in the dialogue that is addressing the critical issues facing the burgeoning Internet industry. As a group we can be a valuable resource and a powerful educational tool for policymakers and the public."

Within a few months, however, the "collective voice" split over the issue of database protection. eBay backed legislation to protect its databases, and other members backed rival legislation that, according to eBay, would provide little if any protection.

LEGISLATION

The "Collections of Information Antipiracy Act" was reintroduced in February 1999 as H.R. 354 by Representative Howard Coble (R-NC), chair of the Subcommittee on Courts and Intellectual Property of the Judiciary Committee. Seventy-five other House members cosponsored the bill. The bill had been redrafted to address concerns with earlier versions, and the Judiciary Committee reported it in October 1999. The bill would provide substantial protection to those who collected information, including those that did so on the Internet. Facts were not protected by the bill and remained in the public domain, but the effect of the bill would be to overturn *Feist*. The bill had not yet been introduced in the Senate, since Senator Orrin Hatch (R-UT), chairman of the Judiciary Committee, had decided to wait until the House acted before taking up the issue.

The Judiciary Committee expressed the basic principle underlying H.R. 354.

> *Developing, compiling, distributing, and maintaining commercially significant collections requires substantial investments of time, personnel, and effort and money. Information companies, small and large, must dedicate massive resources to gathering and verifying factual material, presenting it in a user-friendly way, and keeping it current and useful to customers. . . . But several recent legal and technological developments threaten to derail this progress by eroding the incentives for continued*

[7] They were later joined by EMusic.com.

> *investment needed to maintain and build upon the U.S. lead in world markets for electronic information resources.*[8]

H.R. 354 allowed an injured party to bring a civil action in U.S. court for actual damages as well as for any profits earned by the defendant and attributable to the action in question. An award for actual damages could be trebled by the court. Any person who violated the Act "for purposes of direct or indirect commercial advantage or financial gain" could be subject to a fine not to exceed $250,000 and imprisonment of not more than five years or both.[9]

Interests benefiting from the status quo countered with a rival bill, H.R. 1858, the "Consumer and Investor Access to Information Act of 1999," introduced in May under the sponsorship of Representative Tom Bliley (R-VA), chairman of the Commerce Committee. The bill was referred to the Commerce Committee and reported in October.

H.R. 1858 focused on the value of information to consumers and the benefits to Internet users from being able to obtain comparisons of information from different databases. The bill would proscribe "the sale or distribution to the public of any database that: (1) is a duplicate of another database collected and organized by another person or entity; and (2) is sold or distributed in commerce in competition with that other database."[10] Enforcement responsibility would be assigned to the Federal Trade Commission. The bill also prohibited the misappropriation of real time securities market information, but restricted the ability of market information providers to control that information. This would protect the access of online brokers to financial market information. Yahoo!, America Online, research librarians, telecommunications companies, the U.S. Chamber of Commerce, Consumers Union, Charles Schwab, and Bloomberg L.P. backed H.R. 1858. eBay viewed H.R. 1858 as worse than the current state of the law. Joining eBay in supporting H.R. 354 were Reed Elsevier, Thomson, the American Medical Association, the New York Stock Exchange, and the National Association of Realtors (NAR).

INTERESTS

The e-Commerce Coalition with nearly 300 members was formed to support database protection and H.R. 354 in particular. eBay was a principal member of the Coalition, which argued that H.R. 354 "would strike a balance between protecting the huge investments of e-commerce database developers and maintainers and recognizing the need for continued open access to information. Thus, it is aimed at the misappropriation of collections of information, not at uses that do not effect marketability or competitiveness.

[8] House Report 106-349, September 1999.

[9] A second offense would be subject to a fine of up to $500,000 and not more than 10 years imprisonment. An exemption and relief from monetary damages were provided for a "nonprofit educational, scientific, or research institution, library, or archives, or an employee or agent of such an institution, library, or archives acting within the scope of his or her employment." (Library of Congress, rs9.loc.gov.)

[10] The Act provided exclusions for certain news and sports activities, law enforcement activities, scientific and educational activities, government databases, databases related to Internet communications, computer programs, subscriber lists, certain legal materials, and certain securities market data.

Its goals are to stimulate the creation of even more collections of information and to encourage more competition among those collections."[11]

Online auction companies, Internet service providers, and publishers were not the only ones concerned about their databases. One of the largest and most valuable databases was the multiple listing service of real estate properties. Dennis R. Cronk, president of NAR, stated, "The piracy of online data poses a threat to everyone who is using the Internet to gain real estate information."[12] The NAR was capable of generating considerable grassroots support for, or opposition to, pending legislation.

Companies providing print databases also sought protection. Fifteen companies and associations formed the Coalition Against Database Piracy (CADP) to work in support of H.R. 354 and against H.R. 1858. The CADP argued that H.R. 354 was pro-Internet and pro-consumer, and it established an Internet site www.gooddata.org to provide information on the issue. The CADP argued that "H.R. 1858 only bars thefts that result in duplicative databases (i.e., those substantially similar to the original database). This allowed 'free riders' to avoid liability by the simple contrivance of cutting and pasting the stolen data so that the 'new database' is not a 'duplicate' of the original—a simple task today for anyone with a computer."[13]

In February 2000 the CAPD released a public opinion poll in support of H.R. 354. Gail Littlejohn of Reed Elsevier stated, "This data confirms what we have known all along—the American people share the view that database piracy is a serious problem and that there is an urgent need to enact antipiracy legislation this Congress. . . . Consumer access to accurate information is being compromised when anyone can copy and steal a privately owned database with no fear of penalty. Without protection, databases are in jeopardy, and consumers will lose access to trusted information."[14] Harvard law professor William Fisher, however, said, "There are huge advantages to enabling people when navigating the Internet to have as much information as possible."[15]

The opponents of H.R. 354 argued that it would give too much protection to databases, effectively creating data monopolies. Brokerage companies, for example, were concerned about their ability to obtain and provide to their customers real-time stock quotes. Bloomberg feared that it would be prevented from providing stock price analysis, "The bill would mean they would have absolute ownership right over something as basic as stock quotes." A spokesperson for the Chamber of Commerce said, "Factual data is the nuts and bolts of the information age. If you try to control its use, you're going to stifle commerce."[16]

NetCoalition.com also weighed into the battle. "As Congress considers the database issue, it must balance the objective of preventing database piracy with the equally important objective of preserving legitimate access to information, that does not conflict with the principles [in *Feist*]. Accordingly, additional database protection should be narrowly crafted to address specific, defined problems. NetCoalition.com believes

[11] http://www.theecommercecoalition.org.

[12] The National Association of Realtors had 750,000 members.

[13] http://www.gooddata.org.

[14] Coalition Against Database Piracy, February 3, 2000.

[15] *Fortune*, June 26, 2000, p. 200.

[16] *New York Times*, June 6, 2000.

that H.R. 1858 meets this test and, against the background of the many existing forms of protection, achieves the necessary balance between protection and access."[17] In February 2000 NetCoalition.com wrote to every member of the House urging them to support H.R. 1858 and to oppose H.R. 354.

Frank Politano, trademark and copyright counsel of AT&T, testifying on H.R. 1858, said, "The Internet is in fact a network of databases, and information is made accessible through tables of routers and a standardized system of IP addressing that enables the Internet to work. If the original compilers of those 'databases' exerted monopoly control over, or prohibited, downstream users of the information compiled in those databases, the future operation of the Internet would be threatened."[18]

Matthew Rightmire, director of business development of Yahoo!, argued, "H.R. 1858 has a critical provision which protects Yahoo! and other search engines against liability for linking to or listing categories of data. Absent such a provision, Yahoo! and others could be liable simply for acting like a card catalogue for facts and information available on the Internet."[19] He added, "Yahoo! is somewhat uniquely positioned to comment on this issue. We have spent and continue to spend a great deal of effort developing our own databases. At the same time, we aggregate and disseminate large amounts of information. In our view, legislating on the availability of information is not unlike two porcupines making love: it must be done very carefully. And, in both cases, there are significant unintended consequences which must be avoided."

DATABASE PROTECTION IN THE EUROPEAN UNION

The European Union (EU) adopted a Directive on the Legal Protection of Databases, effective in January 1998.[20] For EU citizens and firms the Directive established copyright protection for "the intellectual creation involved in the selection and arrangement of materials" and established a 15-year *sui generis* right for an investment "in the offering, verification, or presentation of the contents of a data base." This sui generis right effectively established the sweat of the brow doctrine for databases developed within the EU.

Henry Horbaczewski, testifying on behalf of the CADP, argued, "CADP does not advocate adopting a database protection law that mirrors the EU Directive but ignores traditionally accepted U.S. concepts of protecting intellectual property. Nonetheless, the United States database industry cannot endorse enactment of a law [H.R. 1858] whose deficiencies in regard to domestic protection also increase the discrepancies between U.S. and EU law." He also stated, "Without comparable U.S. legislation, U.S. databases will not be protected from piracy in Europe, thereby placing the U.S. database industry at a significant competitive disadvantage in the huge EU market. Each

[17] NetCoalition.com Internet site.

[18] Testimony on H.R. 1858, House Commerce Committee, June 15, 1999.

[19] Testimony on H.R. 1858, House Commerce Committee, June 15, 1999.

[20] Parliament and Council Directive 96/9/EC.

day that passes without fair, balanced, and comparable U.S. legislation gives the EU database-producing industry another leg up on its U.S. competitors."[21]

THE CHALLENGE

Its database and the community it had developed were important strategic assets for eBay, and its challenge was to protect those assets while allowing information to flow freely on the Internet. James Carney, CEO of Bidder's Edge, however, argued, "We're no different from any other search engine. Yahoo! and Lycos garner lots of information every day from sites without exclusive permission. If eBay is right and the courts agree, that would rip the guts out of the Web itself."[22]

Edward Miller, representing the NAR, recognized the reluctance of most members of Congress to regulate the Internet. He said, however, "I don't want to sound flip, but when people tell me, 'The Internet's like the Wild West,' I like to remind them we used to hang cattle rustlers in the Wild West."[23]

EXHIBIT 1 Coalition Against Database Piracy (CADP)*

American Business Press
American Medical Association
The McGraw-Hill Companies
Miller Freeman, Inc.
Newsletter and Electronic Publishers Association
Newspaper Association of America
Phillips Publishing International, Inc.
Reed Elsevier, Inc.
SilverPlatter Information, Inc.
Skinder-Strauss Associates
Software and Information Industry Association
Thomas Publishing Corporation
The Thomson Corporation

*e-Commerce Coalition**

Adweek
AutobytelDirect
DirectAg
eBay
Harris InfoSource,
InsiderSCORES
National Association of Realtors

*Partial list

(continued)

[21] Testimony before the House Commerce Subcommittee on Telecommunications, Trade, and Consumer Protection, July 15, 1999 on H.R. 1858, the Consumer and Investor Access to Information Act of 1999.
[22] *Mass High Tech*, November 8–14, 1999.
[23] *Wall Street Journal*, April 10, 2000.

EXHIBIT 1 *(continued)*

*e-Commerce Coalition**
South-Western College Publishing Thomson Bankwatch
NetCoalition.com
Amazon.com America Online DoubleClick eBay Excite@Home Inktomi Lycos theglobe.com Yahoo! EMusic.com

* Partial list.

STANFORD
GRADUATE SCHOOL OF BUSINESS

INTERNET TAXATION

On May 10, 2000 the House of Representatives passed H.R. 3709, the "Internet Non-Discrimination Act," by a resounding majority of 352–75. The bill provided a five-year extension of an existing moratorium on new Internet taxes that was due to expire in 2001.[1] The bill had been embraced by a diverse coalition of consumer groups, Internet users, and high-tech companies that argued that the imposition of taxes on electronic commerce would slow both the development of the Internet and the growth in the U.S. economy.

In the Senate intense lobbying by a diverse set of interests led Senator John McCain (R-AZ), Chairman of the Senate Commerce Committee, to cancel a hearing on a bill to make the tax moratorium permanent. When questioned about the cancellation, McCain said the topic of Internet taxes was "incredibly complex [and had] not been nearly fleshed out enough."[2] At the same time that the legislation stalled in the Senate, the solidarity of the high-tech community on the Internet taxation issue began to slip. In a June hearing before the Joint Economic Committee, Intel CEO Andy Grove argued for applying sales taxes to transactions on the Web, saying that he felt there was no "justification" for the online tax advantage. At the same hearing, Hewlett-Packard CEO Carly Fiorina warned that "to apply the current system of taxation to the online world would be disastrous." She also, however, criticized those opposed to any Internet taxes, saying that such a stance was "unrealistic."[3] A new report by the General Accounting Office (GAO) claimed that state and local governments stood to lose anywhere between $300 million and $3.8 billion in sales tax revenue in the current year.[4]

This case was written by Alan Wiseman under the supervision of Professor David P. Baron.

[1] The existing moratorium prohibited the imposition of "multiple and discriminatory" taxes on electronic commerce. These taxes would include those that subjected buyers and sellers to taxation in multiple states and localities, as well as taxes on goods specifically sold over the Internet by companies that did not have bricks-and-mortar counterparts in the state. Furthermore, it prohibited the federal government from imposing taxes on Internet access or electronic commerce generally. http://www.house.gov/chriscox/nettax/

[2] *Wall Street Journal*, June 22, 2000.

[3] *Atlanta Journal and Constitution*, June 8, 2000.

[4] Report to Congressional Requesters. "Sales Taxes: Electronic Commerce Growth Presents Challenges; Revenue Losses Are Uncertain," United States General Accounting Office, June, 2000.

PRECEDENTS AND MAIL ORDER SALES

The controversy surrounding Internet taxation resulted from court decisions that exempted from taxes mail order sales to out-of-town residents. In two landmark court cases *National Bellas Hess v. Department of Revenue of the State of Illinois* (386 U.S. 753, 1967) and *Quill v. North Dakota* (504 U.S. 298, 1992), the U.S. Supreme Court concluded that requiring merchants to calculate, collect, and remit the appropriate tax to the appropriate authorities would constitute an undue burden because of the approximately 35,000 state and local tax rates in effect. The Court decided that merchants were only required to collect sales taxes from customers that resided in a state where the merchant had a "nexus." A nexus, loosely defined, is a physical presence, such as a warehouse or retail outlet.

The Supreme Court decisions effectively absolved merchants of their responsibility for tax collection on out-of-state sales, but responsibility for the remittance of the tax remained for consumers. Most states required the remittance of "use" taxes for goods bought from out-of-state vendors. The rate of these use taxes was usually identical to the state sales tax rates for goods sold within the state. It was the responsibility of individual consumers to report to their state government how much tax they owed and pay accordingly.[5] While use taxes provided governments with a legal basis to collect revenue on out-of-state purchases, such collection rarely occurred. Compliance with use tax was very low, as most consumers were unaware that they were required to pay them. Few states attempted to collect them from individual consumers.[6] The inability to collect use taxes on catalog sales had not led to new tax legislation, but the rise of the Internet significantly changed perceptions about the scale of purchases potentially free from state and local taxes. As more transactions migrated to the Web, state and local governments feared a substantial erosion of their tax bases.[7]

Fears of dwindling revenues were accompanied by the concerns of offline main street merchants who felt that the tax advantage of online stores gave them a significant advantage. Online merchants, however, argued that they had to bear delivery costs, which, as with catalog sales, offset the tax exclusion. The online merchants also argued that they did not use state resources other than for delivery and hence should not be required to pay state taxes. These issues led to the introduction of bills in several state legislatures, all of which were aimed at providing some form of tax collection on online sales at least from their own residents.

While state and local governments were clamoring for action, the federal government was effectively putting on the brakes. The Internet Tax Freedom Act (ITFA), introduced in Congress by Representative Christopher Cox (R-CA) and Senator Ron Wyden (D-OR), was passed as part of the Omnibus Appropriations Act of 1998. Plac-

[5] Several states had a minimum purchase threshold (e.g., $100 in Virginia) before consumers were required to pay use taxes on their out-of-state purchases.

[6] States that took measures to collect use taxes met with little success. Several states, such as New Jersey, had a separate line for use taxes on residents' income tax forms. In 1997 less than 1% of New Jersey residents reported use taxes. (Cline, Robert J. and Thomas S. Neubig, 1999, "Masters of Complexity and Bearers of Great Burden: The Sales Tax System and Compliance Costs for Multistate Retailers," Technical Report, Ernst and Young Economics Consulting and Quantitative Analysis.)

[7] All states except Alaska, Delaware, Montana, New Hampshire, and Oregon have a sales tax.

ing a three-year moratorium on new Internet taxes, the ITFA also created the Advisory Commission on Electronic Commerce to study issues related to the taxation of the Internet and to recommend to Congress by April 2000 an appropriate tax policy.[8]

The Advisory Commission consisted of 19 members, eight of whom were from industry and consumer groups, eight from state and local government, and three from the Clinton Administration.[9] Early in its deliberations the Commission separated into three camps. One camp, including executives such as C. Michael Armstrong of AT&T and Theodore Waitt of Gateway, was in favor of taxing electronic commerce, provided that an equitable collection mechanism could be devised. A second group included representatives of state and local governments and was prepared to support any tax regime that would allow recovery of revenues lost to electronic commerce. A third group, represented by Governor James Gilmore (R-VA) and Grover Norquist of the Americans for Tax Reform, opposed any taxes on online commerce.[10]

The Commission considered a variety of alternatives ranging from no taxes to a flat tax on all electronic transactions. One alternative considered would keep the current tax system intact but would require credit card companies to act as trusted third parties in collecting use taxes from consumers and remitting them to the relevant governments.[11] While the Commission was studying the tax options, new measures were being introduced in Congress to address the Internet tax question. Wyden and Cox introduced new legislation asking the World Trade Organization to consider a permanent global moratorium on Internet taxes. Senator McCain introduced legislation to make the ITFA tax moratorium permanent. On the other side of the aisle Senator Ernest Hollings (D-SC) introduced legislation mandating a uniform 5% tax on all remote sales, including Internet and mail order transactions.

As the April deadline approached, the Advisory Commission was unable to reach a consensus for "official" recommendations, which required the agreement of a supermajority of 13 members. A supermajority could not be achieved because the members representing the Clinton Administration and state and local governments abstained on necessary votes, arguing that the Commission had been subverted by industry interests and was not operating with the consensus of the relevant stakeholders.[12] Congressional leaders urged the Advisory Commission to make unofficial policy recommendations nonetheless. Among the unofficial recommendations was an

[8] http://www.ecommercecommission.org.

[9] Representing industry and consumers were Michael Armstrong (AT&T), Grover Norquist (Americans for Tax Reform), Richard Parsons (Time Warner, Inc.), Robert Pittman (America Online), David Pottruck (Charles Schwab and Company), John Sidgmore (MCI Worldcom), Stan Sokul (Association for Interactive Media), and Theodore Waitt (Gateway, Inc.). Representing state and local governments were Dean Andal (California Board of Education), Governor James Gilmore (Virginia), Paul Harris (Virginia state legislature), Delna Jones (county commissioner Oregon), Mayor Ron Kirk (Dallas), Governor Michael Leavitt (Utah), Gene Lebrun (National Conference of Commissioners on Uniform State Laws), and Governor Gary Locke (Washington). Representing the Clinton Administration were Joseph Guttentag (Treasury), Robert Novick (Commerce), and Andrew Pincus (Commerce).

[10] *New York Times*, September 13, 2000.

[11] *Washington Post*, October 4, 1999.

[12] *Washington Post*, March 22, 2000.

additional five-year extension on the existing tax moratorium, which was quickly incorporated into the pending Internet Non-Discrimination Act.

INTERESTS AND THEIR STAKES

Online consumers were, not surprisingly, opposed to the implementation of Internet taxes. According to one poll, 57% of Internet users took tax rates into account when making purchasing decisions.[13] Similarly, 75% of online consumers reported that they would be less likely to purchase goods online if they were required to remit taxes for their purchases.[14] Furthermore, large-sample statistical studies indicated that taxing online sales could reduce online purchases by as much as 30%.[15]

In addition to consumers, many members of the high-tech community opposed online taxes, arguing that instituting taxes on the Web would chill the growth of the Internet in at least two ways. First, if taxes were imposed, consumers might choose not to shop online, constricting the Web's expansion. The demand for many of the companies' products and services was directly proportional to how many people were using the Web. Second, given the high costs associated with collecting and remitting use taxes under the current system, many executives argued that the costs of implementing the taxes would lead to the death of many online firms. A 1998 survey on sales tax compliance costs conducted by the Washington State Department of Revenue offered a plausible picture of the burdens associated with tax compliance. The costs to offline retailers in Washington of collecting and remitting sales taxes ranged from 0.97% for large retailers to 6.47% for small retailers of every tax dollar collected.[16]

The possibility of chilling the Internet's expansion and the high compliance costs had led most high tech companies to support an extended moratorium. They argued that given time more consumers would experiment with, and gain confidence in, online commerce; and during the period some solution might be developed to handle the burdensome compliance costs. Recent research had supported this infant industry argument for an extension of the tax moratorium.[17] Many high tech leaders viewed the Internet as an essential component of the infrastructure of both business and society, and its public goods characteristics warranted as extensive an expansion of the Internet as possible.

Among the groups that had voiced opposition to "discriminatory" taxes (i.e., taxes that targeted online products but had no bricks-and-mortar counterparts) was the Information Technology Association of America (ITAA), which represented over 26,000 companies including Compaq, IBM, MCI-Worldcom, and Microsoft. The American

[13] *Atlanta Journal and Constitution*, July 2, 2000.

[14] http://www.cisco.com/warp/public/779/govtaff/policy/tax/issues/interet_taxation.html.

[15] Goolsbee, Austan, 2000, "In a World Without Borders: The Impact of Taxes on Internet Commerce." *Quarterly Journal of Economics*. 115(2): 561–576. Goolsbee also argued that the implementation of current use taxes online would lead to approximately 20%–25% of the current consumer base choosing not to shop online.

[16] Washington State Department of Revenue, *Retailers' Costs of Collecting and Remitting Sales Tax*, Olympia 1998.

[17] Goolsbee, ibid. For a discussion of other research on these topics, see Wiseman, Alan, 2000, *The Internet Economy: Access, Taxes, and Market Structure*, Washington DC: Brookings Institution Press.

Electronics Association represented over 3,000 companies in the high-tech and electronics industry and had also voiced opposition to new Internet taxes.

To counter the advocates of online taxes, companies also formed several ad hoc coalitions. The Global Business Dialogue on Electronic Commerce was a consortium of several major companies, including Disney, Hewlett-Packard, and IBM, and was cochaired by America Online CEO Steven Case and Time-Warner CEO Gerald M. Levin.

Another ad hoc coalition, the Internet Tax Fairness Coalition (ITFC), was formed in 1998 by 11 companies and associations. ITFC was "committed to ensuring that any taxation imposed on electronic commerce not thwart the development of the Internet marketplace."[18] Mark Nebergall of the ITFC also stressed fairness: "In order to achieve a true 'level playing field,' remote merchants must enjoy the simplicity and predictability of sales tax collection and remittance enjoyed by bricks-and-mortar stores. Otherwise, the burden on remote sellers amounts to a competitive advantage for merchants deciding to stay out of electronic commerce."[19] The ITFC also argued that virtually all sectors of the U.S. economy, including state and municipal governments and main street businesses, had benefited from the growth of the Internet. Furthermore, there was currently no efficient technology to collect taxes under the current tax system. The ITFC argued that any hasty decision on Internet taxation could hinder the country's economic growth.

Opposing the tax moratorium were conventional bricks-and-mortar businesses that felt that the tax advantage available to online retailers resulted in unfair competition and injury to their business. The National Retail Federation (NRF), headquartered in Washington D.C., represented retailers ranging from small independent shops to major department stores. Representing shopping centers hurt by the new economy was the International Council of Shopping Centers, which had 38,000 members. An ad hoc coalition was formed specifically to address the Internet tax question. The E-Fairness Coalition, composed of several interest groups and major retail firms including the International Council of Shopping Centers, the American Booksellers Association, Tandy/Radio Shack, and Wal-Mart, claimed to represent over 350,000 retail outlets. It consistently argued for a "level playing field" where "customers [were] treated fairly regardless of where they [chose] to shop."[20]

State and local governments strongly favored some form of Internet sales taxation. Arguing that online commerce would lower their tax revenues by as much as $20 billion a year by 2002, state governors had begun pressuring their representatives in Washington.[21] The governors were represented by the National Governors Association (NGA), a national lobbying organization representing the interests of the 50 states. A counterpart to the NGA was the National Council of State Legislatures (NCSL), which represented state legislatures.

[18] The members were America Online, Charles Schwab, Cisco Systems, First Data Corporation, and Microsoft, as well as the American Electronics Association, the Information Technology Association, Investment Company Institute, Securities Industry Association, and Software and Information Industry Association.

[19] http://www.nettaxfairness.org.

[20] http://www.e-fairness.org.

[21] *Boston Globe*, December 31, 1998.

City and county governments had voiced their opposition to any tax-moratorium extension. In July 2000 Niles, Illinois, fearing that electronic commerce would lead to a further dwindling of its tax base, launched a $35,000 television advertising campaign aimed at discouraging online commerce. Television commercials appearing on cable channels in the northern suburbs of Chicago warned that "hackers have broken into Web sites for the Pentagon and the FBI. . . . Ask yourself, 'Do I want a chance . . . at becoming a fraud victim?'"[22]

City governments were organized primarily through the U.S. Conference of Mayors, which represented approximately 1,100 cities with populations of at least 30,000. Eighteen thousand smaller cities and towns were represented by the National League of Cities. In legislative matters the National Association of Counties represented over 1,800 counties, almost 75% of the U.S. population.

The June report by the GAO added to the concerns of state and local governments. The GAO estimated that they would lose sales tax revenue up to $3.8 billion in 2000 and up to $12.4 billion in 2003. The GAO also estimated that the losses in 2003 would be $20.4 billion if the taxes not collected on mail-order catalog and telephone sales were included. Forrester Research predicted that online retail purchases would reach $184 billion in 2004.

CONGRESSIONAL ACTIVITY

Any legislation on Internet taxation implicitly dealt with interstate commerce and hence was referred to the relevant committee of jurisdiction in each chamber of Congress. Under the Rules of the House, the Judiciary Committee, chaired by Henry Hyde (R-IL), had jurisdiction over all legislation dealing with "interstate compacts generally," which included Internet taxation.[23] The Standing Rules of the Senate assigned matters dealing with interstate commerce to the Commerce, Science, and Transportation Committee, chaired by John McCain (R-AZ).[24] During his bid for the Republican presidential nomination Senator McCain had come out in favor of a permanent moratorium on all Internet sales taxes.

In addition to H.R. 3709, the Internet Non-Discrimination Act, several related bills had been considered during the current Congress. The House passed legislation in early May that prohibited the Federal Communications Commission from imposing per-minute access charges on ISPs for Internet data transmissions.[25] The House also passed legislation repealing a 3% federal excise tax on telephone usage that had originally been enacted in 1898 to fund the eight-month Spanish-American War.[26] The repeal was recommended by the Advisory Commission on Electronic Commerce.

[22] *Chicago Sun Times*, July 24, 2000.

[23] Rule X: Rules of the House of Representatives, 106th Congress.

[24] Rule 25: Standing Rules of the Senate.

[25] Wisconsin has a tax on Internet access that is collected through ISPs. The tax generates tax revenue of $5.7 million annually.

[26] H.R. 3916 passed the House (420–2). As of July, 2000 it had been reported by the Senate Finance Committee and placed on the legislative calendar.

Congress faced other vexing taxation issues created by technological change. State and local governments impose taxes of between $4 and $7 billion on telephone usage, but with the growth of cellular telephone usage the state and local governments faced the question of which tax rates applied to cellular telephone usage. In July 2000 Congress resolved the issue by enacting legislation specifying that the applicable taxes are those for the address to which the bill is sent. Exceptions were made, for example, for corporations that provide cellular telephones to their employees, allowing the company to designate the area code in which the phone was registered as the location for taxation. Lisa Cowell, executive director, of the E-Fairness Coalition, commented, "A lot of politicians have stopped hiding behind this bogeyman of 'it can't be done' because no one knows where the customer is."[27]

While H.R. 3709 had sailed through the House without serious complications, the procedural differences between the House and the Senate raised possible problems for the moratorium extension. Any senator could filibuster the bill, which if cloture were not invoked, would likely kill the bill, since the Senate had important pending legislation remaining.[28] One senator, in particular, had voiced opposition to an extended moratorium and had proposed an alternative scheme to remedy the problem of multiple and conflicting tax jurisdictions. Senator Byron Dorgan (D-ND) proposed that online sellers be required to collect and remit use taxes at point of sale, and states could join a "compact" to collect and distribute tax revenues. To join the compact, states would have to adopt uniform definitions of taxable products and have a flat use tax rate for the entire state. As of June 2000, several states had announced their participation in this "streamlined sales tax project," a National Governors Association initiative to create uniformity in tax laws so as to facilitate online collection.[29] Working with the National Governors Association, the National Conference of State Legislatures organized a tax project to simplify state sales taxes. Wal-Mart was one of five retailers that volunteered to test a pilot program technology to distinguish among the myriad of state and local tax laws. If successful, the program would be a major step toward making taxation of online sales practical.

STATE ACTIVITY: CALIFORNIA

Legislative activity at the state level was complicating the movement toward a uniform federal solution for the tax issue. In August 2000 the California state legislature passed legislation requiring Internet merchants with bricks-and-mortar stores in California to collect sales taxes on purchases made online by California residents. If enacted, Barnesandnoble.com and Borders.com would have to collect taxes on purchases made by California consumers, since they had retail outlets in California even though their

[27] *New York Times*, July 19, 2000.

[28] Returning from the August 2000 recess, the Senate still needed to pass several appropriations bills and vote on permanent normal trade relations with China in the two months before election day.

[29] Senator Dorgan's proposal would extend the current moratorium on Internet use and access taxes for an additional four years. *Wall Street Journal*, June 29, 2000.

Internet businesses were housed outside California.[30] Barnesandnoble.com and Borders.com claimed that their online companies were separate from their bricks-and-mortar companies and hence were not affected by the nexus principle. Borders.com, however, directed customers to a Borders store if they wanted to return a book. While proponents of the bill hailed it as a "fair and square measure," other parties, such as the American Electronics Association, argued that California was trying to "shoehorn e-commerce business into an old tax system that doesn't make any sense."[31] As the legislation arrived on Governor Gray Davis's desk, observers wondered what its enactment might mean for the future of electronic commerce and state tax autonomy.

INTERNATIONAL ACTIVITY

International developments were also complicating U.S. attempts to resolve the Internet taxation issue. The 1999 Human Development Report of the United Nations made a formal recommendation to impose a $0.01 "bit tax" for every 100 e-mails sent between users. The tax would raise an estimated $70 billion a year for underdeveloped countries. Both the Clinton Administration and Congress urged the WTO to impose bans on the bit tax and similar Internet-specific taxes. Embracing the sentiments of the Clinton Administration at its Seattle meeting in December 1999, the WTO decided to extend for two years an existing moratorium on Internet taxes, effectively striking down the bit tax proposal. The original moratorium on Internet taxes had been established by the WTO in May 1998, when the ministers endowed its General Council with the responsibility for developing a "comprehensive work program to examine all trade-related issues relating to global electronic e-commerce."[32]

Other international organizations were also weighing in on the tax question. In October 1998, the 29-member Organization for Economic Cooperation and Development (OECD) proposed the Ottawa Taxation Framework Conditions. In the hope of developing a uniform taxation scheme for online commerce, the Ottawa Conditions envisioned a tax plan that was economically neutral, efficient, simple, fair, and flexible.[33] The conferees agreed that any taxation scheme should levy taxes on goods based on where they were consumed rather than where they were produced. The flexible nature of Internet commerce, however, raised difficult questions about how to determine where, precisely, goods purchased online were consumed.[34] The OECD established several industry and government working groups to examine these issues in more detail. The United States and the European Union (EU) used the OECD as a forum for their negotiations on Internet taxation.

The member states of the EU imposed a value-added tax (VAT) on electronically delivered goods and services supplied by EU companies to EU residents. In June 2000

[30] Amazon.com does not have a nexus in California and thus does not collect taxes from California residents. It does collect state sales taxes in its home state of Washington.
[31] *San Francisco Chronicle*, August 31, 2000.
[32] *Interpress Service*, December 13, 1999.
[33] OECD Committee on Fiscal Affairs, "Implementing the Ottawa Taxation Framework Conditions," June.
[34] *Financial Times*, 1998, "Plan For Taxing Internet Commerce Outlined," October 9, 2000.

the EU Commission proposed extending the VAT to non-EU companies, despite the existing WTO moratorium. Specifically, the proposal required any firm selling more than 100,000 euro worth of electronic goods into the EU be registered with one of the 15 member states' tax authorities and charge that state's rate. The VAT rates of the EU member states varied from 15% in Luxembourg to 25% in Denmark and Sweden. The VAT accounted for approximately 40% of the tax revenue of the EU member states and financed the entire EU budget.[35]

Despite arguing that the VAT proposal was consistent with the Ottawa conditions, the Commission was heavily criticized by the United States for acting unilaterally despite continued negotiations within the OECD. Stuart Eizenstat, undersecretary of the Treasury Department, argued that the proposal "if implemented, could well hinder the development of [the] global medium of [electronic] commerce." Similarly, Andy Grove came out against the VAT, calling it "e-protectionism."[36] Implementation issues also arose as to how such taxes would be collected, as well as whether the necessary unanimous endorsement of all member states of the European Union could be expected. Mark Bohannon of the U.S.-based Software and Information Industry Association called the Commission report "fatally flawed" because it was impossible to determine where a customer in cyberspace resided.[37]

Freddy Tengberg, CEO of Buyonet, had located his company's head office in Sweden but registered the company in Seattle and sold to European customers primarily from the United States. He called the Commission proposal "primitive and impossible to enforce." He argued that companies in the United States could refuse to register, and if the U.S. government agreed to force registration, the companies would simply move their computers to another country that did not force registration as required by the Commission proposal.[38]

Germany pursued the Internet taxation issue even further by taxing personal Web surfing by employees at work, which the German Finance Ministry viewed as a personal benefit. Andreas Schmidt of Bertelsmann AG commented, "German bureaucrats apparently never run out of ideas to prevent economic growth."

COMPANIES

A variety of companies would be directly affected by an Internet tax, and others would be indirectly affected. A tax would have a major impact on Amazon.com, the largest online retailer. A sale to a customer in California saved the customer the sales tax of approximately 8%, and a sale to a Texas customer saved 8.5%.[39] The tax savings helped compensate for delivery costs, which were paid directly by the customer. Despite not facing sales tax, Amazon.com lost $317 million on sales of $578 million in the quarter

[35] In contrast, sales taxes accounted for approximately 25% of the tax revenue of U.S. states and none of the federal government's tax revenue. The VAT systems in Europe were less complicated than the sales tax systems in many U.S. states.

[36] *Business Week*, June 26, 2000.

[37] *New York Times*, September 30, 2000.

[38] *New York Times*, September 30, 2000.

[39] Customers in the state of Washington were required to pay the sales tax.

ending June 20, 2000, although its loss before special equity arrangements was only $207 million.

Amazon.com had worked behind the scenes to oppose any Internet taxes. Its perspective was revealed in its commentary on the California bill to impose taxes on sales by those online companies that claimed that their Internet companies were separate from their bricks-and-mortar stores. "Paul Misener, vice president for global public policy at Amazon.com, said he does not see any need to tax Internet sales in general since so many state and local governments are running surpluses right now. 'We really have to see the problem first,' he said. 'This is almost a solution in search of a problem.' Misner added that if online sales are taxed, it should be at a lower rate than offline transactions because sales made over the Internet 'use fewer state and local resources.' Amazon opposes the . . . bill because it does not recognize this principle, even though the bill would affect one of the company's biggest competitors: Barnesandnoble.com."[40]

Cisco Systems supported the Internet Non-Discrimination Act based on the recognition that state governments were running surpluses and "the often-confusing tax rules of 7,500 separate jurisdictions could severely impede development of this rapidly expanding medium for global trade, investment, and communication. State and local governments should use an extended moratorium period to simplify their existing, complex tax structures."[41]

Cisco worked on the Internet taxation issue primarily through the Internet Tax Fairness Coalition and the American Electronics Association. Katrina Doerfler of Cisco Systems, testifying on behalf of the American Electronics Association, articulated five principles for any legislative action on Internet taxation. "One, impose no greater tax burden on electronic commerce than other traditional means of commerce. Two, support simplicity in administration. Three, retain and clarify nexus standards. Four, avoid new taxes on the Internet. And, five, consider tax issues in a global context."[42]

[40] *San Jose Mercury News*, September 12, 2000.
[41] http://www.cisco.com/warp/public.
[42] Hearings, House Committee on the Judiciary, Subcommittee on Commercial and Administrative Law, June 29, 2000.

INDEX